D1643469

OXFORD AND CAMBRIDGE CRICKET

The MCC
CRICKET
LIBRARY

OXFORD AND CAMBRIDGE CRICKET

George Chesterton and
Hubert Doggart

INTRODUCTION
by E.W. Swanton

WILLOW BOOKS
Collins
8 Grafton Street, London W1
1989

Willow Books
William Collins Sons & Co Ltd
London · Glasgow · Sydney · Auckland · Toronto · Johannesburg

All rights reserved. No part of this publication
may be reproduced or transmitted in any form or by
any means, electronic or mechanical, including photocopying,
recording or any information storage and retrieval
system now known or to be invented without permission
in writing from the publisher.

First published 1989

© MCC and George Chesterton and Hubert Doggart 1989

BRITISH LIBRARY CATALOGUING IN PUBLICATION DATA

Chesterton, George
Oxford and Cambridge cricket
1. Universities. Activities. Cricket, to 1988
I. Title   II. Doggart, Hubert
796.35'862

ISBN 0 00 218295 5

Typographic design by Tim Higgins

Set in Palatino by Phoenix Photosetting, Chatham
Printed and bound in Great Britain by
Mackays of Chatham PLC, Chatham, Kent

Contents

Introduction
by E. W. Swanton

Oxford and Cambridge cricket and cricketers have had an unparalleled influence on the evolution of the game from the end of its primitive stage until, and certainly not excluding, the present. It is an influence, need one say, wholly for the good both in the playing sense and, just as importantly, in service once active days were past. University cricket runs like a bright thread through the history of the game in England, with blues of both shades instigating the formation of clubs of all kinds, refreshing the counties from their earliest days by the brand and spirit of their play, and adorning Test teams both at home and abroad. There have been to date 126 Test cricketer blues, of whom 30 have been captains of England, 13 of other national sides.

Any self-respecting cricket follower, if he paused to think, should be able to say in which famous fixture over the years most first-class cricketers have taken part. It is, of course, the University Match which since 1827 has now been played 144 times and in which 1,569 blues have appeared. The vast majority of these men have played for their counties, and despite the poor showing of both Universities at the moment of writing it is nevertheless a fact that even in the summer of 1988 some 16 blues were to be seen in county cricket. Over the full spread of years no nurseries of talent can match the respective headquarters of The Parks and Fenner's.

Such a beating of the drum is not superfluous today, though perhaps it might have been in the past when the Universities' place in the scheme of things was taken more for granted. True, the splendour of Lord's Week and the glorification of the blue are things of the past. College entrance policies at Oxford and Cambridge have directed the flow of much sporting talent to the newer universities and to other places of further education. Yet young cricketers of promise – though not enough of them – are still squeezing in and out of Oxford and Cambridge and going on to make the game a career. It would be sad indeed if there ever came a day in which undergraduates no longer aspired to play county cricket, and, equally, if the voices of old Oxford and Cambridge men were to be less clearly heard in the councils of the game. It is perhaps easier for me to say this, who never enjoyed the privilege and advantage of a University education, than either of the distinguished co-authors.

I only hope this regrettable lack does not disqualify me in the eyes of readers from the writing of an introduction to this one and only definitive history of University cricket. For such it is. Much has been written on the subject by distinguished participants. The names of W.J. Ford, A.C.M. Croome, P.F. Warner, R.C. Robertson-Glasgow and J.G.W. Davies will be familiar to most. If that of Geoffrey Bolton is less so, a lifetime of devotion to Oxford cricket and the mind of a classical scholar equipped him to write with rare critical perception his *History of the OUCC* from its beginnings to 1960. George Chesterton here started with a lengthy material advantage over Hubert Doggart, since Ford's admirable *History of the CUCC* ended in 1901. Both authors, of course, have had recourse to, and made ample use of, Volume 1 of the handsome *Fifty Years of Sport* trilogy with its brilliant coverage by Arthur Croome (with the help of many captains and other eye-witnesses) of University cricket between 1861 and 1912. The subject has, of course, been a theme in many autobiographies and other books, several of which are listed in the Bibliography. All the facts and many of the legends of the oldest first-class fixture in the calendar have here been brought together in one book and an obvious gap filled in the noble literature of cricket.

I saw my first University Match in 1926, and first reported it two years later. Thereafter over the half-century span until retirement I saw them all except when, latterly, the fixture collided with a Test match. What with writing and broadcasting (in half-hour spells!), as well as entertaining – the hire of a Tavern box was then more or less within one's pocket – they were almost the busiest as well as the most enjoyable days of the summer's round. Each of the Lord's classics had its distinctive ambience and clientele: the Eton and Harrow, vastly social and vastly popular, with crowds of 20,000 spectators a day; the Oxford and Cambridge and the Gentlemen and Players, both well and more discriminatingly supported; and, annually from 1928 onwards, the Test match.

In my youth and for many years afterwards, the University Match was, as it had always been, very much a festival of public-school cricket – for thence the teams almost exclusively came. Members of Vincent's and the Hawks Clubs, Oxford Authentics, Cambridge Crusaders and undergraduates generally were thick on the ground, as also were the clergy. Dog collars and not a few gaiters were to be seen especially on the Monday, that being then (though scarcely now) recognized as the parson's day off. Most of the crowd were staunchly partisan, though it included regular patrons of Lord's without particular affiliations just in search of a good day's cricket. It is one of the differences between then and now that that sort of uncommitted spectator, more's the pity, is rarely to be found. But if there is one thing my essay must not be, it is a jeremiad.

The public schools have been (until the last few years) the accepted nurseries of University cricket, but in early years most of the players came from only a handful. By the time J.D. Betham published his invaluable *Oxford and Cambridge Scores and Biographies* in 1904, Eton had contributed 60 blues to Oxford, and 84 to Cambridge including six who played in the first match of 1827. Harrow by this date had 52 dark and 54 light blues, Winchester 61 and 17 respectively. Rugby mustered 36 of one and 28 of the other, after which came 32 privately educated, 31 from Marlborough. Westminster, Clifton and Uppingham were the only other schools providing more than 20.

It was the enterprise of a few which first lit the sporting fire of the ancient universities, and at Oxford it was the same heroic figure who inaugurated both the first cricket fixture in 1827 and the first Boat Race two years later. This was none other than Charles Wordsworth, nephew of the poet and, more importantly in this context, son of the then Master of Trinity, Cambridge. Wordsworth was up at

Christ Church, and so with a foot in both camps conceived his happy idea and brought it to fruition. The leading light at Cambridge was an Etonian, Herbert Jenner (later Jenner-Fust), and they had played against one another in the Eton and Harrow. Perhaps these two, who led their University sides on to the field at Lord's on 4 June 1827, should be acclaimed together as the twin progenitors of the great match.

Clearly, before the coming of trains and the telephone, communication was difficult and enthusiasts with a practical turn would have been needed to set things moving. Bolton tells how when the stage-coaches were full, 'private gentlemen' would convey the players to Lord's in their carriages and billet them among their friends. The second match took place at Oxford two years later, immediately after Wordsworth had promoted and rowed in the first Boat Race at Henley. He contributed a few wickets, with his left-underarm off-breaks, to his side's handsome victory, but 'bagged a pair', his hands reputedly still so sore from rowing that he could scarcely hold the bat. He excelled also, incidentally, at tennis, skating, football and rackets. What a Titan! Betham records his taking the top Latin prizes and a First in the 'Schools', and that he was the tutor of Gladstone and Manning. After ordination he taught at Winchester and was Warden of Glenalmond before becoming Bishop of St Andrews. The last of his several published works was an appeal for Christian unity. He lived to the age of eighty-six, and one can only conclude that he must at some stage have declined an archbishopric.

At all events Wordsworth set an example of the true all-rounder ideal which has been faithfully followed by so many University cricketers ever since. His Cambridge rival, Jenner, less illustrious on paper, a barrister by profession, became a leading cricketer for Kent and the Gentlemen and, at the precocious age of twenty-seven, President of MCC. Moreover he lived to be ninety-eight, an age narrowly exceeded among blues, I believe, only by F.A. Mackinnon, 35th Chief of the clan, of Cambridge, Kent and the 1878–9 team to Australia. (At the Canterbury Week of 1946 I met The Mackinnon and we had a lively talk about Australia where I was about to go for the first time. He defied prediction by succumbing in that following hard winter a few weeks short of his ninety-ninth birthday.)

There was a gap of seven years before, in 1836, the third match was held at Lord's. The next was in 1838, after which the only gaps in a century and a half were those caused by the World Wars. That the cricket in these early years must have been as rudimentary as the organization of the sides may perhaps be assumed from the number of byes and wides. Round-arm bowling had only just been legalized, and anyway, the amateurs could scarcely hold a candle to the professionals. Sheep did not give way to the mowing machine until 1850, and the Lord's field was a notoriously rough affair of ridge and furrow. (Perhaps the Rugbeian blue C.S. Bere had Lord's in mind when he included, in his *Garland of Songs*, the famous harvest hymn 'We plough the fields and scatter'.)

If those early University Matches had done nothing else, their contribution would have been important in that they helped to imbue with a love and understanding of cricket men who were to be among the leaders of Church and State. Throughout the reign of Queen Victoria cricket assumed an increasingly significant place in all strata of society. In 1841 the Duke of Wellington ordained that a cricket ground be adjoined to every military barracks.

So far as the last century is concerned, blues of both hues, especially the darker, were drawn to the Church in much greater numbers than from elsewhere. Betham lists a veritable cloud of clerics. Chiefly they became incumbents of parishes, but there were chaplains of various kinds: to the Forces, to bishops, to peers (domestic ones), to prisons and hospitals; there were precentors, minor canons, residentiary canons, perpetual curates, vicars choral, and prebendaries; deans of cathedrals and colleges, mere rural deans in profusion; a Jesuit, and one or two more who crossed over to Rome. Bishops? Fewer perhaps than might have been expected – but mention should be made of one tragic martyr, J.C. Patteson, who played at Lord's for Eton and Oxford in the 1840s, and as the missionary Bishop of Melanesia was murdered by savages in the South Seas, aged forty-four. Nor must we suppose, by the way, that David Sheppard is the first cricket blue to have been appointed to the see of Liverpool. One of his predecessors, Dr J.C. Ryle, who took nine Cambridge wickets in 1838 and died at the crease, as it were, at the age of eighty-four after twenty years in the bishopric, was a prolific writer of Tracts, several of them on temperance. He would appear to have been a zealot after Bishop David's heart.

Of the Oxford blues prior to 1870, almost half (81 out of 182, e and oe) took holy orders. After that date there was a sharp falling-off in favour of the law (easily the most favoured profession) and schoolmastering. There was a fair sprinkling of MPs, but very few medical men or members of the armed services. Around the turn of the century a few well-known names – R.E. ('Tip') Foster, 'Shrimp' Leveson-Gower and F.P. Knox – headed the sporting invasion of the Stock Exchange.

Naturally one finds some empire-builders among the blues, but none with a story to rival the bizarre experiences of H.S. Russell (Oxford 1839), one of the earliest explorers of Queensland, who was taken prisoner by cannibals, condemned to be eaten, but escaped to become in later life a Member of the first Queensland Legislative Assembly. Bathos marked his end, for the intrepid fellow retired to England only to die of a heart attack 'whilst walking to catch a train'. One wonders whether in old age Russell and his captain, G.B. Lee, who took nine Cambridge wickets that year in their only innings, reminisced on their diverse experiences of life. For Lee was one of those ultra-Wykehamical introverted figures who from boyhood onwards never left the cloisters of Winchester and New College, and for the last forty-two of his eighty-five years was Warden of his old school. Of a later Winchester and Oxford captain, H.R. Webbe, it is recorded that his life by contrast came to a devout end before his thirtieth birthday on his recitation of the words 'Thy kingdom come' in the Lord's Prayer at an East End Sunday school.

But it is high time that these esoteric items – intriguing as one may find them – should give place to a broader look at University cricket, and to a salute of some of the great players of other days whose deeds will be noted in these pages. Two men, surprising to say, captained their sides for three years, in each case winning three times. One was T.A. Anson of Cambridge (1840–2), reputedly the finest wicket-keeper of his day. The other was the famous R.A.H. Mitchell, who revived Oxford cricket during the period 1863–5 before returning as a master to Eton and running cricket there for thirty-two summers. Altham names him as the greatest player in the first half-century of the University Match, and the best amateur bat after W.G. Grace. It was said that at Lord's the Eton captain was required to field willy-nilly at long off and long leg to remain within range of the advice of Mitchell in the front row of the pavilion seats. He is still thereabouts as he looks down the Long Room from A. Chevallier Tayler's portrait, a rather dandified figure with buttonhole and I Zingari ribbon round his straw hat. And if Mitchell was a stayer in one field, so was that earlier Etonian, Anson, in another – as rector of Longworth, Derbyshire for forty-nine years.

The year 1878 was a milestone in English cricket because it saw the first Australian visit, the immediate prelude to Test cricket in England. It is noteworthy also as underlining the place the Universities then had in the game, since the Australian side which had made history by beating MCC at Lord's in a single day were themselves overwhelmed by Cambridge by an innings – and that without A.P. Lucas, their best bat.

A special aura has always surrounded Edward Lyttelton's unbeaten Cambridge side of 1878, while that of Oxford under M.C. Kemp in 1884, which also beat the Australians, was accorded a position scarcely less exalted. In addition, Oxford and Cambridge men were by now much to the fore in the birth and growth of the county clubs.

The great figures that proceeded from Fenner's and The Parks to the Test scene now emerge, the first among them A.G. Steel. This young Marlburian was a youthful hero indeed, an all-rounder who was only nineteen when he put both the Australians and Oxford to rout, and twenty-one when he led Cambridge to victory at Lord's and then substantially helped England to win the first ever Test in England. He was an early master of the spun leg-break, and a fine enough batsman to score Test hundreds both at home and 'down under'. Mr Davies, the historian of Cambridge cricket, rated Steel 'the finest all-rounder Cambridge ever produced' – which would place him above that other legendary figure, F.S. Jackson; ahead, too, of S.M.J. Woods, that rumbustious Anglo-Australian who shines through the mists of time as a lovable personality distinctly larger than life.

The stature of Jackson and Woods may be adjudged from the fact that, bowling unchanged through both innings of the Players at Lord's in 1894, they enabled the Gentlemen to win by an innings. Jackson made 63, top score in the match, as well as taking 12 for 77. When he led England in the winning series against Australia in 1905, Jackson headed both the batting and the bowling averages. Just prior to this, an Oxford man, 'Plum' Warner, had brought back the Ashes from Australia – a lesser cricketer than others mentioned here but a lifetime servant of the game and, like H.D.G. Leveson-Gower, his University contemporary, a captain with a gifted touch. C.B. Fry belongs to the same Oxford era, an all-round sportsman and scholar without peer in his age, and if such things are measurable, surely since unsurpassed.

Prince Ranjitsinhji's fame came after his Cambridge days, but G.L. Jessop's genius as a forcing batsman matured through four Fenner's summers (1896–9). The Universities contributed richly, of course, to this Golden Age, the start of which is generally reckoned to be the 1880s with its close (inevitably) in 1914. This pageant of famous names is not by any means exhaustive. No such list, however, can omit the Oxonian R.E. Foster, the finest of the seven Malvern brothers, who died young but not before he had made that record 287 against Australia at Sydney in his first Test match. And one more pre-First World War Malvern and Oxford figure in Foster's class, who also perished young (as an early aviator), was the all-rounder W.H.B. Evans, a Test cricketer *manqué*.

The early post-war years saw a Cambridge preponderance, and indeed the richest vein of talent in relatively modern times, with such names as Chapman, Allen, Gilligan, Marriott, and the Wykehamist trinity of Ashtons – Gilbert, Hubert and Claude. The brothers led Cambridge in three successive years (1921–3), a glorious fluke of nature and a repetition of the famous Eton Studds, G.B., C.T. and J.E.K., who had similarly followed one another in the captaincy forty years earlier. Gilbert's side of 1921 is acclaimed the best in this century and Hubert (only partly because of a subsequent career overseas) the best batsman never to be chosen for England. Oxford, too, had their stars of the early 1920s, among them G.T.S. Stevens, R.H. Bettington and D.R. Jardine. The last named, by the way, was never considered as a University captain.

These reflections can now assume a note of personal reminiscence. Maurice McCanlis and I were contemporaries at Cranleigh and in the same house, but I was able to bask only faintly in his reflected glory since by the time I arrived at Lord's on one particular July morning in 1926 the scorecard told me that the first three Cambridge wickets had fallen to him for 0, 1 and 6 respectively, all caught at second slip by the captain, G.B. Legge. His third victim, Duleep no less, had been missed by Legge the ball before. Late out-swing can confound the best, but this for me was an early illustration of the truth that the higher bowling arts can be more easily lost than those of the batsman and sometimes, as in this case, remain elusive for ever.

In old age the earlier memories are often the clearest. I recall all too plainly the sad, undisciplined way in which in 1930 Oxford on the last day threw away a cast-iron position and finally, despite Ian Peebles' thirteen wickets, went down to a weaker side on paper by 205 runs. The following year Cambridge began the match with a partnership of 149 between George Kemp-Welch and Alan Ratcliffe, and the latter went on to make 201, so beating J.F. Marsh's record 172 not out in 1904. At the close a total of 385 seemed to have put revenge out of Oxford's reach. But Alan Melville's side were made of sterner stuff than their predecessors. The Nawab of Pataudi capped Ratcliffe's effort by (so it was said) nominating that he would beat it and going on to do so. He (238 not out) and Tuppy Owen-Smith (78) created havoc; Oxford declared at 453 for 8 and gave Cambridge half an hour's batting that evening. I can hear now the shout from the Tavern next morning when Robert Scott spreadeagled Ratcliffe's stumps, the prelude to an Oxford victory by eight wickets with time to spare. Such could be the tempo of those days!

I should probably apologize to the authors for putting a disproportionate spotlight on my youthful recollections. I fear, though, that I must confess to an instinctive juvenile leaning towards Oxford, and it is perhaps worth underlining that in those inter-war days such battles were the focus of strong emotions. In any event, not many playing years are to pass before Hubert Doggart and George

Chesterton can themselves give us first-hand accounts, and I can leave the detailed picture safely to them.

Owen-Smith can certainly be accounted a rival to C.B. Fry for the all-rounders' crown if scholarship is not included in the estimation. A Test cricketer for South Africa at twenty and later rugger captain of England, he played for his country before going up – as also in due course did M.P. Donnelly for New Zealand, A.H. Kardar for India (pre-Partition) and E.S.M. Kentish for West Indies. As by far the oldest blue (he was in his fortieth year when he played for Oxford in 1956), Kentish was something of a freak. More significant were the Test caps won by youthful undergraduates while in residence: within my memory there were Tom Killick at Cambridge and N.S. Mitchell-Innes at Oxford. Aidan Crawley got as near a Test cap as twelfth man. Later came the distinguished overlapping post-war quartet, author Doggart, John Dewes, David Sheppard and Peter May. In all between 1948 and 1952 they made 37 hundreds for Cambridge. Strangely, though, only one, by Sheppard, was against Oxford – an illustration perhaps that the University Match was somehow 'different'. More recently Derek Pringle played for England while the Cambridge captain, even though it meant his missing the University Match – a decision (apparently approved by his team) which would have horrified any previous generation, and indeed caused plenty of raised eyebrows even in 1982.

University cricket was healthy enough when the Second World War intervened. Of the undergraduates who took the field at Lord's in 1939 a dozen had already had their first taste of county cricket before hostilities opened in September. Most of the rest played for Minor Counties, including David Macindoe who had opened the Gentlemen's bowling as a freshman. The Gentlemen's eleven which played at Lord's in 1939 included six Cambridge blues: Bryan Valentine, Freddie Brown, Billy Griffith, Kenneth Farnes, Hugh Bartlett and John Brocklebank. Oxford supplied Gerry Chalk, who was killed in the war, as also was Farnes. (A list of casualties can be found in Appendix VII.)

When University cricket was resumed in 1946 Oxford were first into their stride, thanks chiefly to a rich strain from overseas headed by Martin Donnelly. A bright halo surrounds the name of that most delectable of left-handed batsmen who brought to The Parks crowds never seen there before or since. Soon, however, there came to Cambridge the influx of batting talent which has been noted already. As ever, bowlers of quality were harder to find, but the records of Warr, Goonesena and Wheatley for Cambridge in the 1950s speak for themselves. Oxford's attack was generally the weaker – so much so that despite the presence of batsmen of the stature of Colin Cowdrey and M.J.K. Smith, four summers passed without a win. For the latter (captain in 1956) three hundreds, the first a double, against Cambridge in successive years – a unique feat – was at least a sizeable consolation.

There was a certain irony, surely, in the fact that in the four summers preceding the abolition of amateur status in November 1962 every member of the representative Gentlemen's sides at Lord's was a graduate of either Oxford or Cambridge – a sequence unequalled in the history of the ancient fixture. They included a dozen Test cricketers.

In recent years the fortunes of the respective sides have tended very much to reflect the quality of the leadership. A.C. Smith reversed a long Oxford decline. Mike Brearley's achievements at Cambridge presaged his later striking success as a Test captain. Two Pakistanis, Majid Khan at Cambridge and Imran Khan at Oxford, Test players already, radiated experience and self-confidence. In his two-year captaincy of Oxford, Vic Marks made the very best of limited resources. University cricket gave him the grounding that led to good service for England. Since then John Carr (Oxford 1983–5) and Michael Atherton (Cambridge 1987–8) have so profited from University cricket that a future at the highest level seems possible, at the time of writing, for either or both.

From the earliest days Cambridge cricket was generally ahead of that of Oxford in terms of organization. Jack Davies dates the formation of the CUCC at 1820, whereas there was no constituted OUCC until 1862. For many years Oxford were at a disadvantage as to their ground on Cowley Marsh, a common stretching south-east from Magdalen Bridge whereon a few of the colleges also had their allotted space. Parker's Piece at Cambridge was more central and probably provided the better playing surface. In any case, whereas the CUCC was installed at Fenner's in 1846, Oxford's ground in the University Parks did not come into use until 1881. Another advantage held by Cambridge was financial. Although the famous Dr Jowett of Balliol was largely instrumental in gaining a perpetual lease of ten acres within the Parks, on which was built a pavilion, Convocation forbade the taking of gate money. Even today when crowds are small there is at Oxford only a voluntary collection. There were no such inhibitions at Fenner's. Within the last half-century and more I would say that Cambridge undergraduates have been luckier than their counterparts in having found long-serving friends sympathetic to their interests both on the field and off.
   Cyril Coote, who succeeded the patriarchal Dan Hayward as groundsman of Fenner's in 1936 and served until 1980, not only regularly produced some of the best wickets in England but was guide, philosopher and friend to all the cricketing generations within that span. It has similarly been of manifest advantage to Cambridge cricket that such a distinguished figure in the game as Mr Davies, a Treasurer and President of MCC, should have guided their affairs for so long as treasurer of the club, and should be doing so still. I do not at all say that there have not been men at Oxford dedicated to the OUCC. There has, however, been no parallel to the sterling continuity of service of the Davies–Coote partnership.
   The respective tally of Test cricketers reflects no doubt that Cambridge has the larger undergraduate population to draw from in addition to the differences outlined above. Overall, 77 of that select list of 126 have graced Fenner's, as against 49 in The Parks. If one looks at England players only, one finds more than double as many Cantabs as Oxonians – 68 to 31. The fact that twice as many of the latter have played Test cricket for other countries – 18 to 9 is the score here – is to be explained by the strong influence on Oxford games of the Rhodes scholars, who essentially embody the *mens sana in corpore sano* ideal.

This matter of an accent on extra-curricular interests and activities among the credentials for entry brings me to my concluding thoughts on the future of cricket at

Oxford and Cambridge. When I first began to write about University games and to play cricket at both of them, many of the best school sportsmen went up as a matter of course, welcomed by most colleges and more particularly, it seemed, by friendly dons at Brasenose and St Edmund Hall at Oxford and Pembroke and St Catharine's at Cambridge. Pembroke was so full of cricket blues and Crusaders that some of the latter might spill into the college second eleven. The University captain's field of choice would seem incredible today to his counterpart who has to resign himself to a substantial reduction in the source of supply because of the admission of women to men's colleges, as well as the limited availability of talent at his disposal by reason of examination pressure.

The halcyon pre-war times have gone for ever and, unless there is some change of heart regarding admission policies, the very existence of representative elevens at Oxford and Cambridge must be in grave doubt. I am sure that a majority of the TCCB hierarchy looks fondly on University cricket – to which, incidentally, most of the top officers today owe their own start in the game. There may well, however, be a limit to their continuing to accord first-class status to the increasingly uneven fixtures between the Universities and the counties: and if that first-class label were ever to be lost, counties would come no longer to Fenner's and The Parks, and the TCCB could scarcely justify continued support of OUCC and CUCC. Those two lovely grounds would close down and the long and illustrious saga would quietly peter out. Such a tragedy would be an unmistakable signal that the old catholic ethos of university life had been finally submerged.

A more liberal policy in just a few colleges might surely even now do the trick. In a game increasingly controlled in all its aspects by the financial dimension, the desirability of an increased flow of good cricketers from Oxford and Cambridge, both to play and afterwards to fulfil their part in administration and governance, needs no further emphasis.

Authors' Preface

In view of E.W. Swanton's wingéd words, which will give pleasure to many, the authors do not believe that a long preface is required here, but merely a brief indication of our approach to what has been a labour of love.

We have shared equally the accounts of the 144 matches played by Oxford and Cambridge between 1827 and 1988. To be more accurate, we have shared the 143 matches played, since the 1988 match, for the first time, was abandoned because of the sodden state of the ground, without a ball being bowled. Each author has been responsible for the fourteen decades that relate to his own University.

We are both indebted, as all cricket authors are, to many books, but especially to *Wisden*, not least to the *Wisden Book of Obituaries* compiled by Benny Green; to *A History of Cricket* by H.S. Altham and E.W. Swanton; to J.D. Betham's *Oxford and Cambridge Cricket Scores and Biographies*; and to the *Who's Who of Cricketers* by Philip Bailey, Philip Thorn and Peter Wynne-Thomas.

The Cambridge story could not have been begun without W.J. Ford's invaluable *The Cambridge University Cricket Club 1820–1901*, or finished without the knowledgeable help of J.G.W. Davies, Cambridge's guide, philosopher and friend for nearly four decades. Cyril Coote, Cambridge's more-than-groundsman for over four decades, and many past players have given their time and encouragement; and we were able to read reports on nine seasons, written by Leonard Crawley and others, when an earlier book was being planned. The errors and omissions are, of course, ours and not theirs.

From the Oxford angle, especially valuable books have been *Fifty Years of Sport at Oxford, Cambridge and the Great Public Schools*, Volume 1, edited by A.C.M. Croome, and Geoffrey Bolton's scholarly *History of the OUCC*. Many useful contributions have been made by former Oxford players, and also by G.L. Cawkwell, a New Zealander and a don at University College. Particular thanks are due to Samantha Clegg, who typed and retyped the Oxford sections.

The admirably full records at the back have been prepared by Stephen Green, the Curator of MCC, and by those who have worked under him: June Bayliss, Michael Lucy and his recent successor, Glenys Williams. The article on batting by Gerald Brodribb is a delightful bonus.

We would both, finally, like to express our pleasure in being involved in the MCC Cricket Library, under Jim Swanton's aegis and with the helpful co-operation of Michael Doggart, Collins' Sports Commissioning Editor.

GEORGE CHESTERTON   HUBERT DOGGART

1
1827–1844
Wordsworth's Inspiration

OXFORD *Round-arm at Magdalen*

It is probable that the OUCC began in the years immediately preceding Trafalgar, and it is certain that the first Varsity Match took place in 1827, with Waterloo still a vivid memory.

The OUCC did not, as most clubs, come into being through a committee decision or the stroke of a pen. It grew from two other clubs, Bullingdon Green and Magdalen Club, although Pycroft tells us that the Magdalen ground alone was deserving of notice for practice and play. The name was not associated with the College but with Magdalen Choir School; the Headmaster, the Reverend H. Jenkins, handed over part of Cowley Common which he had annexed for his school. Cowley Common stretched from Magdalen Bridge on both sides of the Cowley Road as we now know it, for miles to the foot of Shotover Hill. The Magdalen Club was about a mile along this road on the lower part of the common sometimes known as Cowley Marsh, with 'marsh' often being the operative word. In 1843 the Varsity Match had to be transferred to Bullingdon Green, the Magdalen ground being unplayable.

Such common rights as there were belonged to the Parish of Cowley, but the University's use of the common was encouraged since employment was thus given to local men and boys. Pycroft stated:

Cowley used to supply some useful bowlers, but all underhand. Such rustics as Hoskings, Blucher and Peter (short for Pieria Bancolari) were well-known names.

Describing the play itself, he goes on to say:

On the Magdalen ground we used to practise with six wickets along the upper side, facing at a distance of about fifty yards, six along the lower side. Here we had twelve men batting and twelve men between the rows bowling – no small number for hours daily in danger's way . . . but I never saw any accident of much consequence.

Such practice must have taken place in the roped-off area, since the common was a popular place for undergraduates to exercise their horses. It does not require much imagination to picture the state of the outfield on heavy ground. In his description Pycroft goes on:

We had no pavilion, only a long tent for dinner under the victualling of a very remarkable man – a man who might have made a fortune at Oxford with common prudence, so popular was he and so well did he understand University men – 'Old King Cole'. Few men will ever forget Cole's portly figure, his watch chain and seals plumbing a perpendicular clear of his toes, standing before the tent . . . He would organise the coach for a race at Henley, or for one to take the Eleven to Marylebone, and was to be seen with betting book and pencil – common in those days – under the pavilion at Lord's.

Travel and communication in those early years of the University Cricket Club were major problems, so Cole's services must have been invaluable. True, stage-coaches left Carfax for the six-hour journey to London at regular intervals, but a boisterous cricket eleven could hardly be catered for. The railway link was opened in 1844.

Until 1862 the affairs of the Magdalen Club were managed in a somewhat bizarre manner. There was not an elected captain but there were three treasurers (or stewards) who held equal responsibility although not for a particular office. Each had a right to play for the Club, and indeed was subject to a fine of ten shillings if he failed to do so. The confusion must have been considerable and this divided responsibility was doubtless the reason why Oxford took the field one short at Lord's in 1839. It is not recorded who were the early treasurers, but it can be assumed that Charles Wordsworth was one.

F.B. Wright, who played in the first Varsity Match, kept a scorebook at the Magdalen Club from 1827 to 1829. His grandson presented this, the earliest known such book, to the Library at Lord's in 1949. The recorded matches, probably many of them trials, do not always have titles, or where they do these are somewhat vague, such as 'One side *v* T'other' or 'Outside *v* Inside'. The rain-splattered sheets show the first Club match as 'The Club *v* Kent & Sussex' on 22 May 1827. This was a nine-a-side game, the counties winning by 106–81. The first mention of the University occurs on 21 June when the team so designated was beaten by Wykehamists, who made 138 to 92. There is a fascinating entry in one of the trials which reads: 'Mr Manning Bowld Mr Wright (!!) 12'. What can have happened? Was it a sneak, or dropper, or perhaps an illegal round-arm?

This was the time of the round-arm controversy. In the early years of the century the prevalence of round-arm bowling led to one change of the *Laws* after another. An organized campaign developed between the progressive element, who called themselves the 'March of Intellect', and the diehards who believed the new 'throwing' would ruin the game. In 1827, the year of the first Varsity Match, three experimental 'trial matches' were arranged between Sussex and England. Sussex included Lillywhite, possibly the greatest round-arm bowler. The matches at Sheffield, Lord's and Brighton, if nothing else, proved that the game was not in fact ruined. William Ward, the proprietor of Lord's and the hero of the second trial, stubbornly blocked a change, but the diehards finally gave way in May 1835 and cricket changed its character. The immediate and predictable effect was an astonishing increase in the number of wides. In the Cambridge innings of 287 in the 1839 Varsity Match there were 46 wides, and in the exciting low-scoring match of 1841 Oxford conceded 37 and Cambridge 21.

Charles Wordsworth, largely responsible for the first Boat Race as well as the first Varsity cricket match, in reflecting on these times sixty years later, when Bishop of St Andrews, wrote:

I had a large acquaintance among cricketers who had gone off from Eton, Winchester, Rugby and Harrow (his own school) to both Universities. . . . Nothing came of my wish to bring about a match between the Universities in 1826. But in 1827 the proposal was carried into effect. Though an Oxford man, my home was at Cambridge, my father being Master at Trinity, and this gave me opportunities for communicating with men of that University.

In writing of the need for permission to leave Oxford in term time to play at Lord's, he continues:

My conscience still rather smites me when I remember that in order to gain my end, I had to present myself to the Dean and tell him that I wished to be allowed to go to London – not to play a game of cricket (that would not have been listened to) but to consult a dentist . . . at all events my tutor, Longley – afterwards Archbishop of Canterbury – was privy to it.

In 1829 it would appear there was some sort of festival in Oxford, which would account for Cambridge's visit for the first ever Boat Race, followed two days later by the cricket match. There was then no University Match until 1836, but May 1832 saw the first match against the MCC. Oxford lost by only 14 runs, and in the return match at Lord's they lost again, this time by four wickets.

In 1835 C.M. Gifford (although there is some doubt over his name) recorded Oxford's first hundred: he made 105 against the MCC at Lord's, having earlier taken five wickets. The University lost again, by 42 runs. It was not until 1837 that Oxford defeated the MCC, when E.H. Grimston produced a remarkable all-round performance, making 74 and 28 and taking eight first-innings wickets.

J. Pycroft tells us that in the early years there was little chance of selection for players who had not been at Eton, Winchester or Harrow. In 1836 Pycroft, G. Rawlinson and C.W. Beauclerk, were the only team members not from these schools. There was little inter-school cricket at this time but the schools mentioned competed in a Lord's Week, so these players knew each other, and any others had to achieve recognition by their performances on Cowley Marsh.

Among the great names of the early years, A.J. Lowth of Winchester looms large. He was an exponent of round-arm who bowled left-handed, and he had the rare distinction of playing for the Gentlemen while still at school. He, like so many of his contemporaries, went into the Church and lived to a ripe old age. William Webb Ellis, who batted at number three for Oxford in the first University Match, achieved fame at Rugby when he, 'with a fine disregard for the rules of football played in his time, first took the ball in his arms and ran with it, thus originating the distinctive feature of the Rugby game'. So says the tablet overlooking the Rugby playing fields.

CAMBRIDGE *From the playing fields of Eton*

History may well be only 'a pattern of timeless moments', as T.S. Eliot has suggested, but it must surely be of interest to place in the context of time the early, hesitant beginnings of any cricket club, so rooted is the story of cricket in the heart and soul of England. And this must apply especially to a club whose members, over the years, have made such a signal contribution to the game, some as players, some as administrators, some as authors, and some as enthusiastic supporters.

At a time when cricket was receiving a shot in the arm from the exploits of the Hambledon Club (1750–87) and from the lead given by the Marylebone Club from 1787 onwards, the game at Cambridge seems to have been mainly a pursuit of Old Etonians already in residence, who had acquired at school a taste for the wall game in winter and for cricket in summer. We have a record of the Gentlemen of Eton twice playing the Gentlemen of the University in 1755, and sixty years later King's College, to which Etonians normally passed on since Eton and King's were the twin foundations of Henry VI, took on the rest of the University five times between 1816 and 1820. Organization was beginning.

It is therefore not entirely surprising that the University Cricket Club was founded around this time, or that Etonians were involved in it. The likely date is 1820, five years after the defeat of Napoleon at Waterloo – in an extraordinarily tight finish – and one year before his death on St Helena. This was the year in which the affairs of the club were entrusted to two 'treasurers', Messrs H. Hannington and C. Oxenden, shortly to become a triumvirate with the addition of P. Gurdon. By 1822 the Club was flourishing and mustered no less than 74 members – of whom 29 were honorary – and three dons, whose identity is clear from the prefix 'Mr' and 'who subscribe one guinea to have the privilege of the tent, not being allowed to play on the ground'. Herbert Jenner, the first captain and the doyen of early Cambridge cricket, claims a later date for the club's foundation, 1824–5, with three Etonians, himself included, as the first 'treasurers'; but the original scorebook shows either that his memory was fallible or that in his opinion the first four years were too vestigial to count.

By 1827, the year of the first match against Oxford, the organization was sufficient to arrange fixtures against local clubs such as Cambridge Town and Bury, mainly on the 'tented field' called Parker's Piece, but also on the new ground to the north of Parker's Piece. The dress for cricketers at this time is clear from an early print of Parker's Piece: a comely shirt, knee breeches and silk stockings, soft leather shoes, and surmounting all a stylish Panama hat. Neither the batsmen nor the wicket-keepers wore protective garb – one reason for the profusion of byes in the early matches. The bowling was still underarm until 1835 when round-arm was legalized, and the pitches were unscarified and unrolled. It was a far cry from the Fenner's pitches which Cyril Coote would later so lovingly prepare, much to the ultimate benefit of bowler as well as batsman.

It was not until 1871 that religious tests for admission to the University were finally removed. Admission up to this time was therefore restricted to Anglicans, among whom the cricketers tended to come from the leading public schools, notably Eton as we have seen, Harrow and Winchester – though Wykehamists tended to go to Oxford in view of its relative proximity and the existence of New College, also founded by William of Wykeham. The early Cambridge sides, however, also included undergraduates from the less well-known public schools and from grammar schools, and a fair number who were, for whatever reason, educated privately.

In the early nineteenth century team games did not have an important place in undergraduate life, still less in the thinking of university authorities. It is fair to say that cricket, rowing (the first Boat Race took place two years after the first University Match, in 1829) and rugby football were the three pastimes that spread the new gospel of competitive sport, aided by the educational philosophies of Dr Arnold at Rugby (1828–42) and by the growth of the Muscular Christianity of Charles Kingsley and others of his persuasion.

W.J. Ford's indispensable book *The Cambridge University Cricket Club 1820–1901* depends much, for its early part, on the evidence of Herbert Jenner (later Jenner-Fust), who was born in the reign of George III and lived into the reign of Edward VII, four monarchs later. His memory was most impressive, but twice he seems, like Homer, to have nodded. For not only did he have the date of the Club's inception wrong, but he also claimed at least an equal share with Charles Wordsworth for having instituted the match against Oxford. The chief credit for this must go to Wordsworth, up at Oxford from Harrow, who had unsuccessfully suggested a contest in 1826 but was able to use his Cambridge contacts, through his father's being Master of Trinity, to effect the match in 1827. Strangely, there seem to have been no King's men in this first encounter, even though they were mostly Etonians; less strangely, it was Herbert Jenner, who had captained Eton when Charles Wordsworth had captained Harrow, who enthusiastically took up the challenge.

After the first ten matches Cambridge had established a lead of two victories – won five, lost three, with two matches drawn (in Ford's words these were 'unfinished because of rain') – and it is noticeable how even the struggle has been in subsequent years. The evenness has added an extra ingredient to that competitive edge which, despite friendship off the field, has never lost its flavour. Here, Ford is elaborating on the game's importance to the participants:

It is a trite observation that the Varsity match is a sore trial to the nerves of a batsman who has a reputation to maintain. The affection seems to me so peculiar that I think it will repay closer examination. It is not a general want of courage; men are nervous in this match who are not nervous on other occasions, equally or more important, such as Gentlemen v Players. The germs of this affection of the nerves must be there, but it is the occasion that makes them germinate. I think it is due to over-anxiety not to fail on this occasion, which besets the unfortunate victim at the time of going to the wicket, and continues till – who shall say when? He is under a spell, and it lasts till the spell is dispelled, sometimes by disaster. Paying no heed to the verbal equivoque, this affection may fairly be described as 'blue funk', and there is no more honourable victory than to overcome it.

Five of the Light Blue players of this era deserve special mention. Herbert Jenner's contribution depends in part on his playing ability – he was ranked high as batsman, bowler and wicket-keeper in his short playing career – in part on his accepting Wordsworth's challenge, as we have seen, in part on his longevity and his ability to remember, much in evidence at the dinner to mark the Golden Jubilee of the University Match, and in part on his being appointed President of MCC at the tender age of twenty-seven. He went on playing club cricket until late in life, but strange to relate, he never took the trouble to watch W.G. play, although he lived until his ninety-ninth year.

Another who was still alive at the turn of the century, and who was a stern critic of the modern game, was R.J.P. Broughton, of Harrow and Clare. He played in 1836, 1838 and 1839, and was a sound bat and a magnificent field at cover-point, unquestionably the best of his day. He was one of the originals of I Zingari in 1845 and spent over three decades on the MCC Committee. One of his services to the game was to help in the purchase of Lord's by the MCC from Mr Dark, the owner, who seems to have been a bit of a despot in his later years.

The Reverend J.H. Kirwan, who was unable to play in the 1836 match but eventually won his blue in 1839, deserves recognition for two outstanding feats, and for the imputation by some that his bowling action approached a jerk – though no umpire appears to have 'called' him. His first success was taking all ten wickets, and all of them bowled, for Eton *v* MCC on 9 June 1835; his second was to take fifteen of Cambridge Town's wickets, also all bowled, on 24 May 1836. He was a round-arm bowler of considerable pace, who became a Fellow of King's and made his life as a cleric in Cornwall.

C.G. Taylor, who died at the age of fifty-two, was perhaps the best all-rounder of this period, a description that is not confined to cricket alone for he excelled also at real, or royal, tennis (to distinguish it from its upstart but no longer poor relation), and at billiards. After Eton and Emmanuel, and captaincy of cricket in 1838 and 1839, he continued to play county cricket for Sussex for longer than most, being described at his peak as the finest batsman of the era, as well as a good change bowler and a notable fielder. The print I have of him – found in a Winchester cellar – reflects his style and his confident approach to life.

Last but not least, since he was a distinguished father of distinguished sons, comes Lord Lyttelton, who after Eton played for Cambridge in 1838. He had a successful career, in both politics and public service. He was Under-Secretary of State for the Colonies in Robert Peel's last administration and was one of the Public Schools Inquiry Commission in 1861. He was made a Fellow of the Royal Society in 1840, a Privy Counsellor in 1869 and a KCMG in the same year. He also had time in a busy life to become a noted chess player, and was for many years President of the British Chess Association. And the mention of chess is no bad note on which to close this epoch, for chess and cricket share a satisfying cut and thrust on which their devotees thrive.

4, 5 June
At Lord's[1]

1827

Match drawn

Cricket history was made as a result of a challenge issued and accepted by Charles Wordsworth of Oxford and Herbert Jenner of Cambridge. It enabled them to renew the friendly rivalry initiated when they were captains of Harrow and Eton respectively. It was Wordsworth who seems to have done much of the organizing and to have persuaded the Marylebone Cricket Club, now in its fiftieth year of existence, to allow the match to be played on what had become Thomas Lord's third site in 1814. The organisers could scarcely have imagined that the series would be continuing 162 years later, the year its history would be published.

Half of those taking part were to take holy orders, three died within sixteen years of the match, and one, E. Horsman of Cambridge, fought a duel with a fellow MP whom he had accused of secretly sympathizing with the Chartists and speaking disrespectfully of the Queen. Both emerged unscathed.

Rain, alas!, that scourge of cricket administrators and players alike, restricted the match to one day instead of two, on which Oxford made the unusually high total of 258, and then dismissed Cambridge for 92. Jenner drew first blood by bowling his opposite number for 8 – in passing, he kept wicket at the other end as well – but Wordsworth had the last word by taking 7 for 25 with his underarm off-breaks. R. Price's innings of 71 was especially meritorious in view of the quality of the Lord's pitches of the day.

OXFORD

Charles Wordsworth	*b* Jenner	8
H.E. Knatchbull	*c* Romilly	43
W.W. Ellis	*b* Jenner	12
J. Papillon	*run out*	42
E. Pole	*b* Jenner	11
R. Price	*b* Horsman	71
C.H. Bayly	*b* Kingdon	14
J.W Bird.	*b* Jenner	17
T. Denne	*b* Jenner	4
W. Pilkington	*not out*	12
W.H. Lewis	*b* Horsman	14
EXTRAS	B 10	10
	TOTAL	258

CAMBRIDGE

R.H. Webb	*b* Wordsworth	7
S.N. Kingdon	*b* Wordsworth	5
Herbert Jenner	*c* Bird	47
E.H. Pickering	*b* Wordsworth	3
J. Dolphin	*b* Bayly	6
E. Romilly	*b* Wordsworth	8
J.L. Freer	*b* Wordworth	3
C. Templeton	*run out*	5
W. Gifford Cookesley	*b* Wordsworth	0
E.H. Handley	*b* Wordsworth	0
E. Horsman	*not out*	2
EXTRAS	B 6	6
	TOTAL	92

[1] There is some doubt as to whether the match was actually played on 4 and 5 June. *Bell's Life*, a weekly publication at this date, on Sunday 3 June 1827 stated: 'A Grand Match at cricket will be played tomorrow in Lord's Cricket Ground, between the resident Members of the two Universities of Cambridge and Oxford.' On the following Sunday, 10 June, *Bell's Life* stated: 'owing to the unfavourable state of the weather last Monday, the match between Oxford and Cambridge was postponed to a future day'. Unfortunately, the subsequent issues of *Bell's Life* makes no further reference to the match. Charles Wordsworth, the Oxford captain, who played an important part in getting up the match, stated many years afterwards that he did not remember any postponement, but that it was quite possible that the statement contained in *Bell's Life* was correct.

1829

This was one of five matches between 1829 and 1850 played on a ground in Oxford and resulted in a substantial Dark Blue victory by 115 runs. Since Oxford won four out of five of these matches, it is at least arguable that home advantage played a part in their success. To pour salt on the Light Blue wounds, Oxford two days later won the first Boat Race rowed at Henley.

It was a very low-scoring contest, H.E. Knatchbull of Oxford being the only player to score over thirty in a single innings. C.H. Jenner, brother of the previous year's captain and a scholar of Trinity Hall, took five wickets in Oxford's first innings of 129, but Cambridge could manage only 96 in reply. Oxford's steady batting in the second innings enabled them to set Cambridge 192 to win. The feat was well outside the Cambridge batsmen's compass, and they managed only 76, that due largely to R. Price, who had made his mark as a batsman in the 1827 match.

Charles Wordsworth, the architect of the fixture, poignantly made a pair. His account in the Badminton Library shows that he had made rowing in the Oxford boat his priority and that he was suffering from no practice and hands that made it impossible for him to hold a bat. Two wickets, two catches and a Dark Blue victory were ample compensation.

OXFORD	First innings		Second innings	
H.E. Knatchbull	*b* Jenner	7	*c* Hardy	36
W.M. Musters	*st* Jenner	29	*c* Ellis	24
R. Price	*b* Pickering	5	*b* Gordon	2
F.L. Popham	*c* Horsman	22	*st* Jenner	6
F.B. Wright	*c* Meryweather	5	*st* Jenner	27
Charles Wordsworth	*b* Jenner	0	*b* Meryweather	0
C.H. Bayly	*b* Jenner	0	*c* Gordon	12
J.C. Robertson	*b* Jenner	0	*not out*	10
H. Denison	*c* Grazebrook	16	*b* Pickering	18
J.W. Bird	*b* Pickering	18	*b* Meryweather	3
J. Cooke	*not out*	10	*c* St John	0
EXTRAS	B etc. 17	17	B etc. 20	20
	TOTAL	129	TOTAL	158

CAMBRIDGE				
C.H. Jenner .	*c* Price	2	*c* Wordsworth	12
S. Winthrop	*b* Price	24	*b* Price	2
H.G. Grazebrook	*c* Wordsworth	0	*b* Price	24
E.H. Pickering	*run out*	2	*b* Price	14
C.K. Sivewright	*c* Knatchbull	16	*c* Bird	13
Hon. F.A. Gordon	*run out*	7	*run out*	1
E. Horsman	*c* Wright	1	*not out*	0
E.C. Ellis	*b* Wordsworth	0	*b* Price	0
W.S.T. Meryweather	*not out*	20	*b* Wordsworth	0
E. St John	*b* Price	9	*c* Knatchbull	0
J.R. Hardy	*b* Price	8	*run out*	8
EXTRAS	B etc. 7	7	B 2	2
	TOTAL	96	TOTAL	76

1836

The first match for seven years, played at Lord's, resulted in a decisive victory for Oxford by 121 runs. R.J.P. Broughton, a fine mover at cover-point and later to become a Trustee of MCC, was top scorer for Cambridge in both innings. He has pointed out the casual approach then adopted by Cambridge to the University Match, of which the absence of two players for their second innings seems a ready-made example. It appears from Geoffrey Bolton's *History of the OUCC* that this applied to Oxford also.

Oxford's first-innings score of 100, of which the Hon. E.H. Grimston – who later played for the Hertfordshire County XI when he was a Fellow of All Souls – scored 33, was passed by Cambridge by 27 runs; but their second-innings score of 200, which included no less than 63 extras, put them beyond the opposition's reach. Of this total the Carthusian C.W. Beauclerk made 48 and the Etonian C.D. Yonge 36.

C.G. Taylor, the Cantab who was by common consent the leading gentleman player in England, failed twice with the bat but took four wickets in each of Oxford's innings. J.C. Ryle was the best Oxford bowler, taking six of the eight second-innings wickets to fall. It was surely against the odds that a fine Oxford cricketer like Ryle should later become Select Preacher at Cambridge and subsequently, first, Dean of Salisbury, and later, Bishop of Liverpool.

OXFORD	First innings		Second innings	
J. Pycroft	b Farmer	1	b Farmer	10
G. Rawlinson	run out	12	lbw, b Taylor	6
G.T.W. Sibthorp	c Micklethwait, b Taylor	0	b Farmer	8
G. Vance	c Ponsonby, b Farmer	1	lbw, b Farmer	11
Hon. E.H.Grimston	b Farmer	33	b Farmer	0
C.D. Yonge	b Taylor	17	c Oddie, b Taylor	36
J.C. Ryle	c Farmer, b Taylor	2	b Farmer	7
C. Goring	b Farmer	0	c Long, b Taylor	7
C.W. Beauclerk	not out	7	b Taylor	48
S.E. Bathurst	b Taylor	3	not out	4
C.G. Wynne-Finch	run out	0	hw, b Farmer	0
EXTRAS	B 9, W 12, N-B 3	24	B 36, W 21, N-B 6	63
	TOTAL	100	TOTAL	200

CAMBRIDGE				
W.T. Thompson	b Sibthorp	0	absent	0
F.E. Long	b Ryle	4	b Ryle	0
C.G. Taylor	b Sibthorp	2	c Goring, b Sibthorp	6
H.W. Booth	hw, b Grimston	14	b Sibthorp	7
Hon. F.G.B. Ponsonby	b Goring	11	b Ryle	0
Hon. J.H.M. Sutton	b Goring	4	absent	0
F.N. Micklethwait	b Ryle	6	b Ryle	0
R.J.P. Broughton	b Sibthorp	18	c Pycroft, b Ryle	19
H.H. Oddie	b Ryle	9	b Ryle	3
E.F. Hodgson	not out	4	not out	6
A. Farmer	b Ryle	0	b Ryle	4
EXTRAS	B 45, W 9, N-B 1	55	B 5, W 2	7
	TOTAL	127	TOTAL	52

1838

This was the first of the regular annual sequence of University Matches. It was played at Lord's and Oxford clocked up another easy win, this time by 98 runs. Two Cambridge players and one for Oxford missed one innings each through 'absence caused by the sudden death of Mr Seymour of King's College' – for reasons that cricket history does not relate.

As in each of the first four matches, Oxford batted first and thanks to J.D. Durell's 53 reached 137, six wickets being taken by C.G. Taylor and four by E. Sayres, who played for the Sussex County XI. Cambridge were dismissed for a paltry 57, thanks largely to the bowling of A.J. Lowth,

who took five wickets. Lowth had the unusual distinction of having been to both Eton and Winchester as a boy, and he spent the final twenty years of his life as Rector of St Swithun, Winchester, the parish that boasts the small church in the archway between the College and the Cathedral.

G. Vance made a brave 41 out of 65 in Oxford's second innings, with Taylor and Sayres again sharing the wickets. Cambridge could muster only 47 runs; Lord Lyttelton, bearer of a distinguished Cambridge name, completed an unhappy 'pair' by being run out.

OXFORD	First innings		Second innings	
Hon. R. Grimston	*c and b* Sayres	10	*lbw, b* Taylor	13
R.A. Bathurst	*b* Sayres	0	*c* Massey, *b* Sayres	1
A.J. Lowth	*b* Taylor	4	*b* Taylor	0
C.F. Trower	*lbw, b* Sayres	24	*c* Sayres, *b* Taylor	0
A. Coote	*b* Taylor	10	*c* Bastard, *b* Sayres	0
G. Vance	*b* Taylor	1	*b* Taylor	41
J.D. Durell	*c* Thackeray, *b* Sayres	53	*b* Taylor	1
J.C. Ryle	*b* Taylor	5	*absent*	0
C.W.A. Napier	*b* Taylor	12	*c* Koe, *b* Sayres	0
G.B. Lee	*c* Lyttelton, *b* Taylor	5	*b* Sayres	2
N. Darnell	*not out*	3	*not out*	4
EXTRAS	B 5, W 5	10	W 2, N-B 1	3
	TOTAL	137	TOTAL	65

CAMBRIDGE				
W. Massey	*b* Lowth	3	*b* Lee	0
Lord Lyttelton	*b* Lowth	0	*run out*	0
R.J.P. Broughton	*b* Lee	8	*b* Lowth	2
J. Grout	*b* Lee	5	*b* Lee	15
C.G. Taylor	*c* Bathurst, *b* Lowth	10	*b* Lowth	2
A. Thomas	*b* Darnell	6	*not out*	3
F. Thackeray	*c* Darnell, *b* Lowth	19	*b* Lee	3
E. Sayres	*not out*	2	*b* Lee	0
J.H. Bastard	*b* Lowth	0	*absent*	0
B.D. Koe	*run out*	0	*b* Darnell	11
J. Abercrombie	*absent*	0	*b* Lowth	0
EXTRAS	B 1, W 3	4	B 3, W 8	11
	TOTAL	57	TOTAL	47

1839

Cambridge were a considerable side and, assisted by Oxford's being able to muster only ten men, won convincingly by an innings and 125 runs. J.H. Kirwan, who also opened the Cambridge batting, had established a reputation at Eton for being a very fast bowler and he took five Oxford wickets in their lowly total of 88. His team-mate Broughton later recalled that Kirwan's bowling 'looked something like a jerk', but the umpires do not seem to have called him. Kirwan's most notable performance was bowling out all ten MCC batsmen in their second innings at Eton on 9 July 1835. Kirwan did not have things all his own way, however, for Broughton also claimed that he and Taylor used to stand out of

their ground to Kirwan and hit him 'all over the Piece'.

Cambridge replied with 287, thanks largely to C.G. Taylor's 65 and H. Parker's 43. A total of 46 wides comes as a surprise, but an eye-witness relates that 'the bowlers evidently at times lost their temper at not being enabled to disturb the wickets of their opponents'. All credit to one of the Oxford opening bowlers, G.B. Lee – he became Warden of Winchester College from 1861 until his death – who took nine wickets, all but two of them bowled. Oxford could muster only 74, E. Sayres taking five wickets to add to his three in the first innings.

OXFORD[1]	First innings		Second innings	
G.B. Lee	b Sayres	15	b Sayres	17
R.A. Bathurst	c Maples, b Sayres	1	b Sayres	2
H.J. Torre	b Kirwan	18	not out	13
C.W.A. Napier	b Kirwan	1	b Sayres	1
A. Coote	b Kirwan	11	c Massey, b Sayres	0
G.J. Ford	b Sayres	9	b Thackeray	9
J.H. Wynne	c Kirwan	0	b Kirwan	4
R. Garth	run out	4	b Sayres	5
H.S. Russell	b Kirwan	8	run out	2
N. Darnell	not out	1	b Kirwan	3
EXTRAS	B 12, W 7, N-B 1	20	B 15, W 2, N-B 1	18
	TOTAL	88	TOTAL	74

CAMBRIDGE		
T.A. Anson	b Lee	7
J.H. Kirwan	b Lee	25
W. Massey	b Lee	0
J. Grout	c Darnell, b Lee	18
C.G. Taylor	b Lee	65
H. Parker	b Lee	43
R.J.P. Broughton	c Darnell, b Wynne	20
F. Thackeray	b Lee	22
W. Maples	b Lee	1
W. de St Croix	not out	11
E. Sayres	st Torre, b Lee	5
EXTRAS	B 24, W 46	70
	TOTAL	287

[1] With only 10 men

1840

Cambridge had another good side which fielded well and rose to the occasion, and they beat Oxford by a comfortable 63 runs, despite the Dark Blues being heavily backed. It was a low-scoring match which was decided, after Cambridge had led on the first innings by a mere 10 runs, by a fine second-wicket partnership between W.P. Pickering, one of the original members of the Surrey County Cricket Club and I Zingari, and T.A. Anson, who became the finest wicket-keeper of the day and also rowed in the Cambridge boat that won the Grand Challenge Cup at Henley in 1841. Oxford conceded over three times as many extras as Cambridge.

A.J. Lowth, who had taken eight wickets in the 1838 match for Oxford, this year took ten. H.O. Nethercote, High Sheriff of Northamptonshire in 1872 and author of *The Pytchley Hunt*, took five second-innings Cambridge wickets. For Cambridge W. de St Croix, who was born at Windsor Castle, and E. Sayres, who had come up to Trinity after private education, shared sixteen wickets in the match. G.J. Ford was the only Oxford batsman to score more than twenty. Dark Blue backers who had lost money must have wished for better technique and better temperament.

CAMBRIDGE	First innings		Second innings	
W.P. Pickering	b Spinks	12	b Lowth	27
W. de St Croix	b Spinks	4	b Lowth	0
T.A. Anson	c Garth, b Lowth	6	not out	29
W. Mills	b Lowth	14	b Nethercote	0
F. Thackeray	b Lowth	0	b Lowth	8
Hon. A. Savile	b Lowth	3	b Nethercote	1
G. Barker	b Lowth	0	b Lowth	4
A. Meetkerke	run out	8	b Nethercote	0
E. Sayres	c Wynne, b Spinks	3	b Nethercote	1
G.F. Burr	b Lowth	0	b Nethercote	6
J.H. Bastard	not out	0	b Lowth	5
EXTRAS	b 20, w 12	32	b 2, w 27	29
	TOTAL	82	TOTAL	110

OXFORD				
H.J. Torre	run out	7	b Sayres	1
A.J. Lowth	b Sayres	6	run out	5
W.G. Clarke	c Anson, b St Croix	0	b St Croix	0
A. Coote	run out	10	b Sayres	4
G.J. Ford	b Sayres	18	b Sayres	25
J. Coker	b St Croix	0	not out	8
R. Garth	run out	2	b Sayres	3
H.O. Nethercote	b Sayres	8	c Anson, b St Croix	3
J.H. Wynne	b Sayres	4	b St Croix	2
T. Spinks	b Sayres	0	c Savile, b St Croix	0
N. Darnell	not out	0	b St Croix	4
EXTRAS	b 10, w 7	17	b 2	2
	TOTAL	72	TOTAL	57

1841

This was a close match right to the finish, and when the ninth Oxonian came in in the last innings, only 13 runs were needed. R. Garth, who played for the Surrey County XI in 1844 and became MP for Guildford and, later, the Chief Justice of Bengal, was already top scorer in the match with 36 not out, and he now hit a fine four. At this point, E. Sayres, who took eight wickets in the match, bowled two of his partners for nought. Lord William Ward, who was thus on a hat-trick, made cricket history by being at this dramatic moment 'absent 0'. *Post*, but presumably not *propter*, *hoc*, he became President of MCC.

For Cambridge J.B.R. Bulwer, who was to become MP for Ipswich and to decline the post of Chief Justice of Madras, made 31 and T.A. Anson 30, but their number eleven, H.L. Jenner – ardent botanist, ecclesiologist, and poet in three languages who would later become Bishop of Dunedin in 1856 – was 'absent 0'. The mind boggles at which interest he might have been pursuing! W. de St Croix again proved an effective bowling partner for Sayres. As in the 1840 match, Oxford bowled more wides than Cambridge, for whom E.S.E. Hartopp was a famous long-stop. H.O. Nethercote made history by hitting a 'sixer', a rare feat in those days of low actions and little bounce.

CAMBRIDGE	First innings		Second innings	
E.A.F. Harenc	b Mills	0	b Ward	2
T.A. Anson	run out	15	c Dryden, b Cowburn	30
J.B.R. Bulwer	c Cowburn, b Lowth	31	c and b Lowth	0
A. Hume	b Lowth	0	b Cowburn	16
G.J. Boudier	c Nethercote, b Ward	11	c Loftus, b Mills	24
W. Mills	not out	2	run out	0
W. de St Croix	c Garth, b Ward	6	run out	4
J.B. Turner	c Garth, b Ward	10	b Ward	1
E. Sayres	c Dryden, b Lowth	0	st Garth, b Mills	3
E.S.E. Hartopp	c and b Lowth	0	not out	7
H.L. Jenner	absent	0	b Cowburn	5
EXTRAS	b 12, w 16	28	b 7, w 21	28
	TOTAL	103	TOTAL	120

OXFORD				
A.E. Dryden	c Turner, b Sayres	28	b Mills	7
A.J. Lowth	run out	24	c Jenner, b St Croix	3
H.M. Curteis	b St Croix	0	b Mills	0
R. Garth	b St Croix	16	not out	40
H.O. Nethercote	b Sayres	11	b St Croix	5
G.C. Cherry	b St Croix	1	b Sayres	17
Lord H.Y.A. Loftus	b St Croix	1	b Sayres	0
R. Lowndes	b Sayres	3	b Mills	22
Lord William Ward	c Jenner, b Sayres	1	absent	0
A. Cowburn	not out	2	b Mills	3
B.S.T. Mills	b Sayres	0	b Sayres	0
EXTRAS	b 3, w 13	16	b 7, w 8	15
	TOTAL	103	TOTAL	112

1842

Following on the extremely close match of 1841, this was a surprisingly decisive Light Blue victory by 162 runs – comparable to their innings victory of 1839. Exactly half this deficit consisted of extras. T.A. Anson, Cambridge's Etonian captain for the third year, led from the front with a useful innings of 41, matched by an exactly equal number of byes and wides. It seemed in keeping with his consistency that he became Rector of Longford, Derby, for only one year short of a half-century. B.S.T. Mills, whose forty-one years as Rector of Lawshall, Bury St Edmunds ran him close, was the most successful Oxford bowler.

W. de St Croix, from Eton, had a field day, taking six wickets in the first Oxford innings and five in the second.

After Oxford had been dismissed for 63, Cambridge batted with unusual consistency; the Etonian A. Hume, one day to become Senior Fellow of King's, was the top scorer with 29. A feature of the Light Blue performance in Oxford's second innings was the useful supportive bowling of the Harrovian W. Mills, who was to become a member of the staff of *Law Reports* and to edit several law books.

CAMBRIDGE	First innings		Second innings	
W. Mills	*b* Mills	13	*b* Mills	7
T.L. French	*c* Cherry, *b* Curteis	9	*b* Curteis	10
T.A. Anson	*c* Dryden, *b* Rashleigh	41	*b* Ward	24
W.P. Pickering	*b* Mills	5	*b* Mills	21
W.B. Trevelyan	*c* Dryden, *b* Ward	1	*b* Curteis	1
E.M. Dewing	*not out*	16	*run out*	12
A. Hume	*b* Mills	1	*b* Mills	29
C. Morse	*b* Ward	0	*b* Ward	12
R.N. Blaker	*b* Ward	4	*b* Curteis	22
W. de St Croix	*b* Ward	6	*c* Coker, *b* Ward	2
E.S.E. Hartopp	*b* Mills	1	*not out*	1
EXTRAS	B 24, W 17, N-B 1	42	B 20, W 14, N-B 5	39
	TOTAL	139	TOTAL	180

OXFORD				
W.H. Townsend	*b* Mills	1	*b* Mills	5
A.E. Dryden	*run out*	0	*c* Anson, *b* St Croix	12
J. Rashleigh	*b* St Croix	0	*c* Anson, *b* Mills	2
G.C. Cherry	*b* St Croix	0	*b* St Croix	6
J. Coker	*b* St Croix	21	*b* Mills	5
H.M. Curteis	*c* Trevelyan, *b* St Croix	5	*b* St Croix	5
T. Hughes	*b* St Croix	0	*not out*	15
H.E. Moberly	*c* Morse, *b* St Croix	0	*b* St Croix	5
Lord William Ward	*c* Anson, *b* Mills	11	*run out*	10
R.J.C.R. Ker	*run out*	8	*b* Mills	0
B.S.T. Mills	*not out*	5	*b* St Croix	13
EXTRAS	B 7, W 5	12	B 10, W 6	16
	TOTAL	63	TOTAL	94

8, 9 June
Bullingdon Green, Oxford

1843

Cambridge won by
54 runs

Both Lord's and the Magdalen ground were so waterlogged that the match was played on Bullingdon Green. The ground was as slippery as the wind was high. Despite being for the first time more prodigal of extras than Oxford, Cambridge won convincingly by 54 runs. They owed much in the first innings to W.B. Trevelyan, of Harrow and Caius, who scored 44 not out, and to G.J. Boudier, who contributed a lively 25. He would play an even more responsible role as a chaplain at Sevastopol and Scutari during the Crimean War. T.L. French was the top scorer in the Light Blue second innings; he later returned to Suffolk, the county of his birth, to be Rector of Thrandeston for over fifty years.

Extras were top scorer in both the Oxford innings; W.A. Commerell, an original member of the Surrey County Cricket Club, was the only player to top twenty. For Cambridge R.N. Blaker, of Elizabeth College, Guernsey and St John's, and grandfather of R.N.R. Blaker (Cambridge blue 1900–3), took five wickets in each of the Dark Blue innings; H.E. Moberley, a Wykehamist who became Sub-Warden of both New College and Trinity College, Glenalmond, and returned to Winchester as an Assistant Master at the College and Rector of St Michael's, took fourteen wickets in the match. Their bowling was described as excellent and was clearly the decisive factor.

CAMBRIDGE	First innings		Second innings	
G.J. Boudier	b Ainslie	25	b Mills	18
A.M.W. Christopher	b Moberly	17	c Moberly, b Mills	1
T.L. French	b Moberly	4	c Townsend, b Moberly	32
Hon. F.S. Grimston	c Randolph, b Moberly	6	c Randolph, b Moberly	3
W.B. Trevelyan	not out	44	b Mills	0
C. Morse	b Moberly	0	b Moberly	1
E.M. Dewing	c and b Moberly	6	b Moberly	5
R.N. Blaker	b Ainslie	0	b Moberly	12
W. Mills	b Moberly	0	b Moberly	0
C.D. Crofts	b Ainslie	7	b Moberly	0
S.N. Micklethwait	b Moberly	11	not out	1
EXTRAS	B 4, w 16, N-B 1	21	B 5, w 16	21
	TOTAL	141	TOTAL	94

OXFORD				
A.E. Dryden	b Blaker	2	c Micklethwait, b Mills	7
W.A. Commerell	b Mills	21	b Blaker	0
M.M. Ainslie	b Blaker	11	run out	0
J. Coker	b Mills	5	b Blaker	1
F. Lear	b Blaker	1	b Blaker	6
H.E. Moberly	b Blaker	10	b Mills	11
G.C. Cherry	c Grimston, b Mills	7	b Blaker	7
J. Leslie	b Mills	8	c Trevelyan, b Mills	12
J. Randolph	b Blaker	0	b Blaker	0
W.H. Townsend	run out	2	run out	4
B.S.T. Mills	not out	0	not out	1
EXTRAS	B 10, w 23	33	B 5, w 27	32
	TOTAL	100	TOTAL	81

4, 5 July
At Lord's

1844

Match drawn

Incessant rain on the second day produced the second draw of the series and the last for forty-four years. The wicket was very slow and difficult and Oxford did well to reach 96 in their first innings, V.S.C. Smith and W. Marcon being equal top scorers. Smith would later play frequently for the All-England XI, by whom he was known as 'Podder' after the hero of the Dingley Dell *versus* All-Muggleton XI match to which Charles Dickens brought such realism and life.

Cambridge could manage only 69 in reply, extras being top scorer and the Wykehamist A.M. Hoare, who played one year for the Surrey County XI, being the only player to make double figures. J. Coker, later Fellow of New College, led the way in the Dark Blue second innings with the best score in the match, 27, but G.P. Ottey, one of the few Rugbeians to gain a cricket blue in the early years, took three cheap wickets to keep Cambridge in the game. The contest had then to be left in suspended animation.

OXFORD	First innings		Second innings	
C. Randolph	*b* Ottey	0	*b* Ottey	6
J. Coker	*c* Pell, *b* Sykes	2	*b* Ottey	27
P. Williams	*b* French	13	*b* Ottey	0
V.S.C. Smith	*b* French	24	*run out*	3
W. Marcon	*b* Sykes	24	*not out*	8
H.D. des Vœux	*b* Sykes	3		
F. Lear	*b* Ottey	6		
M.M. Ainslie	*run out*	0	*not out*	2
H.E. Moberly	*run out*	0		
G. Worthington	*run out*	0		
G.E. Yonge	*not out*	2		
EXTRAS	B 11, W 11	22	B 2, W 9	11
	TOTAL	96	TOTAL (4 wkts)	57

CAMBRIDGE		
Hon. F.S. Grimston	*c and b* Yonge	7
E.M. Dewing	*b* Yonge	0
A.M. Hoare	*b* Randolph	11
T.L. French	*b* Randolph	1
H.B. Raymond Barker	*c* Yonge, *b* Moberly	8
W. Sykes	*b* Moberly	7
C. Morse	*b* Moberly	6
O.C. Pell	*not out*	6
T. Dikes	*b* Yonge	2
S.T. Clissold	*b* Yonge	2
G.P. Ottey	*c* Lear, *b* Randolph	0
EXTRAS	B 12, W 5, N-B 2	19
	TOTAL	69

2
1845–1854
New Grounds for Improvement

OXFORD *Enclosure on Cowley Marsh*

The Great Enclosure Act of 1845 released large areas of common land which had previously been protected against enclosure. Cowley Common was put up for auction, and the University paid £2000 to acquire the Magdalen ground. An agreement was signed by Doctor Plumtree, Master of University College and Vice-Chancellor, and William Ridding, steward of the University Cricket Club, whereby the University handed over the Magdalen ground to the OUCC who became permanent lessees of the new enclosed area.

After a further five years, although still without a proper constitution, the OUCC became owners of their ground. This was in 1850, by coincidence the last year that the Varsity Match was played in Oxford; ever since it has been held at Lord's.

The enclosure of much of Cowley Common gave the opportunity for many colleges to establish their own pitches: Exeter, Balliol, Trinity, University, Oriel, New College, Wadham, Queen's, Pembroke and Lincoln leased, shared or bought fields. Christ Church made a ground on the Iffley Road which was rated then, as now, one of the finest in Oxford.

As the Industrial Revolution swept the country, middle-class prosperity leapt forward. In the customary large Victorian families it was a regular practice for the eldest son to succeed to the family estate; the next often found his way to the army, and one or sometimes more of the younger brothers went into the Church. Most young men studied Classics at school, and carried on in this discipline at Oxford and Cambridge. The natural progression was then 'Church' or 'Law'.

Most parishes, no matter how small, would boast at least one curate in addition to the incumbent, and it is not hard to see how the tradition of the sporting parson may have arisen. Much involved in local pursuits, the country rector or vicar might well consider it an added virtue for a curate to offer skill on the cricket field. In the Oxford XI of 1827 there were seven who went into the Church. In the 1840s and '50s there were seldom less than six. The majority went on to be parish priests, and as such were figures of influence and importance in village life.

J. Aitken of Exeter College, a blue from 1848 to 1850, must be considered one of Oxford's finest all-rounders. His greatest distinction was as an oarsman; not only was he a true double blue (cricket and rowing), but he also, with J.W. Chitty (one of four who were later barristers from the 1848 eleven), won the Silver Goblets at Henley. Aitken later became a Canon of Gibraltar Cathedral. J.C. Patteson, from the 1849 side, became a missionary in the New Hebrides, and at the remarkably young age of thirty-four was consecrated Bishop of Melanesia; tragically he was murdered by natives ten years later. Perhaps his early consecration underlines the hazardous nature of this appointment.

Another of the priests who made his mark in this decade was C.S. Bere, from the 1851 eleven, who wrote, collected and translated songs and hymns; among the collections was 'We plough the fields and scatter'. The Jubilee Dinner of 1877 came about through his efforts, and he even composed an ode for the occasion. The first and last verses read as follows:

> Fifty years have sped since first,
> Keen to win their laurel,
> Oxford round a Wordsworth clustered
> Cambridge under Jenner mustered
> Met in friendly quarrel.

> Let us, then, of cricket day
> Long repeat the story;
> Toast we here the noble game,
> Toast we those who made its fame,
> and upheld its glory.

In the spring of 1852, at a dinner in the rooms of C.S. Currer, a Fellow of Merton, the Harlequin Cricket Club was founded. Currer had been in the side in 1847; C.J.B. Marsham (Charlie) was present, also a blue from the previous year, and, one must assume, W. Ridding, the University captain. At least, even if Ridding was not there, it was early accepted that the captain must, *ex officio*, be a member of the Committee and as such has always had an important say in the election of Harlequins. Under the rules there may be no more than twenty members in residence, most of whom will be blues or those who have come close to a Lord's invitation. Freshmen were not normally eligible.

In the earliest days, Harlequins wore shirts of crimson faced with buff, and blue trousers; this dress seems not to have lasted many years, although Harlequin shirts were known into the nineties. Alongside these, even the 'pyjamas' of today's night cricket pale into insignificance. It was many years later that these spectacular colours became familiar to a wider public, most notably through Plum Warner, who was seldom seen in a different cap; later Douglas Jardine wore the colours with dogged courage on the Bodyline tour of Australia.

The Harlequins played their first match shortly after the initial meeting. This was against the Quidnuncs, and was followed, on 24 and 25 May 1852, by a contest with Christ Church. Charlie Marsham was later President of the Club and held this office for thirty-five years; it is worth remembering that among his other achievements he gained a 'double first' in the original meaning of the term, a first in 'Literae Humaniores' followed immediately by another in mathematics.

Among other personalities of this decade V.S.C. Smith, twice captain, deserves a special mention, not only because in 1846 he led Oxford to their first win over Cambridge since 1838, albeit on the Magdalen ground, but also in that he had the distinction of captaining Oxford when, later that year, they defeated the MCC on the first occasion the follow-on rule was introduced.

G.E. Yonge was the first of a small number to play five times in the Varsity Match; bowling fast round-arm, he claimed over-all forty-three Cambridge wickets, of which thirty were clean bowled. The Ridding family also made a significant contribution, although there is some doubt which member of the family was captain in 1849 – it seems most likely to have been Arthur. In that year J.W. Chitty kept wicket in the Varsity Match, yet W. Ridding was selected in this role for the Gentlemen.

A. Cazenove was another formidable bowler of the period; he played with some success at Lord's in 1852, but then in 1853, despite major personal successes before and after the Varsity Match, he did not play against Cambridge. There is no reference to injury, but this must surely have been the cause. He took all ten wickets in one innings against Oxfordshire, clean bowling five in one over – a four-ball over. Umpires made mistakes even then! He had another six wickets in the second innings. Oxford won by 7 runs.

In 1854 the highest individual score made for Oxford was 57; these runs were made by R. Hankey against a United England XI, and yet he was not selected for Lord's. As Geoffrey Bolton said:

Never was the system, or lack of system, in selecting the side more glaringly exposed than in this year. For Chandos-Leigh, who had already failed twice against Cambridge and had in this season made three 0's in five innings, was preferred to an all-rounder of the calibre of Hankey or A.P. Law. The principle seems to have been adopted that Marsham and Payne would get Cambridge out so cheaply that the batting would look after itself.

And so it proved.

It is interesting to reflect on the use of the long-stop. It was said of W. Marcon, in 1844, that he bowled 'so fast as to require two long-stops to keep the byes under'. It may safely be assumed that the importance of this position arose from round-arm bowling and the rustic nature of outfields. C.H. Ridding is described as a famous long-stop as well as a good bat. From his time, byes began to diminish. His younger brother was a talented wicket-keeper.

Old lovers of the game speak with enthusiasm of the time when Mr W. Ridding was wicket-keeper, and Mr C.H. Ridding long-stop behind him; and they were both played for the Gentlemen against the Players at Lord's in 1849.

CAMBRIDGE *The legacy of Fenner and Ward*

If the CUCC's first quarter of a century saw the halting steps of the infant club, counterpointing the halting establishment of an annual University Match itself, then the years between 1845 and 1854 saw an increase in sturdiness and a sense of purpose.

First in time and importance was the opening in 1848 of a new cricket ground, destined to become famous and needed, in the shorter term, for a developing fixture list. F.P. Fenner, a crack batsman of the Town elevens, had two years earlier leased from Gonville and Caius a field to the south of Parker's Piece, and he now, not without an eye to the main chance, sublet it to the University Cricket Club. It will not have escaped the historically minded that the year of the opening of Fenner's was the year also of the birth at Downend, near Bristol, of W.G. Grace – he who, by his personality and his performance, in Ranji's felicitous phrase, 'turned the one-stringed instrument into a many-chorded lyre'.

Two months to the day before W.G.'s arrival, on 18 and 19 May 1848, Cambridge played their opening match at Fenner's, against the MCC, whom they had first played in 1835. A win by six wickets was a happy omen for both the club and the ground. The fact that once again the University Match was played at Oxford suggests that the new square, made of grass and not rolled mud, left something to be desired; that was a view supported by W.S. Deacon, the Cambridge captain in 1850, who was knocked down senseless by a ball in the eye from young Lillywhite (probably referring to James Lillywhite senior, who would have been twenty-five at the time).

A fixture list of eight matches in 1845 – the main ones were against the MCC home and away, the Town and Oxford – remained constant throughout the decade, and it was not until 1855 that the list was extended. The best batting averages during this decade reflected the roughness of the pitches – they were rarely more than, and usually well below, twenty. The two exceptions that prove the rule are worth a reference: an undergraduate by the name of Macniven – whose initial is later listed as E – had an average, after three matches in 1848, of no less than 97.50; and W.M. Leake, after two matches in 1851, had one of 43.50. Bowling averages are not mentioned in Ford's book until the next decade.

There was level-pegging in the first six years of this decade's matches against Oxford – unlike the political balance in Europe, where reaction was signally to triumph over reform. At home, the tragi-comic finale to Chartism, not far from Kennington Oval, seemed to imply that the companionship of cricket was preferable to the conflict of uncivil strife. Oxford's four consecutive victories between 1851 and 1854 ensured that this decade was the only one until after the Second World War in which they had the ascendancy.

The new confidence was marked by the foundation in 1851, the year of the Great Exhibition, of the Quidnunc CC, largely to play holiday and country-house cricket – though Eton and Harrow were to be early opponents. The first officers were: R.T. King, A.W. Baillie and F.H. Whymper. In those days blues were not, as now, automatically elected, but despite this the Quidnunc cap was rated second only to the Light Blue cap as an honour. The Harlequin CC was founded at Oxford around the same time and on the same principles. The revival of the Quidnunc *v* Harlequin match in recent years has given much pleasure, especially since 1986, when Arundel Castle became the delightful venue.

Six players from the second decade of University Matches deserve closer scrutiny. E.W. Blore had a successful academic career at Cambridge from 1862 to the year of his death, 1885, when he was Senior Fellow and Vice-Master of Trinity. Only the year before, he had gladly accepted the posts of both President and Treasurer of the CUCC on the death of the Reverend A.R. Ward – about whom more later – being ready to repay in office the pleasure he had experienced in the sides of 1848 to 1851, the year he was captain. Ford speaks highly of Blore's ability as a slow bowler with a very strong break-back who kept an excellent length. His reputation as 'undoubtedly the best Eton bowler of the day' carries conviction.

R.T. King, already mentioned as one of the first three officers of the Quidnuncs, came up to Emmanuel from Oakham, and during the four years he was in the Cambridge side, 1846 to 1849, he proved himself a fine all-round cricketer. He was a powerful hitter, a fast round-arm bowler and the best point of his day, inevitably dubbed the 'King of Points'. After taking holy orders he found time, in a more leisurely age, to play for Leicestershire, and he was admired as an inspiring coach and a good judge of the game.

Sir Charles (as he later became) Pontifex played for Cambridge in 1851 and 1853, when he was second in the batting averages to A.R. Ward. He was not only a talented batsman but also a left-arm medium-pace bowler good enough to have dismissed Alfred Lubbock, at his best, for a pair. Even that great Etonian player and subsequent cricket master at Eton, R.A.H. Mitchell, never had a season so brilliant as Lubbock did in 1863. After bowling Lubbock for a 'pair', therefore, the bowler had every reason for thinking himself, if only for a fleeting moment, *'Pontifex Maximus'*.

S.M.E. Kempson came up from Cheltenham to Caius and played in the University Match of 1851. His 48 contributed in some measure to the Light Blue victory, but it was as a medium-pace round-arm bowler, with a shuffling run-up and the ability to make the ball fizz off the ground, that he will be remembered, and especially for bowling unchanged with Sir Frederick Bathurst in the 1853 Gentlemen *v* Players match at Lord's. The Gentlemen's victory by 60 runs owed much to this heroic feat. He later pursued a successful academic career in India, and subsequently at Cambridge and the Staff College.

David Buchanan, who played as a fast left-arm bowler in 1850, had considerable success for the Gentlemen of England and the Free Foresters against the Universities, but as a slow bowler. He was the first of the off-theorists who invited indiscretion from the batsmen. His claim to fame rests on his performances for the Gentlemen, for whom he began playing at the age of thirty-nine. During the years 1868 to 1874 he played in ten matches and captured 88 wickets for 1292 runs, with an average of 14.10. He served as captain and treasurer of both the Warwickshire CC and the Rugby CC and was a man whom Mr Jorrocks, who saw the light of day in 1838, would have been pleased to call friend, for he was a fine shot, a clever angler and a first-class man to hounds.

If, finally, one had to select a single individual who was the epitome of loyalty to the CUCC in the middle years of the century, this honour must fall to A.R., later the Reverend A.R. Ward, captain in 1854 but prevented by illness (or indisposition, see match account) from playing against Oxford. He was elected President of the CUCC in 1873 and ensured that the new pavilion, erected in 1877, was handed over to the trustees free of debt. We detect here echoes of his father, William Ward, for some years MP for the City of London, whose generosity ensured the survival of Lord's Cricket Ground at a difficult moment, and whose 278 against Norfolk in 1820 remained a record for that ground until surpassed by Percy Holmes of Yorkshire, who made 315 not out in 1925, and then Jack Hobbs of Surrey, who made 316 not out the following year.

Ward was no great cricketer, but he was a nonpareil supporter and sustainer. He was asked, in gratitude, to manage the new pavilion and to this task he brought a rare singleness of purpose. Walking sticks were strictly forbidden for fear of damage to the oak panels on which the Cambridge sides were, and still are, inscribed in blue and gilt lettering. Dogs too were banned – with the notable exceptions of Hugo and Rollo, the successive companions of the Master of Peterhouse. This liberal patron of cricket had his dogs made life members to escape the ban.

Ward had his fads as well as his fervour. One was not allowed to call Fenner's 'Fenner's', but the 'Cambridge University Cricket Ground'; one must rhyme 'bowl' with 'howl' and not with 'hole'. But he was wondrously hospitable to undergraduates and visitors alike, his favourite meal being breakfast, for which the menu never varied: 'noo-laid eggs, Noomarket sausages and salmon cutlets', all washed down with Bollinger. Ward continued to support the CUCC until he died in 1884.

1845

Cambridge won comfortably by six wickets in a match in which scoring was low and play unsensational. Oxford were dismissed for 66, thanks to three run-outs of early batsmen and the useful bowling of the Rugbeian S.F. Rippingall, who took ten wickets in the match. He was later to show his versatility by winning the Diamond Sculls at Henley in 1853. Cambridge replied with 112, to which another Rugbeian, G.P. Ottey – one day to become MP first for Chippenham and then for North Wilts – contributed a steady 27 and R.P. Long a free-scoring 36. G.E. Yonge, born at Eton

and later to become a barrister and Treasurer of the County of Southampton, had the distinction of taking eight Light Blue wickets in an innings.

The Harrovian the Hon. F.S. Grimston kept wicket impressively and made a rare stumping to end H.E. Moberly's defiant 30. Yonge was 'caught sub' – the first such entry on a University Match scorecard. Thanks to a steady 22 not out by S.C. Campbell, of Bury St Edmunds and Corpus, subsequently a priest, Cambridge had little trouble in knocking off the necessary runs.

OXFORD	First innings		Second innings	
R. Honywood	*b* Wroth	5	*b* Rippingall	5
P. Williams	*run out*	2	*b* Wroth	6
V.S.C. Smith	*run out*	9	*b* Rippingall	8
M.M. Ainslie	*run out*	0	*b* Wroth	3
C. Randolph	*b* Wroth	1	*c* Wroth, *b* Rippingall	8
H.C.T. Hildyard	*b* Rippingall	19	*run out*	0
G.E. Hughes	*c* Hughes, *b* Rippingall	12	*b* Rippingall	0
H.E. Moberly	*b* Wroth	2	*st* Grimston, *b* Rippingall	30
G.E. Yonge	*b* Rippingall	0	*c* sub, *b* Wroth	16
C.H. Ridding	*c* Nicholson, *b* Rippingall	8	*not out*	12
L.C. Randolph	*not out*	0	*b* Rippingall	0
EXTRAS	B 2, W 6	8	B 1, W 5, N-B 2	8
	TOTAL	66	TOTAL	96

CAMBRIDGE				
S.C. Campbell	*b* C. Randolph	11	*not out*	22
G.P. Ottey	*c* Williams, *b* C. Randolph	27	*c* L.C. Randolph, *b* C. Randolph	9
Hon. F.S. Grimston	*b* Yonge	0	*run out*	0
J. Nicholson	*b* Yonge	10	*not out*	7
E.M. Dewing	*c* Ridding, *b* Yonge	5	*b* Yonge	7
O.C. Pell	*b* Yonge	4		
H.T. Wroth	*c* Williams, *b* Yonge	4		
R.P. Long	*b* Yonge	36	*b* C. Randolph	0
F.L. Currie	*b* Yonge	6		
T.F. Hughes	*b* Yonge	0		
S.F. Rippingall	*not out*	0		
EXTRAS	B 6, W 3	9	B 2, W 4	6
	TOTAL	112	TOTAL (4 WKTS)	51

11, 12 June
At Magdalen Ground, Oxford

1846

Oxford won by
3 wickets

This match was played on the Magdalen College ground, and thanks to better bowling and fine fielding Oxford won by three wickets. Having twice defeated MCC, Cambridge were firm favourites, but their cause was not helped by the absence through illness of the captain, A.M. Hoare, and by the fact that J. Walker, who in 1862 made a famous 98 against the Players, did not bat in the first innings. Oxford did well to bowl Cambridge out on the first morning for 75, E. Macniven, a fine all-round games player at Eton, being the only batsman to score over twenty.

Oxford replied with 103, thanks largely to a stout 33 by their captain, V.S.C. Smith, whose fifth year in the Winchester XI had almost included his twenty-second birthday. S.T. Clissold, who was also an oarsman of Eton and Trinity, later to become a barrister and to serve as stipendiary magistrate in Ballarat, Victoria, took six Light Blue wickets. R.P. Long batted excellently for 39 not out in the Light Blues' second innings, in which G.E. Yonge took seven wickets. The 22 not out of C.H. Ridding saw Oxford through; unusually, he had gone to Trinity rather than New College after Winchester, and he would later play several years first for the Oxfordshire and then the Hampshire county elevens.

CAMBRIDGE	First innings		Second innings	
O.C. Pell	b Soames	0	c Williams, b Soames	12
E. Blayds	c Smith, b Yonge	8	b Yonge	0
G.P. Ottey	run out	7	c Hildyard, b Yonge	13
R. Seddon	b Soames	3	b Yonge	18
R.T. King	lbw, b Yonge	15	run out	14
E. Macniven	run out	22	b Davies	0
R.P. Long	run out	0	not out	39
S.T. Clissold	c A. Ridding, b Yonge	1	b Yonge	0
E. Barchard	not out	11	b Yonge	1
J.M. Lee	b Yonge	0	lbw, b Yonge	1
J. Walker[1]	absent	0	b Yonge	1
EXTRAS	B 6, W 2	8	B 16, W 1	17
	TOTAL	75	TOTAL	116

OXFORD				
R.L.J. Bateman	b Clissold	1	b Ottey	8
S. Soames	b Lee	1		
W.H. Davies	b Clissold	0	run out	8
R. Honywood	b Lee	0	b Clissold	11
V.S.C. Smith	b Clissold	33	b Ottey	7
P. Williams	b Clissold	10	not out	6
H.C.T. Hildyard	b Clissold	10	b Ottey	3
C.H. Ridding	b Ottey	18	c Ottey, b Lee	22
G.E. Yonge	b Clissold	4	not out	7
A. Ridding	b Ottey	1		
C.R.F. Loch	not out	5	c Long, b Clissold	1
EXTRAS	B 15, W 3, N-B 2	20	B 8, W 6, N-B 2	16
	TOTAL	103	TOTAL (7 WKTS)	89

[1] There is a conflict of opinion as to who really played. *Bell's Life* gives the name of J. Walker. One or two authorities, however, mention the name of C.D. Goldie.

1847

Cambridge, who arrived at Lord's having won three out of their four preliminary matches, won without difficulty, the margin of 138 runs being especially pleasing to the Rugbeian captain, O.C. Pell. They reached 132 in their first innings thanks to a steady opening partnership by the Rugby–Harrow combination of G.P. Ottey and E. Blayds, and to fine hitting by the Etonian Lord Burghley, bearer of a fine sporting name, who made top score with 45. The indefatigable G.E. Yonge took five Light Blue wickets. Oxford were saved from total disaster by their captain V.S.C. Smith in both innings – his 32 out of 56 in the first innings was 27 more than the score of any other player on his side – and by A. Ridding in the second innings.

The Cambridge victory was notable for the fact that all the Oxford wickets were taken by the two Rugbeians, J.M. Lee and G.P. Ottey. Supporters at Rugby School must have been delighted with the contribution to the Light Blue success made by its former pupils.

CAMBRIDGE	First innings		Second innings	
G.P. Ottey	*b* Yonge	20	*c* Smith, *b* Yonge	0
E. Blayds	*b* Willis	28	*b* Willis	15
O.C. Pell	*b* Yonge	5	*c* A. Ridding , *b* C. Ridding	13
Lord Burghley	*c* Smith, *b* Willis	45	*c* C. Ridding, *b* Yonge	17
J. Walker	*b* Yonge	4	*b* Soames	6
R.T. King	*c* Willis, *b* Yonge	10	*b* Willis	10
R. Seddon	*b* Yonge	0	*b* Yonge	2
T.M. Townley	*run out*	1	*c* Willis, *b* Yonge	22
W.J. Hammersley	*b* Soames	11	*b* Yonge	3
E. Barchard	*c* Currer, *b* Willis	2	*not out*	16
J.M. Lee	*not out*	0	*c* A. Ridding, *b* Willis	15
EXTRAS	B 2, W 4	6	B 2, W 6, N-B 3	11
	TOTAL	132	TOTAL	130

OXFORD				
R. Honywood	*c* Walker, *b* Ottey	2	*c and b* Ottey	2
P. Williams	*b* Lee	0	*c* Townley, *b* Ottey	2
V.S.C. Smith	*b* Ottey	32	*b* Lee	15
C.H. Ridding	*c* Lee, *b* Ottey	0	*c* Barchard, *b* Lee	8
C.S. Currer	*b* Lee	1	*b* Ottey	1
W.H. Davies	*b* Lee	0	*c* Blayds, *b* Ottey	0
G.E. Yonge	*c* Ottey, *b* Lee	2	*not out*	4
A. Ridding	*c* Seddon, *b* Lee	0	*c* Lee, *b* Ottey	22
F.J. Coleridge	*c* Hammersley, *b* Lee	3	*b* Ottey	1
C.F. Willis	*b* Ottey	5	*b* Lee	2
S. Soames	*not out*	2	*c* Seddon, *b* Lee	0
EXTRAS	B 5, W 4	9	B 5, W 6	11
	TOTAL	56	TOTAL	68

1848

This match mysteriously reverted to the Magdalen College ground, even though Lord's was not being used. Oxford made full use of their home advantage and won a satisfying match by 23 runs. The first-innings deficit was only 9 runs, a good innings for Oxford by C.H. Ridding being matched by one from R.T. King for Cambridge. In the Dark Blue second innings Ridding was the only batsman to deal effectively with the bowling of J.M. Lee and E.W. Blore. Blore, who hailed from Eton, was a whole-hearted supporter of Cambridge cricket, a slow right-arm bowler with a very strong break-back from the off – something

of a rarity in an age when round-arm bowling lent itself more naturally to the curl from leg.

The fine all-round batsman W.S. Deacon, like many after him, found runs easier to come by at Fenner's than elsewhere, and Cambridge managed only 96 in their second innings. Much to his pleasure, the Oxford captain, G.E. Yonge, took another six wickets, thereby bringing his five-year total to forty-three. This seemed at the time likely to remain a record, and so it has proved – in part because of the policy, dating from 1865, to allow a player a maximum of four years in the University Match.

OXFORD	First innings		Second innings	
R.L.J. Bateman	c sub, b Blore	1	b Lee	6
F. Bathurst	c King, b Blore	13	b Blore	7
W.H. Davies	c Deacon, b Blore	3	lbw, b Blore	5
A. Wilson	run out	7	c Barchard, b Lee	3
C.H. Ridding	run out	33	run out	26
C.R.F. Loch	b Blore	0	b Blore	13
A. Ridding	b Lee	25	c Lee, b Blore	6
J. Aitken	b Lee	7	run out	17
G.E. Yonge	b Lee	6	not out	0
C.F. Willis	b Lee	0	b Lee	12
J.W. Chitty	run out	8	b King	6
EXTRAS	B 3, w 13	16	B 2, w 7	9
	TOTAL	119	TOTAL	110

CAMBRIDGE				
E. Barchard	b Yonge	6	b Yonge	10
C.T. Calvert	b Yonge	2	not out	4
W.S. Deacon	b Willis	0	b Willis	7
J. Walker	b Willis	0	b Loch	2
J.M. Lee	b Yonge	7	c and b Yonge	19
R.T. King	b Willis	45	c C.H. Ridding, b Willis	12
E. Blayds	b Willis	22	b Yonge	5
J. Leith	not out	13	lbw, b Willis	25
E.W. Blore	b Willis	1	b Yonge	2
J.B.J. Bateman	b Willis	0	b Yonge	0
T.M. Townley	b Willis	5	b Yonge	2
EXTRAS	B 5, w 2, N-B 2	9	B 4, w 2, N-B 2	8
	TOTAL	110	TOTAL	96

21, 22 June
At Lord's

1849

Cambridge won by
3 wickets

Despite Oxford's first-innings score of 198, in which the top scorers were J. Aitken, winner of the Grand Challenge Cup at Henley in 1850 and 1851 and one of the founders of the University Athletic Sports, and C.E. Coleridge, born at Eton and later a barrister, Cambridge won this contest by three wickets. R.T. King, Oakham and Emmanuel, who later played for the Leicestershire County XI and became a first-rate coach and judge of the game, played two captain's innings, and E.W. Blore took five wickets in each innings.

Cambridge were 62 behind on the first innings, but they then decisively bowled Oxford out for 69. The Light Blue fielding, especially that of King – he was dubbed by colleagues the 'King of

Points' – was good. When F. Walker was bowled by M. Jones in the Cambridge first innings, his leg stump was sent twelve yards; the fact that this was recorded suggests that the feat was unusual. W.S. Deacon, the following year's Cambridge captain, has recorded a vignette from this match that anticipates A.G. Macdonell's *England, their England*:

It was in that match that King and the Oxford wicket-keeper, Joe Chitty, came into collision over a very short run. I can distinctly remember the momentary hush and then the roar of laughter when it was seen that Chitty had lost his wig, and was sitting on the ground with the sun shining on his absolutely bald head. It was a very funny sight.

OXFORD	First innings			Second innings	
O.R. Hanbury	b Blore	12		c J. Walker, b Blore	0
J. Aitken	b Blore	36		c Deacon, b Blore	2
C.E. Coleridge	c and b King	34		c Whymper, b Blore	21
J.C. Patteson	b Potter	25		c Blayds, b Blore	2
C.H. Ridding	not out	27		c Fenn, b King	14
J.W. Chitty	lbw, b King	2		not out	9
W. Ridding	c and b Potter	7		b King	0
A. Ridding	run out	11		b Blore	15
A. Wilson	b Blore	11		b King	0
C.F. Willis	b Blore	2		b King	1
M. Jones	b Blore	0		b King	0
EXTRAS	B 18, W 13	31		B 2, W 3	5
	TOTAL	198		TOTAL	69

CAMBRIDGE					
E. Blayds	b Jones	7		c C.H. Ridding, b Willis	13
W.E. Barnett	c Willis, b Jones	14		b Willis	12
W.S. Deacon	b Willis	5		b Hanbury	5
R.T. King	c C.H. Ridding, b Willis	43		not out	49
C.F.G. Jenyns	b Hanbury	27		b Hanbury	23
J. Walker	b Willis	7		c Hanbury, b Jones	0
F.H. Whymper	not out	7		lbw, b Willis	5
E.W. Blore	run out	0		not out	8
F. Walker	b Jones	0		b Willis	4
A. Potter	b Jones	5			
W.M. Fenn	b Willis	3			
EXTRAS	B 11, W 6, N-B 1	18		B 5, W 8	13
	TOTAL	136		TOTAL (7 WKTS)	132

6, 7, 8 June
At Magdalen Ground, Oxford

1850

*Oxford won by
127 runs*

This was the last match to be played away from Lord's, being staged on the Magdalen College ground at the astonishingly early date of 6 June. Cambridge were not a strong batting side, and Oxford, with ground advantage, won by the comfortable margin of 127 runs. Oxford's first-innings total of 211 clinched the match; they owed much to the two Coleridges, both of Eton and Balliol, who made over 90 between them, and to the opener, F.M. Eden, who scored 51. He would later serve with the Oxford Militia in Corfu during the Crimean War, and must be the only cricket blue at Oxford and Cambridge to have been made a 'Count of the Holy Roman Empire'.

For Cambridge, R.S. Edwards, the one early blue from Christ's Hospital, made 65 not out, and W.S. Deacon, a fine Etonian batsman making his top score in the series, 36. The Harrovian M. Jones took six Light Blue wickets. J. Aitken made 31 in Oxford's second innings, helping them to 117. In reply Cambridge could manage a mere 55, the only batsman to reach double figures being W.M. Fenn, who helped First Trinity to Head of the River, and would one day decline the Bishopric of Brisbane offered him by Archbishop Benson, on the grounds that his health was not equal to it. For Oxford, C.E. Coleridge took five wickets to complete a good match.

OXFORD	First innings		Second innings	
M.T.H. Wyatt	*c* Vernon, *b* Buchanan	13	*c* Edwards, *b* Blore	1
F.M. Eden	*c and b* Fenn	51	*b* Blore	5
J. Aitken	*run out*	6	*b* Buchanan	31
W. Ridding	*b* Buchanan	6	*st* Walker, *b* Buchanan	0
C.E. Coleridge	*b* Fenn	43	*b* Buchanan	11
A. Wilson	*c* Buchanan, *b* Blore	0	*b* Fenn	9
A. Ridding	*b* Fenn	0	*not out*	16
Hon. E.V. Bligh	*c* Barnett, *b* Blore	27	*b* Buchanan	0
M. Jones	*b* Blore	7	*absent*	0
F.J. Coleridge	*st* Walker, *b* Blore	22	*b* Fenn	17
E.J. Morres	*not out*	1	*b* Buchanan	10
EXTRAS	B 10, L-B 3, W 21, N-B 1	35	B 9, W 8	17
	TOTAL	211	TOTAL	117
CAMBRIDGE				
W.E. Barnett	*c* Wilson, *b* Jones	8	*c* W. Ridding, *b* C.E. Coleridge	6
H.J. Simonds	*b* C.E. Coleridge	1	*lbw*, *b* Morres	1
R.S. Edwards	*not out*	65	*b* Morres	1
H. Vernon	*c* F.J. Coleridge, *b* Jones	3	*absent*	0
C.F.G. Jenyns	*c* F.J. Coleridge, *b* Jones	3	*b* C.E. Coleridge	1
W.S. Deacon	*b* Morres	36	*c* Eden, *b* C.E. Coleridge	9
F. Walker	*c* C.E. Coleridge, *b* Jones	3	*c* Morres, *b* C.E. Coleridge	1
E.W. Blore	*b* C.E. Coleridge	7	*run out*	5
W.M. Fenn	*c* Eden, *b* Jones	4	*b* C.E. Coleridge	15
E.B. Prest	*lbw*, *b* C.E. Coleridge	0	*b* Morres	1
D. Buchanan	*b* Jones	4	*not out*	1
EXTRAS	B 1, L-B 2, W 9	12	B 1, L-B 1, W 12	14
	TOTAL	146	TOTAL	55

1851

Cambridge took their revenge by inflicting on Oxford a decisive defeat by an innings and 4 runs. In mitigation of the Dark Blue performance, it should be recorded that three of the regular side could not play, including the captain G.W. Ridding. G.R. Dupuis, the Cambridge captain, accepted a mastership at Eton and had to hand over to E.W. Blore.

The bowling and fielding of the Cantabs were very good, Blore taking eight wickets in the match to bring his total of Oxford victims in his four years to thirty-two. It was Cambridge's batting, however, that paved the way for victory. In their 266 W.M. Leake – a Rugbeian who would go to Ceylon as a civil engineer and help to intro-

duce the cultivation of Chinchona and tea – made a fine 66, and the Cheltonian S.M.E. Kempson a hard-hit 48. In the 1853 Gentlemen *v* Players match Kempson bowled unchanged with Sir F. Bathurst, and he later had an academic career in India and at home.

F.D. Longe, of Harrow and Oriel, held the Oxford first innings together with his 46, and his colleague A. Cazenove also had a useful match with bat and ball. Cazenove became an Honorary Canon of Rochester Cathedral in 1877, and sixteen years later died suddenly while playing real tennis – just as J.D. Eggar, an Oxford blue in 1938, died on a lawn tennis court 132 years later.

CAMBRIDGE	First innings		Second innings
W.M. Leake	*run out*	66	
S. Fenn	*c* Longe, *b* Cazenove	25	
W.M. Fenn	*b* Cazenove	1	
H. Vernon	*b* Eden	33	
F. Walker	*b* Marsham	10	
H.K. Boldero	*b* Marsham	9	
C. Pontifex	*run out*	4	
E.W. Blore	*b* Eden	2	
S.M.E. Kempson	*c* Hore, *b* Cazenove	48	
W.A. Norris	*c* Peel, *b* Hore	12	
J.S. Weston	*not out*	0	
EXTRAS	B 29, L-B 5, W 21, N-B 1	56	
	TOTAL	266	

OXFORD					
A. Wallace	*c* Blore, *b* Pontifex	5	*b* Blore	16
M.T.H. Wyatt	*c* W.M. Fenn, *b* Pontifex	0	*c* Walker, *b* Pontifex	14
F.M. Eden	*c* S. Fenn, *b* Pontifex	6	*b* Blore	21
F.D. Longe	*b* Blore	46	*b* Blore	0
C.S. Bere	*c* S. Fenn, *b* Blore	0	*b* Pontifex	20
T.W. Hale	*run out*	5	*b* Pontifex	22
H.R. Peel	*c* Vernon, *b* Blore	8	*run out*	0
A. Cazenove	*hw*, *b* Pontifex	27	*c* Walker, *b* Blore	12
C.J.B. Marsham	*b* Pontifex	13	*b* Pontifex	3
A.H. Hore	*b* Blore	2	*not out*	0
H. Taswell	*not out*	1	*b* Pontifex	13
EXTRAS	B 1, L-B 3, W 5	9	B 7, L-B 5, W 6, N-B 1	19
	TOTAL	122	TOTAL	140

1852

This match began a halcyon period for Oxford, who lost only one match in the next seven years and won four of the others by an innings. This year's margin, an innings and 77 runs, had two mitigating factors, one attributable to erratic management and the other to illness. As a result of the first, Cambridge could muster only ten men; as a result of the second, they were deprived of their two best bowlers, the experienced S.M.E. Kempson and the freshman C. Pontifex, later to become Judge of the High Court at Calcutta and to receive a knighthood. The rest of the Cambridge attack seems to have been decidedly ordinary – apart from E.T. Drake – a fact of which the Oxford batsmen took joyous advantage.

They made 273, thanks largely to the 53 of their captain W. Ridding, a Wykehamist who also captained the Hampshire County XI in 1861 and became a Fellow of New College, and the 43 of W.W. Parker, of Rugby and Merton, who played for four years for the Suffolk County XI. Drake, later to become the best amateur lob bowler of his day, and because of his enthusiasm for the Hunt dubbed the 'Sporting Parson', took five wickets.

When Cambridge batted, the bowling of P.M. Sankey, of King's, Canterbury, and E. Balfour, of Westminster School, was too good for them; only the Harrovian H.K. Boldero, with 50, and F. Walker – who before he developed gout played three times for the Gentlemen – with 36, made any impact.

OXFORD	First innings		Second innings
P.M. Sankey	*b* Drake	27	
Hon. E.C. Leigh	*b* Weston	8	
W.W. Parker	*b* Drake	43	
T.W. Hale	*b* Drake	15	
F.D. Longe	*b* Drake	17	
E.H.L. Willes	*c* Walker, *b* Drake	11	
H.R. Peel	*b* Vernon	7	
W. Ridding	*c* Walker, *b* Vernon	53	
A. Cazenove	*c and b* Vernon	11	
A. Payne	*b* Walker	40	
E. Balfour	*not out*	7	
EXTRAS	B 5, L-B 6, W 18, N-B 5	34	
	TOTAL	273	

CAMBRIDGE[1]				
J.S. Weston	*b* Sankey	0	*run out*	3
C.L. Norman	*b* Payne	0	*c* Payne, *b* Balfour	14
W.M. Leake	*b* Sankey	0	*lbw, b* Sankey	2
H.K. Boldero	*b* Sankey	50	*c* Ridding, *b* Balfour	9
H.G. Southwell	*b* Payne	1	*c* Cazenove, *b* Balfour	0
H. Vernon	*b* Balfour	8	*run out*	6
H.S. White	*run out*	5	*b* Sankey	7
F. Walker	*b* Sankey	13	*b* Balfour	36
E.T. Drake	*not out*	0	*b* Sankey	2
E.A. Fuller	*c* Payne, *b* Sankey	0	*not out*	0
EXTRAS	B 1, L-B 7, W 9, N-B 1	18	B 11, L-B 4, W 5, N-B 2	22
	TOTAL	95	TOTAL	101

[1] With only 10 men.

1853

The University sides of 1853 were considered equally strong, but Oxford, captained by E.H.L. Willes, played distinctly better on the two days and deserved their victory by an innings and 19 runs. Cambridge, led by C. Pontifex, started steadily and finished strongly, thanks to aggressive hitting by F.E. Stacey, of Eton and King's, who was to become Sheriff of Glamorganshire in 1873, but they reached only 155, which paled into insignificance beside Oxford's 297. Four batsmen contributed usefully to this score: R.H. Colley, who came up from Bridgnorth Grammar School and became President of the Shropshire County Club; E. Balfour, one of Oxford's successful bowlers this year; Willes, a Wykehamist who unusually went to Wadham, later became a Scholar and then a Fellow of

Queen's, and showed his catholicity of interest and loyalty by playing for Hampshire as well as for Kent; and R. Hankey, who earned a niche in cricket history by his batting in the Gentlemen *v* Players match in 1857, when he scored 70 in 105 minutes, hitting the Players' bowling to all parts of the field. This total remained a record until 1872.

W. Inge, of Shrewsbury and Worcester, who spent the last twelve years of his life as Provost of his old college, took five Light Blue wickets in the first innings, and E. Balfour, completing a useful all-round performance, took four in the second innings, when Cambridge made only 123. W. Inge, in passing, begat W.R. Inge, a famous Dean of St Paul's, known irreverently as 'the Gloomy Dean'.

CAMBRIDGE	First innings		Second innings	
C. Pontifex	b Inge	27	st Ridding, b Balfour	5
H.G. Southwell	c Armitstead, b Inge	12	lbw, b Balfour	4
S.M.E. Kempson	b Inge	10	b Balfour	0
A.R. Ward	b Aitken	1	c Willes, b Balfour	7
C.L. Norman	b Inge	0	lbw, b Aitken	20
H.K. Boldero	c sub, b Inge	15	b Aitken	11
E.T. Drake	run out	5	b Hankey	10
W.M. Leake	c Ridding, b Hankey	16	b Willes	21
E.M. Reynolds	c Leigh, b Clement	3	b Hankey	1
F.E. Stacey	not out	38	c Balfour, b Inge	9
W. Maule	b Balfour	7	not out	14
EXTRAS	B 2, L-B 8, W 10, N-B 1	21	B 3, L-B 2, W 15, N-B 1	21
	TOTAL	155	TOTAL	123

OXFORD		
W.G. Armitstead	b Drake	26
Hon. E.C. Leigh	b Reynolds	0
R.H. Colley	c and b Kempson	68
R. Hankey	c and b Kempson	33
E. Balfour	st Stacey, b Maule	62
H.M. Aitken	c Drake, b Pontifex	18
W. Inge	st Stacey, b Drake	1
E.H.L. Willes	not out	43
W. Ridding	b Maule	3
W.W. Parker	c Southwell, b Maule	2
R. Clement	c Pontifex, b Kempson	3
EXTRAS	B 6, L-B 11, W 21	38
	TOTAL	297

Cambridge must have been devoutly hoping that they would avoid a hat-trick of crushing defeats. Whether their minds were on events in the Crimea rather than on the cricket at Lord's history does not relate. For whatever reason, Oxford won by an innings for the third year in succession, this time with 8 runs to spare. Cambridge were without their captain, A.R. Ward, absent owing to 'indisposition', caused, it was said, by pique due to some ill-natured chaff from the crowd in the MCC match. J.D. Betham in his *Oxford and Cambridge Cricket Scores and Biographies* twice records that it was illness rather than indisposition. In view of Ward's subsequent devotion to Cambridge cricket, this seems the likelier version. He was, however, able to direct operations from the Pavilion.

But Cambridge's real weakness was their batting and inability to cope with the left-arm quick bowling of C.D.B. Marsham, born at Merton College and later to attend it as an undergraduate after being educated privately; he took nine wickets in the match for 56. He was well supported by A. Payne at the other end. It must have been unusual for two bowlers educated privately to have been so successful. As a result, the Light Blues managed only 70 and 60 in their two innings. For Oxford, E.L. Bateman, who later served on the MCC Committee and became an Auditor of the Club, made 40, and W. Fellows, who was for thirty-eight years the incumbent of St John's, Toorak, Melbourne, 33.

CAMBRIDGE	First innings			Second innings	
C.P. Ingram	*run out*		4	*b* Marsham	2
E.M. Reynolds	*c* Fuller, *b* Payne		7	*b* Payne	7
J. McCormick	*run out*		0	*c and b* Marsham	12
W.M. Leake	*b* Marsham		0	*b* Marsham	1
E.T. Drake	*b* Marsham		10	*b* Marsham	3
R.A. Fitzgerald	*c* Veitch, *b* Marsham		6	*b* Marsham	0
R.A. Clement	*b* Payne		0	*run out*	0
H. Perkins	*b* Payne		5	*c* Fuller, *b* Marsham	27
T.D. Tremlett	*not out*		18	*b* Payne	0
C.W.H. Fryer	*c* Balfour, *b* Fuller		10	*run out*	0
A.R. Du Cane	*run out*		2	*not out*	1
EXTRAS	B 6, L-B 1, W 1		8	B 5, L-B 1, W 1	7
	TOTAL		70	TOTAL	60

OXFORD			
W.G. Armitstead	*run out*		8
Hon. E.C. Leigh	*st* McCormick, *b* Drake		0
R.H. Colley	*b* Drake		0
E. Balfour	*b* Du Cane		7
E.L. Bateman	*c* McCormick, *b* Reynolds		40
W. Fellows	*b* Du Cane		33
E.H.L. Willes	*b* Reynolds		14
C.D.B. Marsham	*b* Du Cane		2
G.P. Fuller	*b* Drake		9
H.G.J. Veitch	*not out*		9
A. Payne	*b* Drake		4
EXTRAS	D 12		12
	TOTAL		138

Oxford bowling	OVERS	RUNS	WKTS	OVERS	RUNS	WKTS
Marsham	30	37	3	22.2	19	6
Payne	23	18	3	20	25	2
Fuller	6	7	1	1	9	0

Cambridge bowling	OVERS	RUNS	WKTS
Du Cane	34	52	3
Drake	22.2	55	4
Reynolds	7	10	2
Fryer	3	9	0

3
1855–1864
Towards W.G. and Wisden

OXFORD *From Marsham to Mitchell*

The pride of the Victorians, which saw an early climax in the Great Exhibition of 1851, took a fall over the incompetent handling of the Crimean War, though this was somewhat restored by the successful outcome of the Indian Mutiny. Against this background, industrial expansion raced ahead, and with the growth of middle-class prosperity leisure activities advanced, not least cricket.

As more undergraduates became involved in the game, the OUCC in 1855 engaged no less than twenty-five professionals for the season. As Geoffrey Bolton puts it: 'One pictures the sagging jaw of the modern Treasurer as he ponders this item.' A match was played and won against a selected eleven from these professionals, which included Julius Caesar, Hillyer and Wells. Similar contests were featured among the trial games for years to come. It is worth noting that for the first time, apart from Oxfordshire, other counties began to figure in the University's programme; Surrey was the first in 1859.

Three great bowlers made their mark during the fifties, all of whom later became parsons – the Hon. W.S. Fiennes, A. Payne and C.D.B. Marsham – and the greatest of these was Marsham. C.D.B., another of the select band who played for five years, was the son of the Warden at Merton. He bowled fast-medium round-arm, combining accuracy with lift off the pitch, and put his success down to 'flexibility of wrist'. His record against Cambridge has certainly never been bettered.

YEAR	BOWLING	RESULT
1854	3 for 37 & 6 for 19	Won by an innings & 8 runs
1855	2 for 47 & 3 for 36	Won by three wickets
1856	6 for 38 & 2 for 37	Lost by three wickets
*1857	5 for 31 & 3 for 58	Won by 81 runs
*1859	5 for 42 & 6 for 17	Won by an innings & 38 runs

*Captain

In his last year C.D.B. played twice against Oxford. Drawing attention to this, Geoffrey Bolton states:

A Captain of today who played for his county rather than for the University and aggravated his offence by taking 8 wickets for 19 would, one fancies, be eyed askance, but nice customs curtsey to great Kings and Marsham could probably get away with anything.

In the ten matches in which he bowled for Gentlemen *v* Players, he delivered 2563 balls for 852 runs and 48 wickets, which gave an average of 17.95.

There were a few years of relative darkness before R.A.H. Mitchell blazed as a glittering star. Incomparably the best batsman who had yet appeared in University cricket, Mitchell is the only man to have captained Oxford three times, an astonishing tribute to his ability and personality. In his four Varsity Matches he had the remarkable average, for the time, of 42. One of the hazards of batting in this period, particularly at Lord's, was the frequency of shooters; with his long reach Mitchell used to smother these dangerous deliveries.

Lord's had a dismal reputation; there was sometimes a search in the playing area to find a satisfactory wicket. Lillywhite commented that the wicket at Lord's did not remotely resemble a billiard table 'except the pockets'. Even in the outfield, where the grass was kept down by as many as four hundred sheep, the old 'ridge and furrow' was still much in evidence. Mitchell not only coped with shooters, but he had a reputation as a tremendous driver and leg-side hitter. The Oxford eleven he led in 1865 (the year following this decade) was certainly among the best ever to take the field, although in practice they did not readily bowl sides out.

It was interesting that R.D. Walker was selected to play in this, his fifth match against Cambridge, despite a mutual understanding that four years should no longer be exceeded. Cambridge's objection was overruled, but during the match the four-year rule was accepted, and this firm understanding remained unchanged for over a hundred years. Walker made only 5 and 0!

Mitchell joined the teaching staff at Eton the year after going down; his personal cricketing career was more or less restricted to the Canterbury Week and occasional appearances for the Gentlemen. For over thirty years he ran Eton's cricket, and in recognition of this long service he was presented with a rose bowl inscribed: 'Presented to Mr R.A.H. Mitchell by the Captains of the Eton Elevens, 1866–1897'. All 'his' captains subscribed except E.O.H. Wilkinson, who had been killed in the Zulu war. Among the great names of Etonians who passed through his hands, to come Oxford's way, C.J. Ottaway and S.E. Butler are the best known.

In 1862 the OUCC was at long last properly constituted. A committee of undergraduates was formed, a report and recommendations were made and it was decided to appoint annually a captain, a secretary and a treasurer. Since 1879 the Treasurer has been a senior member of the University, an admirable arrangement giving the Committee stability and continuity. With minor amendments, notably in 1951, the constitution has remained largely unchanged. In 1862 application was made to the OUBC asking permission for those who played against Cambridge to wear the dark blue colours. The rowing blues alone had that right at the time and, as so often happens, were not eager to share it. Geoffrey Bolton takes up the story:

But by a master-stroke of tact the President of the OUBC (luckily a passable cricketer) was elected to membership of the Harlequins, rightly a most exclusive club. The compliment was so much appreciated that all opposition was withdrawn and the Cricket Blue dates from 1863.

It was during this decade that Law 10 came under fire; this Law did not allow a bowler to raise his hand above the shoulders as it passed the body in the last swing of the arm before delivery. More and more during the late fifties and early sixties the Law was abused and umpires found the enforcement of it difficult. In 1862 John Lillywhite, umpiring in the Surrey *v* England match, staged a showdown. He no-balled Edgar Willsher six times in succession; the England side left the field in protest and play resumed the next day only when Lillywhite was replaced. The MCC Committee realized that if it was to retain authority, the problem must be solved. The Varsity Match was not free from this controversy; in 1863 T. Collins, bowling for Cambridge, was no-balled, and he later wrote:

I went on to bowl at the start at the end away from the pavilion, got R.D. Walker's wicket, and had R.A.H. Mitchell caught off a tremendous hit at long leg (no credit to me!) by A.W.T. Daniel, who was a first-rate field, and took the ball close to the ropes. Then, after being warned that my hand was too high, I was no-balled four or five times, and retired from bowling for the rest of the match.

Much consultation took place, the MCC eventually bowed to the inevitable, and after a general meeting on 10 June 1864 the relevant section of Law 10 was amended to read, succinctly: 'The ball must be bowled. . . . If thrown or jerked, the Umpire shall call No Ball.' The second great bowling revolution had taken place.

Modern cricket is said to date from 1864, when W.G. Grace made his debut on the scene. Strenuous efforts were made by both Universities to persuade him to matriculate, but compulsory Greek stood in the way, for W.G. had no academic bent. 'You don't catch me wasting my time reading,' he once said. To have given him undergraduate status would have reflected little credit on him or on the University.

In the same remarkable year, John Wisden published the first *Cricketer's Almanack* for the price of a shilling. The first issue contained a hotchpotch of information, including even an account of European relations with China and another of the trial of Charles I. It must have been a popular publication among cricketers, because the next edition dropped nearly all non-cricket news and even included scores and results of Varsity Matches from the event's inception.

This had been a decade of interest, truly laying the foundations of modern cricket and opening the doors to the Golden Age.

CAMBRIDGE *Level-pegging at Lord's*

Further progress was made in the CUCC evolution during the decade 1855 to 1864, in which *The Origin of Species* and *Alice in Wonderland* both saw the light of day. The first pavilion, for example, was completed in 1856, and in 1857 F.H. Norman, captain three years later, was able to write, with perhaps the advantage of light blue-tinted spectacles:

A splendid ground it was, and all the UCC matches were played there. The seat of the University cricket was in Parker's Piece: I cannot say that I enjoyed that. The fieldsmen of the different matches were all jumbled up together, long-leg of one match somewhere near cover-point of another, and the hits of one game crossing those of another, which was both disconcerting and dangerous. But it was a splendid lively ground, and not too true – very good to learn on. None of the college grounds were made when I was at Cambridge.

T.E. Bagge, however – a fine, patient batsman who favoured back play and was to make two sixties in the Gentlemen *v* Players match in 1860 – has a slightly different emphasis:

'Fenner's' in '58 did not belong to the Varsity. Ward [A.R.] had secured it for a few years previously, but before 1861 there was a great chance of losing it. There was a debt on the pavilion for some time, nor was there any water in the lavatory except what was fetched by members in a can from a tap close by. The roadway to the ground was often more mud than gravel; but all this was altered in my last year; £300 of debt was wiped off, water was laid on from the town, and the roadway and approaches were properly gravelled. Side-nets were unknown; we only had nets behind the wickets. H.R.H. the Prince of Wales (now of course His Majesty King Edward VII) resided at Madingley Hall, where one of the worst grounds ever played on was made up, and the Prince's pluck in standing up to the bowling, which was as likely to hit the batsman as not, deserves record. A special wicket used to be reserved for the Prince at Fenner's, where he had ample experience of being 'cut over' by his neighbouring batsman. General Bruce, H.R.H.'s Comptroller, was most kind in helping to pay off the pavilion debt – the Prince contributing £10 and promising to make up any amount required at the end of term, but the necessary sum was collected.

The Club's management continued to be in the hands of the three so-called 'treasurers', who were elected, or re-elected, annually. Cambridgeshire professionals were employed on the ground at this time, and we gather that there was 'a little local difficulty' with Hayward – presumably Thomas, uncle of the more famous Tom – and Buttress, mentioned in a poem by C.S. Calverley as a bowler of 'peculiar twisters', Tarrant and Carpenter. Dissatisfied with their terms or their treatment, they apparently threatened, in a show of pique, to transfer their services to Oxford. We know also the names of the successive groundsmen – Tom Parmenter up to 1862, and after him Walter Watts. Finally, we know that in 1855 the fixture list was extended to twelve matches, including the Gentlemen of Cambridgeshire and I Zingari, founded as a wandering club ten years earlier. Alas! only five members of IZ wandered to Cambridge for that first match, and undergraduates had to be found as substitutes. The first match was played at this time between the Perambulators, originally confined to Harrow men but soon extended to include men from Eton, Winchester, Westminster and Rugby, and the Etceteras, covering the other public schools.

The issue of eligibility for the University Match became an issue in this decade; for it was in 1858 that C.D.B. Marsham represented Oxford for the fifth time, as G.E. Yonge had done before him. The following resolution, rather mysteriously worded, was agreed:

That in the annual match between Oxford and Cambridge no member of either University of more than 4 years' standing, such standing to count from the first term of actual residence, be eligible to play unless he be an undergraduate of not more than five years' standing, or have passed his final examination after the Easter preceding the match.

That rule was made at Lord's in 1858. Under it, however, it was possible for a man who had not passed his examination but was still an undergraduate to play a fifth time for his University, and consequently we find that R.D. Walker played for Oxford from 1861 to 1865 inclusive. Another agreement was reached in 1865 in the wake of that feat, which read:

That a man whose name is on the College books be qualified to play in the annual match between Oxford and Cambridge for the four consecutive years dating from the beginning of his first term of residence, and for those years only.

H.M. (later Sir Meredyth) Plowden, who played for Cambridge from 1860 to 1863, believes that the question was settled in 1861 or 1862, but that the rule was not retrospective, thus allowing Walker to play.

One story, the mystery in 1856 of the undergraduate that never was, provides an insight into the generosity of spirit that often prompted the captains of the University sides. On this occasion, magnanimity was displayed by the Oxford captain, who agreed to T.W. Wills taking part, as his name was said to be 'on the books'. In fact he never went up, but would later teach the game to Aborigines working as labourers on his father's sheep stations in New South Wales. He died in 1880 from a self-inflicted wound. Similarly, in 1861 the subsequent Archdeacon of Exeter was allowed by the Cambridge captain a runner and a substitute in the field because of 'the delicate state of his health'.

This decade, as indeed the one following, ended with Oxford and Cambridge each having won five University Matches, leaving them all square after thirty encounters. One factor to emerge clearly was the need to have two fine bowlers in your side to ensure that you bowled sides out and gave your batsmen the chance to win matches. To have three fine bowlers – as Cambridge had in 1860, and has been fortunate to have on several other occasions – is an *embarras de richesses* that no captain worth his salt has ever found an embarrassment.

Cambridge's three fine bowlers in 1861 and 1862 were R. Lang, H.W. Salter and H.M. Plowden, and a formidable combination they were. Lang, a member of the Harrow side for five years, in the opinion of Lord Cobham, better known to cricketers as the Hon. C.G. Lyttelton, 'was in his day perhaps the best University bowler ever seen, being very straight for a bowler of his great pace'; and he had great success for the Gentlemen as well as for Cambridge. He was also a useful bat and a beautiful field. Salter was a bowler above the average, fast-medium with the ability to curl the ball from leg and to keep his length. He had one peculiarity, the power of being able to bowl without running up to the wicket – almost a standing delivery, useful in wet conditions. The third of the trio, Plowden, was a successful off-break bowler, particularly effective on slow wickets. He played a little for Hampshire before being called to the Bar and going out to India, where he was Judge of the Chief Court in the Punjab for seventeen years.

The leading Light Blue batsmen of this era were: J.H. Marshall, also a magnificent long-stop to Lang; T.E. Bagge, already referred to; D.R. Onslow, MP for Guildford for two Parliaments and a member of the Surrey Committee for over half a century; and one celebrated all-rounder, both at Cambridge and afterwards, the Hon. C.G. Lyttelton.

Charles Lyttelton's all-round talent was not confined to cricket, for he was academically able enough to achieve a First-Class Law Tripos, as well as athletic enough to have played in the tennis singles and doubles for Cambridge and to have won the MCC Silver Prize for tennis for five successive years. As is the wont of the Lyttelton family, he had an enviable record of public service: MP for East Worcestershire from 1868 to 1874; Land Commissioner for England, 1881–9; Railway Commissioner, 1891–1905; Chairman of the Royal Commission on Agricultural Depression, 1896–7; Trustee of the National Portrait Gallery from 1893; and the inheritor from his father of both the Lyttelton title and Hagley Hall. As an all-round cricketer, he was a fine driver, leg-hitter and cutter, once cutting a ball from Griffiths for six at The Oval. He imparted considerable spin to the ball when he bowled, and was a fine wicket-keeper and a good field, especially at point. Four years in the Eton side, four in the Cambridge XI and a spell for Worcestershire, plus several periods on the MCC Committee – he was President of MCC in 1886 – gave him ample scope for his cricket skills and commitment. He epitomizes the best sort of amateur tradition, at a time when sport was a fine preparation for service, and service was a natural way of life for the sportsman.

21, 22, 23 June
At Lord's

1855

*Oxford won by
3 wickets*

This was a marvellously close contest which the Dark Blues, captained by R. Hankey, won by three wickets. The standard of hitting, and the cricket generally, was described as brilliant. The odds appear to have been on Cambridge, led by G.R. Johnson, despite their losing four of the regular side, but, as so often in the University Match, being non-favourites had a beneficial effect.

Cambridge batted first, and thanks mainly to the 45 of W.J. Kempson, who later served as a captain in the 99th Foot in the Chinese campaign of 1860 and was present at the surrender of Peking, they reached 139. A. Payne, one of Cambridge's tormentors the previous year, took 7 for

42 and followed this by being top scorer in the Oxford innings despite going in at number ten.

The Cambridge tail wagged, after C.D.B. Marsham and R. Hankey had made early inroads, and they reached 152, setting Oxford 146 to win. G.R. Johnson – good enough to have played for the Cambridgeshire, Norfolk and Suffolk county sides, and respected enough to become a member of the New Zealand legislature – and the Harrovian A.R. Du Cane bowled well, and it was left to the promoted B.M. Randolph, who played for Sussex in 1856 but died of a fever at Christ Church, Oxford, the following year, to make a magnificent 61, while H.G.J. Veitch kept his head in the crisis.

CAMBRIDGE

	First innings		Second innings	
J. Hales	c Fuller, b Marsham	10	b Marsham	0
J.W. Marshall	b A. Payne	0	run out	12
W.J. Kempson	b A. Payne	45	c A. Payne b Hankey	2
O. Hammond	c Randolph, b A. Payne	4	c Colley, b Hankey	10
G.R. Johnson	b A. Payne	0	b Hankey	24
W. Wingfield	b Marsham	10	b Veitch	6
T.W. Bury	b A. Payne	10	b Marsham	4
E.L. Horne	run out	2	b Fellows	0
J.M. Fuller	b A. Payne	17	not out	25
J.S. Gibson	not out	8	c Fuller, b Marsham	23
A.R. Du Cane	b A. Payne	0	b Fellows	17
EXTRAS	B 15, L-B 8, W 10	33	B 24, L-B 1, W 4	29
	TOTAL	139	TOTAL	152

OXFORD

W.W. Parker	run out	18	b Johnson	27
G.P. Fuller	b Johnson	9		
R.H. Colley	c and b Johnson	10	b Johnson	0
E.L. Bateman	b Johnson	2	b Du Cane	5
R. Hankey	b Du Cane	12	run out	11
A.F. Payne	b Horne	20	b Du Cane	0
W. Fellows	b Du Cane	0	b Johnson	5
C.D.B. Marsham	run out	0		
B.M. Randolph	c Fuller, b Johnson	1	c Fuller, b Marshall	61
A. Payne	not out	35	not out	1
H.G.J. Veitch	run out	12	not out	14
EXTRAS	B 8, L-B 9, W 8, N-B 2	27	B 6, L-B 5, W 9, N-B 2	22
	TOTAL	146	TOTAL (7 WKTS)	146

Oxford bowling	OVERS	RUNS	WKTS		OVERS	RUNS	WKTS
Marsham	33	47	2		21.1	36	3
A. Payne	48	42	7		30	19	0
Hankey	9	13	0		22	39	3
Fellows	1.2	4	0		6	2	2
Fuller	—	—	—		5	18	0
Veitch	—	—	—		5	9	1

Cambridge bowling							
Johnson	48.1	39	4		32	53	3
Du Cane	47	61	2		36	48	2
Horne	6	9	1		5	14	0
Marshall	5	6	0		4.2	5	1
Bury	2	4	0		6	4	0

1856

As their captain J. McCormick and his team were well aware, Cambridge had not recorded a victory for four years; but in this match they won by the same margin as Oxford had in 1855. A.R. Du Cane and E.L. Horne, of Shrewsbury and Clare, were unable to play for the victors, who, as happened all too often in the early matches, could muster ten players only. As mentioned earlier, A. Payne, the Oxford captain, agreed to the Rugbeian T.W. Wills taking part, as his name was 'on the books'.

The star of the match for Cambridge was not Wills, but J. Makinson, who was educated in Huddersfield but would later cross the Pennines to play for the Lancashire County XI. He took eight wickets for 40 runs, and scored 31 and 64, and in the current jargon would undoubtedly have won the 'Man of the Match' award. Oxford's main contributors were C.D.B. Marsham, who took 6 for 38 in Cambridge's first innings, and W. Fellows, who made 35 and 30. Fellows was also said to have bowled so fast that even two long-stops often failed to stop the ball. Makinson and Marsham were presented by the MCC with cricket balls, 'the most beautiful ever seen'. Since the balls had been used in the first Light Blue victory for five years, Cambridge must have echoed that sentiment more convincingly than Oxford.

OXFORD	First innings		Second innings	
H.G.J. Veitch	c Fuller, b McCormick	0	not out	6
W.G. Armitstead	b Johnson	0	b Makinson	2
F.W. Oliver	b Johnson	20	c and b Makinson	2
C.D.B. Marsham	b Johnson	10	run out	13
B.M. Randolph	b Johnson	22	b Wills	10
W. Fellows	b Marshall	35	b Makinson	30
C.G. Lane	run out	3	c Fuller, b Makinson	1
A. Payne	c Marshall, b Makinson	30	hw, b Makinson	21
Hon. W.S.T.W. Fiennes	b Makinson	8	b McCormick	3
R.H.B. Marsham	not out	3	b Marshall	13
G. Bennett	b Makinson	0	run out	0
EXTRAS	B 2, W 4	6	B 9, W 7, N-B 1	17
	TOTAL	137	TOTAL	118

CAMBRIDGE				
J. Hales	c Bennett, b C.D.B. Marsham	19	b Fellows	6
J.W. Marshall	c Fiennes, b C.D.B. Marsham	27	not out	13
J. McCormick	b C.D.B. Marsham	5	b Fellows	0
J. Makinson	c Fellows, b C.D.B. Marsham	31	c and b Fiennes	64
W. Wingfield	b Fiennes	6	b C.D.B. Marsham	0
O. Hammond	b Fiennes	2	not out	7
G.R. Johnson	c and b C.D.B. Marsham	1	run out	8
J.M. Fuller	not out	19	b Fiennes	5
T.W. Wills	b C.D.B. Marsham	5		
R.A. Fitzgerald	c Bennett, b Fellows	1		
E.J. Thornewill	run out	1	b C.D.B. Marsham	0
EXTRAS	B 10, L-B 6	16	B 16, L-B 3, W 1	20
	TOTAL	133	TOTAL (7 WKTS)	123

Cambridge bowling	OVERS	RUNS	WKTS		OVERS	RUNS	WKTS
McCormick	39	61	1		24	18	1
Johnson	34	45	4		16	16	0
Marshall	14	21	1		8	17	1
Makinson	9	4	3		28	36	5
Wills	—	—	—		9	14	1

Oxford bowling							
C.D.B. Marsham	29.3	38	6		32	37	2
Fiennes	28	61	2		30	40	2
Fellows	7	5	1		10	9	0
Payne	5	13	0		10	17	2

25, 26, 27 June
At Lord's

1857

Oxford won by
81 runs

Cambridge, led by J.M. Fuller, a Marlburian who became a Fellow of St John's in the same year as this match, had a first-innings lead of 13, thanks to the fine bowling of J. Makinson – he took the first seven Dark Blue wickets for 38 – and to the sensible opening innings of J.W. Marshall. For Oxford, the captain C.D.B. Marsham made 36 and took another five wickets.

It was Oxford's consistent second-innings batting that swung the match decisively their way. A.P. Law, one of the architects of the Harle-quins, who played under his usual sobriquet of 'A. Infelix', made 59. W.H. Bullock and the Harrovian K.E. Digby batted sensibly. W.H. Bullock (later Bullock-Hall) supported the Poles in 1860, and as a special correspondent was under fire with Garibaldi.

Though W. Wingfield batted manfully in the Light Blue second innings for 54, the bowling of Marsham, the Wykehamist H.H. Gillett, and the Hon. W.S.T.W. Fiennes proved too good.

OXFORD	First innings		Second innings	
A.P. Law	b Makinson	0	c Marshall, b Dupuis	59
W.G. Armitstead	b Makinson	14	b Horne	25
H.H. Gillett	c and b Makinson	12	c Johnson, b Makinson	2
W.H. Bullock	c and b Makinson	4	b Makinson	39
C.D.B. Marsham	b Makinson	36	run out	17
W. Fellows	c Johnson, b Makinson	24	b Marshall	3
K.E. Digby	not out	10	run out	38
F.W. Oliver	b Makinson	0	c and b Marshall	14
G.L. Hodgkinson	c Makinson, b Horne	5	b Makinson	3
B.W. Waud	b Horne	3	not out	0
Hon. W.S.T.W. Fiennes	b Horne	0	c Horne, b Johnson	22
EXTRAS	B 6, L-B 2, W 4, N-B 1	13	B 8, L-B 5, W 24, N-B 2	39
	TOTAL	121	TOTAL	261

CAMBRIDGE				
J.W. Marshall	b Marsham	48	b Gillett	4
J.M. Fuller	b Marsham	0	c and b Gillett	13
W. Wingfield	b Law	9	c Law, b Gillett	54
J. Makinson	run out	4	c and b Fiennes	30
O. Hammond	b Marsham	0	b Gillett	0
R.A. Bayford	b Fiennes	7	b Marsham	0
G.R. Dupuis	b Marsham	23	not out	35
G.R. Johnson	run out	6	c Digby, b Fiennes	4
A. Tomblin	b Marsham	12	c Oliver, b Marsham	0
E.L. Horne	b Gillett	0	c Waud, b Marsham	8
Viscount Royston	not out	0	c Oliver, b Gillett	0
EXTRAS	B 2, L-B 13, W 10	25	B 5, L-B 11, W 3	19
	TOTAL	134	TOTAL	167

Cambridge bowling	OVERS	RUNS	WKTS	OVERS	RUNS	WKTS
Makinson	34	38	7	36.3	65	3
Horne	28.3	43	3	37	28	1
Marshall	9	19	0	35	40	2
Hammond	3	8	0	3	6	0
Johnson	—	—	—	33	27	1
Royston	—	—	—	6	12	0
Dupuis	—	—	—	15	32	1
Bayford	—	—	—	5	12	0

Oxford bowling						
Marsham	34	31	5	42	58	3
Law	28.3	44	1	—	—	—
Gillett	9	14	1	27	46	5
Fiennes	5	15	1	10	20	2
Fellows	4	5	0	8	16	0
Oliver	—	—	—	3	8	0

1858

Oxford continued their winning streak – except for 1856 – and Cambridge were roundly defeated by an innings and 38 runs, thanks mainly to the fine bowling of C.D.B. Marsham, their captain, whose 11 for 59 in the match brought his figures over five University Matches to 41 wickets for 362 runs. He was well supported by the Hon. W.S.T.W. Fiennes, who took 6 for 42 in the two innings. F.H. Norman, Eton and Trinity, who was to captain the Kent County XI for six years, made top score when the Light Blues batted first, and in their second innings of 39 W.H. Benthall was the only player to reach double figures. Benthall also played rackets doubles for Cam-

bridge in 1858, and afterwards represented both the Buckinghamshire and the Middlesex county elevens. He was on the MCC Committee and became a précis writer and Assistant Private Secretary to successive Secretaries of State for India.

In between, Oxford had reached the respectable total of 211. W.H. Bullock made 78 before being stumped off C.J. Brereton, after the opener, K.E. Digby, had given his team a good start with 57. Digby became a county court judge and later Permanent Under-Secretary at the Home Office. He became successively a KCB and a KC.

CAMBRIDGE

	First innings			Second innings	
J.M. Fuller	c Digby, b Marsham	28		b Fiennes	0
C.R. Cooke	b Gillett	2		b Marsham	1
J. Makinson	b Marsham	6		b Fiennes	5
G.E. Cotterill	b Marsham	3		b Marsham	2
F.H. Norman	b Fiennes	43		b Marsham	5
W.H. Benthall	b Linton	0		not out	11
R.A. Bayford	b Marsham	6		c Waud, b Fiennes	6
E.L. Horne	not out	17		b Marsham	6
E.J.P. Wilkins	run out	1		b Marsham	0
H. Arkwright	c Traill, b Marsham	3		lbw, b Marsham	0
C.J. Brereton	lbw, b Fiennes	0		c Marsham, b Fiennes	2
EXTRAS	B 16, L-B 3, W 6	25		w 1	1
	TOTAL	134		TOTAL	39

OXFORD

K.E. Digby	b Makinson	57
J. Carpenter-Garnier	b Brereton	3
G.L. Hodgkinson	b Horne	1
C.G. Lane	st Bayford, b Brereton	1
H.H. Gillett	b Brereton	4
W.H. Bullock	st Bayford, b Brereton	78
C.D.B. Marsham	c Makinson, b Cotterill	0
B.W. Waud	b Makinson	21
W.F. Traill	b Horne	8
Hon. W.S.T.W. Fiennes	b Makinson	14
H. Linton	not out	7
EXTRAS	B 5, L-B 3, W 8, N-B 1	17
	TOTAL	211

Oxford bowling	OVERS	RUNS	WKTS	OVERS	RUNS	WKTS
Marsham	53	42	5	17	17	6
Gillett	25	27	1	—	—	—
Linton	17	18	1	—	—	—
Fiennes	13	21	2	16.2	21	4
Traill	3	1	0	—	—	—

Cambridge bowling	OVERS	RUNS	WKTS
Makinson	25	51	3
Horne	25	40	2
Brereton	21	51	4
Arkwright	10	26	0
Cotterill	6	21	1
Wilkins	5	5	0

23, 24 June
At Lord's

1859

Cambridge won by
28 runs

C.G. Lane, of Westminster and Christ Church, and R.A. Bayford, of Kensington Grammar School and Trinity Hall, were the captains of Oxford and Cambridge respectively for the twenty-fifth match of the series. As had often happened in recent contests, it was level-pegging on the first innings, J.H. Marshall of Cambridge, who later became Professor of Landscape Painting at Queen's College, Harley Street, being the only batsman on either side to score over thirty. E.J.P. Cassan took five Light Blue wickets, and G.E. Cotterill five Dark Blue. Cassan, who came from King's School, Bruton, organized the first Gentlemen of Somersetshire team, which

developed into the Somerset County XI, and he became Headmaster of Weybridge School.

The scene was set for an exciting match. Cotterill and W.H. Benthall made 55 and 39 not out respectively for Cambridge in their second innings, Cassan taking 4 for 55. Despite a steady innings of 39 by E.G. Sandford, one day to become Chancellor and Precentor of Exeter Cathedral, and a stout 21 not out at number nine by F. Brandt, who would be Judge of the High Court of Judicature, Madras, Oxford could manage only 139. This useful clerical/legal partnership was not enough to tilt the scales Oxford's way, however, and Cambridge won by 28 runs.

CAMBRIDGE	First innings		Second innings	
T.E. Bagge	b Traill	0	c Brandt, b Cassan	11
R.A. Bayford	b Cassan	0	st Waud, b Sandford	13
W.H. Benthall	b Traill	12	not out	39
E.B. Fawcett	run out	3	c Linton, b Sandford	18
F.H. Norman	b Traill	17	b Traill	0
G.E. Cotterill	b Cassan	17	b Cassan	55
J.H. Marshall	not out	38	c Morley, b Cassan	7
A. Bateman	b Cassan	4	lbw, b Brandt	16
A.E. Northey	b Cassan	13	b Cassan	3
J.E. Harris	b Cassan	0	b Traill	2
F. Nunn	b Brandt	6	b Brandt	0
EXTRAS	B 11, L-B 2, W 1	14	B 4, L-B 3, W 1, N-B 2	10
	TOTAL	124	TOTAL	174

OXFORD				
E.G. Sandford	b Fawcett	13	c Bateman, b Fawcett	39
J.W. Morley	c Bagge, b Fawcett	14	b Harris	1
C.G. Lane	c Nunn, b Cotterill	21	b Fawcett	5
K.E. Digby	b Cotterill	11	b Fawcett	4
B.W. Waud	c Benthall, b Cotterill	2	c Bagge, b Cotterill	11
G.L. Hodgkinson	c Marshall, b Cotterill	0	c Bateman, b Nunn	6
W.F. Traill	b Fawcett	20	c Bagge, b Cotterill	7
H.G. Alington	lbw, b Cotterill	0	b Harris	11
F. Brandt	run out	9	not out	21
E.J.P. Cassan	run out	2	b Cotterill	4
H. Linton	not out	22	c Cotterill, b Fawcett	7
EXTRAS	B 2, L-B 4, W 11	17	B 11, L-B 1, W 11	23
	TOTAL	131	TOTAL	139

Oxford bowling	OVERS	RUNS	WKTS	OVERS	RUNS	WKTS
Traill	31	45	3	39	40	2
Cassan	31	64	5	37	55	4
Brandt	1	1	1	15.2	25	2
Sandford	—	—	—	11	32	2
Linton	—	—	—	2	12	0

Cambridge bowling						
Fawcett	29	41	3	29	39	4
Cotterill	28	23	5	31.2	47	3
Bayford	17	29	0	21	6	0
Nunn	13	16	0	18	15	1
Harris	2	5	0	7	9	2
Bateman	0.3	0	0	—	—	—

25, 26 June
At Lord's

1860

Cambridge won by
3 wickets

This was an extraordinarily low-scoring contest due to the sodden condition of the ground, 16 being the top score made by any batsman. As a result of H.M. Plowden's effective bowling for Cambridge – he took 6 for 29 with his slow off-breaks – and W.F. Traill's for Oxford – he was described as 'a capital round-armed bowler, middle-paced, with an easy delivery', and he took 6 for 35 – Oxford managed a paltry 59 and Cambridge a not much better 76. Traill played several times in the Gentlemen *v* Players match, and eleven times for Kent, and was elected to the MCC Committee at the early age of twenty-five; but Plowden, after a few matches for Hampshire, was called to the Bar and went out to India,

where he became the Senior Judge of the Chief Court of Punjab.

The Light Blue opener, T.E. Bagge, of Eton and Trinity and between 1862 and 1865 the Hon. Sec. of the Norfolk County Club, batted two hours for his 15 runs. However, he fully justified selection for the Gentlemen later that year by scoring 62 and 60 against a strong bowling side. Oxford were hindered by the absence of Price and Sandford. R. Lang, the Harrovian captain in the two previous years, was the most effective Cambridge bowler, with 5 for 10 in seventeen overs. Despite Traill's taking another 5 for 18, Cambridge were the victors by three wickets.

OXFORD	First innings		Second innings	
J.M. Dolphin	c Northey, b Plowden	7	b Lang	2
R.B. Ranken	b Onslow	16	run out	9
B.W. Waud	b Plowden	1	c Lang, b Onslow	9
W.H. Bullock	b Onslow	1	c Fawcett, b Lang	7
C.G. Lane	b Plowden	4	b Lang	0
W. Cator	c Cotterill, b Plowden	2	lbw, b Lang	0
W.F. Traill	c Bateman, b Lang	2	b Plowden	9
R.W. Monro	b Onslow	3	b Lang	0
J.W. Morley	not out	10	b Fawcett	3
C.A. Garnett	c Norman, b Plowden	5	not out	1
F. Brandt	c Cotterill, b Plowden	3	b Plowden	3
EXTRAS	B 3, L-B 1, W 1	5	B 2, L-B 4, W 8	14
	TOTAL	59	TOTAL	57

CAMBRIDGE				
T.E. Bagge	b Traill	15	c Waud, b Brandt	0
D.R. Onslow	c Brandt, b Traill	1	b Traill	11
W.H. Benthall	c Brandt, b Traill	12	run out	2
F. Lee	b Traill	16	c Monro, b Traill	6
F.H. Norman	b Traill	0	b Traill	4
G.E. Cotterill	b Brandt	5	not out	8
A. Bateman	b Brandt	5		
E.B. Fawcett	c Dolphin, b Brandt	0	st Waud, b Traill	1
A.E. Northey	b Traill	0		
H.M. Plowden	b Brandt	5	not out	2
R. Lang	not out	11	b Traill	2
EXTRAS	L-B 1, W 5	6	B 3, W 2	5
	TOTAL	76	TOTAL (7 WKTS)	41

Cambridge bowling	OVERS	RUNS	WKTS	OVERS	RUNS	WKTS
Plowden	26	29	6	11.2	15	2
Onslow	21	16	3	12	12	1
Lang	4	9	1	17	10	5
Fawcett	—	—	—	16	6	1

Oxford bowling	OVERS	RUNS	WKTS	OVERS	RUNS	WKTS
Traill	37	35	6	24	18	5
Brandt	29	22	4	20	16	1
Dolphin	9	13	0	—	—	—
Monro	—	—	—	4	2	0

1861

This was the fourth Match to be played over three days. Thanks to their consistent batting in the second innings, and to the fine fast bowling of their opener H.W. Salter, educated privately before coming up to Clare, who took 9 for 38 in the match, Cambridge won by a decisive margin – 133 runs. They also owed much to three players: H.M. Marshall, who made an invaluable 76 not out in Cambridge's first innings, largely through fine cutting and accurately placed leg hits; D.R. Onslow for his 48 in their second innings; and the Hon. C.G. Lyttelton, first of a

great progeny, who took 7 for 60 in the match.

Oxford's lead of 21 was due to a useful second-wicket partnership between R.D. Walker and H. St J. Reade, who later played for Northamptonshire and became a headmaster three times over: of Beccles, Godolphin School, Hammersmith, and Oundle. In the Oxford second innings, T.P. Garnier and S. Linton were the only batsmen to reach double figures. This was the match in which E.G. Sandford was allowed a runner and a substitute fielder for reasons of ill health.

CAMBRIDGE	First innings		Second innings	
T.E. Bagge	c Reade, b Walker	3	b Daubeny	32
A. Bateman	lbw, b Walker	0	not out	25
H.M. Plowden	b Brandt	1	run out	8
H.M. Marshall	not out	76	b Daubeny	2
W. Bury	b Walker	2	b Walker	11
D.R. Onslow	c and b Inge	17	b Walker	48
A.W.T. Daniel	c Reade, b Daubeny	11	c Garnier, b Inge	18
Hon. C.G. Lyttelton	b Bowden-Smith	7	c Pepys, b Inge	18
W.J. Lyon	c and b Inge	15	b Daubeny	16
R. Lang	b Inge	0	b Daubeny	25
H.W. Salter	b Brandt	10	b Bowden-Smith	1
EXTRAS	B 3, L-B 2, W 4	9	B 2, L-B 7, W 5	14
	TOTAL	151	TOTAL	218

OXFORD				
T.P. Garnier	run out	0	c Daniel, b Salter	24
R.D. Walker	c Plowden, b Daniel	42	run out	6
H. St J. Reade	c Bury, b Daniel	49	c Lang, b Salter	4
E.G. Sandford	c Lyttelton, b Salter	9	b Lyttelton	3
F.G. Inge	lbw, b Lyttelton	16	lbw, b Salter	2
J.A. Pepys	b Salter	0	lbw, b Lyttelton	0
E. Hume	b Lyttelton	2	b Lyttelton	0
S. Linton	c Bateman, b Salter	10	b Salter	17
E.T. Daubeny	b Lyttelton	8	c Bateman, b Salter	2
F. Brandt	lbw, b Lyttelton	0	not out	0
F.H. Bowden-Smith	not out	0	b Salter	2
EXTRAS	B 18, L-B 9, W 7, N-B 2	36	B 1, L-B 3	4
	TOTAL	172	TOTAL	64

Oxford bowling	OVERS	RUNS	WKTS		OVERS	RUNS	WKTS
Brandt	26.2	30	2		3	7	0
Walker	15	21	3		25	60	2
Inge	16	40	3		17.2	45	2
Bowden-Smith	11	21	1		15	40	1
Daubeny	14	30	1		29	52	4

Cambridge bowling							
Lyttelton	31.3	19	4		29	41	3
Lang	26	30	0		—	—	—
Salter	25	19	3		28	19	6
Plowden	18	34	0		—	—	—
Daniel	9	21	2		—	—	—
Onslow	9	13	0		—	—	—

23, 24 June
At Lord's

1862

Cambridge won by
8 wickets

The fixture was again a two-day match, which Cambridge, an immensely strong side with no weak point, and captained by the Harrovian H.M. Plowden, won triumphantly by eight wickets. The side was especially strong in bowling, H.W. Salter taking 4 for 18 in the first innings and R. Lang 9 for 35 in the match. H.M. Marshall made another thirty at Lord's, as did both A.W.T. Daniel, one of the original promoters of the Inter-University Sports, and H.W. Salter. Salter went in at number eleven and took a number eleven's pleasure in being the Light Blue top scorer, with hits 'executed with a bat not rigidly straight'.

Oxford's reply to Cambridge's 171 was 64 and, following on, 158. The finest batting of the match was that of the Dark Blue freshman R.A.H. Mitchell, of Eton and Balliol, who in his innings of 37 and 53 'mirrored the distinction that was awaiting him'. That distinction is fully portrayed in the appropriate Dark Blue section of this book. The Oxford wicket-keeper, J.W. Haygarth, of Winchester and Corpus, 'kept' splendidly.

In this era the 'square' at Lord's left much to be desired, as E.W. Swanton mentions in his introductory essay; innings such as Mitchell's were thus all the more praiseworthy.

CAMBRIDGE

	First innings		Second innings	
C. Booth	*hw, b* Walker	7	*b* Daubeny	0
Hon. T. de Grey	*c* Ridsdale, *b* Daubeny	20	*not out*	22
Hon. C.G. Lyttelton	*b* Daubeny	0		
H.M. Marshall	*c* Haygarth, *b* Reade	31	*not out*	0
W. Bury	*st* Haygarth, *b* Reade	14		
A.W.T. Daniel	*b* Walker	30	*c* Haygarth, *b* Reade	27
H.M. Plowden	*b* Reade	4		
R. Lang	*c and b* Reade	0		
M.T. Martin	*c* Hume, *b* Daubeny	13		
G.F. Helm	*c* Haygarth, *b* Mitchell	0		
H.W. Salter	*not out*	32		
EXTRAS	B 8, L-B 6, W 3, N-B 3	20	W 1, N-B 2	3
	TOTAL	171	TOTAL (2 WKTS)	52

OXFORD

E. Hume	*c* Martin, *b* Salter	2	*b* Lang	0
R.D. Walker	*b* Salter	0	*b* Lyttelton	1
F.G. Inge	*b* Salter	1	*c* Lyttelton, *b* Plowden	22
R.A.H. Mitchell	*b* Plowden	37	*b* Lang	53
T.P. Garnier	*b* Salter	0	*b* Lang	21
H. St J. Reade	*b* Lang	9	*c* Marshall, *b* Lyttelton	19
S.O.B. Ridsdale	*b* Lang	0	*b* Plowden	0
J.W. Haygarth	*not out*	8	*b* Helm	6
S. Linton	*b* Lang	0	*b* Lang	20
C.A. Garnett	*b* Lang	0	*b* Salter	1
E.T. Daubeny	*b* Lang	4	*not out*	0
EXTRAS	B 1, L-B 1, W 1	3	B 4, L-B 4, W 6, N-B 1	15
	TOTAL	64	TOTAL	158

Oxford bowling	OVERS	RUNS	WKTS		OVERS	RUNS	WKTS
Daubeny	42	59	3		8	17	1
Walker	31.1	26	2		7.1	7	0
Reade	22	32	4		8	15	1
Mitchell	17	9	1		—	—	—
Garnett	10	19	0		—	—	—
Inge	2	6	0		7	10	0

Cambridge bowling							
Lyttelton	16	28	0		13	26	2
Salter	13	18	4		14	18	1
Lang	8.2	4	5		24.3	31	4
Plowden	6	11	1		19	38	2
Helm	—	—	—		13	30	1

1863

Oxford gained their revenge for recent defeats by beating Cambridge by eight wickets. The match was played on a very slow pitch – 'with an abundance of sinuous shooters' – on which no batsmen on either side made more than 25 until the Carthusian F.G. Inge hit impressively in the Dark Blue second innings. The bowlers were on top throughout the game, as these bowling analyses show: for Oxford, 7 for 51 in the match by the Etonian A.S. Teape and 8 for 37 by the Marlburian S.C. Voules, Scholar of Lincoln, first captain of the Somerset County XI and Principal of Bath College from 1874 to 1878; and for Cambridge, H.M. Plowden 8 for 62. The Oxford bowler J. Scott's unusual feat was to take 3 for 1,

but to bowl six wides and one no-ball – he was later to have a distinguished career overseas.

Cambridge's fielding reached a high standard, never higher than when R.A.H. Mitchell was superbly caught at long leg by A.W.T. Daniel, off T. Collins. An account of Collins' no-balling appears in the Oxford section of the decade 1855–64. The Hon. T. de Grey was top scorer for Cambridge, and afterwards led a full public life, including being a Trustee of the British Museum and the Royal College of Surgeons. In addition, he formed one of the most important collections of micro-lepidoptera in the world, and his bag of 1070 grouse to his own gun was at that time a record.

CAMBRIDGE	First innings			Second innings	
Hon. T. de Grey	c Bull, b Teape		12	lbw, b Voules	24
G.H. Tuck	run out		7	c Walker, b Voules	0
H.M. Marshall	c Haygarth, b Teape		0	b Voules	3
A.W.T. Daniel	b Scott		7	b Voules	1
Hon. C.G. Lyttelton	not out		19	b Voules	0
T. Collins	b Scott		0	b Teape	1
C. Booth	b Teape		9	b Voules	5
R.D. Balfour	b Teape		0	b Voules	5
H.M. Plowden	b Teape		1	run out	4
G.F. Helm	b Teape		0	b Scott	11
F.C. Hope-Grant	b Voules		0	not out	4
EXTRAS	L-B 2, W 8		10	W 2, N-B 1	3
	TOTAL		65	TOTAL	61

OXFORD					
T.P. Garnier	c Collins, b Plowden		8	hw, b Plowden	2
R.D. Walker	b Collins		10	c Tuck, b Helm	8
F.W. Wright	b Plowden		0		
H.E. Bull	c and b Plowden		1		
R.A.H. Mitchell	c Daniel, b Collins		2		
F.G. Inge	c Lyttelton, b Plowden		5	not out	48
F.R. Evans	b Plowden		25	not out	5
S.C. Voules	b Plowden		4		
J.W. Haygarth	c Lyttelton, b Plowden		0		
A.S. Teape	b Helm		0		
J. Scott	not out		0		
EXTRAS	L-B 1, W 2, N-B 1		4	B 1, L-B 4	5
	TOTAL		59	TOTAL (2 WKTS)	68

Oxford bowling	OVERS	RUNS	WKTS	OVERS	RUNS	WKTS
Teape	21	19	6	26	32	1
Walker	20	24	0	—	—	—
Voules	9	11	1	25	26	7
Scott	6	1	2	0.2	0	1

Cambridge bowling						
Plowden	24	25	7	13	37	1
Collins	15	22	2	4	7	0
Helm	8.1	8	1	4	5	1
Hope-Grant	—	—	—	6	14	0

13, 14 June
At Lord's

1864

Oxford won by
4 wickets

The Etonian R.A.H. Mitchell captained Oxford, and the Rugbeian C. Booth captained Cambridge, in the thirtieth match of the series. As so often, there was nothing in it after the first two innings. Oxford put Cambridge in on a sun-drying wicket not really fit for play, and good bowling by A.S. Teape and W.F. Maitland dismissed the Light Blues for 75, the Hon. C.G. Lyttelton being top scorer with 17. The ground remained sodden throughout the first day, and T.S. Curteis and the Hon. F.G. Pelham were equally effective. The Dark Blue opener, E.W. Tritton, who had the previous year made a perfect 130 for Eton against Winchester, led the way with a sterling 24, but his side could manage only 87.

In a low-scoring match Cambridge may well have been hopeful when they reached 136 in their second innings, thanks largely to A.W.T. Daniel, in fine form throughout the season, R.D. Balfour and C. Booth. But they had already become aware of the special qualities of R.A.H. Mitchell and he did not disappoint his admirers. His stylish and aggressive 55 not out, after carefully playing himself in, turned the game Oxford's way, and Oxford won by four wickets. A contemporary described the enthusiasm in the pavilion as unparalleled but justified, 'for grander batting never was played by an undergraduate than Mr Mitchell's 55'.

CAMBRIDGE	First innings		Second innings	
G.H. Tuck	c Haygarth, b Maitland	4	b Maitland	4
A. Walker	c Haygarth, b Teape	1	b Walker	12
A.W.T. Daniel	c Tritton, b Teape	16	c Voules, b Evans	33
M.T. Martin	b Maitland	3	c Haygarth, b Maitland	0
Hon. C.G. Lyttelton	c Wright, b Teape	17	c Voules, b Maitland	0
C. Booth	b Teape	3	c and b Voules	22
H.M. Marshall	c Tritton, b Maitland	3	c Walker, b Voules	12
T.F. Fowler	not out	7	c Wright, b Maitland	3
R.D. Balfour	b Teape	12	c and b Evans	30
Hon. F.G. Pelham	c Voules, b Teape	4	b Teape	11
T.S. Curteis	b Maitland	5	not out	0
EXTRAS			B 6, W 1, N-B 2	9
TOTAL		75	TOTAL	136

OXFORD				
T. Case	c Balfour, b Fowler	13	b Curteis	5
E.W. Tritton	c Martin, b Curteis	24	b Curteis	2
F.R. Evans	c Martin, b Booth	13	b Pelham	13
J. St J. Frederick	c Daniel, b Curteis	0	c Fowler, b Curteis	1
R.A.H. Mitchell	c and b Curteis	15	not out	55
R.D. Walker	c Lyttelton, b Pelham	5	b Curteis	7
S.C. Voules	b Pelham	2	c Marshall, b Booth	13
F.W. Wright	st Balfour, b Pelham	2		
W.F. Maitland	b Curteis	5	not out	12
J.W. Haygarth	st Balfour, b Pelham	1		
A.S. Teape	not out	0		
EXTRAS	B 3, W 4	7	B 6, L-B 5, W 5, N-B 1	17
TOTAL		87	TOTAL (6 WKTS)	125

Oxford bowling	OVERS	RUNS	WKTS	OVERS	RUNS	WKTS
Maitland	22.3	34	4	12	19	4
Teape	22	41	6	26.2	34	1
R.D. Walker	—	—	—	22	34	1
Voules	—	—	—	19	20	2
Evans	—	—	—	8	20	2

Cambridge bowling						
Curteis	36.1	23	4	39	58	4
Pelham	22	39	4	34.1	28	1
Fowler	9	13	1	2	5	0
Booth	5	5	1	6	11	1
Lyttelton	—	—	—	4	6	0

Score-sheet of the two first innings (handwritten, partially legible)

Oxford		Cambridge	
[Whitehall?] 141 bowled Jenner	7	Jenner 11 caught Price	2
Master 11131121111111231 31 *[...]* Jenner	29	Winthrop 1211214 112 *[...]* 4 bowled Price	24
Price 31 bowled Pickering	4	Graysbrook caught *[...]*	
Pytham 14324113111 caught Horsman	22	Pickering 2 run out	2
Wright 2111 caught Merewether	5	*Twisleton* 1314131 caught *[...]*	16
Wordsworth bowled Jenner		F. Gordon 3A run out	7
Bayly bowled Jenner		Horsman 1 caught Wright	
Robertson bowled Jenner		Elles bowled Wordsworth	
Jamison 1311132A caught Graysbrook	16	Merewether 113311 5232 not out	20
Bull 1131354 bowled Pickering	10	St John 22A1 bowled Price	9
Cook 1114113 not out	10	Handy 111131 bowled Price	8
	129		96
	96		
	33		
Byes 1412 – 9		Byes 121	
Wide Balls 111111 9			

ABOVE Score-sheet of the two first innings of the second match of the series, played on Cowley Marsh, Oxford, in 1829.

BELOW Bullingdon Green, Oxford, where the 1843 match was played and won by Cambridge, clearly attracted pedestrian and equestrian interest.

BELOW Charles Wordsworth, architect of the Boat Race (1829) as well as of the University Cricket Match, was a nephew of the Poet Laureate and became both a headmaster and a bishop.

BELOW R.A.H. Mitchell in his later years. He was an outstanding Oxford batsman, captained the sides from 1863–65, and subsequently coached generations of Etonians to adopt his style and standards.

ABOVE C.B. Fry, whose intellectual and athletic prowess was a by-word in his day, played for Oxford from 1892–95. The Olympian hauteur of this lofted straight-drive has an authentic ring.

The 1884 Oxford side, captained by M.C. Kemp, which defeated the Australians
BACK ROW K.J. Key B.E. Nicholls M.C. Kemp T.C. O'Brien L.d'A. Hildyard
FRONT ROW E.H. Buckland H.V. Page E.W. Bastard H.O. Whitby J.H. Brain
ABSENT T.R. Hine-Haycock

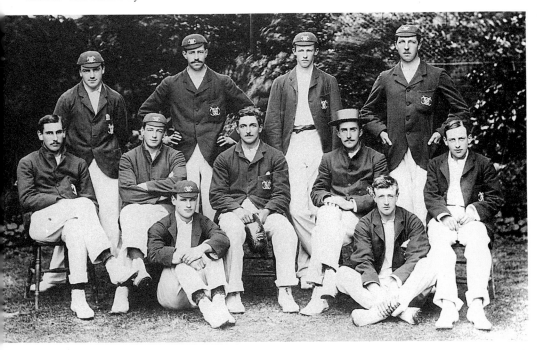

The 1894 Oxford side captained by C.B. Fry
BACK ROW R.P. Lewis G.B. Raikes G.R. Bardswell D.H. Forbes
MIDDLE ROW G.J. Mordaunt L.C.V. Bathurst C.B. Fry R.C.N. Palairet H.D.G. Leveson-Gower
FRONT ROW F.A. Phillips H.K. Foster

The 1878 Cambridge side, captained by Hon. E. Lyttelton, which defeated the Australians
BACK ROW Hon. Ivo F.W. Bligh D.Q. Steel L.K. Jarvis A.F.J. Ford
MIDDLE ROW F.W. Kingston A.P. Lucas Hon. E. Lyttelton Hon. A. Lyttelton P.H. Morton
FRONT ROW H. Whitfield A.G. Steel

The 1890 Cambridge side captained by Sammy Woods
BACK ROW D.L.A. Jephson E.C. Streatfeild R.N. Douglas F.S. Jackson H. Hale A.J.L. Hill
FRONT ROW C.P. Foley F.G.J. Ford S.M.J. Woods R.C. Gosling G. MacGregor

Herbert Jenner (later Jenner-Fust) captained Cambridge in the first match and spoke at the Silver Jubilee dinner held in 1877.

Several cricketers won recognition in the series of cartoons by Spy and others. This is Ape's portrayal of Alfred Lyttelton, the 1879 Light Blue captain.

F.C. Cobden's final over in the 1870 match earned him a special niche in cricket history. Here is its perpetrator wearing his I Zingari cap.

The Studd brothers – J.E.K., C.T., and G.B. – were Cambridge captains in successive years, 1882–83–84. The feat was repeated by the Ashtons in 1921–22–23.

LEFT A.G. Steel, Cambridge captain in 1880, was an all-rounder good enough to be included in a joint University team picked from any age.

BELOW LEFT Hon. Ivo Bligh captained Cambridge in 1881 and the MCC side to Australia in 1882–83. During this tour he was presented with the 'Ashes'.

BELOW RIGHT Sammy Woods was a fine cricketer held in the highest regard. After captaining Cambridge in 1890 he became the inspiration of Somerset cricket.

RIGHT A.J. Webbe was a fine captain of Oxford (1877–78) and Middlesex, and throughout his later life a popular administrator.

BELOW K.J. Key, four years in the Oxford side (1884–87), later captained Surrey. His seventh-wicket partnership with H. Philipson of 340 against Middlesex remains a University record.

ABOVE H.V. Page, Oxford captain 1885–86, had a reputation as a powerful leg-side player. He returned to Cheltenham College, where he taught for thirty-five years.

BELOW C.J. Ottaway was one of Oxford's great all-rounders; he represented the University at cricket (1870–3), football, athletics, rackets and tennis. Impressively, he also took a First in Mods.

ABOVE Cambridge undergraduates on Parker's Piece, 1842. Pads apart, the game has a modern ring – though the marquee seems to be a trifle adjacent!

BELOW The Light Blues batting against the first Australian team to play at Fenner's in 1882. Plenty of spectators, but as yet no College buildings behind the bowler's arm.

4
1865–1874
Cobden catches the Imagination

OXFORD *Fellowes follows on*

Mowing machines were by now in standard use, having been developed by Edwin Bearch, who adapted the spiral cylinder used in textile mills for trimming the nap of cloth to the cutting of grass; overarm bowling was established; the wearing of white was common practice; and field-placing had become an important part of cricket. At Oxford there was bound to be a period of anti-climax after the great days of Mitchell. None the less, in 1866 there were some fine players, W.F. Maitland and E.L. Fellowes contributing more than their share, and a strange record was created: in four matches Oxford enforced the follow-on. The first was a magnificent victory over the Gentlemen, who included W.G. Grace and his brother G.F. at the age of fifteen, and C.D.B. Marsham. They followed this by asking the MCC to bat again, achieving much the better of a drawn match, E. Davenport making a century. Southgate just saved the next match, and then a weak Oxford side defeated the Gentlemen of Warwickshire by an innings.

The narrow win against Cambridge owed much to the weather and to Fellowes' fine use of a wicket which suited him. It is interesting to read that the price of admission for the Varsity Match was increased to one shilling for a person on foot, half a crown to those on horseback, five shillings for a two-wheeled carriage and ten shillings for a four-wheeler.

Under the captaincy of W.F. Maitland, things somehow went wrong. True, a weak Free Foresters side was beaten, but there were two resounding defeats by the MCC. In the second Oxford could manage only 102, 47 of these coming from a bowler's bat, that of E.M. Kenney. Marylebone replied with 163, only for Oxford to lose seven wickets for 9 runs, eventually reaching 32. E.S. Carter was the last Oxford player to win a double blue in the original sense; he rowed in the winning Oxford crews of 1867 and 1868.

Despite having a rather better side in 1868, with a fine pair of opening bowlers in Kenney and E.L. Fellowes, the former bowling fast left-hand round the wicket, and three first-rate batsmen in R. Digby, A.T. Fortescue and B. Pauncefote, they had only one positive success – a low-scoring match against the MCC. A curious feature of the eleven defeated in the Varsity Match was the inclusion of W.H. Lipscombe, whose only claim to a place came from his one previous match for Oxford when he took 1 for 38 and made a 'pair'.

The year 1869 saw the arrival of E.F.S. Tylecote from Clifton. In the previous summer he had made 404 for Classics *v* Moderns, then the world's highest score!

Later he played as a wicket-keeper for England. Sixteen of Oxford did well to draw their first match against an England eleven. The MCC won by an innings, in a match notable for the fact that it was W.G.'s first appearance for the Club, and he took seven wickets and made 117.

In 1870 C.J. Ottaway appeared on the scene. His record compares favourably with that of C.B. Fry, including a First in Mods. He was four years in the cricket team, leading Oxford to victory in 1873; he captained the winning Oxford side in the first Varsity soccer match; he ran in the 100 yards against Cambridge; he played rackets for Oxford over three years in which they swept the board; and he played real tennis for the University. In his few years for Middlesex he averaged over 50, but died tragically young in 1878 only two years after being called to the Bar. As a batsman he was an elegant player with a sound orthodox defence.

He was accompanied by two fine bowlers, C.K. Francis and S.E. Butler, both, like Ottaway, Brasenose men. During this decade not only did BNC provide five captains, but in the years 1871–2 eight of the Oxford side came from the college. Butler was a powerfully built six-footer, who is best remembered for his remarkable performance in Cambridge's first innings of the 1871 Varsity Match, not only taking all ten wickets but hitting the stumps eight times, and retrieving Oxford's honour after defeat in 'Cobden's match' the year before.

It should have been a good year in 1872, with nine old blues available. Cowley Marsh in this wet season was said to resemble a huge sponge, so consequently the batsmen had little practice and only one score of fifty was made in the entire season. The year is notable for a first meeting with Middlesex, a match in which Oxford returned their best performance, saving the game in their second innings against strong opposition.

Under Ottaway in 1873 Oxford won all of their five matches. They made the impressive score of 321 against the MCC – indeed, a huge score for Cowley Marsh in May. Marylebone were made to follow on and Oxford coasted home by seven wickets. Against Middlesex, Oxford needed only 65 in the last innings and made heavy weather of it; Ottaway held firm and they scrambled home by two wickets. W.H. Game, another great name in the University records, made his debut that year; a tremendous hitter, he played a vital part in his first Varsity Match.

The outstanding feature of Lord Harris's eleven in 1874 was the fielding, in a period when the Oxford sides were noted for this aspect of the game. Harris was to become a notable figure in the cricket of his time, second in influence only to W.G. He not only successfully captained England, but raised the fortunes of Kent after years of depression, later becoming President of that county, and his influence was felt strongly at Lord's until his death aged 81.

The most astonishing result of the season was the match with Middlesex at Prince's. The game lasted but six hours (173 overs) and the University bowled out the home team for 61. Oxford, despite losing three batsmen for nought, reached a total of 123. Middlesex then made 47. They might have saved the innings defeat, but V.E. Walker had left the ground, thinking that he would not be wanted that night.

The following year, 1875, if for no other reason would be noteworthy because it saw the first appearance of A.J. Webbe. His is one of the great names of cricket; not only was he a fine batsman and fielder, but he was also a shrewd and popular captain of Oxford and of Middlesex, and as an administrator he has had few equals. He succeeded C.J.B. Marsham as President of the Harlequins. 'Like many Harrow batsmen of the period, he stood at the wicket with legs wide apart, a position well suited to playing back in defence or cutting.' He won a blue as a freshman, playing two innings which helped materially in Oxford's 6-run victory over Cambridge. Later in the year he won high praise from W.G., with whom he shared an opening stand of 203 for the Gentlemen, his contribution being 65.

The Reverend S.C. Voules – a member of three winning Oxford sides in the early sixties, later a master, first at Rossall and then at Marlborough, before moving to a parish – in looking back on the period, drew particular attention to a changing attitude to field-placing.

Easier wickets and, it must be allowed, an improvement in wicket-keeping, have enabled the stumper to dispense with a long-stop, and this time-honoured functionary has practically disappeared . . . men are massed in the slips for fast bowling, or placed just where the bowler wants them in a way that would have staggered the cricketer of earlier days, when, it may be frankly allowed, the methods were rather too stereotyped, and there was little variation or adaptability to a bowler's requirements in placing the field.

During the middle years of the century, Staffordshire potteries were satisfying popular demand for chimney ornaments. It is an indication of cricket's growing influence that from the forties onwards cricket subjects began to appear on the market. Lillywhite, Pilch, Box and Clarke were the first positively identified figures, and a little later Parr and Caesar were modelled. At much the same time, an attractive pair of unidentified figure groups was produced. These comparatively rare cricket figures have appeared in auction catalogues as depicting 'Oxford and Cambridge Cricket'. Almost certainly this is misleading, and probably derives from the fact that at the time the most common underglaze was cobalt blue, which gave an approximation of Oxford blue, but it is a happy thought to believe the description true.

CAMBRIDGE *The era of Yardley and Thornton*

The pattern of the decade from 1865 to 1874 was statistically similar to that of its predecessor, in that the two Universities each finished with five victories, and, correspondingly, five defeats. Thus, after half a century of the combat and companionship implicit in our story, neither had a lead. After two early wins by Oxford, Cambridge came with a convincing run of five wins in six matches between 1867, the year of the second Reform Act, and 1872, when the secrecy of the electoral ballot was safeguarded by Act of Parliament. No secret ballot was needed, however, to record the pleasure felt in Cambridge taverns at the reformed cricket played by the Light Blues in these critical years! Oxford effected a convincing comeback by winning the last two matches of the decade.

The historic Cambridge win of 1878 against the Australians still lies, of course, in the future, but the strength of the Light Blue sides throughout the seventies makes that success seem less improbable. Rather did their supporters in the first few years of this decade look back to 1870 itself – to the remarkable finale, 'the stuff that dreams are made on', of what has justifiably been called 'Cobden's match'. It was notable not only for Cobden's hat-trick with which the game ended, and the failure of Oxford's last five wickets to score the 19 runs needed for victory, but also for William Yardley's becoming the first person to score a hundred in the University Match. It was Cambridge's fourth successive win, and the margin was just 2 runs.

> *Oh the little more and how much it is!*
> *And the little less and what worlds away!*

Cobden's match deserves one last gloss to illustrate Browning's percipient couplet. For a missed catch might so easily have made the difference, as W.B. Money, the Cambridge captain, whose scores at Lord's failed to reflect his ability, afterwards related:

Jack Dale was our point, an excellent one too. All was going well in Oxford's last innings and I didn't feel anxious. One of the Oxford men, either Townshend or Tylecote, in playing forward, sent up a little, gentle catch to point. Jack never even touched it! I was simply astounded, and said 'O Jack, what have you done?' He only replied, 'I'm awfully sorry, Walter; I was looking at a lady getting out of a drag!' I believe it was this that made the match such a near thing.

The Dale Cup is now given at Tonbridge for fielding!

I shall complete this extract from Money's reminiscences, even though it moves away from Cobden's match, since it appears to be the origin of the 'Quid eights' which used to be part of the programme of the May races, and is therefore relevant to our story.

In the same year, 1870, we took a boat manned by 'Varsity-eleven men down to see the May races; needless to say, the rowing was not good, even though we were stroked by a member of the Varsity eight, Jack Dale. In our return Yardley and myself got out, and then pulled the boat over, sending all the crew into the water, when we discovered to our horror that our 'cox' couldn't swim. However, he was promptly and gallantly rescued by Charlie Thornton.

Character has now begun to emerge in plenty in the ranks of Light Blue cricketers – it was almost certainly there earlier, but the records are thinner – and the evidence is clear that from the start many were not cricketers alone. F.G. Pelham, for example, who played from 1864 to 1867, was Amateur Half-Mile Champion in 1871 and 1873, after playing for Sussex for four years. C.A. Absolom, nicknamed the 'Cambridge Navvy' and universally loved, was in the Cambridge XI from 1866 to 1869, went to Australia with the 1878–9 side, did yeoman service for Kent, and was also winner of the high jump in the University sports in 1867. William Yardley, who was regarded as one of the greatest cricketers of his day, and who made two centuries against Oxford, the first in Cobden's match and the second in 1872, showed brilliant promise at rugby football, and was a fine tennis and rackets player also. *Wisden* rates him second only to W.G. Grace as a batsman. He brought distinction also to the theatre in the 1870s, both as an author and as a critic. His early death at the age of fifty-one was a sad blow both to the theatre and to the world of sport.

Others from this era deserve a mention. The Carthusian E.C. Streatfeild not only made a hundred against Oxford and played for the Gentlemen, but was also a soccer blue, and had previously twice been in the winning public schools rackets pair. H.A. Richardson, who was also an excellent billiards player, was a fine batsman who learned his cricket at Tonbridge and for one season was in the top rank. He had a great season in 1868, with an average, high for those days, of 38, including a dazzling 143 in two hours at The Oval, when James Southerton, the distinguished Surrey off-spinner, was made to look decidedly ordinary. Richardson's six victims in the 1869 University Match marked him out as a good, if not great, wicket-keeper. The favourite ground of Money, the Light Blue captain in Cobden's match already quoted, was Lord's, where his performances put him in the top flight, first as a lob bowler, later as a batsman talented enough to achieve an average of 53 in 1870. That year he also had innings of 70 and 109 not out for the Gentlemen at The Oval. C.E. Green, of Uppingham, who led Cambridge to victory in 1868 from the front, since he made 44 and 59, was afterwards the life and soul of Essex cricket.

Three further Cambridge cricketers from these years are worthy of inclusion in the roll of honour. One of these sadly died at the age of forty-three, a sick man then living in Nottingham. He was W.N. Powys, a fast left-arm bowler with a low delivery, who had a bag of 24 Oxford wickets for 153 in his three University Matches, and was chosen to play for the Gentlemen in 1872. After scoring 54 not out against him that year, W.G. held Powys in high regard.

The second player, an octogenarian at the time of his death in 1938, the year of Munich, was G.H. Longman, a stylish batsman who played for the Gentlemen in 1875 and on subsequent occasions, and by dint of immense application became a greatly improved fieldsman after he had left Eton. He represented both Hampshire and Surrey, becoming President of Surrey for three years in 1936. The third, who lived into his nineties, was Charles Tillard, who bowled fast round-arm and very straight for the Cambridge sides of 1873 and 1874, and once had the distinction of clean bowling both W.G. Grace and A.N. Hornby in a match at The Oval – fame indeed! He was also a good hitter and useful fieldsman; after his Cambridge days he taught at Cheltenham.

One of the greatest Cambridge figures of the time, however, was a man who stamped his personality on the game, as on so many other games in which he played, with a rare authority. *Proxime accessit* to Yardley as the personality of the decade, in view of his impact, was C.I. 'Buns' Thornton, the mightiest hitter of his day, and arguably of any other. He too had other strings to his bow: he played rackets and Eton fives with skill, he put the weight and threw the cricket ball with abandon. He was on the winning side at Lord's three years out of four. When his cricketing days were over, he earned the gratitude of many players by establishing and sustaining the Scarborough Festival. I was fortunate enough to play there in 1951, and saw the young Colin Cowdrey make a stylish and composed hundred that belied his youth. Thornton loved the game, preferring to go in first, and jumping quickly to the ball in making his magnificent drives.

Stories of his fast hundreds and towering hits are legion, but few were present to see him hurl an unsuccessful bat over the old wooden pavilion at Fenner's into the adjoining prison-yard, 'for the benefit of his fellow-sinners'. As examples of his hitting power, he hit W.M. Rose, at Canterbury in 1871, for a blow measuring 152 yards. At the nets at Hove he sent the ball 168 yards 2 feet – then the longest authenticated hit. He loved to clear the ring at Lord's and The Oval especially, and once at Scarborough he drove a ball from A.G. Steel over a four-storeyed house into Trafalgar Square.

Thornton treated cricket as a game, firmly believing that a cricket ball was there to be hit, and hit far. He was in the timber business for thirty-five years, and he took pleasure in travel, which was reflected in his book *East and West and Home Again*. In fact, to reach home from the Middle East was made easier during this decade by the opening of the Suez Canal, which would also reduce the time taken for English teams, with players from Oxford and Cambridge to the fore, to reach Australia.

1865

The editor of *Fifty Years of Sport*, writing in 1913, said that by common consent the Oxford team of 1865 was their best ever. Its claim to compare with the Cambridge side of 1878 which defeated the Australians owes much to the fact that four of the team – R.A.H. Mitchell, R.D. Walker, F.R. Evans and W.F. Maitland – assisted the Gentlemen to gain the first victory over the Players at Lord's which had fallen to their lot since 1853. Moreover, two had already played for the Gentlemen, and two more would do so. Both teams were strong, Oxford exceptionally so, and R.A.H. Mitchell was the outstanding player, making 57 and 35. The Hon. F.G. Pelham took 8 for 98 in the match for Cam-

bridge, and W.F. Maitland took 8 for 76 for Oxford.

Oxford batted first and reached 191, Mitchell being well supported by F.R. Evans and S.C. Voules. Cambridge replied with 119, Ashley Walker and R.D. Balfour scoring 38 and 32 respectively, and avoiding the follow-on. Oxford's second innings of 160 proved decisive – it would have been more so had it not been for C. Booth's brilliant fielding at cover – and no Light Blue batsman could manage twenty in the second innings. However, Booth became the first man to hit a ball out of Lord's in the University Match, striking E.L. Fellowes over the Grandstand and into the street.

OXFORD	First innings			Second innings	
T. Case	b Pelham	17		c Walker, b Green	25
E.W. Tritton	b Pelham	10		b Green	12
R.D. Walker	hw, b Pelham	5		c Dyke, b Green	0
F.W. Wright	c Winter, b Green	8		st Balfour, b Walker	27
R.A.H. Mitchell	c and b Pelham	57		c Booth, b Pelham	35
F.R. Evans	c Curteis, b Pelham	43		c Booth, b Walker	1
C.E. Boyle	b Pelham	1		c Pelham, b Walker	0
S.C. Voules	b Walker	24		b Curteis	14
W.F. Maitland	b Dyke	17		not out	27
A.S. Teape	not out	1		b Pelham	0
E.L. Fellowes	st Balfour, b Walker	0		b Green	8
EXTRAS	B 2, L-B 3, W 3	8		B 3, L-B 5, W 3	11
	TOTAL	191		TOTAL	160

CAMBRIDGE					
A.H. Winter	b Fellowes	0		run out	15
E.F. Dyke	b Walker	0		b Maitland	0
A. Walker	not out	38		c Voules, b Teape	3
G.H. Tuck	c Boyle, b Fellowes	7		c Teape, b Maitland	19
R.D. Balfour	b Maitland	32		c Case, b Fellowes	9
E.P. Ash	b Voules	18		c Walker, b Maitland	8
J.S.E. Hood	c Walker, b Voules	4		lbw, b Maitland	5
C. Booth	st Wright, b Maitland	2		b Fellowes	18
Hon. F.G. Pelham	c Case, b Maitland	3		run out	16
C.E. Green	b Voules	1		c and b Fellowes	12
T.S. Curteis	lbw, b Maitland	4		not out	4
EXTRAS	B 6, L-B 3, N-B 1	10		B 2, L-B 5, W 2	9
	TOTAL	119		TOTAL	118

Cambridge bowling	OVERS	RUNS	WKTS	OVERS	RUNS	WKTS
Pelham	53	71	6	23	27	2
Green	30	54	1	26.1	44	4
Dyke	23	26	1	5	16	0
A. Walker	8	18	2	17	53	3
Curteis	8	14	0	8	9	1

Oxford bowling	OVERS	RUNS	WKTS	OVERS	RUNS	WKTS
R.D. Walker	29	28	1	17	28	0
Maitland	25.1	38	4	16	38	4
Fellowes	20	27	2	18	30	3
Voules	17	16	3	—	—	—
Teape	—	—	—	15	10	1
Evans	—	—	—	4	3	0

1866

When Oxford were dismissed for a paltry 62, the Hon. F.G. Pelham having the splendid analysis of 7 for 26, and Cambridge led by 66 runs, the Dark Blue supporters must have wondered whether they were getting value for the increased entrance fee. However, Oxford rallied in the second innings, when the weather was brighter and warmer and the ground faster, to make 171, W.F. Maitland compensating for his earlier duck by playing a beautiful innings of 51 at a critical moment of the match, and O. Spencer Smith making 30. C.A. Absolom and the Hon. G.W.S. Lyttelton each took three wickets. Absolom was winner of the high jump in the 1867

University sports and was a member of the fifth English team to Australia in 1878–9. In 1889 he met an untimely death while Purser of the SS *Muriel*.

The scene was set for an exciting match worthy of the occasion. The Light Blues started steadily, but once E.L. Fellowes, later President of the Cambridgeshire County Club, had bowled A.H. Winter and Pelham, and E.S. Carter, of Durham Grammar School and Worcester, had struck twice, the tail could not cope with Fellowes's speed. He finished with a match analysis of 13 for 88, and Oxford had won for the fourth year in succession, this time by 12 runs.

OXFORD	First innings		Second innings	
E.L. Fellowes	b Pelham	21	not out	5
E. Davenport	b Pelham	8	run out	17
W.F. Maitland	c Winter, b Pelham	0	b Weighell	51
O. Spencer Smith	c Winter, b Pelham	6	c Winter, b Lyttelton	30
E.W. Tritton	c Green, b Pelham	1	b Absolom	7
S.C. Voules	b Green	2	c Richardson, b Weighell	21
G.P. Robertson	c Balfour, b Pelham	0	c Warren, b Lyttelton	5
C.E. Boyle	run out	7	c Pelham, b Absolom	8
E.S. Carter	c Balfour, b Green	4	c Richardson, b Absolom	15
R.T. Reid	not out	5	b Pelham	0
E.M. Kenney	st Balfour, b Pelham	3	c Pelham, b Lyttelton	0
EXTRAS	B 1, W 4	5	B 7, W 5	12
	TOTAL	62	TOTAL	171

CAMBRIDGE				
A.H. Winter	c Kenney, b Fellowes	23	b Fellowes	16
Hon. F.G. Pelham	b Maitland	1	b Fellowes	13
A. Walker	lbw, b Fellowes	1	b Carter	16
J.M. Richardson	b Fellowes	8	b Fellowes	6
R.D. Balfour	c and b Maitland	2	c Maitland, b Carter	11
Hon. G.W.S. Lyttelton	c Kenney, b Fellowes	3	b Kenney	1
C.E. Green	c Voules, b Fellowes	16	c Boyle, b Fellowes	0
C. Warren	not out	37	c Reid, b Fellowes	5
G.H. Tuck	c Boyle, b Fellowes	9	c Voules, b Fellowes	4
C.A. Absolom	c Kenney, b Carter	13	b Fellowes	9
W.B. Weighell	c Robertson, b Carter	3	not out	2
EXTRAS	B 4, L-B 4, W 3, N-B 1	12	B 3, L-B 3, W 4	10
	TOTAL	128	TOTAL	93

Cambridge bowling	OVERS	RUNS	WKTS		OVERS	RUNS	WKTS
Pelham	26	26	7		43	58	1
Weighell	16	17	0		15	25	2
Green	11	14	2		23	35	0
Absolom	—	—	—		14	24	3
Lyttelton	—	—	—		9	17	3

Oxford bowling	OVERS	RUNS	WKTS		OVERS	RUNS	WKTS
Fellowes	23	42	6		32	46	7
Maitland	21	47	2		—	—	—
Carter	9	4	2		15	13	2
Kenney	9	12	0		18	24	1
Voules	3	11	0		—	—	—

1, 2 July
At Lord's

1867

*Cambridge won by
5 wickets*

To no one can Cambridge's success have been more welcome than to their captain, the Hon. F.G. Pelham. For three years he had bowled steadily in a lost cause, but now his 5 for 32 in Oxford's second innings paved the way for the first of four successive wins. Conversely, the Oxford captain, W.F. Maitland, had the mortification of tasting defeat for the first time, despite the fact that his second innings of 45 was comfortably the highest in the match.

Cambridge led by 38 on the first innings, thanks largely to their more consistent batting and to the penetrating bowling of C.A. Absolom and C.J. Brune, of Godolphin School, Hammersmith. The Oxford innings was redeemed by spirited hitting on the part of E.S. Carter, who also rowed in the Dark Blue boat, and R.T. Reid, later Lord Chancellor Loreburn.

The Dark Blue second innings of 147 was restricted by fielding seldom surpassed. Pelham took a hard return from T. Case which would have been out of reach to a normal man, and M.H. Stow at point picked up, with his left hand, a terrific cut by Maitland inches before it would have touched the ground.

E.M. Kenney took three important wickets as Cambridge batted again, but sensible play from A.H. Winter, W.S.O. Warner and the Hon. G.W.S. Lyttelton enabled them to win by five wickets.

OXFORD	First innings			Second innings	
E.W. Tritton	c Warner, b Brune	6		b Absolom	13
T. Case	b Absolom	24		c and b Pelham	19
R. Digby	c and b Brune	9		c Winter, b Lyttelton	7
C.E. Boyle	c Stow, b Brune	4		c J.M. Richardson, b Pelham	16
W.F. Maitland	b Absolom	0		c Stow, b Pelham	45
J. St. J. Frederick	c Warner, b Brune	5		c Green, b Pelham	13
E.S. Carter	b Brune	26		c Pelham, b Absolom	13
E.M. Kenney	b Absolom	11		b Absolom	4
F.H. Hill	b Absolom	0		b Pelham	3
R.T. Reid	b Absolom	23		c Winter, b Absolom	2
R.F. Miles	not out	0		not out	2
EXTRAS	B 2, L-B 1, W 1	4		B 4, L-B 2, W 4	10
	TOTAL	112		TOTAL	147

CAMBRIDGE					
J.M. Richardson	b Kenney	3		c Reid, b Kenney	8
A.H. Winter	b Carter	16		run out	27
H.A. Richardson	c Carter, b Maitland	12		c Reid, ̂arter	0
J.S.E. Hood	b Maitland	0			
C.A. Absolom	b Carter	4			
M.H. Stow	c Hill, b Maitland	25		b Kenney	6
W.S.O. Warner	c Frederick, b Kenney	27		not out	34
Hon. G.W.S. Lyttelton	st Reid, b Miles	17		not out	20
C.E. Green	not out	13		c Reid, b Kenney	6
Hon. F.G. Pelham	b Kenney	10			
C.J. Brune	b Kenney	6			
EXTRAS	B 7, L-B 4, W 4, N-B 2	17		B 1, L-B 6, W 4	11
	TOTAL	150		TOTAL (5 WKTS)	112

Cambridge bowling	OVERS	RUNS	WKTS	OVERS	RUNS	WKTS
Absolom	27.3	64	5	27	45	4
Brune	20	22	5	16	40	0
Lyttelton	4	11	0	16	19	1
Pelham	3	11	0	28.3	32	5
Green	—	—	—	2	1	0

Oxford bowling						
Kenney	36.2	40	4	32.3	40	3
Carter	33	49	2	26	31	1
Miles	15	17	1	12	20	0
Maitland	12	27	3	6	10	0

22, 23, 24 June
At Lord's

1868

Cambridge won by
168 runs

Despite the return of the Oxford fast bowler E.L. Fellowes to captain the side, Cambridge, captained by the Uppinghamian C.E. Green, proved undoubtedly the stronger side. Although they led Oxford by only 23 runs after the first innings, they won in the end handsomely by 168 runs. That they did not score more was due in part to the early run-out of the fine all-rounder J.W. Dale, who played three times at Lord's and rowed twice at Putney, and in part to the very fine bowling of E.M. Kenney, who in the match had the impressive analysis of 14 for 119 in 117 overs. C.E. Green played a captain's innings of 44 in the Cambridge first innings, but it was the bowling of C.A. Absolom and C.J. Brune which ensured the confidence-boosting, though small,

lead. B. Pauncefote, a fine player in the making, was the only Oxford batsman to make more than twenty. He was for some years captain of the 'Butterflies', later settling in Colombo as a merchant.

The Light Blue batting in their second innings was far more consistent, Green's 59 coming out of 86 in an hour and a quarter; W.B. Money, Absolom, J.W. Dale and W.B. Weighell all gave good support. When Oxford batted again, A.T. Fortescue alone made over twenty, and W.B. Money bowled his slows and placed his field with a cunning remarkable in a freshman, taking 5 for 29. R.T. Reid, the Dark Blue number nine, was 'absent (hurt) 0'.

CAMBRIDGE	First innings		Second innings	
J.W. Dale	*run out*	13	c Lipscomb, b Kenney	28
G. Savile	*b* Kenney	10	c Fellowes, b Kenney	8
W.B. Money	c Mathews, *b* Kenney	0	b Fellowes	37
H.A. Richardson	c Reid, *b* Fellowes	1	b Kenney	3
W.S.O. Warner	c Lipscomb, *b* Kenney	13	b Kenney	2
C.E. Green	c and *b* Fellowes	44	c Bartholomew, b Fellowes	59
J.M. Richardson	*b* Fellowes	3	b Kenney	14
M.H. Stow	c Fortescue, *b* Kenney	3	b Kenney	7
C.A. Absolom	*b* Kenney	16	b Kenney	33
C.J. Brune	*b* Kenney	1	c Fellowes, b Kenney	4
W.B. Weighell	*not out*	1	*not out*	22
EXTRAS	B 2, L-B 2, W 2	6	B 7, L-B 2, W 9, N-B 1	19
	TOTAL	111	TOTAL	236

OXFORD				
E. Mathews	c Stow, *b* Absolom	12	b Brune	10
A.T. Fortescue	c Absolom, *b* Brune	12	c and b Money	23
B. Pauncefote	c Stow, *b* Absolom	23	b Absolom	19
R. Digby	c and *b* Absolom	1	b Absolom	0
E.L. Fellowes	*b* Brune	3	c Stowe, b Money	19
W. Evetts	c Green, *b* Absolom	4	b Money	2
A.C. Bartholomew	c Green, *b* Brune	7	*not out*	11
E.M. Kenney	c J.M. Richardson, *b* Absolom	0	b Money	5
R.T. Reid	*b* Brune	3	*absent (hurt)*	0
R.F. Miles	*b* Weighell	11	st H.A. Richardson, b Money	1
W.H. Lipscomb	*not out*	10	c and b Absolom	0
EXTRAS	B 1, W 1	2	W 1	1
	TOTAL	88	TOTAL	91

Oxford bowling	OVERS	RUNS	WKTS		OVERS	RUNS	WKTS
Kenney	38	51	6		79	68	8
Fellowes	31	33	3		51	62	2
Miles	6	21	0		26	39	0
Fortescue	—	—	—		15	17	0
Mathews	—	—	—		9	14	0
Lipscomb	—	—	—		7	17	0

Cambridge bowling							
Brune	30	38	4		12	12	1
Absolom	29	31	5		33	42	3
Weighell	10.2	5	1		6	7	0
Money	5	12	0		14.1	29	5

1869

In 1869 the place of C.E. Green in the Cambridge side was taken by an even more famous hitter, C.I. Thornton, who, like his predecessor, won the match by knocking the Oxford bowlers off their length when they were doing their best to recover a lost advantage. W.B. Money for the second year running bowled skilfully and was supported by first-class fielding and wicket-keeping. Between them the keepers, H.A. Richardson for Cambridge and W.A. Stewart for Oxford, performed impressively, having a pair of hands in fourteen of the dismissals.

On a wet, slippery wicket on which the hitters, Thornton and C.A. Absolom, made over half their side's first-innings total, Cambridge led Oxford by 65 runs. B. Pauncefote was, as in 1868, the Dark Blues' top scorer; Money took 6 wickets for 24.

Cambridge at one time in their second innings lost five wickets for 11 runs, thanks to the bowling of the Etonian A.F. Walter, who took 5 for 35, and the Marlburian R.F. Miles, who took 4 for 42. Thornton it was who prevented a further collapse, aided by a useful 28 from the number ten batsman, W.B. Weighell. The Dark Blues could manage only 98 of the necessary runs, 36 of them coming from R. Digby and 24 from the reliable Pauncefote. Money's 5 for 35 brought his match analysis to 11 for 59. The margin of victory for Cambridge was 58 runs, and they went one ahead in the series.

CAMBRIDGE	First innings		Second innings	
J.W. Dale	c Digby, b Miles	22	b Walter	3
B. Preston	c Stewart, b Miles	5	b Miles	0
W.B. Money	c Stewart, b Pauncefote	1	st Stewart, b Miles	2
H.A. Richardson	c Hill, b Pauncefote	10	c Stewart, b Walter	12
W. Yardley	c Stewart, b Fortescue	19	b Walter	0
C.I. Thornton	st Stewart, b Miles	50	b Walter	36
M.H. Stow	c Stewart, b Walter	10	c Stewart, b Hill	5
C.A. Absolom	c Fortescue, b Hill	30	c Mathews, b Walter	2
C.J. Brune	not out	2	not out	3
W.B. Weighell	c Gibbon, b Hill	0	b Miles	28
T.W. Wilson	run out	4	c Hill, b Miles	0
EXTRAS	B 5, L-B 3, W 3	11		
	TOTAL	164	TOTAL	91

OXFORD				
A.T. Fortescue	b Absolom	8	st Richardson, b Money	8
J.H. Gibbon	c and b Absolom	17	run out	2
R. Digby	c Dale, b Money	6	c Stow, b Wilson	36
E.F.S. Tylecote	lbw, b Wilson	6	c Richardson, b Absolom	3
B. Pauncefote	c Absolom, b Money	33	c Richardson, b Absolom	24
F.H. Hill	b Absolom	4	st Richardson, b Money	9
W. Evetts	st Richardson, b Money	14	c Weighell, b Wilson	3
E. Mathews	c and b Money	4	b Money	4
A.F. Walter	c Absolom, b Money	0	c Richardson, b Money	0
R.F. Miles	c Dale, b Money	0	b Money	0
W.A. Stewart	not out	5	not out	4
EXTRAS	B 2	2	B 2, L-B 3	5
	TOTAL	99	TOTAL	98

Oxford bowling	OVERS	RUNS	WKTS	OVERS	RUNS	WKTS
Miles	30	40	3	28.2	42	4
Pauncefote	26	45	2	—	—	—
Fortescue	20	42	1	6	4	0
Walter	17	24	1	24	35	5
Hill	6.2	2	2	10	10	1

Cambridge bowling						
Absolom	35	39	3	27	26	2
Money	16.3	24	6	22	35	5
Wilson	7	10	1	8	9	2
Brune	6	14	0	16	14	0
Weighell	5	10	0	5	9	0

1870

This has been called 'Cobden's match' because it was F.C. Cobden, the Harrovian Light Blue quick bowler, who bowled the last historic over in the gloaming and clinched the contest. But there were other heroes too: for Oxford, the Etonian C.J. Ottaway – who made 69 in partnership with the Marlburian A.T. Fortescue – and C.K. Francis, who took 12 for 161 in the match; and for Cambridge, W. Yardley – who had the distinction of scoring the first ever century in the series, mainly in partnership with J.W. Dale – and E.E. Harrison-Ward, of Bury St Edmunds and Jesus, whose thirty-two overs and 6 for 29 in the second innings had made victory possible.

Oxford replied with 175 to Cambridge's 147, but it was not until the two second innings that the real excitement began. Cambridge's 206 in the second innings was due almost entirely to the great stand between Yardley, who scored two-thirds of the runs while he was in, and Dale, in the face of hostile bowling by Francis.

Ottaway, Fortescue and the Cliftonian E.F.S. Tylecote, later to play for England, led the Dark Blue charge in a game that was to be finished that night. It proved a fateful decision for Oxford as the drama was to unfold in worsening light. Play proceeded with neither side achieving a clear advantage, and the climax was not reached until well after seven o'clock. Off what was destined to be the last over of the match – it was bowled from the Nursery End – F.H. Hill got a single he would later regret off the first ball; off the second A.A. Bourne made a splendid catch at mid-off to dismiss S.E. Butler; off the third ball Cobden, bowling his fastest in the bad light and pitching the ball up, bowled T.H. Belcher – off his legs, claimed the batsman later, but not the bowler!

Let the Hon. R.H. Lyttelton's *Badminton Library, 1893* take over.

Matters were becoming distinctly grave, and very irritating it must have been to Mr Hill, who was like a billiard-player watching his rival in the middle of a big break; he could say a good deal and think a lot, but he could do nothing. Mr Stewart, spes ultima of Oxford, with feelings that are utterly impossible to describe, padded and gloved, nervously took off his coat in the pavilion. If ever man deserved pity, Mr Stewart deserved it on that occasion. He did not profess to be a good bat, and his friends did not claim so much for him; he was an excellent wicket-keeper, but he had to go in at a crisis that the best bat in England would not like to face. Mr Pauncefote, the Oxford captain, was seen addressing a few words of earnest exhortation to him, and with rather a sick feeling Mr Stewart went to the wicket. Mr Hill looked at him cheerfully, but very earnestly did Mr Stewart wish the next ball well over. He took his guard and held his hands low on the bat handle; for Mr Pauncefote had earnestly entreated Mr Stewart to put the bat straight in the block-hole and keep it there without moving it. This was not by any means bad advice, for the bat covers a great deal of the wicket, and though it is a piece of counsel not likely to be offered to W.G. Grace or Stoddart, it might not have been inexpedient to offer it to Mr Stewart. Here, then was the situation – Mr Stewart standing manfully up to the wicket, Mr Cobden beginning his run, and a perfectly dead silence in the crowd. Whiz went the ball; but alas! – as many other people, cricketers and politicians alike, have done – the good advice is neglected, and Stewart, instead of following his captain's exhortation to keep his bat still and upright in the block-hole, just lifted it: fly went the bails, and Cambridge had won the match by two runs! The situation was bewildering. Nobody could quite realise what had happened for a second or so, but then – up went Mr Absolom's hat, down the pavilion steps with miraculous rapidity flew the Rev. A.R. Ward, and smash went Mr Charles Marsham's umbrella against the pavilion brickwork.

SPORTING INTELLIGENCE.

CRICKET.

OXFORD v CAMBRIDGE.

Viewed in all its bearings, the above match, which was concluded last evening at Lord's, is perhaps the most remarkable since it was first played 33 years ago. To explain this a few brief remarks are necessary. Yesterday Cambridge commenced their second innings at 12.15, with 28 in arrear, and with a prevailing opinion that Oxford were the more effective eleven. First to appear at the wickets were Messrs. Dale and Tobin as on the day previous. Messrs. Francis and Belcher followed Monday's programme in respect to bowling. From the 22d ball Mr. Tobin played on, when six runs only were scored. Mr. Money succeeded, made six singles, and played on also. Mr. Fryer lost his wicket from the first ball presented to him; Mr. Thornton joined Mr. Dale, and cut the second ball into the slips for four. Other runs of less note followed, till 40 were accredited to Cambridge. Mr. Thornton then tried the steeple hit, which Mr. Hadow surveyed with great calmness and judgment. On the retirement of Mr. Thornton came Mr. Scott, but his stay was unexpectedly brief. Five wickets were now down for 40 runs. With Mr. Yardley this dull aspect of affairs changed in

Exciting though "Cobden's match" must have been, this account also provides a striking contrast to present-day coverage as, after a lively introduction, it leaves the reader in doubt as to the outcome until the last few lines.

an extraordinary manner. The leading bowlers were displaced by Messrs. Butler and Hill, but, as no beneficial effect to Oxford was manifest, Messrs. Hadow and Fortescue were brought forward. Mr. Dale occupied his wicket for two hours and a half for 67 runs, and was at length most wonderfully fielded at long leg, very deep, by Mr. Ottaway. His chief hits were six fours (drives), two threes and six twos. Mr. Mackinnon next joined Mr. Yardley, but soon deserted him. Nearly all the subsequent interest centred on Mr. Yardley, who got just 100 runs—a feat which has rarely, if ever, been accomplished in a match of this kind. The innings culminated in 206, thereby leaving Oxford 178 to tie . . .

In two hours and five minutes 100 runs were scored by Oxford; this number was enlarged to 153, when the fourth wicket fell. Mr. Townshend came forward as the clock was striking 7, the time for drawing the stumps, but as the game was considered lost to Cambridge, it was suggested by some that it would be well to finish it. Mr. Ottaway was caught close to the ground after being at the wicket three hours. Mr. Townshend was caught next over in short slip for the smallest contribution possible, and Mr. Francis was given out l.b.w. in the succeeding over. There were now seven wickets down for 176. Mr. Butler came and was caught mid-off without scoring. Mr. Belcher had but one ball, which bowled his leg stump, and Mr. Stewart, the last man, who was only required to make three, failed most signally—bowled also from the first ball, and thus at 7.35 Cambridge were declared winners by two runs. Messrs. Cobden and Ward were the only successful bowlers out of the seven engaged. Mr. Cobden bowled 27 overs (10 maiden) and took four wickets, for 34 runs. Mr. Ward 33 overs (16 maiden), six wickets, 30 runs.

immaculate order on edge of village. 3 reception rooms, study. 5/6 bedrooms. Large garden. £1,700pcm. 0580 753672.

SUSSEX 3 bed farm cottage Horsham 5 miles, central heating, curtains carpets, large garden. £420pcm Box No 8951

TUNBRIDGE WELLS Luxury 1 bed Apart. Own gardens. 50 mins B.Rail to Charing X. £400 pcm. GMK 071 274 8398

OVERSEAS PROPERTY

INT PROPERTY TRIBUNE. Free overseas prop + services magazine. Request line 0483 455254

WORLD OF PROPERTY, more choice than any other. For your Free copy tel: 081 542 9088.

BALEARICS

ILLETAS Mallorca - 2 bed apartment, air cond., CH, pool security. £50,000 or will exchange for boat car or property. Tel: 0704 821818 or 0836 563334.

POLLENSA, MALLORCA Lovely Villa with pool on plot of ½ acre. 6 bedrooms. 2 reception. £500,000. 0886 880685.

TAYLOR WOODROW Mallorca & Menorca. Quality freehold apartments set in outstanding locations from £42,000 to £87,000; also luxury villas in Mallorca from £185,000. 081 575 1150/4830

from £55,000 to £260,000. Daltons 0491 574686

SCOTLAND

COUNTRY HOUSES IN DUMFRIES & GALLOWAY

Manageable Country Homes with Five Bedrooms, Three Public Rooms, Two Bathrooms etc. Attractive situation with easily maintained gardens. To view call

Thomson, Roddick & Laurie
20 Murray St Annan
(0461) 202575
also at Dumfries & Carlisle

SEA/Marina view. Detached 3 beds 2 rec kitchen bath OCH/Solar. Gge space. Inverness/Aberdeen airports 50 mins. £70,000. 0542 832621

SPACIOUS modern 5 bdrm bungalow. Sit. at foot of Five Sisters of Kintail on road to Isle of Skye. Ideal location for B&B business. Offers to 059981584.

SURREY

DARBY GREEN Det character hse on priv 'rd. Access A3. 6 bds. 2 bths, 3 recs. landscaped gdn. £216,000 Mann & Co Thames Valley: 0252 875407.

DORKING 4 bed period character features. Many character features. Gardens. Gge & cellar. 4 receps. Walking distance town centre £289,950 Woolich Property Services 0306 742308.

Vicarage close to town centre and in need of refurbishment. Hall, Cloaks, 3 large Receps, Cellar, Kitchen/ Breakfast, Utility, 4 first floor beds, 2 baths, cloaks, Double garage & walled gardens of about one ¼ acre.

Guide Price £280,000
(0284) 705505

COUNTRY HOUSES in Suffolk & Essex. Peter Andrews Ltd. Long Melford 0787 880660.

ESSEX/SUFFOLK BORDER Beautiful 15th Ct village house. 4 beds. 3 recep, small gdn. 1 hr Liverpool St. £155,000 tel 0206 262393 (day) 262981 (eve).

KINGS LYNN 3mls South. Handsome new house with Vict. Gothic details. 4 good beds, 2 recep. Gge & gdns. High quality house built by craftsmen. £87,500. 0366 384353.

NR DISS Outstanding new high specification bungalow. Close express rail service London. Oil ch. UPVC dble glazing, lux kit, 2 recs. 4 beds (2 e/s), bath dble gge. Attractive gdn £165,000 Sworders 0284 753049

HANTS, DORSET, AND I.O.W.

TEST VALLEY Kings Somborne. Single storey converted cottage; 3 bedr. 2 bathr. living rm. dining hall, fitted kit, walled gdn. shared courtyard access. £139,000. Ring 0962 869859 or write Ashby Guion Assocs. 1 The Broadway, Winchester, SO23 9BE.

Must view 071 381 4998.1

PENTHOUSE Portman Sq. 4 bed dble recep. kit/b'fast, terraces, PBB Gge avail. 68 yr £725,000 Horne & Sons 071-499 9344

WESTMINSTER - 2 bed flat Maunsel St. 86yrs £99,500. 0244 300431/0831 867306

RICHMOND & KINGSTON

VINTAGE RICHMOND 18th and 19th century 3,4, and 5 bedroom classics of much space and elegance, all superbly valued. £250,000–£375,000 F/H Barnes & Barnes 081 940 0093/5

WITH MEWS Cottage at end of tranquil garden, a gracious listed George I res. near Marble Hill Park. Asks £750,000 F/H (Less for main house and garden only) Barnes & Barnes 081 940 0093/5

SOUTH OF THE THAMES

PUTNEY £725,000. 2 superb det period houses in conservation area with 6 beds. One is dble fronted and has garaging for 3 cars. Allen Briegel 081-780 0077 other properties required.

WANDSWORTH SW17. Quick sale required of det. Vic. family house. 4 beds. 2 baths, 3 recep. kit/brkfst rm, gas CH. gdn. O.I.R.O. £210,000. Andrew Milton & Co 081 767 0075

FREE GUIDE to period property for sale in the Cotswolds. Call Barringtons now 0285 862444

DEVON & CORNWALL

BIGBURY-ON-SEA Uniquely sit. character marine residence. Headland posit. 180° sea & island views. 5 beds. £275k. Devon Homesearch 0626 834900

CHURCHWOOD VALLEY. Delightful log cabins set in 45 acres of beautiful wooded valley by Wembury Bay. Situated in coastal conservation area yet close to local attractions, you are ideally placed to enjoy all the South Coast of Devon has to offer. Peaceful & unspoilt surroundings. £13,500 to £40,960. Churchwood Valley, Wembury Bay, Nr Plymouth, South Devon. Tel 0752 862382 and ask for Sales Brochure.

LEWTRENCHARD South Devon. Grade II Listed Rectory. 2 acre grounds. 8 beds, 3 recs, lux kit. coach house, workshop. Gging. J Agents (Hugh Mackenzie 0392 499699) Fulfords 0752 233555.

NR DARTMOUTH Strete. Select det elopement 2 bedroomed houses with views. From £67,500. Tel 0803 770302

TEIGNMOUTH - Detached period residence with many original features in favoured location, enjoying sea and rural views. 4 bedrooms. 2 self-contained apartments. £212,500. Fulfords 0626 770077.

CAMBRIDGE	First innings		Second innings	
J.W. Dale	b Francis	15	c Ottaway, b Francis	67
F. Tobin	b Francis	13	b Belcher	2
W.B. Money	b Belcher	10	b Francis	6
W. Yardley[1]	c Butler, b Francis	2	c and b Francis	100
F.E.R. Fryer	c Stewart, b Hadow	8	b Francis	0
A.T. Scott	b Belcher	45	c Tylecote, b Francis	0
C.I. Thornton	b Belcher	17	c Hadow, b Butler	11
F.A. Mackinnon	not out	17	b Belcher	2
F.C. Cobden[2]	b Francis	7	c Hadow, b Francis	7
A.A. Bourne	b Belcher	3	b Francis	0
E.E. Harrison-Ward	st Stewart, b Francis	2	not out	3
EXTRAS	B 3, L-B 4, W 1	8	B 4, L-B 3, W 1	8
	TOTAL	147	TOTAL	206

OXFORD

	First innings		Second innings	
A.T. Fortescue	b Money	35	b Harrison-Ward	44
W.H. Hadow	b Cobden	17	c Scott, b Cobden	0
C.J. Ottaway	b Bourne	16	c Fryer, b Harrison-Ward	69
B. Pauncefote	c Dale, b Harrison-Ward	15	b Harrison-Ward	5
E.F.S. Tylecote	c Thornton, b Harrison-Ward	25	b Harrison-Ward	29
W. Townshend	st Yardley, b Money	0	c Money, b Harrison-Ward	1
F.H. Hill	b Harrison-Ward	23	not out	13
C.K. Francis	b Cobden	12	lbw, b Harrison-Ward	1
S.E. Butler	b Cobden	18	c Bourne, b Cobden	0
W.A. Stewart	b Cobden	0	b Cobden	0
T.H. Belcher	not out	0	b Cobden	0
EXTRAS	B 10, L-B 2, N-B 1, W 1	14	B 7, L-B 3, W 3, N-B 1	14
	TOTAL	175	TOTAL	176

Oxford bowling	OVERS	RUNS	WKTS		OVERS	RUNS	WKTS
Belcher	45	52	4		29	38	2
Francis	42.2	59	5		42.3	102	7
Butler	11	16	0		2	8	1
Hadow	7	12	1		4	11	0
Hill	—	—	—		13	27	0
Pauncefote	—	—	—		4	5	0
Fortescue	—	—	—		3	7	0

Cambridge bowling							
Bourne	21	36	1		30	41	0
Cobden	19	41	4		27	35	4
Money	17	37	2		7	24	0
Harrison-Ward	16	33	3		32	29	6
Fryer	14	14	0		7	15	0
Thornton	—	—	—		10	13	0
Dale	—	—	—		3	5	0

[1] The first man to score a century in the match.

[2] Finished off the match by performing the hat-trick. His victims were: Butler, Stewart and Belcher. This was the first time that the hat-trick had been performed in the match.

1871

Oxford exacted a sweet and swift revenge for their defeat in Cobden's match, winning by eight wickets thanks to an exceptional bowling performance by S.E. Butler. Not only was he the first bowler in the series to take all ten wickets in an innings – 10 for 38 in the twenty-four overs and one ball needed to bowl Cambridge out in their first innings, eight of his victims being clean bowled – but he also secured five wickets in the second innings. He seemed to be able to make the ball shoot or bump just as he pleased. W.B. Money and W. Yardley were the only Light Blue batsmen to make twenty as their team slumped to 65, in reply to Oxford's healthier 170, of which B. Pauncefote had made 50 and E.F.S. Tylecote

42. E. Bray, of Westminster and St John's, took 5 for 38 and W.N. Powys 4 for 40.

Cambridge were compelled to follow on by the *Laws* of the day, and doubtless the Oxford captain was keen to press home his advantage anyway. The Light Blue batting was more consistent in the second innings, F. Tobin, who played Rugby for England against Scotland the same year, and F.C. Cobden both making thirties, but Butler did not let them off the hook, and the Dark Blues needed only 25 to win. This they did for the loss of two wickets, both openers being bowled by Powys. The Hon. G.R.C. Harris, later Lord Harris, played as a freshman.

OXFORD	First innings		Second innings	
W. Townshend	*b* Bray	22	*b* Powys	6
W. Law	*c* Scott, *b* Cobden	7	*b* Powys	4
C.J. Ottaway	*b* Bray	21	*not out*	13
W.H. Hadow	*c* Yardley, *b* Powys	8	*not out*	0
E.F.S. Tylecote	*b* Powys	42		
B. Pauncefote	*c* sub, *b* Bray	50		
Hon. G.R.C. Harris	*b* Powys	0		
C. Marriott	*b* Bray	0		
C.K. Francis	*not out*	2		
S.E. Butler[1]	*c* Stedman, *b* Bray	4		
S. Pelham	*b* Powys	0		
EXTRAS	B 9, L-B 4, W 1	14	B 1, L-B 1	2
	TOTAL	170	TOTAL (2 WKTS)	25

CAMBRIDGE				
W.B. Money	*b* Butler	23	*b* Butler	5
F. Tobin	*c* Hadow, *b* Butler	5	*b* Hadow	30
F.E.R. Fryer	*b* Butler	1	*c* Marriott, *b* Pelham	2
A.T. Scott	*b* Butler	1	*c* Harris, *b* Butler	15
W. Yardley	*c* Pelham, *b* Butler	25	*b* Butler	2
C.I. Thornton	*b* Butler	4	*b* Butler	12
H.C.P. Stedman	*not out*	1	*b* Butler	22
F.C. Cobden	*b* Butler	0	*not out*	32
E. Bray	*b* Butler	0	*b* Francis	1
W.N. Powys	*b* Butler	0	*b* Law	0
E.E. Harrison-Ward	*b* Butler	0	*b* Law	0
EXTRAS	L-B 5	5	B 4, L-B 2, W 1, N-B 1	8
	TOTAL	65	TOTAL	129

Cambridge bowling	OVERS	RUNS	WKTS		OVERS	RUNS	WKTS	
Harrison-Ward	36	38	0		—	—	—	
Cobden	25	27	1		1.3	10	0	
Powys	24.2	40	4		4	9	2	
Bray	19	38	5		3	4	0	
Thornton	7	13	0		—	—	—	

Oxford bowling								
Butler	24.1	38	10		34	57	5	
Pelham	14	5	0		23	26	1	
Francis	10	17	0		20	34	1	
Law	—	—	—		5.1	2	2	
Hadow	—	—	—		5	2	1	

[1] The only bowler in the history of the match who has captured all the wickets in one innings.

1872

The pendulum swung back with a vengeance, Cambridge winning what was to remain for fifty-one years the record victory of an innings and 166 runs. The Cambridge captain, C.I. Thornton, sent in to open the innings two Etonian freshmen, A.S. Tabor and G.H. Longman, and they responded magnificently, sharing in a partnership of a hundred in a hundred minutes. The Harrovian F.E.R. Fryer hit strongly for his 46, and then W. Yardley followed his century in 1871 with another. He drove with great power and scored twenty fours. The feat was not to be repeated until H.J. Enthoven's two hundreds in 1924 and 1925. C.K. Francis and S.E. Butler bowled 103 overs between them, taking 6 for 236.

Oxford, in reply to Cambridge's 388, were bowled out for 72 by W.N. Powys, who took 6 for 26, and E. Bray, who took 3 for 24. The Rossalian W. Townshend was the only Dark Blue player to reach twenty. Following on on a pitch made dead by a heavy overnight storm, C.J. Ottaway and E.F.S. Tylecote – good enough to have been selected for the Hon. Ivo Bligh's side to tour Australia in 1882, and to have scored 66 in the deciding match, as a result of which the 'Ashes' were regained – showed their experience with forties. Tylecote was one of three batsmen well caught at short leg by Thornton. The tail wagged, but the 7 for 49 by a now experienced Powys was decisive, and Oxford reached 150 but no more.

CAMBRIDGE	First innings		Second innings
A.S. Tabor	c Ridley, b Butler	50	
G.H. Longman	run out	80	
F.E.R. Fryer	c Harris, b Francis	46	
W. Yardley	c Ottaway, b Butler	130	
C.I. Thornton	c Wallroth, b Butler	20	
F. Tobin	b Francis	0	
E.P. Baily	b Francis	4	
F.C. Cobden	c Law, b Ridley	12	
E. Bray	not out	11	
W.N. Powys	c Tylecote, b Ridley	16	
G.S. Raynor	c Law, b Ridley	0	
EXTRAS	B 7, L-B 8, W 4	19	
	TOTAL	388	

OXFORD					
C.J. Ottaway	c Baily, b Powys	11	c Thornton, b Powys	41
W. Townshend	b Powys	20	b Powys	4
W.H. Hadow	b Powys	9	b Powys	0
E.F.S. Tylecote	c Yardley, b Bray	6	c Thornton, b Bray	40
C.A. Wallroth	c Baily, b Bray	15	c Bray, b Powys	1
Hon. G.R.C. Harris	b Powys	5	b Powys	0
C.K. Francis	b Powys	0	c Thornton, b Bray	10
A.W. Ridley	st Baily, b Bray	1	not out	18
W. Law	run out	3	c Raynor, b Powys	8
F.W. Isherwood	b Powys	0	run out	18
S.E. Butler	not out	0	c Fryer, b Powys	0
EXTRAS	B 1, N-B 1	2	B 3, L-B 5, W 1, N-B 1	10
	TOTAL	72	TOTAL	150

Oxford bowling	OVERS	RUNS	WKTS	OVERS	RUNS	WKTS
Francis	58	133	3			
Butler	45	103	3			
Ridley	29	49	3			
Law	20	34	0			
Isherwood	11	36	0			
Hadow	7	14	0			

Cambridge bowling	OVERS	RUNS	WKTS	OVERS	RUNS	WKTS
Powys	17	26	6	47	49	7
Bray	11.1	24	3	38	54	2
Raynor	6	20	0	16	25	0
Cobden	—	—	—	8	12	0

23, 24 June
At Lord's

1873

Oxford won by
3 wickets

This was a close and capital match, Oxford winning by three wickets, thanks largely to the bowling of S.E. Butler and the Etonian J. Maude, who took twelve wickets between them, and the batting of C.J. Ottaway, who scored over ninety, thereby batting for over twelve hours in his four University Matches. He was supported in the first innings by the Shirburnian W.H. Game and in the second by the Carthusian C.E.B. Nepean.

Cambridge batted first and lost five wickets for only 49. At this point W.J. Ford, eldest of a distinguished Reptonian brotherhood, hit strongly to help his side reach 152. Oxford secured a lead of 30, the Harrovian W. Law, Ottaway, Game and Nepean all making important contributions. The

Rugby freshman G.E. Jeffery, a bowler of the Alfred Shaw variety, took 8 for 44 bowling throughout.

A.S. Tabor and the Wykehamist T. Latham – later to be a special pleader at the Shanghai Bar – were the most successful Light Blue batsmen in the second innings, but Maude never allowed them to take complete charge by taking 6 for 39 in twenty-four overs and two balls. C. Tillard, a Reptonian who would later teach at Cheltenham, replied with 6 for 62, making the ball frequently whip back quickly from the pitch. Assisted, however, by fifteen byes as well as by the impressive partnership between Ottaway and Nepean, Oxford won the day.

CAMBRIDGE	First innings		Second innings	
G.H. Longman	c and b Butler	5	b Ridley	20
A.S. Tabor	b Boyle	3	b Ridley	45
W. Blacker	b Butler	24	c Boyle, b Ridley	26
F.E.R. Fryer	c Maude, b Butler	14	b Maude	1
G.E. Jeffery	c Boyle, b Butler	7	b Butler	23
T. Latham	c Ottaway, b Butler	0	c Wallroth, b Maude	48
W.J. Ford	not out	51	c Francis, b Maude	11
C. Tillard	b Francis	13	lbw, b Maude	6
H.A. Douglas Hamilton	b Francis	0	not out	0
H.M. Sims	b Francis	5	b Maude	0
G.H. Hone-Goldney	b Boyle	10	b Maude	0
EXTRAS	B 12, L-B 7, W 1	20	B 18, L-B 3, W 2	23
	TOTAL	152	TOTAL	203

OXFORD				
W. Law	b Jeffery	36	c Tillard, b Sims	27
E.S. Garnier	c and b Jeffery	10	b Tillard	19
C.A. Wallroth	b Jeffery	0	b Tillard	4
C.J. Ottaway	b Tillard	41	b Tillard	52
A.W. Ridley	b Jeffery	8	b Tillard	0
C.E.B. Nepean	c Ford, b Tillard	22	b Tillard	50
W.H. Game	b Jeffery	48	b Tillard	0
C.K. Francis	c Goldney, b Jeffery	4	not out	3
S.E. Butler	lbw, b Jeffery	3	not out	4
C.W. Boyle	b Jeffery	0		
J. Maude	not out	1		
EXTRAS	B 9	9	B 15, L-B 2, W 1	18
	TOTAL	182	TOTAL (7 WKTS)	177

Oxford bowling	OVERS	RUNS	WKTS		OVERS	RUNS	WKTS
Boyle	22.1	42	2		7	21	0
Butler	19	48	5		15	42	1
Francis	13	27	3		11	27	0
Maude	9	15	0		24.2	39	6
Ridley	—	—	—		32	51	3

Cambridge bowling							
Jeffery	45	44	8		28	48	0
Sims	22	74	0		19	36	1
Tillard	19.3	42	2		35.3	62	6
Fryer	3	13	0		—	—	—
Hamilton	—	—	—		4	8	0
Goldney	—	—	—		2	5	0

29, 30 June
At Lord's

1874

Oxford won by
an innings and 92 runs

Oxford were much better suited to the wet conditions and won handsomely by an innings and 92 runs. In fact, Cambridge flattered to deceive, for at one time on the first morning they were 74 for one, A.S Tabor having hit a fine 52, largely by means of his off-drive, which he played with ease and precision. Heavy rain then came down, and after it T.W. Lang, of Clifton and Balliol, and A.W. Ridley, of Eton and Christ Church, proved hard to play, so that the final Light Blue total, also restricted by fine fielding, was only 109. The Dark Blue batsmen, especially D. Campbell – he would score 128 for Fifteen of Victoria against the fifth English team in Australia – T.B. Jones, C.A. Wallroth and that future pillar of the MCC and

Kent, Lord Harris, struck the ball all over Lord's. Harris, in particular, played an innings of high class. Only W.N. Powys, who played for two years for Hampshire after going down, returned decent figures – 5 for 29 in fifteen overs and three balls. Oxford reached the safe haven of 265.

Cambridge fared even more abjectly in the second innings once Tabor was run out; G.H. Longman was the one player to reach twenty in a total of 64. T.W. Lang, the Oxford fast bowler who had already played for Gloucestershire, had a match analysis of 10 for 74. The catch at deep square leg by W.H. Game that sent back the Harrovian G. Macan deserves a special mention.

CAMBRIDGE

	First innings			Second innings	
G.E. Jeffery	b Lang	6		*not out*	2
A.S. Tabor	b Lang	52		*run out*	0
G.H. Longman	b Ridley	14		st Tylecote, b Ridley	24
W. Blacker	b Lang	0		b Ridley	0
G. Macan	b Ridley	6		c Game, b Lang	12
F.F.J. Greenfield	c Jones, b Lang	5		*absent (hurt)*	0
T. Latham	*run out*	1		b Lang	4
E.P. Baily	c and b Ridley	0		c and b Lang	1
H.M. Sims	*not out*	12		b Lang	6
C. Tillard	b Ridley	4		b Ridley	10
W.N. Powys	b Lang	5		c Harris, b Lang	1
EXTRAS	B 1, L-B 1, W 1, N-B 1	4		B 3, L-B 1	4
	TOTAL	109		TOTAL	64

OXFORD

D. Campbell	*run out*	42
W. Law	c Longman, b Powys	26
A.W. Ridley	b Tillard	11
Lord Harris[1]	c Longman, b Jeffery	43
W.W. Pulman	c and b Jeffery	18
C.A. Wallroth	b Sims	44
T.B. Jones	b Powys	38
W.H. Game	b Powys	17
H.G. Tylecote	c Baily, b Powys	0
T.W. Lang	b Powys	1
W. Foord-Kelcey	*not out*	0
EXTRAS	B 15, L-B 8, W 2	25
	TOTAL	265

Oxford bowling	OVERS	RUNS	WKTS		OVERS	RUNS	WKTS
Lang	41.1	49	5		24	25	5
Ridley	29	34	4		19	26	3
Foord-Kelcey	8	11	0		4	9	0
Jones	5	11	0		—	—	—

Cambridge bowling	OVERS	RUNS	WKTS
Tillard	33	69	1
Sims	32	80	1
Jeffery	23	62	2
Powys	15.3	29	5

[1] Played in 1871 and 1872 as Hon. G.R.C. Harris.

5
1875–1884
Fresh Schools enlarge the Scene

OXFORD *To The Parks at last*

The middle of the nineteenth century saw a great expansion of the public-school system. This was due in part to the growing prosperity and ambitions of an expanding middle class. The great reforming headmasters like Arnold at Rugby and Russell at Charterhouse brought back respectability and prestige to these institutions and paved the way for an enormous increase in public-school education. In the 1840s, '50s and '60s a large number of new schools was founded. Moreover, the spidery development of a comprehensive railway network made it easier for parents to send their boys away from home.

For fifty years, University cricket had been fed primarily by young players from Eton, Harrow, Winchester and Rugby. The new schools, modelled very much on the old, came more and more into the reckoning from the fifties onwards. There is no more dramatic way of emphasizing this than to refer to Uppingham's year when no less than four from that school were in the 1876 winning Cambridge side. True, Uppingham, like Shrewsbury, Repton, Charterhouse and others, was a grammar school of ancient foundation, which in the mid-nineteenth century changed course to present a 'public-school' image. Also there were new schools, Cheltenham, Marlborough, Clifton and Malvern being random examples. As all these schools, and others besides, became fully established, the source of supply for the University elevens became wider.

Sherborne School had existed in the eighth century, had been refounded by Edward VI, and was given a new constitution in 1870. From the 'new school' came W.H. Game, the 1876 Oxford captain. While at school he had once made 281 in four-and-a-half hours, and at Oriel, playing against Wadham, he made 234 not out in two-and-a-quarter hours. It is not surprising that he had a reputation as a fine free hitter. Playing for Surrey he once hit the great Spofforth clean out of The Oval. He was also a brilliant fielder and led an eleven which Pycroft described as the finest fielding side ever seen in the University Match. Oxford had not yet taken part in so high-scoring a match as that against Middlesex, when 1217 runs were scored for the loss of twenty-four wickets. Oxford made 612, Webbe scoring 98 and Game a dashing 141. Cambridge were too strong for Oxford, but game to the end, the Oxford captain scored the first hundred against Cambridge.

The great Webbe was captain in 1877 of a side which on paper could not measure up to Cambridge, and yet they won by ten wickets. Sir Pelham Warner wrote of him:

Webbie was clearly an outstanding captain. He was a fine leader, kindness itself, with a rare charm of manner, and no one ever had a more loyal and truer friend. To lame dogs and in troubles which from time to time befall cricketers he was a veritable champion.

F.M. Buckland made his reputation at Eton as a bowler, but at Oxford, although he apparently 'lost the spin from leg', early established himself as an all-rounder. His name will live in cricket history for his fine performances against Cambridge which turned the fortunes of the match in 1877. He learned many of his skills at Eton under the tutorship of R.A.H. Mitchell. After a year or two on the Winchester staff he became headmaster of a preparatory school in Laleham.

The year 1878 was rather a lean one at Oxford; not only did they have to face possibly the best Cambridge side ever, but they went to Lord's lacking practice. For some reason, probably the state of Cowley Marsh, they played only three matches, none of them before June. The one redeeming feature of the season was the appearance of A.H. Evans on the scene; it was he who was going to rebuild Oxford's fortunes. In 1880 he bowled so well as to take 10 for 133 in the Varsity Match, but could not quite turn the tide. In 1881, after a sequence of three Cambridge wins, he at last led Oxford to victory.

Time was running out for Cowley Marsh. The suggestion of a move to the Parks had come in the 1860s. The idea did not find favour at first, because some dons feared a multiplicity of college pavilions, so the project languished. Vice-Chancellor Dr Evans, Master of Pembroke, suggested to Professor T. Case that a petition should be raised among resident MAs, asking Convocation to grant ten acres in the Parks on permanent lease to the OUCC. This petition was well supported, and on 3 May a decree was passed leasing the ground in the Parks to OUCC for ever. The 'Parks' were so named after the original 'parks', which were gun emplacements constructed at the time of the Civil War for the defence of 'Royal' Oxford. Under the guidance of Professor Case the pavilion was built at exactly the same distance from the wicket as is the Pavilion at Lord's.

The Seniors match was played on Cowley Marsh, and then, with much celebration and no doubt a few tears, the move was made in May 1881. The first match was drawn against MCC, and only one other was played in that year, and that was something of a curiosity. One of the great virtues of cricket in The Parks is that, being a public place, no 'gate' may be charged. So prestigious matches, which offered an opportunity for revenue, were moved to where a charge could be made, almost always to the Christ Church ground. The match against the Gentlemen in 1881 began there, but when the Gentlemen were 40 for 3, A.J. Webbe was struck in the face by a ball that lifted off a very rough wicket, whereupon the stumps were uprooted, and it was decided to start again in The Parks, and an excellent match resulted. Oxford made 232 and dismissed the Gentlemen for 146. In the follow-on the Gentlemen raced ahead, finally leaving Oxford needing 330 to win. C.F.H. Leslie put them on the right road, but time not surprisingly ran out when they were 271 for 6.

Leslie had come with a fine reputation from Rugby, being the prime mover in two convincing wins against Marlborough at Lord's, so that it was no surprise when he became a freshman blue. In his first year he more than lived up to expectations. He came off in every match, and stood out with a personal aggregate of

519, averaging 57. He never quite reached these heights again. It is interesting that after his first year he went into business in London, but remained eligible since his name was kept on Oriel's books. This practice, which would not be tolerated today, was not entirely uncommon. T.C. O'Brien, later Sir Timothy, two years a blue, went up to New Inn Hall, resided for one summer and never returned to the University for anything but short periods. He was another fine player. True he made a 'pair' in his first Varsity Match in 1884, but he fared better the following year, although Oxford lost the match.

It was a poor season at Oxford in 1882, but it is notable for the first visit of an Australian team. The following year saw the first visit of Lancashire to The Parks and, indeed, the fixture list was increased to seven matches. M.C. Kemp was an excellent captain and had high expectations against Cambridge, but the weather was against him.

Three undergraduates (Coles Child, A. Acland Wood and H.J. Stone) had all been together at Captain A.M. Bell's cramming establishment and decided with their tutor's encouragement to start a permanent cricket club. The first match of this club was played at Squerryes Court, Kent in 1883. Edward Britten Holmes, a business associate of Child, was the actual founder and being a musician chose the musical term 'Authentic' for the new club. 'Britten' remained secretary until 1915. Professor Case was elected president in 1886 and produced the motto 'By Jove's Authentic Fire', and the colours evolved from this; red for fire, gold for the sun, and blue (light blue until 1898) for the sky. Apart from tours, most notably the famous Northern Tour, the 'Tics' play nearly all their matches in the Trinity term. The captain of OUCC is *ex officio* a vice-president, all blues are elected and there are as many as one hundred members allowed in residence at any one time.

This decade ended in glory. Some claim that the 1884 Oxford side was the best ever – seven of the eight matches were won. The vanquished included Cambridge, the Australians, Lancashire (twice) and Surrey. Oxford's highest total was 251 – there can be no greater tribute to their bowlers. Eight of the team played in every match, and even more striking is the fact that seven of the team were freshmen, this in itself reflecting great credit on Kemp's judgement as captain.

The Australian match was played on Christ Church ground and was the first of the season (the scores are below). The touring side had just crushed a strong team raised by Lord Sheffield, and hardly expected the drubbing they were to receive from Oxford. In Australia's first innings, H.O. Whitby had four caught in the slips in his 8 for 82, bowling unchanged for forty-one overs. The innings ended by four o'clock. Initially, Oxford fared little better, sliding to 25 for 4, but T.C. O'Brien and H.V. Page came together and put on 83 before stumps were drawn. K.J. Key gave O'Brien further help in the morning and Oxford were ahead by 61. This lead looked of even greater value when A.C. Bannerman, W.L. Murdoch and G. Giffen were all back in the pavilion with Australia still 31 behind. There was a recovery but E.W. Bastard bowled superbly to dismiss Australia at the end of the day, leaving 108 for victory.

Next morning O'Brien was dropped in the first over, and T.R. Hine-Haycock should have been run out by the length of the pitch. F.R. Spofforth and H.F. Boyle bowled with the sort of hostility that had taken the 'Ashes' of English cricket to Australia only two years earlier. M.C. Kemp came to the wicket at 24 for 3 to play the innings of a lifetime. At lunch the score was 79. After the interval he cut loose, scoring 25 of the last 31 and winning the match with a slashing blow to leg. Only a week later this powerful Australian eleven won by an innings and 81 runs at Fenner's.

PLAYED AT OXFORD, 15, 16, 17 MAY, 1884
Australians 148 (H.O. Whitby 8 for 82) and 168 (E.W. Bastard 5 for 44)
Oxford 209 (T.C. O'Brien 92) and 110 for 3 (M.C. Kemp 63 not out)
Oxford won by 7 wickets.

CAMBRIDGE *Lytteltons, Studds and Steel scale Olympus*

The years 1875 to 1884 saw not only a new pavilion at Fenner's, which replaced the old low wooden structure adjoining the county gaol (the one that received 'Buns' Thornton's unsuccessful bat!), but also the start of what has been called cricket's Golden Age. That age was to be tragically cut short thirty years later by what Wilfred Owen called 'the pity of war' – when cricket's lights as well as Europe's went out, and the careers of many fine cricketers, both proven and unproven, were extinguished also. The decade opened with a narrow Oxford win, but after it Cambridge gained a decisive advantage, with twice the number of victories, achieved by some fine elevens. *Wisden* goes further by calling the sides of 1878, 1879, 1880 and 1881 great ones. It was, above all, an age made memorable by two great Cambridge families – the Lytteltons and the Studds – whose exploits were rivalled, in the 1920s, by the Ashtons alone, and also by A.G. Steel, *primus inter pares* of the Cambridge cricketers of the era.

Steel played in the sides of 1878, 1879, 1880 and 1881, being captain in his penultimate season and playing under the Hon. Ivo Bligh in his final one. His stock was such that in *The History of Cricket* H.S. Altham places him on the very pinnacle of Olympus for over thirty years. He was a medium-slow bowler who spun the ball both ways, mostly from leg, and a batsman of the highest class, about whom W.G. paid the compliment of saying that he never envied any county the possession of any cricketer as much as he envied the possessors of Steel. He appeared eighteen times for the Gentlemen, taking 99 wickets for something over 15 runs apiece; and he played nine times for England against Australia at home, being captain in 1886 when England won all three, and in 1888 when England were defeated. He also played in four Tests under the Hon. Ivo Bligh in Australia, 1882–3. His two Test hundreds – he made seven in all – were at Sydney in 1883 and at Lord's in 1884. His reputation is well illustrated by the comment of the famous Yorkshire bowler Tom Emmett. On reaching Old Trafford for one Roses match, Emmett was told that Steel was playing, whereupon he turned round to the rest of the side with, 'Let's go home, lads! Mr Steel's playing, and Yorkshire's beat.'

The greatness of the Hon. Alfred Lyttelton, who captained Cambridge in 1879, the year after his brother Edward, was similarly never in doubt. He was picked, as the best amateur wicket-keeper, for the Gentlemen in 1876, his first year at Cambridge; and he kept wicket for England against Australia at The Oval in 1880 and 1882, and at Lord's and The Oval in 1884. As a batsman he represented, in its highest development, the forward style of play taught by R.A.H. Mitchell at Eton, and it brought him seven first-class hundreds, including 181 for Middlesex against Gloucestershire at Clifton in 1883. On his death, *Wisden* waxed lyrical about his personality and his public life – as lawyer, politician and constant worker in philanthropic causes – as well as about his all-round athletic skill. For he was gifted at rackets, Eton fives, tennis and Association football – he played for England at this game also – as well as at cricket. Above all, he was held in the highest esteem for his generosity of spirit.

Whereas Alfred turned to the law and to politics, Edward became an assistant master, both at Wellington and Eton, and was appointed Headmaster first of Haileybury, and later of Eton. He wrote about his life in a fascinating autobiography which was recommended to me by a Cambridge friend long before this book was a gleam in E.W. Swanton's eye. In it he revealed himself as a talented but essentially modest person, with a wide range of interests and a keen understanding of human nature. What I had not fully realized was what a magnificent all-round athlete he was. The memoirs of his son-in-law Dr Cyril Alington, also Headmaster of Eton, ought to have alerted me, since there is in them a chapter headed 'Cricket', and a footnote which records the impression of a young man being interviewed for a post at Haileybury. 'I remember,' the candidate later wrote, 'being much struck by the easy and natural way he passed instantaneously from the subject of the Holy Spirit's work in the young to the excellence of a sudden brilliant stroke by one of the batsmen.'

It would be a culpable omission if I did not add his delightful remark recalled by Lord Home in the Guildhall, on the occasion of the MCC Bicentenary Eve-of-Match dinner. Once, late in life, Alington has told us, his father-in-law was trying to convince a sceptical companion that he was no longer interested in the game. As the short-lived argument proceeded, he flashed out, 'Well, it's certainly a rum thing, but I never go into a church without visualising the spin of the ball up the nave.'

Edward Lyttelton excelled at Eton fives, the field and wall games, the long jump and putting the weight, and like his brother Alfred played Association football for England. But cricket was his true forte, and in his four years at Cambridge he had several outstanding achievements. In the year that his side beat Oxford by 238 runs at Lord's, he helped the Gentlemen to a decisive victory of 206 runs with innings of 44 and 66; but of all that side's achievements – it won all eight matches played – success against the Australians by an innings and 72 runs (the scores are below) must have given him especial pleasure. When Middlesex played them and lost by 98 runs, he went in when the score was 14 for 4 wickets and scored a magnificent hundred, cutting and driving to great effect. He was President of the MCC in 1898.

Played at Lord's, 22, 23 July, 1878
Cambridge 285 (Hon. A. Lyttelton 72, A.G. Steel 59)
Australia 111 and 102 (P.H. Morton 33.2 overs, 12 wickets for 90)
Cambridge won by an innings and 72 runs.

The three Studd brothers of this era also scaled Olympus, as Steel had done, and theirs is a remarkable story. They were all in the 1882 Cambridge side that beat the Australians by six wickets (the scores are below), G.B. and J.E.K. putting on 106 for the first wicket, and C.T. making 118 in the first innings and taking eight wickets in the match. They were successive captains of Cambridge from 1882 to 1884. C.T. was the youngest of the three and the most famous (his obituary appeared in *Wisden* in 1932, the year after his death). He played for England while still at Cambridge, possessing a fine upright batting style and being especially strong on the off-side. He bowled above medium pace, with a high action. His record in 1882 reflected cricket's glorious uncertainty and the even-handedness of fate, even for the most gifted. He had scored 114 for MCC against the strongest bowling side Australia had sent to this country, and 100 at Lord's for the Gentlemen, but in the historic game at The Oval, which the visitors won by 7 runs, he was bowled by Spofforth for nought, and in the second innings, demoted to number ten in the order, he was nought not out at the finish. In three University Matches he took twenty-seven wickets for less than 12 runs each. Unhappily for English cricket, his sense of vocation took him into the missionary field, first to China, and latterly to the Belgian Congo (now Zaire).

PLAYED AT CAMBRIDGE 29, 30, 31 MAY, 1882
Australians 139 (A.C. Bannerman 50; R.C. Ramsay 5 for 61, C.T. Studd 5 for 64) and 291 (G. Giffen 59, T. Horan 51; R.C. Ramsay 7 for 118)
Cambridge 266 (C.T. Studd 118; G.E. Palmer 6 for 65) and 163 for 4
(J.E.K. Studd 66)
Cambridge won by 6 wickets.

G.B., the middle brother, captained Cambridge in 1882 and played a great innings of 120 against Oxford, showing considerable strength in his driving, notably to the off, and saving many runs in the field. His aggregate of 819 runs in a first-class season was high for those days, and he was chosen to go with the Hon. Ivo Bligh's team to Australia in 1882–3. He would have been the first to recognize the exceptional contribution to his team's success not only of C. Aubrey Smith, about whom more later, but also of R.C. Ramsay, 'Twisting Tommy' as he was called, who took 12 for 179, for 15 apiece, against the immensely strong Australians, but went off to work in Ceylon (now Sri Lanka) soon after leaving Cambridge. G.B. also played tennis against Oxford. Like C.T., he too became a missionary, at first in India and China, but from 1891 in Los Angeles, California.

J.E.K., later Sir Kynaston, was captain of Cambridge in 1884, the year Oxford turned the tables during a spell of defeats, but, as already mentioned, he played his part in the great victory over the Australians in 1882. That made it twice in five years! He gained high renown in other walks of life: as Lord Mayor of the City of London in 1928, President of the MCC in 1930 – during his year he took pleasure in entertaining W.M. Woodfull's side at the Merchant Taylors' Hall – and a high officer in the Masonic world, as well as a respected Fruiterer and Merchant Taylor. 'Everything he touched he lifted up,' said Canon F.H. Gillingham, who played for Dulwich and Essex, in his memorial address in St Paul's Cathedral in 1944.

Two other cricketers deserve their place in the hall of fame. These are A.P. Lucas, who played in the Cambridge sides of 1875 to 1878 and toured Australia with the fifth English team in 1878–9 under Lord Harris, and another Uppinghamian, S.S. Schultz, later Storey, who won his blue in 1877. *Wisden* wrote of Lucas: 'He was one of the finest of batsmen – almost unique in his combination of perfect style and impregnable defence.' In 1874, the year that he left Uppingham, coached by H.H. Stephenson, he was picked for the Gentlemen of the South against the Players of the North, and scored 48 and 23. In his career he scored eight centuries, the highest being 145 for England against Cambridge in 1882, and four nineties, including 97 for Middlesex against Gloucestershire in 1883.

The last player to take the stage, and to bring the curtain down on this decade, is Charles Aubrey Smith, who played four times against Oxford, between 1882 and 1885, and was three times on the winning side, achieving bowling figures of 6 for 78 and 6 for 81. He made his name as a cricketer, and as a soccer player for the Corinthians and Old Carthusians, before he became famous on the stage and as a film star, popular for playing archetypal Englishmen with outstanding success. His fifteen years as a Sussex player, three of them as captain, were recently recognized by the unveiling of a plaque on the house he occupied in Brighton. He went to Australia with the side organized by Shaw and Shrewsbury, and in 1888–9 he captained the first English side to visit South Africa. During that tour he took 134 wickets at 7.61 apiece – a modest achievement compared with the 290 wickets of Johnny Briggs at 5.62! While in South Africa, where he stayed as a stockbroker, he helped to initiate the Currie Cup. Over six feet tall, he had an unusual run-up, coming either from deep mid-off or from behind the umpire, and thus acquired the name 'Round the Corner Smith'. He captained the Hollywood side to a ripe old age and was knighted in 1944 in recognition of his support of Anglo-American friendship.

The season of 1878 was a Light Blue *annus mirabilis* – it is worth repeating that it produced a hundred per cent record – and Gilbert Ashton's side in 1921 is the only one that could hold a candle to that of Edward Lyttelton, though a case could be made for Majid's 1971 side. The record over the whole decade, marred somewhat by the 1884 side's winning only one of their matches, is undoubtedly second to none. It reads: Played 75, Won 39, Lost 24, Drew 12. But statistics are but the bare bones; what is more important is that the skill and character of the players of this decade embodied all that was best in the amateur tradition.

1875

This was a wonderful game. The finish was agonizingly close, but the cricket had gone very evenly throughout the match and it was never safe to prophesy who was going to win.

As an interesting aside, tarpaulins were used to cover the wicket; a reference to wicket covers does not appear again for years. Their use in the very wet conditions made play possible by two o'clock on the first day.

A.J. Webbe, of Harrow and Trinity, who only the year before had played two fine innings against Eton at Lord's, made his first appearance for Oxford. He was a fine fielder and batsman, a great captain of Oxford and Middlesex, and few have done more in the administration of the game. His two innings were important, but in catching the Hon. Edward Lyttelton left-handed on the boundary after a chase of twenty yards, not only did he execute one of the great catches of all time but he dashed Cambridge's best hopes of victory. H.M. Sims and W.S. Patterson edged Cambridge nearer to their target, but A.W. Ridley, Oxford's Etonian captain, with quite remarkable courage put himself on to bowl lobs. He immediately bowled Patterson, who hit across a leg-break, and when Smith came to the wicket, bowled him playing for the turn that wasn't there. It was said that Ridley was the only person on the Lord's ground whose calmness was entirely undisturbed by this dramatic finish.

OXFORD	First innings		Second innings	
A.J. Webbe	c Smith, b Sharpe	55	c Blacker, b Sharpe	21
T.W. Lang	b Sims	45	c and b Sharpe	2
D. Campbell	c Smith, b Sharpe	1	b Sharpe	0
A.W. Ridley	b Patterson	21	c Smith, b Patterson	2
R. Briggs	c Smith, b Sharpe	2	b Greenfield	12
W.W. Pulman	c Blacker, b Sharpe	25	st Hamilton, b Sharpe	30
Vernon Royle	b Patterson	1	st Hamilton, b Sharpe	21
F.M. Buckland	b Sims	22	b Patterson	0
W.H. Game	st Hamilton, b Patterson	5	c Lucas, b Patterson	22
H.G. Tylecote	c Greenfield, b Sharpe	1	not out	12
W. Foord-Kelcey	not out	2	c Patterson, b Sharpe	11
EXTRAS	B 15, L-B 3, W 2	20	B 4	4
	TOTAL	200	TOTAL	137

CAMBRIDGE				
F.F.J. Greenfield	c Ridley, b Foord-Kelcey	12	c Campbell, b Royle	14
A.P. Lucas	c Buckland, b Ridley	19	b Buckland	5
G.H. Longman	c Ridley, b Buckland	40	b Royle	23
W. Blacker	b Buckland	19	b Royle	1
Hon. E. Lyttelton	c and b Lang	23	c Webbe, b Buckland	20
H.M. Sims	hw, b Lang	5	c Pulman, b Lang	39
G. Macan	b Lang	2	not out	1
W.S. Patterson	c Ridley, b Buckland	12	b Ridley	18
A.F. Smith	c Royle, b Lang	3	b Ridley	0
C.M. Sharpe	not out	6	b Royle	29
H.A. Douglas Hamilton	st Tylecote, b Lang	5	lbw, b Lang	11
EXTRAS	B 10, L-B 7	17	B 1, L-B 4, N-B 2	7
	TOTAL	163	TOTAL	168

Cambridge bowling	OVERS	RUNS	WKTS		OVERS	RUNS	WKTS
Sharpe	68.2	89	5		37	66	6
Patterson	41	51	3		34	44	3
Sims	26	30	2		5	14	0
Greenfield	7	10	0		7	9	1

Oxford bowling	OVERS	RUNS	WKTS		OVERS	RUNS	WKTS
Lang	35	35	5		14	33	2
Foord-Kelcey	30	48	1		15	23	0
Buckland	28	34	3		22	38	2
Ridley	20	21	1		4.3	16	2
Royle	7	8	0		28	51	4

1876

Four of the victorious Cambridge side were Uppinghamians – A.P. Lucas, D.Q. Steel, W.S. Patterson and H.T.L. Luddington – and between them they contributed 225 runs and were responsible for sixteen wickets. Both sides looked strong in batting but Cambridge had the edge with better bowling, and with Alfred Lyttelton behind the stumps their fielding was sharper.

Oxford were saved from an innings defeat by W.H. Game's fine captain's innings of 109. He

was a Shirburnian at Oriel and had also been awarded blues for rugger and athletics. Three years earlier, at an Oxford athletics meeting, he had thrown a cricket ball 127 yards and 15 inches. His innings was a fine blend of defence and attack. Nevertheless Cambridge eventually needed only 72. They made 32 overnight, and Lyttelton was run out the next morning going for the winning run.

OXFORD	First innings		Second innings	
A.J. Webbe	c Shaw, b Luddington	1	c Greenfield, b Patterson	16
F.M. Buckland	c A. Lyttelton, b Patterson	32	c and b Luddington	0
A.H. Heath	b Luddington	0	b Luddington	0
T.S. Dury	c A. Lyttelton, b Luddington	7	b Luddington	25
R. Briggs	b Luddington	41	b Allsopp	32
A. Pearson	b Patterson	0	b Luddington	14
W.H. Game	c Shaw, b Luddington	4	lbw b Greenfield	109
D. Campbell	c Newton, b Patterson	6	b Greenfield	43
Vernon Royle	c A. Lyttelton, b Patterson	2	not out	11
C.P. Lewis	c Greenfield, b Patterson	15	c Greenfield, b Patterson	1
H.G. Tylecote	not out	0	b Greenfield	0
EXTRAS	B 2, L-B 2	4	B 5, L-B 3, W 2, N-B 1	11
	TOTAL	112	TOTAL	262

CAMBRIDGE				
F.F.J. Greenfield	b Lewis	1		
A.P. Lucas	c Campbell, b Royle	67	not out	23
W. Blacker	b Lewis	0	not out	0
Hon. E. Lyttelton	c Briggs, b Lewis	18		
D.Q. Steel	c and b Royle	24		
Hon. A. Lyttelton	c Briggs, b Pearson	43	run out	47
W.S. Patterson	not out	105		
V.K. Shaw	b Pearson	0		
H.T. Allsopp	b Buckland	21		
S.C. Newton	b Pearson	7		
H.T. Luddington	b Lewis	6		
EXTRAS	B 4, L-B 5, W 1	10	B 4, L-B 1, W 1	6
	TOTAL	302	TOTAL (1 WKT)	76

Cambridge bowling	OVERS	RUNS	WKTS	OVERS	RUNS	WKTS
Patterson	36	42	5	58	110	2
Luddington	26.1	51	5	49	72	4
Shaw	8	15	0	13	18	0
Greenfield	—	—	—	18.1	29	3
Allsopp	—	—	—	5	8	1
Steel	—	—	—	3	8	0
Lucas	—	—	—	1	6	0

Oxford bowling						
Buckland	56	90	1	6	15	0
Lewis	50.1	116	4	11.1	28	0
Royle	20	32	2	2	5	0
Pearson	13	17	3	—	—	—
Heath	9	9	0	6	17	0
Dury	6	10	0	1	5	0
Game	3	7	0	—	—	—
Tylecote	3	11	0	—	—	—

1877

This was the Golden Jubilee year of the Varsity Match, and to celebrate the occasion a dinner was held at the Cannon Street Hotel. Six who played in 1827 were present, including Sir Herbert Jenner-Fust, who had been the Cambridge captain. In an entertaining speech he described the cricketing dress of his youth and deplored the degeneracy of modern wicket-keeping. He was seventy-one and still playing club cricket; he played his last game for the village of Hill in Gloucestershire three years later, and lived on until his ninety-ninth year.

Cambridge were odds on to win this match but lost by ten wickets. Oxford, despite being led by an exceptional captain and fine player in

A.J. Webbe, had a poor batting side. Earlier in the season they had been dismissed for 12 against the MCC, still the lowest score in a first-class match.

For Cambridge, A.P. Lucas was an elegant stylist, and throughout his long career never tired of saying how indebted he was to his teacher H.H. Stephenson. No two players can ever have done more to win a Varsity Match than F.M. Buckland and H.G. Tylecote. They bowled with supreme accuracy and also joined in a match-winning partnership of 142. Tylecote, of Clifton and St John's, formerly a wicket-keeper, had a remarkable analysis for the match. He bowled 93 four-ball overs, unchanged from the Pavilion End, conceding only 122 runs, and took nine wickets.

CAMBRIDGE	First innings		Second innings	
A.P. Lucas	c and b Tylecote	54	b Tylecote	8
Hon. A. Lyttelton	b Tylecote	4	c Jellicoe, b Tylecote	6
W.S. Patterson	lbw, b Tylecote	20	b Jellicoe	7
Hon. E. Lyttelton	b Buckland	7	b Jellicoe	16
D.Q. Steel	c Savory, b Buckland	9	c Fowler, b Buckland	21
L.K. Jarvis	c Greene, b Tylecote	3	b Buckland	30
F.H. Mellor	c Tylecote, b Jellicoe	5	not out	15
H. Pigg	b Jellicoe	0	c Greene, b Buckland	2
S.S. Schultz	b Buckland	18	c Wallington, b Buckland	2
L. Bury	c Buckland, b Tylecote	1	c Greene, b Tylecote	2
H.T. Luddington	not out	1	c and b Tylecote	12
EXTRAS	B 12	12	B 3, L-B 2	5
	TOTAL	134	TOTAL	126

OXFORD				
A.J. Webbe	b Luddington	0	not out	27
H.R. Webbe	st A. Lyttelton, b Patterson	9	not out	19
E.W. Wallington	b Luddington	15		
A.H. Heath	b Patterson	0		
F.M. Buckland	not out	117		
A.D. Greene	b Patterson	5		
J.H. Savory	b Luddington	0		
H.G. Tylecote	c A. Lyttelton, b Luddington	39		
H. Fowler	b Luddington	10		
A. Pearson	b Patterson	9		
F.G.G. Jellicoe.	c Mellor, b Patterson	1		
EXTRAS	B 8, L-B 1	9	N-B 1	1
	TOTAL	214	TOTAL	47

Oxford bowling	OVERS	RUNS	WKTS		OVERS	RUNS	WKTS
Tylecote	58	71	5		35	51	4
Jellicoe	34	28	2		22	41	2
Buckland	24	23	3		13	29	4

Cambridge bowling							
Patterson	37.1	41	5		10	9	0
Luddington	27	90	5		6	24	0
Lucas	11	16	0		—	—	—
Schultz	9	40	0		3.2	13	0
Jarvis	4	9	0		—	—	—
Pigg	3	9	0		—	—	—

1, 2 July
At Lord's

1878

Cambridge won by
238 runs

An already powerful nucleus at Cambridge was strengthened by several freshmen, most notably A.G. Steel, who later played eighteen times for the Gentlemen and thirteen for England. There can have been few stronger Cambridge sides. Oxford, on the other hand, relied on the Webbe brothers, although A.H. Evans, the future Headmaster of Horris Hill, brought all-round ability to the side, and gave Cambridge a foretaste of his later outstanding skill as a bowler, taking at one stage four wickets in eleven balls.

For some reason the prepared area was not used and A.J. Webbe put Cambridge in on a suspect pitch. A total of 168 seemed not too for-

midable, but Oxford struggled to 127. Cambridge then exposed the weakness of Oxford's change bowling, and although Evans came back to destroy the Cambridge tail, a target of 271 was always going to test Oxford. Their second innings started at a quarter to five; Steel had the first three wickets for 2 runs and the whole procession was completed by six o'clock. P.M. Morton bowled well, but it was Steel who ripped the heart out of Oxford's resistance. He had now taken 75 first-class wickets in eight matches. Oxford's 32 is the lowest total ever in a Varsity Match.

CAMBRIDGE	First innings		Second innings	
A.P. Lucas	c Evans, b Knight	4	c Wickham, b Knight	74
Hon. A. Lyttelton	c Kemp, b Evans	5	c Kemp, b Evans	64
Hon. E. Lyttelton	b Evans	53	c Hirst, b Evans	10
H. Whitfeld	b Evans	22	b Evans	5
D.Q. Steel	b Evans	0	b Knight	2
L.K. Jarvis	b Evans	0	b Evans	7
A.G. Steel	not out	44	b Evans	9
F.W. Kingston	c Evans, b Knight	4	c Kemp, b Knight	9
Hon. Ivo F.W. Bligh	c Wickham, b Knight	14	not out	24
P.H. Morton	b Heath	10	b Evans	16
A.F.J. Ford	b Heath	0	c Savory, b Evans	5
EXTRAS	B 6, L-B 6	12	B 1, L-B 2, W 1	4
	TOTAL	168	TOTAL	229

OXFORD				
A.J. Webbe	c E. Lyttelton, b A.G. Steel	11	c and b A.G. Steel	0
H.R. Webbe	c Morton, b A.G. Steel	26	b A.G. Steel	6
A.H. Heath	b A.G. Steel	14	c Whitfeld, b A.G. Steel	8
A.D. Greene	not out	35	c A. Lyttelton, b A.G. Steel	0
E.T. Hirst	c Lucas, b A.G. Steel	0	b Morton	13
A.H. Evans	st A. Lyttelton, b A.G. Steel	0	lbw, b Morton	4
C.W.M. Kemp	b A.G. Steel	2	not out	0
R.L. Knight	b Lucas	3	b Morton	0
A.P. Wickham	b A.G. Steel	1	c Bligh, b A.G. Steel	0
J.H. Savory	b A.G. Steel	19	c Kingston, b Morton	0
G.S. Marriott	c E. Lyttelton, b Lucas	11	b Morton	0
EXTRAS	B 3, L-B 2	5	L-B 1	1
	TOTAL	127	TOTAL	32

Oxford bowling	OVERS	RUNS	WKTS		OVERS	RUNS	WKTS
Evans	40	55	5		50.3	86	7
Knight	30	68	3		40	64	3
Marriott	9	29	0		13	20	0
Heath	1.1	4	2		10	32	0
Kemp	—	—	—		4	8	0
A.J. Webbe	—	—	—		3	15	0

Cambridge bowling							
A.G. Steel	61	62	8		20.1	11	5
Lucas	43.2	27	2		—	—	—
Morton	23	27	0		20	20	5
Ford	3	6	0		—	—	—

30 June, 1, 2 July
At Lord's

1879

*Cambridge won by
9 wickets*

There would have been no justice if Oxford had been saved by rain; they almost were, for a torrential storm broke as Alfred Lyttelton hit the winning blow for Cambridge. A.H. Evans had had a good season for Oxford but otherwise their record was a sorry one. Cambridge were not quite as strong as in the previous year, but G.B., the eldest of the Studd brothers, came up to Trinity from Eton; he and R.S. Jones were useful replacements for Lucas and Edward Lyttelton. The remarkable G.B. Studd was the second of the six brothers; the youngest, R.A., did not win his blue until 1895.

H.R. Webbe and A.H. Heath gave Oxford a decent start, but thereafter only E.T. Hirst showed any confidence, and he was the first victim of a hat-trick by A.G. Steel. Cambridge were just ahead overnight. Tuesday was washed out, and on a dead wicket the next day Steel continued to bat well, but the last five wickets added a mere 43, giving a lead of 49; this proved to be more valuable than the mere figures suggest. Steel and A.F.J. Ford swept Oxford aside, but A.D. Greene showed a dogged defence and was the only Oxonian into double figures, at least ensuring that Cambridge had to bat again.

OXFORD	First innings			Second innings	
H.R. Webbe	c Jones, b Wood		18	c D.Q. Steel, b Ford	7
A.H. Heath	c Bligh, b Ford		45	c Ford, b A.G. Steel	0
A.D. Greene	b Wood		2	c Ford, b A.G. Steel	20
W.A. Thornton	b Wood		2	b Ford	5
J.H.M. Hare	b A.G. Steel		6	c Ford, b A.G. Steel	3
A. Haskett-Smith	b Morton		14	b A.G. Steel	6
E.T. Hirst	st Lyttelton, b A.G. Steel		35	b A.G. Steel	2
H. Fowler	c Lyttelton, b Wood		4	c Studd, b A.G. Steel	5
A.H. Evans	not out		13	c Studd, b A.G. Steel	0
N. McLachlan	b A.G. Steel		0	not out	9
F.G.G. Jellicoe	b A.G. Steel		0	b Ford	6
EXTRAS	B 4, L-B 5, N-B 1		10	B 1	1
	TOTAL		149	TOTAL	64

CAMBRIDGE	First innings			Second innings	
Hon. A. Lyttelton	c Hirst, b Thornton		53	not out	12
H. Whitfeld	b Hare		31	not out	2
A.G. Steel[1]	c Greene, b Thornton		64		
Hon. Ivo F.W. Bligh	b Thornton		1		
D.Q. Steel	c Fowler, b Jellicoe		27		
G.B. Studd	c Greene, b Evans		7		
A.F.J. Ford	b McLachlan		7		
R.S. Jones	b McLachlan		0		
L.K. Jarvis	b McLachlan		0		
H. Wood	b Thornton		5		
P.H. Morton	not out		0	b McLachlan	0
EXTRAS	L-B 2, N-B 1		3	w 1, N-B 1	2
	TOTAL		198	TOTAL (1 WKT)	16

Cambridge bowling	OVERS	RUNS	WKTS		OVERS	RUNS	WKTS
Wood	45	46	4		—	—	—
A.G. Steel	42.2	43	4		38	23	7
Morton	27	38	1		—	—	—
Ford	10	12	1		38	40	3

Oxford bowling	OVERS	RUNS	WKTS		OVERS	RUNS	WKTS
Evans	46	67	1		—	—	—
Jellicoe	35	53	1		2	6	0
McLachlan	27	41	3		3	6	1
Thornton	22.3	29	4		1	2	0
Hare	3	5	1		—	—	—

[1] Performed the hat-trick in Oxford's first innings. His victims were: Hirst, McLachlan and Jellicoe.

28, 29 June
At Lord's

1880

*Cambridge won by
115 runs*

Alfred Lyttelton had gone down from Cambridge, but an equally fine player, the greatest of the Studds, C.T. replaced him. He had a remarkable record as an all-rounder during a short career in first-class cricket; perhaps his finest achievements were the two hundreds he made against the great Australian side of 1882 which included Spofforth.

Oxford had had a poor season in this, their last full year on Cowley Marsh; only H. Fowler had made a score of fifty. There were suspicions about A.H. Evans' action, although these seem to have been allayed and he certainly bowled

with devastating effect in the Varsity Match.

Oxford must have been pleased to see the Cambridge innings close for 166. It was then the turn of A.G. Steel and P.H. Morton to have a field day, the latter inflicting a hat-trick on Oxford, as Steel did the year before. E.T. Hirst, who had never faltered, was joined by N. McLachlan and they saved the follow-on. H. Whitfeld and C.P. Wilson gave Cambridge a good start, the latter being out to a stupendous catch, but Oxford dropped too many chances and a final target of 267 was quite beyond them. Yet again, the great A.G. Steel had the last word.

CAMBRIDGE	First innings			Second innings	
Hon. Ivo F.W. Bligh	c Patterson, b Harrison		59	c Trevor, b Evans	13
H. Whitfeld	b Evans		0	c Fowler, b Harrison	32
A.G. Steel	b Harrison		19	st Fowler, b Evans	4
R.S. Jones	b Evans		1	c Colebrooke, b Harrison	2
C.T. Studd	b Evans		1	c Hirst, b McLachlan	52
G.B. Studd	lbw, b Evans		38	b McLachlan	40
C.P. Wilson	not out		13	c and b Greene	23
A.F.J. Ford	b Evans		1	b Evans	0
O.P. Lancashire	b Evans		5	b McLachlan	29
P.H. Morton[1]	b McLachlan		12	not out	16
C.W. Foley	b Thornton		0	b Evans	3
EXTRAS	B 14, L-B 3		17	B 14, L-B 4	18
	TOTAL		166	TOTAL	232

OXFORD					
E.L. Colebrooke	st Foley, b Steel		3	not out	34
A.H. Trevor	st Foley, b Steel		18	b Steel	4
A.H. Evans	b Morton		12	b Ford	22
A.D. Greene	lbw, b C.T. Studd		14	run out	8
W.A. Thornton	b Morton		0	c G.B. Studd, b Steel	5
W.H. Patterson	b Morton		0	b Steel	2
E.T. Hirst	not out		49	c Ford, b Steel	15
H. Fowler	b Morton		1	c C.T. Studd, b Steel	43
F.L. Evelyn	lbw, b Morton		0	c G.B. Studd, b Steel	1
G.C. Harrison	b Morton		0	c C.T. Studd, b Steel	10
N. McLachlan	b Steel		27	lbw, b Ford	0
EXTRAS	B 6, L-B 2		8	B 5, L-B 2	7
	TOTAL		132	TOTAL	151

Oxford bowling	OVERS	RUNS	WKTS		OVERS	RUNS	WKTS
Evans	57	73	6		56	60	4
Harrison	51	51	2		45	56	2
Thornton	11	18	1		15	34	0
McLachlan	10	7	1		27	30	3
Greene	—	—	—		19	34	1

Cambridge bowling	OVERS	RUNS	WKTS		OVERS	RUNS	WKTS
Steel	31.2	37	3		39.3	61	7
Morton	26	45	6		24	58	0
Wilson	13	24	0		11	18	0
C.T. Studd	9	13	1		2	0	0
Ford	1	5	0		6	7	2

[1] Performed the hat-trick in Oxford's first innings. His victims were: Fowler, Evelyn and Harrison.

1881

With three Studds, A.G. Steel and C.P. Wilson all at the Hon. Ivo Bligh's disposal, Cambridge were again favourites. (Wilson had the rare distinction of playing for England at both Association and Rugby football.) Oxford welcomed two important freshmen in M.C. Kemp and C.F.H. Leslie, the latter having already impressed with a fine 111 not out in his first first-class match against MCC.

Oxford did not prosper in their first innings at Lord's, although a welcome wag of the tail took them to 131, but Cambridge still went comfortably ahead. Honours were even by lunchtime on the second day, Oxford having made up the 48-run deficit. A.H. Trevor was out soon after lunch and Leslie joined Patterson but was soon pavilion-bound, only to be recalled when the umpires, on W.H. Patterson's appeal, adjudged the catch which had caused his departure to be a bump ball. This was crucial; he played a brilliant innings of 70, and Patterson, by now batting with an injured hand, carried his bat, the first to do so in a Varsity Match. Cambridge needed 253, well within their capabilities, but A.H. Evans rounded off his Oxford career with forty-two overs of hostile bowling and added six victims to the seven he had claimed in the first innings.

OXFORD	First innings		Second innings	
W.H. Patterson	c Ford, b Steel	12	not out	107
A.H. Trevor	c Hone, b C.T. Studd	41	b Ford	40
C.F.H. Leslie	st Hone, b Steel	4	c Rowe, b J.E.K. Studd	70
A.H. Evans	c Ford, b C.T. Studd	0	c Bligh, b C.T. Studd	1
W.A. Thornton	c Ford, b C.T. Studd	5	c Wilson, b C.T. Studd	17
A.O. Whiting	c Rowe, b Steel	9	b Spencer	22
E. Peake	c Bligh, b C.T. Studd	0	b C.T. Studd	24
N. McLachlan	c G.B. Studd, b Ford	21	c Steel, b C.T. Studd	0
M.C. Kemp	not out	29	b C.T. Studd	0
G.C. Harrison	run out	1	c Bligh, b C.T. Studd	5
G.E. Robinson	c Ford, b Steel	0	b Spencer	1
EXTRAS	B 8, L-B 1	9	B 17, w 2	19
	TOTAL	131	TOTAL	306

CAMBRIDGE				
Hon. Ivo F.W. Bligh	b Evans	37	c Trevor, b Evans	6
G.B. Studd	b Evans	0	c Kemp, b Harrison	5
C.T. Studd	b Evans	34	c Peake, b Evans	28
A.G. Steel	b Evans	8	c Evans, b Robinson	36
H. Whitfeld	c Evans, b Robinson	29	c McLachlan, b Evans	1
C.P. Wilson	b Evans	0	c and b Evans	6
J.E.K. Studd	c Evans, b Harrison	6	b Peake	13
A.F.J. Ford	b Evans	34	c and b Evans	20
F.C.C. Rowe	b Harrison	12	c Harrison, b Peake	2
R. Spencer	c Robinson, b Evans	10	c sub, b Evans	1
N.T. Hone	not out	0	not out	0
EXTRAS	B 9	9	L-B 5	5
	TOTAL	179	TOTAL	123

Cambridge bowling	OVERS	RUNS	WKTS	OVERS	RUNS	WKTS
Steel	38.3	46	4	46	59	0
Wilson	7	22	0	27	48	0
Ford	11	26	1	25	43	1
C.T. Studd	24	28	4	56	85	6
Spencer	—	—	—	13	27	2
Whitfeld	—	—	—	4	11	0
J.E.K. Studd	—	—	—	6	14	1

Oxford bowling						
Evans	40	74	7	42.2	56	6
Harrison	11.3	23	2	17	31	1
Robinson	15	43	1	16	13	1
Peake	5	4	0	19	18	2
McLachlan	11	16	0	—	—	—
Thornton	1	10	0	—	—	—

26, 27, 28 June
At Lord's

1882

Cambridge won by
7 wickets

Oxford should have saved the match, but with wayward fielding and some inexcusable run-outs they made Cambridge's task easy.

Cambridge welcomed C.A. Smith from Charterhouse, better known later as Sir Charles Aubrey Smith, who raised the banner of cricket in Hollywood and kept it flying for sixty years. He was a fine cricketer, and played in four Varsity Matches. By coincidence the margin of victory in each was seven wickets, three times for Cambridge and once for Oxford. He went on to captain Sussex and led the first English side to tour South Africa, followed by one to Australia.

Oxford collected 165, E.D. Shaw from Forest School holding the innings together. (He later became Bishop of Buckingham.) Early in the Cambridge innings G.B. Studd was badly dropped in the slips, and this probably turned the match. Second time round Oxford had made a good start when A.O. Whiting played the ball to C.T. Studd at cover, and he threw the wicket down. Twice more in the innings there were suicidal runs to this brilliant fielder, and each ended the same way. The target of 148 was too easy for Cambridge.

OXFORD	First innings		Second innings	
E.D. Shaw	st Wright, b Ramsay	63	st Wright, b Ramsay	4
A.O. Whiting	b C.T. Studd	8	run out	38
C.F.H. Leslie	c Gaddum, b Smith	6	b Smith	31
J.G. Walker	b Smith	0	run out	5
W.A. Thornton	c Gaddum, b C.T. Studd	26	lbw, b Gaddum	26
M.C. Kemp	c and b C.T. Studd	4	c and b Gaddum	82
E. Peake	b C.T. Studd	27	b Lacey	21
W.D. Hamilton	c Paravicini, b C.T. Studd	9	run out	0
N. McLachlan	c Ramsay, b C.T. Studd	2	b C.T. Studd	16
J.I. Patterson	not out	8	b C.T. Studd	3
G.E. Robinson	b C.T. Studd	2	not out	9
EXTRAS	B 8, L-B 2	10	B 10, L-B 11, W 1	22
	TOTAL	165	TOTAL	257

CAMBRIDGE				
G.B. Studd	c Hamilton, b Peake	120		
J.E.K. Studd	b Peake	14	b Peake	5
Hon. M.B. Hawke	c Whiting, b Patterson	15	c McLachlan, b Peake	30
F.E. Lacey	c McLachlan, b Robinson	6	not out	39
C.T. Studd	c Whiting, b Robinson	0	c Kemp, b Shaw	69
C.W. Wright	b Robinson	17	not out	1
R.C. Ramsay	b Peake	8		
P.J.T. Henery	lbw, b Thornton	61		
P.J. de Paravicini	not out	9		
C.A. Smith	c Kemp, b Peake	14		
F.D. Gaddum	run out	0		
EXTRAS	B 8, L-B 3	11	B 1, L-B 3	4
	TOTAL	275	TOTAL (3 WKTS)	148

Cambridge bowling	OVERS	RUNS	WKTS	OVERS	RUNS	WKTS
C.T. Studd	66	54	7	72	48	2
Ramsay	29	44	1	23	47	1
Gaddum	6	15	0	24.1	35	2
Smith	25	23	2	32	45	1
de Paravicini	11	19	0	10	19	0
J.E.K. Studd	—	—	—	3	10	0
Lacey	—	—	—	13	31	1

Oxford bowling						
Robinson	39	60	3	25	45	0
Peake	42	81	4	29	66	2
Shaw	29	47	0	13.3	21	1
Patterson	17	31	1	—	—	—
McLachlan	9	24	0	—	—	—
Thornton	7	21	1	4	12	0

25, 26, 27 June
At Lord's

1883

*Cambridge won by
7 wickets*

C.F.H. Leslie was on tour in Australia until the end of May, so handed over the Oxford captaincy to M.C. Kemp. H.V. Page came up to Wadham from Cheltenham with a fine reputation and was in the side for four years, the last two as captain.

C.T. Studd was Cambridge captain and, with a good team under him, had a brilliant season. H.W. Bainbridge writes of him:

C.T. Studd was a fine model for young amateur bowlers: his wonderful accuracy was due entirely to steady application and careful practice. . . . His batting powers are well known, but it is not always

remembered that he used bats, like A.P. Lucas, with specially long handles.

The Lord's match was much influenced by rain. On the first day there were two stoppages, but the wicket remained docile. Overnight, Oxford were 29 for no wicket in reply to Cambridge's 215, but next morning the wicket turned sour, and to add insult to injury there were again three run-outs. Oxford followed on, and only J.G. Walker and Page offered serious resistance. Page's pulled drives 'caused the hair of many in the pavilion to stand on end'. Cambridge cruised to yet another seven-wicket victory.

CAMBRIDGE	First innings		Second innings	
J.E.K. Studd	b Bastard	26	c Walker, b Robinson	4
C.W. Wright	c Robinson, b Peake	102	not out	29
Hon. M.B. Hawke	b Page	0		
C.T. Studd	c Kemp, b Page	31	c Kemp, b Bastard	1
Hon. J.W. Mansfield	b Peake	24	not out	0
P.J. de Paravicini	b Page	1	c Page, b Peake	20
P.J.T. Henery	b Peake	1		
W.N. Roe	b Peake	0		
J.A. Turner	not out	13		
C.A. Smith	b Page	3		
H.G. Topham	c Kemp, b Page	0		
EXTRAS	B 4, L-B 10	14	B 1, L-B 4	5
	TOTAL	215	TOTAL (3 WKTS)	59

OXFORD

	First innings		Second innings	
J.G. Walker	run out	15	b C.T. Studd	51
T.R. Hine-Haycock	b Smith	12	c Topham, b Smith	24
C.F.H. Leslie	c Topham, b Smith	5	b Smith	6
A.G. Grant-Asher	c Smith, b C.T. Studd	0	lbw, b Smith	19
M.C. Kemp	b C.T. Studd	1	b Smith	24
W.E.T. Bolitho	c Smith, b C.T. Studd	1	c Henery, b Smith	10
H.G. Ruggles-Brise	b Smith	5	b Smith	0
H.V. Page	run out	6	c Turner, b C.T. Studd	57
E. Peake	c Smith, b C.T. Studd	0	not out	11
G.E. Robinson	run out	3	b C.T. Studd	0
E.W. Bastard	not out	1	c Smith, b C.T. Studd	5
EXTRAS	L-B 5, N-B 1	6	B 5, L-B 2, N-B 1	8
	TOTAL	55	TOTAL	215

Oxford bowling	OVERS	RUNS	WKTS	OVERS	RUNS	WKTS
Robinson	29	53	0	6	12	1
Page	47.3	67	5	4	10	0
Bastard	32	45	1	7.3	13	1
Leslie	4	9	0	—	—	—
Peake	26	27	4	7	19	1

Cambridge bowling	OVERS	RUNS	WKTS	OVERS	RUNS	WKTS
C.T. Studd	27	14	4	73.2	85	4
Smith	22	28	3	58	78	6
Topham	4	7	0	6	18	0
de Paravicini	—	—	—	10	15	0
Roe	—	—	—	10	7	0
J.E.K. Studd	—	—	—	1	4	0

30 June, 1 July
At Lord's

1884

Oxford won by
7 wickets

Cambridge had a poor build-up to Lord's; Oxford had an exceptionally fine one, especially their bowlers. Kemp chose seven freshmen in a side which some claim as the best ever Oxford eleven. They won seven of their eight warm-up contests, including the Australian match played on Christ Church ground, where a gate could be charged. (*Wisden* records that *only* 11,462 paid gate money on the first day of the Varsity Match!) They won this great match by seven wickets and Geoffrey Bolton describes the ensuing celebrations:

The sides dined at the Mitre that evening and the High was filled with such delirious crowds of Town &

Gown as were not to be seen again until Mafeking night.

Cambridge struggled against E.W. Bastard and H.O. Whitby, and only P.J. de Paravicini batted with any assurance, helping them to reach the meagre total of 111. Poor T.C. O'Brien, after such a good season, was out for the first of two ducks, and Oxford needed a ninth-wicket stand between B.E. Nicholls and Bastard to get a respectable lead.

C.W. Rock was sent in by J.E.K. Studd as night watchman and he truly lived up to his name with a dogged three-and-a-half-hours innings. Oxford, however, were not to be denied.

CAMBRIDGE	First innings		Second innings	
C.W. Wright	b Whitby	16	c Kemp, b Page	34
H.W. Bainbridge	lbw, b Whitby	2	c Kemp, b Bastard	29
J.E.K. Studd	c and b Bastard	4	c and b Buckland	28
P.J. de Paravicini	b Whitby	37	b Whitby	10
D.G. Spiro	c and b Whitby	10	b Bastard	0
Hon. J.W. Mansfield	b Page	18	b Whitby	5
J.A. Turner	b Whitby	1	b Whitby	1
F. Marchant	lbw, b Whitby	0	b Bastard	0
C.W. Rock	c Nicholls, b Bastard	8	c Kemp, b Page	56
C.A. Smith	not out	0	not out	0
H.G. Topham	b Bastard	6	c Kemp, b Whitby	0
EXTRAS	B 8, L-B 1	9	B 9, L-B 4, W 1	14
	TOTAL	111	TOTAL	177

OXFORD				
T.R. Hine-Haycock	b Rock	40	not out	35
J.H. Brain	c and b Smith	42	b Rock	0
T.C. O'Brien	b Bainbridge	0	b Rock	0
H.V. Page	b Turner	25	c Turner, b Topham	38
M.C. Kemp	c Smith, b Rock	2	not out	3
K.J. Key	run out	17		
L. d'Arcy Hildyard	st Wright, b Turner	2		
E.H. Buckland	b Bainbridge	18		
B.E. Nicholls	c Marchant, b Topham	35		
E.W. Bastard	b Smith	17		
H.O. Whitby	not out	3		
EXTRAS	B 5, L-B 1, N-B 1, W 1	8	B 3, W 1	4
	TOTAL	209	TOTAL (3 WKTS)	80

Oxford bowling	OVERS	RUNS	WKTS		OVERS	RUNS	WKTS
Whitby	34	51	6		41	62	4
Bastard	23.3	29	3		46	35	3
Nicholls	13	17	0		20	22	0
Page	3	5	1		23	31	2
Buckland	—	—	—		10	13	1
Cambridge bowling							
Rock	25	37	2		14	13	2
Bainbridge	17	53	2		5.2	14	0
Smith	21.1	36	2		11	29	0
Topham	27	53	1		6	11	1
Turner	11	22	2		6	7	0
Studd	—	—	—		3	2	0

6

1885–1894

Enter the Golden Age

OXFORD *From Page to Fry*

During Victoria's long reign, the near 'feudal' society she had inherited had shown dramatic changes. Country houses and country estates still flourished, but no longer were they supported by agricultural rents; the main income now came from industry and the cities. Moreover, a professional and industrial middle class was growing daily in numbers.

Oxford and Cambridge reflected these changes, but both Universities were influenced by a strange anachronism. No one could hold a scholarship or fellowship in, or be a member of, the Universities of Oxford or Cambridge unless he was a member of the Church of England. This was a survival of the old Tests Act. After a long campaign, the 'religious test' was abolished by the repeal of the Tests Act of 1871. This led to an immediate liberalization and new courses, affecting attitudes and intake to the Universities. The sciences and modern history were encouraged, there were more lay dons, and Fellows were even allowed to be married. Never again would there be six or seven future clerics in a Varsity cricket eleven.

The Varsity Match in *Wisden*'s early years received varied coverage, but in 1885 a rather fuller section was introduced. After their truly splendid season of the previous year, Oxford held pride of place and first mention, and from that day to this that convention has largely prevailed.

H.V. Page was said to be an excellent captain, holding office for two years. Somewhat strangely, for Oxford was hardly changed from the great side of 1884, they did not win a match the following season and lost to Cambridge by seven wickets. Yet in 1886, rather against the odds, they won the Varsity Match. Page had been successful with bat and ball at Cheltenham and to that school he returned as a master, being a stalwart of the common room for thirty-five years.

Page owed much in 1886 to K.J. Key, later Sir Kingsmill Key. He had been in the Clifton XI, making a name for himself at the age of eighteen when he assisted Surrey to a notable victory over Lancashire. His partnership with H. Philipson for Oxford against Middlesex, at Chiswick Park in 1887, still stands as a record for the University; they put on 340 for the seventh wicket, and Key's individual score of 281 has also never been surpassed. Four years after going down, he took the first and last Authentics tour to India. He was later captain of Surrey for six years.

The year 1886 was a remarkable one. Oxford lost to the Australians, but gave them a nasty shock. Spofforth was playing and had 9 for 18 in the first innings, and 6 for 18 in the second; even so, Oxford needed a modest 64 to win but could reach only 38. The 'House' wicket had been a very poor one. They then moved back to The Parks, where there was little improvement, to face Lohmann of Surrey, the other supreme fast bowler of his day; he took 9 for 51, but this time Oxford did win the match. In the last game of term, against the MCC, W.G. defeated Oxford almost on his own; he started by taking two wickets and holding two catches, made 104 out of 260 and then took all ten wickets in the second innings for only 49 runs.

It is sometimes suggested that the players of this great period in Varsity cricket abandoned all for their sport. This was not so. In 1887 E.H. Buckland and H.O. Whitby, the main thrust of Oxford's attack, were not available until after 'Schools'. Until they arrived, J.H. Brain relied on the slow men; fortunately it was such a good batting side that they survived. E.A. Nepean served up a strange but quite successful variety of round-arm leg-breaks. It was this year that Key made his records and W. Rashleigh, later a Canon of Canterbury Cathedral, made over 400 runs.

H. Philipson was a fine wicket-keeper who figured prominently in A.E. Stod-dart's team in Australia, when they won a close rubber in the fifth and deciding Test match. As was then customary, he used to stand up to all bowlers, 'taking the ball with easy grace and certainty'. He represented Oxford at four different ball games. His exact contemporary, Prince Christian, a grandson of Queen Victoria, himself a very useful wicket-keeper, was never quite good enough to replace him.

'Punch' Philipson was elected captain for the 1889 season, and popular though he was, he led a weak side. They drew one match and lost the rest, including their crushing defeat by Cambridge, with Sammy Woods in full cry. It is kinder to remember the season as that in which an over was increased from four balls to five.

The Hon. F.J.N. Thesiger, later Lord Chelmsford, captained the 1890 side and also had a strange University cricket career. Coming up from Winchester with a considerable reputation, he won a blue as a freshman, was unable to play against Cambridge in 1889 because of the ill health of his brother, captained the side in 1890, and in 1891 had to leave the field after lunch on the first day of the Varsity Match with a sprained wrist – the occasion when G. MacGregor sportingly allowed T.B. Case to replace him. Lord Chelmsford went on to important service in public life, being Viceroy of India and First Lord of the Admiralty, and he was elected Warden of All Souls a year before his death.

L.C.H. Palairet came from Repton with a reputation as a bowler rather than a batsman, having taken 56 wickets at only 12 apiece in his last year at school, and having at prep school once taken seven wickets with successive balls. He was a freshman blue who rapidly established himself as a fine player: 'He had almost every good quality as a batsman; combining strong defence with fine cutting and driving, on either side of the wicket he always shaped in classic style.' His best innings were played for Somerset; drives into the river and the churchyard at Taunton were long remembered. He played twice for England against Australia in 1902, when Australia won at Old Trafford by 3 runs and England got home at The Oval by one wicket. He later became a land agent.

In the run-up to the 1890 Varsity Match Oxford had two surprise successes. In the last home match they defeated a strong Lancashire eleven, and although they lost at Old Trafford, they followed this with a fine win against Sussex.

'Schools' interfered with the selection of the eleven in 1891, but it is difficult to believe that the best side was picked. R.C.N. Palairet was given every chance, but V.T. Hill, who achieved such a reputation as a hitter, was not even given a trial. Ernest Smith (later a schoolmaster at Elstree, who did yeoman service for Yorkshire in the school holidays) had a good season, heading both batting and bowling averages. They lost five and drew two matches, and so faced Cambridge with apprehension. This, thanks to Woods, proved justified.

Oxford were a much better side in 1892. There were two outstanding freshmen, F.A. Phillips from Rossall and C.B. Fry from Repton. Phillips appeared for three years against Cambridge, but played his best cricket for Somerset. He served in the Boer War, did a stint as a District Commissioner in Nigeria, won a DSO in the First World War and did long service as a schoolmaster, but even so distinguished an all-rounder could hardly compare with C.B. Fry.

Outside sport, Fry's greatest work was achieved as director of the training ship *Mercury*; he stood in for Ranjitsinhji as a substitute delegate for India at the League of Nations, he published a novel and wrote an intriguing autobiography, *Life Worth Living*, in which he described how he 'very nearly became the King of Albania'. He was for a long period a journalist and once stood as a Liberal Parliamentary candidate in Brighton. He is underestimated as a bowler, for his achievements were considerable: he once took six wickets for 78 in the Varsity Match, took five opening the bowling for the Gentlemen at The Oval, and twice performed a hat-trick at Lord's. He survived an unhappy controversy over his action, being no-balled at Hove nine times in succession. He played in twenty-six Test matches between 1899 and 1912, including eighteen against Australia. In 1901 he scored over three thousand runs, which included six successive centuries – and so the records roll on.

The 1892 Oxford side lost to the Gentlemen, won a thriller against Lancashire by 7 runs and, on tour, another when they defeated Sussex by 10 runs. Other results were not so memorable, however, until the great win at Lord's against a Cambridge eleven which should have out-gunned them in all departments.

'Once more a strange paralysis struck the Oxford side,' writes Geoffrey Bolton of 1893; not a match was won and the Varsity Match was a disaster. Neither H.K. Foster nor P.F. Warner was selected. Despite a great match against the Australians, when Oxford lost by only 19 runs, there followed three crushing defeats on tour before the Varsity Match.

The results of 1894 do not look good on paper, yet Oxford were a side by no means to be despised. Fry, G.J. Mordaunt, H.K. Foster and R.C.N. Palairet were in form with the bat, with Phillips and H.D.G. Leveson-Gower to give useful back-up. The bowling was adequate and the fielding excellent. Although they lost heavily to Lancashire in The Parks, and again at Old Trafford by a smaller margin, a high-scoring draw at Hove, followed by a narrow loss against a powerful MCC side, made people realize that Oxford were to be reckoned with, and so they proved with their eight-wicket victory in the all-important match.

CAMBRIDGE

The greatness of Jackson, MacGregor and Woods

In the decade that embraced Queen Victoria's Golden Jubilee – and there is something very reassuring in the reflection that all but three of the University Matches played to date occurred during one reign – Cambridge continued with its slight advantage, winning six games to Oxford's three, the 1888 match being rained off. Two of the Light Blue victories were decisive ones, that of 1889 by an innings and 105 runs, and that of 1893 by 266 runs. The 1890 and 1891 sides, containing as they did F.S. Jackson, G. MacGregor and S.M.J. Woods, have been ranked by some students of the game as on a par with that of 1878, but their record – 1890, Played 9, Won 4, Lost 3, Drew 2; 1891, Played 8, Won 4, Lost 4 – scarcely supports the claim, added to which several of both sides developed after they had left Cambridge when they were playing for counties.

In the first three years of this decade, 1885 to 1887, Cambridge produced no one who was outstanding at the time, but the whole atmosphere changed with the arrival at Jesus in 1887 of an undergraduate from Brighton College with an impressive cricketing record. In the years ahead he would leave an indelible mark as an all-round sportsman of the highest class. S.M.J. Woods was born at Glenfield, near Sydney, on 14 April 1867 and died at Taunton on 30 April 1931. His cricketing achievements were much talked about, as were his grand physique, cheery disposition, unflinching courage and ability to inspire those with whom he played, especially when he was captain.

When Sammy Woods – for such he was called by all who knew him – was in residence, it was his bowling that won him especial regard. He was fast and accurate, and had at his command not only a deadly yorker and a decided break-back but also a slower ball, cleverly concealed, which proved an immensely successful wicket-taker. In his four years at Cambridge he secured 190 wickets for less than 15 runs each; against Oxford, during the course of three wins and one draw, he obtained 36 wickets for something under 9 apiece. The stark fact is that with Woods in the opposition Oxford never reached two hundred in an innings, and one Dark Blue batsman only, G.L. Wilson, made a fifty. The sight of Sammy Woods bowling, with Gregor MacGregor keeping wicket to him, was one of the most joyous spectacles in the whole of cricket. He took all ten wickets in an innings for 69 against C.I. Thornton's eleven for Cambridge in 1890, and fifteen in the match for 88. His obituary in *Wisden* expresses his skill in these words: 'Unquestionably he reached a measure of excellence which entitled him to a place among the great fast bowlers of all time.'

But he was also a powerful forcing batsman, good enough to have scored nineteen centuries for Somerset, whom he would later serve, first as captain, and later as secretary. They were enjoyable days in Somerset cricket, as R.C. Robertson-Glasgow has attested, not least in his autobiography *46 not out*, and in the *Cricket Print* devoted to Woods himself. He was also capped for England at rugby thirteen times, and such was his versatility that he had the distinction of playing rugby for

Somerset and soccer for Sussex. Playing three times for Australia and three for England puts him in a singular category.

At this time University sides regularly more than held their own against the counties, but rarely did one score as much as 703 for 9, which Cambridge did against Sussex in 1890, the Reptonian F.G.J. Ford making 191, MacGregor 131 and C.P. Foley, who came up to Trinity Hall from Eton in 1888, 117.

The Cambridge sides of 1892 and 1893, the year of the victory over Oxford by 266 runs, were captained by F.S., later Sir Stanley, Jackson, who came up from Harrow whom he had helped to defeat Eton in 1888 by 156 runs. He went from strength to strength, and on his death in 1947 was acclaimed by the editor of *Wisden* as one of the finest cricketers ever seen in England. He was unfortunately never able to go to Australia, because of business commitments. His zenith was reached when he was captain of England against Australia in 1905. He not only made 492 runs against them at an average of 70, including 144 not out at Leeds and 113 at Manchester, but he also took thirteen wickets at 15.46 each. England won the match at Manchester by an innings and 80 runs, and that at Nottingham by 213 runs.

Jackson was once describing the 91 he made in his first Test innings at Lord's, and then he smiled as he recalled the Second Test at The Oval. W.G. Grace, the English captain, had said to him, 'With all these batsmen I don't know where to put you.'

'Anywhere will do,' replied Jackson. 'Then number seven,' said Grace.

'Thanks. That's my lucky number; I was the seventh child.'

He went on to say that it was from this position that he scored his first hundred for England. 'Mold came in last when I was 99. He nearly ran me out, so in desperation I jumped in and drove Giffen high to the seats, reaching 103. Then the bewildered Mold did run me out.'

F.S. Jackson entered Parliament in 1915 and was to serve in various capacities, not least as Governor of Bombay, where he survived an assassination threat. He was President of the MCC in 1921, and chairman of selectors in 1934. He also presided over the special committee appointed by the MCC to consider post-war cricket. His brilliant all-round cricket for Yorkshire and England, serene and self-assured, speaks for itself. Elegant on-side play, lofted straight-driving and effective back-play on difficult wickets were the hallmarks of his batting.

Although he was up for three years, K.S. Ranjitsinhji, who came to Trinity from Rajkumar College, India, played one season only in the Cambridge side, and without success at Lord's. After going down, he could be said to have bridged the turn of the century with batsmanship as brilliant as the game has ever known. In 1895 he scored two hundreds in a day at Hove, against Yorkshire for Sussex; and the following year he had an aggregate of 2870 runs for an average of 57, surpassing W.G.'s record. He made 62 and 154 not out in his first Test against Australia – retaining the same pattern of scoring as in his first match for Sussex, against MCC at Lord's, when he made 77 not out and 150. For A.E. Stoddart's side in Australia, 1897–8, he made 189 in the first match, and 175 in the first Test. His greatest years were 1899 and 1900, in both of which he passed the three thousand, in the latter averaging 87 for forty innings, and scoring over two hundred five times. His top score was 285 not out against Somerset – after being up all the previous night fishing!

H.S. Altham has evoked the skill behind the statistics with his customary eloquence.

Ranji was blest with supreme natural gifts, and an alert and receptive mind, physique that was at once strong, supple, and perfectly co-ordinated, and, as a result, a lightning quickness of conception and excution that no man, not even Victor Trumper, has ever quite equalled.

Some tribute! Some man! I have heard tell that Ranji once late-cut a ball, which would have hit the middle stump, for four in the first over of a Test match. To have seen his superb back-play – not all that common then – and his cutting and gliding, must have been supremely satisfying.

Gregor MacGregor, of Uppingham and Jesus, must not be overlooked, for he was a wicket-keeper of extraordinary ability, even surpassing that of Alfred Lyttelton. His secret was that he could take the ball closer to the wicket than others, thereby enabling him to be a superbly quick stumper. What Woods owed to MacGregor's fearless standing-up cannot be exaggerated. In his five Tests he did himself full justice, but he gave place to Lilley in 1896 and did not play for England again. He was also a member of Lord Sheffield's team in Australia in 1891–92, and played regularly for Middlesex. He was also capped for Scotland in several rugby internationals. He died in 1919, a week short of his fiftieth birthday.

The talents at Cambridge of Woods, MacGregor and Jackson – Ranji, as we have seen, except for his 58 and 37 not out against the Australians, came to his full powers after he had gone down – must not blind us to the skills of other Light Blues in this decade. Five in particular deserve a mention. First (in alphabetical order) is F.G.J. Ford, of Repton and King's, who captained Cambridge in 1889, having played the two previous years, and who for three seasons in county cricket – 1897, 1898 and 1899 – was the equal as an all-rounder of the great Gloucestershire player C.L. Townsend. Lofty achievement, indeed! Ford played for Middlesex for fifteen years, and was another who went with Stoddart's side to Australia.

The second, L.H. Gay of Brighton and Clare, won blues in 1892–3 and was a double international at both soccer and cricket, an achievement that only Alfred Lyttelton, of Cantabs, has matched. Third on the list, A.J.L. Hill of Marlborough and Jesus, played four years for Cambridge and toured South Africa with the MCC in 1895–6, making a hundred at Cape Town.

Fourthly, G.M. Kemp, who arrived at Trinity from Shrewsbury in 1884, was a very fine off-side player, who scored no fewer than three centuries against Yorkshire, two for Cambridge and one for Lancashire for whom he played between 1885 and 1893. He also represented Cambridge in the lawn tennis doubles in 1886 (the first University encounter in this event having taken place in 1881). He became MP for the Heywood division of Lancashire from 1895, and later PPS to the Financial Secretary to the Admiralty, before going off to fight in the Boer War. He subsequently became Lord Rochdale in 1913.

Fifth here only because his name begins with W is C.M. Wells, who represented Dulwich for five years and earned his blue as a freshman in 1891, and played a great part in the Light Blue victory over Oxford by 266 runs in 1893, by taking seven wickets for 66 runs. It was he who, like E.B. Shine in similar circumstances, deliberately gave runs away in order to prevent Oxford following on, which the *Laws* then stipulated if a side was 80 runs behind. (The Law was changed in 1894, so that the follow-on became compulsory after a deficit of 120 runs and in 1900 optional after a deficit of 150 runs.)

Wells played for both Surrey and Middlesex, as well as for the Gentlemen in 1892, 1893 and 1901. He was a free-hitting batsman, whose main asset was his right-arm slow-medium bowling; he usually turned the ball from the off, but also employed the leg-break and the one that went straight on. He was a rugby blue in 1891 and 1892 and was subsequently capped at half-back for England six times. But it may well be his twenty-two years in charge of cricket at Eton, during which time three England captains and eight county captains came under the influence of his dry wit and vast cricketing knowledge, gave him as much pleasure as playing.

Many stories are told about the Wellingtonian Gerry Weigall, also a rackets player and a popularizer of squash, who represented Cambridge in 1891 and 1892, and who later played 127 matches for Kent. He was a colourful character and a great theorist (he once leapt out of a taxi in a traffic jam in Piccadilly, to demonstrate with his umbrella – to his startled companion – the mechanics of a shot), and a worshipper of Frank Woolley, but he seems to have eclipsed himself in the University Match of 1892. Therein he made 63 not out, 'marred only by such responsibility for the run-outs he must bear'; these were three in number, and his partners were described as the victims of 'ludicrous misunderstandings'. One of these was no less a player than Stanley Jackson, who at the time of his misfortune had already started well. Weigall called the great man for a run and then sent him back, uttering the immortal words, 'Get back, Jacker – I'm set.' Further words on this decade would be an 'act of supererogation'!

29, 30 June, 1 July
At Lord's

1885

Cambridge won by
7 wickets

Neither Oxford nor Cambridge won a match in the build-up to Lord's. The Hon. M.B. Hawke returned to the Cambridge XI, having stood down in 1884. It is fitting that he led his University to victory; his fine qualities of leadership were as evident in 1885 as in the twenty-eight years he captained Yorkshire. Hawke was still able to call on the steadfast Rock, and C. Toppin came in to strengthen the attack. Charles Toppin had been six years in the Sedbergh XI and this was his first, and best, of three years for Cambridge. He later made a great reputation as

master and coach at Malvern. Unaccountably, Oxford's established bowlers lost all form, the best figures coming from A.H.J. Cochrane, a freshman from Repton.

The Varsity Match was virtually settled on the first day, when Toppin took 7 for 51, hitting the stumps five times. C.W. Wright and H.W. Bainbridge created a record, destined to last only one year, when they put on 152 for the first wicket. Oxford made a fight of it, but the issue was hardly in doubt.

OXFORD	First innings		Second innings	
J.H. Brain	c Rock, b Toppin	1	lbw, b Rock	0
E.H. Buckland	b Rock	16	b Smith	0
K.J. Key	b Toppin	5	c Hawke, b Toppin	51
T.C. O'Brien	c Smith, b Rock	44	run out	28
H.V. Page	b Smith	22	not out	78
L. d'Arcy Hildyard	b Toppin	13	c Wright, b Buxton	18
W.E.T. Bolitho	b Toppin	24	b Smith	30
A.E. Newton	lbw, b Toppin	1	b Smith	11
A.H.J. Cochrane	b Toppin	1	b Smith	0
H.O. Whitby	b Toppin	1	c Hawke, b Rock	0
E.W. Bastard	not out	4	b Smith	12
EXTRAS	B 2, L-B 2	4	B 6, L-B 5	11
	TOTAL	136	TOTAL	239

CAMBRIDGE				
C.W. Wright	b Whitby	78	c Buckland, b Bastard	15
H.W. Bainbridge	c Cochrane, b Brain	101	lbw, b Bastard	7
Hon. M.B. Hawke	b Cochrane	17	not out	5
C.W. Rock	b Cochrane	6		
J.A. Turner	b Whitby	3		
G. Kemp	c Bolitho, b Whitby	29	b Bastard	26
C.D. Buxton	c Newton, b Whitby	2	not out	36
F. Marchant	run out	8		
P.J. de Paravicini	b Cochrane	0		
C. Toppin	not out	11		
C.A. Smith	c O'Brien, b Bastard	23		
EXTRAS	B 4, L-B 5	9		
	TOTAL	287	TOTAL (3 WKTS)	89

Cambridge bowling	OVERS	RUNS	WKTS		OVERS	RUNS	WKTS	
Rock	34	45	2		41	82	2	
Toppin	27.3	51	7		26	58	1	
Buxton	5	12	0		9	18	1	
Smith	11	24	1		32	57	5	
Turner	—	—	—		3	3	0	

Oxford bowling								
Cochrane	48	49	3		10	14	0	
Whitby	45	96	4		7	28	0	
Bastard	38.3	56	1		22	15	3	
Page	20	33	0		6.2	18	0	
Buckland	10	13	0		10	14	0	
O'Brien	3	8	0		—	—	—	
Brain	9	23	1		—	—	—	

1886

H.V. Page was Oxford's captain again, and a fine job he made of it. His side had given the Australians a shock. Batting on a poor Christ Church wicket, the Australians had made only 70; Oxford replied with 45, and then each eleven made a mere 38 second time round. Spofforth returned figures of 15 for 36 in the match. Cambridge had a sound record, with a fine win against Yorkshire after following on, and were firm favourites at Lord's.

Oxford recovered from 132 for 8 to the acceptable total of 191, C.W. Rock bowling throughout. C.D. Buxton and H.W. Bainbridge put Cambridge on the right road with a stand of 64, but next morning they collapsed dramatically. The next three hours saw Oxford shatter three records: K.J. Key and W. Rashleigh put on 243 for the first wicket – this record still stands; W. Yardley's 1870 figure of 130 was bettered by Key's 143; and Rashleigh scored the first freshman's hundred. A declaration was still not permitted, so Oxford threw their wickets away and left Cambridge 340 to win. That night, in fourteen overs Cambridge scored only 1 run, and that a bye. Next morning E.H. Buckland swung the game decisively Oxford's way.

OXFORD	First innings		Second innings	
K.J. Key	b Toppin	6	c Marchant, b Rock	143
E.H. Buckland	b Rock	15	b Rock	3
W. Rashleigh	b Rock	21	c and b Rock	107
H.V. Page	c Kemp, b Rock	20	c Rock, b Bainbridge	2
J.H. Brain	c Orford, b Rock	17	c Bainbridge, b Rock	8
L. d'Arcy Hildyard	b Toppin	12	lbw, b Bainbridge	5
H.T. Hewett	b Rock	0	b Bainbridge	7
A.R. Cobb	st Orford, b Toppin	50	c Knatchbull-Hugessen, b Rock	9
H.T. Arnall-Thompson	b Toppin	6	b Toppin	4
A.H.J. Cochrane	c Rock, b Buxton	6	c Turner, b Dorman	7
H.O. Whitby	not out	11	not out	0
EXTRAS	B 20, L-B 6, W 1	27	B 6, L-B 1, W 2	9
	TOTAL	191	TOTAL	304

CAMBRIDGE				
C.D. Buxton	c Arnall-Thompson, b Page	30	c Cobb, b Buckland	27
H.W. Bainbridge	c Hildyard, b Cochrane	44	c Arnall-Thompson, b Buckland	79
G. Kemp	b Cochrane	5	c Cobb, b Whitby	19
C.W. Rock	run out	20	b Whitby	27
J.A. Turner	b Cochrane	0	c Brain, b Cochrane	21
F. Thomas	lbw, b Arnall-Thompson	13	c Page, b Buckland	1
F. Marchant	lbw, b Whitby	20	b Arnall-Thompson	3
C. Toppin	c Cobb, b Whitby	8	c Cobb, b Buckland	2
L.A. Orford	c Cobb, b Whitby	8	b Arnall-Thompson	15
Hon. C.M. Knatchbull-Hugessen	c Cobb, b Arnall-Thompson	0	not out	0
A.W. Dorman	not out	0	b Buckland	4
EXTRAS	B 5, L-B 3	8	B 4, L-B 2, W 2	8
	TOTAL	156	TOTAL	206

Cambridge bowling	OVERS	RUNS	WKTS	OVERS	RUNS	WKTS
Rock	59	72	5	50	76	5
Toppin	41.1	62	4	16	57	1
Dorman	16	16	0	20.3	64	1
Buxton	7	14	1	8	40	0
Turner	—	—	—	21	34	0
Bainbridge	—	—	—	17	24	3

Oxford bowling	OVERS	RUNS	WKTS	OVERS	RUNS	WKTS
Whitby	38.3	52	3	41	55	2
Cochrane	32	52	3	32	59	1
Page	20	23	1	40	34	0
Arnall-Thompson	27	21	2	52	31	2
Brain	—	—	—	2	0	0
Buckland	—	—	—	28.1	19	5

4, 5, 6 July
At Lord's

1887

Oxford won by
7 wickets

A remarkable feature of this Varsity Match was
that the rival captains completed their teams only
at the eleventh hour, and each of the men on
whom their final choice fell made a hundred.
Oxford were a strong side, though limited in fast
bowling. Cambridge had not had a good season
and at Lord's their fielding was described as
'unparalleled in its inefficiency'. The number of
runs scored was above the average. Cambridge
started well, but there was a dramatic collapse
after lunch, F.H. Gresson taking the last three
wickets for no runs in nine overs.

Lord George Scott, J.H. Brain's last-minute

choice for Oxford – it is said partly on the advice
of A.J. Webbe – was a fine front-foot player; he
had some good fortune and took part in two
stands, first with the brilliant K.J. Key, and later
with H.W. Forster, before reaching his own
hundred.

Cambridge fought back in their second innings
after early losses. F. Marchant's late selection,
Eustace Crawley, made no mistake, and with
assistance from the tail reached his hundred and
set Oxford 148 to win. Scott made sure of victory,
striking eleven boundaries in knocking off the
runs.

CAMBRIDGE	First innings		Second innings	
F. Marchant	c Whitby, b Buckland	49	st Philipson, b Nepean	32
C.D. Buxton	b Forster	2	b Buckland	1
F. Thomas	b Buckland	22	b Forster	13
E. Crawley	c Ricketts, b Buckland	35	not out	103
A.M. Sutthery	c Gresson, b Nepean	73	c Key, b Buckland	21
F.G.J. Ford	b Buckland	4	b Nepean	8
W.C. Bridgeman	lbw, b Gresson	9	b Buckland	3
L. Martineau	not out	6	b Whitby	5
L.A. Orford	b Gresson	0	c Brain, b Gresson	13
H. Hale	b Gresson	0	st Philipson, b Forster	21
C. Toppin	c and b Nepean	1	c Whitby, b Nepean	18
EXTRAS	B 2, L-B 3, N-B 1	6	B 7, L-B 7	14
	TOTAL	207	TOTAL	252

OXFORD				
F.H. Gresson	c and b Sutthery	33	b Toppin	8
E.A. Nepean	b Hale	0	not out	58
W. Rashleigh	c Sutthery, b Hale	12	c Martineau, b Ford	6
Lord George Scott	c Bridgeman, b Ford	100	c Hale, b Marchant	66
K.J. Key	c Orford, b Ford	64	not out	8
J.H. Brain	c Orford, b Toppin	15		
E.H. Buckland	c Orford, b Toppin	0		
H.W. Forster	not out	60		
G.W. Ricketts	b Hale	17		
H. Philipson	b Hale	0		
H.O. Whitby	c Ford, b Hale	0		
EXTRAS	B 9, L-B 3	12	B 1, W 1	2
	TOTAL	313	TOTAL (3 WKTS)	148

Oxford bowling	OVERS	RUNS	WKTS		OVERS	RUNS	WKTS
Whitby	8	38	0		42	64	1
Forster	41	55	1		40	32	2
Buckland	43	62	4		50	68	3
Nepean	20.3	43	2		55.1	30	3
Gresson	11	3	3		24	40	1
Ricketts	—	—	—		4	4	0

Cambridge bowling							
Hale	37.2	63	5		5	16	0
Ford	56	97	2		20	31	1
Sutthery	36	58	1		6	20	0
Toppin	38	61	2		21	40	1
Martineau	6	20	0		4	13	0
Buxton	1	2	0		11	16	0
Marchant	—	—	—		4	10	1

2, 3, 4, 5 July[1]
At Lord's

1888

Match drawn

This year saw the appearance of Sammy Woods; he was a great all-round sportsman, a hard-hitting batsman and a fast bowler of devastating accuracy. In his four seasons for Cambridge he took 190 wickets.

Arthur Croome, a useful all-rounder and later *The Times'* cricket correspondent, played the first of his two seasons for Oxford. The year before, while fielding for Gloucestershire against Lancashire, he had been impaled through the neck on a boundary railing, and but for Dr W.G. rendering first aid might well have lost his life.

In the Varsity Match the weather was atrocious. It was a source of comment that after Cambridge had won the toss an extension of an extra day was agreed. Lord George Scott played a courageous innings for Oxford which almost certainly saved the follow-on. Oxford bowled really well in the second innings and at 108 for 8 Cambridge were in trouble; but F. Meyrick-Jones and R.C. Gosling put on 43 and Oxford were left needing 218 to win on the extra day. Thanks to further rain they were never put to the test, and the first draw in forty-four years was recorded.

CAMBRIDGE	First innings			Second innings	
H.J. Mordaunt	c and b Croome	14		c Forster, b Croome	7
E. Crawley	b Cochrane	0		b Fowler	1
G. Kemp	b Cochrane	8		c Simpson, b Croome	9
F. Thomas	b Cochrane	36		b Fowler	18
E.M. Butler	b Cochrane	37		c Forster, b Cochrane	26
C.D. Buxton	c Simpson, b Forster	3		b Cochrane	30
S.M.J. Woods	c Rashleigh, b Cochrane	12		b Fowler	7
R.C. Gosling	not out	29		not out	18
F.G.J. Ford	c Philipson, b Cochrane	2		c Fowler, b Croome	3
F. Meyrick-Jones	b Fowler	16		c Nepean, b Forster	36
G. MacGregor	b Fowler	3		lbw, b Cochrane	9
EXTRAS	B 2, L-B 3, W 4, N-B 2	11		B 4, L-B 2	6
	TOTAL	171		TOTAL	170

OXFORD		
E.T.B. Simpson	st MacGregor, b Ford	2
F.H. Gresson	c and b Woods	30
Hon. F.J.N. Thesiger	b Buxton	26
W. Rashleigh	b Woods	12
Lord George Scott	c Mordaunt, b Woods	32
H.W. Forster	b Woods	1
E.A. Nepean	b Woods	1
A.C.M. Croome	b Mordaunt	2
H. Philipson	c Crawley, b Woods	10
A.H.J. Cochrane	b Mordaunt	1
G. Fowler	not out	0
EXTRAS	B 6, L-B 1	7
	TOTAL	124

Oxford bowling	OVERS	RUNS	WKTS		OVERS	RUNS	WKTS
Cochrane	64	62	6		46.2	43	3
Croome	36	33	1		35	41	3
Fowler	12.1	13	2		23	35	3
Forster	33	33	1		36	36	1
Nepean	7	19	0		—	—	—
Gresson	—	—	—		8	9	0

Cambridge bowling	OVERS	RUNS	WKTS
Woods	39	48	6
Ford	20	26	1
Buxton	8	13	1
Mordaunt	21	30	2

[1] There was no play on 2 July owing to incessant rain. And although the captains agreed to play on 5 July if necessary, more rain made the arrangement of no avail.

1889

Two important changes came about this year: overs were increased to five balls, and a declaration on the last day of a three-day match became legal.

H. Philipson, a popular captain, had the misfortune to lead a weak Oxford side, but he was a fine wicket-keeper and at least he ensured good fielding. Cambridge had a useful batting side and Woods spearheaded their bowling. Oxford reached a very low ebb, finding Sammy Woods, who took eleven wickets in the match, almost unplayable.

Oxford lost F.H. Gresson first ball when he lobbed back a friendly catch to Woods off a full toss. Lord George Scott, for the third year running, showed his tenacity, but 105 was a paltry total. The Cambridge innings was a different story, and 'fours were plentiful as blackberries'. H.J. Mordaunt, an Etonian who later played a few years for both Hampshire and Middlesex, achieved the third-highest score in the Varsity Match to date, and E. Crawley, on leave from the army (as by coincidence was Scott), punished Oxford's weak attack. Oxford's second innings was little more than a procession, M.R. Jardine and M.J. Dauglish both registering 'pairs'.

OXFORD	First innings		Second innings	
F.H. Gresson	c and b Woods	0	b Woods	2
H.W. Forster	c MacGregor, b Woods	14	b Woods	10
W. Rashleigh	c Hale, b Ford	9	b Woods	16
A.K. Watson	c Thomas, b Ford	0	c and b Mordaunt	18
Lord George Scott	not out	37	c Hale, b Ford	9
M.R. Jardine	b Woods	0	b Mordaunt	0
A.C.M. Croome	b Woods	1	c MacGregor, b de Little	0
H. Philipson	b de Little	13	not out	26
M.J. Dauglish	b de Little	0	c MacGregor, b Ford	0
H. Bassett	b Woods	10	c Mordaunt, b Woods	0
R.H. Moss	c MacGregor, b Woods	5	b Woods	0
EXTRAS	B 15, W 1	16	B 4, L-B 4, W 1	9
	TOTAL	105	TOTAL	90

CAMBRIDGE		
H.J. Mordaunt	c Philipson, b Bassett	127
C.P. Foley	b Bassett	22
F. Thomas.	c Gresson, b Croome	18
E. Crawley	b Jardine	54
F.G.J. Ford	lbw, b Moss	29
S.M.J. Woods	b Bassett	4
R.C. Gosling	not out	22
E.M. Butler	c Forster, b Bassett	0
H. Hale	b Bassett	4
E.R. de Little	c and b Croome	4
G. MacGregor	b Croome	0
EXTRAS	B 13, L-B 2, W 1	16
	TOTAL	300

Cambridge bowling	OVERS	RUNS	WKTS	OVERS	RUNS	WKTS
Woods	20.4	42	6	24.3	40	5
Ford	27	30	2	13	25	2
de Little	6	13	2	6	5	1
Mordaunt	4	4	0	17	11	2

Oxford bowling			
Forster	26	64	0
Moss	16	52	1
Croome	32.2	58	3
Bassett	37	65	5
Jardine	10	31	1
Gresson	2	14	0

1890

Cambridge had a fine side: S.M.J. Woods could command the services of five other old blues and freshmen of remarkable quality, including R.N. Douglas and E.C. Streatfeild, who played for the Gentlemen later in the season, as well as the great F.S. Jackson. Woods, on being criticized for including H. Hale, a slow bowler, is reputed to have said that he must have someone to bat last!

Oxford looked a useful side, particularly in the bowling department, with G.F.H. Berkeley, H. Bassett and E. Smith all returning good figures. M.J. Dauglish, an eleventh-hour choice in 1889, was again a last-minute selection, and has the rare distinction of having played two of his three matches against Cambridge.

Monday's play was washed out, and nor was play possible after lunch on Tuesday. Tuesday morning saw Oxford dismissed in just over an hour, with five of the middle order out for ducks; Smith collected over half the runs, and Cambridge were only 2 behind at lunch. On Wednesday, C.P. Foley and Jackson added 32 in this low-scoring match, a vital stand, and Cambridge led by 55.

Oxford nosed in front with only three wickets down, but another collapse saw the telegraph read 80 for 7. H.C. Bradby hit bravely but could not survive Woods' return, and Cambridge needed only 54. Despite a jolt in the thirties when three wickets fell, they made short work of it.

OXFORD	First innings		Second innings	
W.D. Llewelyn	b Woods	2	b Streatfeild	3
E. Smith	b Streatfeild	22	b Woods	2
M.R. Jardine	b Streatfeild	3	c MacGregor, b Ford	24
G.L. Wilson	b Streatfeild	0	lbw, b Ford	20
L.C.H. Palairet	b Woods	0	b Hale	17
Hon. F.J.N. Thesiger	b Streatfeild	0	b Hale	4
H.S. Schwann	b Woods	0	b Streatfeild	2
H. Bassett	b Streatfeild	0	c Ford, b Woods	4
H.C. Bradby	not out	2	b Woods	21
M.J. Dauglish	c Jephson, b Woods	9	b Woods	4
G.F.H. Berkeley	run out	1	not out	0
EXTRAS	B 2, L-B 1	3	B 6, L-B 1	7
	TOTAL	42	TOTAL	108

CAMBRIDGE				
R.N. Douglas	hw, b Berkeley	8	b Berkeley	17
F.G.J. Ford	b Smith	8	not out	32
F.S. Jackson	b Berkeley	23	b Smith	1
G. MacGregor	b Smith	4	b Berkeley	1
C.P. Foley	c Wilson, b Bassett	26	not out	1
E.C. Streatfeild	c Jardine, b Berkeley	7		
D.L.A. Jephson	c Jardine, b Thesiger	13		
R.C. Gosling	b Bassett	1		
S.M.J. Woods	c Bradby, b Thesiger	3		
A.J.L. Hill	not out	0		
H. Hale	b Thesiger	0		
EXTRAS	B 2, L-B 2	4	B 1, L-B 1	2
	TOTAL	97	TOTAL (3 WKTS)	54

Cambridge bowling	OVERS	RUNS	WKTS	OVERS	RUNS	WKTS
Woods	14.3	25	4	16.4	31	4
Streatfeild	14	14	5	20	29	2
Jackson	—	—	—	9	17	0
Ford	—	—	—	12	10	2
Hale	—	—	—	7	14	2

Oxford bowling						
Berkeley	21	38	3	13	20	2
Smith	13	29	2	6.2	14	1
Bassett	17	15	2	4	7	0
Palairet	3	5	0	—	—	—
Thesiger	4.1	6	3	3	11	0

29, 30 June
At Lord's

1891

*Cambridge won by
2 wickets*

Cambridge on paper had a side almost as strong as that in 1890. Oxford's preparation had been disappointing and there was some criticism of the side chosen. But M.R. Jardine could hardly have known that Douglas Carr from Sutton Valence, then a freshman in Brasenose, would eighteen years later blossom as an early and skilful exponent of the googly, and that at the age of thirty-seven he would play for England.

The match began with a generous gesture by G. MacGregor when he allowed the Oxford captain to replace the Hon. F.J.N. Thesiger, who sprained a wrist fielding early in the match. Oxford were pleased to dismiss Cambridge for 210. The account in *Fifty Years of Sport* takes up the story:

But their exhilaration was not destined to be long-lasting. Woods bowled like an inspired machine for the rest of the afternoon. A finer spectacle has not often been seen at Lord's than the combination of his energy, MacGregor's consummate skill behind the wicket and Llewelyn's in front of it.

Having followed on, Oxford recovered well, but still left Cambridge needing only 90 to win. At 78 for 5 Cambridge looked home and dry, but a dramatic collapse saw the scores level with only two wickets left to fall. Sammy Woods, padless and gloveless, raced from the Pavilion to the Nursery End, ran down the wicket and struck the ball first bounce to the long-on boundary. A sensational end to the match and to a fine University career.

CAMBRIDGE	First innings			Second innings	
R.N. Douglas	*b* Bassett		4	*b* Berkeley	15
W.I. Rowell	*b* Bassett		3	*b* Smith	1
G.J.V. Weigall	*c* Palairet, *b* Smith		11	*b* Bassett	2
C.P. Foley	*b* Smith		12	*c* Boger, *b* Berkeley	41
A.J.L. Hill	*c* Brain, *b* Smith		62	*c* Berkeley, *b* Bassett	4
F.S. Jackson	*b* Bassett		10	*b* Berkeley	2
G. MacGregor	*b* Berkeley		29	*b* Berkeley	8
E.C. Streatfeild	*b* Berkeley		36	*b* Berkeley	8
C.M. Wells	*st* Brain, *b* Bassett		11	*not out*	0
S.M.J. Woods	*b* Smith		0	*not out*	4
D.L.A. Jephson	*not out*		10		
EXTRAS	B 13, L-B 7, N-B 2		22	B 8	8
	TOTAL		210	TOTAL (8 WKTS)	93

OXFORD					
W.D. Llewelyn	*b* Hill		38	*c* Douglas, *b* Woods	24
H.D. Watson	*c* Streatfeild, *b* Woods		7	*c* Weigall, *b* Woods	17
M.R. Jardine	*b* Woods		0	*c* Hill, *b* Streatfeild	15
L.C.H. Palairet	*c* MacGregor, *b* Jackson		2	*c* Streatfeild, *b* Woods	11
T.B. Case	*c* Rowell, *b* Woods		5	*run out*	2
G.L. Wilson	*c and b* Woods		0	*b* Streatfeild	53
E. Smith	*b* Woods		16	*c* Jephson, *b* Woods	32
A. Boger	*run out*		4	*c* Jackson, *b* Wells	5
H. Bassett	*b* Woods		15	*c* Streatfeild, *b* Jackson	0
W.H. Brain	*c and b* Woods		6	*c* Jephson, *b* Wells	7
G.F.H. Berkeley	*not out*		7	*not out*	8
EXTRAS	B 5, L-B 3		8	B 4, L-B 8, W 3, N-B 2	17
	TOTAL		108	TOTAL	191

Oxford bowling	OVERS	RUNS	WKTS		OVERS	RUNS	WKTS	
Bassett	37	71	4		22	44	2	
Smith	30	81	4		9	21	1	
Berkeley	16	23	2		12.3	20	5	
Wilson	9	13	0		—	—	—	

Cambridge bowling								
Woods	35.3	60	7		32	72	4	
Jackson	21	24	1		22	46	1	
Hill	14	16	1		4	12	0	
Wells	—	—	—		10	18	2	
Streatfeild	—	—	—		15.2	26	2	

1892

R.C.N. Palairet, brother of the Oxford captain, missed most of the season because of a football injury, and M.R. Jardine was only available after the end of term. C.B. Fry, who already had blues in association football and athletics (his great long jump of 23 feet 5 inches stood as a record for twenty-one years), had come from Repton as an all-rounder, but his batsmanship did not fully develop until after his Oxford days.

Cambridge were strong; there were seven old blues, and James Douglas and P.H. Latham were among important freshmen, the latter being the first of a string of Malvern blues. It is astonishing that Ranjitsinhji was not even asked for a trial.

The first innings was decisive. Oxford made a disastrous start but recovered decisively when the left-handed Vernon Hill then joined Jardine – 'from the very start he hit with whole-hearted vigour and a fine contempt for consequences' – and they put on 180 in an hour and forty minutes.

The Cambridge reply was a chapter of accidents, G.J.V. Weigall running out his captain and having a hand in two later run-outs. J.B. Wood's lobs, mesmerized three victims. Following on, Cambridge fared better, E.C. Streatfeild especially, but Oxford won comfortably.

OXFORD	First innings		Second innings	
L.C.H. Palairet	c Gay, b Jackson	0	not out	71
R.T. Jones	lbw, b Streatfeild	0	run out	4
C.B. Fry	c Gay, b Jackson	44	b Jackson	27
M.R. Jardine	b Streatfeild	140	c Gay, b Jackson	39
F.A. Phillips	c J. Douglas, b Bromley-Davenport	10	c Wells, b Jackson	0
T.B. Case	c and b Jackson	29	not out	1
V.T. Hill	c Hill, b Wells	114		
J.B. Wood	c Hill, b Streatfeild	5		
W.H. Brain	c Gay, b Jackson	2		
T.S.B. Wilson	b Streatfeild	8		
G.F.H. Berkeley	not out	1	b Jackson	38
EXTRAS	B 10, L-B 1, N-B 1	12	B 4, L-B 1, W 2	7
	TOTAL	365	TOTAL (5 WKTS)	187

CAMBRIDGE				
R.N. Douglas	b Wood	2	b Wilson	51
J. Douglas	c Jardine, b Berkeley	13	b Wilson	18
G.J.V. Weigall	not out	63	c Brain, b Palairet	25
P.H. Latham	b Wood	5	c Berkeley, b Wood	69
F.S. Jackson	run out	34	b Berkeley	35
C.M. Wells	run out	0	c Hill, b Wilson	29
E.C. Streatfeild	b Berkeley	8	c Palairet, b Berkeley	116
A.J.L. Hill	run out	6	not out	12
D.L.A. Jephson	b Berkeley	3	lbw, b Wood	5
L.H. Gay	b Wood	2	c Jardine, b Wood	4
H.R. Bromley-Davenport	b Berkeley	11	c Jardine, b Wood	3
EXTRAS	B 11, L-B 1, N-B 1	13	B 15, L-B 2, W 4	21
	TOTAL	160	TOTAL	388

Cambridge bowling	OVERS	RUNS	WKTS		OVERS	RUNS	WKTS
Jackson	40	76	4		36	71	4
Streatfeild	36.2	81	4		23	38	0
Wells	27	83	1		8	34	0
Bromley-Davenport	28	41	1		17	37	0
A.J.L. Hill	9	39	0		—	—	—
J. Douglas	7	33	0		—	—	—

Oxford bowling							
Wood	23	53	3		33.3	120	4
Berkeley	25	58	4		54	88	2
Wilson	8	18	0		39	82	3
Palairet	13	18	0		16	40	1
Fry	—	—	—		5	22	0
Jones	—	—	—		4	13	0
V.T. Hill	—	—	—		1	2	0

3, 4 July
At Lord's
1893
Cambridge won by
266 runs

Each University elected the same captain as in the previous year. L.C.H. Palairet at Oxford had a weak side and F.S. Jackson a powerful one, strengthened further by the inclusion of K.S. Ranjitsinhji and A.O. Jones.

This match saw the first of several incidents which led to an improvement in the follow-on Law. In 1893 the Law read as follows: 'The side which goes in second shall follow their innings if they have scored 80 runs less than the opposite side.'

In reply to Cambridge's surprisingly modest total of 182, Oxford were 95 for 9. At this point: 'Brain and Wilson were seen to consult in mid-

wicket and Wells grasped at once that the striker was going to get out on purpose to ensure the follow-on.' It is difficult to see what purpose could have been served, since the Cambridge bowlers were not tired and had their tails up. However, C.M. Wells thwarted the plan by bowling a no-ball and a wide to the boundary. Much discussion, but no demonstration, ensued. The Law was modified, but only to make the follow-on figure 120 runs in a three-day match.

T.T.N. Perkins and L.H. Gay added 71 in half an hour to bring Cambridge's second innings to a dramatic close. This set Oxford 331 to win, a total which was far, far beyond them.

CAMBRIDGE	First innings		Second innings	
F.S. Jackson	c and b Wood	38	b Berkeley	57
J. Douglas	c Bathurst, b Wilson	25	b Berkeley	4
P.H. Latham	c L.C.H. Palairet, b Fry	21	c Bathurst, b Berkeley	54
K.S. Ranjitsinhji	b Berkeley	9	c Wilson, b Bathurst	0
A.J.L. Hill	b Fry	1	c Brain, b Bathurst	8
E.C. Streatfeild	c Brain, b Berkeley	30	c Brain, b Wilson	0
C.M. Wells	c Brain, b Berkeley	8	c Leveson-Gower, b Fry	7
T.T.N. Perkins	c Brain, b Bathurst	18	b Wilson	37
L.H. Gay	b Berkeley	6	b Bathurst	37
A.O. Jones	b Berkeley	2	not out	16
H.R. Bromley-Davenport	not out	2	b Berkeley	9
EXTRAS	B 11, L-B 9, W 2	22	B 18, L-B 5, W 2	25
	TOTAL	182	TOTAL	254

OXFORD				
L.C.H. Palairet	c Gay, b Bromley-Davenport	32	b Jackson	2
R.C.N. Palairet	c Hill, b Wells	4	lbw, b Wells	2
R.W. Rice	c Ranjitsinhji, b Jackson	7	c Gay, b Wells	12
C.B. Fry	b Wells	7	c Bromley-Davenport, b Streatfeild	31
G.J. Mordaunt	b Wells	1	c Jones, b Jackson	5
H.D.G. Leveson-Gower	lbw, b Wells	12	b Jackson	5
L.C.V. Bathurst	c Gay, b Streatfeild	6	b Bromley-Davenport	2
J.B. Wood	c Ranjitsinhji, b Bromley-Davenport	0	b Bromley-Davenport	0
W.H. Brain	not out	10	c Ranjitsinhji, b Bromley-Davenport	0
G.F.H. Berkeley	c Hill, b Wells	14	not out	1
T.S.B. Wilson	st Gay, b Streatfeild	0	b Streatfeild	0
EXTRAS	B 2, L-B 2, W 4, N-B 5	13	B 3, L-B 1	4
	TOTAL	106	TOTAL	64

Oxford bowling	OVERS	RUNS	WKTS		OVERS	RUNS	WKTS
Berkeley	30	38	5		25	56	4
Wood	14	42	1		7	27	0
Wilson	11	26	1		22	52	2
Bathurst	16	27	1		19	68	3
Fry	9	27	2		11	23	1
Leveson-Gower	—	—	—		1	3	0

Cambridge bowling							
Wells	34	39	5		23	27	2
Jackson	14	35	1		23	22	3
Bromley-Davenport	11	9	2		4	2	3
Streatfeild	8.3	10	2		4.4	9	2

1894

Geoffrey Bolton tells us that:

Charles Fry had an exciting year; he had been President of the OUAC which had beaten Cambridge on the same day that Oxford won the Boat Race; he had been captain of the OUAFC which had won all their matches – except that against Cambridge; now he was captain of the OUCC, which did not win a single match – except that against Cambridge.

There had been a remarkable exodus from Cambridge, notably in the bowling department, and there was no one to match up to the skills of F.S. Jackson, E.C. Streatfeild, C.M. Wells, H.R. Bromley-Davenport and A.J.L. Hill. Cam-

bridge's plan was to exploit Fry's supposed weakness on the off-side. An eye witness described his innings in *Fifty Years of Sport*:

It cannot be said that his long innings was extraordinarily good to watch, because though he played magnificently on the leg side, the Cambridge bowlers persistently aimed two feet wide of the off stump; between them they delivered eleven wides, and it is not surprising that Fry was in for half an hour before scoring his first run. He refused almost every off ball until the ninth wicket fell. Then he wanted seventeen for his hundred and R.P. Lewis was opposite him. He got the required number in two overs before Lewis secured his duck.

OXFORD	First innings			Second innings	
R.C.N. Palairet	c Mitchell, b Pope		18	c Douglas, b Mitchell	38
H.D.G. Leveson-Gower	c Field, b Pope		15	c Pope, b Douglas	15
H.K. Foster	c W.G. Druce, b Mitchell		27	not out	19
G.J. Mordaunt	c W.G. Druce, b Mitchell		41	not out	13
C.B. Fry	not out		100		
F.A. Phillips	c Field, b Gray		78		
L.C.V. Bathurst	c and b Robinson		4		
G.B. Raikes	c W.G. Druce, b Mitchell		29		
G.R. Bardswell	c N.F. Druce, b Robinson		0		
D.H. Forbes	b Robinson		0		
R.P. Lewis	b Mitchell		0		
EXTRAS	B 10, L-B 6, W 9, N-B 1		26	L-B 1, W 2	3
	TOTAL		338	TOTAL (2 WKTS)	88

CAMBRIDGE					
J. Douglas	b Bathurst		31	c Fry, b Bardswell	16
F. Mitchell	lbw, b Bathurst		1	c Bathurst, b Leveson-Gower	28
E. Field	b Bathurst		0	b Bardswell	16
J. Du V. Brunton	c Bathurst, b Leveson-Gower		47	c Forbes, b Bathurst	66
P.H. Latham	c Palairet, b Bardswell		21	b Forbes	16
T.T.N. Perkins	c Forbes, b Raikes		23	c Fry, b Bardswell	24
N.F. Druce	c Lewis, b Bathurst		39	c Phillips, b Bardswell	4
W.G. Druce	b Forbes		9	c Fry, b Bardswell	15
C.G. Pope	run out		11	lbw, b Bathurst	0
J.J. Robinson	not out		5	not out	4
H. Gray	b Bardswell		3	c Bathurst, b Bardswell	6
EXTRAS	B 20, L-B 5, W 3, N-B 4		32	B 4, W 1	5
	TOTAL		222	TOTAL	200

Cambridge bowling	OVERS	RUNS	WKTS	OVERS	RUNS	WKTS
Gray	30	71	1	7	14	0
Pope	36	50	2	5	20	0
Robinson	23	72	3	6.4	22	0
Douglas	17	46	0	4	18	1
Mitchell	21.1	44	4	7	11	1
Perkins	9	29	0	—	—	—

Oxford bowling						
Forbes	16	52	1	8	28	1
Bathurst	23	45	4	30	52	2
Bardswell	14.3	25	2	36.2	76	6
Fry	16	32	0	5	19	0
Leveson-Gower	6	23	1	4	10	1
Raikes	9	13	1	5	10	0

7
1895–1904
Jessop and Fry draw the Crowds

OXFORD *A time of mixed fortunes*

It is interesting to reflect on the Oxford story at the turn of the century. The Parks, thanks to good drainage, mowing machines and horse-drawn rollers, was a different proposition to Cowley Marsh, although the tailored perfection made possible by motor machines was still to come. Dress at first glance was comparable with that of the modern game but in detail would be found to be restrictive, and, strangely, white socks were only just appearing; pads and gloves of the day would hardly be considered adequate now. The intake of the 1900 side still came from public schools, but no longer from a select few; there were representatives from Eton, Malvern, Cheltenham, Westminster, Dulwich, Merchant Taylors', Denstone and Exeter GS. Two of this number still went into the Church, and of the rest three went to the Stock Exchange, two to teaching, one to the Civil Service and others into business.

From this decade no less than seven blues went on to represent England at home and abroad. C.B. Fry played twenty-six times for his country and P.F. Warner fifteen. R.E. Foster would no doubt have played more had he not been gradually weakened by diabetes. B.J.T. Bosanquet played at home and away against Australia; H.D.G. Leveson-Gower played three times against South Africa; J.C. Hartley, a medium-paced bowler who played a leading part in Oxford's victory over Cambridge in 1896, not least by dismissing W.G. Grace, son of the famous 'Old Man', for the first of two noughts, went to South Africa with Plum Warner's 1905 side. F.L. Fane, coming up from Charterhouse, was an opening batsman of attractive style who never fulfilled his promise at Oxford, but went on to play for Essex and later in fourteen Test matches, all abroad.

The 1895 Oxford XI was strong in batting but there was weakness in bowling. Sir Foster Cunliffe wrote of the four principal batsmen in the following terms, referring in the first instance to Fry:

Few, I think, then recognised in the laborious style and apparently commonplace methods the batsman who, next after Arthur Shrewsbury, was to become the most original and consistent exponent of the science of modern batting; but his general reputation as an athlete, his insight into the game and its players, and a certain massiveness in his cricket, gave a sense of resource and power which was of great value to the team. Mordaunt, unlike Fry, gave promise of powers which lack of after-opportunity prevented him from fully developing. All through the season up to the Varsity match, he played magnificently, and fully earned his place in the Gentlemen's XI at Lord's. He was a beautiful player to watch; his style commanding, his off-strokes superb, made with precision and power which belong only to great batsmen. He too, like Foster [H.K.], was in the prime of his forcing play, and like Foster, his weakness lay in a somewhat immature defence. But he was the sounder player of the two. The last of the four, Warner, was a very different batsman from the Warner of today. He had already a good defence, but his scoring strokes were mainly on the off-side, and he was, I think, more attractive to watch than he is nowadays. At the wickets he looked small and slight, and I remember with admiration the way he cut balls from Mold off a level with his nose.

He went on to write of H.D.G. Leveson-Gower, F.A. Phillips and G.O. Smith in almost equally glowing terms. Cunliffe himself and H.A. Arkwright bore the brunt of the bowling. They were a fine fielding side. In The Parks they had wins against Somerset and Yorkshire, the first visit from the northern county. At Brighton they made Oxford's highest score ever, 651, which was in reply to 487; G.J. Mordaunt's contribution had been 264 not out, made in four and a half hours. Ranji in reply made Sussex safe. Kent were then defeated, and had they only succeeded at Lord's, this side would have been talked of in the same breath as that of 1884.

Sir Foster Cunliffe believed the eleven of 1896 to be even better, and he wrote of 'Shrimp' Leveson-Gower:

We possessed in Leveson-Gower an ideal Varsity captain. I never played under such a leader; and the team that finds such a one is indeed fortunate. In pluck and nerve, in knowledge of his own team and that of his opponents, in the capacity for getting the utmost out of his team, it will not be easy to find his superior. In the field he never flagged; as a batsman he hardly ever failed; and the great – perhaps one may say the unequalled victory over Cambridge was only his fitting reward.

They lost only two matches, that against the Australians, when the great Trumble took 6 for 17 to destroy Oxford in the second innings, and that against the MCC. They defeated Somerset and Surrey in The Parks, and the latter again at The Oval. Cunliffe more than proved his worth this year with sixty wickets, at only 16.5 apiece, to his credit.

Only four of that fine side were left in 1897, a nucleus on which Bardswell had to build. Cunliffe wrote further:

Our fielding alone was on a level with that of previous years; Champain proved a brilliant fieldsman anywhere. Foster [R.E.] was fast developing into one of the best slips in England, and Fane and Eccles were above average. Considering the rawness of the side and the lack of bowling, we gave a very respectable account of ourselves in the trial matches.

They won against A.J. Webbe's eleven and against the MCC in The Parks. On tour they defeated Sussex, a team which had just routed Cambridge. Perhaps it is from this year that the saying was born, 'Lose at Brighton and win at Lord's', and vice versa.

Geoffrey Bolton, in writing of 1898 writes:

It may be said that this season marked the end of an era. Next year would see the introduc-tion of the six-ball over and, more important, the first Varsity match to be drawn through high scoring. It was fitting that Cunliffe should be captain: the last survivor of the 1895–6 XIs. He was by now a seasoned cricketer, whose knowledge and experience played a great part in Oxford's success at Lord's.

It was a cold wet season in The Parks, and strangely there was a three-week break from 28 May. The batting was disappointing, the big score against Cambridge being by a long way Oxford's highest total. None the less they beat A.J. Webbe's eleven, a strong side, and also the MCC at Lord's. They lost to Somerset, Essex and Surrey.

In 1899 Oxford won only two matches, the first two of the season and against rather weak opposition. A.J. Webbe's eleven were defeated by an innings, and Somerset by seven wickets. Worcestershire, in their first year in the County Championship and led by H.K. Foster, romped home, also by seven wickets. Oxford's best performance was against the Australians, whom they led by 38 in the first innings. Surrey won by five wickets, two former captains, Leveson-Gower and Key, making more than half the total of 415; although Oxford followed on, they still set Surrey 113 to win.

Oxford had a splendid season in 1900. They won five matches, drew four, and in none of the drawn matches had they the worst of the position. Two things account for their success – the batting of 'Tip' Foster and the outstanding performance of H. Martyn behind the stumps. Sussex paid their first visit to The Parks; it was to be 1949 before they came again. Foster made 930 runs, which included four centuries, and he averaged 77.5. Bosanquet, next in the averages, had nearly 600 runs less.

The season of 1901 was as disastrous as the previous year had been successful. The batting figures were reasonably good, the bowling unreasonably bad. F.P. Knox and R.E. More had to do far too much, and they proved expensive. They went down heavily to a strong eleven brought by A.J. Webbe, and the other three matches in The Parks were also lost. On tour, Oxford were defeated by Surrey but then drew the rest.

The next two years were wet and dismal but some fine performances were achieved, notably by W.H.B. Evans. There are those who would support a claim that he be regarded as Oxford's finest all-rounder. What is certain is that he was the first Oxford player to score a thousand runs and take a hundred wickets in his University career. If he had played first-class cricket regularly he would surely have played for England, but little was seen of him after he had gone down.

In 1902 Oxford won three matches, the first against All Ireland, in which Sir Timothy O'Brien, a blue of the eighties, stole the limelight with a swashbuckling innings of 167. Three matches were drawn and four lost, including the vital one. In 1903 the two scores in the Varsity Match were by far the highest of the season. The bowling was good; Evans had fine figures, taking 48 wickets at only 14.2 apiece, and E.G. Martin bowled really fast. A.C. von Ernsthausen overcame a reputation for poor fielding and justified his selection. Apart from the Varsity Match they won only once – the match against Worcestershire. The contest with the Philadelphians was rained off, which was probably just as well, for the awesome pace of J.B. King had disposed of Oxford for 87 in the first innings.

The summer of 1904 provided real cricketing weather, and Oxford, on paper a great side, made a sparkling start. They defeated both the Gentlemen and Somerset, whom they disposed of by an innings. They made 374 against a powerful Yorkshire side in a match which was rained off. After this excellent start came a gap of three weeks. Evans, said to be a temperamental captain, missed two matches just before 'Schools' and Oxford lost confidence. Not until after the Varsity Match, somewhat fortuitously drawn, did they win again, and this to avenge an earlier defeat by Worcestershire.

CAMBRIDGE *Jessop steals the show*

The years 1895 to 1904 are full of moment and interest both at home and abroad – the Jameson Raid, the Queen's Diamond Jubilee followed by her death, the Boer War, the first performance of Edward Elgar's *Enigma Variations*, and so on – but the University Match changed but little, including that competitive level-pegging which has never been far away since the event's inception. Oxford and Cambridge each won three of the matches at Lord's, and for the first time since the series began there were four draws; that of 1899 was helped by a lack of bowling on either side and an over-cautious declaration by Oxford on the last day, and that of 1900 was inevitable after Cambridge had saved the follow-on, in the wake of R.E. Foster's magnificent 171.

Looking again through light blue-tinted spectacles, I note that the Oxford side which was beaten by 134 runs in 1895 included such high-fliers as Plum Warner, H.K. Foster, C.B. Fry, H.D.G. Leveson-Gower and, batting at number eight, that fine Corinthian and Carthusian G.O. Smith. For their part, Cambridge produced during this decade one of the game's most notable adornments in Gilbert Jessop, two great cricketers in S.H. Day and E.R. Wilson, a talented all-round sportsman in Frank Mitchell, and more than useful performers in Norman Druce, C.J. Burnup, C.E.M. Wilson (E.R.'s brother) – all three born in 1875 – L.J. Moon, T.L. Taylor and E.M. Dowson. On the principle of leaving the vintage wine until later, we shall look at these last six first.

Norman Druce came up to Trinity from Marlborough, and so far exceeded expectations that he not only made a considerable impact at Cambridge but was also chosen to tour Australia with Stoddart's side in 1897–8. He was the Light Blue captain in 1897, the year in which he had an unprecedented average of 66, and over his four years he scored nearly 2500 runs, at an average of over fifty – a remarkable achievement for that era. *Wisden* wrote of him: 'He plays his own game without any rigid over-adherence to rule, scoring on the on-side from straight balls in a fashion only possible to a batsman with genius for timing.' In that season he scored four centuries, including 227 not out against C.I. Thornton's side – this was a record at the time, but was beaten by Hubert Ashton's 236 not out against the Free Foresters in 1920, scored in the wake of a May Week Ball.

C.J. Burnup was a distinguished double blue and double international, representing Cambridge and England at both cricket and Association football. He played three years for Malvern and three for Cambridge, 1896 being his best year. In it he scored 666 runs in nine matches, including 80 and 11 in the big match at Lord's. He was a careful player who took no risks, but he possessed strokes which enabled him to score on all types of pitches, and he showed on occasion that he could force the pace. It was for Kent that he achieved most success as an opening batsman, exceeding a thousand runs eight times and having his best season in 1902 when he hit six of his twenty-six centuries. In 1900 he made a double-century against Lancashire at Old Trafford, and he played six times for the Gentlemen, for whom he hit 123 at The Oval.

C.E.M. Wilson stood out as the most promising member of the Uppingham sides of 1893 and 1894, under the inspired coaching of H.H. Stephenson. In 1893 he scored three centuries and averaged 90.25, and though he was less successful the following year, much was expected of him when he came up to Cambridge. An aggregate of 351 in eight innings in the University Match, including 115 in 1898, the year of his captaincy, did not disappoint those hopes. In addition he took five Oxford wickets for 65 in 1895. Though he played a little for Yorkshire after going down, and toured South Africa with Lord Hawke's side in 1898, his ecclesiastical duties prevented his continuing in the first-class game. His hundred in the University Match prepared the way for a fraternal record, equalled for Oxford by H.K. and R.E. Foster, in 1895 and 1900 respectively.

L.J. Moon, who died of wounds on 23 November 1916, came up to Pembroke from Westminster and was invited to play against Oxford in 1899 and 1900. His main feats while still at Cambridge were to make 138 against the Australians in his first year, and to share with J. Stanning in a century partnership for the first wicket at Lord's. It was, however, after his Cambridge days that he blossomed, sharing in a partnership of 248 with P.F. Warner for Middlesex against Gloucestershire in 1903, and in one of 212 with Warner against Sussex five years later. He did well on MCC tours to America and to South Africa. In addition to his cricketing prowess, he was a soccer blue and a Corinthian.

T.L. Taylor was another fine all-round sportsman to come from Uppingham, and he played for Cambridge from 1898 to 1900, being captain in his last year when he scored 74 and 29 not out at Lord's. He also scored a 70 and a 50 in the two previous Varsity Matches. He went on to play successfully for Yorkshire, scoring eight centuries between 1899 and 1906 and having an average of 35.27. *Wisden* made him one of its 'Five Cricketers of the Year' in 1901, and he was President of Yorkshire from 1948 until his death in 1960. Cricket was not his only game. He won hockey blues four years running, and was a winner in the Yorkshire lawn tennis doubles of 1922 and 1923, and in the mixed doubles in 1924.

The last of this sextet is E.M. Dowson, who created something of a surprise when he appeared at Lord's for Harrow against Eton at the age of fifteen, and took 5 for 90 and 3 for 105 with his left-arm slows. After five years in the Harrow side, he played four times for Cambridge, leading them to victory in 1903, having the previous year taken five Oxford wickets in each innings and made 40 and 29. He created a favourable impression as a batsman on Lord Hawke's tour of Australia and New Zealand in 1902–3, finishing second in the averages to P.F. Warner, and in addition taking forty wickets for 8.20 runs apiece. Overall, he made eight centuries, and he never forgot that on one occasion he clean bowled Tom Hayward twice, in the Gentlemen *v* Players match of 1903.

At the start of 'The Golden Age of Batting' – Chapter XXI of *A History of Cricket* – appear the names of that immortal trio: of Ranji (whom we have already discussed), Fry – the responsibility of my co-author (though I may have been the later of the two of us to see him, since he came to the Sussex Martlets Golden Jubilee dinner at the Dudley Hotel, Hove, in the late summer of 1956, shortly before he died), and Jessop. And it is about Gilbert Jessop that I shall now wax lyrical.

It is Altham's view that had C.L. Townsend been able to play regularly for his county in the years when he had become an England batsman, he and Gilbert Jessop might well have played almost as big a role in Gloucestershire cricket as did Ranji and Fry for Sussex. But Jessop had to shoulder most of the burden alone, and since he was by nature a match-winner rather than a match-saver, the county suffered. As a hitter he was in a class of his own; he would unwind from his panther-like stance and, with his remarkable speed of eye, foot and hand, he would despatch even good-length deliveries in directions that surprised the bowlers. Nor must we forget his successful fast bowling and his astonishing fielding.

Jessop came up to Christ's from Beccles GS and Cheltenham GS, and he played in the Cambridge side for four years, from 1896 to 1899, without achieving the impressive results that maturity brought him. He later scored runs at an astonishing rate, including fifty-three hundreds, five of which were double-centuries. His highest score was 286 out of 335 in 175 minutes against Sussex at Brighton in 1903, and four times he scored a hundred in both innings of a match. He played in eighteen Tests, and earned undying fame in the Oval Test of 1902. In conditions supposedly helpful to bowlers, he came in when the score was 48 for 5, with England still needing another 225 to win. Jackson was already there, but it was Jessop who in marvellous fashion made 104 out of 139 in an hour and a quarter, paving the way to victory by one wicket. Twice he hit the ball on to the roof of the Pavilion and from another big hit was caught on the players' balcony by H.K. Foster.

He was a remarkable all-round athlete, being awarded his blue at hockey (but not being well enough to play), playing both rugby and soccer to a decent standard, being prevented from playing in the Varsity billiards match only by being 'gated', running the 100 yards in 10.2 seconds, and becoming a scratch golfer. And added to that virtuosity, he was a man of engaging manner, a charming companion and modest to a degree.

S.H. Day was a stylish batsman who, like many fine Malvernian players before and after him, cut and off-drove with special skill. He played with considerable success for Cambridge for the four years from 1899 to 1903. Though not coming off at Lord's in the year of his captaincy, 1901, he scored prolifically in his other University Matches – 62 and 50 not out in 1899, 55 in 1900, and 117 not out in 1902. He is one of that select band who have scored a century for their county while still at school – his was 101 not out for Kent against Gloucestershire at Cheltenham, on his debut. Between 1897 and 1919 he scored 5893 runs for Kent. He was also a soccer blue, and in 1903, as an excellent inside-forward, he helped the Corinthians to win the Sheriff of London Charity Shield by beating Bury, then a leading club, by 10 goals to 3. In 1906 he played in three internationals for England.

Since Rockley Wilson is the only one of these players whom I met and knew personally, I shall leave him until last, and shall first deal with Frank Mitchell, who has more than one claim to fame. He went to St Peter's, York, where he captained the eleven in his last two seasons, then came up to Cambridge older than most and had four years in the side, also winning blues for rugby and putting the weight. Despite heading the bowling averages in 1894 and making 191 against Somerset in 1895 and 110 against Sussex in 1896, he did not really fulfil his promise until after he had left Cambridge. His later success for Yorkshire brought him recognition as one of the 'Five Cricketers of the Year' in *Wisden*, and he played both for England in South Africa and for South Africa in England. He also won six caps as a forward for the England Rugby XV. To complete the sporting picture, I must mention that he was the captain who instructed E.B. Shine to give runs away in the 1896 Varsity Match to prevent Oxford following on, thus causing a storm of protest, the throwing at him by an irate gentleman of a pair of binoculars, and the loss of confidence in his batsmen when they batted again. *Wisden* defended him; correspondents in *The Times* did not.

Rockley Wilson was a notable personality, full of engaging idiosyncrasies, as well as a notable cricketer. He had a fine record at Rugby, heading both the batting and the bowling averages when captain in 1897. With a highest score of 206 not out, he averaged 51.11 in batting, and he took thirty-one wickets for 14.93 apiece. He too joined the select band of those who scored a hundred against the University, for A.J. Webbe's eleven, before gaining his blue. He played an important part in the University Matches of 1901, when he made 118 (thus the Light Blue fraternal record) and took 5 for 71 and 2 for 38, and of 1902, when he took 5 for 53 and 3 for 66.

Rockley became one of the finest slow bowlers in the country, always bowling a length, always encouraging the batsman to attack, until in the end he deceived him in the flight. His own explanation of his success was entirely in character. 'I have always been a lucky bowler,' he said, 'as my best ball has been the ball which broke from the off when I meant it to break from leg.' He was good enough to have been selected for the 1920–1 tour of Australia, on which he was probably under-bowled. His reports back to the *Daily Express* ruffled a number of feathers, and the MCC took steps to ban such reports from players in future.

Altogether in first-class cricket he took 385 wickets with an average of 21.66 and he scored 3033 runs, with an average of 18.94. That he did not play more first-class cricket is due to his taking up a teaching post at Winchester College, and preferring to play good club cricket instead. It was in one such match – the school were playing the Green Jackets in their final match on the beautiful St Cross ground – that he dismissed D.R. Jardine who, unbeknown to Rockley, had scored 997 runs in the school season, with an average of 66.46. ('Tiger' Pataudi, the future captain of Oxford and India, good enough to have made 203 not out in a Test with one eye, exceeded this figure, making 1068 in the 1959 Winchester season, with an average of 71.20.)

Rockley, who gave his collection of cricket memorabilia to Lord's, was the creator of more *bons mots* than most; these often showed a shrewd understanding of human nature as well as an abundance of cricketing imagery. Since I recollect with considerable pleasure my two terms of French in his class, and seeing him, in his mid-sixties, bowl at net no. 5 with his usual accuracy, I shall end this portrait of him with a perfect example of the genre, which is not staled by repetition. It took place at Lord's after Rockley's return from Australia. He was with friends at one end of the Long Room when Lord Harris, the Treasurer of MCC to whom authority came naturally, appeared at the other end. Rockley waited for him and, wishing to get in his good books, said to him, 'Good morning, your Lordship.' Lord Harris stuck out a limp hand for the shaking, but made no comment. Subsequently relating the incident to a friend, fingering his tie and speaking with his lilting, hesitant voice, Rockley said, 'Lucky to get a touch, da-da. Lucky to get a touch.'

I end the account of this decade with mention of a fine natural sportsman, and one who later reported twenty different sports for *The Times*, after having also written in his earlier days, more racily, for the *Daily Mirror*. He is Freddie Wilson (no relation to the two Wilsons already mentioned), who was captain of Cambridge in 1904, and a fine rackets player as well, and whose sporting interest and judgement were both reflected in his charming book *Sporting Pie*, and inherited by his son Peter, 'the man they can't gag', and his grandson Julian, expert on the 'sport of kings'. One extract from his obituary attracted me when it was brought to my attention, for it epitomizes what sport, cricket in particular, and the University Match not least, has stood for over the years. *Wisden* wrote about him: 'He had an old-world courtesy to his elders, knew to the finest point what was right and what was wrong, was as courageous as a lion, and withal was the jolliest, wittiest person for whom the heart of man could ask.'

1895

Cambridge did not look strong in bowling and yet they dismissed a powerful Oxford batting side twice to win by the handsome margin of 134. G.J. Mordaunt, who captained Oxford well, set an outstanding example in the field. F.H.E. Cunliffe wrote of him:

In Mordaunt we possessed one of the great fieldsmen of cricket history. He was a very fast runner – he played three-quarters for Oxford – he has very long arms and hands, and he possessed the rare gift of being able to pick up a ball when going at full speed. He threw very fast, and almost equally well with either hand; his return from the country or from third man was one of the sights of cricket.

Cambridge recovered somewhat from 137 for 6 to a total of 244. Rain delayed Oxford's start, and in worsening light they struggled to 38 for 4. Several appeals against atrocious visibility went unheeded before the umpires at last relented, but the damage had been done. In the second innings W.G. Druce played a fine captain's innings to set Oxford 331 to win. Oxford looked as though they were to be humbled, but honour at least was restored, with H.K. Foster striking 121 out of 159 in two hours with scarcely a mistake. Sadly, it was not enough to save his team.

CAMBRIDGE	First innings		Second innings	
F. Mitchell	*c and b* Leveson-Gower	28	*c and b* Arkwright	43
W.G. Grace jnr	*c* Mordaunt, *b* Fry	40	*b* Leveson-Gower	28
R.A. Studd	*b* Fry	28	*c* Lewis, *b* Fry	9
N.F. Druce	*b* Fry	0	*c* Arkwright, *b* Cunliffe	22
H.H. Marriott	*b* Fry	7	*b* Leveson-Gower	15
C.E.M. Wilson	*c* Lewis, *b* Fry	13	*b* Raikes	35
W.G. Druce	*c and b* Leveson-Gower	30	*b* Fry	66
W. McG. Hemingway	*c* Cunliffe, *b* Fry	57	*b* Raikes	9
J. Burrough	*c* Lewis, *b* Raikes	8	*c* Arkwright, *b* Raikes	6
W.W. Lowe	*b* Leveson-Gower	13	*b* Cunliffe	20
H. Gray	*not out*	0	*not out*	6
EXTRAS	B 3, L-B 10, W 5, N-B 2	20	B 14, L-B 2, W 4, N-B 9	29
	TOTAL	244	TOTAL	288

OXFORD				
P.F. Warner	*c* N.F. Druce, *b* Wilson	22	*b* Gray	4
G.B. Raikes	*b* Gray	10	*not out*	23
H.K. Foster	*b* Gray	0	*c* Marriott, *b* Gray	121
G.J. Mordaunt	*b* Gray	6	*b* Grace	5
C.B. Fry	*c and b* Wilson	0	*b* Wilson	1
H.D.G. Leveson-Gower	*b* Lowe	73	*b* Lowe	14
F.A. Phillips	*b* Wilson	12	*b* Wilson	3
G.O. Smith	*not out*	51	*b* Lowe	2
F.H.E. Cunliffe	*c* Mitchell, *b* Wilson	9	*b* Lowe	7
H.A. Arkwright	*c* Marriott, *b* Wilson	5	*b* Lowe	10
R.P. Lewis	*b* Gray	2	*b* Lowe	0
EXTRAS	B 7, L-B 2, N-B 3	12	B 1, L-B 1, N-B 4	6
	TOTAL	202	TOTAL	196

Oxford bowling	OVERS	RUNS	WKTS	OVERS	RUNS	WKTS
Arkwright	8	16	0	37	71	1
Cunliffe	25	56	0	23	55	2
Fry	30	78	6	28.1	49	2
Leveson-Gower	19	48	3	21	36	2
Raikes	6	26	1	14	48	3

Cambridge bowling						
Gray	33	76	4	19	77	2
Wilson	25	65	5	19	44	2
Lowe	9	17	1	17.2	48	5
Grace	6	11	0	11	21	1
Burrough	8	21	0	—	—	—

2, 3, 4 July
At Lord's

1896

*Oxford won by
4 wickets*

H.D.G. Leveson-Gower, known almost universally as 'Shrimp', and knighted for his services to cricket in 1953, is recorded as having been a great Oxford captain. He led Oxford to five victories and to this sensational win at Lord's. Cambridge had a good side, with 'Pinky' Burnup, P.W. Cobbold and C.E.M. Wilson all in form, and G.L. Jessop, that great all-rounder, among their freshmen.

Cambridge were at the crease all day in making 319; J.C. Hartley had an analysis of 8 for 161 in all but sixty overs. A contemporary comment on the scoring rate reads: 'the scoring, generally speaking, was deadly slow, not much over 50 runs an hour'!

When Oxford needed 10 runs to save the follow-on, E.B. Shine was directed to bowl no-balls and wides to avoid another session in the field. Whereas in 1893 a similar incident was greeted in silence, on this occasion the Cambridge action was received with hostility. The rights and wrongs of the case gave rise to a long correspondence in *The Times*. Law 53 was later amended to take the form in which it is known today.

The Cambridge batsmen were, it was suggested, upset by the demonstration. Whether or not this was so, they were hopelessly at sea with F.H.E. Cunliffe and Hartley, and lost six wickets for 61. They were saved by a superb innings from N.F. Druce and the brave hitting of E.H. Bray, the close-of-play score being 154 for 8. The last two wickets added 58 and Oxford were set 330 to win in just over five hours.

G.J. Mordaunt and P.F. Warner were dismissed in the way they had been in the first innings, Mordaunt being beaten by Jessop's pace and the luckless Plum Warner being run out. H.K. Foster was showing promise when he was caught and bowled by P.W. Cobbold. After lunch, C.C. Pilkington joined G.O. Smith and the tide began to turn. In an hour and a quarter of first-rate batting, 84 were added, when Pilkington was out. Cunliffe takes up the story:

Through an atmosphere of hope tempered by unbelief, our captain walked to the wicket. Over and over again had he saved the side; was it possible that fortune would again favour the brave? The rate of scoring somewhat slackened, for Smith, playing absolutely the right

game, took no risks, and Leveson-Gower had to play himself in. Time went on and still no wicket fell. People recalled the great stand made by the same men the year before, and felt that the fortunes of Oxford were in worthy hands. Jessop's pace seemed to be lessening, and his short balls – and these were not few – were severely punished by Smith; but Wilson's length and patience were as perfect as ever, and Cobbold occasionally had Smith in difficulties. With that quickness which went to make Leveson-Gower a great captain he agreed with Smith that he should keep as much at Cobbold's end as possible, while Smith devoted himself to knocking Jessop off his length. This policy, imperceptible to the anxious spectator, succeeded admirably. Leveson-Gower was immovable, scoring occasionally in his characteristic way and never making a mistake; Smith, by this time thoroughly at home, seemed to gain in confidence and power every over. As the long afternoon went on, Oxford's supporters began to look beyond a draw. Slowly the moral balance changed with the changing balance of runs, and when, at 241, Leveson-Gower was caught at the wicket off Shine, victory was clearly within reach. Another stage on our long road to victory had been accomplished. In the first the fury of the attack had been broken; in the second it had been exhausted; the time for a general offensive had now come.

Eighty-nine runs were still wanted when Bardswell came in. Had he got out, anything might still have happened, but from his first ball he never made the ghost of a mistake. Jessop went on and was knocked off for the last time; Smith, now scoring brilliantly all round the wicket, passed his hundred; and Mitchell in desperation took off his regular bowlers and tried a series of changes. Burnup, Druce, and himself each had a turn, but in vain. Bardswell began to score freely, the third century went up amongst pavilion-shaking clamour, and for the first time in that long day the Cambridge field began to show some signs of demoralisation.

At last, with the score at 328, Smith, in jumping out to finish the game, was easily caught at short slip; he will be lucky if life ever presents him with a happier moment than that of his entry into the pavilion. Bardswell, the last of his three stalwart partners, finished the match with a difficult chance in the long field which Burnup, usually the safest of fieldsmen, managed to drop.

So ended this famous game, which, to most of the Oxford men who took part in it, was the crowning point of their cricketing career.

CAMBRIDGE	First innings		Second innings	
C.J. Burnup	c Mordaunt, b Hartley	80	c and b Hartley	11
W.G. Grace jnr	b Hartley	0	b Cunliffe	0
H.H. Marriott	c Warner, b Hartley	16	b Cunliffe	1
N.F. Druce	c Smith, b Cunliffe	14	c Pilkington, b Waddy	72
C.E.M. Wilson	c Cunliffe, b Hartley	80	c Lewis, b Hartley	2
W.McG. Hemingway	c and b Hartley	26	b Cunliffe	12
F. Mitchell	c Leveson-Gower, b Hartley	26	b Cunliffe	4
G.L. Jessop	c Mordaunt, b Hartley	0	st Lewis, b Hartley	19
E.H. Bray	c Pilkington, b Cunliffe	49	c Lewis, b Waddy	41
P.W. Cobbold	b Hartley	10	not out	23
E.B. Shine	not out	10	c Hartley, b Waddy	16
EXTRAS	B 4, L-B 1, W 2, N-B 1	8	B 5, W 1, N-B 5	11
	TOTAL	319	TOTAL	212

OXFORD				
P.F. Warner	run out	10	run out	17
G.J. Mordaunt	b Jessop	26	b Jessop	9
H.K. Foster	b Wilson	11	c and b Cobbold	34
G.O. Smith	c Bray, b Wilson	37	c Mitchell, b Cobbold	132
C.C. Pilkington	b Jessop	4	c and b Jessop	44
H.D.G. Leveson-Gower	b Jessop	26	c Bray, b Shine	41
G.R. Bardswell	c and b Cobbold	9	not out	33
P.S. Waddy	st Bray, b Cobbold	0	not out	1
J.C. Hartley	c Marriott, b Wilson	43		
F.H.E. Cunliffe	b Shine	12		
R.P. Lewis	not out	0		
EXTRAS	B 12, L-B 4, N-B 8	24	B 6, L-B 6, W 6, N-B 1	19
	TOTAL	202	TOTAL (6 WKTS)	330

Oxford bowling	OVERS	RUNS	WKTS		OVERS	RUNS	WKTS
Cunliffe	55	87	2		33	93	4
Hartley	59.3	161	8		30	78	3
Waddy	24	35	0		11	28	3
Pilkington	29	24	0		3	2	0
Leveson-Gower	2	4	0		—	—	—

Cambridge bowling	OVERS	RUNS	WKTS		OVERS	RUNS	WKTS
Jessop	37	75	3		30	98	2
Wilson	37	48	3		42	50	0
Shine	12.3	29	1		20	41	1
Cobbold	11	26	2		44.4	96	2
Burnup	—	—	—		2	3	0
Druce	—	—	—		7	11	0
Mitchell	—	—	—		2	12	0

1897

Cambridge's strength was in their attack, with eight blues available from the previous year. At Oxford there were only four left, and of these J.C. Hartley and P.S. Waddy were unable to play the full season, and F.L. Fane and R.E. Foster gave promise of brilliant days ahead. Where Cambridge were strong in bowling, Oxford were weak, relying heavily on F.H.E. Cunliffe. G.R. Bardswell could hardly have known that B.J.T. Bosanquet, of Eton and Oriel, would stamp his name on cricket history; that very year he invented the googly and wrote of it:

Somewhere about the year 1897 I was playing a game with a tennis ball, known as Twisti-Twosti. After a little experimenting, I managed to pitch the ball which broke in a certain direction, then with more or less the same delivery made the ball go in the opposite direction!

So the googly was born, but it was not seen in public for three years. Bosanquet played for Oxford from 1898 to 1900, but as a medium-pace bowler.

Somewhat unexpectedly, Oxford led on the first innings, having bowled Cambridge out on a good fast wicket. G.L. Jessop, bowling very fast indeed, limited their advantage. Cambridge did not fail again, and left Oxford almost the same target as in the previous year – but the class was not there.

CAMBRIDGE

	First innings			Second innings	
C.J. Burnup	b Cunliffe	0		c Waddy, b Cunliffe	58
F. Mitchell	run out	6		c Bardswell, b Hartley	1
H.H. Marriott	c Fox, b Cunliffe	13		c Waddy, b Cunliffe	50
N.F. Druce	c Waddy, b Wright	41		c Waddy, b Cunliffe	0
G.L. Jessop	b Hartley	4		c Fane, b Cunliffe	42
C.E.M. Wilson	c Fox, b Waddy	19		b Wright	77
J.H. Stogdon	c Cunliffe, b Hartley	20		b Cunliffe	0
E.H. Bray	b Cunliffe	6		c Fox, b Waddy	2
H.W. de Zoete	b Hartley	3		b Hartley	29
E.B. Shine	c Foster, b Cunliffe	18		c Bardswell, b Cunliffe	45
A.E. Fernie	not out	9		not out	0
EXTRAS	B 7, L-B 6, N-B 4	17		B 3, L-B 12, W 3, N-B 14	32
	TOTAL	156		TOTAL	336

OXFORD

F.L. Fane	c Bray, b Jessop	12		c Marriott, b Shine	17
F.H.B. Champain	b Jessop	0		c Wilson, b de Zoete	6
G.E. Bromley-Martin	c Shine, b Fernie	14		b Shine	6
R.E. Foster	c and b Jessop	27		b Jessop	6
A. Eccles	b Jessop	2		c Marriott, b de Zoete	12
G.R. Bardswell	c Wilson, b Fernie	35		c Mitchell, b Shine	30
P.S. Waddy	c Mitchell, b Jessop	6		b Wilson	12
J.C. Hartley	b Wilson	27		c Mitchell, b Shine	9
E.C. Wright	c Marriott, b Jessop	2		b de Zoete	11
F.H.E. Cunliffe	not out	24		lbw, b de Zoete	14
R.W. Fox	b Shine	0		not out	3
EXTRAS	B 5, W 2, N-B 6	13		B 8, L-B 10, W 5, N-B 2	25
	TOTAL	162		TOTAL	151

Oxford bowling	OVERS	RUNS	WKTS		OVERS	RUNS	WKTS
Cunliffe	29	58	4		41	101	6
Hartley	22	52	3		32	67	2
Waddy	10	23	1		25	62	1
Wright	4	6	1		24.4	50	1
Bardswell	—	—	—		6	24	0

Cambridge bowling							
Jessop	26	65	6		16	34	1
Wilson	25	32	1		15	16	1
Shine	11.2	26	1		19	28	4
Fernie	12	26	2		15	22	0
de Zoete	—	—	—		17.3	26	4

30 June, 1, 2 July
At Lord's

1898

Oxford won by
9 wickets

In making by far the highest score of the season, A. Eccles ensured for Oxford a convincing victory. It was Cambridge's turn to be light on bowling, particularly as G.L. Jessop had not fully recovered from a winter illness and C.E.M. Wilson had injured his leg and could not bowl at all. G.E. Winter was a lob bowler, only the second in the Varsity Match since 1890. Cunliffe writes:

We were rather afraid of him and before the match got Humphreys, the old Sussex professional, to give us some practice at the nets. . . . In our match against Surrey, Fry had been no-balled by Phillips, and was unable to continue over hand; for our benefit he took to lobs!

In the event, Winter failed and Cunliffe, Oxford's only survivor from 1896, batted well.

Cambridge won the toss for the fourth year running; their innings was held together by Wilson. Cunliffe had generously allowed him to bat with a runner, in fact contrary to the *Laws*, since his injury was sustained before play started. On a fast wicket the next day, Oxford took a firm grip on the match, Eccles, making a hundred in under two hours, hitting sixteen fours. Overnight rain made Cambridge's task doubly difficult; the wicket suited Cunliffe and he finished his Oxford career in deserved triumph!

CAMBRIDGE

	First innings			Second innings	
C.J. Burnup	b Lee	15		c Fox, b Lee	8
A.T. Coode	c Fox, b Bosanquet	1		b Stocks	27
H.H. Marriott	b Cunliffe	9		c Foster, b Cunliffe	16
C.E.M. Wilson	c Stocks, b Lee	115		c Stocks, b Cunliffe	10
G.L. Jessop	c Bosanquet, b Cunliffe	8		st Fox, b Cunliffe	18
T.L. Taylor	c Stocks, b Lee	70		c Stocks, b Lee	15
G.E. Winter	c Champain, b Cunliffe	1		c Champain, b Cunliffe	13
J.H. Stogdon	b Lee	4		run out	24
H.W. de Zoete	lbw, b Lee	0		c Stocks, b Cunliffe	1
A.E. Hind	c Fox, b Bosanquet	17		b Bosanquet	1
H.H.B. Hawkins	not out	14		not out	0
EXTRAS	B 7, L-B 3, N-B 9	19		L-B 2, N-B 5	7
	TOTAL	273		TOTAL	140

OXFORD

F.L. Fane	c Stogdon, b Jessop	10		c Stogdon, b Hind	6
B.D. Bannon	run out	21		not out	21
F.H.B. Champain	c Marriott, b Jessop	4		not out	24
F.H.E. Cunliffe	c and b Jessop	33			
R.E. Foster	c Hind, b Jessop	57			
A. Eccles	run out	109			
G.E. Bromley-Martin	run out	16			
E.C. Lee	b de Zoete	15			
B.J.T. Bosanquet	not out	54			
F.W. Stocks	c Stogdon, b Jessop	21			
R.W. Fox	b Jessop	2			
EXTRAS	B 15, N-B 5	20		N-B 1	1
	TOTAL	362		TOTAL (1 WKT)	52

Oxford bowling	OVERS	RUNS	WKTS		OVERS	RUNS	WKTS
Cunliffe	49	94	3		23	51	5
Bosanquet	29	72	2		16	40	1
Stocks	33	57	0		9.3	16	1
Lee	25.3	31	5		15	26	2

Cambridge bowling							
Jessop	45.2	126	6		6	12	0
Winter	26	66	0		—	—	—
Hind	26	62	0		6	17	1
Hawkins	15	48	0		2	15	0
de Zoete	11	33	1		1	7	0
Burnup	1	7	0		—	—	—

1899

Up to this year only three Varsity Matches had been drawn. That number was to be doubled before either side won again. The chief reasons for this are to be found, first, in the continuing improvement of the wickets at Lord's, and secondly, in the weakness of University bowling in this period. The time when drawn games could be ascribed to unenterprising batting had not yet arrived.

The two captains were Sussex players; not until 1952 did the same county again provide both leaders. This year also saw the almost unheralded advent of the six-ball over.

Both Universities were strong in batting and less so in bowling. Cambridge were further weakened by the fact that G.L. Jessop had to bowl with a strapped-up side. Sam Day, commenting afterwards, said that Oxford batted indifferently, and went on to say of the Cambridge innings:

But we were worse – 89 for 7 – very bad cricket. Bosanquet bowled fast stuff quite well; but some of our side made awful strokes. Then I got 62 by flicking at all the off balls, not knowing any better (or worse).

Cambridge had a handsome lead but Oxford made no mistake the second time, and the first high-scoring draw became inevitable.

OXFORD

	First innings		Second innings	
H.C. Pilkington	c Taylor, b Jessop	0	c Taylor, b Hawkins	93
F.H.B. Champain	c Hawkins, b Jessop	14	c Wilson, b Hind	24
L.P. Collins	b Hind	10	lbw, b Wilson	12
R.E. Foster	c Jessop, b Wilson	21	lbw, b Penn	18
F.P. Knox	b Hind	37	not out	73
A. Eccles	c Hind, b Wilson	32	b Hind	5
A.M. Hollins	b Hind	5	b Jessop	10
R.H. de Montmorency	b Hawkins	25	b Hawkins	62
B.J.T. Bosanquet	c Jessop, b Wilson	4	run out	17
H. Martyn	c Moon, b Hawkins	27	not out	9
F.W. Stocks	not out	4		
EXTRAS	B 6, W 1, N-B 6	13	B 13, L-B 1, W 3, N-B 7	24
	TOTAL	192	TOTAL (8 WKTS DEC.)	347

CAMBRIDGE

L.J. Moon	b Bosanquet	23	lbw, b Knox	13
E.R. Wilson	b Bosanquet	5	c Stocks, b Bosanquet	39
G.E. Winter	b Bosanquet	16		
J.H. Stogdon	lbw, b Bosanquet	27	b de Montmorency	25
G.L. Jessop	c Martyn, b Knox	8	c Champain, b Knox	46
T.L. Taylor	c and b Bosanquet	2	not out	52
S.H. Day	b Bosanquet	62	not out	50
J. Daniell	st Martyn, b Knox	1		
E.F. Penn	c Foster, b de Montmorency	18		
A.E. Hind	not out	52		
H.H.B. Hawkins	b Bosanquet	5		
EXTRAS	B 19, W 3	22	B 4	4
	TOTAL	241	TOTAL (4 WKTS)	229

Cambridge bowling	OVERS	RUNS	WKTS		OVERS	RUNS	WKTS	
Jessop	36	63	2		29	88	1	
Hind	27	36	3		23	26	2	
Wilson	27	53	3		43	80	1	
Hawkins	19	27	2		32	78	2	
Penn	—	—	—		12	36	1	
Winter	—	—	—		4	15	0	

Oxford bowling								
Stocks	29	60	0		23	51	0	
Bosanquet	38	89	7		20	74	1	
Knox	19	48	2		16	47	2	
de Montmorency	12	22	1		8	23	1	
Hollins	—	—	—		3	14	0	
Champain	—	—	—		4	16	0	

5, 6, 7 July
At Lord's

1900

Match drawn

Oxford's bowling in this match fell away so badly that they were unable to capitalize on their magnificent first-innings total. 'Tip' Foster was captain and at last showed his true genius. Geoffrey Bolton says of him:

Foster's batting in this year almost beggars description. Three years previously N.F. Druce at Cambridge had set up a University record by scoring 700 runs with an average of 66. Now Foster made 930 runs with an average of 77, he made the record score in the Varsity Match, and he followed this with two hundreds for the Gentlemen, his second innings of 136 lasting one hour

and three-quarters against the bowling of Rhodes, Trott, Mead and John Gunn. The off-drive and the cut were his chief strokes, but he had no discernible weakness. On figures for Oxford only E.R.T. Holmes, A.M. Crawley, the Nawab of Pataudi and M.P. Donnelly can claim to approach his record for this year.

In Oxford's long innings a mere 4 byes were recorded, and it has been said that when Foster was batting four balls only reached the wicketkeeper. Once Cambridge had saved the follow-on, largely thanks to Foster's former Malvern colleague Sam Day, a draw was the only possible result.

OXFORD	First innings		Second innings	
F.H.B. Champain	c Daniell, b Dowson	2	c Blaker, b Dowson	34
H.C. Pilkington	c Moon, b Fernie	87	c Fernie, b Dowson	45
F.P. Knox	c Wilson, b Fernie	4		
R.E. Foster	c Hind, b Dowson	171	c Fargus, b Dowson	42
C.H.B. Marsham	b Dowson	33		
C.D. Fisher	c Wilson, b Fargus	26		
B.J.T. Bosanquet	c Fernie, b Fargus	42	c Moon, b Hind	23
J.W.F. Crawfurd	c Moon, b Dowson	16	not out	10
H. Martyn	c and b Fargus	94	c Day, b Hind	35
R.E. More	not out	20	b Hind	18
H. White	b Fargus	0		
EXTRAS	B 4, L-B 1, W 1, N-B 2	8	B 9, W 2, N-B 1	12
	TOTAL	503	TOTAL (6 WKTS DEC.)	219

CAMBRIDGE				
L.J. Moon	c More, b Crawfurd	58	b White	60
J. Stanning	c and b More	20	c Bosanquet, b Fisher	60
E.R. Wilson	c Marsham, b White	45	not out	23
T.L. Taylor	c More, b Fisher	74	not out	29
J. Daniell	c Knox, b White	14		
S.H. Day	b Fisher	55		
R.N.R. Blaker	b Knox	15		
E.M. Dowson	b Knox	65		
A.E. Hind	b Bosanquet	30		
A.H.C. Fargus	st Martyn, b Knox	8		
A.E. Fernie	not out	0		
EXTRAS	B 3, L-B 3, W 2	8	B 7, L-B 6, N-B 1	14
	TOTAL	392	TOTAL (2 WKTS)	186

Cambridge bowling	OVERS	RUNS	WKTS		OVERS	RUNS	WKTS
Dowson	44	163	4		26.1	86	3
Fernie	18	72	2		—	—	—
Fargus	27.3	153	4		8	26	0
Wilson	17	55	0		—	—	—
Hind	21	42	0		19	95	3
Moon	2	10	0		—	—	—

Oxford bowling							
Bosanquet	21	46	1		14	28	0
White	25	69	2		15	34	1
Knox	42.3	131	3		9	35	0
More	32	74	1		4	10	0
Crawfurd	15	46	1		8	25	0
Fisher	19	18	2		9	24	1
Pilkington	—	—	—		4	16	0

4, 5, 6 July
At Lord's

1901

Match drawn

For the third year running, a high-scoring match ended in a draw. When Cambridge declared on the third day, Oxford had just over three hours to make the runs. They did not prosper in their task; at 145 for 7, with forty minutes left and with the light poor, they were in some trouble. *Wisden* takes up the story:

At this point a curious and from Cambridge's point of view an unsatisfactory incident occurred. Marsham, well set and batting finely, was joined by Hollins, and the latter, before he had scored, played a ball from Johnson to the slips. Wilson took the ball close to the ground and – clearly under the impression that he had made a catch – threw it up. On appeal to the bowler's umpire, however, W. Hearn could not give Hollins out, owing to Johnson having obstructed his view, and Phillips, on being appealed to, was also unable to give a decision, the wicket-keeper, standing back, having exactly covered Wilson when he secured the ball.

So F.H. Hollins survived. There was clearly no rancour, since in the last over Cambridge fed C.H.B. Marsham's off-drive so that he could reach his hundred – deserved recognition of a fine fighting innings.

CAMBRIDGE	First innings			Second innings	
E.R. Wilson	b Williams		118	c Wyld, b Knox	27
H.K. Longman	b Williams		27	b Knox	34
S.H. Day	b Munn		5	c Knox, b More	12
L.V. Harper	b More		15	b More	84
W.P. Robertson	b More		18	c Williams, b Knox	25
E.M. Dowson	c and b Williams		38	not out	70
J. Daniell	st Findlay, b Dillon		18	c Hollins, b More	14
R.N.R. Blaker	c Wyld, b More		49	c More, b Knox	9
P.R. Johnson	b Dillon		10	not out	3
A.E. Hind	b Dillon		3	b Crawfurd	37
A.H.C. Fargus	not out		17		
EXTRAS	b 2, w 2, n-b 3		7	b 7, l-b 10, w 1, n-b 4	22
	TOTAL		325	TOTAL (8 WKTS DEC.)	337

OXFORD					
C.H.B. Marsham	c Robertson, b Wilson		14	not out	100
E.W. Dillon	c Fargus, b Wilson		30	c Blaker, b Wilson	8
F.H. Hollins	b Dowson		11	not out	6
H.J. Wyld	b Wilson		21	c Wilson, b Johnson	0
F.P. Knox	c Day, b Fargus		81	c Wilson, b Johnson	8
R.E. More	b Wilson		76	b Dowson	0
J.W.F. Crawfurd	c Daniell, b Fargus		6	lbw, b Johnson	10
R.A. Williams	c Daniell, b Dowson		57	c Johnson, b Dowson	23
G.W.F. Kelly	c Harper, b Wilson		7	c Daniell, b Wilson	4
W. Findlay	c Hind, b Johnson		14		
J.S. Munn	not out		5		
EXTRAS	b 5, l-b 2, w 1, n-b 6		14	b 5, l-b 6, w 6, n-b 1	18
	TOTAL		336	TOTAL (7 WKTS)	177

Oxford bowling	OVERS	RUNS	WKTS	OVERS	RUNS	WKTS
More	30.5	62	3	36	109	3
Knox	19	42	0	25	63	4
Kelly	12	48	0	5	12	0
Munn	11	23	1	6	13	0
Williams	25	68	3	20	62	0
Dillon	18	75	3	10	29	0
Crawfurd	—	—	—	8	27	1

Cambridge bowling						
Dowson	44.3	152	2	26	66	2
Fargus	17	51	2	5	10	0
Wilson	45	71	5	15	38	2
Hind	16	25	0	3	4	0
Johnson	7	23	1	18	41	3

After three drawn games in succession, a definite result was achieved, thanks to the Cambridge trio of S.H. Day, E.M. Dowson and the captain, Rockley Wilson. (Wilson later played in one Test match in Australia. Modest and self-effacing though he was, there was some criticism that as a player he sent back reports to the *Daily Express*. This led to a resolution at that year's Annual General Meeting of the MCC deprecating the reporting of matches by players concerned in them.) Wilson went on to be a master at Winchester for forty years and many generations of Wykehamists remember his sound and kindly advice. He was once quoted as saying to a somewhat inept batsman: 'My dear boy, you must hit one ball in the middle of your bat before you meet your maker.'

In the 1902 Varsity Match his 5 for 53 tipped the balance and according to Day, who much admired his gift as a captain, 'He could make Dowson bowl without trying too many tricks.' Dowson and Wilson confined a good Oxford batting side, but still Cambridge needed 272, with most of the last day to get them – no easy task, but Day made light of it.

OXFORD	First innings		Second innings	
E.W. Dillon	*b* E.R. Wilson	85	*b* E.R. Wilson	59
W. Findlay	*c and b* Dowson	45	*c* Baker, *b* Driffield	24
H.J. Wyld	*st* Winter, *b* E.R. Wilson	4	*b* E.R. Wilson	0
W.H.B. Evans	*b* E.R. Wilson	16	*st* Winter, *b* Dowson	67
C.H.B. Marsham	*not out*	30	*c* Winter, *b* F.B. Wilson	44
W.S. Medlicott	*c* Winter, *b* E.R. Wilson	0	*st* Winter, *b* Dowson	18
R.A. Williams	*c* F.B. Wilson, *b* Dowson	1	*lbw, b* Dowson	15
M. Bonham-Carter	*b* Dowson	0	*b* Dowson	0
G.W.F. Kelly	*b* Dowson	1	*b* Dowson	6
A.C. von Ernsthausen	*c* E.R. Wilson, *b* Dowson	1	*c* Gilman, *b* E.R. Wilson	1
R.C.W. Burn	*c* Penn, *b* E.R. Wilson	2	*not out*	0
EXTRAS	B 16, L-B 1, N-B 4	21	B 11, L-B 6	17
	TOTAL	206	TOTAL	254

CAMBRIDGE				
C.H.M. Ebden	*c* Findlay, *b* von Ernsthausen	23	*c* Findlay, *b* Kelly	42
L.V. Harper	*b* von Ernsthausen	0	*c* Burn, *b* Dillon	9
S.H. Day.	*b* von Ernsthausen	4	*not out*	117
E.M. Dowson	*c* Findlay, *b* Kelly	40	*c* Williams, *b* Dillon	29
E.R. Wilson	*st* Findlay, *b* Dillon	13	*c* Findlay, *b* Bonham-Carter	26
E.F. Penn	*c* Evans, *b* Kelly	21	*b* Kelly	4
J. Gilman	*lbw, b* Dillon	0	*not out*	37
R.N.R. Blaker	*c* Medlicott, *b* Bonham-Carter	50		
F.B. Wilson	*b* Kelly	0		
L.T. Driffield	*not out*	29		
C.E. Winter	*b* Bonham-Carter	0		
EXTRAS	L-B 6	6	B 5, L-B 3, W 2	10
	TOTAL	186	TOTAL (5 WKTS)	274

Cambridge bowling	OVERS	RUNS	WKTS	OVERS	RUNS	WKTS
Dowson	34	85	5	36	81	5
E.R. Wilson	35	53	5	26.5	66	3
Penn	13	33	0	13	34	0
Driffield	10	14	0	18	38	1
F.B. Wilson	—	—	—	3	15	1

Oxford bowling						
Burn	23	45	0	3	9	0
von Ernsthausen	22	57	3	8.1	34	0
Dillon	12	38	2	14	60	2
Kelly	13	19	3	19	51	2
Evans	6	11	0	11	26	0
Williams	3	8	0	6	23	0
Bonham-Carter	2.4	2	2	17	61	1

2, 3, 4 July
At Lord's

1903

Oxford won by
268 runs

Cambridge started as favourites this year, but they were unable to deal with W.H.B. Evans, who took eleven wickets in the match.

There were fewer old blues than usual at either University this year. Evans was perhaps the only player in the top flight. He was a very fine all-rounder, bowling this year faster than he had before or did thereafter. It was a sad loss that after his Oxford days a career in the Egyptian Civil Service limited his cricket, and it was a grievous shock when he was killed at Aldershot in 1913 flying with Colonel Cody. He was also a distinguished footballer and rackets player.

The last place in the Oxford side was given to J.E. Raphael, who reminded Findlay, the Oxford captain, of his ability in making runs for Surrey against Oxford the week before. It is hard to picture such an event today. Raphael proved a sound choice being ninth out in Oxford's first use of the wicket – for 130, with the next highest score only 21. A feature of this innings, rare at the time, and unusual even in the present, was a tally of 18 no-balls. Cambridge saved the follow-on, E.M. Dowson playing a brave captain's innings, but Oxford always retained the initiative and deserved their handsome victory.

OXFORD	First innings		Second innings	
J.E. Raphael	c Wilson, b Keigwin	130	c and b Keigwin	19
W. Findlay	lbw, b Dowson	0	c Dowson, b Roberts	10
C.D. McIver	b Dowson	19	c Ebden, b Roberts	51
W.H.B. Evans	c Dowson, b Howard-Smith	21	c Wilson, b Mann	60
K.M. Carlisle	b Roberts	0	lbw, b Roberts	60
H.J. Wyld	c Howard-Smith, b Roberts	19	b McDonell	16
A.C. Pawson	b McDonell	18	b Dowson	7
O.M. Samson	lbw, b McDonell	8	not out	32
E.G. Martin	lbw, b McDonell	0	c Buckston, b Mann	0
A.C. von Ernsthausen	b McDonell	13	b Roberts	19
R.C.W. Burn	not out	0	b McDonell	0
EXTRAS	B 11, L-B 1, W 1, N-B 18	31	B 4, L-B 3, W 5, N-B 5	17
	TOTAL	259	TOTAL	291

CAMBRIDGE				
C.H.M. Ebden	b Evans	5	b Martin	4
R.T. Godsell	b Evans	0	c Pawson, b Evans	59
E.W. Mann	b Burn	9	b Martin	0
E.M. Dowson	c Martin, b Evans	54	b Evans	1
L.V. Harper	c von Ernsthausen, b Evans	8	b Evans	2
F.B. Wilson	b Burn	7	b Evans	42
R.P. Keigwin	not out	30	b von Ernsthausen	9
H.C. McDonell	b Evans	9	c McIver, b von Ernsthausen	2
F.B. Roberts	b Evans	0	b von Ernsthausen	1
G.M. Buckston	c Findlay, b von Ernsthausen	1	c Raphael, b von Ernsthausen	7
G. Howard-Smith	c Carlisle, b Evans	11	not out	0
EXTRAS	B 1, N-B 2	3	B 3, L-B 3, W 5, N-B 7	18
	TOTAL	137	TOTAL	145

Cambridge bowling	OVERS	RUNS	WKTS	OVERS	RUNS	WKTS
Dowson	19	71	2	8	36	1
Roberts	26	60	2	23	93	4
Keigwin	9	21	1	18	32	1
McDonell	19.5	45	4	13	24	2
Howard-Smith	9	31	1	11	55	0
Mann	—	—	—	12	34	2

Oxford bowling						
Martin	10	35	0	18	41	2
Evans	17.4	52	7	19.5	34	4
Burn	9	20	2	8	16	0
von Ernsthausen	7	27	1	13	36	4

30 June, 1, 2 July
At Lord's

1904

Match drawn

A contemporary account of this match in *Fifty Years of Sport* finishes with this comment:

Practical cricketers know that some of the keenest and most enjoyable games in their experience have ended without victory or defeat. But amongst these the University match of 1904 will not be reckoned.

Cambridge had developed into a 'useful and courageous team' but Oxford never fulfilled their potential, despite three wins. At Lord's, Cambridge had a handsome lead after the first innings, although W.H.B. Evans had held a poor Oxford innings from total collapse. It is more than probable that Cambridge sacrificed victory

for an individual record. Their second innings was not declared until Marsh had passed Foster's record of 171.

At the time Cambridge men were keen enough to see Oxford deprived of the record, and Oxford men viewed the possibility of its loss with equanimity, though afterwards they pointed out that it was a pity to sacrifice a chance in order that the score of a great artist should be beaten by a man who held few of his remarkable gifts.

Even so, Oxford looked near to defeat when Evans, supported by a fellow Malvernian, W.S. Bird, played a solid defensive innings to stave it off.

CAMBRIDGE	First innings			Second innings	
J.F. Marsh	c Raphael, b Evans		13	*not out*	172
R.P. Keigwin	c Bird, b Martin		38	c Bird, b von Ernsthausen	7
E.W. Mann	b Burn		42	b von Ernsthausen	19
C.H. Eyre	b Martin		16	b Martin	9
E.S. Phillips	b Burn		9	b von Ernsthausen	12
H.C. McDonell	c Bird, b Martin		36	b von Ernsthausen	7
F.B. Wilson	c Raphael, b Martin		46	b von Ernsthausen	7
K.R.B. Fry	lbw, b von Ernsthausen		28	c Evans, b Martin	57
M.W. Payne	lbw, b von Ernsthausen		6	c Evans, b Branston	21
F.J.V.B. Hopley	c Evans, b Martin		2	*not out*	54
G.G Napier	*not out*		1		
EXTRAS	B 11, L-B 4, N-B 1		16	B 19, L-B 4, N-B 2	25
	TOTAL		253	TOTAL (8 WKTS DEC.)	390

OXFORD					
J.E. Raphael	c Eyre, b Napier		12	c Payne, b McDonell	25
R.W. Awdry	c McDonell, b Napier		22	c Payne, b Mann	36
K.M. Carlisle	c Payne, b Hopley		9	c Mann, b McDonell	12
W.H.B. Evans	c Keigwin, b Napier		65	*not out*	86
G.T. Branston	b McDonell		24	st Payne, b McDonell	7
L.D. Brownlee	lbw, b McDonell		3	b Napier	9
C.D. McIver	lbw, b Napier		1	b McDonell	0
W.S. Bird	b McDonell		6	*not out*	23
A.C. von Ernsthausen	b McDonell		0		
E.G. Martin	b McDonell		0		
R.C.W. Burn	*not out*		2		
EXTRAS	L-B 1, N-B 4		5	B 8, L-B 7, W 2, N-B 6	23
	TOTAL		149	TOTAL (6 WKTS)	221

Oxford bowling	OVERS	RUNS	WKTS	OVERS	RUNS	WKTS
Burn	24	67	2	18	56	0
Evans	22	71	1	13	68	0
Martin	26.2	70	5	39	101	2
von Ernsthausen	18	26	2	34	98	5
Branston	2	3	0	5	42	1

Cambridge bowling						
Napier	23.1	55	4	32	66	1
McDonell	14	49	5	38	76	4
Hopley	7	22	1	18	35	0
Keigwin	3	18	0	3	4	0
Mann	—	—	—	8	17	1

8
1905–1914
Le Couteur hits the Headlines

OXFORD *Rhodes scholars lead to revival*

In the *Wisden*s of this decade, the last of cricket's Golden Age, appear advertisements for motor mowers. Still present none the less are the offers of the 'Pattisson Horse Boot' . . . 'as used for many years in His Majesty's Garden, at Lord's, the Oval and by the principal Cricket Clubs at home and abroad'. This was a time of dramatic change. The confidence, even complacency, and certainly pride at the end of Victoria's long reign had spilled over into Edward's short one with an added touch of gaiety. Life was moving faster, the motor car and even the aeroplane had come to stay, there was a wider and wider application of electricity, and wireless telegraphy now made it possible to gather cricket scores as they happened. There were warnings of approaching crisis, but no one imagined on what a catastrophic scale this was to be.

Cecil Rhodes, through his will, and not quite in the manner he had originally intended, had introduced a revolution to the Oxford world. From 1903 a steady stream of Rhodes scholars has matriculated year by year, from North America, Southern Africa, Australasia, and even for a time from Germany. In his will Rhodes had defined the principles on which he wished his scholars to be selected:

My desire has long been that the students who shall be elected to the scholarship shall not merely be bookworms. I direct that in the election of a student to a scholarship regard shall be had to (i) his literary and scholastic attainments; (ii) his fondness for and success in manly outdoor sports; (iii) his qualities of manhood, truth, courage, devotion to duty, sympathy for and protection of the weak, kindliness, unselfishness and fellowship; and (iv) his exhibition during his school days of moral force of character and of instincts to lead and to take an interest in his schoolmates, for those latter attributes will be likely in after life to guide him to esteem the performance of public duties as his highest aim.

These high ideals have largely been maintained; Rhodes scholars have had a remarkable influence on every aspect of university life, not least, from the very outset of the scheme, on cricket. In 1909 there were R.L. Robinson, later Lord Robinson, P.R. le Couteur and J.A. Seitz, all from Australia, and R.O. Lagden from South Africa. In 1988 there were three Rhodes scholars in the cricket eleven. In very few seasons have there not been Rhodes men at least very close to selection. The Rhodes Trust has not stopped there; as recently as 1979, £30,000 was put up for the construction of indoor cricket nets, a long-felt need.

'Schools' interfered rather more than usual in 1905, but potentially Oxford were a strong side. With the addition of G.N. Foster, the last of the Malvern family to come up to Oxford, and E.L. Wright, another freshman, from Winchester, the batting looked sound.

Blues are awarded to those in receipt of the captain's invitation to play at Lord's, but occasionally through illness or injury a player may be unable to appear in the Varsity Match; he is thus not a blue. One such luckless individual was O.T. Norris, who had been invited to play at Lord's in 1904 and had had to stand down through injury. In 1905 he played nine times but was dropped before the Varsity Match.

Oxford were defeated in the first match, against the Australians, by 200 runs but were by no means disgraced. A weak Gentlemen's side was beaten by 50 runs. W.G., now aged fifty-seven, had made 71 and had had to do much of the bowling. Oxford had a fine win over Kent, having followed on; a ninth-wicket stand of 97 made it possible to set Kent 183 to win, and they fell 50 runs short. This was Oxford's last success of 1905.

W.S. Bird was captain in 1906. He was one of a long line of excellent wicket-keepers, and would certainly have had a blue in his first year had not the great W. Findlay occupied this position. Despite all efforts, his year as captain showed a sad record. Oxford won the first match against a rather weak eleven headed by Leveson-Gower, and thereafter lost the rest.

The discovery of 1907 was H.A. Gilbert, a senior from Charterhouse, who later became a barrister. He was described as a medium-paced bowler also able to spin the ball; perhaps, in modern phraseology, he bowled cutters. He had 8 for 47 against the MCC and 5 for 57 against Leveson-Gower's eleven, quite apart from his 6 for 36 in the Varsity Match. Indeed, his bowling, along with G.N. Foster's batting, was the brightest feature of another poor season. Gilbert's ability with the bat can be gauged from the fact that in his four innings against Cambridge he scored but one run! Foster followed very much in the mould of H.K. and R.E., being particularly an off-side player, and although he always displayed much promise, his best performances came later for Worcestershire. He was also awarded blues for rackets, golf and Association football, going on to represent England as a forward.

Three matches were drawn in 1907, in each case as the result of rain; Oxford's one success was over a below-strength Worcestershire side.

The next seven years witnessed a great revival in Oxford cricket. It is true that they lost to Cambridge in 1912 and 1913; but in 1912 they were unlucky. Of the other University Matches they won four and should have won the fifth. It was a period of good players at both Universities, the majority of them at Oxford. It is useless to speculate what might have been achieved in 1915, 1916 and 1917 by D.J. Knight and the Howell brothers, but it is certain that the Oxford batting would have been strong indeed.

E.L. Wright of Winchester and New College, was captain for a second year in 1908, a rare honour, and he had much to do with breaking Cambridge's run of success. It was another wet summer, the first match being rained off; this was followed by a notable defeat of a Gentlemen's side which included MacLaren and Ranji, H.A. Gilbert taking eight wickets in the match. T. Bowring (228) and H. Teesdale (108) set an Oxford record, which still stands, by putting on 338 for the first wicket. They lost to the MCC and then to Worcester, for whom G.H. Simpson-Hayward, the last of the great lob bowlers, having already made a hundred in the match, took 6 for 13 in the first innings, and Oxford never recovered. The tour was marked by little success, but glory be! Cambridge's long run of victories was halted.

The season of 1909 started with a couple of victories, against Surrey and Leveson-Gower's eleven. The Australian match was spoilt by rain, although Gilbert had a great triumph with 8 wickets for 71, including Trumper and Macartney, and he was picked as a reserve in the First Test. Worcester were beaten by 42 runs, and in the first match of the tour a weak Surrey eleven were despatched by an innings. Thereafter rain and disappointment set in.

The summer of 1910 was the fourth consecutive wet one. It is remarkable that Oxford finished nine of their ten matches, the one draw being due to high scoring. The sensation of the year was Le Couteur. He was a genuine leg-break bowler who could bowl a googly, and he displayed subtle and deceptive changes of pace. He took ten wickets in a dramatic match when the champion county Kent were comfortably defeated. He played a significant part in winning against the Gentlemen in The Parks, and then turned on a prophetically splendid performance against the MCC, making 73 in just over an hour and taking 6 for 22 and 5 for 77. A veil may be drawn over the rest of the tour before Le Couteur resurfaced to destroy a good Cambridge eleven. He became a lecturer in philosophy in Western Australia, and although he played a few times for Victoria he never again achieved such performances.

In 1911 it was a beautiful summer, and Oxford should have made more runs than they did. There were nine old blues available, to whom could be added a freshman of great talent from Repton, I.P.F. Campbell. The Champion County were defeated again, as were All India and Cambridge, who were unlucky again to find Le Couteur on top form after his 'Schools'.

It is claimed that 1912 was the wettest year ever, that is until 1956. Certainly the great triangular experiment was sadly affected by rain. Oxford had to face the South Africans and Australians in one week, their first two matches. The first ended as an honourable draw, the second in a crushing ten-wicket defeat. There were but two successes that year, a 14-run victory over H.K. Foster's eleven and an innings victory over Leveson-Gower's eleven. Hapless fortune with the weather made Cambridge's task easier at Lord's.

The 1913 season was one of frustration. Oxford had plenty of promising material and did well in the home games. From the moment they left The Parks they could do little that was right. Again the bowling was weak, but there were two freshmen of real ability, B.G. Mellé, a South African, a beautiful bowler of the inswing type, and P. Havelock-Davies, a fastish bowler from Brighton College. The batting held a promise which was never quite fulfilled. Several of the batsmen returned quite good figures, but F.H. Knott was disappointing, R.H. Twining fell away badly, and R.V. Bardsley, owing to 'Schools' and injuries, played very little. They won four, lost five and drew one match.

Sadly Mellé broke a finger in 1914 so was not the destroyer he had been in the previous year. Oxford were strengthened by two exceptional batsmen, D.J. Knight of Malvern, a great player on even the most difficult wickets, and

M. Howell from Repton. The season opened with a crushing defeat from Middlesex being followed by a high-scoring draw with Kent. For the first of four occasions Oxford had to face the spin of the South African S.J. Pegler. Pegler assisted the MCC to a narrow win, in which match Oxford made 313 in the second innings, and once more to victory in the return match at Lord's. He also played for Leveson-Gower's eleven at Eastbourne, a match again lost by Oxford. Despite Pegler's 7 for 113, Oxford made 339 and enforced the follow-on against 'Mr Robinson's' eleven, but they could not quite press home their full advantage, and drew the match. A splendid victory at Lord's drew down the curtain on University cricket for the next five years.

CAMBRIDGE *Napier and Morcom point the way*

The decade from 1905 to 1914 was the high noon of the Edwardian summer, during which England and France came closer together in the 'Entente Cordiale', and the countries of Europe, as if in a dream, moved towards war. The even tenor of University life was scarcely affected, and by the end of the ten games at Lord's, Cambridge had achieved an advantage of two wins, having five victories to Oxford's three, with two matches drawn. The two most decisive wins were Oxford's, the first in 1910 when Cambridge lost by an innings and 126 runs, and the second in 1914 when the margin was 194 runs. The first match belonged undoubtedly to Oxford's Le Couteur, since he made 160 and took 11 for 66 in the match. In the second match rain on the second night swung the game Oxford's way, O.C. Bristowe and F.C.G. Naumann shooting Cambridge out summarily.

The three Light Blue victories in 1905, 1906 and 1907 saw the emergence of a pair of bowlers whose performances at Lord's, as well as earlier in the season, matched those of Jackson and Woods in 1891. I was taught from an early age that it is bowlers who win matches, and there is of course a great deal of truth in the assertion. It follows that it is important that their names are remembered in the story of University cricket as readily as those batsmen and all-rounders whose names are apt to come more trippingly off the tongue.

In the three matches G.G. Napier, who died in France on 25 September 1915 from wounds received earlier that day, and A.F. Morcom, bowling medium pace at a fine length, between them took forty-seven of the sixty wickets that fell. Napier, who hailed from Marlborough, had a high and very easy action, and made the ball move away and often make pace; and Morcom, a Reptonian, bowling from the Pavilion End, was able to make the ball break back sharply. They were a fine complementary pair, with Napier probably the senior partner, and were ably supported by P.R. May, a third quick bowler, who in 1906 took 12 for 76 against Yorkshire and 6 for 28 against Gloucestershire, both at Fenner's.

Wisden expresses it emphatically by saying, 'Mr Napier will live in cricket history as one of the best medium-pace bowlers seen in the University Match in his own generation.' His own haul at Lord's was 31 wickets for 544 runs; over his four years at Cambridge he took 283 wickets. He also showed his predilection for the Mecca of cricket in 1906 by taking another six wickets – they were six out of the first seven in the order – for a mere 39 for the Gentlemen in the Players' second innings. In 1913, when home from India, where he held a government appointment at Quetta, he bowled with marked success for MCC against Yorkshire at Scarborough, taking 8 for 44 in one innings.

The victory in 1905 which these two bowlers clinched for Cambridge could not have occurred had it not been for one of the most remarkable innings played in the University Match. But before we look at it, the writer of the account in *Fifty Years of Sport* – Arthur Croome – has pointed out a remarkable correspondence between this match and that of 1870.

In 1870, when William Yardley joined J.W. Dale, Cambridge were in a fair way to lose the game. As all the world knows, Yardley made a hundred. Probably few would back themselves to name Dale's precise score: it was 67. In 1905 Cambridge were deeper in the mire when McDonell came out to partner Colbeck. Between them the pair made 167, Colbeck getting 107 and McDonell 60. Figures are like the actors in 'The Critic' – when they do agree on the stage their unanimity is wonderful. In a second instance history only failed by a single run to repeat itself. Yardley followed his 100 in 1870 with 130 in 1872. Raphael made 130 in 1903, and in 1905 he had made 99 when he got that unstoppable thing from Napier; it came back inches, and turned so fast and low that it looked to unaccustomed eyes as a shooter.

Good writing, to match a good correspondence!

L.G. Colbeck, the hero of that match, died, alas, at sea on 3 January 1918. He had come up to King's with a fine record as a batsman at Marlborough, but nothing in sport could have given him more satisfaction than his innings at Lord's, in which he took all sorts of risks, including cutting balls off the middle stump to the boundary. He had a good season in 1906 also, making 175 not out against W.G. Grace's eleven at Cambridge, scoring 63 and 44 against Oxford, and heading the Cambridge batting with an average of 39. He also played hockey for the University.

To return to the 1905 match, vital fifties had been made in the first innings by two notable all-round sportsmen. R.P. Keigwin, who survived until 1972, captained Clifton in 1901 and 1902, the year he came up to Peterhouse. He represented Cambridge at cricket – he played from 1903 to 1906 – Association football, hockey and rackets. In 1906 he was described thus; 'Keigwin, according to a custom now hallowed by time, played a sound and useful innings.' He later played cricket and football for Essex and Gloucestershire, hockey for Essex and England, and lawn tennis for Gloucestershire. As if that were not enough, he also became an expert in pelota! After coaching at RNC Osborne, he was a master at Clifton for sixteen years and later Warden of Wills Hall, Bristol University. To cap it all, he was rated one of the foremost translators into Danish, and, delightfully, he became an expert on Hans Christian Andersen.

R.A. Young, who for over thirty years taught mathematics at Eton and was master in charge of cricket, was one of the few bespectacled players to represent England at both cricket and Association football. A fine batsman as well as wicket-keeper at Repton, he played four years for Cambridge, distinguishing himself by hitting a match-winning 150 in 1906. He was chosen as a member of the MCC team which toured Australia in 1907–8 under A.O. Jones, who played in the successful Cambridge side of 1893 but did not develop as a batsman until his time in the Nottinghamshire sides at the turn of the century. From 1905 to 1925 Young assisted Sussex as an amateur, his highest score being 220 in a total of 611 against Essex in 1905. In all first-class cricket he scored 6502 runs, including six centuries, for an average of 28.76. He also had 105 victims behind the stumps. He was a speedy outside-right for the Corinthians, and won two amateur international caps.

Michael Falcon, who came up after two years as a batsman in the Harrow sides of 1906 and 1907, did not start bowling until his last year at Cambridge, the year of his captaincy, 1910. From that moment, shrewd observers, though not the selectors in 1921, were aware that an exceptional bowling talent had arrived. With his fast away swing and splendid control, he took 6 for 58 against the Players at The Oval in 1913; and it was his 6 for 67 in the Australian first innings at The Saffrons in 1921 that made victory for A.C. MacLaren's eleven possible. He showed his all-round ability for the Gentlemen in 1924 when, after taking 7 for 78, he helped Arthur Gilligan to put on 134 in an hour for the last wicket. He played thirty-nine years for his beloved Norfolk, becoming chairman, president, then hon. vice-president. And when he presented the caps at Norwich to the English Schools Under-15 side in 1971 – five years before his death – he was the same courteous and friendly person that his contemporaries had known.

J.F. Ireland took 8 for 101 in the 1911 University Match, and the Hon. H.G.H. Mulholland and R.B. Lagden played some important innings, not least in the victory of 1912, but the one Cambridge player in these pre-war years to make a wider impact after the war was E.L. Kidd. He was four years in the Wellington XI and four years in the Cambridge side, being captain in his third, 1912, when he had much to do with leading his side to a three-wicket victory after the teams had tied on the first innings. Not only did he captain well, but he also made 46 and 45, and took 8 for 143 in the match. He did well also for Middlesex and the Gentlemen. In the 1912 Gentlemen *v* Players match at Lord's he took 4 for 97 with his slow leg-breaks, delivered with a high action, his victims being Hobbs, Hayes, Mead and 'Tiger' Smith; and he then played a valuable innings of 37. In all, he scored six hundreds in his career, including 167 against Sussex at Fenner's, and he took 186 wickets at an average of 24.63.

The war interrupted not only cricket itself but the cricketing careers of all those, like Kidd, who were developing as fine players, and for whom, whatever the effects of their particular war, four years was a large slice of life. As we shall see, many of those who survived were able to put their maturity and experience to good effect at Fenner's and at Lord's.

6, 7, 8 July
At Lord's

1905

Cambridge won by
40 runs

The University Match of 1904 had been a game to forget; 1905 was one to remember. Oxford deserved a first-innings lead of 101, achieved on the morning of the second day. Two hours later Cambridge were 77 for 6 and defeat by an innings was on the cards. L.G. Colbeck was then joined by H.C. McDonell, who played a stubborn innings, but Colbeck was inspired. W.H.B. Evans all but bowled him time and again, but he made some amazing strokes, the account in *Fifty Years of Sport* gives a vivid recollection:

Straight balls were cut behind point and went to the boundary like a flash, and it was impossible to place the

field for his off-drive, since no man could say what ball he would select as a suitable medium for the exploitation of it.

Evans displaced the heel of his boot and had to leave the field. Cambridge were able to set a target of 164. K.M. Carlisle juggled his order, with only a few overs to face overnight, and by the time stumps were drawn the score read 15 for 3 – this might have been worse, for F.A.H. Henley survived a ball which hit the stumps and left the bails unmoved. Oxford made a fight of it in the morning, but Cambridge deserved their remarkable success.

CAMBRIDGE	First innings		Second innings	
R.A. Young	lbw, b Henley	51	c Branston, b Evans	9
C.H. Eyre	b Udal	13	b Evans	0
E.W. Mann	c Henley, b Evans	14	c Foster, b Evans	0
C.C. Page	c Bird, b Martin	12	c Bird, b Evans	4
R.P. Keigwin	c Evans, b Udal	50	b Udal	8
M.W. Payne	c and b Udal	36	c Foster, b Evans	26
L.G. Colbeck	b Udal	1	c Burn, b Henley	107
H.C. McDonell	c Branston, b Martin	6	c Branston, b Udal	60
P.R. May	b Martin	0	c Foster, b Henley	10
A.F. Morcom	not out	1	not out	13
G.G. Napier	c and b Udal	18	b Henley	0
EXTRAS	B 9, L-B 2, N-B 5	16	B 14, L-B 5, N-B 8	27
	TOTAL	218	TOTAL	264

OXFORD				
W.H.B. Evans	b McDonell	21	c McDonell, b Napier	8
K.M. Carlisle	lbw, b McDonell	25	run out	1
G.T. Branston	c and b Napier	28	c Payne, b Morcom	0
G.N. Foster	b May	4	c Payne, b Morcom	20
J.E. Raphael	b Napier	99	b Morcom	6
E.L. Wright	b Morcom	95	b Morcom	26
W.S. Bird	lbw, b Napier	2	b Napier	3
N.R. Udal	not out	16	b Morcom	21
F.A.H. Henley	c Payne, b Morcom	1	b Morcom	11
E.G. Martin	c Payne, b Napier	4	b Napier	9
R.C.W. Burn	b Morcom	1	not out	4
EXTRAS	B 16, L-B 5, N-B 2	23	B 8, L-B 4, N-B 2	14
	TOTAL	319	TOTAL	123

Oxford bowling	OVERS	RUNS	WKTS	OVERS	RUNS	WKTS
Burn	6	20	0	4	26	0
Udal	23.4	73	5	18	54	2
Evans	11	50	1	14	66	5
Martin	14	19	3	7	32	0
Henley	9	40	1	6.4	39	3
Branston	—	—	—	3	20	0

Cambridge bowling	OVERS	RUNS	WKTS	OVERS	RUNS	WKTS
Napier	29	92	4	17.4	68	3
Morcom	25.5	69	3	17	41	6
McDonell	15	57	2	—	—	—
May	14	48	1	—	—	—
Keigwin	6	17	0	—	—	—
Mann	2	13	0	—	—	—

1906

Oxford had a weak side. Geoff Foster had much of the family flair, but N.R. Udal, their best bowler, struggled with a severe strain, and G.T. Branston, who had bowled with success at Charterhouse, achieved the rare and dubious honour of conceding a thousand runs and more off his bowling during the University season. It is stated in *Fifty Years of Sport* that Cambridge had the makings of a magnificent side, 'and a magnificent side it would have been if the fielding had been as good as the batting and bowling . . . goodness knows how many they missed at Brighton when they lost to Sussex'.

Among their number they included two unusual all-rounders: R.A. Young, a Reptonian who later taught at Eton, and who played both cricket and amateur football for England; and R.P. Keigwin, from Clifton, who played first-class football, hockey, rackets and lawn tennis, and was even an expert at pelota.

M.W. Payne scored 64 out of 73 for the first wicket, while Young dug himself in for a long and skilful innings. Oxford made a decent start, being 58 for 2, but could not sustain it next morning. Cambridge did not enforce the follow-on and finally left Oxford needing 422 to win in six and a quarter hours. Geoff Foster, dropped twice, batted well, and W.J.H. Curwen and E.G. Martin had a bold 90-run partnership for the last wicket, but Cambridge were much better despite their slack fielding.

CAMBRIDGE	First innings		Second innings	
M.W. Payne	c Foster, b Martin	64	b Martin	21
R.A. Young	c Branston, b Udal	150	lbw, b Udal	31
C.H. Eyre	c Foster, b Udal	20	c Gordon, b Udal	17
J.N. Buchanan	b Udal	8	c and b Udal	47
C.C. Page	b Udal	6	c Bird, b Martin	46
R.P. Keigwin	c Foster, b Martin	27	not out	38
L.G. Colbeck	c Barnes, b Udal	63	c Foster, b Martin	44
H. Mainprice	b Foster	0		
A.F. Morcom	c Branston, b Udal	0		
G.G. Napier	b Udal	0		
P.R. May	not out	7		
EXTRAS	B 9, L-B 2, N-B 4	15	B 4	4
	TOTAL	360	TOTAL (6 WKTS DEC.)	248

OXFORD				
G.N. Foster	b Morcom	41	c Payne, b Napier	77
C.A.L. Payne	c Eyre, b Napier	3	c Payne, b May	5
J.H. Gordon	c Payne, b May	8	c Payne, b Napier	8
R.V. Buxton	c Buchanan, b Napier	33	c Mainprice, b May	28
E.L. Wright	b Morcom	9	c Buchanan, b May	79
R.G. Barnes	b Napier	15	b May	0
G.T. Branston	c Eyre, b May	34	st Payne, b Mainprice	8
W.S. Bird	b Napier	6	b Napier	12
N.R. Udal	c Payne, b Morcom	6	c Payne, b Napier	4
W.J.H. Curwen	not out	12	not out	34
E.G. Martin	c Keigwin, b Napier	7	c Mainprice, b Napier	56
EXTRAS	L-B 1, N-B 12	13	B 5, L-B 3, W 3, N-B 5	16
	TOTAL	187	TOTAL	327

Oxford bowling	OVERS	RUNS	WKTS		OVERS	RUNS	WKTS
Udal	30.5	133	7		17	73	3
Barnes	16	55	0		4	21	0
Martin	14	54	2		22.4	79	3
Branston	20	63	0		12	51	0
Curwen	6	24	0		4	20	0
Foster	4	16	1		—	—	—

Cambridge bowling							
May	19	62	2		23	92	4
Napier	38	68	5		33.1	91	5
Morcom	21	44	3		16	42	0
Mainprice	—	—	—		11	56	1
Buchanan	—	—	—		6	30	0

4, 5, 6 July
At Lord's

1907

Cambridge won by
5 wickets

Oxford were still a weak side; Geoff Foster was in a class of his own as a batsman and H.A. Gilbert, a senior from Charterhouse, gave the bowling respectability. Cambridge were a much better batting side and G.C. Napier and A.F. Morcom were a match-winning pair with the ball. The former, a medium-pace bowler with an easy high action, had a remarkable record in his four Varsity Matches, taking 31 wickets for 544; in 1907 he bowled unchanged. Cambridge strangely had three wicket-keepers playing – M.W. Payne, R.A. Young and A.D. Imlay, the last being chosen for this match, his only appearance.

The weather for the Varsity Match was atro-

cious and Oxford nearly brought off a surprise; indeed, had J.N. Buchanan not been given two chances in the second innings, they probably would have done so. On a restricted first day a feeble effort by Oxford realized 141. At 21 overnight, Cambridge were not able to complete their innings until after lunch on Friday. The wicket was now nasty, and Oxford had an unexpected lead of 33. Oxford struggled to 58 for 4 that night and next day Wright helped them to a modest 112. Young and Buchanan laid the foundations of Cambridge's victory, for C. Palmer to finish it off with three successive boundaries.

OXFORD

	First innings		Second innings	
G.N. Foster	c Buchanan, b Napier	29	c Buchanan, b Napier	0
Hon. C.N. Bruce	c Morcom, b Napier	5	lbw, b Morcom	0
E.L. Wright	b Napier	4	b Morcom	48
J.H. Gordon	b Napier	8	c Payne, b Goodwin	11
C.A.L. Payne	c Buchanan, b Morcom	38	c Napier, b Goodwin	7
C.S. Hurst	c and b Napier	11	c Harrison b Napier	7
T. Bowring	b Morcom	12	not out	18
R.G. Barnes	b Morcom	14	c Payne, b Morcom	1
D.R. Brandt	not out	3	b Napier	4
J.C.M. Lowe	c Imlay, b Morcom	0	c Palmer, b Napier	2
H.A. Gilbert	lbw, b Morcom	0	b Morcom	0
EXTRAS	B 10, L-B 5, N-B 2	17	B 8, L-B 5, N-B 1	14
	TOTAL	141	TOTAL	112

CAMBRIDGE

R.A. Young	c Hurst, b Lowe	6	st Brandt, b Lowe	45
C.C.G. Wright	c Bruce, b Gilbert	13	b Gilbert	17
M.W. Payne	c Payne, b Gilbert	0	c Barnes, b Lowe	5
J.N. Buchanan	c Hurst, b Lowe	2	b Lowe	46
F.H. Mugliston	c Bruce, b Gilbert	0	b Lowe	6
W.P. Harrison	c Foster, b Gilbert	8	not out	1
C. Palmer	b Lowe	16	not out	19
H.J. Goodwin	st Brandt, b Gilbert	26		
A.D. Imlay	b Barnes	7		
A.F. Morcom	c Payne, b Gilbert	15		
G.G. Napier	not out	2		
EXTRAS	B 9, L-B 1, W 3	13	B 4, L-B 1, W 1, N-B 1	7
	TOTAL	108	TOTAL (5 WKTS)	146

Cambridge bowling	OVERS	RUNS	WKTS		OVERS	RUNS	WKTS
Morcom	29	69	5		19	29	4
Napier	28	55	5		29	49	4
Goodwin	—	—	—		11	20	2

Oxford bowling							
Lowe	15	45	3		21	57	4
Gilbert	19.4	36	6		23.1	71	1
Barnes	5	14	1		—	—	—
Bowring	—	—	—		3	11	0

6, 7, 8 July
At Lord's

1908

Oxford won by
2 wickets

After losing for three years running – it was not far from being four – Oxford managed to win in 1908, after a very close and exciting game. In all probability the rain, which fell in considerable quantity on the third morning, had something to do with the result . . . if ever a man deserved to have things go well for him it was Wright, captain of Oxford for the second time. For four years he worked very hard for his University at Lord's, always getting runs in one innings or the other, and never making a mistake in the field through carelessness.

So says the account in *Fifty Years of Sport*.

It is interesting to note that E.L. Wright had previously also been for two years captain of Winchester.

Oxford's narrow lead of 19 was soon overtaken by R.A. Young and M. Falcon, the latter later achieving the remarkable record of playing for Norfolk up until 1946. Oxford were finally set 183 to win. On Wednesday morning R.L. Robinson was out first ball and C.E. Hatfeild was joined by H. Teesdale, with a thumb swathed in bandages, and by 11.30 a.m. the score was 125 for 7; they had added 22. Rain prevented further play until six o'clock when Hatfeild hit out, and although he lost Teesdale, he made the winning run at 6.40 p.m. Ten minutes later the ground was under water.

CAMBRIDGE	First innings		Second innings	
R.A. Young	c Robinson, b Gilbert	20	st Pawson, b Bowring	54
C.C.G. Wright	c Foster, b Gilbert	17	b Lowe	9
F.H. Mugliston	c Foster, b Gilbert	8	c Hurst, b Lowe	0
M. Falcon	b Lowe	10	c Lowe, b Bowring	31
J.N. Buchanan	run out	35	b Gilbert	33
R.E.H. Baily	c Pawson, b Bowring	20	b Robinson	2
J.F. Ireland	b Lowe	1	c Pawson, b Robinson	12
K.G. Macleod	c Bruce, b Lowe	21	c Pawson, b Robinson	4
H.J. Goodwin	c Bruce, b Bowring	40	c Lowe, b Gilbert	21
E. Olivier	c Lowe, b Bowring	0	c Robinson, b Gilbert	25
Hon. C.F. Lyttelton	not out	2	not out	1
EXTRAS	B 7, L-B 6, W 1	14	L-B 4, W 4, N-B 1	9
	TOTAL	188	TOTAL	201

OXFORD				
H. Teesdale	c Lyttelton, b Olivier	15	b Goodwin	18
Hon. C.N. Bruce	b Goodwin	46	c Goodwin, b Lyttelton	0
E.L. Wright	c Ireland, b Lyttelton	0	c Wright, b Olivier	37
G.N. Foster	run out	0	b Olivier	11
T. Bowring	c Goodwin, b Lyttelton	8	b Olivier	6
C.S. Hurst	b Olivier	61	c Young, b Lyttelton	46
R.L. Robinson	c Buchanan, b Olivier	4	b Lyttelton	14
C.E. Hatfeild	c Wright, b Olivier	25	not out	35
A.G. Pawson	not out	8	c Baily, b Olivier	3
J.C.M. Lowe	c Baily, b Olivier	5	not out	0
H.A. Gilbert	b Olivier	0		
EXTRAS	B 16, L-B 6, W 5, N-B 8	35	B 1, L-B 4, W 3, N-B 5	13
	TOTAL	207	TOTAL (8 WKTS)	183

Oxford bowling	OVERS	RUNS	WKTS		OVERS	RUNS	WKTS
Hatfeild	9	20	0		—	—	—
Gilbert	28	64	3		14	35	3
Lowe	24	65	3		15	51	2
Bowring	3.3	10	3		13	34	2
Robinson	6	15	0		23	72	3

Cambridge bowling							
Olivier	28.1	68	6		29	73	4
Lyttelton	14	41	2		22.2	44	3
Goodwin	11	42	1		8	26	1
Macleod	11	21	0		2	11	0
Buchanan	—	—	—		4	16	0

5, 6, 7 July
At Lord's

1909

Match drawn

It was a disappointing Varsity Match. Oxford had much the stronger side and were expected to win. Their openers, A.J. Evans and M.G. Salter, put on 115 for the first wicket in less than an hour and a half; it was thanks to J.H.B. Lockhart that they were able to press home this early advantage, a contemporary wrote in *Fifty Years of Sport*:

No more peculiar bowler had been seen in the University match. Bowling round the wicket he tossed the ball very high in the air with a leg-break action . . . the ball, if allowed to pitch, generally turned from leg . . . he relied mainly on the mistake of the batsman.

He earned his 6 for 96.

Oxford led by 84, and Evans and Salter added to this with another 30 before rain put paid to further play until 12.30 on the third day. This meant that there was no more than five and a half hours' playing time left; with urgency all important, Oxford pottered and, though later on C.V.L. Hooman hit very hard, the innings was not declared until 4.00 p.m. Nobody expected Cambridge to make 276, still less to make them in two hours and three-quarters, and here again Oxford must be condemned for lack of enterprise. Further rain stopped proceedings for good.

OXFORD	First innings		Second innings	
M.G. Salter	c Prest, b Lockhart	53	b Lockhart	15
A.J. Evans	c Tufnell, b Lockhart	79	lbw, b Lockhart	46
J.A. Seitz	b Buchanan	3	c Tufnell, b Olivier	15
C.V.L. Hooman	lbw, b Lockhart	12	c Macleod, b Olivier	44
C.S. Hurst	c Macleod, b Lockhart	6	st Tufnell, b Lockhart	18
P.R. Le Couteur	c Tufnell, b Olivier	25	b Macleod	6
R.O. Lagden	c Prest, b Lockhart	2	c Tufnell, b Macleod	11
A.G. Pawson	run out	22	not out	9
R.L. Robinson	b Buchanan	18	lbw, b Macleod	10
J.C.M. Lowe	b Lockhart	13		
H.A. Gilbert	not out	1		
EXTRAS	B 20, L-B 10, N-B 3	33	B 4, L-B 1, W 9, N-B 3	17
	TOTAL	267	TOTAL (8 WKTS DEC.)	191

CAMBRIDGE				
J.N. Buchanan	b Gilbert	2	c Gilbert, b Lowe	0
J.W.W. Nason	lbw, b Gilbert	4	c Lowe, b Gilbert	9
M. Falcon	c Hurst, b Robinson	13	lbw, b Le Couteur	23
J.F. Ireland	b Evans	65	b Le Couteur	29
F.T. Mann	b Gilbert	0	not out	12
K.G. Macleod	c and b Gilbert	14	not out	6
H.E.W. Prest	c Lagden, b Evans	54		
J.H.B. Lockhart	c Pawson, b Gilbert	8		
N.C. Tufnell	c Hooman, b Robinson	7		
Hon. C.F. Lyttelton	c Evans, b Gilbert	10		
E. Olivier	not out	0		
EXTRAS	B 3, L-B 2, W 1	6	B 1, L-B 6, W 1, N-B 2	10
	TOTAL	183	TOTAL (4 WKTS)	89

Cambridge bowling	OVERS	RUNS	WKTS	OVERS	RUNS	WKTS
Olivier	10	37	1	23	77	2
Lyttelton	20	41	0	—	—	—
Lockhart	37	96	6	24	82	3
Macleod	7	14	0	7.4	15	3
Buchanan	16.5	46	2	—	—	—

Oxford bowling	OVERS	RUNS	WKTS	OVERS	RUNS	WKTS
Gilbert	30	52	6	21	27	1
Robinson	20	53	2	—	—	—
Lagden	1	3	0	2	6	0
Le Couteur	7	29	0	10.1	20	2
Lowe	7	24	0	11	15	1
Evans	5	16	2	4	11	0

1910

After a lot of rain the start was certainly premature, although it was delayed until 4.00 p.m. A.G. Cowie's opening over was a memorable one.

. . . he slipped about in the mud, and the ball flew anywhere at its own sweet will. The first two deliveries were wides; the third one a shoulder high full pitch, Evans tried to hit to leg and skied it to second slip. . . . Salter got a single off the next ball, also a full pitch.

R. Sale was bowled first ball and M.G. Salter survived a confident appeal off the last and eighth delivery. Oxford had expected much from

P.R. Le Couteur, a Rhodes scholar from Melbourne, who bowled leg-breaks. They could hardly have anticipated one of the great all-round performances of all time. He was 94 not out overnight, C.V.L. Hooman having supported him brilliantly, and the next day, with some help from A.G. Pawson and much from J.L.S. Vidler, he reached 160. Cambridge's first innings lasted but two hours, and although they coped better with Le Couteur the second time round, he still had a match analysis of 11 for 66 in this resounding Oxford victory.

OXFORD	First innings		Second innings
A.J. Evans	c Nason, b Cowie	0	
M.G. Salter	c Ireland, b Holloway	15	
R. Sale	b Cowie	0	
C.V.L. Hooman	c Mann, b Holloway	61	
R.L.L. Braddell	c Falcon, b Holloway	0	
P.R. Le Couteur	c Holloway, b Cowie	160	
R.H. Twining	st Tufnell, b Lockhart	5	
R.O. Lagden	c Holloway, b Lockhart	0	
A.G. Pawson	c Falcon, b Ireland	16	
J.L.S. Vidler	b Cowie	32	
F.N. Tuff	not out	10	
EXTRAS	B 7, L-B 5, N-B 2, W 2	16	
	TOTAL	315	

CAMBRIDGE					
N.C. Tufnell	c and b Lagden	6	b Tuff		5
J.W.W. Nason	st Pawson, b Le Couteur	9	not out		10
E.L. Kidd	b Lagden	2	st Pawson, b Le Couteur		26
J.F. Ireland	c and b Lagden	4	c Salter, b Le Couteur		15
M. Falcon	lbw, b Le Couteur	11	b Evans		19
F.T. Mann	lbw, b Le Couteur	2	b Le Couteur		12
D.C. Collins	b Le Couteur	31	b Le Couteur		15
O. Hughes	st Pawson, b Le Couteur	0	b Evans		1
N.J. Holloway	b Le Couteur	2	c Hooman, b Evans		1
J.H.B. Lockhart	c and b Vidler	0	c Vidler, b Evans		0
A.G. Cowie	not out	3	b Le Couteur		0
EXTRAS	B 5, N-B 1	6	B 6, L-B 1, W 1, N-B 1		9
	TOTAL	76	TOTAL		113

Cambridge bowling	OVERS	RUNS	WKTS	OVERS	RUNS	WKTS
Cowie	18	67	4			
Lockhart	22	79	2			
Holloway	27	106	3			
Nason	2	18	0			
Kidd	4	10	0			
Ireland	12	19	1			
Oxford bowling						
Lagden	13	26	3	6	9	0
Vidler	10	24	1	11	21	0
Le Couteur	18.2	20	6	16	46	5
Tuff	—	—	—	7	21	1
Evans	—	—	—	4	7	4

3, 4, 5 July
At Lord's

1911

Oxford won by
74 runs

Harry Altham, although being the first victim of J.F. Ireland's hat-trick in 1911, made an important contribution to Oxford's victory in the second innings. He had already, in earlier years, proved himself at Repton, but it was later as legislator, Test selector, historian and coach that he made his greatest contribution to cricket. He could hold an audience spellbound in passing on his enthusiasm for the history of the game.

This was a beautiful summer and wickets were almost universally good. Oxford started badly and when Ireland had them on their knees with his hat-trick he took himself off. Their total of 203 must be reckoned a poor score, but Cambridge bettered it by only 14. The five Oxford batsmen who failed to score in their first innings more than made amends in the second, and Cambridge were set to get 315. On the last morning they looked to be well on target when P.R. Le Couteur bowled the Hon. H.G.H. Mulholland, and an hour later the match was all but over. Le Couteur had five wickets in quick succession; F.T. Mann and N.J. Holloway showed staunch resistance, but Oxford were not be be denied.

OXFORD	First innings			Second innings	
A.J. Evans	*b* Falcon		0	*c* Ireland, *b* Kidd	43
R.H. Twining	*b* Mulholland		71	*b* Ireland	44
I.P.F. Campbell	*b* Ireland		0	*c* Baggallay, *b* Holloway	33
R.V. Bardsley	*b* Falcon		71	*c* Collins, *b* Ireland	0
P.R. Le Couteur	*b* Falcon		11	*b* Kidd	2
R.L.L. Braddell	*b* Ireland		8	*c* Saville, *b* Kidd	6
H.S. Altham	*b* Ireland		0	*b* Holloway	47
H. Brougham	*lbw*, *b* Ireland		0	*c* Falcon, *b* Ireland	84
R.O. Lagden	*b* Ireland		0	*b* Collins	23
J.L.S. Vidler	*b* Grierson		15	*b* Holloway	18
A.G. Pawson	*not out*		5	*not out*	11
EXTRAS	B 8, L-B 8, W 3, N-B 3		22	B 15, L-B 1, W 1	17
	TOTAL		203	TOTAL	328

CAMBRIDGE					
D.C. Collins	*lbw*, *b* Evans		57	*lbw*, *b* Le Couteur	50
Hon. H.G.H. Mulholland	*c* Bardsley, *b* Lagden		8	*b* Le Couteur	24
S.H. Saville	*lbw*, *b* Le Couteur		15	*lbw*, *b* Le Couteur	21
M. Falcon	*c* Bardsley, *b* Evans		40	*c and b* Le Couteur	5
J.F. Ireland[1]	*c* Evans, *b* Lagden		23	*c and b* Le Couteur	6
H.E.W. Prest	*c* Vidler, *b* Le Couteur		6	*c and b* Lagden	16
F.T. Mann	*b* Le Couteur		12	*lbw*, *b* Le Couteur	32
E.L. Kidd	*b* Evans		16	*b* Le Couteur	1
N.J. Holloway	*lbw*, *b* Lagden		1	*not out*	39
M.E.C. Baggallay	*c* Evans, *b* Lagden		18	*b* Evans	22
H. Grierson	*not out*		4	*b* Le Couteur	6
EXTRAS	B 11, L-B 4, W 2		17	B 15, L-B 2, W 1	18
	TOTAL		217	TOTAL	240

Cambridge bowling	OVERS	RUNS	WKTS	OVERS	RUNS	WKTS
Falcon	20	46	3	16	57	0
Ireland	10	25	5	20	76	3
Grierson	19	37	1	8	23	0
Holloway	8	23	0	12.4	30	3
Kidd	4	33	0	25	92	3
Mulholland	7.1	17	1	4	6	0
Collins	—	—	—	5	27	1

Oxford bowling						
Lagden	19	50	4	20	68	1
Evans	16	39	3	13	37	1
Le Couteur	22	80	3	28.1	99	8
Vidler	7	24	0	6	8	0
Braddell	2	7	0	3	10	0

[1] Performed the hat-trick in Oxford's first innings. His victims were: Altham, Lagden and Brougham.

1912

Not only was this one of the wettest seasons on record but it also saw the one and only Triangular Tournament. The Universities thus had the unique experience of playing South Africa and Australia. Oxford were a good batting side, but then as now those in their final year, with 'Schools' in prospect, were unable to have adequate preparation. Cambridge were a better-looking side; E.C. Baker, it was said, was still able to move the ball in the air when the shine had gone.

Oxford batted first and made 221; their innings was held together we are told in *Fifty Years of Sport*, by G.E.V. Crutchley.

. . . *the grace and ease of his play could hardly have been surpassed, even by such a stylist as Lionel Palairet; and what makes his success the more wonderful is that on his return to the pavilion it was discovered that he was suffering from a severe attack of measles.*

He was unable to take any further part in the match, a sad blow for Oxford.

Cambridge were set 213, a task not easy on a wicket which was kicking badly. J.S.F. Morrison and R.B. Lagden were out on the second evening, but gentle overnight rain bound the wicket together, making the Cambridge task easier, and they won the match soon after lunch.

OXFORD

	First innings		Second innings	
R.H. Twining	b Baker	0	c Riley, b Kidd	22
F.H. Knott	c Mulholland, b Baker	46	b Baker	24
I.P.F. Campbell	c Riley, b Kidd	27	c Kidd, b Baker	9
R.V. Bardsley	c Morrison, b Kidd	2	st Franklin, b Kidd	31
A.J. Evans	c Kidd, b Calthorpe	4	c Kidd, b Lagden	36
G.E.V. Crutchley	not out	99	absent (ill)	0
H.S. Altham	c and b Baker	8	run out	3
E.A. Shaw	c Hopley, b Kidd	4	b Holloway	2
R.O. Lagden	lbw, b Kidd	2	c Mulholland, b Kidd	68
J.L.S. Vidler	c Kidd, b Baker	17	b Baker	2
J.N. Fraser	c Riley, b Kidd	0	not out	0
EXTRAS	B 4, L-B 5, W 3	12	B 11, L-B 5	16
TOTAL		221	TOTAL	213

CAMBRIDGE

W.N. Riley	b Evans	8	run out	30
J.S.F. Morrison	b Evans	19	b Evans	4
S.H. Saville	c Altham, b Evans	0	c Vidler, b Bardsley	3
Hon. H.G.H. Mulholland	c Evans, b Vidler	1	st Shaw, b Bardsley	78
E.L. Kidd	b Fraser	46	b Bardsley	45
Hon. F.S.G. Calthorpe	b Lagden	9	b Vidler	27
R.B. Lagden	run out	61	b Lagden	6
G.W.V.B. Hopley	b Lagden	14	not out	6
W.B. Franklin	b Lagden	0	not out	3
N.J. Holloway	c and b Fraser	34		
E.C. Baker	not out	8		
EXTRAS	B 17, L-B 3, N-B 1	21	B 6, L-B 3, N-B 3	12
TOTAL		221	TOTAL (7 WKTS)	214

Cambridge bowling	OVERS	RUNS	WKTS		OVERS	RUNS	WKTS
Baker	27	41	4		22	51	3
Holloway	17	29	0		21	49	1
Kidd	27.4	75	5		24.2	68	3
Mulholland	8	34	0		5	16	0
Calthorpe	14	30	1		4	12	0
R.B. Lagden	—	—	—		3	1	1

Oxford bowling							
Evans	23	65	3		18.1	47	1
Vidler	17	54	1		11	36	1
R.O. Lagden	17	40	3		22	39	1
Fraser	17.1	37	2		18	65	0
Bardsley	1	4	0		9	15	3

7, 8, 9 July
At Lord's

1913

Cambridge won by
4 wickets

Cambridge were a useful all-round side, although only five of the ten blues in residence were actually selected. Oxford never quite fulfilled themselves after early successes. B.G. Mellé, who had already helped Western Province win the Currie Cup in 1908–9, was an early exponent of leg theory.

His high right-arm medium-pace in-swing to three short-leg fieldsmen so confounded Cambridge that in the Varsity Match he took 6 for 70 in the first innings and 2 for 46 in the second.

A genuine discovery, *Wisden* wrote of him. In the University season he had 55 wickets at 15.90 apiece.

Oxford made a dreadful start, being 17 for 3, and never fully recovered. Cambridge had 44 overnight, and on Tuesday morning Mellé got going, and only R.B. Lagden, who played brilliantly, resisted him. Cambridge's lead, on a difficult wicket, was vital. R.V. Bardsley batted well in Oxford's second innings until, well set, he was unluckily stumped off the wicket-keeper's pads. I.P.F. Campbell was brilliantly run out by S.H. Saville, and Oxford then had little more to offer. Although they made Cambridge fight for the runs, 146 was a target well within their reach.

OXFORD

	First innings			Second innings	
R.H. Twining	b Naumann		3	c Mulholland, b Naumann	9
R.V. Bardsley	c Lagden, b Woodroffe		2	st Lang, b Davies	72
G.R.R. Colman	b Woodroffe		39	b Naumann	1
F.H. Knott	b Woodroffe		0	lbw, b Calthorpe	26
I.P.F. Campbell	c Knott, b Woodroffe		34	run out	13
W.A.C. Wilkinson	c Fairbairn, b Naumann		20	c Calthorpe, b Woodroffe	3
W.G.K. Boswell	c Mulholland, b Davies		22	b Woodroffe	30
B.G. von B. Mellé	c Kidd, b Naumann		0	b Naumann	6
P.H. Davies	c Mulholland, b Davies		0	b Naumann	0
J.N. Fraser	not out		6	not out	3
C.U. Peat	st Lang, b Naumann		4	st Lang, b Davies	4
EXTRAS	B 9, L-B 1, N-B 1		11	B 10, L-B 11, N-B 3	24
	TOTAL		141	TOTAL	191

CAMBRIDGE

B.S. Cumberlege	c and b Mellé		12	c Twining, b Peat	6
A.H. Lang	b Mellé		28	b Mellé	4
R.B. Lagden	c Campbell, b Mellé		71	b Peat	45
Hon. H.G.H. Mulholland	b Peat		7	c Mellé, b Davies	15
E.L. Kidd	lbw, b Mellé		15	c Knott, b Mellé	36
G.B. Davies	run out		0	lbw, b Boswell	14
S.H. Saville	b Davies		9	not out	13
Hon. F.S.G. Calthorpe	c and b Davies		17	not out	2
G.A. Fairbairn	not out		10		
J.H. Naumann	b Mellé		4		
K.H.C. Woodroffe	b Mellé		2		
EXTRAS	B 4, L-B 8		12	B 4, L-B 5, N-B 2	11
	TOTAL		187	TOTAL (6 WKTS)	146

Cambridge bowling	OVERS	RUNS	WKTS	OVERS	RUNS	WKTS
Woodroffe	16	25	4	19	55	2
Naumann	25.3	57	4	17	37	4
Calthorpe	12	22	0	6	12	1
G.B. Davies	7	16	2	8.1	21	2
Mulholland	6	10	0	3	8	0
Kidd	—	—	—	3	34	0

Oxford bowling	OVERS	RUNS	WKTS	OVERS	RUNS	WKTS
Mellé	30.4	70	6	29.4	46	2
P.H. Davies	16	36	2	3	8	1
Fraser	13	47	0	9	24	0
Peat	8	20	1	14	22	2
Boswell	2	2	0	9	35	1

1914

Schoolboy rivals in 1913, Donald Knight of Malvern and Miles Howell of Repton were thrown together as freshmen to open Oxford's innings, and each added an extra touch of class to a good fielding side. *Wisden* described Cambridge as 'a side of unrealised possibilities', but among some fine players was Freddy Calthorpe, who later captained Warwickshire for ten years (he was also a scratch golfer who founded the County Cricketers Golfing Society).

Oxford's 239 was a creditable score on what was not an easy wicket. Cambridge looked like leading them, but collapsed on the second day.

D.J. Knight, always talented on the worst wickets, played the best innings of the match (although he was dropped in the slips before he had scored), and laid a solid enough foundation for F.H. Knott and W.G.K. Boswell to go for quick runs. Cambridge, set 268 to win, had no chance.

Within a month war was declared and it was to be five years before the next Varsity Match. Eight old blues from 1913 or 1914 were to reappear at Lord's; six gave their lives, and at least four others suffered such disability that they could never again play cricket with full enjoyment.

OXFORD	First innings		Second innings	
D.J. Knight	c Vincent, b Baker	11	c Morrison, b Fairbairn	64
M. Howell	b Calthorpe	17	c Wood, b Woodroffe	16
G.R.R. Colman	c Baker, b Calthorpe	30	b Calthorpe	3
F.C.G. Naumann	c Vincent, b Fairbairn	20	b Calthorpe	12
F.H. Knott	c Vincent, b Baker	27	c Wood, b Calthorpe	56
O.C. Bristowe	c Morrison, b Fairbairn	23	c Wood, b Lagden	8
B.G. von B. Mellé	c Vincent, b Baker	24	c Arnold, b Davies	9
W.G.K. Boswell	c Davies, b Fairbairn	5	c Morrison, b Calthorpe	36
E.A. Shaw	not out	57	c Arnold, b Baker	15
C.E.S. Rücker	b Davies	0	not out	2
P.H. Davies	st Wood, b Fairbairn	13	st Wood, b Calthorpe	5
EXTRAS	B 7, L-B 1, W 3, N-B 1	12	B 21, L-B 3, W 3	27
	TOTAL	239	TOTAL	253

CAMBRIDGE				
J.S.F. Morrison	b Davies	54	c Colman, b Mellé	1
A.C.P. Arnold	c Rücker, b Bristowe	22	c Davies, b Bristowe	0
R.B. Lagden	lbw, b Bristowe	20	c Knight, b Bristowe	19
H.G. Vincent	c Colman, b Bristowe	19	b Davies	3
G.E.C. Wood	b Davies	61	b Naumann	14
S.H. Saville	lbw, b Bristowe	3	c Knight, b Davies	0
G.B. Davies	b Bristowe	0	c Howell, b Bristowe	5
Hon. F.S.G. Calthorpe	c Mellé, b Davies	0	not out	16
G.A. Fairbairn	c Colman, b Boswell	13	c Mellé, b Naumann	0
K.H.C. Woodroffe	c Knight, b Mellé	9	b Naumann	0
E.C. Baker	not out	0	c Boswell, b Naumann	3
EXTRAS	B 18, L-B 5, W 1	24	B 12	12
	TOTAL	225	TOTAL	73

Cambridge bowling	OVERS	RUNS	WKTS	OVERS	RUNS	WKTS
Lagden	4	16	0	11	34	1
Baker	26	41	3	13	25	1
G.B. Davies	22	48	1	24	45	1
Calthorpe	12	33	2	23.4	43	5
Fairbairn	24.3	74	4	16	70	1
Woodroffe	7	15	0	5	9	1

Oxford bowling						
Mellé	9.2	20	1	5	4	1
Naumann	6	8	0	4.1	10	4
P.H. Davies	24	75	3	11	13	2
Bristowe	27	70	5	14	30	3
Rücker	7	11	0	—	—	—
Boswell	6	17	1	4	4	0

9
1919–1929
Post-war Quality

OXFORD *Return to sanity*

It is astonishing to record that some 2700 Oxonians lost their lives in the First World War, especially when one remembers that the pre-war undergraduate population numbered only about 3000. Six of those from the Varsity teams of 1905 gave their lives, including the two captains from the 1906 match, who fell in Flanders nine years after they had met at Lord's. The names of thirteen Oxford cricket blues are to be found on the Great War memorials in college chapels.

Happily there were many who had spent a year or two at Oxford before the war and returned after it. The mood was one of relief and there was a determination to recall the relaxed days of 1914. Geoffrey Bolton wrote of this time:

We were anxious to enjoy ourselves again. For those whose enjoyments included watching cricket the OUCC, desperate for funds, made things easy . . . we were besought to join – and we joined in droves. Watching cricket from the pavilion is far more fun than watching it from the ropes, as we were quick to appreciate. Memory can be deceptive, but as one looks back it seems that in 1919 the pavilion was always full.

Stanley Thompson, later Headmaster of Bloxham, and a prolific run-scorer who learned his cricket at Lancing, also recalls those days. He remembers that many joined the OUCC to receive coaching at the nets, even before the University term. He was one of some 2000 freshmen who flooded into Oxford at the war's end. It was impossible to give trials to all who deserved them; L.B. Blaxland, who later played for Derbyshire, had but one trial in his Oxford years; A.E.C. Cornwall, a notable Marlburian cricketer, never had one at all.

College cricket flourished to the extent that a knockout competition was organized. In 1922 the final of 'Cuppers' was played in The Parks between BNC, the eventual victors, and Oriel; the contest had to be completed at 10.00 a.m. on the morning of the University's match with Lancashire.

When fixtures were planned for 1919, what cricket might be possible was unknown, and all dates were provisional. Three old blues returned to Oxford and five to Cambridge. It was agreed that the war years should be discounted; thus, for example, F.C.G. Naumann of Oxford and the Hon. F.S.G. Calthorpe of Cambridge ranked as fourth-year men. The experience which D.J. Knight, Naumann and the captain M. Howell were able to bring was invaluable; all these later went on to play for Surrey.

There was this year the remarkable coincidence of two separate pairs of brothers playing on either side in the Varsity Match. Naumann's brother J.H. played in the Cambridge side alongside A.E.R. Gilligan, whose brother F.W. was an Oxford blue. Not only was Miles Howell a very good player, but he made a major contribution in re-establishing cricket and football at Oxford. For some reason *The Times* led bitter criticisms of Oxford and suggested that they had little chance against Cambridge, particularly when Cambridge trounced the same Sussex side which had comfortably defeated Oxford. An excellent match took place at Lord's and Oxford confounded their critics.

The years after the war saw a procession of fine cricketers going up to Oxford and Cambridge. Gilligan was never the powerful force that his brother Arthur was, but none the less in 1920 he was a good captain and an excellent wicket-keeper; over a period of years he appeared for Essex in the school holidays, but was lost to English cricket when he went to be Headmaster of Wanganui Grammar School in New Zealand.

In 1920 there were a number of strong characters to control. G.T.S. Stevens, who later helped England to regain the Ashes, had come up to Oxford with a considerable reputation, having played for the Gentlemen as a schoolboy. He was known not only as a fine leg-break bowler, close fielder and batsman, but as something of a wit. In his first match he enquired whether he might field in the place he had made famous, to which Gilligan replied, 'Yes, in the deep at both ends.' With Greville Stevens and R.C. Robertson-Glasgow in the side there can hardly have been a dull moment.

Early in the season Robertson-Glasgow earned his nickname when he bowled C. McGahey of Essex with a full toss. McGahey, on enquiry from his captain, pronounced, 'I was bowled by an old — I thought was dead two thousand years ago, called Robinson Crusoe.' The name 'Crusoe' stuck, and somehow suited such a fine cricketer and joyous writer on the game. In the very same match against Essex, D.R. Jardine, so well known as a courageous captain and batsman, took 6 for 6.

Cambridge had an equally good team and it was a tragedy that rain ruined the Varsity Match, despite extra play being agreed on Thursday, when, as Crusoe commented, 'the most interesting sight in that morning's play was the effect of the Cambridge Hawks Ball on the batting of Bettington'.

The year 1921 saw little change in the side, yet not much went right. It has been suggested that Jardine's hostility to the Australians dated from their match with Oxford. V.R. Price, the Oxford captain, had accepted a two-day rather than a three-day match, and when Jardine was 96 not out, with Oxford 174 for 1 in reply to the Australians' 300, it was felt that an extra over might have been allowed, but it was not. Among some remarkable feats was the Free Foresters' achievement in being set 420 to win and getting them in four hours. Another fine batting performance was Oxford's 644 for 8 on the first day of the Sussex match. At Lord's Oxford's limited bowling was soon put to the sword by a strong Cambridge batting side. Hubert Ashton (why did he never play for England?), A.P.F. Chapman and A.G. Doggart, the father of my co-author, were all outstanding, and Oxford deserved to lose.

Another disappointing year followed in 1922, the single discovery being T.B. Raikes, a Wykehamist; he took forty wickets. He and Robertson-Glasgow were batting in the Surrey match at The Oval when the latter played a ball to the deep field at the Pavilion End. Crusoe takes up the story:

. . . we ran one comfortably and when Tom asked if there was another I said 'yes', and we started for a second. Strange things then happened. As we were about to cross over, Tom suddenly turned round and scuttled back to his wicket. I followed him, but thinking this crease overcrowded, I set out for the other. Not to be outdone, Tom did the same. I beat him to it by a head. Meanwhile the fielders, driven temporarily insane by these goings-on, were having a private game of rounders. At length the ball reached Strudwick the wicket-keeper who took off the bails. It was one thing to remove the bails, another to know who was out. We had occupied both ends two or three times each. The umpires Bill Reeves and Frank Chester stood impotent with laughter and doubt. But Tom solved the problem by striding to the pavilion.

A cheerful incident to relieve a gloomy season.

The next year, 1923, was quite different; R.H. Bettington, a fine all-round sportsman who had blues at rugby and golf in addition to his four years in the cricket side, was the first Australian to captain Oxford, and a thoroughly inspiring leader he proved to be. After a lean year, he recovered his skills as an outstanding leg-break and googly bowler, and Stevens and Robertson-Glasgow were also back on form; these three took over a hundred and fifty wickets between them. A highly entertaining batsman, B.H. Lyon, a future captain of Gloucestershire, was in the side, as was C.H. Taylor, a freshman and stylist, who modelled his batting on D.J. Knight, from whom he had learnt so much at Westminster. Oxford won six matches, including their crushing defeat of Cambridge.

The 1924 side never fulfilled its potential; batting was strong, the bowling was ordinary, with Raikes taking most wickets and E.P. Hewetson, a fine all-round sportsman from Shrewsbury, returning the best figures. In this year and the subsequent ones contemporary accounts are critical of the Oxford fielding. Geoffrey Bolton does not mince words: 'There could be no question that in fielding Cambridge year after year outshone Oxford.'

Five matches were won, the most notable of which was a decisive victory at The Oval. Oxford were set 316 to make and won by four wickets, with J.L. Guise playing a truly splendid innings of 154 not out. Despite their reasonable record, Oxford never looked like holding Cambridge at Lord's.

There followed an injection of some very good players. E.R.T. Holmes, G.B. Legge – who both later played for England – and J.W. Greenstock all came from Malvern. I.A.W. Gilliat was an excellent wicket-keeper and a great character, who in a long career as a schoolmaster did much to advance Radley's cricket.

The 1926 season started strangely, with the matches against Kent and Middlesex being abandoned because of the General Strike. Most undergraduates reported to various centres, many of them becoming porters, dock workers, bus drivers and even some engine-drivers. Errol Holmes became a postman in Oxford, delivering mail in his open Darracq.

Jack Hobbs and Andy Sandham put on 428 for the first wicket in the Surrey match at the Oval. Johnnie Greenstock, who took forty-five wickets in the Oxford season, recalls the sense of admiration he felt as Hobbs steered and placed elegant strokes just beyond his reach in the covers.

Errol Holmes was captain in 1927, and he put the experience gained to good use during two spells as leader of Surrey. Errol said of himself: 'What success I had can, I think, be attributed to my natural desire to hit the ball. I hated being kept quiet.' The season was generally one of disappointments, but it did have its moments, as when Holmes and R.E.C. Butterworth put on 236 in an hour and a half to help Oxford to victory over the Free Foresters. P.V.F. Cazalet, better known as the trainer of 250 winners for Her Majesty the Queen Mother, was a good player but never showed his best form. Despite Holmes' fine battling century at Lord's, Cambridge were a better side.

Maurice McCanlis, the 1928 captain, missed all but a few matches through illness, and his absence was keenly felt. D.J. Hill Wood, who had never made the Eton eleven, batted with credit at Lord's, as did his bowler brother C.K., to save Oxford.

In the last season of the twenties Oxford undertook the heaviest programme ever; they played the South Africans and also ten of the counties. They won only twice, the bowling not being of great penetration. A.T. Barber was an excellent captain, A.M. Crawley a very fine attacking batsman who made a superb 204 against Northamptonshire, and H.M. Garland Wells was a genuine all-rounder. The highlight was Pataudi's batting at Lord's. This great player represented England, did great service for Worcestershire and was seen again on the first-class stage as captain of India in 1946. He went with D.R. Jardine on the 1932–3 tour of Australia; his elegantly compiled century in the First Test at Sydney helped England to a ten-wicket victory. He died in 1952 and the subsequent *Wisden* obituary ends: 'He left three daughters besides an 11-year-old son, who has shown promise of developing into a good cricketer.'

This was the year of the Wall Street crash, which marked the end of the roaring twenties. Oxford would never be the same again.

CAMBRIDGE *Ashtons inaugurate a purple patch*

In his poem 'The Islanders' Rudyard Kipling made a deprecating comment about 'flannelled fools' and 'muddied oafs'. Shortly afterwards, many of those he referred to had belied the poetic gibe by their performance on fields other than cricket grounds and football pitches – in France and Flanders. Many of the young platoon officers who did survive – and the odds were fairly short – went up to Oxford and Cambridge, in 1919 and 1920, with two distinct advantages. Firstly, they were older and more mature. Secondly and relatedly, those who had endured the shelling in the final push, or earlier, were not to be deterred by the fire power of Gregory and Macdonald, Australia's fast opening bowlers in 1921, or by their (alas!) less swift English counterparts.

There can never have been such a galaxy of talent as began assembling at Cambridge in the three years immediately after the Armistice. J.S.F. Morrison, a triple blue at cricket, golf and soccer before the war, was eminently suited to the task of welding together the abilities of the freshmen and of seniors like himself. The latter included G.E.C. Wood – a blue also at rugby and hockey, and destined to play for England as a fine wicket-keeper – who was elected secretary, and the Hon.

F.S.G. Calthorpe, later to captain Warwickshire, to tour twice with MCC teams and to found the County Cricketers' Golfing Society. The freshmen included a fine fast bowler from Dulwich, A.E.R. Gilligan – he took part in a tenth-wicket partnership with J.H. Naumann at Hove of 177, and in 1930, with Maurice Tate, he would bowl out South Africa for 30. He later moulded Sussex into a popular and excellent fielding side, and became President of both MCC and Sussex. Another freshman was an attractive batsman, Gilbert Ashton, eldest of three distinguished brothers who, like the Studds before them, captained Cambridge in successive years and earned the side the nickname 'Ashton Villa'. Included in the 1920 side, and later to be a distinguished Somerset batsman who was unlucky not to have been picked more often for England, was J.C.W. MacBryan; he acknowledged a special debt to Sammy Woods for having taught him to play.

The sides reached a peak in the spectacular victories of 1921 and 1922, but also produced several very fine performers later in the decade, who were to bring Light Blue victories in 1924, 1926, 1927 and, just into the next decade, 1930. The statistics of the 1921 and 1922 seasons deserve a place in this story. To wide national interest, and with considerable press coverage, Cambridge's record in 1921 was Played 12, Won 9, Lost 2, Drew 1, and in 1922 it read Played 13, Won 5, Lost 2, Drew 6. This record was achieved by strong leadership and fine all-round play.

By common acclaim – and here I must declare an interest, since he was my godfather – Hubert Ashton, the middle of three brothers whose exceptional contribution to the Corinthians as well as to Cambridge is well attested, was the finest Light Blue batsman of the early twenties. Had he not gone east to work in the Burmah Oil Company, he was a likely England captain, being worth his place both as a close-to-the-wicket fieldsman and as a captain and batsman. He was later knighted, and his career saw him become a popular and respected Member of Parliament for Chelmsford, a Church Commissioner, President of MCC in 1961, and much in demand for his native county of Essex.

The 1921 side also included Percy Chapman, whose brilliant left-handed stroke-play, fine catching and Adonis looks won him many admirers, and who not only, in 1924–5, toured Australia with A.E.R. Gilligan, but also took over from A.W. Carr as captain of England at The Oval in 1926, regaining the Ashes after a lengthy run of Australian supremacy.

Also good enough to play for England in one Test was 'Father' Marriott, who played first for Lancashire and later for Kent, when, at the end of the Dulwich term, he successfully teamed up with another fine leg-spinner, Tich Freeman. R.E.S. Wyatt recently confided to me his view that Marriott was the better bowler against the better players. Of the others, Jack Bryan went on an English tour; M.D. Lyon made two hundreds for the Gentlemen against the Players but batted number seven in the Cambridge side; Clem Gibson was a fine bowler, who played his part in the great defeat of the until then undefeated Australians in 1921 at Eastbourne, but was lost to English cricket through his subsequent life in the Argentine. (In 1959 the MCC tourists were delighted to meet him as the President of the Argentine Cricket Association.) Charles Fiddian-Green was a fine opening bat, and my father, Graham Doggart, who won a full England Association football cap in 1924 and was Chairman of the Football Association at his death, was a more than useful all-rounder. In all, the 1921 side must surely run the exceptional 1878 side a very close second when the quality of Light Blue cricket is assessed.

Hubert Ashton captained the 1922 side and found three freshmen bowlers who took 151 wickets between them in the Cambridge season. Of these, Gubby (now Sir George) Allen would have an influence on cricket comparable to that of Sir Pelham Warner, even surpassing it. Despite his not playing a full season after leaving university, he was good enough to captain England for three series, going two up in Australia in 1936–7 before the rub of the green went against him. He was genuinely fast, with an action answering to classical requirements, and he was a talented batsman also, as his regular visits to Fenner's in the late forties and early fifties showed. His contribution to cricket over fifty years, as player, thinker, selector, administrator, President and Treasurer of the MCC and friend of many, has been unique.

In 1922, Allen's Cambridge haul was 49 wickets; and his feat was statistically surpassed by P.A. Wright, who took 52 wickets – in his three years at Cambridge he took 157 wickets in all – and by F.B.R. Browne with 50. Browne was known from his run-up as 'Tishy', after a horse that crossed its legs at the start of a race. I am extremely fortunate in possessing an original 'Tishy', drawn for me in person by the late Tom Webster.

Cambridge boasted several other players in the decade under discussion who would go on to greater things in the cricket world – three especially, and one other whose cricketing brilliance played second fiddle to his golfing career, both as player and as writer. This was Leonard Crawley, who hit a golf ball further than any other amateur, won a rackets blue, played three years in the cricket side, making 98 at Lord's in 1925, and in 1932 averaged 51.87 for Essex.

Tom Lowry, who captained the Light Blues to victory in 1924, qualified for Somerset – it is said that the authorities cast a benevolent eye over the fact that the Wellington of his birth-place was thousands of miles away from the Wellington he adopted – and was a successful captain of New Zealand as well as a forcing batsman. One of his sisters married Percy Chapman, and the other Reg Bettington, who played for New South Wales after leaving Oxford.

K.S. Duleepsinhji, 'Duleep' as he was affectionately known, Ranji's nephew, who arrived as a freshman from Cheltenham with a fine schoolboy record and scored 75 in the 1925 University Match as a freshman, made a considerable impact as a person as well as a player, until a breakdown in his health forced him to leave cricket – at a time when Sussex were within reach of the Championship. Perhaps his most treasured memory is his 254 not out against Middlesex at Fenner's, which still remains a record; or his 333 for Sussex against Northamptonshire, which inaugurated the new score-board at Hove; or his 173 on his first appearance for England against Australia, at Lord's in 1931. When he was eventually caught in the outfield off a rash stroke, his uncle is said to have remarked: 'He always was a careless boy.' We have reason to be grateful for the charm of his carelessness!

Few cricketers have been as dynamic and enthusiastic as the third of this trio, Walter Robins, who came up from Highgate with an outstanding reputation and had a fine record in the three University Matches of 1926, 1927 and 1928. He was an all-rounder of class, always in the game, whether as an attacking batsman, a bowler of leg-breaks and googlies, or a cover-point who patrolled his area with speed and a reliable pair of hands. He played in nineteen Tests, captaining the home series against New Zealand in 1937, and transformed the Middlesex side immediately before the war leading them to victory in the Championships of 1947 ('O my Compton and my Edrich long ago'!) and 1950. He served as an England selector for seven years in three stints, being chairman for three, and he was also a talented right-winger for the Corinthians.

The top three names in the Cambridge batting averages of 1925 were: H.J. Enthoven, who that year in the match against Oxford equalled William Yardley's special feat of scoring two hundreds in University Matches, and went on to play effectively for Middlesex; K.S. Duleepsinhji, who has been discussed already; and E.W. Dawson, a stylish opening bat from Eton, whose Cambridge side of 1927 defeated the New Zealanders (see scores below), and who later became an outstanding captain of Leicestershire and went with MCC sides to both South Africa and New Zealand, as well as to the West Indies with Sir Julien Cahn in 1929. His last innings for his county was a faultless 91 against the Australians in 1934.

PLAYED AT CAMBRIDGE, 18, 19, 20 MAY 1927
New Zealanders 315 (M.L. Page 134) and 205 (R.C. Blunt 72)
Cambridge 255 (F.J. Seabrook 106, E.W. Dawson 57) and 267 for 5.
Cambridge won by 5 wickets.

The success of the 1925 side captained by the Harrovian Tris Bennett (its record was: Played 13, Won 6, Lost 3, Drew 4), owed much to having two bowlers who took fifty wickets each in the Cambridge season, and one who took forty-one. The first two were R.J.O. Meyer, an exciting and ebullient cricketer, later a bowler of 'Spedigue droppers', who would captain Somerset and found Millfield School, and who maintained a steady length, slightly varied pace and swerve, combined with speed off the pitch and break from off or leg; and Enthoven, who bowled medium pace from the other end and was showing himself to be one of the most improved all-rounders in the country. The third medium-pacer was S.T. Jagger, who played some games for Worcestershire – until it was discovered that he was not qualified for them! He also played rugby fives, and created a fine tradition in squash rackets at Lancing, where he became a house-master. His 4 for 34 made an important contribution to Cambridge's victory by 34 runs in 1926. It should be added that a fourth medium-pacer for Cambridge, R.G.H. Lowe, who also won a soccer blue and one amateur international cap, had his best season in 1925, taking thirty-two wickets and coming third in the Cambridge bowling averages.

Top of the Cambridge bowling averages in 1927 was M.J.C. Allom, who brought the ball off the ground at above medium pace and who took sixty wickets at 22 apiece. He would later play in five Tests, and for Surrey and the Gentlemen, but injury was to prevent his making as great a contribution as he might have done. He was made President of both MCC and Surrey. Top of the Cambridge batting averages in 1928 was E.T. Killick, the second Pauline to win a Cambridge blue, the first having been A.K. Judd in the previous year. (It was Judd's improving second innings of 124 that helped to set up the Light Blue win.) Tom Killick had an average of 104.44 in his last year at school and was chosen to lead the Public Schools against the Australians at Lord's. He made 31 on a difficult pitch. One of his finest innings was his 206 for Middlesex against Warwickshire in 1931, his opening stand with Greville Stevens producing 277 runs. While still in residence in 1929 – the year he made scores of 201 against Essex, 200 not out against Glamorgan and 103 against Surrey – he twice opened for England with Herbert Sutcliffe against South Africa. He was a graceful striker of the ball and a top-rate fielder, Alas, he died at the age of forty-six during a diocesan match between the clergy of St Albans (he was vicar of Bishop's Stortford) and the clergy of Coventry.

Another delightful cricketer who appeared in the Cambridge side of 1929 was Bryan Valentine. He clinched his place with 101 in 85 minutes against a Free Forester attack that included five Cambridge blues in Allom, Meyer, Marriott, Falcon and Graham Doggart. By the mid-thirties he was a potential England player, who scored at an average of fifty runs an hour. Because of the strength of England's batting, he went on two tours only, to India in 1933–4 and to South Africa in 1938–9. In the Second Test in South Africa he made 112 in 2 hours 40 minutes; and in the previous summer he had made 242 for Kent against Leicestershire at Oakham. He made thirty-five centuries in all, and was one of those cricketers for whom the war came at a critical time in his career. His bubbling enjoyment of life was a joy.

It is always pleasing when the captain and secretary both do well, and that was so in 1929. Cambridge's captain was Maurice Turnbull, of Downside and Trinity, who was sadly killed in action in Normandy, serving with the Welsh Guards, on 5 August 1944; and the secretary was J.T. Morgan, who had excited Carthusians by coming in as a fifteen-year-old against Harrow, when the score was 20 for 5, and making 148. Turnbull, like Killick, had an average of over 50 in 1929, and Morgan at Lord's played an astonishing innings of 149, which won high praise from the pundits. In the following year he was equally to be praised for a declaration, both critical and criticized, that led to a swingeing Light Blue victory.

Turnbull was a magnificent sportsman, good enough to have played cricket for England, and rugby and hockey for Wales. He was a fine batsman and an equally fine captain, who raised Glamorgan from the doldrums in both cricketing and financial terms. He had wide interests and could talk knowledgeably about them, not without a subtle sense of humour. With Maurice Allom he wrote *The Book of the Two Maurices* and *The Two Maurices Again*, giving accounts of their tours in New Zealand and South Africa. These are highly civilized books, of which the world has need.

1919

It was a delight for players and spectators alike to be renewing this historic fixture in the first year of peace. The standard was only a little lower than that in 1914, thanks largely to the presence in the match of eight old blues – M. Howell (capt.), D.J. Knight and F.C.G. Naumann for Oxford, and J.S.F. Morrison (capt.), G.E.C. Wood, G.A. Fairbairn, J.H. Naumann and the Hon. F.S.G. Calthorpe for Cambridge – and to the extra maturity of many of the players.

Oxford won the toss on a gloomy day for cricket and batted themselves into a winning position with a total of 387, built on a faultless, though unexciting, 170 by the Reptonian Miles Howell in five hours. He was trebly supported: by a stylish 35 from the Malvernian Donald Knight, one of the most attractive batsmen of the day, who played in two Tests against Warwick Armstrong's Australians; by a useful 40 from another Reptonian, R.L. Holdsworth; and by a swashbuckling 70 from Frank Gilligan, eldest of the three cricketing brothers, in ninety minutes. G.A. Fairbairn, from Geelong Grammar, took 5 for 110 in thirty-three overs and four balls.

For Cambridge, the Cheltonian Wood and the Rugbeian C.P. Johnstone, a stylish left-hander who played for Kent, put on 116 for the first-wicket partnership; but this favourable position had vanished soon after lunch, G.V. Pearse, from Maritzburg, and F.C.G. Naumann, from Malvern, achieving a breakthrough. The tail wagged, Fairbairn and the Rugbeian G.A. Rotherham ensuring the respectable score of 280. Oxford were 98 for 3 at the close, Knight again playing well.

It was a splendid final day, made for Light Blue supporters by Arthur Gilligan's taking six wickets for 52, including Knight's, so that Oxford reached 168, but no more. Wood's wicket-keeping earned the highest praise – his stumping of Naumann on the leg side was described as dazzling – and he was to go on to play three Tests for England against South Africa in 1924. The match was made for Dark Blue supporters by the fine bowling, again, of Frank Naumann, whose 6 for 81 swung the match. The early Cambridge batsmen did not stay long enough to influence matters, and it was left to the Cheltonian G.P. Brooke-Taylor and the Wykehamist Gilbert Ashton to raise Light Blue spirits, followed by brave hitting from Fairbairn. The brilliant running-out of Brooke-Taylor by Howell was the turning point, and Oxford won by 45 runs.

Even more important than the result was the fact that, despite having to play two-day matches in the run-up to the encounter at Lord's (this was an experiment in first-class cricket which lasted only one season), University cricket had got off to a flying start after a war which had more than decimated the flower of British youth. One final point deserves a mention – the fact that the brothers Naumann were on opposite sides, as were the Gilligan brothers. This was not only a happy chance that is unlikely ever to be repeated, but is also indicative of both the kinship that often bound the two teams and the rivalry that over the years this historic series has evoked. That rivalry was reflected by 1919 in the closeness of the results over the eighty-one matches played since the inception of the series in 1827. Of those contests Cambridge had won thirty-eight and Oxford thirty-five, with eight matches drawn.

OXFORD	First innings		Second innings	
M. Howell	*st* Wood, *b* Fairbairn	170	*c* Wood, *b* Gilligan	11
D.J. Knight	*c* Naumann, *b* Rotherham	35	*b* Gilligan	78
F.A. Waldock	*b* Fairbairn	2	*c* Morrison, *b* Fairbairn	3
F.C.G. Naumann	*c* Calthorpe, *b* Fairbairn	15	*st* Wood, *b* Gilligan	21
R.L. Holdsworth	*c* Naumann, *b* Rotherham	40	*b* Fairbairn	11
H.P. Ward	*c* Naumann, *b* Rotherham	6	*lbw, b* Fairbairn	4
G.F. Bell	*b* Calthorpe	10	*b* Gilligan	2
F.W. Gilligan	*c* Brooke-Taylor, *b* Johnstone	70	*run out*	14
G.V. Pearse	*c* Gilligan, *b* Fairbairn	12	*c* Wood, *b* Gilligan	0
V.R. Price	*not out*	9	*b* Gilligan	4
P.W. Rücker	*c and b* Fairbairn	0	*not out*	3
EXTRAS	B 12, L-B 5, N-B 1	18	B 15, L-B 2	17
	TOTAL	387	TOTAL	168

CAMBRIDGE				
G.E.C. Wood	*c* Waldock, *b* Naumann	62	*lbw, b* Naumann	28
C.P. Johnstone	*c* Gilligan, *b* Pearse	78	*lbw, b* Price	13
J.H. Naumann	*run out*	5	*b* Naumann	23
G. Wilson	*b* Naumann	2	*c and b* Naumann	12
J.S.F. Morrison	*c* Bell, *b* Pearse	18	*c* Ward, *b* Naumann	11
G.P. Brooke-Taylor	*c* Knight, *b* Naumann	6	*run out*	55
G. Ashton	*lbw, b* Naumann	7	*c* Naumann, *b* Waldock	43
G.A. Fairbairn	*not out*	47	*b* Naumann	32
Hon. F.S.G. Calthorpe	*b* Naumann	13	*c* Gilligan, *b* Price	0
G.A. Rotherham	*b* Pearse	36	*c* Price, *b* Naumann	5
A.E.R. Gilligan	*st* Gilligan, *b* Pearse	3	*not out*	0
EXTRAS	B 2, L-B 1	3	B 7, w 1	8
	TOTAL	280	TOTAL	230

Cambridge bowling	OVERS	RUNS	WKTS	OVERS	RUNS	WKTS
A.E.R. Gilligan	24	77	0	22.3	52	6
Calthorpe	36	77	1	14	29	0
J.H. Naumann	6	27	0	—	—	—
Fairbairn	33.4	110	5	19	37	3
Rotherham	22	57	3	6	22	0
Johnstone	12	21	1	6	11	0

Oxford bowling						
Price	15	53	0	16	61	2
Waldock	12	32	0	6	26	1
Rücker	12	50	0	3	12	0
Pearse	20	66	4	17	42	0
F.C.G. Naumann	25	76	5	25.2	81	6

Two views of Lord's, the home of the match since 1845
ABOVE The lunch interval in the 1898 match. The view
is from Verity's Pavilion, opened in 1890, towards
the old Tennis Court and Tavern.

BELOW Teams and spectators, of whom a key is extant,
in an Edwardian tableau during the 1908 match.
The view is towards what is now the Warner Stand.

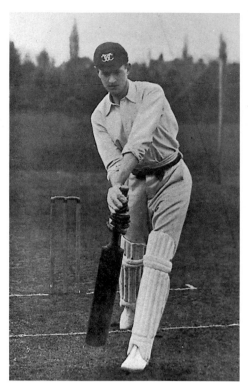

The 'bosey', or googly, has its welcome place in the game's history. Here its inventor, B.J.T. Bosanquet, who played for Oxford from 1898–1900, conceals his secret.

R.E. ('Tip') Foster, one of the Fosters who won Worcestershire the nick-name 'Fostershire', played for Oxford from 1897–1900 and made 287 against Australia at Sydney in 1903.

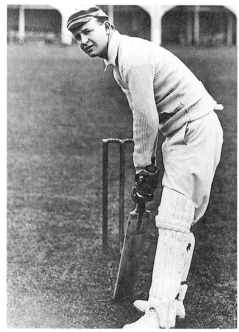

Donald Knight here shows the elegance of style that was evident in his various innings for Oxford (1914 and 1919), Surrey and England.

Plum Warner, knighted in 1937, was an Oxford player in 1895–96, and was for many years the doyen of MCC and Middlesex cricket.

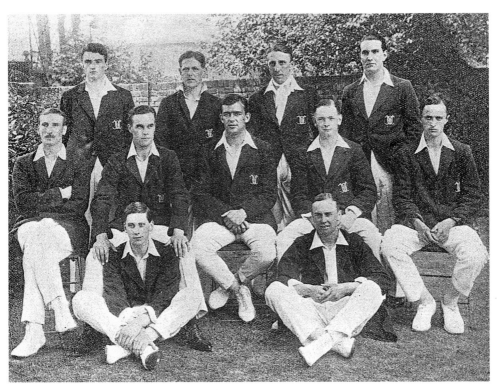

The 1923 Oxford side captained by R.H. Bettington
BACK ROW E.P. Hewetson M. Patten B.H. Lyon T.B. Raikes
MIDDLE ROW D.R. Jardine G.T.S. Stevens R.H. Bettington C.H. Knott R.C. Robertson-Glasgow
FRONT ROW C.H. Taylor H.O. Hopkins

The 1939 Oxford side captained by E.J.H. Dixon
BACK ROW A.J.B. Marsham R. Sale P.H. Blagg S. Pether J. Stanning G. Evans
FRONT ROW E.D.R. Eagar D.H. Macindoe E.J.H. Dixon J.M. Lomas R.B. Proud

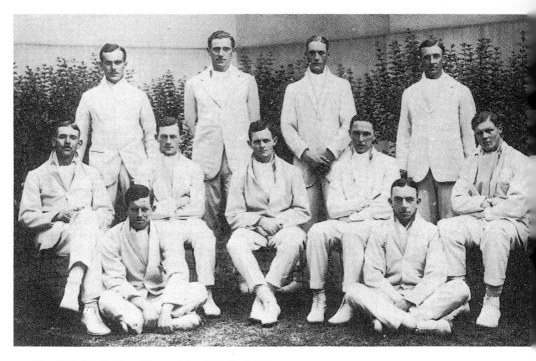

The 1921 Cambridge side captained by G. Ashton
BACK ROW A.G. Doggart M.D. Lyon C.A. Fiddian-Green J.L. Bryan
MIDDLE ROW C.S. Marriott H. Ashton G. Ashton C.H. Gibson A.P.F. Chapman
FRONT ROW C.T. Ashton R.G. Evans

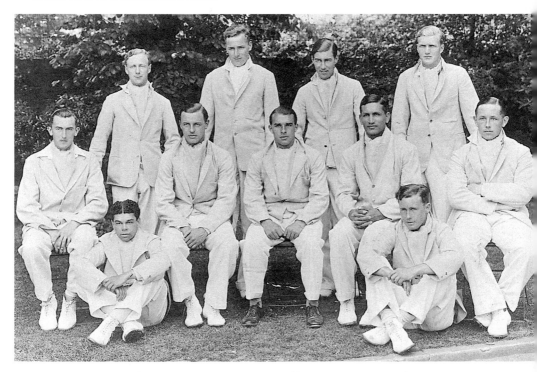

The 1935 Cambridge side captained by G.W. Parker
BACK ROW N.S. Hotchkin W. Wooller N.W.D. Yardley M. Tindall
MIDDLE ROW J.W.T. Grimshaw H.T. Bartlett G.W. Parker M. Jahangir Khan S.C. Griffith
FRONT ROW J.H. Cameron P.A. Gibb

Hon. F. S. Jackson

A Chevallier Tayler 1905.

ABOVE LEFT Gilbert
Jessop's well-known title,
'The Croucher', seems
applicable to his fielding
stance in this Chevallier
Tayler picture as well as to
his batting stance.

ABOVE RIGHT The classical
batsmanship of F.S. Jackson
– for Harrow, Cambridge
(1890–93), Yorkshire and
England – is well caught in
this Chevallier Tayler
picture dated 1905,
Jackson's heroic year.

LEFT Ranji's speed of foot,
eye and wrist, reflected in
this photograph, was the
key to his success for
Cambridge (1893), Sussex
and England.

ABOVE LEFT Talented nephew of talented uncle, Duleep, who played for Cambridge in 1925, '26 and '28 and captained Sussex in 1931 and '32, shows here what a fine hooker he was.

ABOVE RIGHT Proof of Gubby (now Sir George) Allen's fine classical action. His all-round success at Eton and Cambridge (1922–23), and for Middlesex and England, is well-documented, not least in E.W. Swanton's biography.

RIGHT Two perfect positions! The batsman is Don Bradman; the wicket-keeper is Billy Griffith, of Cambridge (1935), Sussex and England, and later Secretary of MCC.

ABOVE LEFT Errol Holmes in full cry in a county match, playing with that *joie de vivre* he showed at Malvern and Oxford (1925–27), and for Surrey and England.

ABOVE RIGHT D.R. Jardine wearing the Harlequin cap that endeared itself to the Sydney 'Hill'. His record as a batsman for Winchester, Oxford (1920, '21 and '23), Surrey and England – and as captain of all but Oxford – is an impressive one.

RIGHT Greville Stevens, an outstanding all-rounder while still at University College School, made a strong contribution to Oxford (1920–23), Middlesex and England.

ABOVE Ian Peebles will be remembered as a coach at Aubrey Faulkner's school, as a class spin-bowler for Oxford (1930), Middlesex and England, and as an accomplished writer.

The only father and son to have captained England – until the Cowdreys – were Frank Mann (ABOVE LEFT) and George Mann (ABOVE RIGHT), here seen in aggressive mood. There was a gap of twenty-nine years between their Cambridge debuts, and they both captained Middlesex in a post-war era.

The Oxford counterpart to the Manns is the two Nawabs of Pataudi, both centurions at Lord's (an understatement in father's case!) and both captains of India. Father (LEFT) also played for England.

5, 6, 7, 8 July
At Lord's# 1920

Match drawn

The weather won decisively, since not a ball could be bowled on either of the first two days, and on the third day only two hours of play were possible. Following the 1888 precedent, play was agreed on the fourth day – but only up to five o'clock because of preparations for the Eton and Harrow match. The curtailment was especially sad since both sides were strong in all departments of the game.

Oxford batted and scored 117 for 1 by the close, thanks largely to the fine off-side play, despite the slowness of the pitch, of the Cliftonian A.F. Bickmore, assisted by the Australian

R.H. Bettington. On the second day, forceful hitting by G.T.S. Stevens, the outstanding schoolboy player from University College School, helped the Dark Blues to 193. C.H. Gibson, from Eton, took 3 for 66 in 32 overs, and C.S. Marriott, from St Columba's, who turned the ball sharply on the drying turf, 7 for 69 in 35.2 overs.

Cambridge's innings was curtailed by a shower in the lunch interval, but they eventually reached 161 for 9, G.E.C. Wood, from Cheltenham, and A.E.R. Gilligan, from Dulwich, both scoring thirties. The rain had certainly had the last laugh.

OXFORD

D.R. Jardine	c MacBryan, b Marriott	13
A.F. Bickmore	b Marriott	66
R.H. Bettington	b Gibson	35
L.P. Hedges	c H. Ashton, b Gibson	0
R.L. Holdsworth	b Gibson	0
F.W. Gilligan	c Johnstone, b Marriott	11
G.T.S. Stevens	c Chapman, b Marriott	39
F.A. Waldock	b Marriott	2
C.H.L. Skeet	b Marriott	6
V.R. Price	b Marriott	10
R.C. Robertson-Glasgow	not out	2
EXTRAS	B 5, L-B 4	9
TOTAL		193

CAMBRIDGE

C.P. Johnstone	b Bettington	14
G.E.C. Wood	c Skeet, b Stevens	30
G. Ashton	c Hedges, b Bettington	9
H. Ashton	b Robertson-Glasgow	0
G.P. Brooke-Taylor	b Stevens	17
J.C.W. MacBryan	st Gilligan, b Bettington	5
A.P.F. Chapman	run out	27
N.E. Partridge	run out	7
A.E.R. Gilligan	not out	35
C.H. Gibson	b Stevens	2
C.S. Marriott	not out	3
EXTRAS	B 12	12
TOTAL (9 WKTS)		161

Cambridge bowling	OVERS	RUNS	WKTS
Gibson	32	66	3
Partridge	13	34	0
Marriott	35.2	69	7
A.E.R. Gilligan	9	15	0

Oxford bowling			
Robertson-Glasgow	17	45	1
Bettington	21	64	3
Stevens	7	18	3
Price	3	16	0
Jardine	2	6	0

1921

Cambridge showed themselves a class above Oxford, and right from the start they called the tune. Gilbert Ashton's superior captaincy, and the fine batting of the Light Blues against an attack whose sting was drawn early on, clinched victory by an innings and 24 runs. Cambridge began quietly and safely, shown the way by the stylish J.L. Bryan. But it was the middle Ashton brother, Hubert, who gave a delightful exhibition of controlled stroke-play in making 118, supported by a partnership between his brother Claude and A.P.F. Chapman. Late in the day A.G. Doggart and C.H. Gibson made light of the tired bowling, and by close of play Cambridge had reached 415 for 9.

The crowd on the second day was comparatively small as Gilbert Ashton declared and Oxford started unconvincingly, until R.L. Holdsworth and L.P. Hedges put together the one main stand. C.S. Marriott, with 5 for 44, and Gibson, with 3 for 44, bowled wonderfully well with spin and seam respectively, to dismiss the Dark Blues for 162.

Following on, Oxford fared little better, except for A.F. Bickmore who drove well until bowled by Doggart. Their eventual total was 229, the wickets being shared.

CAMBRIDGE	First innings		Second innings	
J.L. Bryan	c and b Stevens	62		
C.A. Fiddian-Green	c Lowndes, b Stevens	17		
G. Ashton	c Bettington, b Price	12		
H. Ashton	c Bickmore, b Price	118		
A.P.F. Chapman	c Bettington, b Jardine	45		
C.T. Ashton	b Bettington	48		
M.D. Lyon	st Neser, b Bettington	9		
A.G. Doggart	b Jardine	45		
C.H. Gibson	not out	43		
R.G. Evans	not out	0		
C.S. Marriott	did not bat			
EXTRAS	B 9, L-B 2, W 1, N-B 4	16		
	TOTAL (8 WKTS DEC.)	415		

OXFORD				
D.R. Jardine	c Chapman, b Gibson	5	lbw, b Evans	18
A.F. Bickmore	b Gibson	6	b Doggart	57
R.L. Holdsworth	c Fiddian-Green, b Marriott	45	c Lyon, b Gibson	9
W.G.L.F. Lowndes	c Lyon, b Evans	4	c Chapman, b Bryan	3
H.P. Ward	c Doggart, b Evans	29	c Fiddian-Green, b C.T. Ashton	39
L.P. Hedges	c G. Ashton, b Gibson	36	lbw, b Bryan	26
G.T.S. Stevens	b Marriott	0	c Evans, b Gibson	21
R.H. Bettington	b Marriott	8	c Lyon, b Gibson	31
V.H. Neser	b Marriott	2	c Fiddian-Green, b Marriott	10
V.R. Price	b Marriott	12	lbw, b Marriott	8
R.C. Robertson-Glasgow	not out	0	not out	1
EXTRAS	B 9, L-B 6	15	B 1, L-B 4, N-B 1	6
	TOTAL	162	TOTAL	229

Oxford bowling	OVERS	RUNS	WKTS	OVERS	RUNS	WKTS
Price	30	107	2			
Robertson-Glasgow	27	75	0			
Lowndes	8	25	0			
Stevens	20	75	2			
Bettington	31	90	2			
Jardine	10	27	2			

Cambridge bowling						
Gibson	21	44	3	25	43	3
Evans	7	35	2	15	42	1
Marriott	26.4	44	5	29.4	67	2
Chapman	5	10	0	6	23	0
Doggart	6	14	0	5	22	1
Bryan	—	—	—	3	18	2
C.T. Ashton	—	—	—	3	8	1

10, 11, 12 July
At Lord's

1922

*Cambridge won by
an innings and 100 runs*

Hopes that this would be a Homeric contest were sadly dashed, and this turned out to be a one-sided affair, in which Cambridge led from start to finish and the eventual margin was an innings and 100 runs. Oxford, it must be said, were handicapped by the absence of their best batsman, the Wykehamist D.R. Jardine, and by the fact that their talented captain, G.T.S. Stevens, had had to nurse himself earlier in the season because of illness.

After considerable rain the previous week, the pitch was too soft to help the bowlers, and on winning the toss, Hubert Ashton, the Light Blue captain, elected to bat. By lunch the openers, C.A. Fiddian-Green and W.W. Hill-Wood, had managed only sixty runs, but after lunch, first Hill-Wood and A.G. Doggart put on 118 in an hour and fifty minutes, and then the captain and Percy Chapman batted steadily to the close. On the second morning Chapman reached a cavalier century just before lunch, during which Ashton, who was 90 not out, denied himself the cachet of joining William Yardley as a scorer of two hundreds in successive contests at Lord's. The Wykehamist T.B. Raikes took 3 for 65 in no less than forty-four overs.

For Oxford L.P. Hedges and Stevens played well, but G.O. Allen and P.A. Wright proved irresistible, and Oxford were bowled out for 222 and 81, Allen having match figures of 9 for 78.

CAMBRIDGE	First innings		Second innings
C.A. Fiddian-Green	*b* Raikes	23	
W.W. Hill-Wood	*c* Lyon, *b* Raikes	81	
A.G. Doggart	*b* Raikes	71	
H. Ashton	*not out*	90	
G.O. Shelmerdine	*c* Stevens, *b* Bettington	13	
A.P.F. Chapman	*not out*	102	
EXTRAS	B 15, L-B 4, W 1, N-B 3	23	
	TOTAL (4 WKTS DEC.)	403	

C.T. Ashton, M.D. Lyon, G.O. Allen, P.A. Wright, and F.B.R. Browne did not bat.

OXFORD

R.H. Bettington	*lbw, b* Browne	21	*lbw, b* Wright	1
F.H. Barnard	*c* Doggart, *b* Wright	22	*b* Wright	5
R.L. Holdsworth	*c* H. Ashton, *b* Browne	10	*b* Allen	4
B.H. Lyon	*c* C.T. Ashton, *b* Browne	0	*b* Allen	0
L.P. Hedges	*c* H. Ashton, *b* Allen	44	*lbw, b* Wright	0
G.T.S. Stevens	*b* Wright	41	*b* Browne	29
C.H. Knott	*b* Allen	13	*b* Allen	4
V.R. Price	*b* Allen	1	*lbw, b* Allen	0
M. Patten	*c* Lyon, *b* Allen	8	*c* Allen, *b* Hill-Wood	3
R.C. Robertson-Glasgow	*c* H. Ashton, *b* Allen	5	*not out*	11
T.B. Raikes	*not out*	19	*b* Hill-Wood	12
EXTRAS	B 21, L-B 17	38	B 9, L-B 3	12
	TOTAL	222	TOTAL	81

Oxford bowling	OVERS	RUNS	WKTS	OVERS	RUNS	WKTS
Raikes	44	65	3			
Price	17	61	0			
Robertson-Glasgow	43.1	97	0			
Bettington	44	92	1			
Stevens	19	65	0			

Cambridge bowling						
Allen	33.1	60	5	9	18	4
Wright	30	41	2	11	13	3
Browne	34	35	3	6	18	1
Hill-Wood	16	36	0	2.1	3	2
Doggart	6	2	0	5	17	0
C.T Ashton	3	10	0	—	—	—

1923

Oxford this year took devastating revenge for the heavy defeats of 1921 and 1922 by winning by an innings and a massive 227 runs. They looked the more convincing side and were well led by R.H. Bettington, but Cambridge suffered heavily from the injury to their best bowler, G.O. Allen, and from a thunderstorm which ruined the wicket. It was admirably exploited by two class spinners, Bettington and G.T.S. Stevens – made by his captain to bowl 'offers' – who took eighteen wickets between them for 125.

The Dark Blues were 130 for 1 at lunch, in marked contrast to Cambridge the previous year, thanks to a good partnership between C.H. Taylor and D.R. Jardine. Jardine went to a magnificent catch by Claude Ashton at slip, but Taylor went on to make a cultured 109, scoring equally well on the off and the on. Two further partnerships, the first between H.O. Hopkins, from St Peter's, Adelaide, and the Tonbridgian C.H. Knott, and the second between R.C. Robertson-Glasgow, from Charterhouse, and E.P. Hewetson, from Shrewsbury, set the seal on a successful Dark Blue day. Hewetson's innings was Jessop-like, as his partner has eloquently described in '*46 not out*', including one six off R. Aird, a future MCC Secretary, which went clean over block D and on to a lawn tennis court.

The scorecard tells the story of the mastery of the Oxford bowlers, and of Bettington's 8 for 66, following Stevens' earlier 6 for 20.

OXFORD	First innings		Second innings	
G.T.S. Stevens	c Lowry, b Wright	14		
C.H. Taylor	c Lowry, b Wright	109		
D.R. Jardine	c Ashton, b Wright	39		
B.H. Lyon	lbw, b Tomlinson	14		
H.O. Hopkins	run out	42		
C.H. Knott	b Tomlinson	42		
R.H. Bettington	lbw, b Wright	12		
R.C. Robertson-Glasgow	c Allen, b Enthoven	53		
E.P. Hewetson	c Aird, b Ashton	57		
T.B. Raikes	c Aird, b Enthoven	16		
M. Patten	not out	0		
EXTRAS	B 23, N-B 1	24		
	TOTAL	422		

CAMBRIDGE				
C.T. Bennett	b Stevens	5	b Bettington	5
H.F. Bagnall	b Stevens	9	b Bettington	4
G.O. Allen	b Raikes	8	lbw, b Stevens	28
T.C. Lowry	c Lyon, b Stevens	1	c Stevens, b Bettington	3
C.T. Ashton	b Stevens	15	b Bettington	21
R. Aird	c Lyon, b Stevens	1	b Bettington	5
L.G. Crawley	st Patten, b Bettington	1	c Bettington, b Robertson-Glasgow	20
H.J. Enthoven	b Bettington	2	c and b Bettington	16
W.J.V. Tomlinson	c Knott, b Bettington	4	c Taylor, b Bettington	19
N.B. Sherwell	c and b Stevens	8	b Bettington	0
P.A. Wright	not out	1	not out	5
EXTRAS	L-B 2, N-B 2	4	B 10	10
	TOTAL	59	TOTAL	136

Cambridge bowling	OVERS	RUNS	WKTS		OVERS	RUNS	WKTS
Allen	15	37	0				
Wright	38	113	4				
Enthoven	14	45	2				
Ashton	28	92	1				
Tomlinson	23	79	2				
Aird	7	32	0				

Oxford bowling	OVERS	RUNS	WKTS		OVERS	RUNS	WKTS
Robertson-Glasgow	3	4	0		10	22	1
Raikes	7	12	1		6	18	0
Stevens	14.3	20	6		11	20	1
Bettington	10	19	3		14.4	66	8

7, 8, 9 July
At Lord's

1924

*Cambridge won by
9 wickets*

The first day's play, which did not start until twenty past twelve, went in Cambridge's favour after Oxford won the toss and batted. They were 10 for 3 wickets after half an hour, including that of the previous year's centurion for nought. The one stand of note was between F.H. Barnard, from Charterhouse, and H.W.F. Franklin, from Christ's Hospital; eight of the side mustered a mere 16 runs between them. By the close of play Cambridge had reached 181 for 4, T.C. Lowry giving a brilliant display of aggressive batting in scoring 68 in less than an hour. On the second day Cambridge carried their score to 361,

thanks to a spirited hundred from the Harrovian H.J. Enthoven in a little over two hours. He received useful support from H.M. Austin, from Melbourne G.S. – he would be in the 1924 Australian Olympics team – and the Tonbridgian N.B. Sherwell. The Wykehamist J.L. Guise was brought into an undistinguished Dark Blue attack late in the day and took 4 for 19.

Oxford batted more resolutely in the second innings, and escape seemed a possibility. On the third morning, however, the Wellingburian P.A. Wright bowled superbly.

OXFORD	First innings			Second innings	
C.H. Taylor	c Shirley, b White	0		run out	26
J.E. Frazer	b Shirley	5		c Shirley, b White	20
J.L. Guise	c Sherwell, b White	21		b Wright	50
K.G. Blaikie	b Shirley	0		c Mann, b Austin	48
F.H. Barnard	b White	61		b Wright	0
C.H. Knott	b Meyer	3		st Sherwell, b Wright	18
H.W.F. Franklin	not out	29		c and b Wright	4
E.H. Sinclair	b Wright	2		b Wright	37
E.P. Hewetson	b White	1		c Shirley, b Austin	18
T.B. Raikes	c Dawson, b Austin	5		not out	0
G.E.B. Abell	run out	0		st Sherwell, b Wright	10
EXTRAS	B 2, L-B 3, N-B 1	6		B 10, L-B 4, N-B 3	17
	TOTAL	133		TOTAL	248

CAMBRIDGE					
W.R. Shirley	run out	15			
E.W. Dawson	b Blaikie	20		not out	7
T.C. Lowry	c Barnard, b Sinclair	68			
L.G. Crawley	c Hewetson, b Sinclair	8			
J.E.F. Mann	b Hewetson	21		not out	12
H.M. Austin	lbw, b Sinclair	51			
H.J. Enthoven	c Franklin, b Guise	104			
N.B. Sherwell	c Abell, b Guise	29		b Blaikie	0
R.J.O. Meyer	b Guise	8			
A.H. White	c Barnard, b Guise	5			
P.A. Wright	not out	1			
EXTRAS	B 19, L-B 11, N-B 1	31		L-B 5	5
	TOTAL	361		TOTAL (1 WKT)	24

Cambridge bowling	OVERS	RUNS	WKTS	OVERS	RUNS	WKTS
Shirley	6	11	2	9	27	0
Wright	16	21	2	29.3	49	6
White	11	32	3	23	57	1
Austin	9	34	1	17	45	2
Enthoven	2	9	0	1	0	0
Meyer	6	20	1	16	53	0

Oxford bowling						
Hewetson	21	43	1	3	3	0
Blaikie	19	50	1	3	16	1
Raikes	14	63	0	—	—	—
Sinclair	34	132	3	—	—	—
Knott	5	23	0	—	—	—
Guise	7.2	19	4	—	—	—

6, 7, 8 July
At Lord's

1925

Match drawn

The match ended in a draw with honours even. In beautiful weather, and before a crowd of around 15,000, Oxford made 316 for 7, the openers, J.L. Guise and P.H. Stewart-Brown, putting on 110 in even time and J.S. Stephenson and J.V. Richardson also having a fruitful partnership.

Oxford added 34 runs on the second morning and their opening bowlers, E.P. Hewetson and E.R.T. Holmes, then proved lively. E.W. Dawson played a good innings, preparing the way for K.S Duleepsinhji's fine knock of 75, in which he was particularly strong on the on-side. He found

a confident partner in H.J. Enthoven, who the next day joined W. Yardley in scoring two hundreds in University Matches. L.G. Crawley too played with great panache and reached 98 not out by lunch, only to be caught at the wicket off Holmes by the exceptional I.A.W. Gilliat without adding to his score.

Oxford in their second innings, with a draw inevitable, made 214 for 4, which included a fine partnership between Stewart-Brown and Holmes, the former making 125 runs in the match.

OXFORD

	First innings		Second innings	
J.L. Guise	b Enthoven	58	c Sherwell, b Meyer	5
P.H. Stewart-Brown	c Francis, b Jagger	56	c Crawley, b Jagger	69
G.W.F. Lyon	c Jagger, b Meyer	7	b Jagger	3
E.R.T. Holmes	c Bennett, b Lowe	24	b Lowe	68
C.H. Taylor	b Jagger	41	c Bennett, b Duleepsinhji	11
G.B. Legge	c Duleepsinhji, b Meyer	38	c Crawley, b Meyer	15
J.V. Richardson	c Jagger, b Duleepsinhji	28	not out	12
J.S. Stephenson	c Crawley, b Meyer	31	not out	13
I.A.W. Gilliat	c Duleepsinhji, b Enthoven	22		
E.P. Hewetson	c Jagger, b Meyer	15		
J.W. Greenstock	not out	1		
EXTRAS	B 17, L-B 10, N-B 2	29	B 17, L-B 1	18
	TOTAL	350	TOTAL (6 WKTS)	214

CAMBRIDGE

E.W. Dawson	b Hewetson	29
T.E.S. Francis	b Greenstock	15
K.S. Duleepsinhji	st Gilliat, b Guise	75
C.T. Bennett	b Hewetson	12
H.J. Enthoven	c Gilliat, b Holmes	129
L.G. Crawley	c Gilliat, b Holmes	98
R.J.O. Meyer	b Holmes	28
N.B. Sherwell	c Greenstock, b Hewetson	9
A.U. Payne	b Hewetson	4
R.G.H. Lowe	c Stephenson, b Holmes	0
S.T. Jagger	not out	0
EXTRAS	L-B 5, W 2, N-B 3	10
	TOTAL	409

Cambridge bowling	OVERS	RUNS	WKTS		OVERS	RUNS	WKTS
Enthoven	28	56	2		15	25	0
Meyer	43	96	4		19	59	2
Lowe	23	40	1		10	23	1
Jagger	31	76	2		9	34	2
Duleepsinhji	21	53	1		10	55	1

Oxford bowling	OVERS	RUNS	WKTS
Hewetson	38	86	4
Holmes	31.1	99	4
Greenstock	30	92	1
Stephenson	15	45	0
Richardson	4	18	0
Guise	14	49	1
Taylor	2	10	0

5, 6, 7 July
At Lord's

1926

Cambridge won by
34 runs

The match was contested for the most part under depressing weather conditions and ended in a win for Cambridge late on the third afternoon by 34 runs. Rain delayed the start until half past two and Cambridge began shakily, M.A. McCanlis taking three wickets for nought – the point at which his fellow Cranleighan E.W. Swanton arrived at the ground! It was now also that H.J. Enthoven added a fifty to his two previous centuries, and R.W.V. Robins and R.J.O. Meyer played with a refreshing freedom to score 37 in twenty minutes. The final score was 178, McCanlis returning 5 for 59 and G.B. Legge taking four catches.

Oxford started their innings steadily, but after lunch on the second day, R.G.H. Lowe and H.J. Enthoven, turning the ball sharply, took eight wickets between them for 61 runs. Lowe had the distinction of completing the innings with a hat-trick, joining a select band of Cobden (1870), Steel (1879), Morton (1880) and Ireland (1911).

J.W. Greenstock took 5 for 77, but Cambridge's enterprise paid off, F.J. Seabrook and K.S. Duleepsinhji making quick thirties, and R.W.V. Robins and S.T. Jagger adding 37 in twenty minutes. Oxford, needing 208 for victory, lost eight wickets for 108, but the Salopian J.S. Stephenson made 52 with exhilarating power before being bowled by Enthoven. Jagger had the creditable figures of 4 for 34.

CAMBRIDGE	First innings		Second innings	
E.W. Dawson	c Legge, b McCanlis	0	c Legge, b Greenstock	12
F.J. Seabrook	c Legge, b McCanlis	1	c McBride, b Taylor	38
K.S. Duleepsinhji	c Legge, b McCanlis	6	c Stephenson, b Greenstock	36
M.J. Turnbull	c McCanlis, b McBride	18	b McBride	20
H.J. Enthoven	b McCanlis	51	b McCanlis	23
R.G.H. Lowe	c Legge, b McBride	16	lbw, b Greenstock	1
R.W.V. Robins	hw, b Greenstock	37	not out	21
R.J.O. Meyer	c Holmes, b McCanlis	23	b Greenstock	0
S.T. Jagger	c Stephenson, b Greenstock	7	lbw, b McBride	15
R.H. Riddell	c Abell, b McBride	7	b McBride	0
L.G. Irvine	not out	0	lbw, b Greenstock	0
EXTRAS	B 6, L-B 6	12	B 17, L-B 6, W 1, N-B 1	25
	TOTAL	178	TOTAL	191

OXFORD				
P.H. Stewart-Brown	c Meyer, b Irvine	26	b Enthoven	6
J.A. Nunn	b Jagger	30	c Turnbull, b Jagger	33
E.R.T. Holmes	b Lowe	28	b Lowe	9
C.H. Taylor	c Turnbull, b Enthoven	14	b Lowe	4
G.B. Legge	b Lowe	14	b Jagger	16
G.C. Newman	c Turnbull, b Enthoven	4	c Lowe, b Jagger	2
J.S. Stephenson	lbw, b Enthoven	5	b Enthoven	52
G.E.B. Abell	not out	13	c and b Enthoven	3
W.N. McBride	c Seabrook, b Lowe	6	lbw, b Lowe	1
M.A. McCanlis	b Lowe	0	not out	15
J.W. Greenstock	b Lowe	0	b Jagger	13
EXTRAS	B 16, L-B 1, N-B 5	22	B 16, L-B 2, N-B 1	19
	TOTAL	162	TOTAL	173

Oxford bowling	OVERS	RUNS	WKTS		OVERS	RUNS	WKTS
McCanlis	22	59	5		17	28	1
Holmes	6	9	0		6	5	0
Greenstock	27	45	2		27.4	77	5
McBride	14.2	48	3		16	52	3
Taylor	3	5	0		2	4	1

Cambridge bowling	OVERS	RUNS	WKTS		OVERS	RUNS	WKTS
Meyer	14	29	0		18	39	0
Enthoven	13	39	3		15	40	3
Irvine	9	41	1		1	7	0
Jagger	6	9	1		15	34	4
Lowe	15	22	5		21	34	3

1927

This was the eighty-ninth match of the series, played one hundred years after the first. Cambridge won this one by 116 runs and now led by forty-three wins to thirty-six. Cambridge's first innings of 178 was largely the result of two attractive fifties by R.W.V. Robins and F.J. Seabrook, countering the promising quick bowling of R.I.F. McIntosh, who took 5 for 60. E.R.T. Holmes played well but the other Dark Blue batsmen found the bowling of T.C. Longfield, who made the ball break back sharply, and L.G. Irvine, an effective spinner, too much for them.

E.F. Longrigg and A.K. Judd retrieved the setback of the early loss of E.W. Dawson. Judd's

124, improving as it went on, paved the way for a Light Blue victory. After two early escapes, Robins played another enterprising innings, and Longfield and Lowe made hay in the closing overs. The Cranleighan M.A. McCanlis bowled well for his 4 for 47.

There was much good cricket on the final day, none better than the exciting partnership between Holmes, who made a hundred in two hours, and A.T. Barber. But the Cambridge fielding and the accurate bowling of M.J.C. Allom, Longfield and Irvine convincingly won the day.

CAMBRIDGE	First innings		Second innings	
E.W. Dawson	*c and b* Greenstock	16	*st* Abell, *b* McIntosh	5
E.F. Longrigg	*b* McIntosh	7	*c* McCanlis, *b* Greenstock	57
A.K. Judd	*st* Abell, *b* Greenstock	8	*b* Holmes	124
R.W.V. Robins	*b* Holmes	55	*b* McIntosh	41
R.H. Cobbold	*lbw, b* Butterworth	3	*c* Holmes, *b* McIntosh	3
F.J. Seabrook	*not out*	51	*b* McCanlis	18
T.C. Longfield	*c* Nunn, *b* McIntosh	8	*b* McCanlis	48
R.G.H. Lowe	*b* McIntosh	3	*c* Barber, *b* McCanlis	20
R.S. Machin	*b* McIntosh	0	*b* McCanlis	6
M.J.C. Allom	*c* McCanlis, *b* McIntosh	1	*not out*	5
L.G. Irvine	*b* Holmes	10		
EXTRAS	B 9, L-B 3, N-B 4	16	B 9, L-B 7, W 2, N-B 4	22
	TOTAL	178	TOTAL (9 WKTS DEC.)	349

OXFORD				
A.M. Crawley	*c* Lowe, *b* Longfield	9	*c* Machin, *b* Longfield	0
P.V.F. Cazalet	*c* Longrigg, *b* Irvine	19	*b* Allom	0
A.T. Barber	*lbw, b* Irvine	18	*st* Machin, *b* Longfield	62
E.R.T. Holmes	*b* Longfield	47	*c* Longfield, *b* Allom	113
J.A. Nunn	*b* Longfield	7	*b* Allom	16
G.C. Newman	*b* Longfield	11	*lbw, b* Allom	15
R.E.C. Butterworth	*b* Longfield	0	*c* Robins, *b* Irvine	12
G.E.B. Abell	*b* Allom	11	*st* Machin, *b* Irvine	2
M.A. McCanlis	*st* Machin, *b* Irvine	3	*b* Longfield	14
J.W. Greenstock	*c* Seabrook, *b* Irvine	5	*c* Cobbold, *b* Irvine	15
R.I.F. McIntosh	*not out*	1	*not out*	1
EXTRAS	B 6, L-B 11, N-B 1	18	B 6, L-B 4, N-B 2	12
	TOTAL	149	TOTAL	262

Oxford bowling	OVERS	RUNS	WKTS		OVERS	RUNS	WKTS
Holmes	11.3	18	2		20	53	1
McIntosh	23	60	5		32	96	3
McCanlis	14	18	0		23.4	47	4
Greenstock	11	24	2		16	34	1
Butterworth	11	42	1		18	88	0
Newman	—	—	—		3	9	0
Cambridge bowling							
Allom	10	26	1		24	60	4
Longfield	15	35	5		30	58	3
Irvine	14.5	55	4		19.1	80	3
Lowe	7	14	0		15	35	0
Robins	1	1	0		—	—	—
Cobbold	—	—	—		3	17	0

9, 10, 11 July
At Lord's

1928

Match drawn

This match was played in delightful weather, and it ended in a draw to make the nerves tingle, with Oxford narrowly holding out. Winning the toss for the third year running, Cambridge made 292, owing much to that fine trio K.S. Duleepsinhji, R.W.V. Robins and E.T. Killick. For Oxford the Etonian C.K. Hill-Wood, their fastest bowler, a left-hander, did most damage, taking 6 for 79.

Oxford batted consistently, an opening stand of 66 leading the way, and P.G.T. Kingsley, N.M. Ford and H.M. Garland-Wells all batted with aggressive intent. Robins was the most successful Light Blue bowler. By close of play on the second day Cambridge had made 82 for 2.

The third day's play was full of interest. Duleepsinhji and F.J. Seabrook, the Cambridge captain, shared in an attacking partnership of 62 in thirty-five minutes, and then Robins indulged in some fine hitting, scoring 101 not out in one hour and three-quarters. Seabrook declared, leaving Oxford to make 335 in three hours and thirty-five minutes. T.C. Longfield and Robins ensured that they were 87 for 5. Garland-Wells batted gloriously, making 70 out of 97 in seventy-five minutes, and Hill-Wood stayed in for an hour and forty minutes to save the match.

CAMBRIDGE	First innings		Second innings	
M.J. Turnbull	c Benson, b C.K. Hill-Wood	2	b McCanlis	19
E.F. Longrigg	b McCanlis	2	c Garland-Wells, b McIntosh	20
K.S. Duleepsinhji	c McCanlis, b C.K. Hill-Wood	52	c Garland-Wells, b McCanlis	37
E.T. Killick	c Skene, b C.K. Hill-Wood	74	lbw, b Garland-Wells	20
R.W.V. Robins	b Crawley	53	not out	101
F.J. Seabrook	c Benson, b McCanlis	44	c Skene, b McCanlis	83
T.C. Longfield	c and b C.K. Hill-Wood	8	run out	9
J.T. Morgan	b C.K. Hill-Wood	18	c Skene, b Garland-Wells	17
N.G. Wykes	c Benson, b C.K. Hill-Wood	24	not out	19
M.J.C. Allom	b Garland-Wells	1		
E.D. Blundell	not out	0		
EXTRAS	B 4, L-B 7, W 1, N-B 2	14	B 2, L-B 1, W 1	4
	TOTAL	292	TOTAL (7 WKTS DEC.)	329

OXFORD				
D.J. Hill-Wood	b Allom	23	c Duleepsinhji, b Robins	23
A.T. Barber	b Allom	36	c Killick, b Robins	14
A.M. Crawley	st Morgan, b Robins	14	b Longfield	29
N.M. Ford	b Longfield	40	b Longfield	0
P.G.T. Kingsley	c Wykes, b Robins	53	b Robins	11
R.W. Skene	run out	18	lbw, b Longfield	11
H.M. Garland-Wells	not out	64	c Allom, b Longfield	70
M.A. McCanlis	b Blundell	7	b Robins	1
C.K. Hill-Wood	c Robins, b Blundell	0	not out	20
R.I.F. McIntosh	b Robins	2	b Allom	7
E.T. Benson	b Robins	1	not out	1
EXTRAS	B 11, L-B 10, W 5, N-B 3	29	B 22, L-B 7, W 9, N-B 2	40
	TOTAL	287	TOTAL (9 WKTS)	227

Oxford bowling	OVERS	RUNS	WKTS	OVERS	RUNS	WKTS
C.K. Hill-Wood	36	79	6	35	118	0
McCanlis	24	56	2	25	81	3
Garland-Wells	19.1	40	1	26	89	2
McIntosh	21	67	0	9	29	1
Skene	9	28	0	—	—	—
Crawley	4	8	1	1	8	0

Cambridge bowling						
Allom	27	99	2	12	47	1
Blundell	20	43	2	12	22	0
Robins	27.4	91	4	25	60	4
Longfield	11	25	1	23	49	4
Seabrook	—	—	—	3	9	0

This match ended in a draw that was less exciting than that in 1928. It was marked by two fine centuries, one for Cambridge by J.T. Morgan, the first Welshman and the first wicket-keeper to have achieved this feat, and the other for Oxford by the Nawab of Pataudi, who was to become one of the few international cricketers to play for more than one country. A pencilled entry in my copy of *Wisden* states that M.J. Turnbull had received over a hundred anonymous letters before the match telling him he should not have picked J.T. Morgan! The Cheltonian E.M. Wellings was the most successful bowler, making the ball move both ways and taking 5 for 118 off forty-five overs in Cambridge's first innings.

S.A. Block, the first president of the revived Quidnuncs, and G.D. Kemp-Welch scored 73 for the opening stand when Cambridge took first innings, but Morgan apart their batting disappointed. When Oxford batted, A.T. Barber, a future Yorkshire captain and Headmaster of Ludgrove, and A.M. Crawley, whose autobiography, *Leap Before You Look*, nearly sixty years later would reflect his all-round ability and interests, gave them a sound start, but the Nawab of Pataudi's innings was dominant. Strong batting by both sides in their second innings ensured that there would be no conclusive result, despite a brave partnership of 165 in two hours in Oxford's second innings between Crawley and Pataudi.

CAMBRIDGE

	First innings			Second innings	
S.A. Block	c Garland-Wells, b Wellings	36		b Wellings	55
G.D. Kemp-Welch	c Barber, b Garthwaite	57		c Ford, b Garthwaite	29
E.T. Killick	c Kingsley, b Wellings	0		lbw, b Garland-Wells	31
B.H. Valentine	b Hill-Wood	11		run out	52
G.C. Grant	c Benson, b Wellings	6			
M.J. Turnbull	b Wellings	27		not out	32
J.T. Morgan	c Kingsley, b Wellings	149		not out	14
W.K. Harbinson	b Garland-Wells	37			
H.R.W. Butterworth	b Garland-Wells	10			
A.H. Fabian	not out	16			
E.D. Blundell	b Hill-Wood	20			
EXTRAS	B 6, L-B 1, W 1	8		B 3, L-B 3, N-B 1	7
	TOTAL	377		TOTAL (4 WKTS DEC.)	220

OXFORD

	First innings			Second innings	
A.T. Barber	lbw, b Butterworth	17		b Blundell	6
A.M. Crawley	c Morgan, b Blundell	33		c Valentine, b Butterworth	83
Nawab of Pataudi	b Blundell	106		c Kemp-Welch, b Blundell	84
P.G.T. Kingsley	c Harbinson, b Kemp-Welch	6		not out	6
N.M. Ford	c Grant, b Fabian	5		not out	4
P.J. Brett	c Butterworth, b Kemp-Welch	24			
H.M. Garland-Wells	c Valentine, b Kemp-Welch	13			
E.T. Benson	b Grant	9			
C.K. Hill-Wood	c Grant, b Fabian	9			
E.M. Wellings	b Blundell	4			
P.F. Garthwaite	not out	0			
EXTRAS	B 15, L-B 3, W 1, N-B 1	20		B 16, L-B 1, W 1, N-B 1	19
	TOTAL	246		TOTAL (3 WKTS)	202

Oxford bowling	OVERS	RUNS	WKTS		OVERS	RUNS	WKTS
Hill-Wood	50.2	116	2		12	58	0
Wellings	45	118	5		20	61	1
Garland-Wells	25	54	2		10	48	1
Garthwaite	18	63	1		7	40	1
Brett	8	18	0		0.3	6	0

Cambridge bowling							
Blundell	39	63	3		18	30	2
Kemp-Welch	24	52	3		11	27	0
Fabian	24.3	40	2		8	25	0
Butterworth	19	49	1		15	89	1
Grant	5	22	1		8	12	0

10
1930–1939
Elation not Depression

OXFORD *From despair to recovery*

In the last decade before Hitler's war, University cricket was largely unaffected by the widespread growth of a negative spirit in sport. The sinister events in Germany and Italy, the slow recovery from the Depression, the Spanish Civil War, the Munich crisis and, in Oxford itself, the infamous 'King and Country' debate all had their influence on general attitudes, but did not upset the cheerful enjoyment of cricket in The Parks – and even the arrival of Bodyline bowling in the Varsity Match of 1933 could not destroy the spirit in which the game was played.

The period between the wars was a time when both Oxford and Cambridge supplied many common rooms with most of their schoolmasters, and among these would be a fair sprinkling of blues. The numbers of these future schoolmasters who were members of Oxford cricket elevens never approached the multitude of future clerics of the mid-nineteenth century; none the less, in this decade alone at least two were to be found each year.

Among these was F.G.H. Chalk, whose wit brightened the Malvern common room for some years. On announcing one morning, as he proceeded to teach Latin to the Lower Fourth, that he was going to give them all he had got, he replied to the question, 'What will they do for the last twenty minutes?' by saying, 'I shall ask them to revise.' He was an outstanding cricket coach who did what he could to pass on his own ability to hit the ball, to move his feet and never to be tied down. He left Malvern to captain Kent for the last two years before the war. In 1943 he was lost on a fighter sweep over France.

The captain of the English hockey team in 1948, M.M. (Micky) Walford, a rugby blue in 1937 and a cricket blue in 1936 and 1938, who went on the combined Oxford and Cambridge cricket tour of Jamaica, opened the batting for Somerset in August, during some of the years of a long career at Sherborne.

J.D. Eggar became a Repton house master before going on to be Headmaster of Shiplake. When in charge of cricket he did much to enhance Repton's reputation. No bat looked broader than his when he was settled at the wicket. A second-wicket partnership of 340, made with C.S. Elliott in 1947 for Derbyshire against Nottinghamshire, still stands as a Derbyshire record; John Eggar's part was 173.

Two years later, when playing against Lancashire at Old Trafford in Dick Pollard's benefit match, Eggar went to meet Dick Sale, his Repton colleague, as he came to the wicket. 'On no account run to Cyril Washbrook at cover,' he warned. Dick slashed his first ball straight to cover and called his partner for a run.

Washbrook's throw missed the stumps by inches and went for four over-throws, and Dick Sale went on to make 146. (There was a third Oxonian playing for Derbyshire in this match – Donald Carr.) Dick Sale had blues in 1939 and 1946, and went on from Repton to be Headmaster, first of Oswestry and later of Brentwood; throughout a long playing career he was noted for his relentless determination on both cricket and football fields.

Another schoolmaster whose university career spanned the war years was D.H. Macindoe; he did for Oxford in 1946 what Miles Howell had done in 1919. He was a tireless bowler and was selected for the Gentlemen in 1937. After the war he became a master at Eton, where he rose to be Vice-Provost. For nearly twenty years he was seen leading the Harlequin attack, seldom bowling less than twenty overs in a day.

Sussex were able to call on the services of R.G. Stainton in school holidays. He was a blue in 1933 and was for many years a prep school headmaster, before becoming a professional artist. Among other blues of the decade who went on to make their mark in teaching were W.H. Bradshaw, R.F.H. Darwall-Smith, D.E. Young and S. Pether.

Despite a positive galaxy of stars, both seniors and freshmen, the 1930 eleven never settled to become a team. Geoffrey Bolton remembers with heartfelt sadness:

Unhappily it was soon apparent that, whatever individuals might do, there was little like-lihood of Oxford becoming a real team. Dissident elements were at work and it became pain-fully clear to the humblest observer that the side was being run by a faction which, to put it mildly, did not regard cricket qualifications as the most necessary attribute of a blue.

Oxford, it was thought, had done well to score 374 against Gloucester, who replied with 627 for 2; 206 of these runs coming from the bat of D.N. Moore, who had been dropped from the Oxford side. He was recalled, and joined such fine players as the Nawab of Pataudi, Alan Melville and A.M. Crawley, who added two more scores of over a hundred, to bring his tally to nine during his four Oxford years. Add to these I.A.R. Peebles, one of the best leg-break and googly bowlers of his day, and Oxford looked a formidable side. Ian Peebles wrote modestly of the wicket at The Parks in a season when he took seventy wickets: 'though inclined to slowness, it always gave promise of a little turn'. It was hardly a surprise when he was picked for the Gentlemen and for the Old Trafford Test. Despite his thirteen wickets at Lord's, the match was lost.

D.N. Moore was the elected captain in 1931; most unluckily, having proved his worth, he became ill and handed over to A. Melville. Both were in their second year; this was the first time since 1863 that such an honour had fallen on men so junior. B.W. Hone and H.G. Owen-Smith were new faces who did much to raise morale. Owen-Smith 'had an electrifying effect on any side for which he played', he was a hard-hitting batsman, deadly spinner and magnificent fielder. He seemed to climb along the turf, head low, with that sense of balance which stood Oxford and England in such good stead at Twickenham.

Pataudi made four hundreds on the 1931 tour, and after an exhausting day in the field at Lord's cheered his colleagues by assuring them that he would pass Ratcliffe's record total of 201. He made good this promise within twenty-four hours, scoring an unbeaten 238, an innings of graceful brilliance which assured victory. Oxford had to wait six years before winning again.

Alan Melville was elected captain in his own right for the 1932 season. He had announced his arrival in Oxford two years earlier by making 132 not out, never before having batted on turf; two weeks later he made 118 against Yorkshire. His classical upright style of batting was always a delight to watch. Subsequently he proved a shrewd leader at Oxford, which prepared him for the captaincy of South Africa, an office which he graced before and after the war. At Oxford he developed into a true all-rounder; his best performance as a bowler was against Leveson-Gower's eleven at Eastbourne, when he had a hat-trick. With Owen-Smith, E.A. Barlow and A.R. Legard, who bowled a highly individual variety of out-swing and off-breaks, the attack was well balanced.

D.C.H. Townsend, yet another Wykehamist who owed much to H.S. Altham, was a very correct player who made three hundreds in 1933, in preparation for his great innings of 193 at Lord's the following year. David Townsend has the rare distinction of playing for England without appearing for a first-class county, preferring to stay with his native Durham.

It is a feature of this period that most cricketers also had blues in other sports. In 1933 there was a remarkably versatile spread of talent: there were four football blues, two rugby, three hockey and, for good measure, also a lawn tennis and a boxing blue.

A.P. Singleton, a future captain of Worcestershire, and yet another who spent some years in teaching, came up to Brasenose in 1933 and won a blue as a freshman. His experience exemplifies what is best in the severe school of cricket education at Oxford. He came up with a good, though not outstanding, reputation from Shrewsbury. In the freshmen's trials he made it quite clear that he preferred not to take the advice of Frank Gilligan, who had come to help with early season coaching. Singleton remembers:

He told me that my run-up to the wicket was too long for an off-spinner, and that I must cut it down. I replied that I had copied Verity's run, and refused to change it. So I was somewhat surprised to be selected for the first match against Gloucestershire.

He was in and out of the side until, having taken four wickets against Leicestershire in the last match in The Parks, he was invited to play at Lord's. Over four seasons he learned the hard way against the best in the land, and in his last year had the added experience of captaincy – a year in which he became the fourth Oxonian to make a thousand runs and take a hundred wickets for the University, and led Oxford to victory at Lord's. Sandy goes on to recall:

First-class cricket was rather like a sort of brotherhood, and I still remember how I was accepted into this in my first season. Players who had been my idols in my schooldays suddenly became my friends, and I was thrilled to be, so to speak, a member. I can still remember the great moment when Herbert Sutcliffe called me Sandy, and when Walter Hammond talked to me as an equal.

Of his introduction to the press, he remembers:

The rather too keen atmosphere in The Parks lasted for a week or two, but suddenly cleared with the arrival of a sunburned and jovial figure dressed in a rough coat which had seen hard work in its time, grey flannels at half mast, a tie which had blown over his shoulder, and black dancing shoes. This was Raymond Robertson-Glasgow, known to one and all as Crusoe, who was the cricket correspondent of the Morning Post. *He carried a small red memo book, which he referred to as 'the washing book' and in which he occasionally made notes. Wherever he was, one could hear his bellow of laughter, and the whole scene brightened up at once, and cricket became fun.*

Also living in Oxford during these years was Jim Swanton, who wrote, I think, for the Evening Standard, *and also did an amusing column for the* Sporting and Dramatic! *We had a lot of fun at his digs in Long Wall Street over this column. It should be mentioned that in those days most of the cricket journalists were responsible men who had played good cricket, or at any rate knew about it. Most of the papers carried detailed accounts of the first-class matches, and there was no 'muck-raking'.*

There were usually good crowds to watch the games, The Parks being a delightful ground, with big trees all round it, and deck chairs all along the boundary. Quite a few of the dons and schoolmasters were members of the club, and would come whenever possible to watch the games. Apart from Sonners (Dr Stallybrass) I can remember J.C. Masterman, Philip Landon, Geoffrey Bolton, Captain D.V. Hill, known to all as Hooky. There were many others who were devoted followers of the Oxford team, and schools used to bring their boys to watch.

He goes on to describe aspects of the tour.

There were four matches on the tour, and the Varsity match. We stayed in a hotel for the Sussex match and for the Varsity match, but otherwise stayed in private houses. There were a good many loyal and generous people who were willing to put up members of the team. I remember staying at a big hotel in Eastbourne, where there was a Hall Porter of imposing stature, decked out like an admiral, with a row of First World War medals. We were debating how small a tip we could get away with, when the match against Sussex was over, when the local paper published an obituary of the previous Hall Porter. It mentioned that he had left £15,000 – this was very big money in those days – and we had an entirely clear conscience in giving him a five-shilling tip. I also remember a match at Reigate where Sir Jeremiah Colman, the mustard king, had a magnificent Georgian mansion. He put up not only both teams, but also a few friends, for the three nights, and nobody shared a room.

But the greatest pleasure was our stay at the Cumberland Hotel in London for the Varsity match. This hotel was comparatively new, and was pure luxury for us, undergraduates with very little money to spare.

The account of this decade would be incomplete without further mention of two outstanding players. One was N.S. Mitchell-Innes, who first played in 1934, missing a thousand runs by only two. The following year he had three hundreds, including 168 against the South Africans. This fine innings prompted the England selectors to pick him for the First Test at Trent Bridge; it was a cruel blow that during the match he was miserable with hay fever and did himself little justice.

R.C.M. Kimpton, from Melbourne, was a quick-footed, wristy player of small stature, and a very sound wicket-keeper who had been awarded his blue as a freshman. In 1936 he began by scoring two separate hundreds against Gloucestershire, and almost repeated his performance against the Free Foresters when he made 110 and 85, following this with a further hundred against Lancashire. An injury at the eleventh hour caused him to withdraw at Lord's.

In the face of some adversity Oxford did fairly well in 1938. They defeated Middlesex in The Parks and Sussex on tour, when they also had a fine win over the MCC, Micky Walford making 201, driving and hooking with assurance. J.M. Lomas, a freshman from Charterhouse who played such an excellent innings at Lord's, topped the averages and made over 900 runs.

The decade finished with a very good win in the Varsity Match of 1939. The nucleus which would have gone forward to 1940 might well have been part of an exceptional team, but this was not to be.

CAMBRIDGE *Victory in 1930 to glory in defeat in 1939*

Old newsreels, with their sepia tints and their exaggerated speed of hand, foot and face, always tell a distorted and selective story, and those of the thirties are no exception. Reminiscent pictures can be found in them of the Jarrow March, of the so-called 'Bodyline Tour' of Australia in 1932–3, of a beflannelled Fred Perry winning the men's tennis singles at Wimbledon three years running, of the Olympic Games of 1936, when the victories of Jesse Owens were to dent the Führer's racial theories, of the bombing of Guernica in the Spanish War, of the return of Neville Chamberlain from Munich, waving at Heston Airport his tragic piece of paper and hoping against hope that it would bring 'peace in our time', and so on.

What they do not show is that University cricket continued with unabated skill and enthusiasm. In the words of T.E.B. Howarth, Senior Tutor of Magdalene after being High Master of St Paul's, in his *Cambridge Between the Wars*: 'All in all, it was undoubtedly a period when athletic prowess was much valued, though without the grimness of dedication which today tends to turn games into a professional treadmill.'

There is no newsreel, as far as I know, that shows the fine 136 of Tom Killick in the 1930 University Match, including an opening partnership of 139 with the Carthusian George Kemp-Welch, who scored 270 runs in his three University Matches, with an average of 45, and was killed when the Guards Chapel was destroyed by enemy action in June 1944. This paved the way for a famous Light Blue victory by an innings and 205 runs – one which had looked unlikely when Oxford had seven wickets in hand and there were only seventy minutes left to ensure a draw. Nor is there a reel of the aggressive all-round play of Freddie Brown, who in his last season at The Leys, not far from Fenner's, took sixty wickets and had a batting average of 65, and who won a place in the MCC party to tour Australia in 1932–3.

A class leg-spinner and a punishing striker of the ball, Brown owed much, from his early days, to Aubrey Faulkner, South Africa's greatest all-rounder, and was of a type of cricketer in short supply today. In 1950 he won the captaincy of the MCC team to Australia, in part through a glorious innings in the Gentlemen *v* Players match, and he there earned the respect of friend and foe alike. Originally a Surrey player, for a few years he lifted Northamptonshire by his captaincy, and he was later appointed President, first of the MCC, and then of the National Cricket Association, becoming also an Honorary Life Vice-President of the MCC for his services to the Club.

Nor can a cinematic re-enactment be found of two historic moments at Fenner's in 1934 involving the Tonbridgian Jack Davies, a scholar as well as an athlete, who also played with distinction for Kent, not least as a cover-point, was a winner of the amateur rugby fives singles championship, became Treasurer, President and Honorary Life Vice-President of the MCC and for nearly four decades from 1952 was the overseer of Cambridge cricket. The first of these was when Davies, much to the CUCC treasurer's dismay, bowled the great Don Bradman for nought, with a ball that he must have assumed would turn but did not. The second was when, a few days later, he brilliantly ran out Len Hutton, from cover, for nought, on the latter's debut in first-class cricket.

We again have to rely on imagination to recapture the cultured wicket-keeping of the Carthusian Adam Powell, or the Alleynian Billy Griffith, or Paul Gibb, from St Peter's, York, a talented opener also, who made four hundreds in 1938, including 122 against Oxford, and was chosen to play for England that year. He flew Sunderlands during the war, and he later became an umpire on the first-class list.

Griffith later kept wicket for England in all five 'Victory Tests' in 1945, and toured Australia and New Zealand in 1935–6, South Africa in 1947 when he was preferred to Godfrey Evans in two Tests, and West Indies in 1948, during which he made his maiden hundred at Trinidad. In the wake of injuries, the captain, Gubby Allen, had organized a competitive net practice, and from it had selected Griffith to open. Billy, it was said, was frightened of meeting Gubby after the one really experienced batsman, Jack Robertson, had been run out for nought, so that survival was thus vital. He recently told me that it was the only time in his career that he had seen sweat coming right through pads worn by a batsman!

From 1930 Griffith had been able to see at close quarters the glorious stroke-play of Hugh Bartlett, first at Dulwich and later in three innings especially – in 1935, 183 for Cambridge against Nottinghamshire, in 1938, a hundred for Sussex against the Australians at Hove in 57 minutes, thus winning the Lawrence Trophy that year, and an equally distinguished hundred in the Gentlemen *v* Players match of 1938. Griffith and Bartlett, incidentally, were close friends at Pembroke as well as at Dulwich, both took part as experienced glider pilots in the Arnhem landing in 1944, and both gave excellent service to Sussex as players and administrators. Griffith also became a much-loved Secretary of the MCC from 1962 to 1974, and President in 1980, and was until recently Chairman of the Friends of Arundel Castle Cricket Club.

Are there, I wonder, moving pictures that I have not seen of the effortless quick bowling of Jahangir Khan, famous father of famous son, whose 11 for 133 against Yorkshire in 1933 helped Cambridge to a victory of 19 runs, their first against that county since 1921. He played in four Tests for India, and was a guiltless accessory in the death of the sparrow – killed in mid-flight when he was bowling to Tom Pearce, of Essex, at Lord's – which rests in peace in the Memorial Gallery. Are there pictures also of the menacing sight of the tall Ken Farnes, from Royal Liberty, Romford, one of the two best amateur fast bowlers of the thirties, when roused (and his colleagues learned the trick of rousing him when the moment was ripe), who shared the opening attack in 1932 with R.C. Rought-Rought, who played for Norfolk until his early death in an accident in 1937, taking ninety-six wickets between them? Few who were at Lord's will not remember Farnes' spell one evening in the gloaming in the 1938 Gentlemen *v* Players match, after he had been dropped from the Test side, when his bowling was said to have been awesome in its speed and power. Farnes was killed in 1941 shortly after qualifying as a pilot in the RAF.

To complete a distinguished trio, is there no flash-back to the wily spin bowling of John Cameron, from Taunton School, who, for the Rest against the Public Schools at Lord's in 1931, took all ten wickets in an innings for 49 in 19.1 overs, and who would tour England with the West Indies in 1939, when he had changed from leg-spin to off-spin? His 9 for 99 in the two innings against Oxford in 1935 played a vital part in the Light Blue victory by 195 runs.

Fine sportsmen also were two brothers who were to play for the West Indies as well as for Cambridge, one of whom would also win an amateur international soccer cap. This was Rolph Grant, the younger brother, a Corinthian goalkeeper, who won his cricket blue in 1933, dismissing three out of the first four Oxford batsmen for 44 and brilliantly catching Gerry Chalk at short leg. He also captained the West Indies in England in 1939. Both brothers were born in Port of Spain, and the elder brother, G.C. (Jack), played for Cambridge in 1929 and 1930, and captained the West Indies in each of the twelve Tests in which he played. He must have enjoyed the convincing Light Blue victory of 1930, to which Rought-Rought's overall 5 for 74 and the 7 for 66 of Arthur Hazlerigg, captain of Cambridge in 1932 and of Leicestershire in 1934, greatly contributed. Jack once declared twice against Australia and won, showing, perhaps, the same spirit of adventure as when he later became a missionary.

It is a tragedy that there should be no taped record of the astonishing remark of the senior Nawab of Pataudi, in the wake of Alan Ratcliffe's fine 201 for the Light Blues in 1931 (after a last-minute recall to the side), giving no chance until he was 179. The Noob's 'They threw the runs at him; I shall beat it' quite takes the breath away, and his 238 not out, in eighty minutes less, is no less remarkable. The following year Ratcliffe, who had been at Rydal School, equalled the feat of W. Yardley and H.J. Enthoven by scoring a second hundred for Cambridge at Lord's.

There were two batsmen in the early thirties, both freshmen in 1932, whose approach to the game epitomized amateur cricket at its best. The first is the Wykehamist Roger Winlaw, who scored five hundreds in 1934, including a hundred in each innings against Glamorgan at Cardiff, and made 977 runs that year at an average of 57.47. He later played a few games for Surrey, but appeared mainly for Bedfordshire, whom he captained successfully from 1935. He also won three soccer blues against Oxford and was a good rugby fives player. Tragically, he was killed in 1942, in an accident in which Claude Ashton was also involved, between a Wellington bomber and the Beaufighter in which they were flying, near Speke aerodrome. The case in the MCC Memorial Gallery which holds the Ashes urn was donated in their memory.

The second of the two batsmen is the Reptonian John Human, who scored four hundreds in 1933 and five in 1934, several of them glorious displays which reflected both his excellent technique and the same bubbling enthusiasm which I had the pleasure of experiencing when I called on him in his Sydney flat over-looking Rose Bay, in February 1988, in order to discuss this book. His memory was in top working order, and he conveyed to me not only the exhilaration of the cricket of this era, but also one or two moments that deserve a place in this story. For instance, what a sensible, old-fashioned sense of priorities that Geoffrey Fisher, his headmaster (and later to become Archbishop of Canterbury), should arrange with Henry Thirkell at Clare, later to become President both of the College and the CUCC, for John to take his Cambridge entrance examination paper later, since the Public Schools match with The Army clashed with it! He recalled with affection, when illness had kept him out of several of the matches on the MCC tour of India in 1933–4, the sympathetic handling of his captain, Douglas Jardine, and with amused horror the time that he had left half a tumbler of gin on the washstand, and his room-mate Billy Griffith had used it to wash his teeth in, and thinking it was water had swallowed the lot. His exclamation, 'I nearly killed Billy', carried conviction over half a century later! He remembered vividly the time he took 2 for 0, with the leg-spinners that he bowled with such skill, in a Gentlemen *v* Players match, including the wicket of the great Wally Hammond, who was heard later asking what the little so-and-so had bowled.

There were several other notable all-round sportsmen in this decade who must now be acknowledged, three of them in the successful 1935 side. First, by reason of his captaincy, is Grahame Parker, from the Crypt School, Gloucester, who also played full-back at rugby for England as well as for Cambridge, and who maintained his links with Gloucestershire cricket, first as a player, and later, after teaching at Blundells, as secretary-manager, until 1976.

The second would take over the mantle of Glamorgan cricket from Maurice Turnbull and John Clay, leading them from the front with considerable skill to their first Championship win in 1948, and becoming a Test selector from 1955 to 1962. This was another Rydalian, Wilf Wooller, who formed with Cliff Jones a brilliant combination, the one in the centre, the other at fly-half, for Wales as well as for Cambridge.

The third, from St Peter's, York is Norman Yardley, a fine hockey and squash player as well as a cricketer, who captained England in the post-war years, having gone to Australia on the 1946–7 tour as Hammond's vice-captain and surprised the opposition, including Bradman thrice running, with his medium-pace seam bowling. At Cambridge he was mainly an aggressive stroke-player, who made 90 in the 1936 Varsity Match and 101 in 1937. He served Yorkshire well, both as captain and administrator, and after his playing days became a broadcaster with balanced views on the game.

The second England captain from this era, who has continued to serve the game with integrity as Chairman of the TCCB and, more recently, as both President and a Trustee of the MCC, is George Mann. He and his father Frank were the only father and son to captain their country until Colin and Chris Cowdrey, and in addition they both captained Middlesex. George captained Eton in 1936 and had two years in the Cambridge side, in the second of which, 1939, he and another talented stroke-player, John Thompson – for whom, as for so many, the war came at a crucial moment in his sporting career – put on 262 for the first wicket against Leicestershire, beating the 259 by D.C. Collins and the Hon. H.G.H. Mulholland against the Australians in 1911. (It was a record twice defeated by Dewes and Sheppard in 1950.) Thompson played for Warwickshire in the school holidays from Marlborough, and had considerable success at other games, rackets and squash in particular, being in the winning pair in the amateur rackets doubles on ten occasions and the singles on four.

Mann played for several years after the war and will probably have taken most pleasure in the general enjoyment, as well as the victory, of the MCC side in South Africa in 1948–9, and in particular in his series-winning 136 not out in the Fifth Test, when MCC were one up in the series. That first win was, in passing, made even more memorable by Cliff Gladwin's scrambled winning leg-bye off the last ball of the match, and his subsequent dictum, 'cometh the hour, cometh the man'. The side was unbeaten and widely acclaimed as one of the best fielding sides ever seen.

No impressionistic review such as this can hope to do justice to all the cricket or all the cricketers. Beating Yorkshire in 1933 can be contrasted with being bowled out in 1932 by Larwood and Voce for 34. The victories at Lord's of 1930 and 1935 have to be weighed against the defeats of 1931, 1937 and 1939; but there was glory in defeat in 1939, under the much-respected captaincy of Peter Studd, who would carry on a family tradition by becoming Lord Mayor of the City of London. Having fielded with distinction throughout the match, and indeed throughout the season, they were set 430 to win, and, thanks mainly to the hundred of Pat Dickinson, from KCS Wimbledon, described by Plum Warner as one of the finest in the history of the match, lost by 45 runs only.

Regular watchers at Fenner's were impressed by the batting of three future county captains. These were: Denys Wilcox, who had already played for Essex when he arrived at Cambridge, and who made 157 at Lord's in 1932; Basil Allen, top Light Blue scorer at Lord's in 1933 with 53, who became a captain of Gloucestershire spanning the war; and Robert Nelson, from St Alban's and St George's, Harpenden, who captained Northamptonshire in 1938 and 1939, leading the county to its first victory, against his old university, since May 1935, and was sadly killed while serving with the Royal Marines. Spectators also saw three hundreds in 1937 from John Pawle, amateur singles rackets champion, whose good fortune did not continue at Lord's.

Cambridge supporters enjoyed the style of the Etonian Tony Allen, who liked Lord's, scoring a hundred there for Eton before lunch, and then 115 for Cambridge in 1934, and they saw the Harrovian Mark Tindall score over a thousand runs for Cambridge and Middlesex in 1936. They also enjoyed in 1939 the evident promise of the Aldenhamian John Blake, who played for Hampshire while still at school but did not survive the war; and the sweet off-driving of the Malvernian Podge Brodhurst, who headed the averages in 1939, scoring a hundred against Yorkshire in two and a half hours, and another against Leicestershire. Brodhurst later enthusiastically ran the cricket at Winchester in two different eras, and he can also claim cricket historian Harry Altham as his father-in-law.

The Fenner's crowd only once viewed the bowling, off the wrong foot, of John Brocklebank, who took 10 for 139 against Oxford in 1936 and was chosen for the MCC tour of India in 1939–40, which in fact never came off (he was also the chairman of Cunard who placed the order for the QE2). In 1939 they could enjoy that of Jack Webster, a lively fast-medium bowler with a whippy action, who also played sixty matches for Northamptonshire during the school holidays from Harrow.

Other sporting all-rounders who showed promise early in the decade were two

Cholmeleians: Howard Fabian, never dismissed in a University Match, who also played soccer for Derby County and the Corinthians, and won the Kinnaird Cup for Eton fives; and Tagge Webster, who played forty-five matches for Middlesex, became President of the MCC and won six soccer amateur international caps. He took over from Graham Doggart as the Cambridge University representative on the Football Association, and handed over to Doug Insole. Sporting all-rounders who were showing promise as the covers came out for what came to be termed 'the duration' were a pair of fine golfers – John Langley, a golf international at the time of the 1938 University Match, and Gethyn Hewan, also a hockey blue, and one day to become Headmaster of Cranbrook, Sydney, as well as of Allhallows, Rousden, where we were colleagues in the Headmasters' Conference (South-West Division). The Alleynian Alan Shirreff, who played for three different counties, but mainly for the Combined Services and the RAF, was also demonstrating great potential when war intervened. Several Light Blues did not survive it, and their names are recorded in Appendix VIII.

Let us pause here to recap on the table of results in the University Match as, for the second time in a quarter of a century, 'the lights went out all over Europe'. Since Wordsworth and Jenner-Fust (as he became) had first tossed for innings in 1827, Cambridge had won forty-six matches to Oxford's thirty-nine, with sixteen draws.

7, 8, 9 July
At Lord's

1930

Cambridge won by
205 runs

The ignominious defeat of a highly talented Oxford eleven caused Geoffrey Bolton to write of this match many years later: 'More than thirty years on, the recollection of this game still has power to sting.'

Oxford were set 307 to win in two hours and twenty minutes on the last afternoon. J.T. Morgan, when praised for his declaration, stated with disarming honesty that he never believed Oxford would go for the runs, let alone get themselves out, and he had thought it 'indecent to go on batting'. After the Nawab of Pataudi was out with the score at 78, Oxford lost their last seven wickets for 23 runs in fifty minutes.

Cambridge again won the toss; G.D. Kemp-

Welch and E.T. Killick gave them an excellent start, putting on 139 in under two hours. But against superb bowling by I.A.R. Peebles after lunch, only F.R. Brown and Morgan saved Cambridge from total collapse.

Oxford led on the first innings despite early losses, including the run out of A.M. Crawley in the first over.

In Cambridge's second innings, Killick put together a match-winning score. Despite the stirling efforts of Melville and Peebles, Oxford put down catch after catch (including a simple chance from Killick behind the wicket), thereby setting the scene for their final demoralising defeat.

CAMBRIDGE	First innings		Second innings	
G.D. Kemp-Welch	c Mayhew, b Hill-Wood	61	c Kingsley, b Bradshaw	8
E.T. Killick	b Peebles	75	b Bradshaw	136
A. Ratcliffe	b Peebles	11	b Peebles	9
G.C. Grant	b Peebles	0	c and b Garland-Wells	11
H.E. Carris	b Hill-Wood	4	c Melville, b Peebles	25
R.H.C. Human	c Peebles, b Hill-Wood	21	c Melville, b Peebles	8
J.T. Morgan	c Hill-Wood, b Peebles	39	c Melville, b Peebles	1
F.R. Brown	b Peebles	42	c and b Peebles	29
A.G. Hazlerigg	lbw, b Peebles	0	c Melville, b Peebles	17
A.H. Fabian	not out	12	not out	33
R.C. Rought-Rought	lbw, b Peebles	5	not out	18
EXTRAS	B 10, L-B 1, W 1, N-B 6	18	B 15, L-B 8, N-B 14	37
	TOTAL	288	TOTAL (9 WKTS DEC.)	332

OXFORD				
A.M. Crawley	run out	0	c Ratcliffe, b Kemp-Welch	13
D.N. Moore	c Rought-Rought, b Hazlerigg	59	c Hazlerigg, b Brown	29
Nawab of Pataudi	b Human	5	b Hazlerigg	20
P.G.T. Kingsley	c Rought-Rought, b Hazlerigg	13	c Ratcliffe, b Kemp-Welch	13
N.M. Ford	c Human, b Rought-Rought	53	not out	9
A. Melville	c and b Brown	3	c Hazlerigg, b Brown	0
H.M. Garland-Wells	lbw, b Hazlerigg	53	b Hazlerigg	1
C.K. Hill-Wood	c Fabian, b Rought-Rought	47	c Hazlerigg, b Rought-Rought	0
W.H. Bradshaw	c Hazlerigg, b Rought-Rought	7	c Kemp-Welch, b Hazlerigg	0
I.A.R. Peebles	not out	26	lbw, b Rought-Rought	0
J.F.N. Mayhew	c Fabian, b Brown	6	c Kemp-Welch, b Hazlerigg	1
EXTRAS	B 26, L-B 13, W 1, N-B 2	42	B 12, L-B 2, N-B 1	15
	TOTAL	314	TOTAL	101

Oxford bowling	OVERS	RUNS	WKTS		OVERS	RUNS	WKTS
Hill-Wood	31	102	3		36	79	0
Bradshaw	11	37	0		14	25	2
Peebles	31.1	75	7		50	162	6
Garland-Wells	14	37	0		20	29	1
Melville	2	19	0		—	—	—

Cambridge bowling							
Rought-Rought	26	64	3		7	10	2
Human	19	62	1		2	13	0
Hazlerigg	24	49	3		11	17	4
Brown	33.5	81	2		14	36	2
Fabian	11	16	0		2	0	0
Kemp-Welch	—	—	—		6	10	2

6, 7, 8 July
At Lord's

1931

Oxford won by
8 wickets

It is stated in *Wisden* that over 30,000 spectators paid to see this match; they certainly had value for money, with a record being broken in one innings, only to have it surpassed in the next, followed by a surprise result.

A.T. Ratcliffe was recalled to the Cambridge side on the morning of the match, after an injury to J.G.W. Davies. Not only did he take part in a stand of 149 with G.D. Kemp-Welch in under two hours, but raced past J.F. Marsh's 1904 record of 172.

The next day the Nawab of Pataudi equalled Ratcliffe's total in eighty minutes less time, and went on to better it by 37 runs. This was Pataudi's fifth three-figure innings from his last six, and he

also joined the small but select band who had made two separate hundreds in the Varsity Match. On this occasion Pataudi's runs were made all round the wicket with delightful freedom, and he gave no absolute chance. H.G. Owen-Smith for a time almost outshone Pataudi, and certainly made a declaration practical.

Despite Oxford's remarkable innings, a draw seemed likely. Kemp-Welch and A.G. Hazlerigg took Cambridge to 49 without loss on the third morning. Once Owen-Smith separated these two, Cambridge collapsed to the medium pace of E.M. Wellings, for the further addition of only 77 runs, making Oxford's final task an easy one.

CAMBRIDGE	First innings		Second innings	
G.D. Kemp-Welch	c Scott, b Owen-Smith	87	b Owen-Smith	28
A.T. Ratcliffe	c Melville, b Scott	201	b Scott	9
A.G. Hazlerigg	c Raikes, b Wellings	20	c Melville, b Owen-Smith	29
J.C. Christopherson	b Scott	9	c Lindsay, b Wellings	7
D.R. Wilcox	lbw, b Scott	0	c Melville, b Scott	4
D.M. Parry	c Hone, b Wellings	13	c Bradshaw, b Wellings	2
F.R. Brown	c Hone, b Owen-Smith	3	c Pataudi, b Wellings	1
R.H.C. Human	b Scott	8	b Owen-Smith	17
A.H. Fabian	not out	14	not out	11
J.T.H. Comber	b Scott	22	c Raikes, b Wellings	1
K. Farnes	b Scott	1	b Wellings	0
EXTRAS	B 5, L-B 2	7	B 7, L-B 6	13
	TOTAL	385	TOTAL	122

OXFORD				
B.W. Hone	b Farnes	6	not out	25
W.O'B. Lindsay	c Fabian, b Brown	13	c Human, b Brown	2
Nawab of Pataudi	not out	238	c Comber, b Brown	4
A. Melville	b Hazlerigg	47	not out	14
F.G.H. Chalk	c Comber, b Hazlerigg	10		
H.G. Owen-Smith	c Christopherson, b Brown	78		
R.S.G. Scott	c Hazlerigg, b Brown	6		
E.M. Wellings	b Brown	2		
T.M. Hart	c Ratcliffe, b Brown	14		
EXTRAS	B 32, L-B 5, W 2	39	B 4, L-B 5, N-B 1	10
	TOTAL (8 WKTS DEC.)	453	TOTAL (2 WKTS)	55

W.H. Bradshaw and D.C.G. Raikes did not bat

Oxford bowling	OVERS	MDNS	RUNS	WKTS	OVERS	MDNS	RUNS	WKTS
Bradshaw	12	5	26	0	3	1	2	0
Scott	33.2	11	64	6	20	10	23	2
Wellings	40	11	106	2	23.4	11	25	5
Owen-Smith	51	12	141	2	20	5	59	3
Melville	12	1	41	0	—	—	—	—

Cambridge bowling								
Farnes	28	5	79	1	8	2	18	0
Human	17	2	59	0	—	—	—	—
Brown	43.5	4	153	5	10.2	4	18	2
Hazlerigg	28	3	86	2	3	0	9	0
Fabian	7	1	37	0	—	—	—	—

UMPIRES A. Morton and H. Young

4, 5, 6 July
At Lord's

1932

Match drawn

In three days there was some highly creditable batting, with three hundreds being scored. Rain was about and a draw always seemed the most likely result. Cambridge won the toss, yet again. An ordinary Oxford attack was for several hours treated with boring respect. Once A.T. Ratcliffe and D.R. Wilcox appreciated that there were few hazards, they put on 132 together in two hours. Ratcliffe joined the illustrious when he registered a second hundred in the Varsity Match, William Yardley, H.J. Enthoven and the Nawab of Pataudi being the others to have achieved this feat. Cambridge went on to make 431, their highest total at Lord's.

Oxford started badly, there being four wickets down for 78. H.G. Owen-Smith then came to the rescue and gave B.W. Hone the confidence he seemed to need, and they added 58 in thirty-five minutes before rain closed proceedings for the day. Hone was inspired next morning, and with help from T.M. Hart and E.A. Barlow took Oxford's total to within 63 of their opponents. K. Farnes had bowled impressively, but he was a great 'dragger' and gave away 21 no-balls.

Only three hours' play was left, and although the stylish Wilcox batted well for the second time and J.H. Human showed his class, rain finally put paid to further play at 6.15 p.m.

CAMBRIDGE

	First innings		Second innings	
A.G. Hazlerigg	b Legard	45	c and b Legard	20
W.H. Webster	b Owen-Smith	12	b Owen-Smith	12
D.R. Wilcox	c Evans, b Barlow	157	c Evans, b Legard	44
A.W.G. Hadingham	b Owen-Smith	8	st Oldfield, b Owen-Smith	2
A.T. Ratcliffe	c Van der Bijl, b Legard	124	c Van der Bijl, b Owen-Smith	0
R. de W.K. Winlaw	lbw, b Legard	15	c Oldfield, b Melville	34
J.H. Human	b Owen-Smith	35	st Oldfield, b Melville	28
E. Cawston	c and b Barlow	2	c Owen-Smith, b Barlow	7
R.C. Rought-Rought	b Barlow	3	c Brooke, b Melville	1
K. Farnes	c Barlow, b Legard	11	not out	0
J.T.H. Comber	not out	0	not out	1
EXTRAS	B 13, L-B 3, N-B 3	19	B 10, L-B 3, W 1	14
	TOTAL	431	TOTAL	163

OXFORD

F.G.H. Chalk	c Cawston, b Human	7
R.H.J. Brooke	c Comber, b Farnes	10
B.W. Hone	c Winlaw, b Cawston	167
P.G. van der Bijl	c Rought-Rought, b Farnes	7
A. Melville	b Farnes	3
H.G. Owen-Smith	c Wilcox, b Farnes	67
E.N. Evans	lbw, b Rought-Rought	9
T.M. Hart	c Winlaw, b Farnes	26
E.A. Barlow	not out	43
P.C. Oldfield	c Hazlerigg, b Cawston	0
A.R. Legard	b Cawston	4
EXTRAS	B 6, L-B 7, N-B 12	25
	TOTAL	368

Oxford bowling	OVERS	MDNS	RUNS	WKTS		OVERS	MDNS	RUNS	WKTS
Hart	24	10	46	0		7	1	12	0
Barlow	58	21	111	3		19	6	28	1
Owen-Smith	56	7	165	3		19	4	69	3
Melville	9	1	36	0		4.3	0	16	3
Legard	22.3	2	40	4		11	2	24	2
Brooke	4	0	14	0					

Cambridge bowling				
Farnes	32	3	98	5
Rought-Rought	30	11	73	1
Hazlerigg	23	3	70	0
Human	19	4	52	1
Cawston	19.1	4	50	3

UMPIRES A. Morton and J. Hardstaff

10, 11, 12 July
At Lord's

1933

Match drawn

R.G. Stainton, who later played for Sussex, remembers the 1933 match:

The University match was still, for all the traditional determination of each side to win, a social occasion. Dark and light blue ribbon swathed the grandstand boxes and a decorative perambulation took place round the square during the lunch interval. Partisan cheers, though not mutual embraces, acclaimed a boundary or the fall of a wicket. There was neither TV nor radio broadcast. 'The Brasenose Bar' and the Tavern did for both.

B.W. Hone, known as 'Nippy', who had earlier caused some feeling by standing down from some matches to win a tennis blue, successfully chose the great Welsh rugby full-back V.G.J. Jenkins instead of A.R. Legard.

D.R. Wilcox had the services of Ken Farnes, by now a seasoned fast bowler, and Jahangir Khan, a freshman from the Indian touring side of 1932.

Many interruptions from rain carried Oxford's first innings to the end of the second day. Fast leg-theory tactics were employed, first by Farnes, who bowled with four short-legs, and then by Jahangir Khan and R.S. Grant. After Cambridge's useful score F.G.H. Chalk and Jenkins defended courageously on a nasty wicket to stave off defeat.

OXFORD

	First innings			Second innings	
D.F. Walker	c Human, b Grant	46		c Davies, b Farnes	4
D.C.H. Townsend	lbw, b Grant	9		hw, b Farnes	3
B.W. Hone	c B.O. Allen, b Jahangir Khan	26		c Comber, b Farnes	8
A. Melville	c Comber, b Grant	15		b Jahangir Khan	14
F.G.H. Chalk	c Grant, b Jahangir Khan	0		not out	19
R.G. Stainton	c Wilcox, b Jahangir Khan	1		c B.O. Allen, b Farnes	0
H.G. Owen-Smith	c Davies, b Jahangir Khan	14		b Jahangir Khan	1
V.G.J. Jenkins	c Comber, b Farnes	25		not out	24
R.G. Tindall	b Farnes	10			
E.A. Barlow	not out	4			
P.C. Oldfield	b Farnes	0			
EXTRAS	B 8, L-B 3, N-B 3	14		B 3, L-B 3	6
	TOTAL	164		TOTAL (6 WKTS)	79

CAMBRIDGE

A.W. Allen	c Stainton, b Barlow	25
A.S. Lawrence	b Owen-Smith	20
D.R. Wilcox	lbw, b Barlow	3
B.O. Allen	c Stainton, b Owen-Smith	53
R. de W.K. Winlaw	c Walker, b Owen-Smith	20
J.H. Human	c and b Owen-Smith	26
J.G.W. Davies	b Owen-Smith	1
M. Jahangir Khan	c Hone, b Barlow	34
R.S. Grant	not out	9
J.T.H. Comber	c and b Melville	0
K. Farnes	c Tindall, b Melville	0
EXTRAS	B 12, L-B 5, N-B 1	18
	TOTAL	209

Cambridge bowling	OVERS	MDNS	RUNS	WKTS		OVERS	MDNS	RUNS	WKTS
Farnes	24.4	9	44	3		16	7	27	4
Jahangir Khan	43	19	54	4		22	13	21	2
Grant	22	10	44	3		—	—	—	—
Human	3	0	8	0		7	0	20	0
Lawrence	—	—	—	—		5	1	5	0

Oxford bowling				
Tindall	12	5	19	0
Townsend	12	5	21	0
Owen-Smith	30	5	93	5
Barlow	24	8	51	3
Melville	4.3	1	7	2

UMPIRES A. Morton and J. Hardstaff

9, 10, 11 July
At Lord's

1934

Match drawn

Both Oxford and Cambridge were strong in batting. J.H. Human was much criticized for the handling of his attack, particularly for not using J.G.W. Davies until Oxford had over 300 in the first innings, and for taking off A.G. Pelham, in the second, when he had reduced Oxford to 19 for 2.

Oxford lost two wickets quickly, but D.C.H. Townsend and F.G.H. Chalk took control, despite the latter having trouble with bats; by the time he had made 40 he was on to his fourth! He played a glorious innings, hitting sixteen fours, but it was Townsend who ensured a high total.

G.W. Parker and A.W. Allen set a Cambridge record opening partnership, putting on 205, and Allen joined the select few who have made a century in the Eton and Harrow and Varsity matches. R. de W.K. Winlaw, who played a fine attacking innings, and J.W.T. Grimshaw kept up the momentum.

J.W. Seamer and A.P. Singleton ensured Oxford's safety on the last afternoon after they were 135 for 6.

The *poor* attendance of *only* 24,000 was said to have been caused by a clash with the Old Trafford Test.

OXFORD	First innings		Second innings	
D.F. Walker	c Pelham, b Jahangir Khan	7	b Davies	30
D.C.H. Townsend	st Powell, b Davies	193	b Pelham	6
F.C. de Saram	c Powell, b King	18	c Human, b Pelham	0
N.S. Mitchell-Innes	c Pelham, b Jahangir Khan	27	c Powell, b Davies	42
F.G.H. Chalk	b Davies	108	c Allen, b Grimshaw	12
J.W. Seamer	c Powell, b Davies	0	not out	24
R.G. Tindall	c Human, b Grimshaw	27	lbw, b Davies	15
K.L.T. Jackson	c Bartlett, b Davies	2	b Jahangir Khan	16
N.S. Knight	b Grimshaw	1	b Jahangir Khan	1
E.A. Barlow	not out	2	c King, b Grimshaw	11
A.P. Singleton	c Human, b Davies	1	c Powell, b Pelham	9
EXTRAS	B 16, L-B 7, W 1, N-B 5	29	B 6, L-B 8, N-B 2	16
TOTAL		415	TOTAL	182

CAMBRIDGE				
A.W. Allen	c de Saram, b Barlow	115	run out	37
G.W. Parker	run out	94	c Barlow, b Singleton	27
R. de W.K. Winlaw	lbw, b Singleton	56	not out	12
J.G.W. Davies	b Barlow	1		
J.H. Human	b Jackson	8	not out	6
H.T. Bartlett	c and b Tindall	12		
A.G. Powell	b Tindall	11		
M. Jahangir Khan	c Townsend, b Singleton	3	lbw, b Singleton	1
A.G. Pelham	c Barlow, b Jackson	17		
J.W.T. Grimshaw	b Mitchell-Innes	40		
F. King	not out	14		
EXTRAS	B 17, L-B 2, W 2, N-B 8	29	B 8, L-B 2, N-B 1	11
TOTAL		400	TOTAL (3 WKTS)	94

Cambridge bowling	OVERS	MDNS	RUNS	WKTS	OVERS	MDNS	RUNS	WKTS
Pelham	19	5	46	0	9.2	5	6	3
Jahangir Khan	33	7	82	2	31	10	46	2
King	20	4	55	1	—	—	—	—
Grimshaw	31	6	93	2	36	23	33	2
Human	5	0	37	0	—	—	—	—
Parker	13	3	30	0	1	1	0	0
Davies	14.4	1	43	5	42	15	81	3

Oxford bowling								
Tindall	29	2	90	2	3	0	14	0
Barlow	32	11	70	2	13	3	24	0
Jackson	22	3	55	2	6	0	28	0
Singleton	36	7	127	2	10	1	17	2
Townsend	6	2	15	0	—	—	—	—
Mitchell-Innes	7.3	2	14	1	—	—	—	—

UMPIRES A. Morton and J. Newman

1935

This match was a triumph for G.W. Parker, the Cambridge captain. He had shown considerable skill and judgement in building a new side, and he made the second highest score in the match, bowled tidily and took three important catches.

Cambridge were very slow before lunch in the first innings, being only 78 for 1. Soon after lunch M. Tindall, with some glorious square-cuts and strokes through the covers, showed that the attack was not all that formidable, and set the scene for Parker's innings.

Oxford struggled against the leg-breaks of J.H. Cameron, a West Indian who three years earlier,

as a Taunton schoolboy, had taken ten wickets in an innings for The Rest against The Lord's Schools, and was later, in 1939 to represent his country against England. In seven overs before lunch he disposed of A. Benn, N.S. Mitchell-Innes and R.C.M. Kimpton at a cost of only 20 runs. F.C. de Saram, with a fine 85, and A.P. Singleton staged a recovery, but the damage had been done.

Despite an excellent bowling performance by A.R. Legard, Oxford were left with 305 to make in five hours and forty minutes; not for a moment did they look like winning, or indeed saving, the match.

CAMBRIDGE

	First innings			Second innings	
N.S. Hotchkin	b Singleton	29		b Legard	30
P.A. Gibb	c Mitchell-Innes, b Darwall-Smith	43		c Halliday, b Singleton	26
M. Tindall	lbw, b Ballance	53		b Legard	12
N.W.D. Yardley	st Kimpton, b Ballance	19		run out	36
H.T. Bartlett	b Ballance	0		c Kimpton, b Legard	24
G.W. Parker	not out	76		b Darwall-Smith	14
W. Wooller	b Darwall-Smith	20		c Ballance, b Legard	35
M. Jahangir Khan	c Benn, b Singleton	30		c Mitchell-Innes, b Legard	26
S.C. Griffith	b Legard	0		b Legard	6
J.H. Cameron	c Halliday, b Singleton	14		lbw, b Legard	0
J.W.T. Grimshaw	b Darwall-Smith	1		not out	1
EXTRAS	B 5, L-B 7, W 1, N-B 4	17		B 7, L-B 2, N-B 4	13
	TOTAL	302		TOTAL	223

OXFORD

D.F. Walker	c Grimshaw, b Jahangir Khan	15		c Griffith, b Jahangir Khan	4
A. Benn	c and b Cameron	46		c Parker, b Wooller	1
F.C. de Saram	c and b Cameron	85		c Hotchkin, b Jahangir Khan	22
N.S. Mitchell-Innes	lbw, b Cameron	1		lbw, b Parker	0
J.W. Seamer	c Parker, b Cameron	4		st Griffith, b Grimshaw	3
R.C.M. Kimpton	lbw, b Cameron	4		lbw, b Cameron	39
J.G. Halliday	b Jahangir Khan	5		b Jahangir Khan	6
A.P. Singleton	b Grimshaw	33		c Parker, b Jahangir Khan	1
R.F.H. Darwall-Smith	b Cameron	7		c Jahangir Khan, b Wooller	14
T.G.L. Ballance	c Jahangir Khan, b Cameron	8		not out	3
A.R. Legard	not out	4		c Gibb, b Cameron	8
EXTRAS	B 5, L-B 4	9		B 3, L-B 5	8
	TOTAL	221		TOTAL	109

Oxford bowling	OVERS	MDNS	RUNS	WKTS		OVERS	MDNS	RUNS	WKTS
Legard	18	8	33	1		25.1	10	36	7
Darwall-Smith	30.3	6	75	3		25	3	59	1
Mitchell-Innes	3	1	3	0		3	2	1	0
Singleton	36	14	66	3		17	5	39	1
Ballance	38	12	92	3		26	7	75	0
Halliday	6	1	16	0		—	—	—	—

Cambridge bowling									
Jahangir Khan	26	4	62	2		25	10	31	4
Wooller	12	2	25	0		7	2	19	2
Grimshaw	20	6	42	1		6	0	11	1
Cameron	25	3	73	7		11.3	2	28	2
Parker	6	3	10	0		11	5	12	1

UMPIRES J. Hardstaff and J. Newman

6, 7, 8 July
At Lord's

1936

*Cambridge won by
8 wickets*

R.C.M. Kimpton, who had made four centuries, sprained an ankle and could not play. This was a cruel blow to Oxford, as was the loss of the toss. Cambridge were a strong all-round team and deserved to win by 3.15 p.m. on the third day.

After lunch on Monday, R.P. Nelson and N.W.D. Yardley put on over a hundred. Nelson was out to a remarkable catch, when M.M. Walford was knocked over at short leg by a full-blooded blow and caught the ball on the rebound. Yardley played superbly, but when he left, Oxford's agony was but half over; by seven o'clock Cambridge had passed their previous record score.

N.S. Mitchell-Innes was out just before lunch on the second day, having batted with skill and courage, and although B.H. Belle showed tenacity and Micky Walford struck the ball well, a follow-on looked inevitable, and so it proved.

For the second time, Oxford found the leg-breaks of J.M. Brocklebank their undoing. Later Sir John Brocklebank, he was selected for the MCC tour of India in the winter of 1939–40, which was cancelled. He had ten wickets for 139 in this match. Mitchell-Innes played another brave captain's innings and J.W. Seamer resisted sternly, but to no avail, and Cambridge needed only 17 to win.

CAMBRIDGE	First innings		Second innings	
N.P. Nelson	c Walford, b Dyson	91	b Darwall-Smith	1
A.F.T. White	hw, b Dyson	19	b Mitchell-Innes	5
M. Tindall	c and b Murray-Wood	10	not out	9
N.W.D. Yardley	c Singleton, b Darwall-Smith	90	not out	2
H.T. Bartlett	c Matthews, b Dyson	0		
P.A. Gibb	c Matthews, b Singleton	46		
J.H. Pawle	b Murray-Wood	40		
M. Jahangir Khan	c Dyson, b Mitchell-Innes	49		
W. Wooller	c Dyson, b Seamer	37		
J.H. Cameron	not out	28		
J.M. Brocklebank	not out	4		
EXTRAS	B 15, L-B 2, W 1	18		
	TOTAL (9 WKTS DEC.)	432	TOTAL (2 WKTS)	17

OXFORD				
N.S. Mitchell-Innes	c and b Cameron	43	c Cameron, b Jahangir Khan	84
M.R. Barton	b Jahangir Khan	4	b Brocklebank	28
B.H. Belle	st Gibb, b Brocklebank	48	st Gibb, b Brocklebank	26
J.N. Grover	c White, b Cameron	12	c Gibb, b Jahangir Khan	19
J.W. Seamer	lbw, b Jahangir Khan	11	b Brocklebank	43
M.M. Walford	c Yardley, b Brocklebank	40	lbw, b Brocklebank	12
W. Murray-Wood	b Jahangir Khan	0	c Gibb, b Jahangir Khan	0
A.P. Singleton	b Wooller	32	c Yardley, b Brocklebank	6
M.H. Matthews	c Yardley, b Brocklebank	0	lbw, b Brocklebank	13
J.H. Dyson	c White, b Brocklebank	3	c Gibb, b Wooller	5
R.F.H. Darwall-Smith	not out	5	not out	0
EXTRAS	B 6, L-B 3, W 2	11	L-B 1, W 2	3
	TOTAL	209	TOTAL	239

Oxford bowling	OVERS	MDNS	RUNS	WKTS	OVERS	MDNS	RUNS	WKTS
Darwall-Smith	25	6	54	1	3	0	3	1
Mitchell-Innes	22	8	53	1	2.4	0	14	1
Singleton	47	10	118	1	—	—	—	—
Dyson	28	3	94	3	—	—	—	—
Murray-Wood	19	1	73	2	—	—	—	—
Seamer	4	0	22	1	—	—	—	—

Cambridge bowling								
Wooller	17.5	6	33	1	23	11	46	1
Jahangir Khan	29	12	33	3	36	15	50	3
Brocklebank	30	12	47	4	27.3	7	92	6
Cameron	24	3	85	2	14	2	40	0
Nelson	—	—	—	—	7	5	8	0

UMPIRES J. Hardstaff and J. Newman

1937

For the first two days it was a ding-dong affair. N.W.D. Yardley made a century for Cambridge, and J.N. Grover did the same for Oxford. In the second innings, apart from P.A. Gibb, Cambridge collapsed against accurate and aggressive bowling and top-class fielding, leaving Oxford needing 160 to win. M.R. Barton and R.C.M. Kimpton ended the match in what *Wisden* described as a 'sensational and brilliant finish'. Roger Kimpton's winning hit went first bounce into the Pavilion. A.P. Singleton takes up the story:

Mark Tindall, the Cambridge captain, and I and a few others were having a beer or two when I was told that I was wanted on the telephone. It was the television experimental station at Alexandra Palace, asking if Mark Tindall and I would go and be interviewed. . . . They sent a car for us. Gordon Harker was on set when we arrived, and when he finished we were on live. We had no briefing at all. Neither of us could remember the scores in the match, and not much of the detail, and the interview developed into arguments between us, and a good deal of laughter. It was not a success.

CAMBRIDGE	First innings		Second innings	
P.A. Gibb	c Macindoe, b Darwall-Smith	0	run out	87
W.E.G. Payton	b Macindoe	10	c Ballance, b Darwall-Smith	3
J.H. Pawle	lbw, b Macindoe	0	lbw, b Macindoe	0
N.W.D. Yardley	c Matthews, b Singleton	101	lbw, b Mitchell-Innes	6
M. Tindall	c Matthews, b Kimpton	10	b Macindoe	8
J.H. Cameron	lbw, b Kimpton	48	c Mitchell-Innes, b Macindoe	22
P.M. Studd	c Matthews, b Mitchell-Innes	18	c Mitchell-Innes, b Ballance	12
R.G. Hunt	c Matthews, b Darwall-Smith	29	c Barton, b Macindoe	2
D.C. Rought-Rought	b Darwall-Smith	11	c Matthews, b Darwall-Smith	16
B.C. Khanna	not out	6	b Ballance	1
T.W. Fraser	c Matthews, b Darwall-Smith	1	not out	1
EXTRAS	B 15, L-B 3, N-B 1	19	B 5, L-B 9, N-B 1	15
	TOTAL	253	TOTAL	173

OXFORD				
M.R. Barton	c Hunt, b Rought-Rought	8	not out	74
E.J.H. Dixon	lbw, b Cameron	61	c Gibb, b Rought-Rought	3
N.S. Mitchell-Innes	b Yardley	19	c and b Fraser	29
R.C.M. Kimpton	c Gibb, b Yardley	6	not out	52
A.P. Singleton	c and b Hunt	9		
J.N. Grover	lbw, b Cameron	121	c Gibb, b Hunt	1
K.B. Scott	c Gibb, b Cameron	10		
R.F.H. Darwall-Smith	b Cameron	0		
M.H. Matthews	c Gibb, b Khanna	13		
D.H. Macindoe	b Hunt	3		
T.G.L. Ballance	not out	8		
EXTRAS	L-B 4, W 5	9	N-B 1	1
	TOTAL	267	TOTAL (3 WKTS)	160

Oxford bowling	OVERS	MDNS	RUNS	WKTS		OVERS	MDNS	RUNS	WKTS
Darwall-Smith	23.3	7	70	4		15.1	4	28	2
Macindoe	25	9	50	2		24	8	42	4
Mitchell-Innes	9	3	16	1		7	3	15	1
Kimpton	14	3	35	2		1	0	9	0
Singleton	11	4	32	1		7	4	7	0
Ballance	9	1	29	0		23	7	43	2
Scott	2	1	2	0		9	4	14	0

Cambridge bowling									
Rought-Rought	20	5	32	1		7.1	3	19	1
Khanna	13.4	3	32	1		3	2	1	0
Hunt	25	8	51	2		16	2	45	1
Yardley	20	9	34	2		4	1	21	0
Fraser	23	6	43	0		14	4	35	1
Cameron	24	4	66	4		6	0	38	0

UMPIRES J. Hardstaff and J. Newman

2, 4, 5 July
At Lord's

1938

Match drawn

The Match was played for the first time on Saturday, Monday and Tuesday. But only 6,372 paid at the gate on Saturday.

Cambridge boasted three future England players. The first was P.A. Gibb, who had already been selected for the Third Test against Australia, which was abandoned through rain. The two others were future England captains, N.W.D. Yardley and F.G. Mann.

Rain deprived Cambridge of probable victory. Oxford were given a good start by E.J.H. Dixon and M.M. Walford, and an attractive innings by J.M. Lomas enabled them to reach 317.

On Monday, Paul Gibb and J.R. Thompson, the one mostly on the back foot and the other mostly on the front, put on 146. Another century stand followed when Yardley joined Gibb, and later M.A.C.P. Kaye livened up the final overs.

Rain prevented a start before tea on Tuesday and there was nothing for Oxford to play for but a draw; at 69 for 5 even this seemed in doubt.

OXFORD	First innings		Second innings	
E.J.H. Dixon	c Wild, b Hewan	73	c Thompson b Hewan	14
M.M. Walford	c Langley, b Hewan	34	c Carris, b Rees-Davies	0
J.M. Lomas	c Rees-Davies, b Kaye	94	c Thompson, b Kaye	3
R.C.M. Kimpton	c Carris, b Kaye	25	c Yardley, b Wild	2
J.D. Eggar	run out	2	lbw, b Hewan	29
J.N. Grover	b Kaye	2	b Carris	35
P.M. Whitehouse	c Thompson, b Hewan	36	not out	26
D.E. Young	lbw, b Hewan	26	not out	9
D.H. Macindoe	c Gibb, b Hewan	0		
R.F.H. Darwall-Smith	c Yardley, b Hewan	9		
W.J. Pershke	not out	1		
EXTRAS	B 7, L-B 4, W 2, N-B 2	15	B 6, L-B 2	8
	TOTAL	317	TOTAL (6 WKTS)	126

CAMBRIDGE		
P.A. Gibb	c Eggar, b Young	122
B.D. Carris	lbw, b Macindoe	4
J.R. Thompson	b Pershke	79
N.W.D. Yardley	c Young, b Macindoe	61
J.D.A. Langley	c Young, b Pershke	15
F.G. Mann	c Grover, b Macindoe	25
P.M. Studd	c Whitehouse, b Pershke	0
G.E. Hewan	b Macindoe	35
J.V. Wild	b Macindoe	3
M.A.C.P. Kaye	not out	55
W.R. Rees-Davies	c Macindoe, b Darwall-Smith	1
EXTRAS	B 12, L-B 8, N-B 5	25
	TOTAL	425

Cambridge bowling	OVERS	MDNS	RUNS	WKTS		OVERS	MDNS	RUNS	WKTS
Rees-Davies	20	3	64	0		10	4	9	1
Kaye	24	5	60	3		11	8	4	1
Wild	21	7	40	0		15	7	25	1
Hewan	36.5	7	91	6		31	13	60	2
Yardley	13	2	30	0		3	2	4	0
Carris	7	1	17	0		7	1	16	1

Oxford bowling	OVERS	MDNS	RUNS	WKTS
Macindoe	45	15	132	5
Darwall-Smith	26.1	7	87	1
Young	36	10	80	1
Pershke	24	8	54	3
Whitehouse	14	4	47	0

UMPIRES J. Newman and J. Hardstaff

1939

Oxford batted most of the first day, with R. Sale displaying an attractive freedom of stroke. They looked set for a big score until A.C. Shirreff returned and the last five wickets fell for few runs.

Only B.D. Carris and A.H. Brodhurst offered much resistance against a skilful medium-pace attack, and Oxford had a handsome lead. E.J.H. Dixon did not enforce the follow-on. J.M. Lomas and R.B. Proud gave a fine display of batting for Oxford, whereupon Cambridge were set 430 to win in five hours. When they were 155 for 5 the match seemed all but over, with D.H. Macindoe in full cry. But this was reckoning without Podge Brodhurst and P.J. Dickinson, for they put on 84 in an hour. G. Evans bowled Podge and

followed this with two more victims, and once again the match seemed over. Not so – J. Webster joined Dickinson, and Oxford began to flag. As *Wisden* describes:

At six o'clock Dixon called for drinks when Dickinson was 98. The interruption did not worry Dickinson at the moment, but he cracked his bat in placing the stroke that completed his hundred, and, after doubt about changing it, he gave short-leg an easy catch off the next ball.

This had been a fine innings, but Cambridge were still not done. J. Webster, who had defended stubbornly, now hit out until S. Pether at last beat him at 7.05 p.m. and the brave fight was over.

OXFORD

	First innings		Second innings	
J.M. Lomas	lbw, b Webster	8	c Blake, b Gillespie	91
R. Sale	c Studd, b Gillespie	65	lbw, b Webster	19
R.B. Proud	c and b Shirreff	19	run out	87
J. Stanning	b Webster	38	not out	39
E.J.H. Dixon	b Shirreff	75		
E.D.R. Eagar	c Mann, b Webster	31	not out	27
G. Evans	c Studd, b Shirreff	59		
A.J.B. Marsham	c Carris, b Shirreff	0		
D.H. Macindoe	c Studd, b Shirreff	0		
S. Pether	lbw, b Dickinson	6		
P.H. Blagg	not out	0		
EXTRAS	B 12	12	B 9, W 1	10
	TOTAL	313	TOTAL (3 WKTS DEC.)	273

CAMBRIDGE

B.D. Carris	lbw, b Macindoe	44	b Pether	36
F.G. Mann	b Evans	13	c Sale, b Pether	57
J.R. Thompson	b Evans	2	b Evans	22
J.P. Blake	lbw, b Macindoe	1	c Stanning, b Macindoe	23
A.H. Brodhurst	c Macindoe, b Marsham	34	b Evans	45
P.M. Studd	b Marsham	7	c Blagg, b Macindoe	0
P.J. Dickinson	run out	26	c Pether, b Evans	100
K.D. Downes	b Evans	3	not out	7
A.C. Shirreff	c Lomas, b Evans	2	c Stanning, b Evans	0
D.W. Gillespie	not out	16	c and b Evans	8
J. Webster	c Blagg, b Macindoe	4	b Pether	60
EXTRAS	L-B 3, N-B 2	5	B 15, L-B 7, N-B 4	26
	TOTAL	157	TOTAL	384

Cambridge bowling	OVERS	MDNS	RUNS	WKTS	OVERS	MDNS	RUNS	WKTS
Webster	19	2	73	3	11	0	50	1
Dickinson	18	2	65	1	8	1	36	0
Shirreff	25.6	9	64	5	17	4	66	0
Gillespie	13	1	52	1	12	0	50	1
Carris	11	4	24	0	19	5	61	0
Brodhurst	4	1	23	0				

Oxford bowling	OVERS	MDNS	RUNS	WKTS	OVERS	MDNS	RUNS	WKTS
Macindoe	16.2	4	32	3	28	6	81	2
Evans	18	2	55	4	33	8	127	5
Pether	8	3	23	0	22.3	6	39	3
Marsham	9	2	42	2	20	2	106	0
Eagar	—	—	—	—	2	1	5	0

UMPIRES J. Hardstaff and J. Newman

11
1946–1955
Swift Recovery

OXFORD *The glorious return*

On a chill April day in 1946 cricket returned to The Parks. In 1914 the Universities had emptied at once and few undergraduates were left save the unfit or the unworthy; the situation was handled better in 1939. Young men were encouraged to continue their education until they were needed, and an imaginative scheme of short courses was introduced. For many, these gave a taste of University life which they were able to renew after their demobilization.

A most generous gesture in the form of a Further Education Grant made possible a University education to many young men returning from the navy, army and air force. Many of these were married, but proper allowance was made for wives and children. The University authorities themselves made an important concession to ex-servicemen – they were excused one subject in the entry requirements. Such a multitude poured into Oxford, including the return to a normal teenage entry, that for a few years 'Schools' took place in June and December to work off the backlog. For cricketers this offered a joyous choice!

Some cricket was played during the war years. Huts were built on part of the Balliol ground, although cricket continued in the middle; the Magdalen ground became a hayfield; some college fields were partly maintained by clubs; North Oxford used the St John's ground, a liaison which continues to the present day. Baseball practice occurred from time to time in The Parks, but largely this most beautiful of grounds lay fallow awaiting happier days.

A great effort was made to keep some sort of University eleven in being, and matches were played at Lord's against Cambridge sides from 1941 to 1945. Of this wartime series, Cambridge won four of the five one-day matches played. The gate money was given to the Red Cross; in 1945 the sum so raised was £475, from a crowd of 11,000. A notable guest on this occasion was F.A. Mackinnon, who had played in 'Cobden's match' in 1870. Apart from these matches at Lord's, Oxford cricket was kept alive under the banner of the Authentics. Some notable names are to be found: E.K. Scott, later a doctor in Cornwall and captain of England's rugby side, played early in the war; L.L. Toynbee, the distinguished sporting artist, played in 1942; and G.A. Wheatley, who captained the later sides, also played at this time.

Before the war, more or less anyone who had the money could get into Oxford provided he had the minimum brains necessary for 'Responsions'. It was not unknown to find places filled as late as early October. In a world where athletic attainments were so highly esteemed, and a blue was regarded as both highly admirable and distinctly useful (especially for admission to the Colonial Service, hence the quip that we had 'an empire of blacks ruled by a handful of blues'), inevitably the athletically gifted aspired to Oxford, which was pleased to have them. Such great Oxford figures as Philip Landon, Dr Stallybrass ('Sonners') and J.C. Masterman were among those dons who would seek out cricketers, even finding funds to help where necessary, although always demanding academic attainment as well.

The war changed all that; the Further Education Grants and, more permanently, R.A. Butler's 1944 Education Act, made money available for all who aspired to University education and could win a place.

Oxford were fortunate indeed that D.H. Macindoe was able and ready to restart cricket in The Parks. He built a good and happy side under his truly inspired leadership. He chose G.A. Wheatley, a wartime player, as his secretary. His greatest good fortune was that M.P. Donnelly came into residence. This name was already known, for Donnelly had toured with the New Zealanders in 1937, and in 1945 had made a memorable hundred for the Dominions against England at Lord's. There was no stroke of which Donnelly was not the master. His off and straight drives were near perfection, he was an elegant and quick-footed cutter, and he murdered anything loose on the leg side. In his two glorious years in The Parks, the word that Donnelly was at the wicket would spread like wildfire, and lecture halls would empty, for the crowds to pack three deep round the ropes.

R.H. Maudsley was a sound player who had already established a reputation at Malvern and Birmingham University, and he gave solid support to Donnelly. Against the Indians they put on 171 together, and in the Lancashire match they shared partnerships of 218 and 124, Donnelly's contributions being 106, 139 and 95 respectively. Macindoe was the best of the bowlers, but J.N. Bartlett, who bowled a tantalizing variety of slow left-arm, had much success, notably in the Varsity Match when, in the first innings, he mesmerized Cambridge's lower order – a performance which deservedly earned him a place for the Gentlemen ten days later.

Donnelly was an admirable captain in 1947, and an injection of established players came up as freshmen – H.A. Pawson and W.G. Keighley as batsmen, A.H. Kardar and A.W.H. Mallett as all-rounders (Kardar had toured with the Indians the previous year), and P.A. Whitcombe as a bowler. Donnelly's batting was again a joy to watch and for the second year he topped a thousand runs. The match against Leicester in The Parks started a run of five wins. In this match, after fine bowling by Mallett and Whitcombe, Oxford needed 239 runs in three hours; they won by five wickets, Donnelly striking seventeen fours in his 95 not out. Cambridge were much stronger this year, and with some assistance from rain, earned a draw.

H.A. Pawson led Oxford to crush Cambridge by an innings, to follow his father's leadership to the same result in Le Couteur's match of 1910. Not only was Pawson a fine cricketer but he was a key figure in the brief but glorious story of the Cup-winning Pegasus football side, and he also played for Charlton as an amateur. (He was the last amateur to play both county cricket and First Division football.) As if this were not enough, as recently as 1984 he successfully represented England in the World Fly Fishing Championships. Pawson led Oxford to a fine victory over Middlesex in The Parks. Kardar made 138 not out and took, in all, nine wickets for 83. Whitcombe had seven of the rest for 76. These two, with C.B. van Ryneveld, also made short work of Somerset.

Contrary to custom, the secretary was not elected captain for the following year; C.B. van Ryneveld was preferred. The strong Commonwealth element of B.H. Travers, who also won a blue for Rugby football, A.H. Kardar and H.B. Robinson, a sharp spinner of off-breaks from Vancouver, carried the day. As it turned out, Whitcombe suffered so much from a back injury that he was seldom at his best in 1949, except in the New Zealand match.

New Zealand suffered the one defeat of their 1949 tour in The Parks when Oxford compiled 247, with M.B. Hofmeyr placidly surviving the whole innings. New Zealand were 67 for 3 overnight. A heavy storm the next morning created conditions which were extremely difficult. Whitcombe and M.H. Wrigley, each over 6 feet 4 inches tall, were for a period almost unplayable. On this remarkable day twenty-two wickets fell for 160. W.M. Wallace for the tourists and C.E. Winn for Oxford both played important innings of character. When the New Zealanders had lost half their wickets for 45 by the second evening, the issue seemed settled; Wallace and Donnelly, kept back until the wicket improved, made a fight of it, but Whitcombe and Wrigley were again in commanding form.

PLAYED AT THE PARKS, 25, 26, 27 May 1949
OXFORD 247 (M.B. Hofmeyr 95 not out, C.E. Winn 58, D.B. Carr 34; G.O. Rabone 5 for 60) and 72 (C.E. Winn 37; G.O. Rabone 6 for 18)
NEW ZEALAND 110 (W.M. Wallace 43; P.A. Whitcombe 4 for 45, M.H. Wrigley 5 for 28) and 126 (W.M. Wallace 37, M.P. Donnelly 32; P.A. Whitcombe 4 for 65, M.H. Wrigley 3 for 23)
Oxford won by 83 runs.

Yorkshire and Middlesex were defeated in The Parks. The author of these words received his introduction to the press when, having taken 5 for 22 against Yorkshire, he was greeted by a young reporter, who called to his mate 'Don't bother with the camera, Charley, he's twenty-seven not seventeen!' Six wins and then defeat at Lord's – such is cricket.

Donald Carr first hit the cricket headlines as an eighteen-year-old in one of the 'Victory Tests', and the year after going down from Oxford played for England in India. He is perhaps best known as the first Secretary of the TCCB, where his tact and diplomacy have been invaluable. Carr led a very useful Oxford side in 1950. Yorkshire were beaten again, with Hofmeyr and B. Boobbyer putting on 131 to pave the way to victory. Hofmeyr made three other hundreds, his captain two, and there were ten in the season.

In 1950 the interior of the pavilion in The Parks was refurbished in memory of Lt F.C. Boult, who gave his life in Tunisia, having led Oxford's wartime XI in 1941.

It was decided in 1951 to put the affairs of the OUCC on a more businesslike footing. Under the guidance of H.S. Altham and R.H. Twining, a new constitution was drawn up. The undergraduate officers were to continue to have full responsibility for the selection and running of the sides; but graduate officers were to share responsibility for money and general guidance.

Apart from Oxford's splendid victory at Lord's, the only other win was against the Free Foresters; a notable feature of this match was the 143 scored by M.C. Cowdrey, not yet an undergraduate, and the 162 in the Foresters' second innings by E.R.T. Holmes of considerably greater seniority. R.V. Divecha had fifty-two wickets in the season, being invaluable to his captain, as he proved in the Varsity match, by turning from a new-ball bowler to be an off-spinner when the shine was gone.

The next four years record the fact that not a single match was won, and this despite the superb batting of Colin Cowdrey and M.J.K. Smith. Rain robbed Oxford of two victories in The Parks in 1953. The bowling improved, and no one could have had a more astonishing and distinguished start to his career than J.M. Allan. Against Yorkshire he bowled seven maidens (five of them to Sir Leonard Hutton) for one wicket, and in the next match against the Australians, he dismissed Miller and Craig in his first over, still without a run from his bowling. Cowdrey stood out head and shoulders above his colleagues as a batsman, but J.C. Marshall played some very good innings and remembers how easy it was to bat at the other end to Cowdrey. The South African H.B. Birrell with 114, and the Australian A.L. Dowding, the very popular captain, with 99, put Oxford on the road to 422 for 9 against Yorkshire.

Apart from Pakistan's easy victory, the defeats in 1954 were narrowly incurred. Worcestershire won by 11 runs, J.P. Fellows-Smith playing a very good innings; Hampshire won by 22 runs in a match involving three declarations; and Warwickshire scraped home by one wicket after a sporting declaration by Cowdrey. A great match was played against Sussex in The Parks. G.H.G. Doggart, by now the Sussex captain, made a hundred in each innings. Allan and Cowdrey both had three-figure scores in the first innings, and Oxford were content to draw with eight wickets gone on the last day. M.J.K. Smith was now on the scene, making even more runs than his captain.

The last year of this decade was a miserably wet one. Allan put in some good performances and coupled with his time for Kent, only just missed doing the 'double'. D.C.P.R. Jowett for the fourth year running bowled his heart out, but still never found himself on a winning side. Oxford, resplendent in their blazers, which for the first time carried the Oxford crowns on the pocket, were content to settle for a draw at Lord's.

CAMBRIDGE *Exciting days again at Fenner's*

In the post-war years Oxford were strengthened by a number of talented overseas players, and despite Cambridge's having a rich vein of home-grown talent who would represent England in this period, they rarely fulfilled their considerable promise at Lord's. Oxford won convincingly in 1946, with a more experienced side, in 1948, when they played much the better cricket, and in 1951, when they brought off a remarkable victory by 21 runs against the odds. Cambridge upset the form book with a stirring win in 1949, and they won an exciting match in 1953, the year which that year's captain sees as something of a watershed, when the post-war boom was over. Thus it can be seen that the Dark Blues had the edge by three victories to two, at a time when the record of the Light Blues against the counties was superior. The inference is obvious – that previous results count for little when Lord's is reached, and that the atmosphere of the big match often produces an outcome that neither the astrologers nor the 'experts' can predict.

There were several preliminary matches that any faithful recorder of these exciting years must include. But before these are evoked, it is worth making the same obvious point that was made about the attributes of the players, and the atmosphere of the play, as first-class cricket re-started after the First World War. To a certain extent in 1946, but in the following years especially, most of the blues had done National Service, some had experienced the vagaries of war (though not all, as I did, had led a platoon attack on a farmhouse in the middle of Europe, and luckily found it empty on arrival!), and all were older, more mature and more experienced cricketers than those who came up direct from school. The excitement of playing against household names, and the thrill of being invited to play at Lord's, and then of actually doing so, were as vivid to me in 1948 as they had been to my father Graham in 1921, and were to be to my son Simon in 1980. (There was, in passing, one person, Douglas Piggott – son of Percy, who was an integral part of Cambridge cricket when I was in residence – who was on the ground at Fenner's either helping in the score-box or scoring, for the debuts of all three of us. Since no other family has had three generations, father to son, of University cricket blues Cambridge can claim a piece of cricket history.)

I shall begin with a personal recollection and then return to four players from the two earlier years of this decade who merit a mention. There are two matches at Fenner's in 1950 that deserve a fuller recollection, once I have made reference to three matches in 1949, and to one in 1948. In the first match of the 1948 season against Lancashire, after play was washed out on the first day – and I include this not to boast, but to set the record straight – the author made 215 not out on debut. 'What's this dangerous relative of yours doing to our Lancashire?' said an eminent cranio-surgeon to my eminent opthalmic surgeon uncle!

The first of the three matches in 1949 was against Essex, in which John Dewes, a left-handed opener from Aldenham, with strong forearms, an ability to hook and cut well, and a thirst for runs, who played in five Tests – and was once, at Hove, heard to call on the fifth ball of an over, 'Come one, three or five'! – and the author, who played in two Tests, set up an unfinished English second-wicket partnership record of 429 in five hours ten minutes. It was a record which was not surpassed until twenty-five years later, by John Jameson and Rohan Kanhai, for Warwickshire. The fact that Doug Insole declared overnight, and did not allow an attempt at the world record 29 runs away, was hailed by the magazine *Truth* as a splendid example of the amateur tradition. The reporters and photographers who came from afar, on Monday morning, to observe a possible world record did not share the same view!

The second match in 1949 to which I refer was against Yorkshire, in which Cambridge gave a trial to J.J. Warr, who had played the previous match for the Arabs, who were one short, against the Crusaders, and been strongly recommended by two Arabs, Allen and Swanton (their founder), over dinner at the University Arms Hotel. It was also the match in which, in the words of *Wisden*, 'Yorkshire gave a trial to three young players, Lowson, an opening bat, Close, an allrounder, and Trueman, a spin bowler [*sic*]'. It was not, as it turned out, a lucky debut for J.J.

The third match, the next one, was against Lancashire, when J.J., who might not have been selected had Peter Hall, a useful opener from Geelong GS, now been fit, took 6 for 35 in twenty-one impressive overs – and was chosen to go to Australia and New Zealand in 1950–1.

The two matches I have chosen from 1950 are the one against the West Indies and that against Leicestershire. The West Indies match was remarkable for the almost total domination of bat over ball. First, John Dewes and David Sheppard put on 343 for the first wicket in four hours forty minutes (they were to put on 349 later in the season, against Sussex at Hove), and Cambridge finished up with 594 for four wickets declared. The tourists then made 730 for three wickets – end of match! When Everton Weekes, who with Frank Worrell put on 350 in three hours and three-quarters, was in the 290s, the Cambridge wicket-keeper for that match, Wynne Denman, heard him mumbling to himself, as he tapped the hard, unyielding Fenner's pitch on a length. He leaned forward to hear the great man's repeated words: 'Play carefully, Weekes man, in the nineties.' The scorecard of this fulfilling yet unfulfilled match makes bizarre reading. As an aside, it was the last occasion when covers were used at Fenner's, until the official introduction of covering.

Played at Cambridge 17, 18, 19 May
Cambridge 594 for 4 dec. (D.S. Sheppard 227, J.G. Dewes 183, G.H.G. Doggart 71, M.H. Stevenson 53 not out)
West Indies 730 for 3 (E.D. Weekes 304 not out, F.M. Worrell 160, R.J. Christiani 111, J.B. Stollmeyer 83, K.B. Trestrail 56 not out)

The second match was the first one to be won by Cambridge at Fenner's after the war. I remember it well for several aspects: for the first 'pair' made by that stalwart Leicestershire opener Les Berry; for J.J.'s 9 for 104 in the match; for the quality of the Light Blue catching in the Leicestershire first innings, in the wake of the talented Australian all-rounder Bill Hayward's superb catch in the first over of the match; and for the fact that I was taking the important examination in my 'Certificate of Competence to teach Latin' on the second morning of the match – and I was not out overnight! Drawing to a close that I hoped would imply further knowledge of the subject at five minutes past eleven o'clock – the examination did not technically finish until noon – I made for the exit from the Mill Lane examination hall. There I found my tutor, Patrick Wilkinson, who was also one of the two examiners, with a broad grin on his face, saying, 'I thought you might be leaving at this time.' Thereupon we mounted our bicycles and rode up to Fenner's, I to continue batting – in partnership with the Rydalian Mike Stevenson, who played many good innings over four years – he to watch the match, and at the same time to look over my undoubtedly inadequate script.

These were enjoyable days at Fenner's, when Cyril Coote prepared pitches that gave aspiring players the ideal conditions in which to learn the arts of batting and bowling; when there was a loyal following at Fenner's and much good cricket to enjoy; when the number of blues selected for the Gentlemen, and for England, added an extra interest and attraction; and when, as in other eras also, there was much 'laughter and the love of friends'. One instance stays in my memory. Fenner's is about a hundred or so yards from Parker's Piece, where Cambridge had once played, and the great Jack Hobbs and Tom Hayward had learned their craft, and where there were usually dozens of matches going on at the same time. In one county match at Fenner's the author had been calling, decisively or indecisively according to choice, but certainly not short on decibels. On returning to the pavilion, he was greeted by J.J.'s, 'Well done, Hubert! You've just run out twenty-seven batsmen on Parker's Piece.'

Then there was a latter-day 'Miller's Tale', when the Australians returned to Fenner's in 1953. Keith, as is well known, had sporting interests other than cricket, and the proximity of Newmarket proved irresistible. He made a quick 20 going in first, and after his dismissal – *c* Bushby *b* Hare – he was spirited away to the Heath in a taxi ordered by Cyril Coote. The tourists were dismissed by tea-time – Marlar 5 for 139 – and Neil Harvey, captaining the tourists, had Miller summoned over the tannoy. Arriving back, he raced into the pavilion, saw a plate of cakes in front of the Pickwickian figure of Sir Henry Thirkill, the much-loved President of the CUCC, and whipped them from in front of his startled gaze. 'No lunch, no tea, and I have lost my shirt,' were Keith's hurried words of justification, as he ran on to the field.

Thirdly, there was the occasion of the ex-Middlesex captain and the walking stick. Les Berry's 'pair' at Fenner's, recently referred to, raised no attendant smile, but the 'pair' experienced by Walter Robins in the Cambridge *v* Free Foresters match of 1951 evoked, for justifiable reasons, an outbreak of laughter that those who were there recall to this day with unalloyed pleasure. Robbie had ribbed G.O. Allen about how he used to go regularly to Fenner's and make a hundred, assisted by the kindness of the pitch. 'One could make a hundred there with a walking stick,' Robbie claimed, and responded to the suggestion that he too should play for the Foresters in 1951 and make good his boast.

Wisden makes no bones about what happened. In the first innings it states, 'G.O. Allen *c* Popplewell *b* Warr 103', but also 'R.W.V. Robins *b* Wait 0'. What it does not record is that his dismissal came off the first ball he received, an inducker from the Alleynian and fellow Kingsman of mine John Wait – on his day a fine bowler, who later taught at Mill Hill but sadly died relatively young – and that Robbie tried to hit it past cover's left hand. George Unwin went in on a hat-trick, 'in the know' about Robbie's boast and savouring what had happened. Come the second innings, Allen had made but 55 when he was out and passed Robbie coming in on a 'pair'. 'It is customary,' Robbie said as he passed J.J. Warr, the Cambridge captain, 'to give someone on a pair one off the mark, especially if he is an old blue.' Warr bowled him an away-swinger which he tried to hit wide of mid-on, and he was comprehensively bowled, thus completing an imperial royal pair. All knew of the claim about the walking stick and collapsed with mirth, except perhaps the outgoing batsman and his incoming colleague, George Unwin, on a hat-trick for the second time in the match, who was heard to say, 'I'm getting rather fed-up with this.'

The cricketing faithful at Fenner's had much to savour throughout the decade. The 1946 side was captained by the Bradfieldian Peter Bodkin, a medic who was equally good at soccer and cricket; and the 1947 side by the talented left-handed opener from Repton, Guy Willatt, also a soccer blue, who had been unlucky not to play at Lord's in 1939. He went on to play, first for Nottinghamshire, but mainly for Derbyshire, whom he captained from 1951 to 1954, before his school-mastering, including as headmaster twice over, curtailed his availability. Other talented games-players of this period were Barry Trapnell, chosen to play for the Gentlemen in 1946, an outstanding rugby fives player and, like Willatt, a head-master twice over, and Guy Shuttleworth, who subsequently taught at St Peter's, York, a fine cover-point and more than useful batsman, and a good enough wing-half also to have won a soccer international cap.

There was much to admire in the fine play of Trevor Bailey, who became an indispensable member of the England side, and one of the country's greatest all-rounders. Who will forget, for example, his heroic stand with Willie Watson at Lord's in 1953, which saved England from defeat and virtually regained the Ashes, or his 7 for 34 against the West Indies at Kingston, Jamaica, on the 1953–4 tour? He obtained the 'double' more times than any amateur bar two, and showed a champion's style in other sports by winning an FA Amateur Cup medal for Walthamstow. He was either Essex captain or secretary, or both, for many years, and he now writes and summarizes on radio with considerable analytical skill.

Another man of Essex, from Sir George Monoux, Walthamstow, Doug Insole also pleased with his outstanding fielding and unorthodox but effective batting. He led Cambridge to a surprise victory against Oxford in 1949, and went on to play twelve Tests for England, to captain Essex, and to serve the game disinterestedly as a top administrator, for Essex, the TCCB and the MCC. He too was a fine soccer player, playing for Corinthian Casuals and winning a runner-up's medal at Wembley in 1956. I had the pleasure of being his secretary for soccer in 1948, and for cricket in 1949.

Those who were present at Fenner's also enjoyed the successful partnerships of Peter May, arguably the finest English post-war batsman, and David Sheppard, now Bishop of Liverpool. Described by J.J Warr in his Foreword to May's *A Game Enjoyed* as 'a great performer in the classical tradition' and as 'the supreme professional in the ranks of the amateurs, just as Denis Compton was the supreme amateur in the ranks of the professionals', P.B.H. led England in 41 Tests, 35 of them consecutively, and made over four thousand runs in Test cricket. He also scored five double-centuries in his career, including 285 not out in a famous partnership, at Edgbaston, in 1957, with his friend Colin Cowdrey. What is sometimes forgotten is that as a seventeen-year-old he made 146 for the Public Schools against the Combined Services, and 138 on debut against the South Africans at Headingley in 1951, his second season at Cambridge. He also won soccer blues, and the Kinnaird Cup, the amateur championship for Eton fives. In the third edition of *Barclay's World of Cricket* Richie Benaud pays tribute to May as both a fine and an extremely pleasant cricketer, and believes that his second hundred between lunch and tea on the third day of the MCC match against the Australian eleven, at Sydney in 1958, can rarely have been bettered by an English player anywhere in the world. Subsequent to his all too early retirement in the early sixties, he has given much back to the game – on behalf of Surrey, whom he captained to two Championship wins; for the TCCB, as chairman of selectors 1982–88; and for the MCC, both as Chairman of the Cricket Committee, and as President in 1980–1.

Sheppard was chosen to tour Australia and New Zealand in 1950–1, at the end of his first Cambridge season, which had seen those two remarkable partnerships of over three hundred with Dewes, and he created a record in the 1952 Cambridge season, in which he was captain, by scoring no less than 1581 runs, with seven centuries, including one in the University Match, at an average of 79.05. Cyril Coote has recently recalled his straight six off Sonny Ramadhin on to the roof of the old pavilion, over the pavilion clock, photographed all the way by the delightful E.A. Wood, who was most generous in his gifts of photographs. Cyril claimed that the three batting positions revealed in this stroke were an ideal model for the young.

Sheppard made a considerable impact, by both his personality and his play, as captain of Sussex in 1953, when the Championship depended on the final match against Surrey, which Sussex had to win, and which rain unfortunately curtailed. By application and an exceptional commitment he became a talented opener in demand by England, before, like Tom Killick before him, his priestly vocation cut short his cricketing career, although it did not prevent a number of successful returns. After taking holy orders he served the Mayflower Family Centre both before and after his second tour in Australia, and was then made Suffragan Bishop of Woolwich, before being translated to Liverpool.

The supporters also saw some fine attacking bowling in the early fifties. First, already mentioned, there was J.J. Warr, a future captain of Middlesex and President of the MCC in 1988, who took 169 wickets as a Cambridge bowler over four years, by universal consent a raconteur and wit of unusual talent. His 1951 side, in passing, contained two future England hockey players – Pat Mathews, of Felsted and Clare, and John Cockett, Aldenham and Trinity Hall, who lived his teaching life at Mathews' old school. Secondly there was Robin Marlar, now a lively and articulate cricket correspondent of the *Sunday Times*, and founder of an international firm of headhunters. In three years he took 147 wickets as an off-spinner, captained Sussex for several years and was unlucky not to have played for England. He recalls with a wistful pleasure Len Hutton's remark to him in 1951, at lunch, after he had had Len stumped by Oliver Popplewell: 'I suppose you'll be thinking you'll get a blue now you've got me out.'

In his one year in the Cambridge side, that of 1952 – the side included Raman Subba Row, who was also rugby fives captain and became, by temperament and technique, a successful England opener and administrator – the South African fast bowler Cuan McCarthy, wearing a home international blazer dyed light blue, and with the top pocket removed, headed the bowling averages, taking 44 wickets at an average of 17.20 each. Few who were at Worcester that year, when Cambridge won by six wickets, will forget the delayed lunch on the first day, when several no-balls were called by Paddy Corrall, the square-leg umpire, as he paid especial attention to McCarthy's action. *Wisden* preserves a curious silence about this episode, but records Sheppard's fine 239 not out in the second innings, and his partnership with Subba Row of 202 in two and a quarter hours for the third wicket.

There were, of course, several other Light Blue players to catch the eye during this decade. Three were to become judges – the Carthusian Hugh Griffiths, who opened the bowling with Trevor Bailey in 1947 and 1948, and played for Glamorgan, also becoming its President; Oliver Popplewell, at Charterhouse with May, a more than useful wicket-keeper in the sides of 1949, 1950 and 1951, now a judge and author of the report on the Bradford City Fire Disaster in 1986, which was to lead to legislation to improve the safety at sports grounds, and a Trustee of MCC; and John Slack, from University College School, Hampstead, who made 135 against Middlesex at Fenner's on his debut, and subsequently played for Buckinghamshire at cricket and for Middlesex at rugby. Gerry Alexander, a talented wicket-keeper/batsman who played twenty-five Tests for the West Indies and headed the batting averages on their Australian tour of 1960–1, has become a veterinary surgeon working for the World Bank. Brian Parsons, from Brighton College, was to turn professional and play 119 matches for Surrey. Vic Lumsden, who had his moment of glory when Worcestershire were beaten at Worcester by four wickets, scoring 93 and 107, returned to the West Indies.

Several blues in this decade other than those already mentioned were to become schoolmasters: six, for example, of the 1950 side, including three headmasters – Tom Wells, also a rugby blue, at Wanganui, Bill Hayward at Brisbane Church of England Grammar School, and me at King's School, Bruton – and two of the 1954 side, including the strong opening partnership of Mike Bushby, the captain and a fine cover-point who ran the cricket at Tonbridge for several years, and Dennis Silk, a talented rugby and rugby fives player and still a celebrated Warden of Radley after twenty years, who achieved the distinction of scoring a century twice at Lord's in successive years and who would later captain MCC in New Zealand. Reference to the Cambridge captain of 1955, the poor man's Clark Gable in the film *Radley*, as he was flatteringly described in one after-dinner speech, is a strong note on which to end the story of this decade.

1946

Three Dark Blues, in particular, gave their side an edge over less experienced opponents: M.P. Donnelly, a left-handed batsman of rare skill and experience, D.H. Macindoe, the Oxford captain, who would one day become Vice-Provost of Eton, and R. Sale, a future Headmaster of Brentwood.

Cambridge made a disastrous start, the analysis of B.H. Travers, future Headmaster of Sydney Grammar, at one time reading 13–8–17–2. N.M. Mischler, a Pauline, checked the rot,

aided by two fine games-players, G.M. Shuttleworth and B.M.W. Trapnell, but J.N. Bartlett, the slow left-armer, tidied up the tail.

Of the Oxford batsmen nobody except Donnelly and Sale reached twenty, thanks largely to the hostile bowling of W.H. Griffiths, later to play for Glamorgan and become a High Court Judge. On Monday morning Donnelly reigned supreme; his brilliant 142 came in two hours and fifty-five minutes. A crowd of 23,000 watched, recapturing pre-war interest.

CAMBRIDGE	First innings		Second innings	
G.L. Willatt	c Newton-Thompson, b Travers	9	c Newton-Thompson, b Travers	6
D.G. Lacy-Scott	c Rumbold, b Travers	0	c Travers, b Macindoe	11
P.E. Bodkin	lbw, b Macindoe	3	c Maudsley, b Travers	2
N.M. Mischler	b Sutton	42	lbw, b Bartlett	16
G.M. Shuttleworth	c Wheatley, b Bloy	33	lbw, b Bartlett	16
J. Pepper	b Travers	33	b Bartlett	3
E.R. Conradi	b Bartlett	12	c Maudsley, b Sutton	22
B.M.W. Trapnell	b Bartlett	41	c Wheatley, b Sutton	8
J.M. Mills	not out	10	c Bartlett, b Macindoe	11
B.S. Hobson	b Bartlett	2	b Travers	6
W.H. Griffiths	lbw, b Bartlett	0	not out	0
EXTRAS	B 10, L-B 5, N-B 1	16	B 21, L-B 4, N-B 1	26
	TOTAL	201	TOTAL	127

OXFORD	First innings		Second innings	
R. Sale	c Conradi, b Trapnell	42	c Mischler, b Mills	10
J.S. Rumbold	b Griffiths	9	lbw, b Mills	10
R.H. Maudsley	b Trapnell	3	c Shuttleworth, b Trapnell	15
M.P. Donnelly	b Griffiths	142	c Hobson, b Griffiths	1
N.C.F. Bloy	b Bodkin	19	not out	26
J.O. Newton-Thompson	b Griffiths	4	not out	1
G.A. Wheatley	c Conradi, b Trapnell	10		
B.H. Travers	lbw, b Griffiths	8		
D.H. Macindoe	c Mischler, b Griffiths	13		
M.A. Sutton	st Mischler, b Bodkin	6		
J.N. Bartlett	not out	1		
EXTRAS	B 1, L-B 2, N-B 1	4	B 4, L-B 2	6
	TOTAL	261	TOTAL (4 WKTS)	69

Oxford bowling	OVERS	MDNS	RUNS	WKTS	OVERS	MDNS	RUNS	WKTS
Macindoe	26	11	52	1	29	18	30	2
Travers	26	16	30	3	12.5	4	27	3
Maudsley	1	0	3	0	—	—	—	—
Sutton	18	4	39	1	8	1	28	2
Bloy	12	1	49	1	—	—	—	—
Bartlett	11	5	12	4	24	15	16	3

Cambridge bowling	OVERS	MDNS	RUNS	WKTS	OVERS	MDNS	RUNS	WKTS
Griffiths	28.4	7	84	5	13	5	18	1
Lacy-Scott	8	2	23	0	—	—	—	—
Trapnell	24	12	41	3	6.5	1	19	1
Mills	18	1	52	0	4	0	10	2
Bodkin	13	7	40	2	4	0	16	0
Hobson	2	0	17	0	—	—	—	—

UMPIRES G. Beet and H.W. Lee

5, 7, 8 July
At Lord's

1947

Match drawn

Oxford arrived at Lord's with three old blues, Cambridge with six; Oxford with five first-class wins to their credit, Cambridge with two. Oxford batted on until nearly one o'clock on the second day, and thereby limited their chance of victory. W.G. Keighley, and H.A. Pawson put on a fine 226 for the second wicket, to which outstanding running between the wickets contributed. M.P. Donnelly played excitingly, and was well supported by A.H. Kardar and D.F. Henley. T.E. Bailey took three important wickets, but J.M. Mills, a leg-spinner, had the best figures, with 53–11–137–4.

Cambridge's reply centred on H.E. Watts and D.J. Insole. Kardar and the Canadian H.B. Robinson both bowled well. Cambridge followed on, and G.L. Willatt made 90 in three hours fifty minutes and, together with B.G.M. Cangley, Bailey and Insole, helped Cambridge survive. Over 20,000 watched the match.

OXFORD	First innings		Second innings	
W.G. Keighley	*b* Bailey	99		
N.C.F. Bloy	*b* Griffiths	9		
H.A. Pawson	*run out*	135		
M.P. Donnelly	*lbw, b* Bailey	81		
A.H. Kardar	*b* Bailey	46		
D.F. Henley	*c* Bailey, *b* Mills	52		
R.H. Maudsley	*b* Mills	12		
A.W.H. Mallett	*b* Mills	10		
P.A. Whitcombe	*lbw, b* Mills	6		
H.B. Robinson	*b* Griffiths	1		
W.M. Davidson	*not out*	0		
EXTRAS	B 5, L-B 1	6		
	TOTAL	457		

CAMBRIDGE				
G.L. Willatt	*c* Pawson, *b* Whitcombe	1	*lbw, b* Kardar	90
J. Pepper	*b* Kardar	13	*c* Mallett, *b* Kardar	20
B.G.M. Cangley	*b* Kardar	23	*b* Mallett	38
H.E. Watts	*c* Mallett, *b* Robinson	65	*c* Keighley, *b* Robinson	1
T.E. Bailey	*c* Donnelly, *b* Robinson	9	*not out*	60
G.M. Shuttleworth	*c* Donnelly, *b* Robinson	9	*not out*	27
D.J. Insole	*run out*	38	*c* Davidson, *b* Robinson	44
P.B. Datta	*b* Robinson	19		
N.M. Mischler	*c* Davidson, *b* Kardar	8		
J.M. Mills	*b* Kardar	3		
W.H. Griffiths	*not out*	1		
EXTRAS	B 3, L-B 8, W 1	12	B 30, L-B 3, N-B 1	34
	TOTAL	201	TOTAL (5 WKTS)	314

Cambridge bowling	OVERS	MDNS	RUNS	WKTS	OVERS	MDNS	RUNS	WKTS
Bailey	36	10	112	3				
Griffiths	30	7	78	2				
Datta	31	6	80	0				
Mills	53	11	137	4				
Willatt	6	1	20	0				
Insole	3	0	24	0				

Oxford bowling								
Mallett	27	9	45	0	38	21	39	1
Whitcombe	16	5	35	1	18	4	31	0
Henley	4	0	8	0	—	—	—	—
Kardar	25.3	9	50	4	36	19	50	2
Robinson	17	5	51	4	30	6	99	2
Pawson	—	—	—	—	11	3	19	
Donnelly	—	—	—	—	6	2	23	0
Bloy	—	—	—	—	2	0	18	0
Maudsley	—	—	—	—	2	1	1	0

UMPIRES H.G. Baldwin and D. Davies

1948

Oxford had eight old blues – including an experienced captain in H.A. Pawson, and a bowler, P.A. Whitcombe, who had that season dismissed Hutton (twice), Hassett, Dollery and Robertson – and a fine South African freshman all-rounder in C.B. van Ryneveld. Cambridge had five old blues, including the all-rounder T.E. Bailey, plus the returning J.G. Dewes, and successful freshmen in B.C. Elgood and the author.

In the event, Oxford showed marked superiority. The key to the match lay in Cambridge's managing a paltry 209, in good conditions, on the whole of the first day, and then, in the nets on Monday morning, losing the seamer J.R. Urquhart without his bowling a ball. But fine bowling by Whitcombe, with his high action and splendid control – he took 7 for 51 in 34.2 overs – had pointed the way. Dewes, Bailey and G.M. Shuttleworth, made the only worthwhile scores.

The Oxford innings was dominated by a brilliant 145 not out in two hours fifty minutes by H.E. Webb, also a fine rackets player, in partnerships first with the admirable Pawson and later with A.W.H. Mallett. Spinning the ball beautifully, van Ryneveld completed the rout.

CAMBRIDGE	First innings		Second innings	
J. Pepper	c Travers, b Whitcombe	21	lbw, b van Ryneveld	7
J.G. Dewes	c Davidson, b Mallett	54	hw, b van Ryneveld	14
G.H.G. Doggart	b Whitcombe	3	b van Ryneveld	5
B.C. Elgood	c Webb, b Whitcombe	19	b Kardar	10
T.E. Bailey	c Davidson, b Whitcombe	55	b Whitcombe	18
G.M. Shuttleworth	not out	46	st Davidson, b van Ryneveld	10
D.J. Insole	c Davidson, b Whitcombe	2	b van Ryneveld	29
J.M. Mills	c Davidson, b Whitcombe	1	c Davidson, b van Ryneveld	0
B.J.K. Pryer	b Travers	3	b van Ryneveld	18
J.R. Urquhart	run out	0	not out	1
W.H. Griffiths	b Whitcombe	0	c Webb, b Kardar	19
EXTRAS	L-B 5	5	B 9, L-B 3, W 1	13
	TOTAL	209	TOTAL	144

OXFORD

W.G. Keighley	c Griffiths, b Bailey	13
C.E. Winn	c Griffiths, b Bailey	16
C.B. van Ryneveld	c Insole, b Bailey	31
H.A. Pawson	b Griffiths	59
A.H. Kardar	c Pryer, b Bailey	6
H.E. Webb	not out	145
B.H. Travers	not out	21
P.A. Whitcombe	c Doggart, b Bailey	13
A.W.H. Mallett	c Insole, b Pryer	57
H.B. Robinson	c Doggart, b Pryer	1
EXTRAS		9
	TOTAL (9 WKTS DEC.)	361

W.W. Davidson did not bat

Oxford bowling	OVERS	MDNS	RUNS	WKTS		OVERS	MDNS	RUNS	WKTS
Whitcombe	34.2	14	51	7		18	6	27	1
Mallett	31	16	37	1		24	7	33	0
Travers	23	10	32	1		—	—	—	—
van Ryneveld	25	10	47	0		34	14	57	7
Kardar	17	9	27	0		13.1	7	14	2
Robinson	3	1	10	0		—	—	—	—

Cambridge bowling									
Bailey	26	3	110	5					
Griffiths	35	9	106	1					
Pryer	17.3	3	54	2					
Mills	15	0	64	0					
Doggart	3	0	18	0					

UMPIRES A.R. Coleman and C.N. Woolley

1949

Oxford came to Lord's with six first-class victories under their belt, including one against the New Zealanders, and Cambridge with a solitary win over Somerset at Bath. The tables were now turned with a vengeance.

Put in to bat, the Light Blues did so with a welcome consistency. J.G. Dewes and R.J. Morris had an opening partnership of 84, and M.H. Stevenson and the author had a third-wicket partnership of 111. A.G.J. Rimell also batted forcefully. Cambridge eventually made 359, the spinners A.H. Kardar and C.B. van Ryneveld both bowling well.

Oxford batted disappointingly against the spirited Light Blue attack, of which J.J. Warr and O.J. Wait were the pick. M.B. Hofmeyr played throughout the innings – the first time since W.H. Patterson in 1881 – taking four hours five minutes to make 64 runs. Warr's sustained bowling and impressive out-cricket limited Oxford in their second innings. It was touch and nearly go when Warr took the final wicket – leaving Cambridge to make 133 in ninety-five minutes. Dewes led the way with some good hooking.

CAMBRIDGE	First innings			Second innings	
J.G. Dewes	c Carr, b Kardar	48		c Campbell, b Carr	45
R.J. Morris	b Wrigley	46		st Campbell, b van Ryneveld	25
M.H. Stevenson	c Boobbyer, b Wrigley	70		c Hofmeyr, b van Ryneveld	37
G.H.G. Doggart	b Whitcombe	60		not out	6
A.G.J. Rimell	c Kardar, b Chesterton	57		not out	8
D.J. Insole	c van Reyneveld, b Kardar	5			
A.C. Burnett	b Kardar	0			
P.J. Hall	c and b van Ryneveld	12			
O.B. Popplewell	st Campbell, b van Ryneveld	17			
J.J. Warr	not out	15			
O.J. Wait	c and b van Ryneveld	2			
EXTRAS	B 10, L-B 17	27		B 5, L-B 5, W 2	12
	TOTAL	359		TOTAL (3 WKTS)	133

OXFORD					
M.B. Hofmeyr	not out	64		c Doggart, b Rimell	54
B. Boobbyer	b Wait	10		c Burnett, b Doggart	17
C.E. Winn	c Doggart, b Wait	2		b Warr	30
C.B. van Ryneveld	run out	12		c Popplewell, b Warr	47
D.B. Carr	c Burnett, b Hall	13		run out	35
A.H. Kardar	lbw, b Doggart	25		c Doggart, b Wait	11
I.P. Campbell	c Popplewell, b Doggart	0		b Doggart	16
C.R.D. Rudd	b Hall	5		b Warr	0
P.A. Whitcombe	c Popplewell, b Warr	14		lbw, b Doggart	47
G.H. Chesterton	b Warr	9		not out	39
M.H. Wrigley	b Warr	0		c Burnett, b Warr	11
EXTRAS	B 10, L-B 3, W 1, N-B 1	15		B 3, L-B 7, W 2, N-B 3	15
	TOTAL	169		TOTAL	322

Oxford bowling	OVERS	MDNS	RUNS	WKTS		OVERS	MDNS	RUNS	WKTS
Whitcombe	21	4	48	1		1	0	5	0
Wrigley	18	3	67	2		5	0	22	0
Chesterton	18	4	40	1		4	0	20	0
Kardar	49	21	79	3		7.5	0	41	0
van Ryneveld	38.1	9	98	3		8	1	28	2
Carr	—	—	—	—		1	0	5	1

Cambridge bowling									
Warr	21.3	7	43	3		33.2	6	91	4
Wait	18	6	31	2		20	5	66	1
Hall	17	3	46	2		19	4	64	0
Rimell	12	9	7	0		10	3	29	1
Doggart	8	3	10	2		21	7	57	3
Stevenson	4	0	17	0		—	—	—	—

UMPIRES F. Chester and E. Cooke

8, 10, 11 July
At Lord's

1950

Match drawn

This was a well-contested match, spoilt by the loss of Monday's play after lunch. Cambridge had arrived at Lord's with a reputation for high scoring – the freshman D.S. Sheppard and J.G. Dewes twice put on over 340 for the first wicket, and P.B.H. May had also arrived. Oxford had four first-class wins to their credit, under their talented captain D.B. Carr. When Cambridge batted, Sheppard was the only one of the four to enhance his reputation. C.B. van Ryneveld, in a long spell took 5 for 78 in 32.1 overs.

M.B. Hofmeyr played with more freedom than in 1949 and J.J. Warr again bowled well.

On the final day R.V. Divecha took 4 for 82 in 31 overs and prevented Cambridge from getting away, despite a sterling partnership of 81 for the fifth wicket by May and M.H. Stevenson. Cambridge played safe, setting Oxford 225 in two hours ten minutes. They were never in touch, but Carr excelled until his surprising dismissal.

CAMBRIDGE	First innings		Second innings	
J.G. Dewes	c Divecha, b Jose	23	c Campbell, b Divecha	25
D.S. Sheppard	b Carr	93	c Carr, b Henderson	26
G.H.G. Doggart	c Campbell, b van Ryneveld	27	b Divecha	14
P.B.H. May	run out	7	b Divecha	39
A.G.J. Rimell	b van Ryneveld	0	c Carr, b Divecha	2
M.H. Stevenson	lbw, b Carr	8	not out	64
T.U. Wells	st Campbell, b van Ryneveld	6	c Blake, b Henderson	3
W.I.D. Hayward	st Campbell, b van Ryneveld	3	run out	0
O.B. Popplewell	lbw, b van Ryneveld	11	not out	5
J.J. Warr	b Divecha	4		
P.A. Kelland	not out	0		
EXTRAS	B 9, L-B 5, N-B 4	18	B 7, L-B 7, N-B 1	15
	TOTAL	200	TOTAL (7 WKTS DEC.)	193

OXFORD				
M.B. Hofmeyr	b Stevenson	75	lbw, b Stevenson	11
B. Boobbyer	lbw, b Warr	6	c Sheppard, b Hayward	26
P.D.S. Blake	run out	1	b Hayward	0
C.B. van Ryneveld	c Popplewell, b Kelland	0	not out	8
D.B. Carr	b Warr	22	b Doggart	55
A.D. Jose	c May, b Warr	8		
C.E. Winn	c Sheppard, b Rimell	9	b Popplewell, b Warr	4
H.J. Potts	b Kelland	19	not out	8
R.V. Divecha	c Doggart, b Stevenson	2		
I.P. Campbell	not out	19		
D. Henderson	c Doggart, b Warr	1		
EXTRAS	B 1, L-B 1, W 2, N-B 3	7	B 4, L-B 4, W 2	10
	TOTAL	169	TOTAL (5 WKTS)	122

Oxford bowling	OVERS	MDNS	RUNS	WKTS	OVERS	MDNS	RUNS	WKTS
Jose	11	3	28	1	9	2	25	0
Divecha	22	12	22	1	31	7	82	4
Henderson	11	3	22	0	22	7	31	2
van Ryneveld	32.1	8	78	5	12	2	26	0
Carr	7	0	32	2	3	0	14	0

Cambridge bowling								
Warr	21.5	7	44	4	13	2	49	1
Kelland	10	1	32	2	5	1	13	0
Hayward	6	0	20	0	6	2	13	2
Rimell	21	9	32	1	6	3	5	0
Doggart	11	6	21	0	6	1	12	1
Stevenson	6	2	13	2	5	1	12	1
May	—	—	—	—	1	0	8	0

UMPIRES H. Elliott and K. McCanlis

1951

Cambridge came to Lord's with three victories, on tour under their belt, and with four players who later the same season played for the Gentlemen. Oxford arrived with only one victory to their credit – and with what critics called a less prestigious side. Such, however, is cricket's glorious uncertainty that the Dark Blues achieved a remarkable win.

Wisden suggests that the victory was due as much as anything to the number of runs that Oxford, by brilliant fielding, saved, and Cambridge, by occasional slackness, gave away. Cambridge's having to bat last on a wearing wicket must also have told against them – as also

the fact that, whereas the Uppinghamian B. Boobbyer made a cautious but important 80 in Oxford's second innings, neither Sheppard nor May, although batting stylishly, played the really long innngs that they, and their captain, must have hoped for. For Oxford, D.B. Carr twice played well.

Warr's 4 for 31, opening for Cambridge, was matched by the Australian A.D. Jose's 4 for 46, opening for Oxford; but class spin-bowling played an important part, Marlar's 5 for 41 and R. Subba Row's 5 for 21 being surpassed by R.V. Divecha's splendid 7 for 62 in Cambridge's second innings.

OXFORD	First innings		Second innings	
M.B. Hofmeyr	*lbw*, b Warr	40	*run out*	19
B. Boobbyer	c May, b Marlar	17	c and b Subba Row	80
P.J. Whitcombe	c Subba Row, b Marlar	10	c Subba Row, b Wait	5
D.B. Carr	c Popplewell, b Marlar	34	c Subba Row, b Marlar	50
P.D.S. Blake	c Subba Row, b Marlar	24	c Cockett, b Subba Row	1
C.E. Winn	c Warr, b Stevenson	6	st Popplewell, b Subba Row	0
D.J. Lewis	c Hayward, b Warr	19	c Popplewell, b Subba Row	0
R.V. Divecha	b Warr	0	c Sheppard, b Warr	14
W.M. Mitchell	c May, b Warr	9	*not out*	17
A.D. Jose	b Marlar	1	c Marlar, b Subba Row	0
J.N. Bartlett	*not out*	4	c Popplewell, b Warr	0
EXTRAS	B 11, L-B 2, W 1	14	B 14, L-B 2, W 5, N-B 1	22
	TOTAL	178	TOTAL	208

CAMBRIDGE				
D.S. Sheppard	c Whitcombe, b Divecha	23	c Boobbyer, b Divecha	42
K.P.A. Mathews	*lbw*, b Mitchell	25	*lbw*, b Divecha	15
W.I.D. Hayward	*lbw*, b Jose	9	c Whitcombe, b Divecha	35
P.B.H. May	c sub., b Divecha	30	c Whitcombe, b Bartlett	33
J.A. Cockett	b Jose	0	c Carr, b Divecha	0
R. Subba Row	*not out*	37	b Bartlett	4
M.H. Stevenson	c Jose, b Mitchell	0	c Carr, b Divecha	7
O.B. Popplewell	*run out*	10	b Divecha	1
J.J. Warr	*lbw*, b Jose	5	b Divecha	28
R.G. Marlar	b Jose	0	c Whitcombe, b Bartlett	17
O.J. Wait	*run out*	2	*not out*	0
EXTRAS	B 22, L-B 5	27	B 8, L-B 6, W 1	15
	TOTAL	168	TOTAL	197

Cambridge bowling	OVERS	MDNS	RUNS	WKTS	OVERS	MDNS	RUNS	WKTS
Warr	21	12	31	4	29	9	45	2
Wait	14	2	26	0	19	5	32	1
Hayward	9	1	28	0	12	3	16	0
Marlar	26	11	41	5	26	8	64	1
Subba Row	14	5	31	0	9.1	2	21	5
Stevenson	5	2	7	1	6	3	8	0

Oxford bowling								
Jose	16.4	4	46	4	5	0	17	0
Divecha	23	10	36	2	43.2	19	62	7
Mitchell	17	5	45	2	16	5	42	0
Carr	3	2	2	0	6	0	14	0
Bartlett	11	7	12	0	34	16	47	3

UMPIRES D. Davies and F. Chester

5, 7, 8 July
At Lord's

1952

Match drawn

Oxford came to Lord's with a poor record, despite the arrival of M.C. Cowdrey. Cambridge, although beating only Worcestershire and the Free Foresters, had a strong side, in which the captain D.S. Sheppard and P.B.H. May had averages into the seventies, and C.N. McCarthy, the South African Test bowler, J.J. Warr and R.G. Marlar had taken well over a hundred wickets between them. They also had a future West Indian wicket-keeper in F.C.M. Alexander.

Cambridge established the expected advantage, but Oxford gallantly staved off impending defeat, thanks mainly to a fine innings for two and a half hours by the Australian A.L.

Dowding, and deservedly shared the honours. Sheppard's hundred, the first by a Light Blue batsman since the renewal of matches after the war, and Marlar's nine wickets for 129 in the two innings were the outstanding performances, but credit must also go to R. Subba Row, to D.C.P.R. Jowett, who took 6 for 133, and to the three Dark Blue scorers of fifty, Dowding, Cowdrey and the opener J.E. Bush.

I watched Oxford's rear-guard action and recall A.J. Coxon, Oxford's number nine, heading a short-pitched ball from McCarthy, with remarkable insouciance to cover-point.

OXFORD	First innings		Second innings	
B. Boobbyer	*lbw, b* Marlar	29	*lbw, b* McCarthy	1
J.E. Bush	*b* Marlar	62	*c* Alexander, *b* McCarthy	9
W.G.E. Wiley	*b* Warr	5	*st* Alexander, *b* Marlar	7
M.C. Cowdrey	*b* Marlar	55	*st* Alexander, *b* Kenny	7
A.L. Dowding	*b* Kenny	19	*b* McCarthy	52
P.D.S. Blake	*run out*	20	*c* Alexander, *b* Warr	2
P.J. Whitcombe	*c* Sheppard, *b* Marlar	0	*c* Alexander, *b* McCarthy	12
W.M. Mitchell	*c and b* Marlar	48	*c* McCarthy, *b* Kenny	25
A.J. Coxon	*c and b* Marlar	13	*not out*	43
I.D.F. Coutts	*not out*	5	*b* Marlar	6
D.C.P.R. Jowett	*b* Marlar	1	*not out*	0
EXTRAS	B 10, L-B 4, W 1	15	B 12, L-B 3	15
	TOTAL	272	TOTAL (9 WKTS)	179

CAMBRIDGE		
D.S. Sheppard	*lbw, b* Jowett	127
M.H. Bushby	*b* Jowett	19
P.B.H. May	*c* Dowding, *b* Jowett	10
C.G. Tordoff	*run out*	10
M.H. Stevenson	*b* Coutts	25
R. Subba Row	*c* Mitchell, *b* Jowett	94
F.C.M. Alexander	*b* Jowett	7
J.J. Warr	*b* Jowett	19
R.G. Marlar	*not out*	48
C.N. McCarthy	*not out*	20
EXTRAS	B 20, L-B 9	29
	TOTAL (8 WKTS DEC.)	408

C.J.M. Kenny did not bat

Cambridge bowling	OVERS	MDNS	RUNS	WKTS		OVERS	MDNS	RUNS	WKTS
McCarthy	32	9	57	0		23	7	38	4
Warr	26	13	35	1		20	5	45	1
Kenny	17	3	40	1		17	4	43	2
Marlar	49.2	20	104	7		16	7	25	2
Subba Row	13	7	20	0		5	0	13	0
Tordoff	1	0	1	0		—	—	—	—

Oxford bowling	OVERS	MDNS	RUNS	WKTS
Coutts	24	6	58	1
Coxon	13	2	32	0
Mitchell	38	10	112	0
Jowett	52	13	133	6
Cowdrey	16	5	44	0

UMPIRES A. Skelding and K. McCanlis

4, 6, 7 July
At Lord's

1953

Cambridge won by
2 wickets

This proved to be a thrilling encounter at the end of a season in which Cambridge had beaten Middlesex, Kent and MCC but Oxford had no victory to its name. There were only three minutes to spare when D.R.W. Silk, who had batted five hours and a quarter for his 116 not out, negotiated victory, like Nelson at Copenhagen.

Oxford's 312, made in good time on the first day, owed most to M.C. Cowdrey, who gave a masterly display of stroke-play. The Cambridge captain, who captured his wicket in both innings, was the only bowler to trouble him. With a first-

innings lead of 121 runs, the Oxford captain A.L. Dowding must have had high hopes of repeating the success of 1951.

That it was not to be, despite the stroke-play of J.P. Fellows-Smith, owed most to Marlar's fine command of flight and spin, allied to his competitive urge and to the quality of the Cambridge catching. His bowling figures deserve to be included in this account: 62–26–143–12. Fine defensive bowling from the Oxford spinners was almost decisive, but Silk had other ideas.

OXFORD

	First innings			Second innings	
H.B. Birrell	c Alexander, b Hayward	6		b Hayward	0
J.C. Marshall	c Alexander, b Marlar	21		c Alexander, b Dickinson	26
C.C.P. Williams	lbw, b Marlar	40		c Hayward, b Marlar	5
M.C. Cowdrey	c Silk, b Marlar	116		c Alexander, b Marlar	0
A.L. Dowding	lbw, b Marlar	7		c Subba Row, b Marlar	9
J.P. Fellows-Smith	b Dickinson	33		c Alexander, b Marlar	49
J.M. Allan	run out	2		c Lumsden, b Marlar	7
A.P. Walshe	c Marlar, b Dickinson	29		b Marlar	2
G.H. McKinna	c Crookes, b Hayward	0		c Bushby, b Marlar	3
D.K. Fasken	b Marlar	20		c Lumsden, b Hayward	3
D.C.P.R. Jowett	not out	6		not out	0
EXTRAS	B 18, L-B 12, N-B 2	32		B 8, L-B 2, N-B 2	12
	TOTAL	312		TOTAL	116

CAMBRIDGE

M.H. Bushby	c Dowding, b Allan	10		b Jowett	21
D.R.W. Silk	c Fellows-Smith, b Allan	22		not out	116
V.R. Lumsden	c Fellows-Smith, b Fasken	16		c Williams, b Fasken	14
R. Subba Row	c Marshall, b Jowett	6		lbw, b Jowett	28
F.C.M. Alexander	b McKinna	31		c Marshall, b Allan	7
W. Knightley-Smith	c Cowdrey, b McKinna	20		c Williams, b Fasken	10
L.K. Lewis	b Jowett	22		c Williams, b McKinna	2
D.V. Crookes	c Fasken, b Cowdrey	25		st Walshe, b Allan	5
W.I.D. Hayward	not out	6		run out	6
D.C. Dickinson	b Jowett	0			
R.G. Marlar	b Allan	11		not out	9
EXTRAS	B 16, L-B 3, W 2, N-B 1	22		B 19, L-B 1	20
	TOTAL	191		TOTAL (8 WKTS)	238

Cambridge bowling	OVERS	MDNS	RUNS	WKTS		OVERS	MDNS	RUNS	WKTS	
Hayward	34	11	88	2		22.4	10	27	2	
Dickinson	21.5	4	58	2		5	1	10	1	
Marlar	37	14	94	5		25	8	49	7	
Lumsden	3	1	6	0		—	—	—	—	
Subba Row	6	0	26	0		6	3	18	0	
Crookes	1	0	8	0		—	—	—	—	

Oxford bowling										
McKinna	17	9	14	2		20	4	45	1	
Fasken	17	7	28	1		22	5	48	2	
Jowett	31	11	57	3		32	15	50	2	
Allan	30.3	13	65	3		33.5	12	61	2	
Cowdrey	2	1	3	1		—	—	—	—	
Fellows-Smith	2	1	2	0		1	0	3	0	
Birrell	—	—	—	—		5	2	11	0	

UMPIRES F. Chester and H.G. Baldwin

3, 5, 6 July
At Lord's

1954

Match drawn

Again Oxford came without a victory to Lord's, but their performance in the big match belied their earlier lack of success. Cambridge had beaten Worcestershire and MCC on tour, but they were to suffer the loss through injury, after a few overs of the first day's play, of M.N. Morgan, one of their two opening bowlers.

Double-centuries in the University Match have been rare, but on the first day M.J.K. Smith made 201 not out in a faultless display of polished batsmanship. He was helped in an opening partnership of 145 by J.M. Allan, and by M.C.

Cowdrey in a third-wicket stand of 180 in two hours.

Cambridge's sterling reply owed much to J.F. Pretlove, and most to D.R.W. Silk's second century in successive University Matches, equalling the feat, for Cambridge, of W. Yardley, H.J. Enthoven and A.T. Radcliffe, and for Oxford of the senior Nawab of Pataudi.

The best bowling in the match was in the two second innings. For Cambridge, G. Goonesena took 6 for 71, and for Oxford, H.B. Birrell added 5 for 20 to his useful batting.

OXFORD

	First innings		Second innings	
M.J.K. Smith	*not out*	201	c Goonesena, b Estcourt	20
J.M. Allan	c Smith, b Goonesena	86	c Parsons, b Morgan	0
H.B. Birrell	c Parsons, b Smith	27	b Pretlove	64
M.C. Cowdrey	c Smith, b Goonesena	66	st Melluish, b Goonesena	5
J.P. Fellows-Smith			c Silk, b Goonesena	30
G.P. Marsland			c Melluish, b Goonesena	2
C.C.P. Williams			b Goonesena	14
D.K. Fasken			c Silk, b Goonesena	2
J.A. Arenhold			st Melluish, b Goonesena	2
A. Kamm			*not out*	0
EXTRAS	B 13, L-B 2, N-B 6	21	B 9	9
	TOTAL (3 WKTS DEC.)	401	TOTAL (9 WKTS DEC.)	148

D.C.P.R. Jowett did not bat

CAMBRIDGE

	First innings		Second innings	
M.H. Bushby	c Smith, b Allan	24	b Birrell	15
D.R.W. Silk	b Allan	118	lbw, b Birrell	15
J.K.E. Slack	lbw, b Birrell	12	b Arenhold	0
V.R. Lumsden	lbw, b Jowett	20	c Smith, b Jowett	47
J.F. Pretlove	c Smith, b Fasken	73	c Smith, b Birrell	7
G. Goonesena	c Williams, b Fasken	39	c Fasken, b Allan	26
A.B.D. Parsons	c Marsland, b Birrell	1	*not out*	1
C.S. Smith	c Fellows-Smith, b Jowett	3	c Allan, b Birrell	10
N.S.D. Estcourt	*not out*	20	c Cowdrey, b Birrell	19
M.E.L. Melluish	b Allan	8	*not out*	1
M.N. Morgan	*not out*	2		
EXTRAS	B 15, L-B 7, W 1, N-B 1	24	B 13, L-B 6	19
	TOTAL (9 WKTS DEC.)	344	TOTAL (8 WKTS)	160

Cambridge bowling	OVERS	MDNS	RUNS	WKTS	OVERS	MDNS	RUNS	WKTS
C.S. Smith	38	3	144	1	4	1	8	0
Morgan	6	1	20	0	3	2	6	1
Goonesena	31	10	79	2	19	3	71	6
Estcourt	7	2	31	0	4	1	16	1
Silk	8	1	35	0	—	—	—	—
Pretlove	17	2	71	0	16	4	38	1

Oxford bowling	OVERS	MDNS	RUNS	WKTS	OVERS	MDNS	RUNS	WKTS
Arenhold	14	3	32	0	7	2	17	1
Fasken	21	2	65	2	3	1	11	0
Fellows-Smith	4	3	3	0	—	—	—	—
Birrell	38	11	89	2	14	7	20	5
Allan	39	16	64	3	16	4	59	1
Jowett	26	9	62	2	8	3	18	1
Cowdrey	1	0	5	0	3	0	6	0
M.J.K. Smith	—	—	—	—	2	0	10	0

UMPIRES P. Corrall and E. Canning

2, 4, 5 July
At Lord's

1955

Match drawn

Whereas Oxford came to Lord's with no wins under their belt, Cambridge had come with a rush on tour. Cambridge were well placed by the second evening, thanks to the 114 of J.F. Pretlove, and to the bowling of G. Goonesena and Swaranjit Singh. For Oxford, J.P. Fellows-Smith's 5 for 83 and A.C. Walton's fluent 57 were indispensable.

Cambridge batted on until shortly past one o'clock on the third day. Oxford needed 313 to win in four and a quarter hours, and while M.J.K. Smith and C.C.P. Williams were together in a cultured fourth-wicket partnership of 103 in 90 minutes, victory was a possibility. Once Smith, who had equalled A.T. Ratcliffe's feat of scoring a double-century and a hundred in successive Varsity Matches, was caught at long-on, the game swung in Cambridge's favour. Like Leonidas against the Persians, however, the Oxford captain barred the way.

CAMBRIDGE	First innings		Second innings	
R. O'Brien	b Fellows-Smith	34	b Fasken	24
A.B.D. Parsons	c Allan, b Fellows-Smith	31	lbw, b Fasken	0
G. Goonesena	c Williams, b Gibson	23	c and b Fasken	21
V.R. Lumsden	lbw, b Fasken	14	c Smith, b Allan	25
J.F. Pretlove	c Smith, b Allan	114	c Walshe, b Fasken	40
S. Singh	c Williams, b Fellows-Smith	2	c and b Phillips	11
P.D. Croft	lbw, b Allan	9	c Fasken, b Gibson	1
D.R.W. Silk	lbw, b Fellows-Smith	23	c Gibson, b Phillips	6
C.S. Smith	run out	7	not out	26
M.E.L. Melluish	c Allan, b Fellows-Smith	12	not out	13
D.J. Smith	not out	4		
EXTRAS	B 18, L-B 10, W 1, N-B 2	31	B 8, L-B 3	11
	TOTAL	304	TOTAL (8 WKTS DEC.)	178

OXFORD				
M.J.K. Smith	c Melluish, b C.S. Smith	25	c Singh, b Goonesena	104
J.M. Allan	c Pretlove, b D.J. Smith	9	b Goonesena	11
A.C. Walton	st Melluish, b Goonesena	57	c Silk, b D.J. Smith	2
C.C.P. Williams	b Goonesena	18	not out	47
A.P. Walshe	b Singh	20	not out	5
G.P.S. Delisle	c Silk, b Goonesena	0	c Melluish, b Singh	15
I. Gibson	c Pretlove, b Singh	24	b D.J. Smith	8
J.P. Fellows-Smith	not out	24	lbw, b C.S. Smith	23
D.K. Fasken	c Lumsden, b Goonesena	4		
D.C.P.R. Jowett	b Singh	0		
J.B. Phillips	lbw, b Singh	2		
EXTRAS	B 9	9	B 12, L-B 3	15
	TOTAL	170	TOTAL (6 WKTS)	230

Oxford bowling	OVERS	MDNS	RUNS	WKTS	OVERS	MDNS	RUNS	WKTS
Phillips	21	3	54	0	21	4	46	2
Fasken	22	6	39	1	18	6	38	4
Fellows-Smith	37	9	83	5	6	2	20	0
Jowett	9	3	22	0	10	4	14	0
Allan	14.2	4	36	2	17	6	21	1
Gibson	13	5	39	1	6	1	28	1
Cambridge bowling								
C.S. Smith	18	1	49	1	23	9	47	1
D.J. Smith	13	3	30	1	18	5	46	2
Singh	17	7	20	4	14	2	49	1
Goonesena	12	5	62	4	18	4	73	2
Pretlove	—	—	—	—	3	3	0	0

UMPIRES A.E. Pothecary and N. Oldfield

12
1956–1965
East and West meet at Lord's

OXFORD *A decade of stars from the East*

This was a decade of mixed fortunes. The heights were reached in 1959 when A.C. Smith led Oxford to victory at Lord's, and the depths were plumbed when Oxford lost twelve matches in 1962. A series of excellent captains, notably M.J.K. Smith, A.C. Smith, J.A. Bailey and the Nawab of Pataudi, gave OUCC a sense of purpose and optimism. At last some bowlers of real class presented themselves for selection; there were Jack Bailey, J.M. Allan, A.J. Corran, D.M. Sayer and J.D. Piachaud, all in the top flight. The batsmen included players of immense ability; M.J.K. Smith, D.M. Green, and a trio from the East – the Nawab of Pataudi, J. Burki and A.A. Baig, who all rank with the best.

Mike Smith must take pride of place in 1956 by virtue of his remarkable achievement of making a third hundred against Cambridge; moreover, he passed the elder Pataudi's record aggregate for the Varsity Match of 457. (This in turn was to be surpassed by R.J. Boyd-Moss in 1983, but in one match more.) A.C. Walton made three hundreds, including, against Sussex, the fastest of the season and the fastest since 1949, in 61 minutes. A fine front-foot player, he captained Oxford in 1957, then played a few years for Middlesex before being lost to English cricket when he went to Australia. Allan became the sixth Oxonian to do a University 'double' (1000 runs and 100 wickets) and went on to play for the Gentlemen.

At last Oxford learned what it was like to win again; no match had been won since 1951. Yet it was a lost match in 1956 which created the greatest excitement. Set to get 305 at fifty an hour by Hampshire the University reached 303 for 8 with two balls remaining; Cannings bowled Bailey with the fifth ball, and then uprooted Kentish's middle stump with the last.

Geoffrey Bolton writes of 1958:

Oxford were a different side now. Well led by a cheerful captain [J.A. Bailey], who had to battle with misfortune and never bowed to it, they fielded with the utmost keenness and the atmosphere both in The Parks and at Lord's was alive with determination and enthusiasm.

It must be admitted that the batting was bad. A.C. Smith, M.A. Eagar, R.L. Jowett and J. Burki always looked good but none of them was really reliable and there were some sad collapses for which the vile summer of 1958 cannot wholly be blamed.

Bailey, who bowled on the fast side of medium, also had a remarkable record, with figures of forty-eight wickets for 14.12 apiece. He took 6 for 28 against the New Zealanders, and in the match against Lancashire 12 for 54.

Corran bowled at much the same pace; D.M. Green writes of him:

Andrew Corran was tall and angular, possessed of boundless stamina, and moved the ball in the air and off the wicket at fast-medium pace. . . . He had firm opinions on a wide variety of subjects; the freedom and frequency with which he expressed them caused him to be known as 'Oracle'.

A.C. Smith succeeded Jack Bailey and carried on where he had left off, leading Oxford to victory at Lord's for the only time in this decade. He was unanimously re-elected captain in 1960, when but for the weather the record might have surpassed that of the previous year. Smith again had a fine attack, with only Bailey having gone down. David Green writes of Piachaud:

The off-spinner was the slim, red-haired Dan Piachaud from Ceylon. Though Dan bowled fairly quickly, he had a peculiar looping flight and skilful change of pace, so that he was effective on flat wickets as well as when the ball turned.

David goes on to write modestly of himself:

When all else failed, I rushed up with optimistic in-swing. In my view, my pace was well on the hasty side of medium, and I was therefore somewhat chagrined when the late Denys Rowbotham, writing in The Guardian, *expressed the view that 'Green pushed his off-spinners through too quickly to expect any great degree of turn.'*

Abbas Baig added to the success of 1959. He was a neat, wristy player and a master of the square-cut. In 1960, during an innings of 150 against Yorkshire on a slow-turning wicket, he forced Ray Illingworth to bowl with cover-point on the fence and a deep squarish third-man as well. Javed Burki was his chief support, although Alan Smith and David Green were not far behind. Burki went on to captain Pakistan in 1962, and scored a century in the Lord's Test.

The batting line-up was completed by C.A. Fry, M.A. Eagar and R.L. Jowett. David Green writes:

Charles Fry had to operate under the considerable handicap of being his grandfather's grandson . . . the press, in order to slip in the phrase 'grandson of the great C.B.', would comment favourably on an innings of a dozen or so by Charlie while ignoring a knock of 60 or 70 by another player . . .

Mike Eagar, a fine hockey player, was a good batsman, though one prone to excessive theorising. At one stage he worked out that the only safe attacking shot was the 'lap'. This obsession, which was the cause of some strange-looking innings, was fortunately dominant only for a few weeks.

Smith had to cope with an unusual problem in 1960. There were well-grounded fears that there might be some form of demonstration in advance of, or during, the South African match. For some nights, therefore, the pitch was under constant surveillance by members of the OUCC, who made up bridge parties (dummy's duty being to patrol the wicket). As it happened, the South African match was ruined by rain.

The match against the Free Foresters in The Parks in 1960 caused something of a sensation when Alan Smith handed over his wicket-keeping gloves to Charles Fry and proceeded to take nine wickets for 77. Fry and Pataudi each made a hundred.

Few would doubt that the Nawab of Pataudi, now officially Mohammed Mansur Ali Khan, would have gone on to be one of the 'greats' of all time had he not lost an eye the following year. Though small in stature, he could drive powerfully and was strong off his legs, and his cutting has seldom been bettered. The violence and certainty of his hooking discouraged several bouncer-happy fast men from bowling at him at all. Overshadowing all else in the events of Oxford cricket in 1961 was his car accident at Hove. Up to the time of the accident Pataudi had made 1216 runs, which included hundreds in each innings against Yorkshire. It is often forgotten that R.H.C. Waters was in this year denied a blue as a result of the injuries he sustained in the same accident.

C.D. Drybrough who, bowling slow left-arm, delivered over seven hundred overs in the season with sixty wickets to his credit, took over the captaincy. He was also elected captain the following year, a year in which he struggled to find bowlers. The fact that no Oxford bowler hit the stumps in four thousand deliveries gave ammunition to the cartoonists. Roy Ullyett in the *Express* drew a coconut shy displaying a notice which said: '3 balls for 6d – Oxford University bowlers 10 balls for 6d'. 'Schools' made unprecedented inroads into Drybrough's available strength. For the first time since 1928 there were brothers in the team, with the inclusion of M.A. Baig to join Abbas, his elder brother.

Pataudi was back in 1963 and there was an upsurge in the University's fortunes, with the match against the West Indies raising great expectations. As *Wisden* put it:

After making only 119 in their first innings the dark blues caused something of a sensation in the cricketing world by dismissing the touring team for 107, thanks to an inspired piece of medium-fast swing bowling by P.N.G. Mountford, who took seven wickets for 47. The Oxford second innings produced a memorable knock of 94 by J.L. Cuthbertson and left a target of 232. With two wickets captured for 25 Oxford's hopes ran high. On the third day the wicket dried out and Nurse and Hunte saw the West Indies home by six wickets.

M. Manasseh, a very good player, had failed to find form in the previous two years but in 1964 fully justified his selection, relieving a drab season on the very last day at Lord's. His match-saving innings stood at 99, with I.G. Thwaites to bowl the last over; M.G.M. Groves, the non-striker, came down the wicket and told Maurice to push for one and he would run for anything. 'No,' said Maurice, 'I have waited three years for this, and I am going to get my hundred with a four and if necessary, I'll claim the extra half-hour.' Five balls later; still no score. The field scattered for the last ball, Maurice cut it to third man and Groves ran; only when he reached the striker's end did Maurice set off with reluctance. The return to the bowler comfortably preceded Maurice but Ian Thwaites let it go through. Maurice Manasseh got his hundred, but not with a four.

The decade finished with promise somewhat dashed by wretched weather. Oxford had a well-balanced side; M.G.M. Groves, R.M.C. Gilliat and P.J.K. Gibbs returned some solid performances on the rare occasions that the sun shone. J.D. Martin found A.G.M. Watson a useful partner with the new ball and unusually he included two left-arm spinners, A.H. Barker and G.N.S. Ridley. But the weather had the last say even at Lord's.

During these years the OUCC was experiencing anxiety over finances. Ever-rising costs of the tour and declining revenues from the Varsity Match were leading to crisis. Relief came from two different quarters: the MCC voted an annual grant of £2000 (since increased several times by the TCCB) in recognition of the outstanding contribution made by the University to English cricket; and the University authorities took over the payment of the ground staff. It is important also to remember the generosity of the counties; the visits of these first-class teams cost the OUCC not a penny.

CAMBRIDGE *Dexter, Lewis and Brearley fly the flag*

The decade from 1956 to 1965 – which began politically with the humiliation of Suez and ended with the death of Winston Churchill – began for our purposes with a draw at Lord's, and finished with six draws, something previously unheard of in the history of the University Match. In terms of personality rather than of results, the decade started with the arrival as a freshman from Radley of Ted Dexter, one of the most exciting Light Blue cricketers to play for England in the post-war years, and finished with the appointment to the captaincy for 1966 of Deryck Murray, from Queen's Royal, Trinidad, who had kept wicket for the West Indies in all five Tests on their English tour of 1963 – during which, by a neat juxtaposition, Dexter had played a famous innings at Lord's. Of the three University Matches that did not end in a draw, Cambridge, under Gamini Goonesena, won decisively in 1957, by an innings and 186 runs, the largest margin in Cambridge's favour since the inception of the match; and under Dexter in 1958, when David Green from Burton GS played well in both innings, by 99 runs, with only six minutes of the extra half-hour remaining. Oxford's one victory was in 1959, by 85 runs, after a well-fought and evenly-balanced contest.

University cricket has produced many batsmen, and a goodly number of all-rounders, who have made their impact on the game, but fewer bowlers who have risen above the challenge of the Fenner's 'square' and later gone on to make a signal contribution to their county, or even their country. In this decade there was one outstanding bowling performance which deserves a special place in the story of Cambridge cricket. The perpetrator was Ossie Wheatley, a tall fast-medium bowler from King Edward's, Birmingham, who showed a fine control of direction and length, making the ball move late, usually away from the right-handed batsman. In the 1958 season – described by Cyril Coote as a 'green' one – he broke an eighty-year-old record by surpassing the seventy-five wickets taken in 1878 by A.G. Steel. Of his astonishing tally of eighty wickets, forty were taken at Fenner's, where three counties had one innings only, his best bowling figures being: 8 for 22 in 21.5 overs in Kent's first innings; 7 for 86 in 33.1 overs in Lancashire's first innings; and 7 for 78 in 31.1 overs in Warwickshire's first innings. He played sixty-three matches for Warwickshire, and two hundred and six for Glamorgan whom he has served in different capacities, and he is the current Chairman of the TCCB Cricket Committee.

There were other bowlers in this decade who topped fifty wickets in a Cambridge season. The first, chronologically, was Colin Smith (later Stansfield-Smith), who played for Lancashire for several seasons, and designed the more functional pavilion at the Hughes Hall end of the ground which took over from its engaging Victorian counterpart at the other end. The 1956 side was captained by Mike Melluish, from Rossall, a wicket-keeper good enough to be selected that year for the Gentlemen, and included five batsmen who shared seven centuries between them. Two were future England players – Bob Barber, from Ruthin, in his second year, and the freshman Ted Dexter. Heading the batting averages was John Pretlove, also a fine soccer player and rugby fives amateur champion. There was an outstanding all-rounder in that side from Royal College, Colombo, Gamini Goonesena, who took 7 for 98 in the 1956 University Match, made an outstanding 211 at Lord's in 1957, sharing in a partnership of 289 with the Alleynian Geoff Cook, took most wickets in a Cambridge career, 208, and later played successfully for Nottinghamshire. Swaranjit Singh, from northern India, whose turban changes added considerable colour to the Fenner's scene, performed usefully and later played twenty-seven matches for Warwickshire.

In 1957 Smith repeated the feat, taking fifty-four wickets – Wheatley, his opening partner, took forty-one and when opponents had seen off the pace bowlers, they were confronted by Goonesena, who leg-spun the ball to such good effect that he took fifty-three wickets, and Cook, who took thirty. This was also the year in which two Australians from Adelaide made their mark – Ian MacLachlan, an opening bat and useful leg-spinner who was chosen as twelfth man for Australia, and has recently been the President of the National Farmers' Federation, and Brian Swift, a promising wicket-keeper whose promise was sadly cut short by a fatal motor-cycle accident in Suffolk in 1958.

When Wheatley took his record toll in 1958, he was well supported by Ian Pieris, from St Thomas, Colombo, whose hat-trick at Eastbourne against D.R. Jardine's eleven he continues to treasure, Dexter and Alan Hurd, a fine off-spinner from Chigwell, who would play regularly for Essex, and who took fifty-eight wickets for Cambridge in 1959, and fifty-nine in 1960. The Cliftonian medic Richard Bernard, and David Kirby, from St Peter's York, who captained Leicestershire in 1962 and later became a schoolmaster, made useful contributions as all-rounders in this period.

Two more bowlers took over fifty wickets in a Cambridge season in this decade, taking them in the same year, 1962. The first, Tony Pearson, a medic from Downside, captured fifty-one wickets and was well supported by the other opener, the Harrovian Mark Weedon, and two all-rounders, the Reptonian Richard Hutton, about whom more later, and the Cliftonian Tony Windows, an especially fine striker of the ball in his first year, and an increasingly useful medium-pace bowler, who was chosen to tour Pakistan with the Under-25 team captained by Mike Brearley. The second was Andrew Benke, a third-year off-spinner from Cheltenham, whose arm was not as high as some; he was found by the Cambridge captain of his year on the Corpus Christi ground, and he took exactly fifty wickets.

The year 1961, the third season of the extremely useful all-rounder Mike Willard, from the Judd, Tonbridge, was the only season of the Wykehamist Richard Jefferson, a promising fast-medium bowler and clean striker of the ball who took forty-four wickets and later played 76 matches for Surrey. It was also the year that Pearson had excitingly taken 10 for 78 in a single innings against

Leicestershire at Loughborough, thereby equalling the feat of the only other Light Blue to have taken all ten, the great S.M.J. Woods, whose 10 for 69 was against C.I. Thornton's eleven at Fenner's in 1890. The match at Loughborough was notable also for a fine partnership of 185 by Eddie Craig and the Marlburian Tony Goodfellow, as well as for Maurice Hallam's first hundred of the season, in which he opened for Leicestershire and was last out.

It is rare for two spinners to head the Cambridge averages, as happened in the 1963 season, when Roy Kerslake, from Kingswood, who captained Somerset in 1968, took twenty-six wickets, and Martin Miller, from Prince Henry GS, Hohne, West Germany, took thirty-three, including 6 for 89, in 56 overs, 27 of them maidens, against Middlesex at Fenner's, the six wickets being the first six batsmen.

Turning to batsmen, no faithful history of the CUCC can omit the remarkable innings of Mike James, a freshman from St John's, Leatherhead, who in his second innings in first-class cricket made a brilliant hundred against the Australians in 1956. He scored 116 out of 151 in three hours eight minutes, before being 'stumped Langley bowled Benaud'. He later played for Wellington, NZ, in the 1964–5 season.

Three Cambridge and England captains of this era, one an all-rounder and two of them pure batsmen – Dexter, Brearley and Tony Lewis – each deserve a paragraph to themselves. Meanwhile, there are three future England players – Bob Barber, Hutton and the Tonbridgian Roger Prideaux – who also merit a reference.

Barber was an outstanding schoolboy cricketer who did the 'double' at Ruthin in 1953, played for Cambridge in 1956 and 1957, although with less brilliance than his schoolboy record suggested, and went on to play for Lancashire and subsequently, with a new aggressive style, for Warwickshire. He played in twenty-eight Tests between 1960 and 1968, but the innings for which he will be especially remembered was his 185 at Sydney on the 1965–6 tour, a virtuoso performance in cavalier style and one of the finest of modern Test innings.

Hutton did yeoman service for Yorkshire in 208 matches, and was chosen to play for England in five Tests. At Cambridge his best season was in 1963, when he scored 843 runs at an average of 35.12, including 163 not out against Surrey at Guildford and a masterly 73 at Lord's; he also took over thirty wickets at brisk pace. He is a great supporter of MCC cricket, and was player/manager of the team to Bermuda in 1987.

Prideaux won blues in 1958, 1959 and 1960, the year in which Chris Howland was a lively captain and a more than useful wicket-keeper and middle-order batsman. Prideaux had his most prolific season in his second year, when he scored 1311 runs at an average of 38.55, hitting four centuries and making, with the freshman Lewis, a formidable opening pair. He played first for Kent, but at greater length for Northamptonshire, whom he captained for three seasons, and was selected to represent England in three Tests.

At the risk of staling a theme by repetition, cricket blues of this era were often proficient at other sports also. The Wellingtonian Robin O'Brien, for instance, who died tragically young, not only made a splendid hundred on the first day of the 1956 University Match, but won a golf blue also. Mike Griffith, son of Billy, a talented wicket-keeper/batsman from Marlborough in the 1963–5 sides, who went on to play 232 games for Sussex, captaining them for five years, also played hockey for England as well as for Cambridge, and won his blue for rackets. Several further examples could be found.

Two other batsmen made a particular mark at this time: Eddie Craig and Ray White. Craig, a Lancastrian who played three matches for Lancashire, was an outstanding schoolboy player at Charterhouse, who achieved a First in both parts of the Moral Sciences Tripos. It is not mere rumour that one or two others in the Cambridge side found the philosophical exchanges between Craig, first slip, and Brearley, keeping wicket, very heavy going! Craig scored 1342 runs in 1961, including a hundred at Lord's after a duck in the first innings, and 1113 runs in 1962. He was a good timer, a thoughtful, watchful player, avid for runs – so thoughtful in fact that at one time, so the story goes, when his undergraduate days were over, he had a ceremonial burning of his cricket gear, also impaling one large cricket boot, which he had preserved, on the outside door of his room in Churchill College, to the surprise of his pupils. He has taught at Cambridge for many years and gives visiting Quidnunc sides, for which he has occasionally played, a warm welcome.

Ray White came from Hilton, South Africa, and won blues for four years, making an impact as an attacking batsman of considerable power, especially for his hundred at Fenner's in 1965, when New Zealand were forced to follow on, and a superlative fifty against the West Indies, including Wes Hall. He returned to South Africa, there making a top score of 205 against Griqualand West, and has made a marked success of his business career. He recently paid a particularly warm tribute to his first Light Blue captain, Tony Lewis.

A word about the three England captains makes a suitable finale to these reflections and again makes the point about the immense contribution that Light Blue cricketers have made to the English cricket scene, not least to the ranks of captains. Many, by pen, voice, time and talent, have given back to the game what they as players received from it. Dexter is a classic example of this, for he is an analyst of style and of the fashions of the day (a theorist by any other name shall smell as sweet, or as sour, according to taste!), and he has a deep affection for the game that he graced with such distinction. Mind you, he has graced rackets courts and golf courses with equal distinction, particularly the latter, as recent successes in the President's Putter show, but it is as a striker of a cricket ball that he will be especially remembered, above all perhaps for his superb 70 against the West Indies at Lord's in 1963.

Dexter played longer innings – the 180, for instance, that saved the Edgbaston Test against Australia in 1961; the 174 in eight hours that again saved England against the 'old enemy' at Old Trafford in 1964; his 185 for Cambridge against Lancashire at Fenner's in 1957; and two double-centuries for Sussex – but the 70 at Lord's caught the imagination in a different way. At Cambridge, he has said, it was Cyril Coote who coaxed him into playing an innings with judgement, and tempering with defence his natural instinct to belt into outer space any ball that came his way. In 1957 he took 5 for 8 and 3 for 47 for the Gentlemen, and he became a lively and dangerous bowler when in the mood, always liable to break an important partnership.

Lewis, in whose Welsh home can now be found (purchased, not purloined) the

Munsey of Cambridge clock that used to hang on the panelled wall above the large fireplace of the old pavilion, was chosen to play for Glamorgan while still a boy at Neath Grammar School – perhaps to ensure that his elegant style would manifest itself on the cricket field rather than in the concert hall. He has written in his auto-biography of the delights of going up to Cambridge after National Service – this stopped in 1958, making him one of the last to begin his cricketing career at a more mature age – and of playing as a freshman both at Twickenham, as full-back, and at Lord's. There he made an elegant 95 in the second innings of the 1960 University Match against one of Oxford's strongest sides ever, and had the misfortune to find two Glamorgan umpires 'standing', neither of whom thought that he should have got out.

Lewis's team-mate Brearley has paid tribute to his warmth as an indigenous Welshman and to his experience in the Combined Services team as well as for Glamorgan. His rugby was ended early by an injury to his knee, but he captained Glamorgan for six seasons and led them to their second Championship victory in 1969. The climax of his cricketing career was captaincy of England on the tour of India, Sri Lanka and Pakistan in 1972–3, making 70 not out in the vital First Test that England won, and 125 in the Fourth Test at Kanpur. He has made a success of his career in journalism and broadcasting, bringing a strong line and a sense of humour to his articles as cricket correspondent of the *Sunday Telegraph*, and carrying out with flair the commission from the MCC to write the official history of the Club, *Double Century*, in its Bicentenary year. Music and mirth are regular features, including the recollection of Craig's recently arriving for a match at Margam with his golf clubs, and of golf's being forsaken for Bach and Beethoven, as Lewis played his beloved violin and his friend played the piano throughout the day. It is an idyllic note on which to end this sketch of one who was also a member of the Welsh Youth Orchestra, and had to make a difficult career decision. Neville Cardus would perhaps not have minded either way!

Last of the three, but from his record certainly not least, comes Brearley, described in the caption over a photograph of him 'placing a man just-so' (in the third edition of *Barclay's World of Cricket*) as 'the captain who was both philosopher and tactician'. Coming up to Cambridge from City of London School, where his father was on the staff, he has ensured a unique niche for himself in this story by the sum of his achievements. For he not only captained two years running – others have done that – and was, as *Wisden* put it, 'by example and astute leadership an inspiration to his side' – others have been that – but he scored in his four seasons 4310 runs and – and here's the point – he achieved in addition a First in Classics, a good Second in Moral Sciences, and a lacrosse blue as well.

The intelligence that he brought to captaincy – and, in passing, to his book *The Art of Captaincy*, which the Cricket Society chose as the best cricket book of its year – is reflected in his success. In the twelve years he captained Middlesex, from 1971 to 1982, they won three County Championships and shared another, won two Gillette Cups and narrowly missed a number of other one-day titles. As captain of England he won six rubbers, halved three and lost only one, and at times had to overcome the fact that his batting scarcely merited his inclusion. It is a great testimony to his temperament as well as to his intellectual acumen that his value was rarely doubted, and that England's results were so favourable. His psychological insight and the value he places on personal qualities were reflected when we spoke on the third day of the Sri Lanka Test at Lord's in 1988.

It was from Mike Brearley on this occasion, but from various people on others, that I heard an especially warm tribute to Cyril Coote, BEM, Cambridge's more-than-groundsman from 1938 to 1980 (and even in the late 1980s he has been called in to advise on the Fenner's 'square'). Cyril's feel for Cambridge cricket, as well as his technical know-how (he once made 89 not out, out of 130, against the great Sydney Barnes, for Cambridgeshire against Staffordshire), were the secret of his influence, coupled with a devotion to the art of groundsmanship second to none. He would throw balls from half-way in a net, and continually emphasize the basics: 'Hit straight into the V, sir' and 'Get on the back foot, sir, and play it with a broomstick, sir.' The 'sir' was the result of having graduated through the college system, and was bestowed on the best players as well as on the worst. He would often hark back to the late forties and the early fifties: 'There he is, sir,' – pointing to the appropriate gold-leafed panel – 'Mr May, sir . . . Y'see, sir, with Mr May, sir, county bowlers dreaded coming here.'

His model captain was undoubtedly from the seventies – Majid Khan, he who so wished to emulate his father, even to the extent of standing on the pavilion steps and throwing the ball to hit the far stumps full toss, from a standing start. The son did not, in this side-show, match the father. Cambridge cricket's debt to Cyril Coote has been immense – as it has also been to Jack Davies, who has watched over affairs since 1952 with judgement, humour and imperturbability, and to his predecessors, and to the various coaches who have helped in pre-season training and with knowledgeable advice during it.

If that is too serious a note on which to end this decade, let us recount, in conclusion, an anecdote concerning a particular cable and its riposte. The cable contains the pungent message of Santosh Reddy, he of the thick pebbled spectacles, from Madras, who later played for Hyderabad. On receiving the conclusive cable 'Failed all exams', he sent a reciprocal one. 'Reddy is a fighter, see you next term.' And he did!

7, 9, 10 July
At Lord's

1956

Match drawn

Pride of place for individual honours must go to M.J.K. Smith, captain of Oxford and later of England. He scored a third successive century in the Varsity Match, and his aggregate of 477 runs scored against Cambridge took him 20 runs past Pataudi's record, and in one year less.

The Cambridge first innings was dominated by a splendid hundred from Robin O'Brien, who was eventually bowled by E.S.M. Kentish. (Kentish, who had played twice for the West Indies against England, was, at thirty-nine, the oldest ever blue.) E.R. Dexter gave a delightful taste of things to come, and Cambridge declared.

J.M. Allan and I.M. Gibson survived the last twenty minutes, but weekend rain boded ill for Oxford. The Cambridge spinners reduced them to 76 for 5 and a follow-on looked in prospect, until M.A. Eagar joined his captain. In a fine stand these two added 141 and made a declaration possible.

The two captains dispensed with a tea interval and Cambridge declared, offering Oxford the task of making 191 at nearly two runs a minute. Wickets fell rapidly and at 33 for 5 defeat seemed imminent. However, Allan and Eagar held firm, and Cambridge were deprived of victory.

CAMBRIDGE	First innings		Second innings	
R.W. Barber	*c and b* Allan	35	*c* Smith, *b* Allan	7
R. O'Brien	*c* Clube, *b* Kentish	146	*c* Delisle, *b* Kentish	0
B.C.G. Wilenkin	*b* Bailey	7	*c* Eagar, *b* Allan	20
E.R. Dexter	*c* Walton, *b* Clube	46	*st* Walshe, *b* Gibson	17
J.F. Pretlove	*run out*	16	*not out*	34
R.M. James	*c* Walshe, *b* Kentish	8	*not out*	24
S. Singh	*run out*	1	*c and b* Kentish	26
C.S. Smith	*not out*	13		
G. Goonesena	*not out*	18		
EXTRAS	B 3, L-B 8, W 1, N-B 1	13	B 2, L-B 1, N-B 3	6
	TOTAL (7 WKTS DEC.)	303	TOTAL (5 WKTS DEC.)	134

D.J. Smith and M.E.L. Melluish did not bat

OXFORD				
J.M. Allan	*b* C.S. Smith	6	*not out*	14
I.M. Gibson	*c* Melluish, *b* Goonesena	19	*b* C.S. Smith	5
A.C. Walton	*lbw, b* Singh	13	*lbw, b* C.S. Smith	0
M.J.K. Smith	*c* Melluish, *b* Goonesena	117	*c* Pretlove, *b* Goonesena	10
G.P.S. Delisle	*b* Singh	7	*c* D.J. Smith, *b* Goonesena	2
S.G. Metcalfe	*st* Melluish, *b* Goonesena	7	*b* C.S. Smith	16
M.A. Eagar	*not out*	55	*not out*	7
A.P. Walshe	*c* D.J. Smith, *b* Goonesena	5		
S.V.M. Clube	*b* Goonesena	0		
J.A. Bailey	*run out*	5		
EXTRAS	B 6, L-B 6, N-B 1	13	B 4	4
	TOTAL (9 WKTS DEC.)	247	TOTAL (5 WKTS)	58

E.S.M. Kentish did not bat

Oxford bowling	OVERS	MDNS	RUNS	WKTS	OVERS	MDNS	RUNS	WKTS
Bailey	24	2	76	1	3	1	6	0
Kentish	24	6	83	2	12	6	15	2
Allan	34	10	82	1	18	7	36	2
Clube	12	0	49	1	11	4	20	0
Gibson	—	—	—	—	11	2	51	1

Cambridge bowling	OVERS	MDNS	RUNS	WKTS	OVERS	MDNS	RUNS	WKTS
C.S. Smith	29	5	83	1	13	6	22	3
D.J. Smith	20	6	34	0	3	0	7	0
Goonesena	31	8	77	5	14	9	21	2
Singh	18	6	40	2	3	3	0	0
Barber	—	—	—	—	2	1	4	0
Pretlove	—	—	—	—	1	1	0	0

UMPIRES P. Corrall and E. Davies

6, 8, 9 July
At Lord's

Cambridge won by
an innings and 186 runs

1957

Cambridge won by an innings and 186 runs. The margin was their biggest in the history of the Varsity Match. G. Goonesena's 211 was a Cambridge record, and his stand of 289 with G.W. Cook was the highest for either side in the whole series.

It is no disparagement of the skilful bowling by Cambridge to say that the Oxford batting was unbelievably bad. At lunch they were 48 for 8; R.W. Wilson and the future MCC Secretary J.A. Bailey bravely took this score to 92.

By the close of play Cambridge were 108 for 5, but after the fall of the sixth wicket on Monday morning Goonesena and Cook came together. The Cambridge captain spent four hours over his first hundred, surviving a half-chance as he reached three figures, and then with a fine range of cuts, drives and pulls raced to his second in ninety minutes. Cook played almost as well, hitting thirteen fours in his 111.

I.M. Gibson and J.A.D. Hobbs safely played out the evening but the story was different next morning when Smith and Goonesena bowled well. The only thing that could save Oxford was rain, but there would have been no justice had it done so.

OXFORD	First innings		Second innings	
I.M. Gibson	c Barber, b Wheatley	8	run out	63
J.A.D. Hobbs	lbw, b Wheatley	0	b Smith	19
A.C. Walton	run out	4	st Swift, b Goonesena	7
C.D. Melville	b Pieris	9	lbw, b Smith	6
M.A. Eagar	c Dexter, b Wheatley	0	lbw, b Smith	2
R.G. Woodcock	c Swift, b Wheatley	11	retired hurt	5
R.L. Jowett	c Swift, b Pieris	0	lbw, b Goonesena	0
M.D. Scott	c Swift, b Smith	0	b Goonesena	22
R. Bowman	b Goonesena	17	c Swift, b Goonesena	0
R.W. Wilson	not out	17	b Smith	6
J.A. Bailey	b Wheatley	21	not out	4
EXTRAS	B 3, L-B 1, N-B 1	5	B 8, L-B 3, N-B 1	12
	TOTAL	92	TOTAL	146

CAMBRIDGE		
R.W. Barber	lbw, b Woodcock	36
I.M. McLachlan	b Bowman	11
D.J. Green	c Gibson, b Bowman	20
E.R. Dexter	b Gibson	7
R.M. James	lbw, b Gibson	15
G. Goonesena	c Jowett, b Woodcock	211
C.S. Smith	lbw, b Gibson	8
G.W. Cook	not out	111
EXTRAS	L-B 3, W 1, N-B 1	5
	TOTAL (7 WKTS DEC.)	424

P.L. Pieris, B.T. Swift, O.S. Wheatley did not bat

Cambridge bowling	OVERS	MDNS	RUNS	WKTS	OVERS	MDNS	RUNS	WKTS
Smith	12	3	26	1	30	13	42	4
Wheatley	15	8	15	5	13	4	17	0
Pieris	14	4	31	2	7	4	16	0
Dexter	1	0	3	0	—	—	—	—
Goonesena	5	2	12	1	17.2	6	40	4
Barber	—	—	—	—	4	0	19	0

Oxford bowling	OVERS	MDNS	RUNS	WKTS
Bailey	36	5	146	0
Bowman	39	10	101	2
Melville	4	0	12	0
Woodcock	13.5	2	40	2
Gibson	17	4	48	3
Wilson	22	11	51	0
Jowett	6	0	21	0

UMPIRES H.G. Baldwin and T.W. Spencer

1958

Cambridge achieved their fiftieth victory with six minutes remaining. J.A. Bailey, the Oxford captain's, serious ankle injury in his first over on the last morning was a cruel blow to his side.

The first day, shortened by an hour, was dreary; D.J. Green played an attractive innings and R.M. Prideaux occupied the crease for three hours. E.R. Dexter declared at the Saturday-night total.

E.M. Dyson and that astonishingly versatile cricketer A.C. Smith set Oxford off to a good start, but A. Hurd, bowling off-breaks, tore the heart out of Oxford's batting.

On Tuesday morning, G.W. Cook and Green cut and drove well, and Dexter made a sparkling 58 which included three sixes. His declaration followed, with Oxford needing 251.

R.L. Jowett and M.A. Eagar staged a rally from 11 for 4, but a further collapse saw Oxford with their backs to the wall at 105 for 7. A.J. Corran put up a stubborn defence until Dexter, also injured, returned to have him caught behind. Bailey, supported by Eagar, his runner, and filled with pain-killing injections, bravely resisted for another quarter of an hour before C.B. Howland took his fourth catch at the wicket.

CAMBRIDGE

	First innings			Second innings	
D.J. Green	b Sayer	47		b Conran	70
J.R. Bernard	b Bailey	6		c Smith, b Bailey	9
G.W. Cook	c Jowett, b Gibson	12		c and b Piachaud	71
E.R. Dexter	c Smith, b Sayer	15		b Sayer	58
R.M. Prideaux	not out	26		c Smith, b Woodcock	10
I.M. MacLachlan	c Bailey, b Piachaud	22		lbw, b Bailey	0
R.M. James	c Burki, b Bailey	22		c Jowett, b Sayer	18
C.B. Howland	c Sayer, b Gibson	2		not out	12
P.I. Pieris	not out	3		lbw, b Sayer	0
O.S. Wheatley	did not bat			not out	0
EXTRAS	N-B 6	6		B 12, L-B 6, N-B 3	21
	TOTAL (7 WKTS DEC.)	161		TOTAL (8 WKTS DEC.)	269

A. Hurd did not bat

OXFORD

A.C. Smith	b James	45		b Wheatley	0
E.M. Dyson	b Hurd	34		c Howland, b Dexter	6
I.M. Gibson	lbw, b Pieris	7		b Dexter	5
J. Burki	c MacLachlan, b Hurd	16		b Dexter	0
R.L. Jowett	st Howland, b Hurd	0		c Howland, b Dexter	56
M.A. Eagar	c Howland, b Hurd	17		c Dexter, b Hurd	54
R.G. Woodcock	c Green, b Wheatley	19		b Hurd	0
J.D. Piachaud	lbw, b Wheatley	5		c and b Pieris	7
A.J. Corran	c Prideaux, b Dexter	18		c Howland, b Wheatley	7
J.A. Bailey	b Dexter	3		c Howland, b Hurd	1
D.M. Sayer	not out	1		not out	3
EXTRAS	B 6, L-B 4, W 1, N-B 4	15		B 8, L-B 3, W 1	12
	TOTAL	180			151

Oxford bowling	OVERS	MDNS	RUNS	WKTS		OVERS	MDNS	RUNS	WKTS
Bailey	26	10	33	2		13	5	18	2
Sayer	23	3	79	2		16	2	49	3
Corran	3	0	4	0		17	2	56	1
Gibson	13	4	25	2		13	2	40	0
Piachaud	15	9	14	1		6	0	47	1
Woodcock	—	—	—	—		8	2	38	1

Cambridge bowling									
Wheatley	27	11	39	2		20	2	47	2
Pieris	22	11	38	1		12	5	21	1
Dexter	24	4	51	2		7	3	14	4
Hurd	19	10	35	4		15.3	9	17	3
James	2	1	2	1		3	1	8	0
McLachlan	—	—	—	—		7	2	32	0

UMPIRES John Langridge and L.H. Gray

11, 13, 14 July
At Lord's

1959

*Oxford won by
85 runs*

A.C. Smith led a talented Oxford side to their first victory at Lord's in eight years. Cambridge were rather weak in bowling and Oxford should certainly have made more than 217. C.A. Fry and M.A. Eagar had pulled them up from 68 for 4.

Cambridge lost four for 60 by the close of play. On the second morning, Smith both surprised and impressed early spectators by holding a fielding practice at the Nursery End. Once the two left-handers M.J.L. Willard and N.S.K. Reddy were removed Cambridge were soon undone.

Oxford quickly lost their first pair, enabling their stars from the Indian sub-continent to come together. A.A. Baig, who later in the month made a valiant century for India at Old Trafford, hit ten fours in his 50, and J. Burki, who only a season later was to play for Pakistan, shared an important stand, both finally falling to J.R. Bernard. Oxford collapsed to 154 for 8, but the last two wickets yielded 84, and Cambridge needed 282.

D.M. Sayer, genuinely quick off a shortish run, and A.J. Corran again bowled well and took fifteen wickets between them in the match. D. Kirby and Bernard were the only two to face them with confidence, but to no avail as Oxford won with two hours to spare.

OXFORD

	First innings		Second innings	
A.C. Smith	c Prideaux, b Bernard	12	c and b Douglas-Pennant	19
D.M. Green	b Douglas-Pennant	26	b Hurd	11
A.A. Baig	run out	15	b Bernard	50
J. Burki	b Hurd	13	c Howland, b Bernard	26
C.A. Fry	c Bernard, b Hurd	37	c Prideaux, b Hurd	19
M.A. Eagar	b Wheelhouse	39	lbw, b Kirby	2
R.L. Jowett	b Willard	13	c Wheelhouse, b Bernard	41
J.D. Piachaud	c Howland, b Douglas-Pennant	14	b Hurd	2
J.G. Raybould	b Wheelhouse	29	b Kirby	1
A.J. Corran	not out	11	lbw, b Bernard	30
D.M. Sayer	b Wheelhouse	5	not out	17
EXTRAS	B 1, L-B 2	3	B 9, L-B 9, W 2	20
	TOTAL	217	TOTAL	238

CAMBRIDGE

D. Kirby	b Corran	6	b Piachaud	52
H.C. Blofeld	c Smith, b Sayer	2	b Corran	1
M.J.L. Willard	b Piachaud	65	c Baig, b Sayer	26
D.J. Green	lbw, b Corran	4	c Eagar, b Sayer	0
R.M. Prideaux	b Green	0	lbw, b Raybould	11
N.S.K. Reddy	b Sayer	45	c Jowett, b Corran	25
J.R. Bernard	b Sayer	21	c Smith, b Corran	51
C.B. Howland	b Corran	0	c Piachaud, b Sayer	11
A. Hurd	c Piachaud, b Sayer	5	run out	2
S. Douglas-Pennant	b Sayer	2	not out	2
A. Wheelhouse	not out	9	c Baig, b Corran	13
EXTRAS	B 11, L-B 2, W 2	15	L-B 1, W 1	2
	TOTAL	174		196

Cambridge bowling	OVERS	MDNS	RUNS	WKTS	OVERS	MDNS	RUNS	WKTS
Douglas-Pennant	23	9	33	2	19	5	43	1
Wheelhouse	21.3	5	57	3	17	0	54	0
Bernard	18	4	55	1	16	4	44	4
Hurd	21	6	61	2	23	8	52	3
Kirby	1	0	5	0	20	10	25	2
Willard	4	2	3	1	—	—	—	—

Oxford bowling								
Sayer	23	5	41	5	22	3	74	3
Corran	24	3	62	3	24.3	7	47	4
Green	6	1	7	1	1	0	3	0
Raybould	7	0	35	0	14	4	39	1
Piachaud	3	0	14	1	10	1	31	1

UMPIRES D. Davies and H. Yarnold

6, 7, 8 July
At Lord's   # 1960   *Match drawn*

Batting first, Cambridge were out for a moderate score, A.J. Corran bowling splendidly. At 32 for 3 it looked as though Oxford might fare worse, until J. Burki and the Nawab of Pataudi came together. The following day, these two put on a further 142 at a run a minute. Burki was solid in defence, cutting the ball firmly whenever it was dropped short; Pataudi's innings, though not chanceless, was as elegant and skilful as his father's first century thirty-one years before, and established this unique father and son record. Oxford later collapsed, only a last-wicket stand of 36 taking them past 300.

It is strange that the Cambridge order for the second year running should have included an opening bat whose commentator voice is now known to millions of listeners. In 1959 H.C. Blofeld was one of the openers, and his place was taken in 1960 by A.R. Lewis. Lewis, on this occasion accompanied by M.J.L. Willard, batted with power and assurance, only holing out in the deep, off A.R. Duff, five short of his century. On this third day, shortened by rain, three more wickets fell before the innings defeat was safely avoided, and further dogged resistance by G. Atkins made sure that Cambridge were safe.

CAMBRIDGE	First innings		Second innings	
R.M. Prideaux	c Fry, b Corran	9	b Corran	5
A.R. Lewis	c Smith, b Corran	24	c Burki, b Duff	95
M.J.L. Willard	c Pataudi, b Green	30	c Fry, b Corran	48
D. Kirby	run out	16	b Sayer	16
N.S.K. Reddy	c Smith, b Corran	1	c Smith, b Corran	3
J.R. Bernard	c Smith, b Corran	30	b Corran	0
G. Atkins	b Corran	0	c Smith, b Sayer	37
C.B. Howland	c Smith, b Sayer	15	c Smith, b Corran	2
J.B. Brodie	b Corran	10	not out	17
T.B.L. Coghlan	not out	9	b Corran	10
A. Hurd	c Pataudi, b Sayer	2	not out	0
EXTRAS	B 4, L-B 3	7	B 7, L-B 2, W 1	10
	TOTAL	153	TOTAL (9 WKTS)	243

OXFORD		
A.C. Smith	lbw, b Brodie	6
D.M. Green	b Brodie	13
A.A. Baig	c Howland, b Willard	8
J. Burki	c Howland, b Coghlan	79
Nawab of Pataudi	c Lewis, b Kirby	131
C.A. Fry	c Prideaux, b Coghlan	1
C.D. Drybrough	c and b Hurd	9
A.R. Duff	c Coghlan, b Hurd	2
D.M. Sayer	c Howland, b Willard	17
A.J. Corran	c Bernard, b Hurd	18
J.D. Piachaud	not out	15
EXTRAS	B 3, L-B 5, W 1, N-B 2	11
	TOTAL	310

Oxford bowling	OVERS	MDNS	RUNS	WKTS	OVERS	MDNS	RUNS	WKTS
Corran	29	13	48	6	46	21	70	6
Sayer	21	5	48	2	33	10	81	2
Green	17	5	43	1	—	—	—	—
Piachaud	3	0	7	0	10	4	22	0
Duff	1	1	0	0	7	3	15	1
Drybrough	—	—	—	—	16	4	45	0

Cambridge bowling				
Brodie	29	9	71	2
Coghlan	25	5	74	2
Willard	31	5	87	2
Hurd	24.2	8	53	3
Atkins	1	0	4	0
Kirby	5	2	10	1

UMPIRES D. Davies and E. Davies

15, 17, 18 July
At Lord's

1961

Match drawn

Oxford were still reeling from the recent injury to their captain, the Nawab of Pataudi, who had lost an eye in a motor accident at a Hove crossroads only a week before. The match proved an undistinguished draw. Two thunderstorms restricted the first day's play, in which Cambridge scored 90 for 6. The Oxford bowlers continued their good work on Monday until R.I. Jefferson, a six-foot-seven Wykehamist, coming in at number nine, stroked the ball with comfort to all parts of the field, making 54 of Cambridge's last 61.

Oxford were 104 for 1 at tea, apparently well set for a big total when D. Kirby, the Cambridge captain, had an inspired spell of medium-pace bowling, so that at the close Oxford were but six runs ahead with only four wickets left. A.R. Duff, with a splendid display of free hitting, next morning made a declaration possible. Duff later recorded a remarkable tally of minor MCC tours, including North and South America, Bangladesh twice, and several trips to Ireland.

A solid century by E.J. Craig, in four hours, placed Cambridge out of danger, but Kirby was never in a position to set Oxford a target. *Wisden* tells us that 6,250 paid at the gate over the three days.

CAMBRIDGE	First innings		Second innings	
E.J. Craig	b Potter	0	b Pithey	105
A. Goodfellow	c Pithey, b Piachaud	22	b Duff	34
M.J.L. Willard	c Fry, b Potter	5	lbw, b Duff	4
A.R. Lewis	c Worsley, b Piachaud	20	c Pithey, b Drybrough	32
N.S.K. Reddy	b Jakobson	14	b Green	13
J.M. Brearley	lbw, b Potter	27	c Duff, b Green	23
D.E. Kirby	c Fry, b Jakobson	4	not out	21
R.H. Thomson	c Green, b Jakobson	3	not out	4
R.I. Jefferson	c Jakobson, b Piachaud	54		
P.D. Brodrick	not out	11		
A.J.G. Pearson	c Baig, b Jakobson	8		
EXTRAS	B 1, L-B 3, N-B 1	5	B 15, L-B 3	18
	TOTAL	173	TOTAL (6 WKTS)	254

OXFORD		
D.R. Worsley	c Willard, b Kirby	43
D.B. Pithey	c Brearley, b Pearson	22
A.A. Baig	b Willard	65
D.M. Green	c Brearley, b Brodrick	1
F.W. Neate	c Craig, b Kirby	24
C.A. Fry	b Kirby	2
C.D. Drybrough	b Jefferson	16
A.R. Duff	b Kirby	40
J.D. Piachaud	not out	11
EXTRAS	B 3, L-B 5	8
	TOTAL (8 WKTS DEC.)	232

T.R. Jakobson and I.C. Potter did not bat

Oxford bowling	OVERS	MDNS	RUNS	WKTS		OVERS	MDNS	RUNS	WKTS
Jakobson	24.3	10	42	4		25	5	58	0
Potter	30	15	45	3		9	3	24	0
Green	13	4	17	0		19	6	29	2
Piachaud	27	15	30	3		10	5	12	0
Drybrough	17	8	30	0		10	5	17	1
Pithey	3	2	4	0		18	10	32	1
Duff	—	—	—	—		25	7	59	2
Baig	—	—	—	—		1	0	5	0

Cambridge bowling				
Jefferson	18	2	51	1
Pearson	19	1	58	1
Willard	15	5	35	1
Brodrick	21	8	39	1
Kirby	26	9	41	4

UMPIRES J.G. Langridge and N. Oldfield

11, 12, 13 July
At Lord's

1962

Match drawn

The pattern for a draw was set by Cambridge's first innings; in four hours they scored 180 runs off eighty-five overs. J.M. Brearley, with his unruffled temperament, scored eighteen boundaries. D.B. Pithey dislocated a finger when he dropped the left-handed A.R. Goodfellow at slip, a double blow to Oxford since Pithey was unable to bowl and Goodfellow with Brearley added 115.

Sir Leonard's son R.A. Hutton bowled D.R. Worsley with the first ball of Oxford's innings. The brothers Baig, M.A. and A.A. then batted with fluency until the former ran himself out. An

Oxford collapse to 128 for 6 persuaded Pithey, against his doctor's advice, that he must bat. He played a fine innings, bringing Oxford close to the Cambridge total.

One of the features of the third day was the steady bowling for Oxford of J.L. Cuthbertson and J.D. Martin; with seventy-one overs between them they conceded only 148 runs. A.R. Lewis was never able to bat with freedom. Oxford needed 213 in two and a half hours; they accepted the challenge until Murtuza Baig twisted an ankle and had to retire – thereafter they played out time.

CAMBRIDGE	First innings		Second innings	
E.J. Craig	b Pithey	35	c Majendie, b Cuthbertson	3
R.H. Thomson	c Worsley, b Potter	12	c Majendie, b Martin	0
J.M. Brearley	not out	113	c Majendie, b Martin	31
A.R. Lewis	c Majendie, b Martin	21	not out	103
R.C. White	c M.A. Baig, b Martin	0	c Majendie, b Cuthbertson	1
A.R. Goodfellow	c Neate, b Cuthbertson	53	b Cuthbertson	0
A.R. Windows	c Martin, b Potter	9	c Worsley, b Cuthbertson	42
R.A. Hutton	not out	8	not out	6
EXTRAS	B 2, L-B 4, W 1, N-B 1	8	B 2, W 1, N-B 1	4
	TOTAL (6 WKTS DEC.)	259	TOTAL (6 WKTS DEC.)	190

A.F. Benke, M.J.H. Weedon and A.J.G. Pearson did not bat

OXFORD				
D.R. Worsley	c Brearley, b Hutton	0	c Hutton, b Pearson	8
M.A. Baig	run out	30	retired hurt	10
A.A. Baig	c Brearley, b Windows	43	c Brearley, b Pearson	42
F.W. Neate	lbw, b Pearson	6	c Pearson, b Windows	10
J.L. Cuthbertson	c White, b Windows	27	c and b Benke	36
R.E.F. Minns	c and b Hutton	4	not out	17
C.D. Drybrough	c White, b Windows	25	not out	3
D.B. Pithey	c White, b Windows	67	c Brearley, b Pearson	3
N.L. Majendie	lbw b Benke	28		
I.C. Potter	not out	2		
J.D. Martin	b Benke	2		
EXTRAS	L-B 2, W 1	3	B 2, L-B 3, W 1, N-B 1	7
	TOTAL	237	TOTAL (5 WKTS)	136

Oxford bowling	OVERS	MDNS	RUNS	WKTS		OVERS	MDNS	RUNS	WKTS
Potter	23	10	54	2		8	2	19	0
Martin	27	10	66	2		34	11	71	2
Pithey	14	5	26	1		3	1	7	0
Cuthbertson	25	8	66	1		37	16	77	4
Drybrough	8	1	19	0		8	2	12	0
Worsley	7	3	11	0		—	—	—	—
M.A. Baig	3	1	9	0		—	—	—	—

Cambridge bowling									
Hutton	23	6	53	2		8	0	36	0
Pearson	26	12	65	1		18	5	41	3
Weedon	11	4	28	0		—	—	—	—
Windows	17	6	49	4		4	0	14	1
Benke	7.1	0	33	2		11	4	33	1
White	1	0	6	0		—	—	—	—
Lewis	—	—	—	—		2	1	5	0

UMPIRES F.S. Lee and F. Jakeman

<table>
<tr><td>13, 15, 16 July
At Lord's</td><td style="text-align:center"># 1963</td><td style="text-align:right">*Match drawn*</td></tr>
</table>

The Nawab of Pataudi and J.M. Brearley, both future international captains, set a fine example of enterprise in a rain-interrupted match.

J.D. Martin retired ill with a high temperature after bowling only five overs for Oxford. This, coupled with some excellent batting by the sons of the two former England players R.A. Hutton and M.G. Griffith, saw Cambridge to a total of 246. Hutton played particularly well.

Pataudi and J.L. Cuthbertson rallied the Oxford cause from 77 for 4, putting on 89 together. Much of the second day was lost through rain, so Pataudi declared 45 behind. Cambridge responded with a positive chase for runs. E.W.J. Fillary, Oxford's leg-spinner, was the ideal bowler for the occasion, and he finished with 6 for 77.

The challenge to Oxford, of making 195 in two hours and twenty minutes, was taken up, but despite some fine strokes by M.A. Baig, the chase for runs was a failure, and at 101 for 6 it was called off. Cuthbertson and F.J. Davis safely played out time, and Brearley bowled two overs of lobs before calling it a day.

CAMBRIDGE

	First innings		Second innings	
E.J. Craig	c Worsley, b Cuthbertson	43	c Majendie, b Fillary	17
J.M. Brearley	c Cuthbertson, b Mountford	3	b Mountford	0
R.A. Hutton	c sub, b Davis	73	c Pataudi, b Fillary	35
R.C. White	c Majendie, b Davis	14	c sub, b Fillary	33
M.G. Griffith	c Sabine, b Fillary	58	c Worsley, b Davis	19
A.R. Windows	c Sabine, b Davis	11	b Fillary	5
M.H. Rose	c Sabine, b Davis	5	not out	16
R.C. Kerslake	run out	12	c Pataudi, b Fillary	17
A.J.G. Pearson	c Cuthbertson, b Fillary	17	b Fillary	0
M.E. Miller	lbw, b Davis	1		
M.C. Kirkman	not out	7		
EXTRAS	L-B 1, W 1	2	B 2, L-B 2, N-B 2	6
	TOTAL	246	TOTAL (8 WKTS DEC.)	148

OXFORD

D.R. Worsley	c Kirkman, b Windows	37	c White, b Hutton	4
M.A. Baig	b Hutton	16	st Griffith, b Kerslake	30
P.N.B. Sabine	c Brearley, b Kerslake	15	c Griffith, b Pearson	12
Nawab of Pataudi	c Brearley, b Kerslake	51	c White, b Miller	0
R.E.F. Minns	c Griffith, b Hutton	5	c Miller, b Kirkman	21
J.L. Cuthbertson	c Windows, b Kerslake	62	not out	43
E.W.J. Fillary	not out	4	c Brearley, b Kirkman	9
F.J. Davis	not out	4	not out	9
EXTRAS	B 1, L-B 3, N-B 3	7	B 4, L-B 2, W 1, N-B 1	8
	TOTAL (6 WKTS DEC.)	201	TOTAL (6 WKTS)	136

N.L. Majendie, P.N.G. Mountford and J.D. Martin did not bat

Oxford bowling	OVERS	MDNS	RUNS	WKTS		OVERS	MDNS	RUNS	WKTS
Martin	5	2	9	0		—	—	—	—
Mountford	15	1	52	1		8	2	17	1
Cuthbertson	37	8	88	1		5	2	7	0
Davis	33	14	67	5		25	12	41	1
Sabine	5	2	19	0		—	—	—	—
Fillary	3.3	0	9	2		22.4	5	77	6
Cambridge bowling									
Hutton	26	11	51	2		3	0	13	1
Pearson	18	5	34	0		8	2	13	1
Miller	12	6	19	0		8	3	25	1
Kirkman	13	5	35	0		14	5	33	2
Windows	12	4	23	1		3	0	11	0
Kerslake	12	5	28	3		13	6	24	1
Brearley	1	0	4	0		2	2	0	0
White	—	—	—	—		2	0	9	0

UMPIRES H.E. Hammond and F.S. Lee

8, 9, 10 July
At Lord's

1964

Match drawn

For the fifth year running the match was drawn, and again it was a rain-affected contest.

Oxford lost their captain D.R. Worsley without a run on the board when play began in mid-afternoon. Only M. Manasseh, who had been Oxford Secretary in 1963 and had been luckless enough not to obtain a blue, and E.W.J. Fillary batted with any confidence, and although the latter hung on, with the overnight score 126 for 5, Oxford collapsed next morning on 142.

When Brearley was joined by M.G. Griffith, they demonstrated, in a third-wicket stand of 167, that the wicket held no terrors. Brearley, in his second Varsity Match hundred, struck seventeen fours in an attractive innings, and Griffith almost matched him with fourteen boundaries. R.C. White handed out further punishment and Cambridge were 155 ahead overnight.

Cambridge added 66 and left Oxford the task of making 221 to save an innings defeat. M.A. Baig, R.M.C. Gilliat, later captain of Hampshire, and Manasseh rose to the occasion, and with Oxford 22 ahead and six wickets standing, Brearley did not claim the extra half-hour.

OXFORD	First innings		Second innings	
D.R. Worsley	*lbw, b* Hutton	0	*b* Hutton	18
P.J.K. Gibbs	*c* Hutton, *b* Windows	27	*c* Griffith, *b* Kerslake	12
M.A. Baig	*c* Griffith, *b* Windows	14	*c* Brearley, *b* Hutton	44
R.M.C. Gilliat	*c* White, *b* Pritchard	5	*c* Griffith, *b* Windows	57
M. Manasseh	*c* Brearley, *b* Kerslake	45	*not out*	100
E.W.J. Fillary	*b* Windows	35		
M.G.M. Groves.	*c* White, *b* McLachlan	8	*not out*	10
M.R.J. Guest	*c* Griffith, *b* Pritchard	0		
A.H. Barker	*c* Griffith, *b* Pritchard	0		
C.J. Saunders	*not out*	2		
C.R. Harris	*lbw, b* McLachlan	0		
EXTRAS	L-B 4, W 1, N-B 1	6	N-B 2	2
	TOTAL	142	TOTAL (4 WKTS)	243

CAMBRIDGE		
J.M. Brearley	*c and b* Worsley	119
D.M. Daniels	*c* Fillary, *b* Guest	11
R.A. Hutton	*lbw, b* Groves	6
M.G. Griffith	*c* Mannasseh, *b* Worsley	82
R.C. White	*not out*	89
R.C. Kerslake	*c* Manasseh, *b* Guest	11
M.H. Rose	*run out*	10
I.G. Thwaites	*c* Barker, *b* Manasseh	22
A.R. Windows	*c* Fillary, *b* Manasseh	6
EXTRAS	L-B 1, W 4, N-B 2	7
	TOTAL (8 WKTS DEC.)	363

A.A. McLachlan and G.C. Pritchard did not bat

Cambridge bowling	OVERS	MDNS	RUNS	WKTS		OVERS	MDNS	RUNS	WKTS
Hutton	17	6	39	1		19	3	62	2
Pritchard	16	8	29	3		15	2	47	0
Windows	19	9	38	3		15	8	36	1
Kerslake	14	6	12	1		15	8	25	1
Thwaites	6	4	6	0		5	1	16	0
McLachlan	7.2	3	12	2		15	7	55	0
Rose	—	—	—	—		1	1	0	0

Oxford bowling				
Harris	20	0	90	0
Guest	23	5	70	2
Worsley	15	7	48	2
Groves	19	3	55	1
Manasseh	15.2	2	52	2
Barker	12	4	41	0

UMPIRES F. Jakeman and W.E. Phillipson

7, 8, 9 July
At Lord's

1965

Match drawn

Oxford came very close to success, but after an uninspiring first day's batting hardly deserved it. At the end of the pre-lunch period, Oxford's score stood at 60 for 2. At one stage, M.G.M. Groves and M.R.J. Guest played fifteen consecutive maidens bowled by Cambridge spinners. Bad light and rain stopped play three-quarters of an hour early.

J.D. Martin, who had returned as Oxford captain, backed his overnight declaration with accurate bowling, and half the Cambridge players were dismissed for 65. D.L. Murray, their wicket-keeper, already launched on a distinguished Test career with the West Indies, batted

so aggressively that R.C. White was able to declare, albeit behind.

By close of play Oxford were four down and 116 ahead. A sparkling innings by R.M.C. Gilliat on the last morning put Oxford on the way to a total of 196. Cambridge needed 220 to win in just under four hours. A.G.M. Watson and J.D. Martin bowled with considerable fire and reduced them to 114 for 6. After an interruption for rain, only twenty minutes remained. A.A. McLachlan was snapped up at short leg, G. Hughes was lbw, and S.G. Russell was caught in the slips. An appeal against the light was dismissed and R. Roopnaraine safely played out the last over.

OXFORD	First innings		Second innings	
P.J.K. Gibbs	c Murray, b Russell	4	c McLachlan, b Roopnaraine	39
R.J.A. Thomas	b Russell	22	c Hughes, b Russell	5
R.M.C. Gilliat	c Close, b Hughes	30	c Daniels, b Hughes	51
E.W.J. Fillary	c Murray, b Harvey	2	b Hughes	16
M.G.M. Groves	lbw, b Harvey	45	c Griffith, b Hughes	5
M.R.J. Guest	c Roopnaraine, b Hughes	20	c sub, b Harvey	29
G.N.S. Ridley	b Russell	9	c Daniels, b McLachlan	20
A.H. Barker	b Russell	16	not out	4
A.G.M. Watson	not out	14	c Murray, b Russell	4
A.W. Dyer	not out	9	c McAdam, b Russell	12
J.D. Martin	did not bat		c Murray, b Russell	0
EXTRAS	L-B 2, N-B 3	5	B 6, L-B 3, N-B 2	11
	TOTAL (8 WKTS DEC.)	176	TOTAL	196

CAMBRIDGE				
D.M. Daniels	c Gilliat, b Martin	7	lbw, b Watson	12
K.P.W.J. McAdam	c Groves, b Ridley	12	lbw, b Watson	22
P.A. Close	c Fillary, b Martin	0	b Martin	3
R.C. White	c Dyer, b Watson	31	c Thomas, b Martin	9
D.L. Murray	c and b Martin	50	c Gilliat, b Ridley	33
M.G. Griffith	c Fillary, b Watson	0	c Dyer, b Watson	9
G. Hughes	b Barker	14	lbw, b Watson	18
A.A. McLachlan	c Barker, b Fillary	19	c Ridley, b Martin	1
R. Roopnaraine	not out	12	not out	0
S.G. Russell	not out	7	c Martin, b Watson	0
J.R.W. Harvey	did not bat		not out	0
EXTRAS	N-B 1	1	B 3, L-B 12, W 1, N-B 1	17
	TOTAL (8 WKTS DEC.)	153	TOTAL (9 WKTS)	124

Cambridge bowling	OVERS	MDNS	RUNS	WKTS		OVERS	MDNS	RUNS	WKTS
Harvey	27	9	61	2		17	6	37	1
Russell	23	9	50	4		17.2	6	32	4
White	3	0	10	0		—	—	—	—
Roopnaraine	28	19	19	0		28	14	42	1
Hughes	24	16	23	2		29	7	61	3
McLachlan	2.4	0	8	0		3	0	13	1
Oxford bowling									
Martin	20	6	43	3		22	8	40	3
Watson	15	5	29	2		19	5	44	5
Ridley	26	9	48	1		17	11	17	1
Fillary	7	1	30	1		5	2	6	0
Barker	3.3	2	2	1		1	1	0	0

UMPIRES T.W. Spencer and W.E. Phillipson

13
1966–1975
Majid and Imran take the Honours

OXFORD *The Rhodesian years*

In the long history of Oxford and Cambridge cricket, pressure of academic work and the demands of examinations have understandably figured large. It is now not uncommon for the captain to lead sides in The Parks which are sadly below strength. In 1966, for example, R.M.C. Gilliat could call upon only five of the final team against Hampshire and six against Gloucestershire. Certainly this gave an important opportunity for experiment, but in an era when reserve strength was not as deep as in days gone by, it made the captain's task more difficult. To build a team into a cohesive unit, with a preparation based mainly on matches against seasoned professionals, demands very high standards of leadership, and these were provided by Gilliat in 1966. Not only did he captain Oxford to crush Cambridge by an innings, but for the first time in twenty years they defeated Lancashire.

Gilliat's achievement was recognized when he was chosen to lead the MCC President's XI against the West Indies, before going on to captain Hampshire with notable success throughout most of the seventies. He was also far and away Oxford's most consistent batsman, seldom failing to give solidarity in the middle order. P.J.K. Gibbs and F.S. Goldstein made a sound opening pair, R.W. Elviss, from Leeds Grammar School, developed as an off-spinner, and G.N.S. Ridley, the 1967 captain, took forty-two first-class wickets.

The next six years saw Oxford led by Rhodesians, all of whom were Rhodes scholars, and with the exception of Ridley all took further degrees at Oxford – a modern trend with most Rhodes scholars. Ridley was presented with an unusual problem in the match against Northamptonshire in The Parks, a match in which the Northants captain, R.M. Prideaux, was the first victim of a hat-trick by J.N.C. Easter when on 99. Oxford failed with the bat early on the last day, the second having been totally washed out. Confusion then arose when Oxford were asked to follow on 117 behind, after the umpires had incorrectly applied the two-day ruling. The Dark Blues went for the runs in the mistaken belief that Prideaux had forfeited the second innings. Two telephone calls to Lord's cleared any doubt and Ridley wisely called the batsmen in twenty minutes from time, but still 40 runs behind. Oxford had a fine nine-wicket win over Somerset, a match in which A.H. Barker took 9 for 67 bowling slow left-arm, to win back the place he had lost the previous year. Gilliat rejoined the side after 'Schools' and celebrated with two hundreds.

F.S. Goldstein in his first year as captain was able to call on only three old blues until after 'Schools'. The weakness of the batting was well demonstrated against Surrey, when half the side was out for 2, and one of those was a no-ball. They recovered to make 50, but six had failed to score. More frequently Goldstein, who finished only 55 short of a thousand runs, saw Oxford off to a good start. Not possessed of much patience, he was a fine player of fast bowling. He carried on the next year much where he had left off, causing excitement when he thrashed the West Indian attack, scoring 78 out of 90 in a match which saw two innovations. These were the first combined Oxford and Cambridge team to play the West Indies, and Sunday play, which had never been seen before in The Parks. The match was ruined by rain.

Oxford had a nail-biting win over Kent; set to score 258 to win they reached their target off the fifth ball of the last over. With the scores level, R.A. Niven lofted A.J. Hooper to deep mid-off, where S.E. Leary dropped the catch and the batsmen raced through to win the match. This result reflects great credit on M.H. Denness, who declared twice and ensured a gripping match by keeping on his spinners.

The year of 1969 will be recalled as that in which vandals dug a five-foot trench along one end of the square in The Parks, to prevent play against a South African touring team. In fact, rapid and expert repair work allowed play to start on time, and no permanent damage ensued.

Three defeats by an innings in 1970, and two of them in two days, makes depressing reading. This must surely have been a year when cloud banks from behind Keble Chapel, the rainy quarter, were considered a good omen. Poor D.J. Hone, bowling against Worcester, started with an over of full tosses prompting Syd Buller, one of the umpires, to ask 'Is the wicket doing anything?'

Against Northamptonshire R.M. Ridley achieved a remarkable performance of stamina. He carried his bat in the first innings for 70 and then, as Oxford followed on, was at the wicket again ten minutes later. This time he made 66, batting altogether for seven hours and forty minutes. Northamptonshire still won by eight wickets.

There was something of a revival the following year. B. May, at the age of twenty-seven, already a hockey blue, led with cheerful determination, and with his drive, and the enthusiasm and expertise of Jim Stewart, the coach, Oxford developed into a very good fielding side. The batting was unaccountably brittle, and this inconsistency was underlined in two matches: against Sussex they made 81 and 340, and in their second match against Warwickshire 309 and 81.

A.R. Wingfield Digby played in the first of his four Varsity Matches in 1971. These were somewhat strangely spread over a long period, and he next played against Cambridge in 1975. In his book *A Loud Appeal* Andrew remembers being asked to act as night watchman at the end of the first day at Lord's: 'Phil Edmonds slipped in a quicker ball and yet another bowler's ambition of making a hundred was dashed. Getting back to the changing room full of anger and disappointment, I discovered my team-mates falling about laughing.' Nevertheless, he had a tally of thirty-two first-class wickets and fifty-nine overall.

In 1972, for the sixth year running the captain was a Rhodesian – surely a unique record in the history of Varsity cricket. It was a damp chill season in The Parks. *Wisden* tells us:

*. . . the good moments were few, the bad moments many, but account must be taken of the
unusually large number of players who were not available until late in the season due to
pressures of tutors and examinations.*

The high spot of the season was in the second match, when A.C. Smith set Oxford
to get 218 in just under three hours, and a good opening stand by A.K.C. Jones
and D. Williams put the Dark Blues on the road to a two-wicket win. An innings
defeat at Lord's came as no great surprise.

Never were Oxford bowled out for under a hundred, nor did they lose a match
by an innings in a season of promise and improvement in 1973. In the first ever
combined Oxford and Cambridge side against New Zealand, victory was only
four runs away. Imran Khan, Oxford's star freshman, already with a Pakistan tour
under his belt, was top scorer in each innings for the Universities. Played in glorious weather at Fenner's, New Zealand set a target of 211 in two hours and forty
minutes; at the beginning of the last over 11 were needed; R.P. Hodson and
C.R.V. Taylor, two Cambridge players, managed 7 and the match was drawn
with the Universities nine wickets down. The same year saw Oxford's first
success in the Benson and Hedges Cup, the first match to be won by a non-
Championship eleven. Oxford, set to score 173 by Northamptonshire, won by
two wickets with four balls to spare.

For the greater part of the 1974 University season Imran Khan virtually took on
the opposition single-handed. In his first book, *Imran*, he acknowledged the debt
he owed to Oxford; although he had already toured England, when he came up,
he was still an immature player. Like C.B. Fry, his greatest achievements were to
follow his Oxford days. It was his misfortune that the Oxford eleven he led had
few players of class. He made more than twice as many runs as anyone else – his
innings including five three-figure scores – and in making 106 against Nottinghamshire he joined the small list of University players to score two hundreds in a
match. As a bowler he was not as accurate as he later became, but he still took
forty-five first-class wickets. In 1975 pressure of work allowed him few opportunities for cricket, although he helped to bring the best out of the Oxbridge combination which won two matches in the Benson and Hedges competition, against
Worcester and Northamptonshire.

Imran and E.D. Fursdon made major contributions to the exciting contest with
the 1974 Indian eleven. Fursdon, bowling out-swingers in a sustained hostile spell
of bowling, claimed six wickets for 60. A fine innings of 160 from Imran ensured a
handsome lead for Oxford. The final target set for the home side in The Parks proved too much, and Oxford lost by 59 runs.

There was some anxiety in 1975 over the state of the wickets in The Parks,
accentuated by a very wet season. T.R. Glover, of Lancaster Royal Grammar
School, had to rely on a large intake of freshmen; the most notable of these were
two future England players, C.J. Tavaré and V.J. Marks, who made 215 against
the Army at Aldershot. Fursdon scored one of only two hundreds in the season in
the best Varsity Match at Lord's for years.

There had been talk in the early sixties of reviving 'Cuppers', the inter-college
competition, which had lapsed over thirty years before. It is said that the actual
cup was discovered in the Brasenose beer cellar, but it took the initiative of Felix

Stephens, Secretary of the Authentics, and now Father Felix, a Housemaster at Ampleforth, to relaunch the competition. Backed by typical Catholic hospitality, he persuaded the captains of College elevens that a one day knock-out programme was practical and 1967 saw 'Cuppers' revived. B.N.C. won the cup that year in a final played on the Christ Church Ground and the competition is now an established feature of the Oxford cricketing calendar.

CAMBRIDGE *The Majid era*

The decade between 1966 and 1975 saw more draws at Lord's than in any previous decade, though to get the matter in perspective, in three of them fielders were clustered vainly round the bat to achieve the final breakthrough. It saw also both the introduction of Oxford and Cambridge, playing as separate sides, into the new 55-over competition sponsored by Benson and Hedges, and, less importantly but more significantly, the end of admission charges when the Varsity sides were playing on county grounds.

The Cambridge representative of *Wisden*, in his report on the 1968 season, was looking for reasons for what he saw as a decline in University cricket, and in particular for the fact that, for the first time since the war, no Light Blue batsman had managed to score five hundred runs. Apart from the very wet start to this particular season, the writer thought that two main causes stood out – the abolition of National Service, which had given players two more years in which to mature, and the understandable reluctance of undergraduates in those days to sacrifice academic studies for the game.

To these causes I would add, as mentioned in the account of the previous decade, the decline of the admissions tutor who was highly sympathetic to sportsmen, and the new emphasis on the Norrington league table of examination prowess at Oxford, and its later Cambridge equivalent. In the earlier heyday of the amateur, an easy place was found for the likes of several to whom I have spoken who, frankly, were following, to a greater or lesser degree, the advice of W.G. Grace: 'Never read print; it spoils your eye for batting.'

We must now come down from the mountain-top of theory into the marketplace of practice and of personalities. For the record, Oxford's innings victory in 1966, their first by an innings since 1948 (when Hughie Webb, to whom I had given his colours at Winchester, batted so gloriously), was countered by Cambridge's innings win in 1972, and it is to the Light Blue captain on that occasion, as in 1971, that I wish to turn.

This decade was notable for the arrival of a Test and county player who was able, by his play and his personality, to counter the decline that the *Wisden* writer described, and to revive the interest, excitement and confidence which the loyal supporters at Fenner's have especially felt in certain eras. They felt these particularly from 1878 to 1882; in the S.M.J. Woods era; from 1919 to 1922; in certain years during the early thirties; from 1948 to 1952; in the Dexter and the Lewis–Brearley years . . . and they were now to feel them again. Majid Khan, for such was the reviver's name, famous son of famous father, Jahangir Khan – to repay the compliment paid in the 1929 decade section – had already played for Pakistan at a young age, as well as for Glamorgan, and it was his Glamorgan friends Wilf Wooller and Tony Lewis who suggested that he should go to Cambridge, and helped him to get there.

At Cambridge, Majid immediately showed how early he saw the ball, and how sweetly he timed it, off both the front and the back foot. Over the three years he was in residence, he had an aggregate of 2545 runs, at an average of a little over 52, and in 1970 he joined the select band of those who have scored a double-century in the historic match – bringing the total to three for Cambridge, Ratcliffe, Goonesena and Majid, and two for Oxford, the Nawab of Pataudi senior and M.J.K. Smith. On this occasion he shared in a second-wicket partnership of 225 with Philip Carling, from Kingston GS and now the secretary of Glamorgan, against whom he had scored a hundred earlier in the term. Majid's two hundred at Lord's was his fifth century of the season, the previous four having been watched by a procession of undergraduates who flocked to Fenner's when they heard that he was at the crease.

It was, however, as a captain – rated, as mentioned, by Cambridge's celebrated groundsman as the best he saw – that Majid's influence was greatest, for he also had the ability to raise the performance of those around him. It was 1971, the first of Majid's two years as captain, that was the golden year, when Cambridge defeated the Pakistanis, Leicestershire and Sussex, as well as the MCC, D.H. Robins' eleven and the Combined Services. A case could be made for saying that, though there may have been better batting sides, and better bowling sides, this side, taken all in all, was the equal of any other after the Second World War. We shall later look at other members of that side, whose skills benefited from Majid's nurturing, but we include here the scores of the Pakistan match to mark the achievement, with the reflection that in 1972 Majid was the only batsman to pass two thousand runs for the full season.

Played at Cambridge 15, 17, 18 May 1971
Pakistan 126 (J. Spencer 6 for 40) and 235 (Zaheer Abbas 62; J. Spencer 5 for 58)
Cambridge 360 (Majid Khan 94, D.R. Owen-Thomas 77, H.K. Steele 73) and 2 for no wicket.
Cambridge won by 10 wickets.

To return to the first half of the decade, Deryck Murray's 1966 side was limited, by the captain's decision, to those who could, or would, play the whole time. Thus the two bowlers Angus McLachlan, from St Peter's, Adelaide, and Mark Whitaker, from Bryanston, the former a blue in 1964 and 1965, and the latter a quick bowler doing well in 1965 until illness intervened, were not considered. The opening bowler Stephen Russell, from Tiffin School, had most success; his forty-one wickets over the Cambridge season, and his 5 for 60 in 25 overs in Oxford's only innings at Lord's, reflected his speed, line and length. Apart from Murray, who showed his class with his 133 against Sussex but was not as consistent as his experience should have made him, the performance that gave most satisfaction and hope for the future was that of Nick Cosh, a freshman from Dulwich, who had toured South Africa with the MCC Schools team in 1965. In his first year he finished top of the batting averages; his technique and temperament brought him almost 700 runs in 1966, including a fine 98 against the West Indies, and 664 runs in 1967, including a hundred at Lord's. He played six matches for Surrey, was a noted rugby footballer, playing for Blackheath as well as for Cambridge, and is now finance director of MAI plc.

Joining Cosh as a class batsman in 1967, when Russell was a good captain and again did well at Lord's, was the left-handed batsman and right-handed bowler Roger Knight, who arrived from Dulwich with a considerable schoolboy reputation. He did not belie this, making 86 on debut against Essex in the second innings, being run out, presumably to his considerable chagrin, and following this with 140 against Middlesex. Knight's best season at Cambridge was in 1969, when he made over 600 runs with an average of 33.73, six times made fifty, and played well at Lord's. Perhaps he will remember with especial pleasure his performance against Essex in 1970, when he made 0 and 164 not out, and took 6 for 65 in 30 overs. He has successfully combined his teaching with cricket, playing in turn for Sussex, Gloucestershire and Surrey, whom he captained for several years, and he must have more than once been close to winning an England cap. The schoolmaster cricket blue is, alas, a declining breed.

There is a continuing theme in our story of cricketers being successful at other sports, and this decade is no exception. The Brentwoodian David Acfield, for instance, won his blue as a talented off-spinner in 1967 and 1968, has recently retired from first-class cricket after playing 310 games for Essex, and was a noted fencer, representing Great Britain as well as Cambridge and becoming British sabre champion. Tony Jorden, from Monmouth School, who won cricket blues from 1968 to 1970 and who played 60 matches for Essex, was also a talented rugby full-back for Cambridge, Blackheath and England. He was one of those who captained Cambridge successfully two years running; in his first year, 1969, his side was close to beating a county – Nottinghamshire won by one wicket only – and held the initiative at Lord's. The Marlburian Christopher Pyemont, who played several useful innings in 1967, was also a hockey and a rackets blue.

One of those players who benefited from Majid's presence was Dudley Owen-Thomas, born in Mombasa, Kenya, who went to King's College School, Wimbledon and whom I first saw, as also Chris Old, in the Colts match between ESCA and my eleven at Southampton in 1964. He made an impact in the 1969 season, making 182 not out against Middlesex, 101 against Warwickshire in the next match, and 78 at Lord's. After a less good year in 1970, he was second to Majid in the 1971 batting averages, his own being 49.80, with a top score of 146 not out, happily reserved for Lord's. In his final year he again topped forty in the averages, and, proudest claim of all, he joined that small band of Light Blue cricketers who have made hundreds against Oxford in two succeeding years. He played 73 matches for Surrey.

One unusual incident occurred in 1969, Tony Jorden's first year as captain, when the Eastbournian Mike Barford made a hundred on debut for Cambridge as a freshman against the MCC – only for the match to be declared non-first-class a few weeks later. He went on to win blues in 1970 and 1971, became one of the most prolific batsmen in club cricket, and has been for several years the honorary treasurer of the Quidnunc CC. The captain's disappointment in just failing to beat Nottinghamshire that year was forgotten in his pleasure at the defeat in 1970 of County Champions Glamorgan, by eight wickets. He was helped this year by the arrival, from Brighton and Hove GS, of John Spencer, who took eighty-nine wickets in his three seasons as an opening bowler who could make the ball run away late and break back sharply. At Lord's in the innings win of 1972, he had analyses of 16–7–21–5 and 17–8–36–2. He played 186 matches for Sussex, and now teaches at Brighton College. The other opening bowler in the period 1971–3 was the medic R.J. Hadley, a genuinely fast left-armer from Neath, who took 5 for 70 at Lord's in 1973 and played two matches for Glamorgan. Mike Selvey, a quick bowler who played three Tests for England and who represented both Middlesex and Glamorgan, whose captain he became in 1983, won his blue in 1971, and now has a successful writing and broadcasting career.

Two other players who were to contribute to the Majid era, whom I shall discuss shortly, were Peter Johnson, from Nottingham High School, and Philippe Edmonds, of Gilbert Rennie HS Lusaka and Cranbrook School, who captained the 1973 side. This was the side in which Chilton Taylor, from Birkenhead School, who played one match registered for Warwickshire, and two matches unregistered for Middlesex, for which they were penalized, proved himself a fine wicket-keeper, and in which Bill Snowden, from Merchant Taylors', Crosby, captain in 1974 and now running the cricket at Harrow, and Phillip Hodson, from Queen Elizabeth GS, Wakefield, after initial disappointments, came good with an opening partnership of 202 against Kent. Chris Aworth, from Tiffin School, to be captain in 1975, also showed good technique as a freshman in 1973. Hodson, in passing, was pressed into service as a seam-bowler in 1975 and finished top of the averages.

I now return to Peter Johnson and Philippe Edmonds. Johnson had a remarkable record at school, as both a stylish batsman and a leg-break and googly bowler of ability. He won blues from 1970 to 1972, went on to play 58 matches for Nottinghamshire, and later played also for Lincolnshire and Cambridgeshire. He began slowly, but in 1971 and 1972 he started to show something of why he had been awarded the Sir Frank Worrell Memorial Award for the Young Cricketer of the Year in 1969. He must have particularly enjoyed sharing with Owen-Thomas at Lord's, in 1971, a partnership of 150 at a run a minute, as well as being awarded a First in his final examination.

Edmonds was a talented and in some ways idiosyncratic cricketer who, at Cambridge, earned much respect from his opponents as a left-arm bowler who could both spin and flight the ball, bringing much-needed variety to his craft. In those days he was also no mean batsman, but this aspect of his cricket never fully developed afterwards. He went on to play successfully for Middlesex and for England, being first summoned to Headingley in August 1975 and promptly dismissing five Australians for 17 runs in 12 overs. That he played only 32 internationals in his first decade is attributable, Vic Marks suggests in the third *World of Cricket*, in part to the presence of Derek Underwood and in part to his fiercely independent streak, which did not always win him the approval of those who mattered (although they may not always have mattered to him). In India, under David Gower, in 1984 he became the linch-pin of the attack; he again played well against the Australians in 1986, and he bowed out at the end of the 1987 season. His ambitions were never fully realized, as he has made clear in his autobiography, for he was never appointed captain of either Middlesex or England, and he believes that he would have done both jobs well.

After the five wins while Majid was in residence, Cambridge had to wait for several years for another. In Edmonds' year they had Oxford on the run, thanks to the fine bowling of Hadley, of the unusually tall Wykehamist James Roundell – who now works for Christie's – of the captain himself and of Hodson, and to the batting of Snowden and Murrills. In 1974, in a low-scoring match which seems not to have pleased the writer in *Wisden*, Aworth made the only fifty in the match, and the opening bowlers Max Field of Bablake, who took twenty-four wickets in the Cambridge season of that year and played three matches for Warwickshire, and Geoff Moses of Cwmtawe bowled best, and also shared in an important last-wicket partnership of 47 at Lord's.

In the 1975 University Match, Peter Roebuck and Alastair Hignell had a glorious partnership of 161, and the Wykehamist Edward Jackson, bowling quick left-arm, had the best analysis: 29–7–98–7 and 28–6–62–3. It was in this year that the Brightonian Peter Hayes, now teaching at Framlingham and playing for Suffolk, won the Benson and Hedges Gold Award, when the Combined Universities beat Worcestershire by 66 runs. He made nought and took no wicket, but fielded well, caught Glenn Turner off a stunning catch, and bowled so tightly at the crisis of the match that the adjudicator showed no hesitation with his decision. Such an adjudication makes a suitable finale to the account of this decade.

1966

Cambridge came to Lord's with one of the weakest sides for twenty years, in part because of their West Indian captain D.L. Murray's decision to play only those who were available throughout the term. Murray showed his own class on several occasions, the promising Alleynian opener N.J. Cosh made over 700 runs, and S.G. Russell took forty-one wickets at 25.24 each. Oxford had been moulded into a strong side by R.M.C. Gilliat. They had very useful opening batsmen in the Rhodesian F.S. Goldstein and P.J.K. Gibbs, later to play for Derbyshire, and successful spinners in G.N.S. Ridley, also a Rhodesian, and R.W. Elviss, from Leeds GS.

In the event, Oxford played aggressive and effective cricket and won convincingly by an innings and 9 runs, thereby bringing to an end a run of six draws. Oxford's 300 for 7 wickets declared owed most to an attractive innings of 86 by their captain, who put on 135 with the much-improved Tonbridgian D.P. Toft, and to a militant 80 by the South African M.G.M. Groves. Russell deservedly took 5 for 60 in twenty-five overs. Cambridge lost two wickets overnight and never recovered. Their captain played the one long innings, 72 not out in three and a quarter hours. Twelve of the wickets fell to the two Oxford spinners.

OXFORD	First innings		Second innings	
P.J.K. Gibbs	c Murray, b Russell	25		
F.S. Goldstein	c Hays, b Cottrell	25		
D.P. Toft	b Russell	61		
R.M.C. Gilliat	c Hays, b Murray	86		
M.G.M. Groves	*not out*	80		
M.R.J. Guest	c Cosh, b Russell	6		
A.W. Dyer	c and b Russell	1		
G.N.S. Ridley	*lbw, b Russell*	0		
A.G.M. Watson	*not out*	8		
EXTRAS	B 5, L-B 3	8		
	TOTAL (7 WKTS DEC.)	300		

R.W. Elviss and R.B. Hiller did not bat

CAMBRIDGE

K.P.W.J. McAdam	b Ridley	13	c Dyer, b Watson	0
R.E.J. Chambers	b Elviss	4	c and b Hiller	20
G.A. Cottrell	b Hiller	4	c Goldsmith, b Hiller	21
N.D. Sinker	c Dyer, b Watson	9	b Elviss	0
D.L. Hays	c Guest, b Ridley	35	b Watson	20
D.L. Murray	*lbw, b Ridley*	20	*not out*	72
N.J. Cosh	*not out*	38	c Hiller, b Ridley	6
V.P. Malalasekera	c Watson, b Ridley	0	*lbw, b Elviss*	2
A.B. Palfreman	c Hiller, b Elviss	5	c Dyer, b Hiller	0
R. Roopnaraine	c Dyer, b Watson	0	c Watson, b Elviss	0
S.G. Russell	*lbw, b Elviss*	1	b Ridley	0
EXTRAS	B 11	11	B 4, L-B 5, N-B 1	10
	TOTAL	140	TOTAL	151

Cambridge bowling	OVERS	MDNS	RUNS	WKTS					
Russell	25	8	60	5					
Palfreman	21	8	68	0					
Cottrell	10	2	19	1					
Sinker	18	3	48	0					
Roopnaraine	19	7	51	0					
Murray	6	1	46	1					

Oxford bowling	OVERS	MDNS	RUNS	WKTS		OVERS	MDNS	RUNS	WKTS
Watson	11	5	31	2		10	2	26	2
Hiller	8	2	37	1		15	5	48	3
Ridley	22	8	35	4		21.5	12	29	2
Elviss	19.2	10	26	3		34	20	26	3
Guest	—	—	—	—		5	2	12	0

UMPIRES C.S. Elliott and C.G. Pepper

8, 10, 11 July
At Lord's

1967

Match drawn

Both teams came to the big match with shaky records, but with a fair sprinkling of talent. Two future county captains, for Oxford Richard Gilliat (Hampshire) and for Cambridge Roger Knight (Surrey), played in the match, but without the impact they later made in county cricket.

The match got off to a quick tempo, with the Oxford opening batsmen – the Tonbridgian D.P. Toft and F.S. Goldstein, from Falcon, Rhodesia – scoring at a run a minute for the first hour and a half. Toft batted for over five hours for his 145, and shared in partnerships with Goldstein,

A.R. Garofall and the Rhodesian captain G.N.S. Ridley. Cambridge's reply to Oxford's 316 for 7 declared owed most to the composed batting of the Alleynian N.J. Cosh, before Ridley and R.W. Elviss caused a collapse with spin.

Good Cambridge bowling by S.G. Russell, G.A. Cottrell and D.L. Acfield kept Oxford in check, but useful innings were played by D.R. Walsh, A.H. Barker and R.A. Brooks. Once Oxford declared, Cosh and V. Malalasekera, one of two batsmen from Colombo, started splendidly, but the task was too much.

OXFORD

	First innings		Second innings	
D.P. Toft	c Knight, b Aers	145	lbw, b Cottrell	2
F.S. Goldstein	b Cottrell	59	b Russell	4
R.M.C. Gilliat	b Russell	3	c Malalasekera, b Russell	11
A.R. Garofall	run out	44	b Cottrell	17
D.R. Walsh	b Acfield	0	not out	41
A.H. Barker	b Acfield	12	b Cottrell	33
G.N.S. Ridley	b Aers	46	b Aers	6
R.A. Brooks	not out	0	c Paull, b Knight	44
R.W. Elviss	did not bat		not out	0
EXTRAS	B 2, L-B 3, W 2	7	W 1	1
	TOTAL (7 WKTS DEC.)	316	TOTAL (7 WKTS DEC.)	159

N.W. Gamble and J.N.C. Easter did not bat

CAMBRIDGE

C.E.M. Ponniah	c Goldstein, b Elviss	21	not out	20
V.P. Malalasekera	c Elviss, b Easter	35	c and b Ridley	29
R.D.V. Knight	b Elviss	36	b Ridley	12
N.J. Cosh	b Barker	100	c Toft, b Elviss	46
C.P. Pyemont	c Brooks, b Ridley	41	run out	13
R.K. Paull	b Elviss	0	c Toft, b Ridley	21
G.A. Cottrell	lbw, b Ridley	6	not out	6
D.R. Aers	b Barker	7		
D.W. Norris	c Walsh, b Ridley	1		
D.L. Acfield	b Ridley	0		
S.G. Russell	not out	0		
EXTRAS	B 2, L-B 8, W 1	11	B 1, L-B 4	5
	TOTAL	258	TOTAL (5 WKTS)	152

Cambridge bowling	OVERS	MDNS	RUNS	WKTS		OVERS	MDNS	RUNS	WKTS
Russell	25	3	97	1		16	4	52	2
Cottrell	26	5	88	1		17	6	35	3
Acfield	35	14	70	2		27	11	35	0
Paull	2	0	16	0		3.2	1	12	0
Aers	17.4	6	38	2		11	7	10	1
Pyemont	—	—	—	—		3	0	8	0
Knight	—	—	—	—		2	0	6	1

Oxford bowling									
Easter	17	8	42	1		3	0	17	0
Gamble	13	1	56	0		2	0	14	0
Elviss	35	14	51	3		20	5	48	1
Ridley	36	19	57	4		20	7	43	3
Barker	25	9	41	2		4	1	10	0
Goldstein	—	—	—	—		5	2	7	0
Gilliat	—	—	—	—		1	0	8	0

UMPIRES C.S. Elliott and O.W. Herman

6, 8, 9 July
At Lord's

1968

Match drawn

Poor weather was contributory to both sides arriving at Lord's with disappointing records, but this match was notable for fighting, spirited cricket throughout. Oxford set the tempo with an exciting innings of 155 by F.S. Goldstein, their captain from Falcon, Rhodesia, a hundred coming in boundaries, mostly fierce pulls and on-drives, in addition to three sixes. He received strong support from D.R. Walsh and A.R. Garofall. Apart from one run-out, the wickets were shared by the opener A.M. Jorden, and the captain, G.A. Cottrell.

After a poor start, Cambridge were revived by

a fine partnership between two Alleynian left-handers who would both later play for Surrey, N.J. Cosh and R.D.V. Knight. D.C. Haywood, from Nottingham HS, also made an important contribution; and A.G.M. Watson and J.N.C. Easter were the most effective bowlers.

Goldstein and Garofall again led the way when Oxford went for quick runs, and Cambridge were set 242 in two hours and three quarters. At 78 for 6, at the hands of two fine spinners, G.N.S. Ridley and A.J. Khan, they seemed doomed; but Cosh and Jordan batted for seventy minutes to save the day.

OXFORD	First innings		Second innings	
F.S. Goldstein	c Knight, b Jorden	155	c and b Acfield	54
R.M. Ridley	b Jorden	26	c Norris, b Jorden	0
D.R. Walsh	b Cottrell	65	c and b Acfield	28
A.R. Garofall	c and b Cottrell	58	c and b Jorden	61
A.J. Khan	b Jorden	23		
P.R.B. Wilson	c Haywood, b Cottrell	10	not out	29
A.G.M. Watson	run out	1	c Knight, b Jorden	0
G.N.S. Ridley	b Cottrell	12	b Jorden	1
S.A. Westley	not out	3	b Acfield	3
EXTRAS	L-B 9, N-B 1	10	B 5, L-B 3	8
	TOTAL (8 WKTS DEC.)	363	TOTAL (7 WKTS DEC.)	184

R.N. Niven and J.N.C. Easter did not bat

CAMBRIDGE				
C.E.M. Ponniah	c Wilson, b Watson	17	b Khan	31
P.G. Carling	b Niven	14	c Khan, b G.N.S. Ridley	32
G.A. Cottrell	c Goldstein, b Watson	0	c G.N.S. Ridley, b Khan	0
N.J. Cosh	c Khan, b G.N.S. Ridley	59	not out	24
R.D.V. Knight	c Westley, b Easter	69	c sub, b G.N.S. Ridley	2
D.L. Hays	st Westley, b Easter	16	c Garofall, b G.N.S. Ridley	1
D.C. Haywood	c Westley, b Niven	62	c Garofall, b Khan	9
D.W.W. Norris	lbw, b G.N.S. Ridley	0		
A.M. Jorden	c sub, b Easter	21	not out	22
D.L. Acfield	c Niven, b Watson	16		
J.F. Fitzgerald	not out	17		
EXTRAS	B 10, L-B 4, N-B 1	15	B 6, L-B 2, N-B 2	10
	TOTAL	306	TOTAL (6 WKTS)	131

Cambridge bowling	OVERS	MDNS	RUNS	WKTS		OVERS	MDNS	RUNS	WKTS
Acfield	37	14	107	0		13.4	1	63	3
Jorden	33.4	8	100	3		12	1	52	4
Knight	21	5	53	0		4	0	13	0
Ponniah	8	2	30	0		2	0	7	0
Fitzgerald	15	8	32	0		3	0	6	0
Cottrell	14	5	31	4		8	1	35	0

Oxford bowling									
Watson	16.1	1	52	3		5	1	16	0
Niven	24	1	87	2		3	1	7	0
G.N.S. Ridley	33	10	84	2		23.3	11	32	3
Khan	26	18	36	0		23	7	54	3
Wilson	4	2	6	0		4	2	6	0
Easter	15	6	32	3		5	4	6	0

UMPIRES A.E. Fagg and A.E. Rhodes

12, 14, 15 July
At Lord's

1969

Match drawn

Several Dark and Light Blue batsmen had more than respectable batting averages in the season; D.R. Walsh made 207 for Oxford against Warwickshire, and for Cambridge D.R. Owen-Thomas made 182 not out against Middlesex and 101 against Warwickshire, and R.D.V. Knight scored over 600 runs. The record of the bowlers was less impressive.

At Lord's there was a re-run of last year's pattern, with Cambridge making the running in a fluctuating, absorbing contest. Knight looked a class player and Owen-Thomas was in punishing form. F.S. Goldstein, the Oxford captain, was less commanding than in 1968, but Oxford scored consistently.

On the third morning, Knight and C.E.M. Ponniah, from St Thomas, Colombo, made 123 in ninety-two minutes. Positive captaincy by A.M. Jorden allowed Oxford three hours and twenty minutes to score 249. While Goldstein and the Stoic J.W.O. Allerton were scoring freely, Oxford looked well set for victory, but when 59 were needed from ten overs, with three wickets in hand, they called off the chase. H. Pearman, from King Alfred's, took 4 for 56.

CAMBRIDGE	First innings		Second innings	
H. Pearman	c Goldstein, b Millener	4	b Millener	24
J.I. McDowell	c Khan, b Niven	32	lbw, b Millener	35
R.D.V. Knight	c Westley, b Heard	55	not out	88
C.E.M. Ponniah	lbw, b Heard	27	not out	50
D.R. Owen-Thomas	c Goldstein, b Millener	78		
J.E. Hall	b Burton	12		
R.L. Short	c Westley, b Heard	5		
N.P.G. Ross	not out	9		
A.N. Bhatia	c Ridley, b Burton	43		
EXTRAS	B 1, L-B 6, N-B 1	8	B 7, L-B 6	13
	TOTAL (8 WKTS DEC.)	273	TOTAL (2 WKTS DEC.)	210

A.M. Jorden and M.R.S. Nevin did not bat.

OXFORD				
F.S. Goldstein	c Bhatia, b Knight	43	c McDowell, b Pearman	69
R.M. Ridley	c Cross, b Knight	26	c McDowell, b Pearman	18
D.R. Walsh	c Nevin, b Pearman	12	c Ross, b Bhatia	17
J.W.O. Allerton	c Ross, b Pearman	8	c Owen-Thomas, b Jorden	48
A.J. Khan	lbw, b Jorden	24	st McDowell, b Pearman	16
A.H. Morgan	c Owen-Thomas, b Jorden	33	not out	15
M.St.J.W. Burton	c Owen-Thomas, b Ross	21	c Knight, b Ross	11
S.A. Westley	b Pearman	32	c sub, b Pearman	11
H. Heard	b Nevin	0	not out	8
D.J. Millener	c Jorden, b Ross	20		
R.A. Niven	not out	13		
EXTRAS	W 1, N-B 2	3	B 3, L-B 5	8
	TOTAL	235	TOTAL (7 WKTS)	221

Oxford bowling	OVERS	MDNS	RUNS	WKTS		OVERS	MDNS	RUNS	WKTS
Millener	22	9	43	2		31	16	57	2
Heard	24	4	66	3		7	1	35	0
Niven	19	8	49	1		4	0	22	0
Burton	25.2	8	49	2		20	7	56	0
Khan	17	2	58	0		7	1	27	0

Cambridge bowling									
Jorden	20	3	59	2		7	0	34	1
Nevin	17	1	50	1		5	0	27	0
Owen-Thomas	13	5	22	0		4	1	13	0
Knight	17	6	45	2		6	1	23	0
Pearman	25	14	31	3		23	6	56	4
Bhatia	5	3	3	0		16	4	38	1
Ross	4.1	0	22	2		4.4	1	22	1

UMPIRES J.F. Crapp and O.W. Herman

11, 13, 14 July
At Lord's
1970
Match drawn

The arrival at Cambridge of the Pakistan Test player Majid Khan, after helping Glamorgan to their Championship win in 1969, was a great tonic, increasing interest and helping to raise the performance of others. He scored 1216 in the short University season of twelve matches, capping his form with a remarkable double-century, in four hours and forty minutes, at Lord's. The Cambridge attack was strengthened by the arrival of J. Spencer, from Brighton and Hove GS.

Oxford reached Lord's without a victory, but B. May, from Prince Edward's, had made a hun-

dred against Glamorgan, and the Cliftonian R.M. Ridley had batted for seven hours and forty minutes against Nottinghamshire.

The match was ruined by rain on the third day, when Cambridge were 136 ahead with all their wickets intact. On the first day, P.G. Carling and R.D.V. Knight had given good support to Majid in Cambridge's 337 for 8 wickets declared. Oxford replied with 254, thanks mainly to A.N. Campbell and R. Johns. The fast-medium attack of Jorden, Spencer and Knight proved economical and effective.

CAMBRIDGE

	First innings		Second innings	
P.G. Carling	c Millener, b Burton	44	not out	25
M.T. Barford	b Heard	13	not out	26
Majid Khan	c Johns, b Millener	200		
R.D.V. Knight	c Burton, b Millener	33		
D.R. Owen-Thomas	c Burchnall, b Burton	6		
P.D. Johnson	c May, b Heard	8		
R.C. Bromley	c Heal, b Heard	13		
T.E.N. Jameson	not out	8		
A.M. Jorden	b Millener	5		
EXTRAS	B 2, L-B 4, W 1	7	B 2	2
	TOTAL (8 WKTS DEC.)	337	TOTAL (0 WKTS)	53

C.L. Wilkin and J. Spencer did not bat

OXFORD

R.M. Ridley	c Jameson, b Knight	31
R.L. Burchnall	lbw, b Spencer	9
B. May	b Knight	13
P.R.B. Wilson	c and b Wilkin	8
A.N. Campbell	c Khan, b Jorden	57
M.G. Heal	b Johnson	18
R. Johns	not out	61
M.St.J.W. Burton	b Jorden	8
H. Heard	c Khan, b Owen-Thomas	2
D.J. Millener	c Bromley, b Knight	24
D.F. Allison	c Bromley, b Spencer	0
EXTRAS	B 11, L-B 8, W 3, N-B 1	23
	TOTAL	254

Oxford bowling	OVERS	MDNS	RUNS	WKTS	OVERS	MDNS	RUNS	WKTS
Millener	28.3	5	86	3	19	0	30	0
Heard	28	5	101	3	4	0	19	0
Burton	24	7	66	2	4	3	2	0
Johns	19	4	59	0				
Wilson	1	0	18	0				

Cambridge bowling	OVERS	MDNS	RUNS	WKTS
Jorden	23	11	38	2
Spencer	15.5	4	48	2
Knight	19	10	37	3
Owen-Thomas	13	6	23	1
Wilkin	14	5	35	1
Johnson	13	2	46	1
Jameson	2	1	4	0

UMPIRES W.E. Alley and A.E. Rhodes

10, 12, 13 July
At Lord's

1971

Match drawn

Oxford came to the University Match with a new spirit, induced by their Rhodesian captain, B. May, and victories to their credit against Derbyshire and MCC. Cambridge had what several pundits thought was their best side since the Second World War; but three wins, against Pakistan – no University side had defeated the tourists since Oxford beat the New Zealanders in 1949 – and Leicestershire and Sussex, do not tell the full story of the Light Blue revival. Fuelled by Majid, it was reflected also in the impressive batting of D.R. Owen-Thomas and the freshman P.D. Johnson, from Nottingham HS, and in the bowling achievements of J. Spencer and the freshman from Gilbert Rennie, Lusaka and Cranbrook, P.H. Edmonds.

This match, like those of 1968 and 1969, reached a tense climax, with fieldsmen clustered round the last three Dark Blue batsmen, who held out for an hour. Majid made a cultured 73, and declared Cambridge's innings closed at tea on the first day. J.M. Ward, from Newcastle-under-Lyme, held the Oxford innings together with a sterling 71, but the analysis of the orthodox left-hander, Edmonds, read 33.4–13–56–7. When Cambridge batted again, Owen-Thomas made a decisive 146 in just under four hours, and shared in a partnership of 150 at a run a minute with Johnson. Shortly afer tea Oxford were 134 for 8, but A. Wingfield Digby and S.C. Corlett hung on heroically.

CAMBRIDGE

	First innings		Second innings	
Majid Khan	c Carroll, b Hamblin	73	b Hamblin	2
M.T. Barford	c Ward, b Hamblin	0	c Robinson, b Hamblin	22
D.R. Owen-Thomas	b Hamblin	0	b Corlett	146
P.D. Johnson	c Robinson, b Hamblin	34	c Carroll, b Burton	62
C.P. Seager	c Burton, b Wingfield Digby	23	b Hamblin	19
H.K. Steel	lbw, b Burton	27	not out	7
P.H. Edmonds	c and b Burton	0		
M.W.W. Selvey	not out	5		
J. Spencer	not out	12		
EXTRAS	B 3, L-B 2, N-B 1	6	B 4, L-B 3, N-B 1	8
	TOTAL (7 WKTS DEC.)	180	TOTAL (5 WKTS DEC.)	266

C.R.V. Taylor and R.J. Hadley did not bat

OXFORD

A.K.C. Jones	b Edmonds	20	c Majid, b Edmonds	28
G.A. Robinson	b Edmonds	29	run out	18
R.L. Burchnall	c Majid, b Edmonds	6	run out	1
A. Wingfield Digby	b Edmonds	0	c Spencer, b Selvey	26
C.B. Hamblin	c Hadley, b Edmonds	19	not out	4
B. May	b Spencer	2	b Majid	26
P.R. Carroll	b Majid	13	b Edmonds	5
J.M. Ward	c Majid, b Edmonds	71	b Edmonds	9
M.St.J.W. Burton	b Edmonds	18	b Majid	10
P.C.H. Jones	b Majid	13	b Majid	9
S.C. Corlett	not out	1	not out	19
EXTRAS	L-B 4, W 1, N-B 6	11	B 17, L-B 4, N-B 4	25
	TOTAL	203	TOTAL (9 WKTS)	180

Oxford bowling	OVERS	MDNS	RUNS	WKTS		OVERS	MDNS	RUNS	WKTS
Wingfield Digby	20	9	41	1		26	7	73	0
Hamblin	13	5	32	4		20.3	3	62	3
Burton	33	12	60	2		20	1	74	1
Corlett	15	5	41	0		13	2	49	1

Cambridge bowling									
Spencer	14	7	11	1		10	3	15	0
Hadley	10	2	25	0		6	4	4	0
Majid Khan	34	12	60	2		38	15	47	3
Edmonds	33.4	13	56	7		35	12	73	3
Selvey	10	0	40	0		6	2	16	1

UMPIRES A.G.T. Whitehead and W.I. Budd

1972

Each team arrived at Lord's with one victory against a county to its credit, but whereas Oxford had had a dispiriting season in The Parks, Cambridge were basking in the climax of the Majid era, during which he not only made 2545 runs at an average of over 52, but also raised standards to surprising heights. It was fitting that he crowned his University career with victory over Oxford, the first since 1958, by an innings and 25 runs.

The key to the Light Blue success was the ability of their fast–medium trio to extract bounce and movement from a lively Lord's pitch. Thus, in reply to Cambridge's total of 280 for 6 declared, Oxford could manage only 121 and 134. Their match analysis tells the tale: J. Spencer 33–15–57–7;

R.J. Hadley 33–14–77–6; and M.P. Kendall 39–16–77–7. Oxford were 10 for 6 in their first innings when C.B. Hamblin, from King's, Canterbury, and R.J. Lee, from Sydney University, fashioned a recovery; in the second innings M.G. Heal, from St Brendan's, batted defiantly.

After a sound opening partnership by W. Snowden, from Merchant Taylors', Crosby, and R.P. Hodson, from Queen Elizabeth GS, Wakefield, D.R. Owen-Thomas plundered the bowling and scored 114 not out in three hours and twenty-five minutes. He had thus joined the distinguished band of those who scored centuries in more than one University Match.

CAMBRIDGE	First innings		Second innings
R.P. Hodson	*lbw, b* Corlett	12	
W. Snowden	*c and b* Lee	51	
Majid Khan	*c and b* Wagstaffe	16	
D.R. Owen-Thomas	*not out*	114	
P.D. Johnson	*lbw, b* Lee	12	
H.K. Steele	*c* Wagstaffe, *b* Corlett	44	
P.H. Edmonds	*c and b* Corlett	7	
C.R.V. Taylor	*not out*	11	
EXTRAS	B 5, L-B 5, N-B 3	13	
	TOTAL (6 WKTS DEC.)	280	

J. Spencer, M.P. Kendall and R.J. Hadley did not bat

OXFORD			
A.K.C. Jones	*b* Hadley	1	*c* Majid, *b* Hadley	9
B. May	*lbw, b* Hadley	0	*c* Edmonds, *b* Hadley	0
M.G. Heal	*c* Taylor, *b* Spencer	0	*c* Taylor, *b* Kendall	39
M.C. Wagstaffe	*c* Snowden, *b* Spencer	0	*c* Majid, *b* Spencer	19
M.J.J. Faber	*b* Hadley	1	*c* Hodson, *b* Kendall	3
J.M. Ward	*lbw, b* Spencer	0	*c* Hodson, *b* Kendall	0
C.B. Hamblin	*c* Taylor, *b* Spencer	45	*c* Owen-Thomas, *b* Kendall	2
R.J. Lee	*c* Edmonds, *b* Hadley	38	*lbw, b* Kendall	21
P.C.H. Jones	*not out*	16	*lbw, b* Spencer	13
R.C. Kinkead-Weekes	*c* Edmonds, *b* Spencer	0	*c* Majid, *b* Kendall	9
S.C. Corlett	*b* Kendall	0	*not out*	11
EXTRAS	L-B 3, N-B 17	20	N-B 8	8
	TOTAL	121	TOTAL	134

Oxford bowling	OVERS	MDNS	RUNS	WKTS				
Hamblin	16	5	42	0				
Corlett	22	5	53	3				
Lee	27	3	92	2				
Wagstaffe	33	11	80	1				

Cambridge bowling	OVERS	MDNS	RUNS	WKTS	OVERS	MDNS	RUNS	WKTS
Spencer	16	7	21	5	17	8	36	2
Hadley	17	9	30	4	16	5	47	2
Kendall	14	4	34	1	25	12	43	6
Steele	4	1	16	0	2	2	0	0

UMPIRES R. Aspinall and D.L. Evans

7, 9, 10 July
At Lord's

1973

Match drawn

After a wet May in The Parks, Oxford were heartened by a three-day victory against Warwickshire, and by a one-day win over Northamptonshire in the Benson and Hedges Cup – the first success in a one-day competition by a non-Championship side. They were strengthened by the Pakistan all-rounder Imran Khan, who, it is said, failed to gain admission at Cambridge. It was predictable that the Light Blue captain P.H. Edmonds, who had played for Middlesex after the University season in 1972, would have much rebuilding to do, since six members of the victorious 1972 side had gone down.

Both sides in their first innings started badly and never fully recovered the lost momentum.

After T.R. Glover scored a mere 7 in two hours and ten minutes, Imran, J.M. Ward and V.G.B. Cushing raised the tempo, as Oxford made 188. The wickets were shared, with the Cambridge captain taking 3 for 72 in 38 overs and the Wykehamist J. Roundell ending the innings, with the new ball, in a spell of 3 for 3. Cambridge too took a while to recover, but an aggressive partnership by W. Snowden and T.J. Murrills, from The Leys, helped Cambridge to a 50-run lead.

R.J. Hadley broke through when Oxford batted again, and it was Cushing who saved the day. The effective bowling of the Salopian T.M. Lamb and the accuracy of Imran Khan put paid to Cambridge's attempt to score 160 in 105 minutes.

OXFORD	First innings		Second innings	
R.J. Lee	*b* Hadley	9	*b* Edmonds	30
T.R. Glover	*lbw, b* Edmonds	7	*c* Baker, *b* Hadley	11
A.K.C. Jones	*b* Hadley	2	*lbw, b* Hadley	4
Imran Khan	*c* Taylor, *b* Edmonds	51	*lbw, b* Hadley	2
J.M. Ward	*st* Taylor, *b* Edmonds	28	*b* Hadley	2
C.B. Hamblin	*lbw, b* Hodson	10	*lbw, b* Edmonds	13
V.G.B. Cushing	*lbw, b* Roundell	44	*not out*	77
R.G.L. Paver	*c* Murrills, *b* Hadley	8	*c* Taylor, *b* Hodson	26
S.R. Porter	*not out*	6	*lbw, b* Hodson	8
R.A. Niven	*b* Roundell	0	*c* Aworth, *b* Hadley	1
T.M. Lamb	*c* Smythe, *b* Roundell	2	*not out*	9
EXTRAS	B 6, L-B 10, W 4, N-B 1	21	B 6, L-B 17, W 1, N-B 2	26
	TOTAL	188	TOTAL (9 WKTS DEC.)	209

CAMBRIDGE				
R.P. Hodson	*lbw, b* Lamb	3	*c* Jones, *b* Lamb	33
S. Wright	*lbw, b* Lamb	18	*b* Lamb	16
C.J. Aworth	*c* Paver, *b* Lee	26	*c* Jones, *b* Lee	17
R.I. Smythe	*c* Cushing, *b* Porter	40	*not out*	0
P.H. Edmonds	*lbw, b* Imran	7	*c* Ward, *b* Lamb	11
W. Snowden	*c and b* Imran	52	*c* Hamblin, *b* Lamb	6
T.J. Murrills	*c* Lee, *b* Niven	53	*not out*	5
R.K. Baker	*b* Imran	4		
C.R.V. Taylor	*not out*	21		
R.J. Hadley	*not out*	3		
EXTRAS	L-B 3, W 1, N-B 7	11	L-B 1	1
	TOTAL (8 WKTS DEC.)	238	TOTAL (5 WKTS)	89

J. Roundell did not bat

Oxford bowling	OVERS	MDNS	RUNS	WKTS		OVERS	MDNS	RUNS	WKTS
Hadley	24	9	46	3		23	6	70	5
Roundell	14.5	7	12	3		6	2	22	0
Edmonds	38	17	72	3		35.3	15	50	2
Hodson	21	9	37	1		17	7	41	2

Oxford bowling	OVERS	MDNS	RUNS	WKTS		OVERS	MDNS	RUNS	WKTS
Imran Khan	34	5	81	3		8	0	16	0
Lamb	22	4	50	2		11	3	29	4
Niven	8	2	19	1		4	4	0	0
Lee	21	6	48	1		5	1	24	1
Porter	25	14	29	1		7	3	19	0

UMPIRES J. Langridge and H. Yarnold

6, 8, 9 July
At Lord's

1974

Match drawn

Oxford's preparations for the University Match were obstructed by academic commitments, but at full strength they beat Northamptonshire, and Imran Khan played heroically, scoring five centuries, two in the same match against Nottinghamshire and taking forty-five wickets at 26.28 each. Cambridge had a poor season, apart from the encouraging form of their secretary, C.J. Aworth, and the impressive bowling of M.N. Field and E.J.W. Jackson.

At Lord's no side reached two hundred, despite three fine days. Cambridge's first innings of 139 – Imran took 5 for 44 in 20 overs – was matched by Oxford's 127 – in which G. Moses,

from Cwmtawe, took 5 for 31 in 15 overs, and, crucially, Imran was run out after receiving one ball. Cambridge fared little better, but a critical dropped c & b reprieved D.P. Russell, from West Park, St Helens, and he and Aworth brought respectability to the total. Jackson spent eighty-one minutes on 0 – a record then outside Tests – and the last pair added a crucial 47. Imran and Tim Lamb shared nine wickets.

Oxford needed 205 in four hours forty minutes; T.R. Glover and R.J. Lee gave them a flying start, sustained by Imran. Oxford needed 62 in the last twenty overs and P.R. Thackeray's lack of enterprise was critical.

CAMBRIDGE	First innings			Second innings	
S.P. Coverdale	b Imran	24		b Imran	0
R.I. Smyth	run out	46		lbw, b Lamb	17
C.J. Aworth	lbw, b Imran	5		b Lamb	51
W. Snowden	c Paver, b Imran	9		c Paver, b Lamb	3
T.J. Murrills	b Fursdon	1		c Imran, b Lamb	8
R.K. Baker	c Botton, b Imran	9		lbw, b Imran	3
D.P. Russell	b Lamb	13		c Botton, b Fursdon	31
E.J.W. Jackson	b Imran	1		c Paver, b Imran	4
P.J. Hayes	not out	21		lbw, b Imran	5
M.N. Field	b Lee	0		hw, b Imran	24
G. Moses	b Lamb	3		not out	24
EXTRAS	B 3, L-B 4	7		B 6, L-B 7, W 5, N-B 4	22
	TOTAL	139		TOTAL	192

OXFORD					
T.R. Glover	b Moses	4		b Jackson	26
R.J. Lee	b Moses	22		c Murrills, b Field	42
G. de W. Waller	lbw, b Moses	2		c Coverdale, b Jackson	0
P.R. Thackeray	c Baker, b Field	2		not out	42
Imran Khan	run out	0		c Baker, b Moses	46
R.G.L. Paver	lbw, b Moses	34		lbw, b Field	3
N.D. Botton	run out	6		b Field	9
M.F.D. Lloyd	c Baker, b Moses	14		lbw, b Field	0
E.D. Fursdon	lbw, b Jackson	10		not out	6
M.J.D. Stallibrass	b Jackson	15			
T.M. Lamb	not out	13			
EXTRAS	B 1, L-B 2, N-B 2	5		L-B 5, W 5	10
	TOTAL	127		TOTAL (7 WKTS)	184

Oxford bowling	OVERS	MDNS	RUNS	WKTS		OVERS	MDNS	RUNS	WKTS
Imran Khan	20	4	44	5		37.4	14	69	5
Lamb	13.4	4	30	2		33	12	68	4
Fursdon	21	8	31	1		12	6	16	1
Stallibrass	9	2	21	0		4	3	7	0
Lee	3	1	6	1		5	2	10	0
Botton	—	—	—	—		5	5	0	0

Cambridge bowling									
Field	23	3	59	1		33	9	76	4
Moses	15	3	31	5		20	8	33	1
Hayes	5	1	7	0		1	0	2	0
Jackson	5.4	0	25	2		22	7	53	2
Aworth	—	—	—	—		2	0	10	0

UMPIRES H. Horton and G.H. Pope

1975

Match drawn

Oxford were handicapped by the dreadful weather in March and April, which affected the preparation of pitches. Imran Khan was not available until late in the season, but promising freshmen arrived in V.J. Marks, C.J. Tavaré, and G. Pathmanathan, from Royal College, Colombo. Cambridge profited from the arrival of P.M. Roebuck, who averaged 40.14, and A.J. Hignell, from Denstone.

This match concluded, once again, with tail-end batsmen playing out time. Cambridge held out, but it had looked as if their captain's decision to put Oxford in had been justified when E.J.W. Jackson, in a devastating spell, took 5 for 30 in his first 10.5 overs. Sanity was, however, restored by the combination of the wristy Pathmanathan and the strong E.D. Fursdon. For a number nine to make a century at Lord's as Fursdon did, must be every bowler's dream!

The next day Roebuck and Hignell featured in a fine retrieving stand of 161 at a run a minute. Roebuck's 158 followed his maiden 146 not out against Glamorgan the previous Friday. In Oxford's second innings Marks, Pathmanathan and D.W. Jarrett all played well, and Cambridge were left to score 206 in two and a quarter hours. They never looked like succeeding against a belligerent Imran.

OXFORD

	First innings			Second innings	
T.R. Glover	*lbw, b* Jackson	4	*c* Roebuck, *b* Wookey	38
A.C. Hamilton	*c* Coverdale, *b* Jackson	0	*c* Hignell, *b* Jackson	7
V.J. Marks	*b* Jackson	28	*c* Aworth, *b* Wookey	56
Imran Khan	*b* Jackson	19	*lbw, b* Jackson	9
C.J. Tavaré	*b* Hayes	4	*c* Hignell, *b* Jackson	0
G. Pathmanathan	*lbw, b* Allbrook	50	*c* Hayes, *b* Wookey	72
D.W. Jarrett	*b* Jackson	2	*st* Coverdale, *b* Roebuck	35
E.D. Fursdon	*not out*	112	*c* Allbrook, *b* Roebuck	7
A.R. Wingfield Digby	*c* Coverdale, *b* Jackson	23	*not out*	14
P.B. Fisher	*lbw, b* Jackson	3	*not out*	3
EXTRAS	B 1, L-B 8, W 1, N-B 1	11	B 3, L-B 6, N-B 1	10
	TOTAL (9 WKTS DEC.)	256	TOTAL (8 WKTS DEC.)	251

C.P.T. Cantlay did not bat

CAMBRIDGE

W. Snowden	*c* Tavaré, *b* Imran	10	*lbw, b* Imran	31
R.I. Smyth	*c* Fisher, *b* Marks	5	*c* Fisher, *b* Fursdon	7
C.J. Aworth	*b* Fursdon	5	*c* Wingfield Digby, *b* Fursdon	11
P.M. Roebuck	*c* Fisher, *b* Cantlay	158	*lbw, b* Marks	33
A.J. Hignell	*b* Marks	60	*c* Fisher, *b* Imran	2
S.P. Coverdale	*retired hurt*	2	*not out*	12
D.P. Russell	*c* Fisher, *b* Imran	28	*not out*	30
E.J.W. Jackson	*c* Fisher, *b* Imran	0		
S. Wookey	*not out*	21		
EXTRAS	B 5, L-B 4, W 1, N-B 3	13	B 5	5
	TOTAL (7 WKTS DEC.)	302	TOTAL (5 WKTS)	131

P.J. Hayes and N.E. Allbrook did not bat

Cambridge bowling

Wookey	12	4	31	0	24	3	75	3
Jackson	29	7	98	7	28	6	62	3
Hayes	19	6	33	1	13	3	46	0
Roebuck	12	5	25	0	17	6	35	2
Russell	2	0	11	0	4	0	23	0
Allbrook	24	5	47	1	—	—	—	—

Oxford bowling

	OVERS	MDNS	RUNS	WKTS	OVERS	MDNS	RUNS	WKTS
Imran Khan	30	5	89	3	17	3	40	2
Cantlay	21.3	4	61	1	1	1	0	0
Marks	14	3	48	2	14	3	55	1
Fursdon	14	3	56	1	6	2	11	2
Wingfield Digby	5	0	35	0	4	0	20	0

UMPIRES J.G. Langridge and A.G.T. Whitehead

14
1976–1988
Fresh Dawn or Dire Finale?

OXFORD *First-class honours or first-class status?*

Oxford hearts were lifted by the successes in the first year of this decade. Seven of the 1976 eleven later played first-class cricket other than at Oxford: G. Pathman-athan, J.A. Claughton, D.R. Gurr, P.B. Fisher, R. Le Q. Savage, V.J. Marks and C.J. Tavaré, the last two going on to play for England. This was a year in which the Treasurer expressed 'a certain embarrassment' over a financial surplus of £4000, a rare event indeed.

Vic Marks proved an excellent captain. John Claughton recalls:

He was the best captain I ever played under and I suspect not one of the team would say otherwise. He had to do nothing to inspire loyalty and commitment. . . . He was immensely supportive and level-headed when things were going badly. Despite the flair of Pathman-athan, and Vic Marks' invention as a batsman, our stability rested largely upon Chris Tavaré's outstanding season (775 runs in 10 first-class matches). After a dreadful start he played with extraordinary precision and concentration. I was enthralled at pre-season nets by the unhurried simplicity of his technique and timing. During the season he played some outstanding innings, coping in difficult circumstances when the rest of us could not, and destroying anything slightly less threatening. His hundred in the second innings at Pag-ham where 100 would have been a good score for all 11, was a remarkable innings.

Claughton, who made two hundreds himself in 1976, goes on to refer to the bowlers.

David Gurr arrived at Oxford with almost no past form, but he was tall, brisk and could swing the ball. . . . Andrew Wingfield-Digby, despite his apparently innocuous appear-ance as a bowler, still managed to get good players out. He once had E.J. Barlow caught in the gully in his first over by Gaj Pathmanathan. Gaj said that he was thinking about dropping it, because he wanted to see Barlow bat.

Richard Savage bowled fast off-spinners and on bad pitches could bowl out county players as fast as their spinners could bowl us out. . . . At Pagham (the first first-class match played there) he was close to unplayable; it was a joy to see county players unable to cope.

Savage had 12 for 99 in the match, which was won by Sussex, the margin being only 19 runs. A further high spot of 1976 was the Oxford and Cambridge combined victory over Yorkshire in the Benson and Hedges Cup at Barnsley.

An interesting feature of the great ten-wicket win at Lord's was the selection of D.W. Jarrett for Cambridge, having been in the Oxford camp for the two previous years. His appearance made history, but was not really of his choosing. After a successful conclusion to a course in Greats, he had hoped to continue in Oxford for a Post-Graduate Certificate in Education. The OU Department of Education did not welcome him, so he turned to the other place, which did. The precedent he created was followed by S.M. Wookey, who had blues at Cambridge in 1975 and 1976, moving to Oxford to continue in his path towards ordination at Wycliffe Hall, and winning a blue in 1978. G. Pathmanathan was the third to change allegiance, playing for Oxford between 1975 and 1978 and donning light blue in 1983; there will doubtless be others.

In 1977 many of the same players survived, but exams loomed large and Chris Tavaré was hardly available. An unusual occurrence in a first-class match was the absence of one umpire on the third day of the Surrey match in The Parks. P.B. Wight officiated at the bowler's end while players stood in at square leg. The weather had been so foul that the missing umpire believed no play could be possible. In a three-declaration match, Oxford hung on for a draw with nine wickets down.

Although Oxford did not win at all in 1978 they were well led, the captain John Claughton making his highest first-class score, 130, in a drawn match against Sussex. The Yorkshire match was also drawn. Stephen Wookey, in the year of his ordination, dismissed G. Boycott for nought, and when he let slip later that he thought the return catch was a bump ball, Alan Gibson was prompted to say 'This is the sort of pusillanimity that is getting the Church of England such a bad name.' Oxford was the only first-class side in the country against whom Boycott never scored a hundred. After he had been dismissed, there was not another wicket until the score read 217. Boycott left Oxford 549 to win; thanks to Claughton, Oxford held on with comfort. The proposal that the twelfth man should be awarded a blue was turned down at the 1978 AGM.

The unfortunate G.V. Marie dislocated a shoulder in a Benson and Hedges match and had to stand down as captain. S.M. Clements, from Ipswich and Trinity, took over for the rest of the 1979 season. This was a wet and dismal year, Oxford's lack of success being underlined by the fact that the lowest bowling average exceeded the highest batting average.

The passage into the eighties emphasized the problems of University cricket. In 1980 only two players were able to appear in all matches; C.J. Ross had to rely on inexperienced players – very often a testing experience for young men facing professional bowlers for the first time, often bowling yards faster than anything they have previously known. The following year saw a shorter programme, with only eight matches in this, the hundredth season in The Parks. Norman Morris retired as groundsman, having officiated for half this period. One of his last tasks was to repair damage by vandals in advance of the drawn match against the Sri Lankans. S.P. Sutcliffe, bowling off-breaks, and T.J. Taylor, slow left-arm, were the leading wicket-takers.

One of the driest seasons ever experienced in The Parks led to high scores in 1982. No less than twenty-one hundreds, five for the University, were registered in eight first-class matches. R.S. Cowan and R.G.P. Ellis were the most prolific run-scorers, but the bowlers suffered heavy punishment. Ellis, also a fine rackets player, was joined by his fellow Haileyburian A.J.T. Miller in 1983; these two proved the best opening pair for years, both averaging over forty. R.P. Moulding found his way into the record books by playing in his sixth University Match. This led to lengthy discussions between the two Universities. The problem had arisen through a difference in the definition of *in statu pupillari*. From 1983 it was agreed that blues should be awarded only to those in residence, paying fees and studying for a degree, diploma or certificate, and that the limit should be four years.

The following season saw the University authorities coming nobly to the rescue of OUCC. The scoreboard had been in a state of dilapidation and never had there been satisfactory covers in The Parks; these deficiencies were made good at no expense to the club. J.D. Carr began to make his presence felt, making hundreds against Lancashire and Somerset. Miller and G.J. Toogood saved their three-figure contributions for Lord's. Only the Varsity Match was won.

John Carr continued where he had left off in 1984 with another hundred against Somerset, but with 'Schools' in prospect he had to wait until mid June for his next appearance, which he celebrated with 101 against Yorkshire in a drawn match. D.A. Thorne scored Oxford's other hundred in The Parks, having earlier been denied a three-figure score against Glamorgan as he saw six wickets fall at the other end for only 8 runs; he finished with 98. He was remarkably consistent with the bat, ten of his seventeen innings being over fifty. Oxford were unlucky to be caught on a pig of a wicket by Leicestershire, eight of the side failing to score in the first innings as they totalled 24, their second-lowest score ever. They recovered well next time round, but still lost by an innings.

In every phase, says *Wisden*, of the 1986 season, Oxford were no match for the counties, several of which lessened the margin of victory by preferring batting practice to enforcing the follow-on. A deterioration in out-cricket emphasized the need for a coach. However, despite a lean season the Dark Blues did play their part in a memorable match at Lord's, D.A. Thorne contributing an unbeaten hundred, and Cambridge won only on the seventh delivery of the last over.

The following year saw but little improvement, in another depressingly wet season. C.D.M. Tooley gained some encouragement from an intake of useful freshmen – P.G. Edwards, R.D. Sardesai, son of the former Indian Test player, and most markedly M.A. Crawley from Manchester Grammar School. None the less, the counties reaped a plentiful harvest of runs; Glamorgan saw a second-wicket record established when S.P. James and H. Morris together put on 249. For the second year running Oxford reserved their best performance for Lord's in the drawn match against Cambridge.

There was a positive improvement in 1988, M.J. Kilborn from New South Wales, the captain, giving middle-order stability and Mark Crawley, the captain-elect for 1989, showing his class in a sound innings of 98 against Nottinghamshire. The eleven chosen to play against Cambridge won their blues, but never took the field at Lord's; unrelenting rain over three days established this damp record for the 144th match in this great long-running series. Cambridge have won fifty-four matches and Oxford forty-six, with the rest drawn or abandoned.

First-class honours or first-class status? Happily these two are not mutually exclusive, but there is none the less some relationship. From the academic standpoint it is hardly surprising that tutors responsible for entrance view cricketers with suspicion, some sadly with outright hostility. Many schools list the colleges, and in some cases the individuals, who offer some sympathy to the cricketer or, indeed, to applicants with any interests outside their academic work. It is an unhappy reflection on entry procedures that ability at sport by an individual is often played down in his application, for fear that such skills may be considered an actual handicap to a place being offered. It is unlikely that there will be any significant change in this process, although there could be a swing of the pendulum. Fortunately a few fine players will still find a place at Oxford, and the numbers of sympathetic dons may increase, but unless the overall standard of cricket can be raised, first-class status must be in jeopardy. Among the many who have contributed their thoughts on this subject, none puts the whole problem more clearly than G.L. Cawkwell, a Fellow of University College, New Zealand Rhodes scholar, fine rugby player and enthusiastic cricketer. Referring to the period following R.A. Butler's Education Act, he writes:

So began the long process whereby entrance became ever more hotly and widely sought and academic promise accorded an ever greater and greater influence on College's choices. We are now so far along that road that it is probably the case that no Oxford college would admit a man simply because he can hit or kick a ball or move an oar better than the rest of the candidates. It is not the case, as old Blues are prone to grumble, that Oxford no longer cares about non-academic attainments. At least, in this college, efforts are made to assess the all-round abilities of candidates. But these are not just athletic. Great value is put by many of my colleagues on musical interest and skill (indeed the college contains a great many undergraduates who play to a very high level), and the life of the college is rich and diverse. But the essential requirement is academic ability.

This attitude took time to develop and in the decade or so after the war Entrance Examination in Colleges (which was quite separate from Scholarship Examinations) was conducted in a very casual fashion, and so whoever was in charge of admissions was able, if he were so minded, to admit the athletically able but academically not strong (or idle). But the shades of the prison house were closing in. As the Entrance Exams became more efficient and thorough and the separate Scholarship exam was abandoned, the interest of tutors in whom they were to teach became ever greater, and gradually the real responsibility for admissions passed from central control to tutors who finally could not be coerced into teaching someone they violently objected to.

At the same time there was ever more effort put into attracting more and more candidates from all sorts and conditions of schools. When one had only a few candidates for a place, an athlete might be preferred on the grounds of his being a good all-rounder and having a lot to contribute to the common life of a college, but when there were many candidates for a small number of places and a good number of those to be rejected were of high academic standard, it seemed monstrous for anyone who was not of high academic standard to be given a place.

One particularly solemn development was the ordering of colleges according to results obtained in the Schools, the so-called Norrington Table. Its effect has been quite disastrous. Tutors are now very sensitive to examination results, and will take no avoidable risk in admissions, I mean risk of taking an interesting person who may not get at least a Second. All tutors profess to deplore such a narrow conception of a college's worth, but many privately preen themselves on their pupils' performance and in any case it cannot be stopped. It began as an expression of an increasing concern with academic performance, and it has in time produced an oppressive preoccupation with examinations as the be-all and end-all of university life. I loathe and despise it, but it will never go away, not in the fore-seeable future.

Another factor is the great increase in the number of women. To my mind that has been generally beneficial, but it does mean that competition for places for other than the highly gifted is the more severe. Good athletes tend to fall in the bracket of the not so gifted academi-cally, and so their chances of getting in are disproportionately reduced by the admission of women to all colleges.

Finally, one must note a very great change in the esteem for athletic ability. When I was an undergraduate, a great number of undergraduates, male and female, would go to Iffley Road to watch the OURFC or to the Parks to watch the OUCC. That is no longer the case, and having frequently discussed with undergraduates, male and female, their attitude to athletic prowess, I have come to the conclusion that games have lost a good deal of their esteem. Indeed I have known good games-players give up the game when they reached Oxford. I have heard of this happening even at school. Academic requirements seem to be rising and good A-levels are a necessary step to a successful life. No wonder that the OUCC is not what it was, and it is not likely to return to the golden days. Sic transit gloria.

As if this somewhat depressing picture is not enough, John Woodcock, writing after one early Oxford defeat, concluded in the spring of 1988:

First-class status has become an embarrassment, as much to the county players, because the runs and wickets which they enter into their records are of such dubious value, as to the University sides, who are so hopelessly out of their depth.

Again, depressing reading, although not entirely fair; this last decade has intro-duced a string of fine players to the first-class game, including six from Oxford and Cambridge who have moved up to the England side, among whom is V.J. Marks. He recalls, 'University cricket was far more valuable than three or four years in a county second eleven, an excellent bridge between second- and first-team cricket.' The latest Oxonian to be well on the way up the cricketing ladder is John Carr of Middlesex. Mark Crawley next? Why not? Retain first-class status, and first-class honours will follow.

CAMBRIDGE *Pringle and Atherton hold the fort*

There are various factors that militate against sporting achievement at the two ancient Universities. They include: a less unimpeded cricket season at school because of the retiming of summer examinations; an unsympathetic admissions policy which, in most colleges, appears to place little emphasis on anything other than academic criteria (and sometimes, as in one recent instance when a fine sportsman with three A grades in A level was turned down by a Cambridge college, seems actually to discriminate against those who play games); the effects of admitting women to men's colleges without commensurate expansion; and the importance of gaining a good degree in an increasingly competitive world. Thus, at a time when the counties are uniformly stronger, the Oxford and Cambridge sides have in general become weaker than in the days when National Service was in action, and when admissions tutors, such as Lucan Pratt of Christ's and Vivian Fisher at Jesus in the fifties, and those of Magdalene for many years, looked with favour on the sportsman because of his contribution to the balance of college life as well as to the reputation of that college, and indeed of the University itself, in the outside world.

Despite these and other more general factors that the reader can interpret for himself, both Oxford and Cambridge produced several players in this extended decade who held their own in county sides, and a select few who went on to play for England. There were a number of Cambridge sides able to give their opponents testing competition, though, as has happened so many times in the past, the bowling has rarely been good enough to win matches against the counties. The occasional calls for an early end to the first-class status of Oxford and Cambridge, on the grounds that the sides are too often below par, will, it is to be hoped, be refutable on merit rather than on sentiment. It will be a sad day indeed if the words of Tony Lewis, in his engaging autobiography *Playing Days*, come true. He writes:

It is probable that first-class cricket and rugby will soon end at Fenner's and Grange Road and the Boat Race will be no more than a spring scuffle between overgrown schoolboys. Cambridge will only have impact on the narrow world of academic achievement, not on the wider world. It will shrink by its own myopia.

What of course is crucial is the realization by admission tutors that colleges benefit from the presence of undergraduates who are interested in activities other than the academic – sporting, theatrical and so on – and that such people not only add to the richness of college life, but also usually gain a decent degree as well.

To return to the years in question, once again there were too many draws at Lord's for satisfaction, though the match in 1980 was ruined by rain alone; of the four games that were decided, Cambridge won those in 1979 and 1982, and lost those in 1976 and 1984. It was in 1979 that the Cambridge bowling began to bowl sides out again, and it was a fitting climax to Ian Greig's year of captaincy that Oxford were defeated by an innings and 52 runs. In 1982, victory came in the wake of an Oxford declaration – the first ever such victory in the history of the University Match – and was notable both for the winning century by Robin Boyd-Moss, of Bedford School, who the following year would make history, and for the absence, with the approval of his team, of Derek Pringle, who chose to play for England rather than for Cambridge. That he should do so, whereas Majid Khan a decade earlier had made the reverse decision, is perhaps a commentary both on the decline in importance of the University Match, and on a more modern, and perhaps questionable, sense of priorities.

Four Light Blues of this time have to date received international recognition. Paul Parker, who played for Cambridge in 1976, 1977 and 1978, became captain of Sussex in 1988 and has played one Test; he is a stylish batsman in the classical mould and an outstanding fielder. Sustaining an honourable tradition, he joined the unhappy breed of those invited to play rugby against Oxford but having to withdraw because of injury. He was one of three members of the successful 1973 English Schools team, which defeated the Indian Schools 2–0, to be reading classics in the sixth form – a rare statistic in these days, when even a school with Latin in its title has recently dropped Latin from the curriculum. He shares with George Cox, another Sussex stalwart, famous son of famous father, and coach at Cambridge for several seasons, the status of being an old boy of Collyer's School, Horsham; and he had the pleasure of having made 215 against Essex at Fenner's.

Ian Greig, who had spent a long time in the shadow of his brother Tony, also played three seasons in the Cambridge side – 1977, 1978 and 1979 – and won a rugby blue. In his first year in the side he proved himself to be a more than useful all-round cricketer, who went on to play 58 games for Sussex, but much to their loss was not kept on. After a short break, he was invited in 1987 to captain Surrey, who were glad to have signed on so experienced a player, with two Test caps to his name.

Derek Pringle, whose father represented East Africa in the 1975 ICC Trophy but was sadly killed in a motor accident not long afterwards, was born in Nairobi and went to school at Felsted, where he played on excellent pitches and won recognition as a fine schoolboy all-rounder. He had considerable success at Cambridge; he not only won his first England cap while still an undergraduate, but he also had marked success in the 1981 Light Blue season, leading Cambridge to their first win against a county (Lancashire) since Majid had inspired three such wins. His batting average of 74.42 in 1982 followed figures of 54.50 in 1980 and 40.00 in 1981, and in all three years he headed the bowling averages. He remains an important contributor to Essex's continuing success, and he is still in the England side as I write this, a more seasoned and experienced performer than when he was first summoned to play at Old Trafford.

The fourth Light Blue to have received the selectors' nod is Tim Curtis, who was at RGS Worcester and, like Stephen Henderson, that year's captain, had first gone to Durham University, breeding-ground of a host of talented cricketers, lured there both by the excellence of the University itself and by the sympathetic scouting of Dr Grenville Holland. Curtis opened the Cambridge innings in 1983 and was second to Boyd-Moss in the batting averages; but it was not until he matured into a technically sound and reliable opener with Worcestershire that he attracted notice. The full story of his England career, as that, one hopes, of Pringle and – who knows? – of Parker also, has yet to be written.

Several other Cambridge players of this generation have made an impact on the county scene, and one has succeeded as a writer, not least in *Slices of Cricket*, a most readable book about the current county circuit. Peter Roebuck, for such it is, had already established himself as a fine batsman at Millfield, where both his parents taught, when he arrived at Cambridge. I can vouch for his early tactical awareness, as well as for his cricketing skill, from personal experience. For he captained my Under-15 side to victory against the ESCA Colts two years running, at Norwich and at Aigburth. Apart from achieving a First in the Law Tripos, he headed the batting averages as a freshman, improving once the examinations were over and making an impressive 158 at Lord's. He was less successful in the two following seasons, but went on to play for, and to captain, Somerset during the next decade, opening the innings with a good technique that never quite brought him England honours.

Alastair Hignell, captain in 1977 – in the wake of Chris Aworth, an attractive batsman from Tiffin, and Tim Murrills from The Leys – was a talented games-player, who also played at Aigburth, and who won several rugby caps for England at full-back. Hignell came up to Fitzwilliam from Denstone, and had his two best seasons as captain, a role in which he excelled. His top score in 1977 was his 149 against Glamorgan, scored in 93 balls and ninety-nine minutes, which he followed up with two fifties at Lord's; and in 1978 he scored a hundred in both innings against Surrey, the first to achieve the feat since Roger Prideaux, and the first to do so at Fenner's since David Sheppard. He played for Gloucestershire in 137 matches, and now devotes himself to broadcasting and writing.

In the sides of the late seventies, the Harrovian Matthew Fosh was a member of the England Young Cricketers party to the West Indies, captained by Chris Cowdrey, in 1976. He played well out there, and on occasions for Essex as well as for Cambridge, but he gave up sport regrettably early, and cricket and rugby were the losers. Nigel Popplewell won blues as a useful all-rounder in 1977–9, but reserved his best performances for Somerset, for whom he played 78 matches between 1979 and 1983. It was a great loss to the county when he put the law before cricket.

The 1980 side had behind it the inspiration of the victory at Lord's in 1979 of the side captained by Greig and including in it a successful opening bowler in David Surridge, who played for Hertfordshire and Gloucestershire. Ian Peck's side gave a good account of itself against the counties, never scoring less than 250 in a first innings at Fenner's, and on four occasions declaring, to bowl at the opposition the same evening. Peter Mills, Oundelian son of the Light Blue captain in 1948, who had the unusual experience of being dismissed lbw off a gentle full toss from John Lever before the 1981 season had technically begun (at 11.29 a.m. precisely), and Aziz Mubarak, from Royal College, Colombo, proved a balanced opening pair. Mubarak's 80 against a West Indies side that included Colin Croft deserves a special mention.

They were followed, in the batting order, not only by Pringle, but also by Robin Boyd-Moss, a talented freshman, who was to play regularly for Northamptonshire at the end of the University term. It is a disappointment that he has decided to give up first-class cricket in 1988, having found it hard to make his mark with the county side, in part because of injury and illness, and in part because of the strength of the side. It was in the 1982 and 1983 seasons that Boyd-Moss came good for Cambridge, scoring 717 runs at an average of 44.81 the first year, and 733 runs at an average of 38.57 in the second. His entry into the record books comes from his scores at Lord's these two years – his match-winning 100 not out in the second innings in 1982 being followed in 1983 by scores of 139 and 124, the first time two hundreds in a match had been scored in this fixture. In his four University Matches, in one of which rain denied him an innings, he scored 489 runs, a record aggregate for either University.

Decent players were not in short supply in the early eighties. A useful all-rounder, for instance, in the 1980 and 1981 sides was Neil Russom, of Richard Huish's School, Taunton, their only product to gain a cricket blue, who played four matches for Somerset and finished with a career batting average of 32.05. Another in the 1981–3 sides was Ian Hodgson, an Oundelian, also a squash blue, who went on to play successfully for Buckinghamshire. He will look back with pleasure on the first day of the 1982 season when he took the first eight wickets against Glamorgan. That was the year also that the left-handed Stephen Henderson, from Downside and hot-foot from Durham University, made a memorable 209 not out against a strong Middlesex attack, although he never fully recaptured that form. He was a popular captain in 1983 and went on to play, all too briefly, for both Worcestershire and Glamorgan, finishing with an average of 24.24. Another opening partner of Mills, in 1982, was David Varey, from Birkenhead – Cambridge twin brother of Oxford twin brother – who made 156 not out against Northamptonshire and subsequently played successfully for Lancashire for three seasons.

There was an interesting gloss on the regulations governing University cricket. In 1975 there was a change to accepting any student in residence, enabling, *mirabile dictu*, Roger Moulding to play no less than six years for Oxford. In 1982 agreement was reached that only those in residence, and studying, and paying fees, could play at Lord's. History of a kind was made in the 1976 University Match, when David Jarrett, who had played for Oxford in 1975, played for Cambridge. It happened again, when Gajanand Pathmanathan, who had played four years for Oxford, represented Cambridge in 1983, and, in passing, scored a half-century in the match. History was made again when Ian Peck, of Bedford School, was elected captain of both cricket and rugby, for the Twickenham match in 1979 and the Lord's match in 1980, without having won his blue the previous year. Peck, who captained successfully two seasons running, surfaced again in the 1984 season, for when it was known that the appointed captain, the Salopian Angus Pollock, would not be available until after his examinations, he was given leave from teaching at Bedford School to captain for the first part of the season. Brearley, similarly, had played during examinations after he had gone down, and had made a hundred against Yorkshire in 1966.

Credit is due in the later years to Rob Andrew, cricket captain in 1985 and stand-off half for England as well as Cambridge; to David Price, from Haberdashers' Aske's, who captained the 1986 and 1987 sides with assurance; and to Paul Bail, of Millfield, who made an attractive 174 at Lord's in 1986 and 90 in 1987. Bail and John Davidson, of Penglais, a quick bowler who took 9 for 150 in the match, played the vital roles in the Light Blue victory of 1986. The three seamers

ABOVE Oxford normally play in the Parks, and this photograph shows that the word 'Parks' in its modern sense is no misnomer.

Martin Donnelly was one of the game's finest left-handed batsmen, as his record of scoring a hundred at Lord's for Oxford, the Gentlemen and New Zealand shows.

Colin Cowdrey here plays an effortless cover-drive. He is wearing his Kent cap, but it could just as well have been his Oxford or England one.

RIGHT The first of three international captains on this page. Hafeez Kardar was a talented all-rounder, who played for Oxford from 1947–49 and captained Pakistan on his return. Here he is seen batting against Worcestershire in 1954; Hugo Yarnold is the wicket-keeper.

BELOW Imran Khan's athleticism and sideways action are vividly portrayed. Oxford (1973–75), Sussex and Pakistan owed much to his all-round skill.

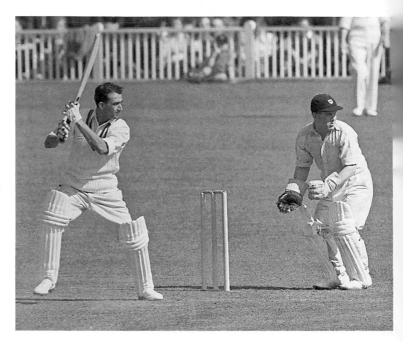

ABOVE M.J.K. Smith was a respected captain – of Oxford (in 1956), Warwickshire and England – and a particularly strong on-side player, as this picture shows.

The 1949 Oxford side, captained by C.B. Van Ryneveld, which beat the New Zealanders
BACK ROW M.B. Hofmeyr C.R.D. Rudd G.H. Chesterton M.H. Wrigley I.P. Campbell B. Boobbyer
FRONT ROW P.A. Whitcombe C.E. Winn C.B. Van Ryneveld A.H. Kardar D.B. Carr

The 1959 Oxford side on tour captained by A.C. Smith
STANDING J. Burki J.G. Raybould A.A. Baig A.R. Duff C.A. Fry A.J. Corran E.M. Dyson D.M. Green
SITTING J.D. Piachaud R.L. Jowett A.C. Smith M.A. Eagar D.M. Sayer

The 1952 Cambridge side captained by D.S. Sheppard
BACK ROW F.C.M. Alexander R. Subba Row C.N. McCarthy G.G. Tordoff C.J.M. Kenny
M.H. Bushby
FRONT ROW P.B.H. May R.G. Marlar D.S. Sheppard J.J. Warr M.H. Stevenson

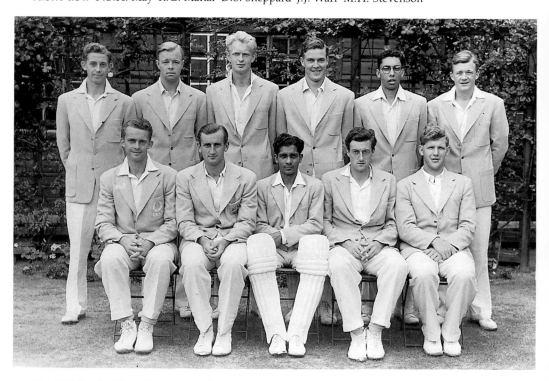

The 1957 Cambridge side captained by G. Goonesena
BACK ROW D.J. Green I.M. McLachlan O.S. Wheatley G.W. Cook P.I. Pieris B.T. Swift
FRONT ROW R.W. Barber E.R. Dexter G. Goonesena C.S. Smith R.M. James

Trevor Bailey, who became a substantial all-rounder for Cambridge (1947–48), Essex and England. It is sometimes forgotten what a fine forcing batsman he could be.

Hubert Doggart and John Dewes in front of the Cambridge scoreboard showing their record University, and then English, 2nd-wicket partnership of 429 v Essex on 7 May, 1949.

Peter May, finest English post-war batsman, shows several important facets of batsmanship, not least the stillness of the head. Don Tallon is the 'keeper'.

Few have hit both the cricket and golf ball better than the Light Blue captain of 1958, Ted Dexter. This majestic leg-hit was made at Lord's against Oxford.

ABOVE One of the younger recent Oxonians (1983–85) to have made the grade in first-class cricket, John Carr is here batting positively for Middlesex.

BELOW Chris Tavaré, of Oxford (1975–77), Kent and England, shows that he is an aggressive as well as a defensive player.

ABOVE Vic Marks, captain of Oxford in successive years, 1976–77, has made frequent all-round, match-winning contributions for his native Somerset. Here he uses the crease interestingly.

ABOVE Mark Crawley, a talented sportsman, is Oxford's captain in 1989. He and his opposite number, Michael Atherton, both come from Manchester Grammar School.

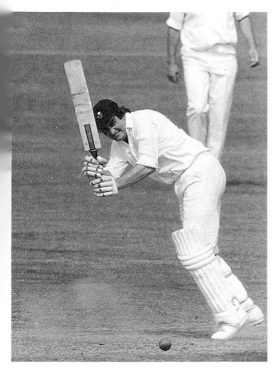

Tony Lewis, of Cambridge (1960–62), Glamorgan and England, stylishly forces a ball off his toes.
He is equally at home at cricket, rugby football and as a musician.

Majid Khan transformed the Cambridge sides of the early seventies – and had a similar influence on the Pakistan and Glamorgan sides.

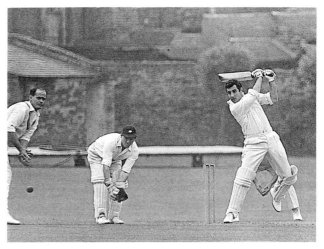

Michael Atherton, Cambridge captain in 1989, has already made his mark in a strong Lancashire side and is one of the most promising of the younger generation.

Watched by Jimmy Binks and Brian Close, Mike Brearley forces the ball off the back foot.
A strategist as well as a tactician, he became a successful captain of Cambridge (1963–64), Middlesex and England.

ABOVE Fenner's at its best, in early May, looking towards the Victorian pavilion, of many memories, and to the Roman Catholic church.
BELOW Robin Boyd-Moss, of Cambridge (1980–84) and Northants, has the highest aggregate of runs in the Varsity match. His retirement to Kenya is a loss to the first-class game.

Derek Pringle bowling for England in front of a full house. His all-round ability has benefited Cambridge (1979–82) and Essex as well as his country.

were the source of the improved performance that year; for in addition to Davidson, Alistair Scott, of Seaford Head, who took 5 for 97 in 33.3 overs at Lord's in 1987, and the Tonbridgian Charles Ellison, the first cricket blue from Homerton, both made an impact. It is worth adding that both Davidson and Scott each achieved a First in the Tripos.

The arrival of Michael Atherton, of Manchester Grammar School, in the 1987 season was a welcome reversal of the depressing unreadiness of admission tutors to accept class cricketers into their colleges. At the end of his first season at Cambridge he found himself batting at number three in a Lancashire side that was in the running for the Championship – a clear indication of the quality of a player that had been evident in Schools cricket for several years. He has an old head on young shoulders, and he has already shown himself to be a batsman and a captain of considerable ability, being awarded in 1987 the Cricket Society's award for 'The Most Promising Young Cricketer of the Year', and captaining the Young England side to play in Adelaide in the Youth competition to mark Australia's Bicentennial. He was the fourth English batsman in the 1988 averages, and there seems little doubt that he has a promising career in front of him. Let us hope that he will play for England for many years, and that he will not go down in history as the last Cambridge captain to play for his country.

<table>
<tr><td>30 June, 1, 2 July
At Lord's</td><td style="text-align:center">1976</td><td style="text-align:right">Oxford won by
10 wickets</td></tr>
</table>

The 1976 Varsity Match was a considerable triumph for V.J. Marks, a popular and astute captain from Blundells. His side was in excellent spirits and the good players all played well, even surviving the oddity of G. Pathmanathan being bowled trying to sweep the third ball. Marks and C.J. Tavaré added 149 in even time, the latter playing particularly well off his legs until he was out one shot off his hundred. S.M. Clements hit with enterprise and helped the score along to Oxford's highest total in eight years.

D.R. Gurr yorked A.J. Hignell at the end of the first day and had two early wickets the next morning. P.W.G. Parker fell to R. Le Q. Savage with the last ball before lunch. Savage took three wickets in five balls, with his sharpish off-breaks, to destroy the Cambridge tail, as they slid from 113 for 6 to be 116 all out.

Following on, Cambridge took encouragement from a second-wicket stand of 87 between Hignell and P.M. Roebuck, but on the third morning Gurr broke through with two wickets. D.W. Jarrett fought well to deny his former teammates, but Oxford were left only 83 to make in just under two hours. Marks, who made runs when needed, took important wickets in Cambridge's second innings and led Oxford with enthusiasm, thoroughly earned the Man of the Match award.

OXFORD

	First innings		Second innings	
G. Pathmanathan	*b* Brooker	0	*not out*	57
J.A. Claughton	*b* Wookey	7	*not out*	18
C.J. Tavaré	*c* Brooker, *b* Bannister	99		
V.J. Marks	*c* Jackson, *b* Allbrook	80		
S.M. Clements	*not out*	73		
R.D.M. Topham	*c* Murrills, *b* Wookey	6		
EXTRAS	B 4, L-B 14, W 3, N-B 11	32	B 4, L-B 2, W 2, N-B 3	11
	TOTAL (5 WKTS DEC.)	297	TOTAL (NO WKT)	86

A.R. Wingfield Digby, P.B. Fisher, D.R. Gurr, K. Siviter and R. Le Q. Savage did not bat

CAMBRIDGE

S.P. Coverdale	*b* Gurr	11	*c* Pathmanathan, *b* Gurr	2
A.J. Hignell	*b* Gurr	6	*c* Pathmanathan, *b* Wingfield Digby	57
E.J.W. Jackson	*c* Fisher, *b* Savage	22	*c* Wingfield Digby, *b* Marks	26
P.M. Roebuck	*b* Gurr	0	*b* Wingfield Digby	41
P.W.G. Parker	*c* Clements, *b* Savage	37	*c* Marks, *b* Gurr	7
T.J. Murrills	*b* Savage	21	*c* Fisher, *b* Gurr	2
D.W. Jarrett	*lbw, b* Siviter	2	*lbw, b* Marks	56
C.S. Bannister	*c* Wingfield Digby, *b* Savage	3	*c* Siviter, *b* Marks	0
S.M. Wookey	*c* Marks, *b* Savage	0	*lbw, b* Savage	48
M.E. Allbrook	*lbw, b* Gurr	2	*lbw, b* Gurr	1
M.E.W. Brooker	*not out*	1	*not out*	0
EXTRAS	B 3, W 1, N-B 7	11	B 8, L-B 5, N-B 10	23
	TOTAL	116	TOTAL	263

Cambridge bowling

Brooker	20	7	60	1	7	3	18	0
Jackson	14	2	50	0	4	0	14	0
Wookey	15	5	42	2	—	—	—	—
Bannister	16	5	34	1	7	2	20	0
Allbrook	17	2	65	1	6	1	13	0
Roebuck	6	1	14	0	—	—	—	—
Parker	—	—	—	—	1.4	0	10	0

Oxford bowling

	OVERS	MDNS	RUNS	WKTS	OVERS	MDNS	RUNS	WKTS
Gurr	16.5	7	29	4	23	8	66	4
Siviter	14	4	25	1	15	4	23	0
Marks	3	1	2	0	26	6	54	3
Wingfield Digby	11	6	17	0	18	4	41	2
Savage	13	3	32	5	32.1	10	56	1

UMPIRES K.E. Palmer and T.W. Spencer

29,30 June, 1 July
At Lord's

1977

Match drawn

Oxford made fine progress on the last afternoon, having been set a target of 241 in two hours and twenty minutes. G. Pathmanathan, Oxford's Sri Lankan opener, who six years later appeared in this match wearing light blue, set Oxford on the right road with a brisk 52. With only three wickets down, Oxford required 122 at the start of the last twenty overs. J.A. Claughton, having been the linch-pin, fell in the eighth of these, within ten minutes; and only 21 runs nearer the target, three more wickets had gone and it was left to M. L'Estrange and D.N. Brettell to play out time.

Cambridge had batted first in this, the 150th anniversary match, and after an uncertain start had compiled a good score. A.J. Hignell played a captain's part, and I.A. Greig and P.W.G. Parker put on 90 together. Parker was finally caught off R. Le Q. Savage, who had been warned twice for following through down the wicket.

Oxford lost wickets at regular intervals until D.A. Kayum, from Guyana, and D.R. Gurr staged a revival, the latter making the highest score of his first-class career.

Hignell set a fine example on the last morning, with two sixes in his 51, but Cambridge's progress was slow – they added only 164 in three hours before Hignell felt in a position to declare.

CAMBRIDGE

	First innings		Second innings	
M.K. Fosh	b Savage	29	lbw, b Gurr	4
A.C.D. Moylan	b Wingfield Digby	16	c Fisher, b Gurr	23
P.M. Roebuck	run out	31	b Gurr	1
A.J. Hignell	b Marks	52	c Marks, b Savage	51
P.W.G. Parker	c Wingfield Digby, b Savage	44	b Brettell	58
I.A. Greig	b Wingfield Digby	70	c Fisher, b Brettell	6
S.P. Coverdale	not out	18	run out	54
P.J. Hayes	lbw, b Wingfield Digby	4	not out	2
N.F.M. Popplewell	not out	1		
EXTRAS	B 5, L-B 8, N-B 3	16	L-B 6, N-B 1	7
	TOTAL (7 WKTS DEC.)	281	TOTAL (7 WKTS DEC.)	206

M. G. Howat and M.E. Allbrook did not bat

OXFORD

	First innings		Second innings	
G. Pathmanathan	c Hignell, b Greig	22	lbw, b Hayes	52
J.A. Claughton	lbw, b Greig	20	c Allbrook, b Hayes	54
V.J. Marks	c Roebuck, b Hayes	36	run out	1
C.J. Tavaré	b Allbrook	26	b Hayes	29
M.G. L'Estrange	b Allbrook	7	not out	23
A.R. Wingfield Digby	b Allbrook	0	run out	1
D.N. Brettell	lbw, b Roebuck	0	not out	2
D.A. Kayum	c Hignell, b Hayes	57	c Allbrook, b Hayes	13
D.R. Gurr	not out	46	b Allbrook	2
P.B. Fisher	c Greig, b Roebuck	6		
R. Le Q. Savage	b Allbrook	13		
EXTRAS	L-B 9, N-B 5	14	L-B 19, W 5, N-B 2	26
	TOTAL	247	TOTAL (7 WKTS)	203

Oxford bowling	OVERS	MDNS	RUNS	WKTS		OVERS	MDNS	RUNS	WKTS
Gurr	24	6	70	0		20	7	52	3
Wingfield Digby	23	9	63	3		8	2	21	0
Savage	24	6	59	2		22	8	46	1
Brettell	14	3	45	0		17	6	41	2
Marks	17	7	31	1		13	6	39	0

Cambridge bowling	OVERS	MDNS	RUNS	WKTS		OVERS	MDNS	RUNS	WKTS
Howat	7	2	27	0		1	0	1	0
Greig	15	1	54	2		5	0	36	0
Hayes	20	7	48	2		11	0	53	4
Roebuck	28	10	66	2		4.4	2	9	0
Allbrook	16.5	8	26	4		15	0	56	1
Popplewell	8	3	22	0		5	0	22	0

UMPIRES D.G.L. Evans and K.E. Palmer

28, 29, 30 June
At Lord's

1978

Match drawn

This was a very wet season, in which Oxford did not win a match and Cambridge had but one victory. A.J. Hignell captained Cambridge for a second year, highlighting his season with a hundred in each innings against Surrey – the first time such a feat had been achieved at Fenner's since David Sheppard's fine performance in 1951 against Middlesex. Thereafter Hignell, as *Wisden* put it, 'left his form in the examination room'. J.A. Claughton led a largely unchanged Oxford side, but almost to a man they were faced with 'Schools', and arrived at Lord's sadly short of practice.

Cambridge were bowled out cheaply, with C.J. Ross, a New Zealander from Wellington, taking early wickets, followed by R. Le Q. Savage and V.J. Marks having three each with off-breaks. Savage, bowling at near-medium pace, contrasted with the more orthodox flighted deliveries from Marks.

Marks decided that attack was the best form of defence on a doubtful pitch and 90 were put on for the third wicket, of which his contribution was 60. Oxford were a hundred ahead at the close of the first day.

No play was then possible until 3.30 p.m. on the third afternoon. P.W.G. Parker removed any chance that Oxford had by hitting a sparkling 61 out of 89 for Cambridge's second wicket, thus ensuring the seventh draw of the seventies.

CAMBRIDGE	First innings		Second innings	
M.K. Fosh	c Pathmanathan, b Ross	5	not out	27
A.M. Mubarak	c Savage, b Ross	16	lbw, b Marks	9
P.W.G. Parker	c Kayum, b Savage	24	c Pathmanathan, b Marks	61
A.J. Hignell	c Savage, b Ross	8	not out	20
I.A. Greig	st Fisher, b Marie	10		
D.J. Beaumont	lbw, b Savage	0		
A.R. Dewes	c Moulding, b Savage	5		
N.F.M. Popplewell	lbw, b Marks	2		
S.J. Gardiner	st Fisher, b Marks	2		
D.J. Littlewood	c Kayum, b Marks	0		
M.E. Allbrook	not out	1		
EXTRAS	L-B 18, N-B 1	19	N-B 1	1
	TOTAL	92	TOTAL (2 WKTS)	118

OXFORD		
G. Pathmanathan	b Allbrook	14
J.A. Claughton	c Hignell, b Gardiner	10
V.J. Marks	c Fosh, b Allbrook	60
D. Kayum	c Parker, b Allbrook	27
J.O.D. Orders	c Littlewood, b Gardiner	32
R.P. Moulding	lbw, b Allbrook	6
P.B. Fisher	c Gardiner, b Allbrook	0
S.M. Wookey	lbw, b Gardiner	1
G.V. Marie	b Allbrook	18
R. Le Q. Savage	c Parker, b Gardiner	8
C.J. Ross	not out	0
EXTRAS	B 10, L-B 4, N-B 2	16
	TOTAL	192

Oxford bowling	OVERS	MDNS	RUNS	WKTS	OVERS	MDNS	RUNS	WKTS
Wookey	8	1	12	0	—	—	—	—
Ross	11	3	26	3	2	2	0	0
Savage	13	7	21	3	13	4	56	0
Marie	4	1	10	1	2	0	8	0
Marks	5.3	3	4	3	13	4	53	2

Cambridge bowling				
Greig	3	0	10	0
Popplewell	3	0	9	0
Allbrook	22	3	81	6
Gardiner	17.1	4	52	4
Dewes	4	0	24	0

UMPIRES W.E. Alley and R.T. Wilson

4, 5, 6 July
At Lord's

1979

*Cambridge won by
an innings and 52 runs*

Cambridge won by an innings and 52 runs, their first win for seven years and the most decisive victory since 1957, when they had won by an innings and 186.

Oxford batted first on a humid morning and were dismissed for 97 in 41 overs. Two future England players did much of the damage – I.A. Greig and D.R. Pringle had three wickets apiece – but D. Surridge, on a one-year post-graduate course, an opening bowler from Hertfordshire who later played for Gloucestershire, had four victims.

By the time stumps were drawn on the first day, Cambridge were 131 for 4. The next day Pringle raised the tempo of the match, dealing severely with a moderate Oxford attack. The last 49 of his 103 came in sixty-five minutes and there were three sixes in an innings which made a declaration practical.

The same combination of Cambridge bowlers again had Oxford in difficulty; only S.M. Clements, the captain, gave Dark Blue supporters any cause for optimism, and this was short-lived. His opposite number, Ian Greig, it later transpired, had bowled and batted with a fractured bone in his hand.

OXFORD	First innings		Second innings	
J.A. Claughton	*lbw, b* Surridge	7	*c* Mills, *b* Greig	6
J.J. Rogers	*b* Surridge	22	*c* Cottrell, *b* Greig	4
S.M. Clements	*c* Cottrell, *b* Greig	1	*c* Greig, *b* Pringle	30
R.P. Moulding	*b* Greig	0	*c* Greig, *b* Surridge	1
J.O.D. Orders	*c* Cottrell, *b* Greig	1	*b* Popplewell	15
M.G. L'Estrange	*c* Holliday, *b* Surridge	24	*c* Cottrell, *b* Popplewell	18
N.D. Morrill	*c* Cooper, *b* Pringle	14	*c and b* Surridge	20
A. Hameed	*c* Greig, *b* Pringle	11	*c and b* Surridge	34
C.J. Ross	*not out*	3	*not out*	9
J.M. Knight	*c* Holliday, *b* Surridge	1	*b* Pringle	9
J.P. Pearce	*b* Pringle	0	*b* Surridge	0
EXTRAS	L-B 9, W 2, N-B 2	13	B 3, L-B 4	7
	TOTAL	97	TOTAL	153

CAMBRIDGE		
N.H.C. Cooper	*c* Orders, *b* Ross	54
A.M. Mubarak	*b* Ross	25
J.P.C. Mills	*b* Knight	6
B.W.P. Bennett	*lbw, b* Knight	0
N.F.M. Popplewell	*lbw, b* Hameed	40
D.R. Pringle	*not out*	103
I.A. Greig	*b* Ross	10
D.C. Holliday	*b* Knight	16
N.C. Crawford	*c* Claughton, *b* Hameed	13
P.R. Cottrell	*b* Knight	7
D. Surridge	*not out*	1
EXTRAS	B 4, L-B 9, W 7, N-B 7	27
	TOTAL (9 WKTS DEC.)	302

Cambridge bowling	OVERS	MDNS	RUNS	WKTS		OVERS	MDNS	RUNS	WKTS
Surridge	14	4	22	4		23.4	8	56	4
Greig	9	1	33	3		6	1	19	2
Crawford	7	2	19	0		—	—	—	—
Pringle	11	4	10	3		22	12	27	2
Cooper	—	—	—	—		3	0	9	0
Popplewell	—	—	—	—		11	2	35	2

Oxford bowling				
Knight	30	4	69	4
Hameed	28	3	85	2
Ross	26.3	4	78	3
Pearce	11	2	43	0

UMPIRES A. Jepson and T.W. Spencer

28, 30 June, 1 July
At Lord's

1980

Match drawn

I.G. Peck, late of Bedford School, led an enthusiastic well-balanced Cambridge side and they moved to Lord's confident of a second successive victory. D.R. Pringle, of Felsted and Essex, showed his class as an all-rounder in the trial matches, making two hundreds. Much interest focused on the performance of S.J.G. Doggart, son of my co-author G.H.G. Doggart, captain in 1950, and grandson of A.G. Doggart, who played in 1921 and 1922. Like his father, also from Winchester, he proved well worth his place in the side. Another freshman was R.J. Boyd-Moss, due to break records in the years ahead.

At Oxford, C.J. Ross had to rely on relatively inexperienced players, despite the fact that there was an unusually large number of blues in residence. Examinations and injury had taken a heavy toll. They arrived at Lord's not having won a match.

The weather for the 136th Varsity Match was almost as depressing as it was to be in 1988, and only four hours and ten minutes' play was possible. The first and last days were washed out. Oxford made 206 for 6; S.P. Sutcliffe, I.J. Curtis and J.F.W. Sanderson all won blues without taking the field. J.J. Rogers and R.S. Cowan, a tall player who was also a footballer, gave Oxford a promising start as Simon Doggart bowled his off-breaks well to take 3 for 54.

OXFORD	First innings	
R.A.B. Ezekowitz	c Doggart, b Pringle	11
J.J. Rogers	c Pringle, b Crawford	49
R. Cowan	b Doggart	61
J.O.D. Orders	b Doggart	6
S.J. Halliday	c Pringle, b Doggart	19
R.P. Moulding	c Odendaal, b Boyd-Moss	16
C.J. Ross	*not out*	23
T.E.O. Bury	*not out*	0
EXTRAS	B 7, L-B 5, W 3, N-B 6	21
	TOTAL (6 WKTS)	206

S.P. Sutcliffe, I.J. Curtis and J.F.W. Sanderson did not bat

Cambridge bowling	OVERS	MDNS	RUNS	WKTS
Howat	6	1	20	0
Russom	21	6	49	0
Pringle	14	2	30	1
Crawford	11	3	22	1
Doggart	23	5	54	3
Boyd-Moss	2	1	10	1

UMPIRES T.W. Spencer and A.G.T. Whitehead

No play was possible on the first and third days.

The Cambridge side, in batting order, was:
A.M. Mubarak, J.P.C. Mills, A. Odendaal, R.J. Boyd-Moss, D.R. Pringle, S.J.G. Doggart, N. Russom. I.G. Peck, D.C. Holliday. N.C. Crawford, M.G. Howat

20, 22, 23 June
At Lord's

1981

Match drawn

I.G. Peck, the Cambridge captain had an experienced side, selecting R.J.A. Huxter at the eleventh hour to use the new ball with Pringle.

At Oxford, R.P. Moulding shared the same problem. J.M. Knight had the misfortune to be left out at the last moment, his name even appearing on the scorecard. N.V.H. Mallett, from South Africa, the son of A.W.H., a fine all-rounder of the later forties, won his blue after an excellent performance against Glamorgan.

Oxford, put in to bat, were reduced to 54 for 3 by Pringle, but J.O.D. Orders and K.A. Hayes staged a recovery in a stand of 65, Hayes once hitting Pringle into the grandstand. A further partnership between J.J. Rogers and Moulding was broken only when S.J.G. Doggart ran out the Oxford captain with a direct throw from third man.

Cambridge lost Mills at once, and C.F.E. Goldie seized the opportunity as night watchman to dominate a positive partnership and make the highest score of the innings, more than doubling his previous personal best.

On the third morning, R.S. Cowan and R.A.B. Ezekowitz, from Durban, produced the most purposeful batting of the match in a stand of 143, but an unadventurous declaration made a draw inevitable.

OXFORD	First innings		Second innings	
R.A.B. Ezekowitz	*lbw, b* Pringle	18	*b* Hodgson	93
R.G.P. Ellis	*b* Pringle	6	*c* Boyd-Moss, *b* Pringle	26
R.S. Cowan	*c* Edwards, *b* Pringle	15	*b* Boyd-Moss	87
K.A. Hayes	*lbw, b* Doggart	56	*b* Pringle	38
J.O.D. Orders	*b* Hodgson	25	*not out*	9
J.J. Rogers	*c* Edwards, *b* Huxter	54		
R.P. Moulding	*run out*	23		
N.V.H. Mallett	*lbw, b* Doggart	1		
T.J. Taylor	*lbw, b* Russom	5		
S.P. Sutcliffe	*lbw, b* Russom	2		
P.N. Huxford	*not out*	0		
EXTRAS	B 8, L-B 1, N-B 8	17	B 3, L-B 12, N-B 6	21
	TOTAL	222	TOTAL (4 WKTS DEC.)	274

CAMBRIDGE				
J.P.C. Mills	*c* Ezekowitz, *b* Mallett	2	*c* Cowan, *b* Taylor	34
I.G. Peck	*b* Sutcliffe	30	*c* Cowan, *b* Taylor	29
C.F.E. Goldie	*lbw, b* Sutcliffe	77		
T.D.W. Edwards	*c* Cowan, *b* Sutcliffe	21	*not out*	30
R.J. Boyd-Moss	*b* Sutcliffe	58	*c* Ezekowitz, *b* Sutcliffe	27
D.R. Pringle	*b* Taylor	2		
N. Russom	*c* Cowan, *b* Taylor	3		
S.J.G. Doggart	*not out*	13		
D.C. Holliday	*not out*	13		
K.I. Hodgson	*did not bat*		*not out*	30
EXTRAS	B 10, L-B 3, W 1, N-B 3	17	L-B 5	5
	TOTAL (7 WKTS DEC.)	236	TOTAL (3 WKTS)	155

R.J.A. Huxter did not bat

Cambridge bowling	OVERS	MDNS	RUNS	WKTS	OVERS	MDNS	RUNS	WKTS
Russom	20	9	45	2	15	0	56	0
Pringle	28	9	64	3	22	2	59	2
Hodgson	14	2	37	1	12.2	0	54	1
Huxter	19.3	5	30	1	8	0	25	0
Doggart	17	7	29	2	15	3	35	0
Boyd-Moss	—	—	—	—	10	2	24	1

Oxford bowling								
Mallett	7	1	22	1	5	1	13	0
Orders	7	1	17	0	5	0	14	0
Taylor	29	7	69	2	19	4	56	2
Sutcliffe	38	8	91	4	19	2	67	1
Cowan	10	3	20	0	—	—	—	—

UMPIRES R. Julian and K.E. Palmer

26, 29, 30 June
At Lord's

1982

Cambridge won by
7 wickets

Before the war it would have been unthinkable to arrange Test-match dates which clashed with the Oxford and Cambridge match. But times change, and although there was much criticism, D.R. Pringle, the Cambridge captain, cannot fairly be blamed for accepting an invitation to play in the Second Test against India. His personal performances during the season gave confidence to his Cambridge team-mates, and they did him proud at Lord's under the leadership of J.P.C. Mills, his Oundelian stand-in.

Oxford had had a good season in The Parks, enjoying the benefits of a dry summer. Five hundreds were scored, but the bowling figures underline their weakness. I.J. Curtis had the best

average, taking fifteen wickets at 43.93 a piece in the University season.

This was a notable match in that it was the first ever won on a declaration in the 138 years of the series. R.G.P. Ellis set Cambridge to score 272 in 210 minutes. A dashing hundred by R.J. Boyd-Moss, and a sparkling fifty by S.P. Henderson, son of Derek from the Oxford 1950 side, saw them home with five overs to spare and with seven wickets in hand.

D.W. Varey of Cambridge was dismissed off the bowling of his twin brother J.G. to give the 1982 match another place in history. These two had played together for Birkenhead School.

OXFORD	First innings		Second innings	
R.G.P. Ellis	c Goldie, b Hodgson	86	c Henderson, b Pollock	14
R. Marsden	lbw, b Palmer	13	b Boyd-Moss	39
K.A. Hayes	retired hurt	13		
R.S. Cowan	c Goldie, b Hodgson	33	c Mills, b Pollock	4
G.J. Toogood	c Henderson, b Hodgson	31	c Barrington, b Boyd-Moss	38
R.S. Luddington	b Boyd-Moss	6	c Henderson, b Boyd-Moss	7
R.P. Moulding	not out	20	c Mills, b Boyd-Moss	8
J.G. Varey	not out	32	not out	12
S.P. Ridge	did not bat		not out	2
EXTRAS	L-B 10, W 1, N-B 4	15	B 6, L-B 4, N-B 2	12
	TOTAL (5 WKTS DEC.)	249	TOTAL (6 WKTS DEC.)	136

I.S. Curtis and T.J. Taylor did not bat

CAMBRIDGE				
J.P.C. Mills	c sub, b Ellis	9	lbw, b Ridge	11
D.W. Varey	c Cowan, b Varey	22	retired hurt	16
R.J. Boyd-Moss	not out	41	c sub, b Curtis	100
S.P. Henderson	not out	39	c Ridge, b Taylor	50
N.E.J. Barrington	did not bat		not out	48
K.I. Hodgson	did not bat		not out	36
EXTRAS	L-B 1, W 1, N-B 1	3	B 1, L-B 9, N-B 1	11
	TOTAL (2 WKTS DEC.)	114	TOTAL (3 WKTS)	272

S.J.G. Doggart, A.J Pollock, C.F.E. Goldie, R.M.W. Palmer and C.C. Ellison did not bat

Cambridge bowling	OVERS	MDNS	RUNS	WKTS	OVERS	MDNS	RUNS	WKTS
Palmer	17	2	52	1	10	0	35	0
Pollock	3	1	19	0	7	1	16	2
Hodgson	26	4	89	3	3	0	20	0
Ellison	6	1	23	0	2	0	7	0
Boyd-Moss	11	1	51	1	9	0	42	4
D.W. Varey	—	—	—	—	1	0	4	0
Oxford bowling								
Cowan	7	0	49	0	6	0	42	0
Ridge	6	0	14	0	8	1	33	1
Ellis	4	0	18	1	1	0	2	0
Taylor	5	0	17	0	16	4	46	1
J.G. Varey	2	0	13	1	3	0	19	0
Curtis	—	—	—	—	22	2	119	1

UMPIRES J. Birkenshaw and W.L. Budd

29, 30 June, 1 July
At Lord's

1983

Match drawn

Three entries for the record books come out of this drawn match. R.J. Boyd-Moss was the first batsman ever to score two separate hundreds in the same Varsity Match and also to make three successive hundreds, having just reached three figures in the 1982 victory. He also passed M.J.K. Smith's aggregate of 477 with a total 12 runs higher. Oxford's contribution to the history books is less spectacular. R.P. Moulding, of Haberdashers' Aske's, played in his sixth successive match, a figure unlikely to be possible again.

Three declarations were not enough to produce a result. T.S. Curtis, a post-graduate from Durham and later of Worcestershire and England, and G. Pathmanathan, formerly of Oxford, strengthened an experienced Cambridge side. Oxford made a spirited reply, declaring 39 runs behind. Boyd-Moss was well supported in a lively second innings by Pathmanathan, and left Oxford 304 to win in 265 minutes. Oxford put on 123 for the first wicket in quick time, but wickets began to fall and they had to be content with a draw. Boyd-Moss, bowling slow left-arm, added to his batting triumphs with a match analysis of 7 for 68.

CAMBRIDGE	First innings			Second innings	
T.S. Curtis	b Petchey		75	b Hayes	0
D.W. Varey	c Cullinan, b Hayes		6	b Carr	32
R.J. Boyd-Moss	c Carr, b Petchey		139	c Heseltine, b Petchey	124
S.P. Henderson	not out		51	retired hurt	8
G. Pathmanathan	b Carr		5	c Carr, b Rawlinson	64
S.J.G. Doggart	not out		31	b Carr	18
K.I. Hodgson	did not bat			not out	6
T.A. Cotterell	did not bat			c Heseltine, b Rawlinson	4
EXTRAS	B 4, L-B 4, W 2, N-B 5		15	L-B 4, W 2, N-B 2	8
	TOTAL (4 WKTS DEC.)		322	TOTAL (6 WKTS DEC.)	264

A.J. Pollock, C.C. Ellison and P.G.S. Hewitt did not bat

OXFORD					
R.G.P. Ellis	lbw, b Hodgson		18	c Curtis, b Cotterell	83
A.J.T. Miller	c Ellison, b Boyd-Moss		62	b Boyd-Moss	48
P.G. Heseltine	lbw, b Doggart		13	c Pollock, b Boyd-Moss	29
G.J. Toogood	c Doggart, b Boyd-Moss		14	lbw, b Hodgson	5
K.A. Hayes	c Varey, b Cotterell		45	b Hodgson	11
R.P. Moulding	lbw, b Cotterell		66	c Ellison, b Boyd-Moss	27
J.G. Varey	not out		40	c Doggart, b Boyd-Moss	0
J.D. Carr	not out		16	lbw, b Boyd-Moss	0
H.T. Rawlinson	did not bat			not out	18
M.R. Cullinan	did not bat			not out	2
EXTRAS	B 1, L-B 7, W 1		9	L-B 7, W 1, N-B 5	13
	TOTAL (6 WKTS DEC.)		283	TOTAL (8 WKTS)	236

M.D. Petchey did not bat

Oxford bowling	OVERS	MDNS	RUNS	WKTS	OVERS	MDNS	RUNS	WKTS
Petchey	26	3	127	2	25	3	129	1
Hayes	9.5	1	57	1	6	3	9	1
Varey	9	1	37	0	—	—	—	—
Rawlinson	11	3	43	0	9	1	32	2
Carr	25	7	43	1	28	7	84	2
Moulding	—	—	—	—	1	0	2	0

Cambridge bowling								
Hodgson	15	2	61	1	26	5	64	2
Pollock	7.2	1	24	0	4	1	6	0
Ellison	3	2	6	0	6	0	26	0
Doggart	35	11	74	1	14	4	48	0
Cotterell	23	7	57	2	16	4	43	1
Boyd-Moss	20	9	41	2	12	4	27	5
Curtis	1	0	11	0	6	2	9	0

UMPIRES D.G.L. Evans and B.J. Meyer

1984

Cambridge were more than usually hard-hit by exam requirements; indeed, A.J. Pollock, the captain, was able to play only twice during the term. I.G. Peck, the 1980–1 captain, was invited back to hold the fort, being excused for four matches from his teaching duties at Bedford School. A precedent for such an arrangement had been set by J.M. Brearley in 1966.

Oxford deserved their five-wicket victory at Lord's. Although they failed to bowl Cambridge out in the first innings, they made up good time with A.J.T. Miller, from Haileybury, making his highest first-class score – the first left-hander to make a hundred in the Varsity Match since M.P. Donnelly in 1946. Miller had had a good season,

winning the Gold Award in limited-overs matches against both Surrey and Gloucestershire.

At the end of the second day, Cambridge were 191 ahead, with seven wickets standing. Some very tight bowling by J.D. Carr – son of D.B., the 1950 captain – who delivered sixty-nine overs in the match, and by D.A. Thorne restricted Cambridge and they managed only another 69 runs.

Oxford had three hours and forty minutes to make 261. Carr rounded off a splendid performance by adding 102 with G.J. Toogood in only thirteen overs, to put Oxford ahead of the clock. Toogood carried on to make a maiden first-class hundred and to ensure his side's victory.

CAMBRIDGE	First innings		Second innings	
A.E. Lea	b Thorne	39	lbw, b Thorne	10
I.D. Burnley	c Thorne, b Carr	86	b Carr	70
M.N. Breddy	c Edbrooke, b Carr	61	c and b Rawlinson	17
P.G.P. Roebuck	c Carr, b Toogood	31	c Franks, b Thorne	6
C.R. Andrew	c Thorne, b Carr	0	lbw, b Thorne	30
D.G. Price	c Miller, b Carr	25	c and b Lawrence	20
A.G. Davies	not out	17	c and b Carr	8
A.J. Pollock	c Carr, b Lawrence	4	c Carr, b Hayes	9
T.A. Cotterell	did not bat		c Franks, b Thorne	14
A.D.H. Grimes	did not bat		lbw, b Thorne	0
P.L. Garlick	did not bat		not out	4
EXTRAS	B 3, L-B 5	8	B 1, L-B 6	7
	TOTAL (7 WKTS DEC.)	271	TOTAL	195

OXFORD				
A.J.T. Miller	not out	128	b Garlick	5
R.M. Edbrooke	c Davis, b Garlick	20	b Andrew	15
G.J. Toogood	not out	52	c Price, b Pollock	109
J.D. Carr	did not bat		st Davies, b Andrew	68
D.A. Thorne	did not bat		run out	3
K.A. Hayes	did not bat		not out	35
W.R. Bristowe	did not bat		not out	15
EXTRAS	L-B 5, N-B 1	6	B 1, L-B 8, W 2	11
	TOTAL (1 WKT DEC.)	206	TOTAL (5 WKTS)	261

M.R. Cullinan, J.G. Franks, H.T. Rawlinson and M.P. Lawrence did not bat

Oxford bowling	OVERS	MDNS	RUNS	WKTS	OVERS	MDNS	RUNS	WKTS
Thorne	23	8	60	1	26.1	12	39	5
Hayes	12	5	33	0	15	3	50	1
Carr	34	9	93	4	35	16	49	2
Rawlinson	6	3	14	0	5	1	21	1
Lawrence	31.2	10	62	1	17	5	25	1
Toogood	1	0	1	1	4	3	4	0
Cambridge bowling								
Garlick	12	0	46	1	9	2	17	1
Grimes	6	1	21	0	6	2	13	0
Pollock	10	2	32	0	11	2	60	1
Andrew	20.1	6	38	0	20.2	2	75	2
Cotterell	14	5	48	0	12	9	85	0
Lea	2	0	15	0	—	—	—	—

UMPIRES N.T. Plews and D.R. Shepherd

3, 4, 5 July
At Lord's

1985

Match drawn

Having outplayed Cambridge on the first two days, Oxford were denied a likely victory when torrential rain ended play shortly after lunch on the third. This was Toogood's match. Not since P.R. Le Couteur's performance in 1910 had one man so dominated the University Match.

Cambridge, put in, started steadily, but G.J. Toogood, who had come up from North Bromsgrove High School, bowled at medium pace and destroyed their innings. Next day, well supported by his captain A.J.T. Miller, with whom he put on 150, and by J.D. Carr in a stand of 146, he put Oxford in a dominant position. Miller declared to give Cambridge fifty minutes'

batting; two wickets fell, both to the bowling of Toogood.

On the last morning Cambridge gave their supporters grounds for optimism. A.E. Lea and S.R. Gorman combined in a stand which took the score to 96 before the latter was caught, by none other than Toogood, off the bowling of Rutnagur. This was the last wicket to fall before rain had the final say.

In Toogood's four Varsity Matches he scored 398 runs at an average of over 66. Only in 1983 did he fail to make a major contribution, perhaps owing to the cares of captaincy.

CAMBRIDGE

	First innings			Second innings	
A.E. Lea	c Carr, b Toogood	41		*not out*	47
C.R. Andrew	b Toogood	12		c Franks, b Toogood	12
D.J. Fell	b Lawrence	8		lbw, b Toogood	0
P.G.P. Roebuck	c Thorne, b Toogood	2		*not out*	34
D.C. Price	lbw, b Toogood	12			
A.G. Davies	lbw, b Toogood	11			
T.A. Cotterell	lbw, b Toogood	24			
S.R. Gorman	b Toogood	6		c Toogood, b Rutnagur	43
C.C. Ellison	c Franks, b Toogood	4			
A.M.G. Scott	c Franks, b Thorne	5			
J.E. Davidson	*not out*	1			
EXTRAS	B 3, L-B 1, W 3, N-B 1	8		B 2, L-B 3	5
	TOTAL	134		TOTAL (3 WKTS)	141

OXFORD

A.J.T. Miller	b Andrew	78
W.R. Bristowe	c Lea, b Ellison	16
G.J. Toogood	c Andrew, b Ellison	149
J.D. Carr	*not out*	84
D.A. Thorne	c Davies, b Ellison	17
J.G. Franks	c Gorman, b Andrew	0
P.C. MacLarnon	b Andrew	2
EXTRAS	B 3, L-B 8, W 5, N-B 2	18
	TOTAL (6 WKTS DEC.)	364

C.D.M. Tooley, R.S. Rutnagur, J.D. Quinlan and M.P. Lawrence did not bat

Oxford bowling	OVERS	MDNS	RUNS	WKTS	OVERS	MDNS	RUNS	WKTS
Thorne	9.3	1	23	1	9	3	14	0
Quinlan	13	5	18	0	7	3	21	0
MacLarnon	4	1	13	0	—	—	—	—
Toogood	24	7	52	8	13	3	41	2
Lawrence	13	8	8	1	—	—	—	—
Carr	11	4	16	0	11	5	25	0
Rutnagur	—	—	—	—	13	2	35	1

Cambridge bowling				
Davidson	10	1	40	0
Ellison	27	6	76	3
Scott	11	1	43	0
Cotterell	25	8	78	0
Gorman	4	0	14	0
Lea	1	0	1	0
Andrew	25.4	5	101	3

UMPIRES B. Leadbeater and K.E. Palmer

1986

Cambridge won by five wickets in one of the most dramatic finishes of the whole series, D.W. Browne and A.K. Golding scampering a leg-bye off the last ball of the match.

Oxford were put in to bat and struggled their way to 163 for 5 at tea. Within twenty minutes of the interval they were all out for 167. J.E. Davidson had taken 4 for 13 in twenty-five balls.

P.A.C. Bail, a freshman from Millfield, took advantage of a weak Oxford attack. He drove through the covers with freedom, hitting two sixes and twenty fours in his innings of 174, the seventh-highest ever figure in the Varsity Match. This put D.G. Price in a position to declare.

Oxford's hopes of saving the match were raised by a stubborn and watchful innings from their captain, D.A. Thorne. This was the only three-figure score by any Oxford player in the whole season. When he ran out of partners, Cambridge needed 106 in sixteen overs.

With eighteen balls left, and 30 runs still required, Oxford looked to be safe. J.E. Davidson, promoted for the occasion, laid about him, being run out only on the fourth ball of the last over, with but 4 still wanted. R.S. Rutnagur's fifth delivery was adjudged a wide; D.W. Browne hit 2 off the next ball and the scores were level. Then came the leg-bye.

OXFORD

	First innings			Second innings	
D.A. Hagan	c Lea, b Davidson	12		c Lea, b Ellison	31
A.A.G. Mee	c Brown, b Ellison	41		c Bail, b Davidson	0
M.J. Kilborn	c Brown, b Ellison	28		c Brown, b Scott	59
D.A. Thorne	b Davidson	61		not out	104
C.D.M. Tooley	c Bail, b Golding	2		b Davidson	31
R.S. Rutnagur	b Golding	5		b Golding	5
N.V. Salvi	run out	7		c Browne, b Davidson	10
R.A. Rydon	c Bail, b Davidson	2		c Browne, b Golding	2
J.E.B. Cope	lbw, b Davidson	1		c Lea, b Golding	0
T.A.J. Dawson	not out	1		c Brown, b Davidson	0
M.P. Lawrence	b Davidson	0		lbw, b Scott	0
EXTRAS	L-B 6, N-B 1	7		B 3, L-B 16, W 4, N-B 3	26
	TOTAL	167		TOTAL	268

CAMBRIDGE

P.A.C. Bail	lbw, b Rydon	174		c Tooley, b Thorne	7
M.S. Ahluwalia	lbw, b Thorne	9		did not bat	
D.J. Fell	lbw, b Rutnagur	22		c Lawrence, b Rutnagur	20
D.W. Browne	c Cope, b Rutnagur	2		not out	13
D.G. Price	lbw, b Thorne	0		c Tooley, b Rutnagur	7
A.E. Lea	c Lawrence, b Dawson	19		b Rutnagur	19
A.K. Golding	b Dawson	47		not out	0
A.D. Brown	b Dawson	4		did not bat	
J.E. Davidson	not out	41		run out	26
A.M.G. Scott	not out	1		did not bat	
EXTRAS	L-B 7, W 3, N-B 1	11		B 1, L-B 12, W 1	14
	TOTAL (8 WKTS DEC.)	330		TOTAL (5 WKTS)	106

C.C. Ellison did not bat

Cambridge bowling	OVERS	MDNS	RUNS	WKTS		OVERS	MDNS	RUNS	WKTS
Davidson	19.1	3	58	5		30	4	92	4
Scott	15	4	36	0		17.5	6	43	2
Ellison	10	5	19	2		11	5	21	1
Golding	22	8	39	2		30	10	51	3
Lea	13	0	9	0		10	0	42	0

Oxford bowling	OVERS	MDNS	RUNS	WKTS		OVERS	MDNS	RUNS	WKTS
Thorne	32	11	42	2		8	0	43	1
Rydon	21	4	89	1		—	—	—	—
Rutnagur	26	3	69	2		8	0	50	3
Dawson	28	4	92	3		—	—	—	—
Lawrence	10	2	31	0		—	—	—	—

UMPIRES M.J. Kitchen and D.O. Oslear

1, 2, 3 July
At Lord's

1987

Match drawn

The arrival of M.A. Atherton as a freshman from Manchester Grammar School brightened an otherwise undistinguished Fenner's season. Cambridge were dismissed for 207, T. Firth and I.M. Henderson doing the early damage.

M.A. Crawley, Atherton's former team-mate at Manchester, patiently developed a maiden hundred, hitting thirteen boundaries and batting for almost three and three-quarter hours in his innings of 140. He followed M.J.K. Smith and the Nawab of Pataudi in becoming the third Oxford freshman since the war to score a hundred against Cambridge. At 135 for 5 he was joined by S.D. Weale, who played a determined part in the sixth-wicket stand of 191. A.M.G. Scott, the quickish left-arm bowler, returned figures of 5 for 97.

For the second time in the match T. Firth had Atherton lbw, but Cambridge lost no further wickets on the second evening. The next morning, despite trying eight bowlers, the Oxford captain, C.D.M. Tooley, was able to make little impression on stolid performances by a succession of Cambridge batsmen. His opposite number made a token declaration shortly before the end.

CAMBRIDGE

	First innings			Second innings	
P.A.C. Bail	lbw, b Henderson	5		c Kilborn, b Weale	90
M.A. Atherton	lbw, b Firth	7		lbw, b Firth	0
A.M. Hooper	b Edwards	15		c Tooley, b Edwards	89
D.J. Fell	c Kilborn, b Henderson	0		not out	67
D.G. Price	b Firth	46		c Kilborn, b Tooley	57
S.R. Gorman	c Cope, b Crawley	26			
J.M. Tremellen	b Edwards	28		b Edwards	39
G.A. Pointer	lbw, b Firth	33			
J.N. Perry	b Weale	10			
A.M.G. Scott	not out	11			
T.R. Middleton	b Crawley	6			
EXTRAS	B 1, L-B 6, W 3, N-B 10	20		B 2, L-B 8, W 2, N-B 13	25
	TOTAL	207		TOTAL (5 WKTS DEC.)	367

OXFORD

R.E. Morris	lbw, b Scott	0		not out	13
A.R. Beech	c Fell, b Perry	1		c Fell, b Pointer	6
M.J. Kilborn	c and b Scott	59		not out	6
C.D.M. Tooley	lbw, b Scott	5			
R.D. Sardesai	lbw, b Atherton	40			
M.A. Crawley	b Scott	140			
S.D. Weale	b Scott	76			
I.M. Henderson	not out	4			
EXTRAS	B 7, L-B 7, W 2, N-B 6	22		L-B 2, N-B 2	4
	TOTAL (7 WKTS DEC.)	347		TOTAL (1 WKT)	29

J.E.B. Cope, P.G. Edwards and T. Firth did not bat

Oxford bowling	OVERS	MDNS	RUNS	WKTS		OVERS	MDNS	RUNS	WKTS
Firth	21	4	64	3		26	6	101	1
Henderson	9	0	29	2		12	1	75	0
Edwards	22	7	50	2		22	9	63	2
Weale	13	4	27	1		11	2	25	1
Crawley	7.1	1	30	2		17	6	38	0
Kilborn	—	—	—	—		3	0	23	0
Tooley	—	—	—	—		5.3	1	21	1
Morris	—	—	—	—		2	0	11	0

Cambridge bowling									
Scott	33.3	7	97	5		—	—	—	—
Perry	19	3	50	1		3	0	14	0
Pointer	23	2	61	0		5	1	9	1
Middleton	15	1	47	0		—	—	—	—
Atherton	22	0	66	1		1	0	4	0
Tremellen	2	0	12	0		—	—	—	—

UMPIRES J.H. Harris and J.A. Jameson

<table>
<tr><td>2, 3, 4 July
At Lord's</td><td># 1988</td><td align="right">*Match abandoned*</td></tr>
</table>

This was the first time in 144 Varsity Matches that not a ball was bowled throughout the three days. The teams were:

Oxford   M.J. Kilborn, S.D. Weale, D.A. Hagan, M.A. Crawley, P.G. Edwards, F.D. Reynolds, M.E.O. Brown, J.D. Duttall, M.R. Sygrove, T.B. Jack, F.A. Almaer.

Cambridge M.A. Atherton, G.A. Pointer, P.A.C. Bail, J.M. Tremellen, J.N. Perry, R. Bate, G.J. Noyes, R.J. Turner, N.C.W. Fenton, J.C.M. Atkinson, S.D. Heath.

UMPIRES R.A. White and P.B. Wight

Envoi

The *envois* of cricket books should be like the envoys of Lilliput – decidedly short and sparing of words. We have come to the end of our collection – a gross of University Matches, bar that one, in 1988, that never was, and fourteen decades that have taken our story from 1827 to 1988 – and we are conscious of the constraints imposed by the length of the book, and of a subsequent need to be selective that will not please all readers. The names, and the numbers, and the records, and the Roll of Honour, all come after this envoi.

From a Cambridge viewpoint, I shall end with two nuggets, and with two regrets. W.G. Grace, who never went to Oxford or Cambridge, must have been delighted that his son, W.G. Grace junior, not only won his Cambridge blue in 1895 and 1896, but also, on 1st June, 1896, with C.S. Graham-Smith, put on 337 for the first wicket for Pembroke *v* Caius. And, secondly, your 1916 *Wisden* – if, that is, you have one, which is most unlikely – contains the obituaries, not only of W.G. and Victor Trumper, but also of a keen cricketing Kingsman, though not a Cambridge blue, Sub-Lieutenant Rupert C. Brooke. By the time that he died of sunstroke on Lemnos in 1915, he had gained a reputation as a poet more considerable than that suggested by the final lines of his poem, *The Old Vicarage, Grantchester*:

> *Stands the Church clock at ten to three?*
> *And is there honey still for tea?*

The two Light Blue regrets are straightforward: they are that, although Cambridge may have produced more England captains and England players (but not as many overseas captains and players) as Oxford, they cannot boast a 12th man on tour who is now the Australian Prime Minister, Bob Hawke, nor a Quidnunc that became the British Prime Minister, as did the Harlequin Alec Douglas-Home, now Lord Home of the Hirsel.

This small extra space gives an Oxford man the opportunity for a few personal recollections of The Parks in 1949 – such as: the superb catch when Clive van Ryneveld ran twenty-five yards to dismiss Tom Graveney; or the devastating finesse of Hafeez Kardar in bowling out Sussex; or the sparkling fielding of Chris Winn in the covers; or the defeats of the joint-holders of the County Championship, Yorkshire and Middlesex; or, most dramatically, the famous weather-assisted victory over the New Zealanders. A few elm trees have gone, some buildings have been added to the skyline, but this beautiful ground remains unspoilt.

The one hundred and sixty-one years that this story has encompassed have seen a wealth of change – social, economic, military, educational, even personal. What, we believe, has remained constant has been the simple pride and enjoyment experienced by all who have worn the Dark Blue or Light Blue cap – or even, since the end of the second world war, a variety of caps and other headgear not previously countenanced! – and the especial thrill of taking part in the historic encounters at Lord's.

GEORGE CHESTERTON   HUBERT DOGGART

Appendix

I Results of University Matches

1827 Drawn	1883 Cambridge won by 7 wickets
1829 Oxford won by 115 runs	1884 Oxford won by 7 wickets
1836 Oxford won by 121 runs	1885 Cambridge won by 7 wickets
1838 Oxford won by 98 runs	1886 Oxford won by 133 runs
1839 Cambridge won by an innings and 125 runs	1887 Oxford won by 7 wickets
1840 Cambridge won by 63 runs	1888 Drawn
1841 Cambridge won by 8 runs	1889 Cambridge won by an innings and 105 runs
1842 Cambridge won by 162 runs	1890 Cambridge won by 7 wickets
1843 Cambridge won by 54 runs	1891 Cambridge won by 2 wickets
1844 Drawn	1892 Oxford won by 5 wickets
1845 Cambridge won by 6 wickets	1893 Cambridge won by 266 runs
1846 Oxford won by 3 wickets	1894 Oxford won by 8 wickets
1847 Cambridge won by 138 runs	1895 Cambridge won by 134 runs
1848 Oxford won by 23 runs	1896 Oxford won by 4 wickets
1849 Cambridge won by 3 wickets	1897 Cambridge won by 179 runs
1850 Oxford won by 127 runs	1898 Oxford won by 9 wickets
1851 Cambridge won by an innings and 4 runs	1899 Drawn
1852 Oxford won by an innings and 77 runs	1900 Drawn
1853 Oxford won by an innings and 19 runs	1901 Drawn
1854 Oxford won by an innings and 8 runs	1902 Cambridge won by 5 wickets
1855 Oxford won by 3 wickets	1903 Oxford won by 268 runs
1856 Cambridge won by 3 wickets	1904 Drawn
1857 Oxford won by 81 runs	1905 Cambridge won by 40 runs
1858 Oxford won by an innings and 38 runs	1906 Cambridge won by 94 runs
1859 Cambridge won by 28 runs	1907 Cambridge won by 5 wickets
1860 Cambridge won by 3 wickets	1908 Oxford won by 2 wickets
1861 Cambridge won by 133 runs	1909 Drawn
1862 Cambridge won by 8 wickets	1910 Oxford won by an innings and 126 runs
1863 Oxford won by 8 wickets	1911 Oxford won by 74 runs
1864 Oxford won by 4 wickets	1912 Cambridge won by 3 wickets
1865 Oxford won by 114 runs	1913 Cambridge won by 4 wickets
1866 Oxford won by 12 runs	1914 Oxford won by 194 runs
1867 Cambridge won by 5 wickets	1919 Oxford won by 45 runs
1868 Cambridge won by 168 runs	1920 Drawn
1869 Cambridge won by 58 runs	1921 Cambridge won by an innings and 24 runs
1870 Cambridge won by 2 runs	1922 Cambridge won by an innings and 100 runs
1871 Oxford won by 8 wickets	1923 Oxford won by an innings and 227 runs
1872 Cambridge won by an innings and 166 runs	1924 Cambridge won by 9 wickets
1873 Oxford won by 3 wickets	1925 Drawn
1874 Oxford won by an innings and 92 runs	1926 Cambridge won by 34 runs
1875 Oxford won by 6 runs	1927 Cambridge won by 116 runs
1876 Cambridge won by 9 wickets	1928 Drawn
1877 Oxford won by 10 wickets	1929 Drawn
1878 Cambridge won by 238 runs	1930 Cambridge won by 205 runs
1879 Cambridge won by 9 wickets	1931 Oxford won by 8 wickets
1880 Cambridge won by 115 runs	1932 Drawn
1881 Oxford won by 135 runs	1933 Drawn
1882 Cambrige won by 7 wickets	1934 Drawn

1935 Cambridge won by 195 runs
1936 Cambridge won by 8 wickets
1937 Oxford won by 7 wickets
1938 Drawn
1939 Oxford won by 45 runs
1946 Oxford won by 6 wickets
1947 Drawn
1948 Oxford won by an innings and 8 runs
1949 Cambridge won by 7 wickets
1950 Drawn
1951 Oxford won by 21 runs
1952 Drawn
1953 Cambridge won by 2 wickets
1954 Drawn
1955 Drawn
1956 Drawn
1957 Cambridge won by an innings and 186 runs
1958 Cambridge won by 99 runs
1959 Oxford won by 85 runs
1960 Drawn
1961 Drawn
1962 Drawn
1963 Drawn
1964 Drawn
1965 Drawn
1966 Oxford won by an innings and 9 runs
1967 Drawn
1968 Drawn
1969 Drawn
1970 Drawn
1971 Drawn
1972 Cambridge won by an innings and 25 runs
1973 Drawn
1974 Drawn
1975 Drawn
1976 Oxford won by 10 wickets
1977 Drawn
1978 Drawn
1979 Cambridge won by an innings and 52 runs
1980 Drawn
1981 Drawn
1982 Cambridge won by 7 wickets
1983 Drawn
1984 Oxford won by 5 wickets
1985 Drawn
1986 Cambridge won by 5 wickets
1987 Drawn
1988 Match abandoned – no play

Summary   Oxford 46 wins, Cambridge 54 wins, Drawn 43, Abandoned 1

II Captains

OXFORD

1827 C. Wordsworth (Harrow and Christ Church)
1829 C. Wordsworth (Harrow and Christ Church)
1836 Unknown
1838 A. Coote (Eton and Brasenose)
1839 G.B. Lee (Winchester and New College)
1840 R. Garth (Eton and Christ Church)
1841 R. Garth (Eton and Christ Church)
1842 J. Coker (Winchester and New College)
1843 J. Coker (Winchester and New College)
1844 M.M. Ainslie (Eton and Christ Church)
1845 M.M. Ainslie (Eton and Christ Church)
1846 V.S.C. Smith (Winchester and New College)
1847 V.S.C. Smith (Winchester and New College)
1848 G.E. Yonge (Eton and Trinity)
1849 W. Ridding (Winchester and New College)
1850 J. Aitken (Eton and Exeter)
1851 W. Ridding (Winchester and New College)
1852 W. Ridding (Winchester and New College)
1853 E.H.L. Willes (Winchester and Wadham)
1854 E.H.L. Willes (Winchester and Wadham)
1855 R. Hankey (Harrow and Balliol)
1856 A. Payne (Private and Trinity)
1857 C.D.B. Marsham (Private and Merton)
1858 C.D.B. Marsham (Private and Merton)
1859 C.G. Lane (Westminster and Christ Church)
1860 C.G. Lane (Westminster and Christ Church)
1861 F. Brandt (Cheltenham and Brasenose)
1862 H.S. Reade (Tonbridge and University)
1863 R.A.H. Mitchell (Eton and Balliol)
1864 R.A.H. Mitchell (Eton and Balliol)
1865 R.A.H. Mitchell (Eton and Balliol)
1866 E.W. Tritton (Eton and Christ Church)
1867 W.F. Maitland (Harrow and Christ Church)
1868 E.L. Fellowes (Marlborough and Brasenose)
1869 B. Pauncefote (Rugby and Brasenose)
1870 B. Pauncefote (Rugby and Brasenose)
1871 E.F.S. Tylecote (Clifton and St John's)
1872 E.F.S. Tylecote (Clifton and St John's)
1873 C.J. Ottaway (Eton and Brasenose)
1874 W. Law (Harrow and Brasenose)
1875 A.W. Ridley (Eton and Christ Church)
1876 W.H. Game (Sherborne and Oriel)
1877 A.J. Webbe (Harrow and Trinity)
1878 A.J. Webbe (Harrow and Trinity)
1879 H.R. Webbe (Winchester and New College)
1880 A.D. Greene (Clifton and Exeter)
1881 A.H. Evans (Rossall, Clifton and Oriel)
1882 N. McLachlan (Loretto and Keble)
1883 M.C. Kemp (Harrow and Hertford)
1884 M.C. Kemp (Harrow and Hertford)
1885 H.V. Page (Cheltenham and Wadham)
1886 H.V. Page (Cheltenham and Wadham)
1887 J.H. Brain (Clifton and Oriel)
1888 W. Rashleigh (Tonbridge and Brasenose)
1889 H. Philipson (Eton and New College)
1890 The Hon. F.J.N. Thesiger (Winchester and Magdalen)
1891 M.R. Jardine (Fettes and Balliol)
1892 L.C.H. Palairet (Repton and Oriel)
1893 L.C.H. Palairet (Repton and Oriel)
1894 C.B. Fry (Repton and Wadham)
1895 G.J. Mordaunt (Wellington and University College)
1896 H.D.G. Leveson-Gower (Winchester and Magdalen)
1897 G.R. Bardswell (Uppingham and Oriel)
1898 F.H.E. Cunliffe (Eton and New College)
1899 F.H.B. Champain (Cheltenham and Hertford)

1900 R.E. Foster (Malvern and University College)
1901 F.P. Knox (Dulwich and Corpus Christi)
1902 C.H.B. Marsham (Eton and Christ Church)
1903 W. Findlay (Eton and Oriel)
1904 W.H.B. Evans (Malvern and Oriel)
1905 K.M. Carlisle (Harrow and Magdalen)
1906 W.S. Bird (Malvern and New College)
1907 E.L. Wright (Winchester and New College)
1908 E.L. Wright (Winchester and New College)
1909 C.S. Hurst (Uppingham and Exeter)
1910 A.G. Pawson (Winchester and Christ Church)
1911 A.J. Evans (Winchester and Oriel)
1912 R.H. Twining (Eton and Magdalen)
1913 I.P.F. Campbell (Repton and Hertford)
1914 F.H. Knott (Tonbridge and Brasenose)
1919 M. Howell (Repton and Oriel)
1920 F.W. Gilligan (Dulwich and Worcester)
1921 V.R. Price (Bishop's Stortford and Magdalen)
1922 G.T.S. Stevens (University College School and Brasenose)
1923 R.H. Bettington (King's School, Parramatta and New College)
1924 C.H. Knott (Tonbridge and Brasenose)
1925 J.L. Guise (Winchester and Brasenose)
1926 G.B. Legge (Malvern and Brasenose)
1927 E.R.T. Holmes (Malvern and Trinity)
1928 M.A. McCanlis (Cranleigh and St Edmund Hall)
1929 A.T. Barber (Shrewsbury and Queen's)
1930 P.G.T. Kingsley (Winchester and New College)
1931 D.N. Moore (Shrewsbury and Queen's) did not play owing to illness.
     A. Melville (Michaelhouse, South Africa and New College) was captain for the match.
1932 A. Melville (Michaelhouse, South Africa and New College)
1933 B.W. Hone (Adelaide University and New College)
1934 F.G.H. Chalk (Uppingham and Brasenose)
1935 D.F. Walker (Uppingham and Brasenose)
1936 N.S. Mitchell-Innes (Sedbergh and Brasenose)
1937 A.P. Singleton (Shrewsbury and Brasenose)
1938 J.N. Grover (Winchester and Brasenose)
1939 E.J.H. Dixon (St Edward's and Christ Church)
1946 D.H. Macindoe (Eton and Christ Church)
1947 M.P. Donnelly (New Plymouth BHS, Canterbury University and Worcester)
1948 H.A. Pawson (Winchester and Christ Church)
1949 C.B. van Ryneveld (Diocesan College, South Africa and University College)
1950 D.B. Carr (Repton and Worcester)
1951 M.B. Hofmeyr (Pretoria, South Africa and Worcester)
1952 P.D.S. Blake (Eton and Brasenose)
1953 A.L. Dowding (St Peter's, Adelaide and Balliol)
1954 M.C. Cowdrey (Tonbridge and Brasenose)
1955 C.C.P. Williams (Westminster and Christ Church)
1956 M.J.K. Smith (Stamford and St Edmund Hall)
1957 A.C. Walton (Radley and Lincoln)
1958 J.A. Bailey (Christ's Hospital and University College)
1959 A.C. Smith (King Edward's, Birmingham and Brasenose)

1960 A.C. Smith (King Edward's, Birmingham and Brasenose)
1961 Nawab of Pataudi (Winchester and Balliol) did not play owing to an accident.
     C.D. Drybrough (Highgate and Worcester) was captain for the match.
1962 C.D. Drybrough (Highgate and Worcester)
1963 Nawab of Pataudi (Winchester and Balliol)
1964 D.R. Worsley (Bolton and St Edmund Hall)
1965 J.D. Martin (Magdalen College School and St Edmund Hall)
1966 R.M.C. Gilliat (Charterhouse and Christ Church)
1967 G.N.S. Ridley (Milton, Rhodesia and Pembroke)
1968 F.S. Goldstein (Falcon, Rhodesia and St Edmund Hall)
1969 F.S. Goldstein (Falcon, Rhodesia and St Edmund Hall)
1970 M. St. J.W. Burton (Umtali BHS, Rhodesia and Mansfield)
1971 B. May (Prince Edward's, Rhodesia and Brasenose)
1972 P.C.H. Jones (Milton HS, Rhodesia and St Edmund Hall)
1973 A.K.C. Jones (Solihull and St Edmund Hall)
1974 Imran Khan (Worcester RGS and Keble)
1975 T.R. Glover (Lancaster RGS and Lincoln)
1976 V.J. Marks (Blundell's and St John's)
1977 V.J. Marks (Blundell's and St John's)
1978 J.A. Claughton (King Edward's, Birmingham and Merton)
1979 G.V. Marie (University of Western Australia and Wolfson)
1980 C.J. Ross (Wellington University and Magdalen)
1981 R.P. Moulding (Haberdashers' Aske's and Christ Church)
1982 R.G.P. Ellis (Haileybury and St Edmund Hall)
1983 G.J. Toogood (North Bromsgrove HS and Lincoln)
1984 K.A. Hayes (Queen Elizabeth's GS, Blackburn and Merton)
1985 A.J.T. Miller (Haileybury and St Edmund Hall)
1986 D.A. Thorne (Bablake and Keble)
1987 C.D.M. Tooley (St Dunstan's and Magdalen)
1988 M.J. Kilborn (University of NSW and St John's)

CAMBRIDGE

1827 H. Jenner (Eton and Trinity Hall)
1829 E.H. Pickering (Eton and St John's)
1836 H.W. Booth (Eton and Christ's)
1838 C.G. Taylor (Eton and Emmanuel)
1839 C.G. Taylor (Eton and Emmanuel)
1840 T.A. Anson (Eton and Jesus)
1841 T.A. Anson (Eton and Jesus)
1842 T.A. Anson (Eton and Jesus)
1843 G.J. Boudier (Eton and King's) } (joint captains)
     T.L. French (Winchester and Emmanuel)
1844 E.M. Dewing (Harrow and Trinity)
1845 E.M. Dewing (Harrow and Trinity)

1846	A.M. Hoare (Private and St John's)
1847	O.C. Pell (Rugby and Trinity)
1848	J. Walker (Private and Trinity)
1849	R.T. King (Oakham and Emmanuel)
1850	W.S. Deacon (Eton and Trinity)
1851	E.W. Blore (Eton and Trinity)
1852	H. Vernon (Harrow and Trinity)
1853	C. Pontifex (Private and Trinity)
1854	A.R. Ward (Private and St John's)
1855	G.R. Johnson (Bury St Edmund's and Clare)
1856	J. McCormick (Liverpool College, Bingley and St. John's)
1857	J.M. Fuller (Marlborough and St John's)
1858	J.M. Fuller (Marlborough and St John's)
1859	R.A. Bayford (Kensington GS and Trinity Hall)
1860	F.H. Norman (Eton and Trinity)
1861	T.E. Bagge (Eton and Trinity)
1862	H.M. Plowden (Harrow and Trinity)
1863	H.M. Plowden (Harrow and Trinity)
1864	C. Booth (Rugby and Trinity)
1865	G.H. Tuck (Eton and Trinity)
1866	The Hon. F.G. Pelham (Eton and Trinity)
1867	The Hon. F.G. Pelham (Eton and Trinity)
1868	C.E. Green (Uppingham and Trinity)
1869	M.H. Stow (Harrow and Trinity)
1870	W.B. Money (Harrow and Trinity)
1871	W. Yardley (Rugby and Trinity)
1872	C.I. Thornton (Eton and Trinity)
1873	F.E.R. Fryer (Harrow and Gonville & Caius)
1874	G.H. Longman (Eton and Trinity)
1875	G.H. Longman (Eton and Trinity)
1876	F.F.J. Greenfield (Hurstpierpoint and Peterhouse)
1877	W.S. Patterson (Uppingham and Trinity)
1878	The Hon. E. Lyttelton (Eton and Trinity)
1879	The Hon. A. Lyttelton (Eton and Trinity)
1880	A.G. Steel (Marlborough and Trinity Hall)
1881	The Hon. Ivo Bligh (Eton and Trinity)
1882	G.B. Studd (Eton and Trinity)
1883	C.T. Studd (Eton and Trinity)
1884	J.E.K. Studd (Eton and Trinity)
1885	The Hon. M.B. Hawke (Eton and Magdalene)
1886	H.W. Bainbridge (Eton and Trinity)
1887	F. Marchant (Eton and Trinity)
1888	C.D. Buxton (Harrow and Trinity)
1889	F.G.J. Ford (Repton and King's)
1890	S.M.J. Woods (Brighton and Jesus)
1891	G. MacGregor (Uppingham and Jesus)
1892	F.S. Jackson (Harrow and Trinity)
1893	F.S. Jackson (Harrow and Trinity)
1894	P.H. Latham (Malvern and Pembroke)
1895	W.G. Druce (Marlborough and Trinity)
1896	F. Mitchell (St Peter's, York and Gonville & Caius)
1897	N.F. Druce (Marlborough and Trinity)
1898	C.E.M. Wilson (Uppingham and Trinity)
1899	G.L. Jessop (Beccles, Cheltenham GS and Christ's)
1900	T.L. Taylor (Uppingham and Trinity)
1901	S.H. Day (Malvern and Queens')
1902	E.R. Wilson (Rugby and Trinity)
1903	E.M. Dowson (Harrow and Trinity)
1904	F.B. Wilson (Harrow and Trinity)
1905	E.W. Mann (Harrow and Trinity)
1906	C.H. Eyre (Harrow and Pembroke)
1907	M.W. Payne (Wellington and Trinity)
1908	R.A. Young (Repton and King's)
1909	J.N. Buchanan (Charterhouse and Trinity)
1910	M. Falcon (Harrow and Pembroke)
1911	J.F. Ireland (Marlborough and Trinity)
1912	E.L. Kidd (Wellington and Pembroke)
1913	The Hon. H.G.H. Mulholland (Eton and Trinity)
1914	S.H. Saville (Marlborough and Trinity)
1919	J.S.F. Morrison (Charterhouse and Trinity)
1920	G.E.C. Wood (Cheltenham and Pembroke)
1921	G. Ashton (Winchester and Trinity)
1922	H. Ashton (Winchester and Trinity)
1923	C.T. Ashton (Winchester and Trinity)
1924	T.C. Lowry (Christ's College, Christchurch, New Zealand and Jesus)
1925	C.T. Bennett (Harrow and Pembroke)
1926	H.J. Enthoven (Harrow and Pembroke)
1927	E.W. Dawson (Eton and Magdalene)
1928	F.J. Seabrook (Haileybury and St John's)
1929	M.J. Turnbull (Downside and Trinity)
1930	J.T. Morgan (Charterhouse and Jesus)
1931	G.D. Kemp-Welch (Charterhouse and Sidney Sussex)
1932	A.G. Hazlerigg (Eton and Trinity)
1933	D.R. Wilcox (Dulwich and Pembroke)
1934	J.H. Human (Repton and Clare)
1935	G.W. Parker (Crypt, Gloucester and Selwyn)
1936	H.T. Bartlett (Dulwich and Pembroke)
1937	M. Tindall (Harrow and St Catharine's)
1938	N.W.D. Yardley (St Peter's, York and St John's)
1939	P.M. Studd (Harrow and Clare)
1946	P.E. Bodkin (Bradfield and Gonville & Caius)
1947	G.L. Willatt (Repton and St Catharine's)
1948	J.M. Mills (Oundle and Corpus Christi)
1949	D.J. Insole (Sir George Monoux and St Catharine's)
1950	G.H.G. Doggart (Winchester and King's)
1951	J.J. Warr (Ealing CGS and Emmanuel)
1952	D.S. Sheppard (Sherborne and Trinity Hall)
1953	R.G. Marlar (Harrow and Magdalene)
1954	M.H. Bushby (Dulwich and Queens')
1955	D.R.W. Silk (Christ's Hospital and Sidney Sussex)
1956	M.E.L. Melluish (Rossall and Gonville & Caius)
1957	G. Goonesena (Royal College, Colombo and Queens')
1958	E.R. Dexter (Radley and Jesus)
1959	D.J. Green (Burton GS and Christ's)
1960	C.B. Howland (Dulwich and Clare)
1961	D. Kirby (St Peter's, York and Emmanuel)
1962	A.R. Lewis (Neath GS and Christ's)
1963	J.M. Brearley (City of London and St John's)
1964	J.M. Brearley (City of London and St John's)
1965	R.C. White (Hilton, South Africa and Jesus)
1966	D.L. Murray (Queen's Royal College, Trinidad and Jesus)
1967	S.G. Russell (Tiffin and Trinity)
1968	G.A. Cottrell (Kingston GS and St Catharine's)
1969	A.M. Jorden (Monmouth and Fitzwilliam)
1970	A.M. Jorden (Monmouth and Fitzwilliam)
1971	Majid Jahangir Khan (Aitcheson's, Lahore and Emmanuel)

1972 Majid Jahangir Khan (Aitcheson's, Lahore and Emmanuel)
1973 P.H. Edmonds (Gilbert Rennie, Lusaka, Cranbrook and Fitzwilliam)
1974 W. Snowden (Merchant Taylors', Crosby and Emmanuel)
1975 C.J. Aworth (Tiffin and St Catharine's)
1976 T.J. Murrills (Leys and Emmanuel)
1977 A.J. Hignell (Denstone and Fitzwilliam)
1978 A.J. Hignell (Denstone and Fitzwilliam)
1979 I.A. Greig (Queen's College, South Africa and Downing)
1980 I.G. Peck (Bedford and Magdalene)
1981 I.G. Peck (Bedford and Magdalene)

1982 D.R. Pringle (Felsted and Fitzwilliam) did not play as he was representing England.
      J.P.C. Mills (Oundle and Corpus Christi) was captain for the match.
1983 S.P. Henderson (Downside and Magdalene)
1984 A.J. Pollock (Shrewsbury and Trinity)
1985 C.R. Andrew (Barnard Castle and St John's)
1986 D.G. Price (Haberdashers' Aske's and Homerton)
1987 D.G. Price (Haberdashers' Aske's and Homerton)
1988 M.A. Atherton (Manchester GS and Downing)

III Hundreds in University Matches

238*	Nawab of Pataudi (Snr) (Ox)	1931
211	G. Goonesena (Cam)	1957
201*	M.J.K. Smith (Ox)	1954
201	A.T. Ratcliffe (Cam)	1931
200	Majid Khan (Cam)	1970
193	D.C.H. Townsend (Ox)	1934
174	P.A.C. Bail (Cam)	1986
172*	J.F. Marsh (Cam)	1904
171	R.E. Foster (Ox)	1900
170	M. Howell (Ox)	1919
167	B.W. Hone (Ox)	1932
160	P.R. Le Couteur (Ox)	1910
158	P.M. Roebuck (Cam)	1975
157	D.R. Wilcox (Cam)	1932
155	F.S. Goldstein (Ox)	1968
150	R.A. Young (Cam)	1906
149	J.T. Morgan (Cam)	1929
149	G.J. Toogood (Ox)	1985
146	R. O'Brien (Cam)	1956
146	D.R. Owen-Thomas (Cam)	1971
145*	H.E. Webb (Ox)	1948
145	D.P. Toft (Ox)	1967
143	K.J. Key (Ox)	1886
142	M.P. Donnelly (Ox)	1946
140	M.R. Jardine (Ox)	1892
140	M.A. Crawley (Ox)	1987
139	R.J. Boyd-Moss (Cam)	1983
136	E.T. Killick (Cam)	1930
135	H.A. Pawson (Ox)	1947
132	G.O. Smith (Ox)	1896
131	Nawab of Pataudi (Jnr) (Ox)	1960
130	W. Yardley (Cam)	1872
130	J.E. Raphael (Ox)	1903
129	H.J. Enthoven (Cam)	1925
128*	A.J.T. Miller (Ox)	1984
127	H.J. Mordaunt (Cam)	1889
127	D.S. Sheppard (Cam)	1952
124	A.K. Judd (Cam)	1927
124	A.T. Ratcliffe (Cam)	1932
124	R.J. Boyd-Moss (Cam)	1983
122	P.A. Gibb (Cam)	1938
121	H.K. Foster (Ox)	1895
121	J.N. Grover (Ox)	1937
120	G.B. Studd (Cam)	1882
119	J.M. Brearley (Cam)	1964
118	E.R. Wilson (Cam)	1901
118	H. Ashton (Cam)	1921
118	D.R.W. Silk (Cam)	1954
117*	F.M. Buckland (Ox)	1877
117*	S.H. Day (Ox)	1902
117	M.J.K. Smith (Ox)	1956
116*	D.R.W. Silk (Cam)	1953
116	E.C. Streatfeild (Cam)	1892
116	M.C. Cowdrey (Ox)	1953
115	C.E.M. Wilson (Cam)	1898
115	A.W. Allen (Cam)	1934
114*	D.R. Owen-Thomas (Cam)	1972
114	V.T. Hill (Ox)	1892
114	J.F. Pretlove (Cam)	1955
113*	J.M. Brearley (Cam)	1962
113	E.R.T. Holmes (Ox)	1927
112*	E.D. Fursdon (Ox)	1975
111*	G.W. Cook (Cam)	1957
109	W.H. Game (Ox)	1876
109	A. Eccles (Ox)	1898
109	C.H. Taylor (Ox)	1923
109	G.J. Toogood (Ox)	1984
108	F.G.H. Chalk (Ox)	1934
107*	W.H. Patterson (Ox)	1881
107	W. Rashleigh (Ox)	1886
107	L.G. Colbeck (Cam)	1905
106	Nawab of Pataudi (Snr) (Ox)	1929
105*	W.S. Patterson (Cam)	1876
105	E.J. Craig (Cam)	1961
104*	D.A. Thorne (Ox)	1986
104	H.J. Enthoven (Cam)	1924
104	M.J.K. Smith (Ox)	1955
103*	E. Crawley (Cam)	1887
103*	A.R. Lewis (Cam)	1962
103*	D.R. Pringle (Cam)	1979
102*	A.P.F. Chapman (Cam)	1922
102	C.W. Wright (Cam)	1883
101*	R.W.V. Robins (Cam)	1928
101	H.W. Bainbridge (Cam)	1885
101	N.W.D. Yardley (Cam)	1937
100*	C.B. Fry (Ox)	1894
100*	C.H.B. Marsham (Ox)	1901
100*	M. Manasseh (Ox)	1964
100	W. Yardley (Cam)	1870
100	Lord George Scott (Ox)	1887
100	P.J. Dickinson (Cam)	1939
100	N.J. Cosh (Cam)	1967
100	R.J. Boyd-Moss (Cam)	1982

* not out

IV Records

OXFORD
Wicket Partnerships

1st	338	T. Bowring & H. Teesdale v Gentlemen, Oxford 1908
2nd	226	W.G. Keighley & H.A. Pawson v Cambridge, Lord's 1947
3rd	273	F.C. de Saram & N.S. Mitchell-Innes v Gloucestershire, Oxford 1934
4th	276	P.G.T. Kingsley & N.M. Ford v Surrey, The Oval 1930
5th	256*	A.A. Baig & C.A. Fry v Free Foresters, Oxford 1959
6th	270	D.R. Walsh & S.A. Westley v Warwickshire, Oxford 1969
7th	340	K.J. Key & H. Philipson v Middlesex, Chiswick Park 1887
8th	160	H. Philipson & A.C.M. Croome v MCC, Lord's 1889
9th	157	H.M. Garland-Wells & C.K. Hill-Wood v Kent, Oxford 1928
10th	149	F.H. Hollins & B.A. Collins v MCC Oxford 1901

Highest Total

For Oxford, 651 v Sussex, Hove 1895
Against Oxford, 679 for 7 declared, Australians, Oxford 1938

Lowest Total

For Oxford, 12 v MCC, Oxford 1877
Against Oxford, 24 by MCC, Oxford 1846

Highest Innings

For Oxford, 281 K.J. Key v Middlesex, Chiswick Park 1887
Against Oxford, 338 W.W. Read for Surrey, The Oval 1888

Best Bowling in an Innings

For Oxford, 10 for 38 S.E. Butler v Cambridge University, Lord's 1871
Against Oxford, 10 for 49 W.G. Grace for MCC, Oxford 1886

Best Bowling in a Match

For Oxford, 15 for 65 B.J.T. Bosanquet v Sussex, Oxford 1900
Against Oxford, 16 for 225 J.E. Walsh for Leicestershire, Oxford 1953

Most Runs in a Season

1307 Nawab of Pataudi (Snr) (av 93.35), 1931

Most Runs in a Career

3319 N.S. Mitchell-Innes (av. 47.41), 1934–7

Most Hundreds in a Season

6 Nawab of Pataudi (Snr), 1931

Most Hundreds in a Career

9 A.M. Crawley (1927–30)
  Nawab of Pataudi (Snr) (1928–31)
  N.S. Mitchell-Innes (1934–7)
  M.P. Donnelly (1946–7)

Most Wickets in a Season

70 I.A.R. Peebles (av. 18.15), 1930

Most Wickets in a Career

182 R.H. Bettington (av. 19.38), 1920–3

University Match Records

Highest total: 503, 1900
Lowest total: 32, 1878
Highest innings: 238* Nawab of Pataudi (Snr), 1931
Best bowling in an innings: 10 for 38 S.E. Butler, 1871
Best bowling in a match: 15 for 95 S.E. Butler, 1871
Match doubles: 160 & 11 for 66 P.R. Le Couteur, 1910
149 & 10 for 93 G.J. Toogood, 1985

Three Centuries at Lord's in Different Fixtures

M.P. Donnelly:	1946 in the University Match	142
	1947 for Gentlemen v Players	162*
	1949 for New Zealand v England	206

(M.P. Donnelly shares this distinction with A.P.F. Chapman for Cambridge.)

* not out

CAMBRIDGE

Wicket Partnerships

1st 349 J.G. Dewes & D.S. Sheppard *v* Sussex, Hove 1950

2nd 429* J.G. Dewes & G.H.G. Doggart *v* Essex, Cambridge 1949

3rd 284 E.T. Killick & G.C. Grant *v* Essex, Cambridge 1929

4th 275 R. de W.K. Winlaw & J.H. Human *v* Essex, Cambridge 1934

5th 220 R. Subba Row & F.C.M. Alexander *v* Nottinghamshire 1953

6th 245 J.L. Bryan & C.T. Ashton *v* Surrey, The Oval 1921

7th 289 G. Goonesena & G.W. Cook *v* Oxford, Lord's 1957

8th 145 H. Ashton & A.E.R. Gilligan *v* Free Foresters, Cambridge 1920

9th 200 G.W. Cook & C.S. Smith *v* Lancashire, Liverpool 1957

10th 177 A.E.R. Gilligan & J.H. Naumann *v* Sussex, Hove 1919

Highest Total

For Cambridge, 703 for 9 declared *v* Sussex, Hove 1890

Against Cambridge, 703 for 3 declared by West Indies, Cambridge 1950

Lowest Total

For Cambridge, 30 *v* Yorkshire, Cambridge 1928

Against Cambridge, 32 by Oxford, Lord's 1878

Highest Innings

For Cambridge, 254* K.S. Duleepsinhji *v* Middlesex, Cambridge 1927

Against Cambridge, 304* E. de C. Weekes for West Indies, Cambridge 1950

Best Bowling in an Innings

For Cambridge, 10 for 69 S.M.J. Woods *v* C.I. Thornton's XI, Cambridge 1890

Against Cambridge, 10 for 38 S.E. Butler for Oxford, Lord's 1871

Best Bowling in a Match

For Cambridge, 15 for 88 S.M.J. Woods *v* C.I. Thornton's XI, Cambridge 1890

Against Cambridge, 15 for 95 S.E. Butler for Oxford, Lord's 1871

Most Runs in a Season

1581 D.S. Sheppard (av 79.05), 1952

Most Runs in a Career

4310 J.M. Brearley (av. 38.48), 1961–4

Most Runs in a Career in the University Match

489 R.J. Boyd-Moss, 1980–3 (including two hundreds in a match and three in successive seasons)

Most Hundreds in a Season

7 D.S. Sheppard, 1952

Most Hundreds in a Career

14 D.S. Sheppard 1950–2

Most Wickets in a Season

80 O.S. Wheatley (av. 17.63), 1958

Most Wickets in a Career

208 G. Goonesena (av. 21.82), 1954–7

University Match Records

Highest total: 432 for 9 declared, 1936
Lowest total: 39, 1858
Highest innings: 211 G. Goonesena 1957
Best bowling in an innings: 8 for 44 G.E. Jeffery, 1873
Best bowling in a match: 13 for 73 A.G. Steel, 1878
Hat-tricks: F.C. Cobden (1870)
           A.G. Steel (1879)
           P.H. Morton (1880)
           J.F. Ireland (1911)
           R.G.H. Lowe (1926)

Three Centuries at Lord's in Different Fixtures

A.P.F. Chapman: 1922 in the University Match 102*
               1922 for Gentlemen *v* Players 160
               1930 for England *v* Australia 121

(A.P.F. Chapman shares this distinction with M.P. Donnelly for Oxford.)

Double-Century in England on Debut

G.H.G. Doggart 215* *v* Lancashire, 1948
(No other player has scored a double-century on his debut in England.)

* not out

V Oxford Blues

Aamer Hameed (Central Model HS, Punjab U and University)	1979
Abell G.E.B. (Marlborough and Worcester)	1924, 1926–7
Ainslie M.M. (Eton and Christ Church), captain in 1844–5	1843–5
Aitken H.M. (Eton and Exeter)	1853
Aitken J. (Eton and Exeter), captain in 1850	1848–50
Alington H.G. (Rugby and Magdalen)	1859
Allan J.M. (Edinburgh Academy and Worcester)	1953–6
Allerton J.W.O. (Stowe and Hertford)	1969
Allison D.F. (Greenmore College and Brasenose)	1970
Almaer F.A. (Ilford County HS and St Catherine's)	1988
Altham H.S. (Repton and Trinity)	1911–12
Arenhold J.A. (Diocesan College, S. Africa and University)	1954
Arkwright H.A. (Eton and Magdalen)	1895
Armitstead W.G. (Westminster and Christ Church)	1853–4, 1856–7
Arnall-Thompson H.T. (Rugby and Brasenose)	1886
Asher A.G.G (Loretto and Brasenose)	1883
Awdry R.W. (Winchester and New College)	1904
Baig A.A. (Aliya and Osmania U, India and University)	1959–62
Baig M.A. (Osmania U, India and New College)	1962–4
Bailey J.A. (Christ's Hospital and University), captain in 1958	1956–8
Balfour E. (Westminster and Christ Church)	1852–4
Ballance T.G.L. (Uppingham and Brasenose)	1935–7
Bannon B.D. (Tonbridge and Oriel)	1898
Barber A.T. (Shrewsbury and Queen's), captain in 1929	1927–9
Bardsley R.V. (Shrewsbury and Merton)	1911–13
Bardswell G.R. (Uppingham and Oriel), captain in 1897	1894, 1896–7
Barker A.H. (Charterhouse and Keble)	1964–5, 1967
Barlow E.A. (Shrewsbury and Brasenose)	1932–4
Barnard F.H. (Charterhouse and Brasenose)	1922, 1924
Barnes R.G. (Harrow and Balliol)	1906–7
Bartlett J.N. (Chichester and Lincoln)	1946, 1951
Bartholomew A.C. (Marlborough and Trinity)	1868
Barton M.R. (Winchester and Oriel)	1936–7
Bassett H. (Bedford House, Oxford and Non-collegiate)	1889–91
Bastard E.W. (Sherborne and Wadham)	1883–5
Bateman E.L. (Repton, Marlborough and University)	1854–5
Bathurst F. (Winchester and Merton)	1848
Bathurst L.C.V. (Radley and Trinity)	1893–4
Bathurst R.A. (Winchester and New College)	1838–9
Bathurst S.E. (Winchester and Christ Church)	1836
Bayly C.H. (Winchester and New College)	1827, 1829
Beauclerk C.W. (Charterhouse and Christ Church)	1836
Beech A.R. (John XXIII College, Perth, U of Western Australia and Magdalen)	1987
Belcher T.H. (Magdalen College School and Queen's)	1870
Bell G.F. (Repton and Balliol)	1919
Belle B.H. (Forest and Keble)	1936
Benn A. (Harrow and Christ Church)	1935
Bennett G. (Winchester and New College)	1856
Benson E.T. (Blundell's and Merton)	1928–9
Bere C.S. (Rugby and Christ Church)	1851
Berkeley G.F.H. (Wellington and Keble)	1890–3
Bettington R.H. (King's School Parramatta and New College), captain in 1923	1920–3
Bickmore A.F. (Clifton and Magdalen)	1920–1

Bird J.W. (Winchester and Wadham) — 1827, 1829
Bird W.S. (Malvern and New College), captain in 1906 — 1904–6
Birrell H.B. (St Andrews, S. Africa and Lincoln) — 1953–4
Blagg P.H. (Shrewsbury and Oriel) — 1939
Blaikie K.G. (Maritzburg and St John's) — 1924
Blake P.D.S. (Eton and Brasenose), captain in 1952 — 1950–2
Bligh E.V. (Eton and Christ Church) — 1850
Bloy N.C.F. (Dover and Brasenose) — 1946–7
Boger A.J. (Winchester and Magdalen) — 1891
Bolitho W.E.T. (Harrow and Trinity) — 1883, 1885
Bonham-Carter M. (Winchester and Balliol) — 1902
Boobbyer B. (Uppingham and Brasenose) — 1949–52
Bosanquet B.J.T. (Eton and Oriel) — 1898–1900
Boswell W.G.K. (Eton and New College) — 1913–14
Botton N.D. (King Edward's, Bath and Hertford) — 1974
Bowden-Smith F.H. (Rugby and Trinity) — 1861
Bowman R.C. (Fettes and University) — 1957
Bowring T. (Rugby and Exeter) — 1907–8
Boyle C.E. (Charterhouse and Christ Church) — 1865–7
Boyle C.W. (Clifton and University) — 1873
Bradby H.C. (Rugby and New College) — 1890
Braddell R.L. (Charterhouse and Oriel) — 1910–11
Bradshaw W.H. (Malvern and Trinity) — 1930–1
Brain J.H. (Clifton and Oriel), captain in 1887 — 1884–7
Brain W.H. (Clifton and Oriel) — 1891–3
Brandt D.R. (Harrow and Balliol) — 1907
Brandt F. (Cheltenham and Brasenose), captain in 1861 — 1859–61
Branston G.T. (Charterhouse and Hertford) — 1904–6
Brett P.J. (Winchester and Trinity) — 1929
Brettell D.N. (Cheltenham and Trinity) — 1977
Briggs R. (Winchester and St John's) — 1875–6
Bristowe O.C. (Eton and Christ Church) — 1914
Bristowe W.R. (Charterhouse and St Edmund Hall) — 1984–5
Bromley-Martin G.E. (Eton and New College) — 1897–8
Brooke R.H.J. (St Edward's, Oxford and St John's) — 1932
Brooks R.A. (Quintin, Bristol U and St Edmund Hall) — 1967
Brougham H. (Wellington and Brasenose) — 1911
Brown M.E.O. (Diocesan College, Cape Town and Worcester) — 1988
Brownlee L.D. (Clifton and Oriel) — 1904
Bruce C.N. (Winchester and New College) — 1907–8
Buckland E.H. (Marlborough and New College) — 1884–7
Buckland F.M. (Eton and University) — 1875–7
Bull H.E. (Westminster and Christ Church) — 1863
Bullock-Hall W.H. (Rugby and Balliol) — 1857–8, 1860
Burchnall R.L. (Winchester and Lincoln) — 1970–1
Burki J. (St Mary's Rawalpindi, Punjab U and Christ Church) — 1958–60
Burn R.C.W. (Winchester and Oriel) — 1902–5
Burton M. St J.W. (Umtali HS, Rhodes U and Mansfield), captain in 1970 — 1969–71
Bury T.E.O. (Charterhouse and St Edmund Hall) — 1980
Bush J.E. (Magdalen College School and Magdalen) — 1952
Butler S.E. (Eton and Brasenose) — 1870–3
Butterworth R.E.C. (Harrow and Christ Church) — 1927
Buxton R.V. (Eton and Trinity) — 1906

Campbell A.N. (Berkhamsted and New College) — 1970
Campbell D. (Melbourne U and Christ Church) — 1874–6
Campbell I.P. (Canford and Trinity) — 1949–50
Campbell I.P.F. (Repton and Hertford), captain in 1913 — 1911–13
Cantlay C.P.T. (Radley and Oriel) — 1975

Carlisle K.M. (Harrow and Magdalen), captain in 1905	1903–5
Carpenter-Garnier J. (Harrow and Christ Church)	1858
Carr D.B. (Repton and Worcester), captain in 1950	1949–51
Carr J.D. (Repton and Worcester)	1983–5
Carroll P.R. (Newington College, Sydney U and Mansfield)	1971
Carter E.S. (Durham GS and Worcester)	1866–7
Case T. (Rugby and Balliol)	1864–5, 1867
Case T.B. (Winchester and Magdalen)	1891–2
Cassan E.J.P. (King's School, Bruton and Magdalen)	1859
Cator W. (Bromsgrove and St John's)	1860
Cazalet P.V.F. (Westminster and Christ Church)	1927
Cazenove A. (Private and Exeter)	1851–2
Chalk F.G.H. (Uppingham and Brasenose), captain in 1934	1931–4
Champain F.H.B. (Cheltenham and Hertford), captain in 1899	1897–1900
Chandos-Leigh Hon. E. (Harrow and Oriel)	1852–4
Cherry G.C. (Harrow and Christ Church)	1841–3
Chesterton G.H. (Malvern and Brasenose)	1949
Chitty J.W. (Eton and Balliol)	1848–9
Clarke W.G. (Winchester and Oriel)	1840
Claughton J.A. (King Edward's, Birmingham and Merton), captain in 1978	1976–9
Clement R. (Rugby and University)	1853
Clements S.M. (Ipswich and Trinity), captain in 1979	1976, 1979
Clube S.V.M. (St John's, Leatherhead and Christ Church)	1956
Cobb A.R. (Winchester and New College)	1886
Cochrane A.H.J. (Repton and Hertford)	1885–6, 1888
Coker J. (Winchester and New College), captain in 1842–3	1840, 1842–3
Colebrooke E.L. (Charterhouse and Exeter)	1880
Coleridge C.E. (Eton and Balliol)	1849–50
Coleridge F.J. (Eton and Balliol)	1847, 1850
Colley R.H. (Bridgnorth GS and Christ Church)	1853–5
Collins L.P. (Marlborough and Keble)	1899
Colman G.R.R. (Eton and Christ Church)	1913–14
Commerell W.A. (Harrow and Corpus Christi)	1843
Cooke J. (Winchester and Balliol)	1829
Coote A. (Eton and Brasenose), captain in 1838	1838–40
Cope J.E.B. (St John's, Leatherhead and Keble)	1986–7
Corlett S.C. (Worksop and Exeter)	1971–2
Corran A.J. (Gresham's and Trinity)	1958–60
Coutts I.D.F. (Dulwich and Lincoln)	1952
Cowan R.S. (Lewes Priory CS & Magdalen)	1980–2
Cowburn A. (Winchester and Exeter)	1841
Cowdrey M.C. (Tonbridge and Brasenose), captain in 1954	1952–4
Coxon A.J. (Harrow CS and Lincoln)	1952
Crawford J.W.F. (Merchant Taylors' and St John's)	1900–1
Crawley A.M. (Harrow and Trinity)	1927–30
Crawley M.A. (Manchester GS and Oriel)	1987–8
Croome A.C.M. (Wellington and Magdalen)	1888–9
Crutchley G.E.V. (Harrow and New College)	1912
Cullinan M.R. (Hilton College, S. Africa and Worcester)	1983–4
Cunliffe F.H.E. (Eton and New College), captain in 1898	1895–8
Currer C.S. (Harrow and Balliol)	1847
Curteis H.M. (Westminster and Christ Church)	1841–2
Curtis I.J. (Whitgift and Lincoln)	1980, 1982
Curwen W.J.H. (Charterhouse and Magdalen)	1906
Cushing V.G.B. (King's College School, Wimbledon and Oriel)	1973
Cuthbertson J.L. (Rugby and Worcester)	1962–3
Darnell N. (Winchester and Exeter)	1838–40
Darwall-Smith R.F.H. (Charterhouse and Brasenose)	1935–8

Daubeny E.T. (Bromsgrove and Exeter) 1861–2
Dauglish M.J. (Harrow and Magdalen) 1889–90
Davenport E. (Rugby and Trinity) 1866
Davidson W.W. (Brighton and Wadham) 1947–8
Davies P.H. (Brighton and Queen's) 1913–14
Davies W.H. (Charterhouse and Christ Church) 1846–8
Davis F.J. (Blundell's and St John's) 1963
Dawson T.A.J. (Mill Hill and Linacre) 1986
Delisle G.P.S. (Stonyhurst and Lincoln) 1955–6
de Montmorency R.H. (Cheltenham, St Paul's and Keble) 1899
Denison H. (Eton and Christ Church) 1829
Denne T. (Private and Christ Church) 1827
de Saram F.C. (Royal College, Colombo and Keble) 1934–5
Des Voeux H.D. (Harrow and Balliol) 1844
Digby K.E. (Harrow and Corpus Christi) 1857–9
Digby R. (Harrow and New College) 1867–9
Dillon E.W. (Rugby and University) 1901–2
Divecha R.V. (Podar HS, Bombay U and Worcester) 1950–1
Dixon E.J.H. (St Edward's Oxford and Christ Church), captain in 1939 1937–9
Dolphin J.M. (Marlborough and Oriel) 1860
Donnelly M.P. (New Plymouth BHS, Canterbury U and Worcester), captain in 1947 1946–7
Dowding A.L. (St Peter's, Adelaide and Balliol), captain in 1953 1952–3
Drybrough C.D. (Highgate and Worcester), captain in 1961–2 1960–2
Dryden A.E. (Winchester and Trinity) 1841–3
Duff A.R. (Radley and Lincoln) 1960–1
Durell J.D. (Westminster and New Inn Hall) 1838
Dury T.S. (Harrow and St John's) 1876
Dyer A.W. (Mill Hill and St Catherine's) 1965–6
Dyson E.M. (QEGS, Wakefield and Keble) 1958
Dyson J.H. (Charterhouse and Christ Church) 1936

Eagar E.D.R. (Cheltenham and Brasenose) 1939
Eagar M.A. (Rugby and Worcester) 1956–9
Easter J.N.C. (St Edward's, Oxford and Christ Church) 1967–8
Eccles A. (Repton and Trinity) 1897–9
Edbrooke R.M. (Queen Elizabeth's Hospital and Hertford) 1984
Eden F.M. (Rugby, Eton and Christ Church) 1850–1
Edwards P.G. (Canford and Christ Church) 1987–8
Eggar J.D. (Winchester and Trinity) 1938
Ellis R.G.P. (Haileybury and St Edmund Hall), captain in 1982 1981–3
Ellis W.W. (Rugby and Brasenose) 1827
Elviss R.W. (Leeds GS and Trinity) 1966–7
Evans A.H. (Rossall, Clifton and Oriel), captain in 1881 1878–81
Evans A.J. (Winchester and Oriel), captain in 1911 1909–12
Evans E.N. (Haileybury and Wadham) 1932
Evans F.R. (Cheltenham, Rugby and Exeter) 1863–5
Evans G. (St Asaph and Brasenose) 1939
Evans W.H.B. (Malvern and Oriel), captain in 1904 1902–5
Evelyn F.L. (Rugby and Oriel) 1880
Evetts W. (Harrow and Brasenose) 1868–9
Ezekowitz R.A.B. (Westville BHS, Durban, Cape Town U and Wolfson) 1980–1

Faber M.J.J. (Eton and Balliol) 1972
Fane F.L. (Charterhouse and Magdalen) 1897–8
Fasken D.K. (Wellington and Trinity) 1953–5
Fellowes E.L. (Marlborough and Brasenose), captain in 1868 1865–6, 1868
Fellows W. (Westminster and Christ Church) 1854–7
Fellows-Smith J.P. (Durban HS, S. Africa and Brasenose) 1953–5
Fiennes Hon. W.S.T.W. (Winchester and New College) 1856–8

Fillary E.W.J. (St Lawrence, Ramsgate and Oriel)   1963–5
Findlay W. (Eton and Oriel), captain in 1903   1901–3
Firth T. (Stockport GS and Oriel)   1987
Fisher C.D. (Westminster and Christ Church)   1900
Fisher P.B. (St Ignatius, Enfield and Christ Church)   1975–8
Foord-Kelcey W. (Chatham House, Ramsgate and Exeter)   1874–5
Forbes D.H. (Eton and Christ Church)   1894
Ford G.J. (King's College School and Exeter)   1839–40
Ford N.M. (Harrow and Oriel)   1928–30
Forster H.W. (Eton and New College)   1887–9
Fortescue A.T. (Marlborough and Christ Church)   1868–70
Foster G.N. (Malvern and Worcester)   1905–8
Foster H.K. (Malvern and Trinity)   1894–6
Foster R.E. (Malvern and University), captain in 1900   1897–1900
Fowler G. (Clifton and Oriel)   1888
Fowler H. (Clifton and New College)   1877, 1879–80
Fox R.W. (Wellington and Merton)   1897–8
Francis C.K. (Rugby and Brasenose)   1870–3
Franklin H.W.F. (Christ's Hospital and Christ Church)   1924
Franks J.G. (Stamford and St Edmund Hall)   1984–5
Fraser J.N. (C of E GS Melbourne, Melbourne U and Magdalen)   1912–13
Frazer J.E. (Winchester and Balliol)   1924
Frederick J. St J. (Eton and Christ Church)   1864, 1867
Fry C.A. (Repton and Trinity)   1959–61
Fry C.B. (Repton and Wadham), captain in 1894   1892–5
Fuller G.P. (Winchester and Christ Church)   1854–5
Fuller-Maitland W. (Harrow and Christ Church), captain in 1867   1864–7
Fursdon E.D. (Sherborne and St John's)   1974–5

Gamble N.W. (Stockport GS and St Edmund Hall)   1967
Game W.H. (Sherborne and Oriel), captain in 1876   1873–6
Garland-Wells H.M. (St Paul's and Pembroke)   1928–30
Garnett C.A. (Cheltenham and Trinity)   1860–2
Garnier E.S. (Marlborough and University)   1873
Garnier T.P. (Winchester and Balliol)   1861–3
Garofall A.R. (Latymer Upper and St Edmund Hall)   1967–8
Garth R. (Eton and Christ Church), captain in 1840–1   1839–41
Garthwaite P.F. (Wellington and Brasenose)   1929
Gibbon J.H. (Harrow and Brasenose)   1869
Gibbs P.J.K. (Hanley GS and University)   1964–6
Gibson I.M. (Manchester GS and Brasenose)   1955–8
Gilbert H.A. (Charterhouse and Christ Church)   1907–9
Gillett H.H. (Winchester and Exeter)   1857–8
Gilliat I.A.W. (Charterhouse and Magdalen)   1925
Gilliat R.M.C. (Charterhouse and Christ Church), captain in 1966   1964–7
Gilligan F.W. (Dulwich and Worcester), captain in 1920   1919–20
Glover T.R. (Lancaster RGS and Lincoln), captain in 1975   1973–5
Goldstein F.S. (Falcon, Rhodesia and St Edmund Hall), captain in 1968–9   1966–9
Gordon J.H. (Winchester and Magdalen)   1906–7
Goring C. (Winchester and Christ Church)   1836
Green D.M. (Manchester GS and Brasenose)   1959–60
Greene A.D. (Clifton and Exeter), captain in 1880   1877–80
Greenstock J.W. (Malvern and Brasenose)   1925–7
Gresson F.H. (Winchester and Oriel)   1887–9
Grimston Hon. E.H. (Harrow and Christ Church)   1836
Grimston Hon. R. (Harrow and Christ Church)   1838
Grover J.N. (Winchester and Brasenose), captain in 1938   1936–8
Groves M.G.M. (Diocesan College, S. Africa and St Edmund Hall)   1964–6
Guest M.R.J. (Rugby and Magdalen)   1964–6

Guise J.L. (Winchester and Brasenose), captain in 1925	1924–5
Gurr D.R. (Aylesbury GS and Regent's Park)	1976–7
Hadow W.H. (Harrow and Brasenose)	1870–2
Hagan D.A. (Trinity, Leamington and St Edmund Hall)	1986, 1988
Hale T.W. (Rugby and St John's)	1851–2
Halliday J.G. (City of Oxford HS and Merton)	1935
Halliday S.J. (Downside and St Benet's)	1980
Hamblin C.B. (King's, Canterbury and Keble)	1971–3
Hamilton A.C. (Charterhouse and St Peter's)	1975
Hamilton W.D. (Haileybury and Queen's)	1882
Hanbury O.R. (Rugby and Trinity)	1849
Hankey R. (Harrow and Balliol), captain in 1855	1853, 1855
Hare J.H.M. (Uppingham and Exeter)	1879
Harris C.R. (Buckingham RLS and Keble)	1964
Harris Hon. G.R.C. (Eton and Christ Church)	1871–2, 1874
Harrison G.C. (Clifton and Oriel)	1880–1
Hart T.M. (Strathallan and Brasenose)	1931–2
Hartley J.C. (Tonbridge and Brasenose)	1896–7
Haskett-Smith A. (Eton and Non-Collegiate)	1879
Hatfeild C.E. (Eton and New College)	1908
Hayes K.A. (QEGS, Blackburn and Merton), captain in 1984	1981–4
Haygarth J.W. (Winchester and Corpus Christi)	1862–4
Heal M.G. (St Brendan's, Bristol and St Edmund Hall)	1970, 1972
Heard H. (Queen Elizabeth Hospital School and Exeter)	1969–70
Heath A.H. (Clifton and Brasenose)	1876–9
Hedges L.P. (Tonbridge and Trinity)	1920–2
Henderson D. (St Edward's, Oxford and Trinity)	1950
Henderson I.M. (Laxton and Pembroke)	1987
Henley D.F. (Harrow and Trinity)	1947
Henley F.A.H. (Forest and Oriel)	1905
Heseltine P.G. (Holgate GS and Keble)	1983
Hewetson E.P. (Shrewsbury and Pembroke)	1923–5
Hewett H.T. (Harrow and Trinity)	1886
Hildyard H.C.T. (Eton and Merton)	1845–6
Hildyard L.d'A. (Private and Magdalen)	1884–6
Hill F.H. (Bradfield and Oriel)	1867, 1869–70
Hill V.T. (Winchester and Oriel)	1892
Hill-Wood C.K. (Eton and Christ Church)	1928–30
Hill-Wood D.J. (Eton and Christ Church)	1928
Hiller R.B. (Bec and St Edmund Hall)	1966
Hine-Haycock T.R. (Wellington and New College)	1883–4
Hirst E.T. (Rugby and Balliol)	1878–80
Hobbs J.A.D. (Liverpool College and St Peter's)	1957
Hodgkinson G.L. (Harrow and Pembroke)	1857–9
Hofmeyr M.B. (Pretoria, S. Africa and Worcester), captain in 1951	1949–51
Holdsworth R.L. (Repton and Magdalen)	1919–22
Hollins A.M. (Eton and Hertford)	1899
Hollins F.H. (Eton and Magdalen)	1901
Holmes E.R.T. (Malvern and Trinity), captain in 1927	1925–7
Hone B.W. (Adelaide U and New College), captain in 1933	1931–3
Honywood R. (Eton and Trinity)	1845–7
Hooman C.V.L. (Charterhouse and Brasenose)	1909–10
Hopkins H.O. (St Peter's, Adelaide and Magdalen)	1923
Hore A.H. (Tonbridge and Trinity)	1851
Howell M. (Repton and Oriel), captain in 1919	1914, 1919
Hughes G.E. (Rugby and Oriel)	1845
Hughes T. (Rugby and Oriel)	1842
Hume E. (Marlborough and Trinity)	1861–2

Hurst C.S. (Uppingham and Exeter), captain in 1909   1907–9
Huxford P.N. (Richard Hale and Christ Church)   1981

Imran Khan (Aitchison College, Lahore, Worcester RGS and Keble), captain in 1974   1973–5
Inge F.G. (Charterhouse and Christ Church)   1861–3
Inge W. (Shrewsbury and Worcester)   1853
Isherwood F.W. (Rugby and Brasenose)   1872

Jack T. (Aquinas College, Perth and Keble)   1988
Jackson K.L.T. (Rugby and Trinity)   1934
Jakobson T.R. (Charterhouse and University)   1961
Jardine D.R. (Winchester and New College)   1920–1, 1923
Jardine M.R. (Fettes and Balliol), captain in 1891   1889–92
Jarrett D.W. (Wellington and Worcester)   1975
Jellicoe F.G.G. (Haileybury and New College)   1877, 1879
Jenkins V.G.J. (Llandovery and Jesus)   1933
Johns R.L. (St Albans, Keele U and St Edmund Hall)   1970
Jones A.K.C. (Solihull and St Edmund Hall), captain in 1973   1971–3
Jones M. (Harrow and University)   1849–50
Jones P.C.H. (Milton HS, Rhodesia, Rhodes U and St Edmund Hall), captain in 1972   1971–2
Jones R.T. (Eton and New College)   1892
Jones T.B. (Dublin U and Jesus)   1874
Jones-Bateman R.L. (Winchester and Trinity)   1846, 1848
Jose A.D. (Adelaide U and Brasenose)   1950–1
Jowett D.C.P.R. (Sherborne and St John's)   1952–5
Jowett R.L. (Bradford GS and Magdalen)   1957–9

Kamm A. (Charterhouse and Worcester)   1954
Kardar A.H. (Islamia College, Punjab U and University)   1947–9
Kayum D.A. (Selhurst GS, Chatham House GS and Lincoln)   1977–8
Keighley W.G. (Eton and Trinity)   1947–8
Kelly G.W.F. (Stonyhurst and Lincoln)   1901–2
Kemp C.W.M. (Harrow and Oriel)   1878
Kemp M.C. (Harrow and Hertford), captain in 1883–4   1881–4
Kenny-Herbert E.M. (Rugby and Merton)   1866–8
Kentish E.S.M. (Cornwall College, Jamaica and St John's)   1956
Ker R.J.C.R. (Eton and Corpus Christi)   1842
Key K.J. (Clifton and Oriel)   1884–7
Khan A.J. (Aitchison College, Lahore; Punjab U and Keble)   1968–9
Kilborn M.J. (Farrer Agricultural College, New South Wales U and St John's), captain in 1988   1986–8
Kimpton R.C.M. (Melbourne GS and Brasenose)   1935, 1937–8
Kingsley P.G.T. (Winchester and New College), captain in 1930   1928–30
Kinkead-Weekes R.C. (Eton and Lincoln)   1972
Knatchbull H.E. (Winchester and Wadham)   1827, 1829
Knight D.J. (Malvern and Trinity)   1914, 1919
Knight J.M. (Oundle and Worcester)   1979
Knight N.S. (Uppingham and Wadham)   1934
Knight R.L. (Clifton and Corpus Christi)   1878
Knott C.H. (Tonbridge and Brasenose), captain in 1924   1922–4
Knott F.H. (Tonbridge and Brasenose), captain in 1914   1912–14
Knox F.P. (Dulwich and Corpus Christi), captain in 1901   1899–1901

Lagden R.O. (Marlborough and Oriel)   1909–12
Lamb Hon. T.M. (Shrewsbury and Queen's)   1973–4
Lane C.G. (Westminster and Christ Church), captain in 1859–60   1856, 1858–60
Lang T.W. (Clifton and Balliol)   1874–5
Law A.P. (Rugby and Corpus Christi)   1857
Law W. (Harrow and Brasenose), captain in 1874   1871–4
Lawrence M.P. (Manchester GS and Merton)   1984–6

Lear F. (Winchester and Christ Church) 1843–4
Le Couteur P.R. (Warrnambool Academy and University) 1909–11
Lee E.C. (Winchester and University) 1898
Lee G.B. (Winchester and New College), captain in 1839 1838–9
Lee R.J. (Sydney GS, Sydney U and Worcester) 1972–4
Legard A.R. (Winchester and Trinity) 1932, 1935
Legge G.B. (Malvern and Brasenose), captain in 1926 1925–6
Leigh E.C. (Harrow and Oriel) 1852–4
Leslie C.F.H. (Rugby and Oriel) 1881–3
Leslie J. (Harrow and Christ Church) 1843
L'Estrange M.G. (St Aloysius College, Sydney U and Worcester) 1977, 1979
Leveson-Gower H.D.G. (Winchester and Magdalen), captain in 1896 1893–6
Lewis C.P. (Llandovery, King's Gloucester and Jesus) 1876
Lewis D.J. (Cape Town U, S. Africa and Corpus Christi) 1951
Lewis R.P. (Winchester and University) 1894–6
Lewis W.H. (Harrow and Trinity) 1827
Lindsay W.O'B. (Harrow and Balliol) 1931
Linton H. (Harrow and Wadham) 1858–9
Linton S. (Rugby and Wadham) 1861–2
Lipscombe W.H. (Marlborough and University) 1868
Llewelyn W.D. (Eton and New College) 1890–1
Lloyd M.F.D. (Magdalen College School and Magdalen) 1974
Loch C.R.F. (Edinburgh Academy, Rugby and University) 1846, 1848
Loftus Lord H.Y.A. (Harrow and Oriel) 1841
Lomas J.M. (Charterhouse and New College) 1938–9
Longe F.D. (Harrow and Oriel) 1851–2
Lowe J.C.M. (Uppingham and Oriel) 1907–9
Lowndes R. (Winchester and Christ Church) 1841
Lowndes W.G.L.F. (Eton and New College) 1921
Lowth A.J. (Eton, Winchester and Exeter) 1838, 1840–1
Luddington R.S. (KCS, Wimbledon and St Edmund Hall) 1982
Lyon B.H. (Rugby and Queen's) 1922–3
Lyon G.W.F. (Brighton and Wadham) 1925

McBride W.N. (Westminster and Christ Church) 1926
McCanlis M.A. (Cranleigh and St Edmund Hall), captain in 1928 1926–8
Macindoe D.H. (Eton and Christ Church), captain in 1946 1937–9, 1946
McIntosh R.I.F. (Uppingham and University) 1927–8
McIver C.D. (Forest and Hertford) 1903–4
McKinna G.H. (Manchester GS and Brasenose) 1953
McLachlan N. (Loretto and Keble), captain in 1882 1879–82
MacLarnon P.C. (Loughborough GS and St Peter's) 1985
Maitland W.F. (Brighton, Harrow and Christ Church), captain in 1867 1864–7
Majendie N.L. (Winchester and Christ Church) 1962–3
Mallett A.W.H. (Dulwich and Brasenose) 1947–8
Mallett N.V.H. (St Andrew's College, Cape Town U and University) 1981
Manasseh M. (Epsom and Oriel) 1964
Marcon W. (Eton and Worcester) 1844
Marie G.V. (Western Australia U, Reading U and Wolfson), captain in 1979 but did not play 1978
Marks V.J. (Blundell's and St John's), captain in 1976–7 1975–8
Marriott C. (Winchester and Brasenose) 1871
Marriott G.S. (Winchester and Brasenose) 1878
Marsden R. (Merchant Taylors' and Christ Church) 1982
Marshall J.C. (Rugby and Brasenose) 1953
Marsham A.J.B. (Eton and Christ Church) 1939
Marsham C.D.B. (Private and Merton), captain in 1857–8 1854–8
Marsham C.H.B. (Eton and Christ Church), captain in 1902 1900–2
Marsham C.J.B. (Private and Merton) 1851
Marsham R.H.B. (Private and Merton) 1856

Marsland G.P. (Rossall and Lincoln)	1954
Martin E.G. (Eton and New College)	1903–6
Martin J.D. (Magdalen College School and St Edmund Hall), captain in 1965	1962–3, 1965
Martyn H. (Exeter GS and Exeter)	1899–1900
Mathews E. (Harrow and Brasenose)	1868–9
Matthews M.H. (Westminster and Christ Church)	1936–7
Maude J. (Eton and Lincoln)	1873
Maudsley R.H. (Malvern and Brasenose)	1946–7
May B. (Prince Edward's, Salisbury, Cape Town U and Brasenose), captain in 1971	1970–2
Mayhew J.F.N. (Eton and Brasenose)	1930
Medlicott W.S. (Harrow and Magdalen)	1902
Mee A.A.G. (Merchant Taylors' and Oriel)	1986
Mellé B.G. von B. (S. African College School, Cape Town and Brasenose)	1913–14
Melville A. (Michaelhouse, S. Africa and Trinity), captain in 1931–2	1930–3
Melville C.D.M. (Michaelhouse, S. Africa and Trinity)	1957
Metcalfe S.G. (Leeds GS and Pembroke)	1956
Miles R.F. (Marlborough and Trinity)	1867–9
Millener D.J. (Auckland GS, Auckland U and St Catherine's)	1969–70
Miller A.J.T. (Haileybury and St Edmund Hall), captain in 1985	1983–5
Mills B.S.T. (Harrow and Christ Church)	1841–3
Minns R.E.F. (King's, Canterbury and Corpus Christi)	1962–3
Mitchell R.A.H. (Eton and Balliol), captain in 1863–5	1862–5
Mitchell W.M. (Dulwich and Merton)	1951–2
Mitchell-Innes N.S. (Sedbergh and Brasenose), captain in 1936	1934–7
Moberly H.E. (Winchester and New College)	1842–5
Monro R.W. (Harrow and Balliol)	1860
Moore D.N. (Shrewsbury and Queen's), captain in 1931 but did not play	1930
Mordaunt G.J. (Wellington and University), captain in 1895	1893–6
More R.E. (Westminster and Christ Church)	1900–1
Morgan A.H. (Hastings GS and St Edmund Hall)	1969
Morley J.W. (Marlborough and Brasenose)	1859–60
Morres E.J. (Winchester and Trinity)	1850
Morris R.E. (Dyffryn Conwy, Llanrwst and Oriel)	1987
Morrill N.D. (Sandown GS, Millfield and Lincoln)	1979
Moss R.H. (Radley and Keble)	1889
Moulding R.P. (Haberdashers' Aske's and Christ Church), captain in 1981	1978–83
Mountford P.N.G. (Bromsgrove and Keble)	1963
Munn J.S. (Forest and Hertford)	1901
Murray-Wood W. (Mill Hill and Oriel)	1936
Musters W.M. (Eton and Corpus Christi)	1829
Napier C.W.A. (Harrow and Christ Church)	1838–9
Naumann F.C.G. (Malvern and Trinity)	1914, 1919
Neate F.W. (St Paul's and Brasenose)	1961–62
Nepean C.E.B. (Charterhouse and University)	1873
Nepean E.A. (Sherborne and University)	1887–8
Neser V.H. (S. African College, Cape Town and Brasenose)	1921
Nethercote H.O. (Charterhouse, Harrow and Balliol)	1840–1
Newman G.C. (Eton and Christ Church)	1926–7
Newton A.E. (Eton and Pembroke)	1885
Newton-Thompson J.O. (Diocesan College, Cape Town and Trinity)	1946
Nicholls B.E. (Winchester and Magdalen)	1884
Niven R.A. (Berkhamsted and New College)	1968–9, 1973
Nunn J.A. (Sherborne and New College)	1926–7
Nuttall J.D. (Pocklington and St Peter's)	1988
O'Brien T.C. (St Charles' College, Notting Hill and New Inn Hall)	1884–5
Oldfield P.C. (Repton and University)	1932–3
Oliver F.W. (Westminster and Christ Church)	1856–7

Orders J.O.D. (Winchester and Trinity) — 1978–81
Ottaway C.J. (Eton and Brasenose), captain in 1873 — 1870–3
Owen-Smith H.G. (Diocesan College, S. Africa and Magdalen) — 1931–3

Page H.V. (Cheltenham and Wadham), captain in 1885–6 — 1883–6
Palairet L.C.H. (Repton and Oriel), captain in 1892–3 — 1890–3
Palairet R.C.N. (Repton and Oriel) — 1893–4
Papillon J. (Winchester and University) — 1827
Parker W.W. (Rugby and Merton) — 1852–3, 1855
Nawab of Pataudi (Snr) (Chief's College, Lahore and Balliol) — 1929–31
Nawab of Pataudi (Jnr) (Winchester and Balliol), captain in 1961 when he did not play, and in 1963 — 1960, 1963
Pathmanathan G. (Royal College Colombo, Sri Lanka U and University) — 1975–8
Patten M. (Winchester and Christ Church) — 1922–3
Patterson J.I. (Chatham House, Ramsgate and Pembroke) — 1882
Patterson W.H. (Chatham House, Ramsgate; Harrow and Pembroke) — 1880–1
Patteson J.C. (Eton and Balliol) — 1849
Pauncefote B. (Rugby and Bransenose), captain in 1869–70 — 1868–71
Paver R.G.L. (Fort Victoria HS, Rhodes U and Pembroke) — 1973–4
Pawson A.C. (Winchester and Christ Church) — 1903
Pawson A.G. (Winchester and Christ Church), captain in 1910 — 1908–11
Pawson H.A. (Winchester and Christ Church), captain in 1948 — 1947–8
Payne A. (Private and Trinity), captain in 1856 — 1852, 1854–6
Payne A.F. (Private and Trinity) — 1855
Payne C.A.L. (Charterhouse and New College) — 1906–7
Peake E. (Marlborough and Oriel) — 1881–3
Pearce J.P. (Ampleforth and St Benet's) — 1979
Pearse G.V. (Maritzburg College, Natal and Brasenose) — 1919
Pearson A. (Loretto, Rugby and Balliol) — 1876–7
Peat C.U. (Sedbergh and Trinity) — 1913
Peebles I.A.R. (Glasgow Academy and Brasenose) — 1930
Peel H.R. (Eton and Christ Church) — 1851–2
Pelham S. (Harrow and Magdalen) — 1871
Pepys J.A. (Eton and Christ Church) — 1861
Pershke W.J. (Uppingham and Brasenose) — 1938
Petchey M.D. (Latymer Upper and Christ Church) — 1983
Pether S. (Magdalen College School and St Peter's) — 1939
Philipson H. (Eton and New College), captain in 1889 — 1887–9
Phillips F.A. (Rossall and Exeter) — 1892, 1894–5
Phillips J.B.M. (King's, Canterbury and St Edmund Hall) — 1955
Piachaud J.D. (St Thomas', Colombo and Keble) — 1958–61
Pilkington C.C. (Eton and Magdalen) — 1896
Pilkington H.C. (Eton and Magdalen) — 1899–1900
Pilkington W. (Midhurst and Trinity) — 1827
Pithey D.B. (Plumtree HS, Cape Town U and St Edmund Hall) — 1961–2
Pole E. (Winchester and Exeter) — 1827
Popham F.L. (Harrow and University) — 1829
Porter S.R. (Peers School, Littlemore and St Edmund Hall) — 1973
Potter I.C. (King's, Canterbury and Corpus Christi) — 1961–2
Potts H.J. (Stand GS and Keble) — 1950
Price R. (Winchester and New College) — 1827, 1829
Price V.R. (Bishop's Stortford and Magdalen), captain in 1921 — 1919–22
Proud R.B. (Winchester and Brasenose) — 1939
Pulman W.W. (Marlborough and St John's) — 1874–5
Pycroft J. (Bath and Trinity) — 1836

Quinlan J.D. (Sherborne and St Peter's) — 1985

Raikes D.C.G. (Shrewsbury and Queen's) — 1931

Raikes G.B. (Shrewsbury and Magdalen)	1894–5
Raikes T.B. (Winchester and Trinity)	1922–4
Randolph B.M. (Charterhouse and Christ Church)	1855–6
Randolph C. (Eton and Christ Church)	1844–5
Randolph J. (Westminster and Brasenose)	1843
Randolph L.C. (Westminster and Christ Church)	1845
Ranken R.B. (Edinburgh Academy and Balliol)	1860
Raphael J.E. (Merchant Taylors' and St John's)	1903–5
Rashleigh J. (Harrow and Balliol), fielded substitute for R. Garth (who batted) and was allowed to bowl	1842
Rashleigh W. (Tonbridge and Brasenose), captain in 1888	1886–9
Rawlinson G. (Ealing and Trinity)	1836
Rawlinson H.T. (Eton and Christ Church)	1983–4
Raybould J.G. (Leeds GS and New College)	1959
Reade H. St J. (Tonbridge and University), captain in 1862	1861–2
Reid R.T. (Cheltenham and Magdalen)	1866–8
Reynolds G.D. (Wellington and University)	1988
Rice R.W. (Cardiff and Jesus)	1893
Richardson J.V. (Uppingham and Brasenose)	1925
Ricketts G.W. (Winchester and Oriel)	1887
Ridding A. (Winchester and New College)	1846–50
Ridding C.H. (Winchester, Trinity and Magdalen)	1845–9
Ridding W. (Winchester and New College), captain in 1849 and 1852, and also in 1851 when he did not play	1849–50, 1852–3
Ridge S.P. (Dr Challenor's GS and Worcester)	1982
Ridley A.W. (Eton and Christ Church), captain in 1875	1872–5
Ridley G.N.S. (Milton HS, Rhodesia and Pembroke), captain in 1967	1965–8
Ridley R.M. (Clifton and St Edmund Hall)	1968–70
Ridsdale S.O.B. (Tonbridge and Wadham)	1862
Robertson G.P. (Rugby and Trinity)	1866
Robertson J.C. (Winchester and University)	1829
Robertson-Glasgow R.C. (Charterhouse and Corpus Christi)	1920–3
Robinson G.A. (Preston Catholic College and Pembroke)	1971
Robinson G.E. (Burton and Jesus)	1881–3
Robinson H.B.O. (North Shore College, Vancouver and Oriel)	1947–8
Robinson R.L. (St Peter's, Adelaide, Adelaide U and Magdalen)	1908–9
Rogers J.J. (Sedbergh and University)	1979–81
Ross C.J. (Wanganui CS, Wellington U and Magdalen), captain in 1980	1978–80
Royle V.P.F.A. (Rossall and Brasenose)	1875–6
Rücker C.E.S. (Charterhouse and University)	1914
Rücker P.W. (Charterhouse and University)	1919
Rudd C.R.D. (Eton and Trinity)	1949
Ruggles-Brise H.G. (Winchester and Balliol)	1883
Rumbold J.S. (St Andrew's College, NZ and Brasenose)	1946
Russell H.S. (Harrow and Christ Church)	1839
Rutnagur R.S. (Westminster and New College)	1985–6
Rydon R.A. (Sherborne and Pembroke)	1986
Ryle J.C. (Eton and Christ Church)	1836, 1838
Sabine P.N.B. (Marlborough and Hertford)	1963
Sale R. (Repton and St John's)	1910
Sale R. (Repton and Oriel)	1939, 1946
Salter M.G. (Cheltenham and Hertford)	1909–10
Salvi N.V. (Rossall and Christ Church)	1986
Samson O.M. (Cheltenham and Hertford)	1903
Sanderson J.F.W. (Westminster and New College)	1980
Sandford E.G. (Rugby and Christ Church)	1859, 1861
Sankey P.M. (King's, Canterbury and Corpus Christi)	1852
Sardesai R.D. (St Xavier's College, Bombay, Bombay U and University)	1987

Saunders C.J. (Lancing and Wadham)	1964
Savage R. Le Q. (Marlborough and Pembroke)	1976–8
Savory J.H. (Winchester and Trinity)	1877–8
Sayer D.M. (Maidstone GS and Brasenose)	1958–60
Schwann H.S. (Clifton and Corpus Christi)	1890
Scott Lord George (Eton and Christ Church)	1887–9
Scott J. (Bruce Castle and Pembroke)	1863
Scott K.B. (Winchester and Trinity)	1937
Scott M.D. (Winchester and Worcester)	1957
Scott R.S.G. (Winchester and Magdalen)	1931
Seamer J.W. (Marlborough and Brasenose)	1934–6
Seitz J.A. (Scotch College, Melbourne U and Merton)	1909
Shaw E.A. (Marlborough and Brasenose)	1912, 1914
Shaw E.D. (Forest and Oriel)	1882
Sibthorp G.T.W. (Harrow and Oriel)	1836
Simpson E.T.B. (Harrow and Pembroke)	1888
Sinclair E.H. (Winchester and Brasenose)	1924
Singleton A.P. (Shrewsbury and Brasenose), captain in 1937	1934–7
Siviter K. (Liverpool and Keble)	1976
Skeet C.H.L. (St Paul's and Merton)	1920
Skene R.W. (Sedbergh and New College)	1928
Smith A.C. (King Edward's, Birmingham and Brasenose), captain in 1959–60	1958–60
Smith E. (Clifton and University)	1890–1
Smith G.O. (Charterhouse and Keble)	1895–6
Smith M.J.K. (Stamford and St Edmund Hall), captain in 1956	1954–6
Smith V.S.C. (Winchester and New College), captain in 1846–7	1844–7
Soames S. (Rugby and Trinity)	1846–7
Spencer-Smith O. (Eton and Oriel)	1866
Spinks T. (Merchant Taylors' and St John's)	1840
Stainton R.G. (Malvern and Brasenose)	1933
Stallibrass M.J.D. (Lancing and Magdalen)	1974
Stanning J. (Winchester and Christ Church)	1939
Stephenson J.S. (Shrewsbury and University)	1925–6
Stevens G.T.S. (University College School and Brasenose), captain in 1922	1920–3
Stewart W.A. (Winchester and Oriel)	1869–70
Stewart-Brown P.H. (Harrow and Magdalen)	1925–6
Stocks F.W. (Lancing, Denstone and New College)	1898–9
Sutcliffe S.P. (King George V GS, Southport and Lincoln)	1980–1
Sutton M.A. (Ampleforth and Worcester)	1946
Sygrove M.R. (Lutterworth GS and St John's)	1988
Taswell H.J. (Rugby and Christ Church)	1851
Tavaré C.J. (Sevenoaks and St John's)	1975–7
Taylor C.H. (Westminster and Christ Church)	1923–6
Taylor T.J. (Stockport GS and Magdalen)	1981–2
Teape A.S. (Eton and Exeter)	1863–5
Teesdale H. (Winchester and Oriel)	1908
Thackeray P.R. (St Edward's, Oxford, Exeter U and Keble)	1974
Thesiger F.J.N. 1st Viscount Chelmsford (Winchester and Magdalen), captain in 1890. Began to play in 1891 game but was injured soon after the start. His place was taken by T.B. Case	1888, 1890
Thomas R.J.A. (Radley and Corpus Christi)	1965
Thorne D.A. (Bablake and Keble), captain in 1986	1984–6
Thornton W.A. (Winchester and St John's)	1879–82
Tindall R.G. (Winchester and Trinity)	1933–4
Toft D.P. (Tonbridge and University)	1966–7
Toogood G.J. (N. Bromsgrove HS and Lincoln), captain in 1983	1982–5
Tooley C.D.M. (St Dunstan's and Magdalen), captain in 1987	1985–7
Topham R.D.N. (Shrewsbury, Australian National U and St Edmund Hall)	1976

Torre H.J. (Harrow and University)	1839–40
Townsend D.C.H. (Winchester and New College)	1933–4
Townsend W.H. (Rugby and Lincoln)	1842–3
Townshend W. (Rossall and Brasenose)	1870–2
Traill W.F. (Merchant Taylors' and St John's)	1858–60
Travers B.H. (Sydney U and New College)	1946, 1948
Trevor A.H. (Winchester and Corpus Christi)	1880–1
Tritton E.W. (Eton and Christ Church), captain in 1866	1864–7
Trower C.F. (Winchester and Exeter)	1838
Tuff F.N. (Malvern & Brasenose)	1910
Twining R.H. (Eton and Magdalen), captain in 1912	1910–13
Tylecote E.F.S. (Clifton and St John's), captain in 1871–2	1869–72
Tylecote H.G. (Clifton and New College)	1874–7
Udal N.R. (Winchester and New College)	1905–6
Vance G. (Eton and Exeter)	1836, 1838
van der Bijl P.G. (Diocesan College, S. Africa and Brasenose)	1932
van Ryneveld C.B. (Diocesan College, S. Africa and University), captain in 1949	1948–50
Varey J.G. (Birkenhead and St Edmund Hall)	1982–3
Veitch H.G.J. (Twyford and Balliol)	1854–6
Vidler J.L.S. (Repton and Oriel)	1910–12
von Ernsthausen A.C. (Uppingham and Balliol)	1902–4
Voules S.C. (Marlborough and Lincoln)	1863–6
Waddy P.S. (King's School, Parramatta and Balliol)	1896–7
Wagstaffe M.C. (Rossall, Exeter U and St Edmund Hall)	1972
Waldock F.A. (Uppingham and Hertford)	1919–20
Walford M.M. (Rugby and Trinity)	1936, 1938
Walker D.F. (Uppingham and Brasenose), captain in 1935	1933–5
Walker J.G. (Loretto and Trinity)	1882–3
Walker R.D. (Harrow and Brasenose)	1861–5
Wallace A. (Winchester and Trinity)	1851
Waller G. de W. (Hurstpierpoint and Worcester)	1974
Wallington E.W. (Sherborne and Oriel)	1877
Wallroth C.A. (Harrow and Brasenose)	1872–4
Walsh D.R. (Marlborough and Brasenose)	1967–9
Walshe A.P. (Milton HS, Rhodesia and Wadham)	1953, 1955–6
Walter A.F. (Eton and Christ Church)	1869
Walton A.C. (Radley and Lincoln), captain in 1957	1955–7
Ward H.P. (Shrewsbury and St John's)	1919, 1921
Ward J.M. (Newcastle-under-Lyme HS and Mansfield)	1971–3
Ward Lord (Eton and Christ Church)	1841–2
Warner P.F. (Rugby and Oriel)	1895–6
Watson A.G.M. (St Lawrence, Ramsgate and Corpus Christi)	1965–6, 1968
Watson A.K. (Harrow and Balliol)	1889
Watson H.D. (Harrow and Balliol)	1891
Waud B.W. (Eton and University)	1857–60
Weale S.D. (Westminster City and Keble)	1987–8
Webb H.E. (Winchester and New College)	1948
Webbe A.J. (Harrow and Trinity), captain in 1877–8	1875–8
Webbe H.R. (Winchester and New College), captain in 1879	1877–9
Wellings E.M. (Cheltenham and Christ Church)	1929, 1931
Westley S.A. (Lancaster RGS and Corpus Christi)	1968–9
Wheatley G.A. (Uppingham and Balliol)	1946
Whitby H.O. (Leamington and Lincoln)	1884–7
Whitcombe P.A. (Winchester and Christ Church)	1947–9
Whitcombe P.J. (Worcester RGS and Hertford)	1951–2
White H. (Denstone and Keble)	1900

Whitehouse P.M. (Marlborough and New College)   1938
Whiting A.O. (Sherborne and Merton)   1881–2
Wickham A.P. (Marlborough and New College)   1878
Wiley W.G.E. (Diocesan College, S. Africa and Lincoln)   1952
Wilkinson W.A.C. (Eton and University)   1913
Willes E.H.L. (Winchester and Wadham), captain in 1853–4   1852–4
Williams C.C.P. (Westminster and Christ Church), captain in 1955   1953–5
Williams P. (Winchester and New College)   1844–7
Williams R.A. (Winchester and University)   1901–2
Willis C.F. (Tonbridge and Brasenose)   1847–9
Wilson A. (Rugby and Exeter)   1848–50
Wilson G.L. (Brighton and Hertford)   1890–1
Wilson P.R.B. (Milton HS, Rhodesia, Cape Town U and St Edmund Hall)   1968, 1970
Wilson R.W. (Warwick and Brasenose)   1957
Wilson T.S.B. (Bath College and Trinity)   1892–3
Wingfield Digby A.R. (Sherborne, Keble and Wycliffe Hall)   1971, 1975–7
Winn C.E. (King's College School, Wimbledon and Exeter)   1948–51
Wood J.B. (Marlborough and Balliol)   1892–3
Woodcock R.G. (Worcester RGS and Keble)   1957–8
Wookey S.M. (Malvern, Cambridge U and Wycliffe Hall)   1978
Wordsworth Charles (Harrow and Christ Church), captain in 1827, 1829   1827, 1829
Worsley D.R. (Bolton and St Edmund Hall), captain in 1964   1961–4
Worthington G. (Tonbridge and St John's)   1844
Wright E.C. (Clergy Orphan School and Keble)   1897
Wright E.L. (Winchester and New College), captain in 1907–8   1905–8
Wright F.B. (Winchester and Queen's)   1829
Wright F.W. (Rossall and St John's)   1863–5
Wrigley M.H. (Harrow and Worcester)   1949
Wyatt M.T.H. (Private and Exeter)   1850–1
Wyld H.J. (Harrow and Magdalen)   1901–3
Wynne J.H.G. (Eton and Christ Church)   1839–40
Wynne-Finch C.G. (Eton and Christ Church)   1836

Yonge C.D. (Eton and St Mary Hall)   1836
Yonge G.E. (Eton and Trinity), captain in 1848   1844–8
Young D.E. (King's College School, Wimbledon and Brasenose)   1938

VI Cambridge Blues

Abercrombie J. (Tonbridge and Gonville & Caius)   1838
Absolom C.A. (Private and Trinity)   1866–9
Acfield D.L. (Brentwood and Christ's)   1967–8
Aers D.R. (Tonbridge and Queens')   1966–8
Ahluwalia M.S. (Latymer Upper and Emmanuel)   1986
Aird R. (Eton and Clare)   1923
Alexander F.C.M. (Wolmer's College, Jamaica and Gonville & Caius)   1952–3
Allbrook M.E. (Tonbridge and Trinity Hall)   1975–8
Allen A.W. (Eton and Magdalene)   1933–4
Allen B.O. (Clifton and Gonville & Caius)   1933
Allen G.O. (Eton and Trinity)   1922–3
Allom M.J.C. (Wellington and Trinity)   1927–8
Allsopp H.T. (Cheltenham and Trinity Hall)   1876
Andrew C.R. (Barnard Castle and St John's), captain in 1985   1984–5
Anson T.A. (Eton and Jesus), captain in 1840–2   1839–42
Arkwright H.A. (Harrow and Trinity)   1858
Arnold A.C.P. (Malvern and Magdalene)   1914
Ash E.P. (Rugby and Gonville and Caius)   1865

Ashton C.T. (Winchester and Trinity), captain in 1923	1921–3
Ashton G. (Winchester and Trinity), captain in 1921	1919–21
Ashton H. (Winchester and Trinity), captain in 1922	1920–2
Atherton M.A. (Manchester GS and Downing), captain in 1988	1987–8
Atkins G. (Dr Challenor's GS and Emmanuel)	1960
Atkinson J.C.M. (Millfield and Downing)	1988
Austin H.M. (Melbourne C of E GS and St Catharine's)	1924
Aworth C.J. (Tiffin and St Catharine's), captain in 1975	1973–5
Baggallay M.E.C. (Eton and Trinity)	1911
Bagge T.E. (Eton and Trinity)	1859–61
Bagnall H.F. (Harrow and Pembroke)	1923–5
Bail P.A.C. (Millfield and Downing)	1986–8
Baily E.P. (Harrow and Gonville & Caius)	1872, 1874
Baily R.E.H. (Harrow and Pembroke)	1908
Bailey T.E. (Dulwich and St John's)	1947–8
Bainbridge H.W. (Eton and Trinity), captain in 1886	1884–6
Baker E.C. (Brighton and St Catharine's)	1912, 1914
Baker R.K. (Brentwood and Fitzwilliam)	1973–4
Balfour R.D. (Westminster, Bradfield and Magdalene)	1863–6
Bannister C.S. (Caterham and Downing)	1976
Barber R.W. (Ruthin and Magdalene)	1956–7
Barchard E. (Winchester and Trinity)	1846–8
Barford M.T. (Eastbourne and St Catharine's)	1970–1
Barker G. (Bury St Edmund's and Trinity)	1840
Barnett W.E. (Eton and Trinity)	1849–50
Barrington W.E.J. (Lancing and St Catharine's)	1982
Bartlett H.T. (Dulwich and Pembroke), captain in 1936	1934–6
Bastard J.H. (Winchester and Trinity)	1838, 1840
Bate R. (Haberdashers' Aske's and Pembroke)	1988
Bateman A. (Repton, Brighton and St John's)	1859–61
Bayford R.A. (Kensington GS and Trinity Hall), captain in 1859	1857–9
Beaumont D.J. (West Bridgford GS, Bramshill College and Wolfson)	1978
Benke A.F. (Cheltenham and Sidney Sussex)	1962
Bennett B.W.P. (Welbeck, RMA Sandhurst and Queens')	1979
Bennett C.T. (Harrow and Pembroke), captain in 1925	1923, 1925
Benthall W.H. (Westminster, Marlborough and Clare)	1858–60
Bernard J.R. (Clifton and St John's)	1958–60
Bhatia A.N. (Doon School, India and Emmanuel)	1969
Blacker W. (Harrow and Trinity)	1873–6
Blake J.P. (Aldenham and St John's)	1939
Blaker R.N. (Elizabeth College, Guernsey and St John's)	1842–3
Blaker R.N.R. (Westminster and Jesus)	1900–2
Blayds E. (Harrow and Trinity)	1846–9
Bligh Hon. I.F.W. (Lord Darnley) (Eton and Trinity), captain in 1881	1878–81
Block S.A. (Marlborough and Pembroke)	1929
Blofeld H.C. (Eton and King's)	1959
Blore E.W. (Eton and Trinity), captain in 1851	1848–51
Blundell E.D. (Waitaki, New Zealand and Trinity Hall)	1928–9
Bodkin P.E. (Bradfield and Gonville & Caius), captain in 1946	1946
Boldero H.K. (Harrow and Trinity)	1851–3
Booth C. (Rugby and Trinity), captain in 1864	1862–5
Booth H.W. (Eton and Christ's), captain in 1836	1836
Boudier G.J. (Eton and King's), joint captain with T.L. French in 1843	1841, 1843
Bourne A.A. (Rugby and St John's)	1870
Boyd-Moss R.J. (Bedford and Magdalene)	1980–3
Bray E. (Westminster and St John's)	1871–2
Bray E.H. (Charterhouse and Trinity)	1896–7
Brearley J.M. (City of London and St John's), captain in 1963–4	1961–4

Breddy M.N. (Cheltenham GS and Fitzwilliam)	1984
Brereton C.J. (Marlborough and St John's)	1858
Bridgeman W.C. (Eton and Trinity)	1887
Brocklebank J.M. (Eton and Magdalene)	1936
Brodie J.B. (Union HS, S. Africa and Fitzwilliam)	1960
Brodhurst A.H. (Malvern and Pembroke)	1939
Brodrick P.D. (Royal GS, Newcastle and Gonville & Caius)	1961
Bromley R.C. (Christ's College, Canterbury U, NZ and St Catharine's)	1970
Bromley-Davenport H.R. (Eton and Trinity Hall)	1892–3
Brooke-Taylor G.P. (Cheltenham and Pembroke)	1919–20
Brooker M.E.W. (Lancaster RGS, Burnley GS and Jesus)	1976
Broughton R.J.P. (Harrow and Clare)	1836, 1838–9
Brown A.D. (Clacton HS and Magdalene)	1986
Brown F.R. (Leys and St John's)	1930–1
Browne D.W. (Stamford and St Catharine's)	1986
Browne F.B.R. (Aldro School, Eastbourne and Emmanuel)	1922
Brune C.J. (Godolphin School, Hammersmith and Trinity)	1867–9
Brunton J. du V. (Lancaster GS and Pembroke)	1894
Bryan J.L. (Rugby and St John's)	1921
Buchanan D. (Rugby and Clare)	1850
Buchanan J.N. (Charterhouse and Trinity), captain in 1909	1906–9
Buckston G.M. (Eton and Trinity)	1903
Bulwer J.B.R. (King's College, London and Trinity)	1841
Burghley, Lord (Eton and St John's)	1847
Burnett A.C. (Lancing and Pembroke)	1949
Burnley I.D. (Queen Elizabeth, Darlington and Churchill)	1984
Burnup C.J. (Malvern and Clare)	1896–8
Burr G.F. (Maidstone and St John's)	1840
Burrough J. (King's Bruton, Shrewsbury and Jesus)	1895
Bury L. (Eton and Trinity)	1877
Bury T.W. (Winchester and Emmanuel)	1855
Bury W. (Private and Trinity)	1861–2
Bushby M.H. (Dulwich and Queens'), captain in 1954	1952–4
Butler E.M. (Harrow and Trinity)	1888–9
Butterworth H.R.W. (Rydal and Jesus)	1929
Buxton C.D. (Harrow and Trinity), captain in 1888	1885–8
Calthorpe Hon. F.S.G. (Repton and Jesus)	1912–14, 1919
Calvert C.T. (Shrewsbury and St John's)	1848
Cameron J.H. (Taunton and St Catharine's)	1935–7
Campbell S.C. (Bury St Edmund's and Corpus Christi)	1845
Cangley B.G.M. (Felsted and Trinity Hall)	1947
Carling P.G. (Kingston GS and St Catharine's)	1968, 1970
Carris B.D. (Harrow and St John's)	1938–9
Carris H.E. (Mill Hill and St John's)	1930
Cawston E. (Lancing and Pembroke)	1932
Chambers R.E.J. (Forest and Queens')	1966
Chapman A.P.F. (Oakham, Uppingham and Pembroke)	1920–2
Christopher A.W.M. (Private and Jesus)	1843
Christopherson J.C. (Uppingham and Pembroke)	1931
Clement R.A. (Rugby and Trinity)	1854
Clissold S.T. (Eton and Trinity)	1844, 1846
Close P.A. (Haileybury and Gonville & Caius)	1965
Cobbold P.W. (Eton and Trinity)	1896
Cobbold R.H. (Eton and Magdalene)	1927
Cobden F.C. (Harrow and Trinity)	1870–2
Cockburn-Hood J.S.E. (Rugby and Trinity Hall)	1865, 1867
Cockett J.A. (Aldenham and Trinity)	1951
Coghlan T.B.L. (Rugby and Pembroke)	1960

Colbeck L.G. (Marlborough and King's)	1905–6
Collins D.C. (Wellington College, NZ and Trinity)	1910–11
Collins T. (Bury St Edmund's and Christ's)	1863
Comber J.T.H. (Marlborough and Pembroke)	1931–3
Conradi E.R. (Oundle and Gonville & Caius)	1946
Coode A.T. (Fauconberge School, Beccles and Jesus)	1898
Cook G.W. (Dulwich and Queens')	1957–8
Cooke C.R. (Eton, Ipswich and Clare)	1858
Cookesley W.G. (Eton and King's)	1827
Cooper N.H.C. (St Brendan's, Bristol, East Anglia U and Fitzwilliam)	1979
Cosh N.J. (Dulwich and Queens')	1966–8
Cotterell T.A. (Downside and Peterhouse)	1983–5
Cotterill G.E. (Brighton and St John's)	1858–60
Cottrell G.A. (Kingston GS and St Catharine's), captain in 1968	1966–8
Cottrell P.R. (Chislehurst & Sidcup GS and Trinity)	1979
Coverdale S.P. (St Peter's, York and Emmanuel)	1974–7
Cowie A.G. (Charterhouse and Gonville & Caius)	1910
Craig E.J. (Charterhouse and Trinity)	1961–3
Crawford N.C. (Shrewsbury and Magdalene)	1979–80
Crawley E. (Harrow and Trinity)	1887–9
Crawley L.G. (Harrow and Pembroke)	1923–5
Croft P.D. (Gresham's and Jesus)	1955
Crofts C.D. (Winchester and St John's)	1843
Crookes D.V. (Michaelhouse, S. Africa and Jesus)	1953
Cumberlege B.S. (Durham and Emmanuel)	1913
Currie F.L. (Rugby and Christ's)	1845
Curteis T.S. (Bury St Edmunds and Trinity)	1864–5
Curtis T.S. (Worcester RGS and Magdalene)	1983
Dale J.W. (Tonbridge and St John's)	1868–70
Daniel A.W.T. (Harrow and Trinity)	1861–4
Daniell J. (Clifton and Emmanuel)	1899–1901
Daniels D.M. (Rutlish and Gonville & Caius)	1964–5
Datta P.B. (Asutosh College, Calcutta and Trinity Hall)	1947
Davidson J.E. (Penglais and Trinity)	1985–6
Davies A.G. (Birkenhead and Robinson)	1984–5
Davies G.B. (Rossall and Selwyn)	1913–14
Davies J.G.W. (Tonbridge and St John's)	1933–4
Dawson E.W. (Eton and Magdalene), captain in 1927	1924–7
Day S.H. (Malvern and Queens'), captain in 1901	1899–1902
de Grey Hon. T. (Eton and St John's)	1862–3
de Little E.R. (Geelong GS and Jesus)	1889
de Paravicini P.J. (Eton and Trinity)	1882–5
de St Croix W. (Eton and St John's)	1839–42
de Zoete H.W. (Eton and Trinity)	1897–8
Deacon W.S. (Eton and Trinity), captain in 1850	1848–50
Dewes A.R. (Dulwich and St John's)	1978
Dewes J.G. (Aldenham and St John's)	1948–50
Dewing E.M. (Harrow and Trinity), captain in 1844–5	1842–5
Dexter E.R. (Radley and Jesus), captain in 1958	1956–8
Dickinson D.C. (Clifton and Trinity Hall)	1953
Dickinson P.J. (King's College School, Wimbledon and St John's)	1939
Doggart A.G. (Bishop's Stortford and King's)	1921–2
Doggart G.H.G. (Winchester and King's), captain in 1950	1948–50
Doggart S.J.G. (Winchester and Magdalene)	1980–3
Dolphin J. (Eton and Trinity)	1827
Dorman A.W. (Dulwich and Corpus Christi)	1886
Douglas J. (Dulwich and Selwyn)	1892–4
Douglas R.N. (Dulwich and Selwyn)	1890–2

Douglas-Hamilton H.A. (Wellington and Trinity)   1873, 1876
Douglas-Pennant S. (Eton and Clare)   1959
Downes K.D. (Rydal and Christ's)   1939
Dowson E.M. (Harrow and Trinity), captain in 1903   1900–3
Drake E.T. (Westminster and Magdalene)   1852–4
Driffield L.T. (St John's, Leatherhead and St Catharine's)   1902
Druce N.F. (Marlborough and Trinity), captain in 1897   1894–7
Druce W.G. (Marlborough and Trinity), captain in 1895   1894–5
Du Cane A.R. (Harrow and Trinity)   1854–5
Duleepsinhji K.S. (Cheltenham and Clare)   1925–6, 1928
Dupuis G.R. (Eton and King's)   1857
Dyke E.F. (Eton and Trinity Hall)   1865
Dykes T. (Kingston College, Hull and Clare)   1844

Ebden C.H.M. (Eton and Trinity)   1902–3
Edmonds P.H. (Gilbert Rennie HS, Lusaka, Cranbrook and Fitzwilliam), captain in 1973   1971–3
Edwards R.S. (Huntingdon GS, Christ's Hospital and St John's)   1850
Edwards T.D.W. (Sherborne and St John's)   1981
Elgood B.C. (Bradfield and Pembroke)   1948
Ellis E.C. (Private and Trinity)   1829
Ellison C.C. (Tonbridge and Peterhouse and Homerton)   1982–3, 1985–6
Enthoven H.J. (Harrow and Pembroke), captain in 1926   1923–6
Estcourt N.S.T. (Plumtree, S. Rhodesia and Corpus Christi)   1954
Evans R.G. (King Edward, Bury St Edmunds and Peterhouse)   1921
Eyre C.H. (Harrow and Pembroke), captain in 1906   1904–6

Fabian A.H. (Highgate and Pembroke)   1929–31
Fairbairn G.A. (Geelong C of E GS and Jesus)   1913–14, 1919
Falcon M. (Harrow and Pembroke), captain in 1910   1908–11
Fargus A.H.C. (Clifton, Haileybury and Pembroke)   1900–1
Farmer A.A. (Winchester and Gonville & Caius)   1836
Farnes K. (Royal Liberty School, Romford and Pembroke)   1931–3
Fawcett E.B. (Brighton and Trinity)   1859–60
Fell D.J. (John Lyon and Trinity)   1985–7
Fenn S. (Blackheath and Trinity)   1851
Fenn W.M. (Blackheath and Trinity)   1849–51
Fenton N.C.W. (Rugby and Magdalene)   1988
Fernie A.E. (Wellingborough and Clare)   1897, 1900
Fiddian-Green C.A. (Leys and Jesus)   1921–2
Field E. (Clifton and Trinity)   1894
Field M.N. (Bablake and Emmanuel)   1974
Fitzgerald J.F. (St Brendan's, Bristol and Churchill)   1968
Fitzgerald R.A. (Harrow and Trinity)   1854, 1856
Foley C.P. (Eton and Trinity Hall)   1889–91
Foley C.W. (Eton and King's)   1880
Ford A.F.J. (Repton and King's)   1878–81
Ford F.G.J. (Repton and King's), captain in 1889   1887–90
Ford W.J. (Repton and St John's)   1873
Fosh M.K. (Harrow and Magdalene)   1977–8
Fowler T.F. (Uppingham and Christ's)   1864
Francis T.E.S. (Tonbridge and Pembroke)   1925
Franklin W.B. (Repton and Trinity)   1912
Fraser T.W. (Jeppe, S. Africa and Pembroke)   1937
Freeman-Thomas F. (Lord Willingdon) (Eton and Trinity)   1886–9
Freer J. (Eton, Winchester and Trinity)   1827
French T.L. (Winchester and Emmanuel), joint captain with Boudier G.J. 1843   1842–4
Fry K.R.B. (Cheltenham and Clare)   1904
Fryer C.W.H. (Rugby and Trinity)   1854
Fryer F.E.R. (Harrow and Gonville & Caius), captain in 1873   1870–3

Fuller E.A. (Rugby and Emmanuel)	1852
Fuller J.M. (Marlborough and St John's), captain in 1857–8	1855–8
Gaddum F.D. (Uppingham, Rugby and St John's)	1882
Gardiner S.J. (St Andrew's, Bloemfontein and St John's)	1978
Garlick P.L. (Sherborne and Jesus)	1984
Gay L.H. (Marlborough, Brighton and Clare)	1892–3
Gibb P.A. (St Edward's, Oxford and Emmanuel)	1935–8
Gibson C.H. (Eton and Clare)	1920–1
Gibson J.S. (Harrow and Trinity)	1855
Gillespie D.W. (Uppingham and Clare)	1939
Gilligan A.E.R. (Dulwich and Pembroke)	1919–20
Gilman J. (St Paul's and Jesus)	1902
Godsell R.T. (Clifton and Trinity)	1903
Goldie C.D. (Kensington GS and St John's)	1846
Goldie C.F.E. (St Paul's and Pembroke)	1981–2
Golding A.K. (Colchester GS and St Catharine's)	1986
Goodfellow A. (Marlborough and Magdalene)	1961–2
Goodwin H.J. (Marlborough and Jesus)	1907–8
Goonesena G. (Royal College, Colombo and Queens'), captain in 1957	1954–7
Gordon Hon F.A. (Charterhouse and Trinity)	1829
Gorman S.R. (St Peter's, York and Emmanuel)	1985, 1987
Gosling R.C. (Eton and Trinity)	1888–90
Grace W.G. (Jnr) (Clifton and Pembroke)	1895–6
Grant G.C. (Queen's Royal, Trinidad and Christ's)	1929–30
Grant R.S. (Queen's Royal, Trinidad and Christ's)	1933
Gray H. (Perse and Jesus)	1894–5
Grazebrook H.G. (Winchester and Jesus)	1829
Green C.E. (Uppingham and Trinity), captain in 1868	1865–8
Green D.J. (Burton GS and Christ's), captain in 1959	1957–9
Greenfield F.F.J. (Hurstpierpoint and Peterhouse), captain in 1876	1874–6
Greig I.A. (Queen's College, S. Africa and Downing), captain in 1979	1977–9
Grierson H. (Bedford GS and Pembroke)	1911
Griffith M.G. (Marlborough and Magdalene)	1963–5
Griffith S.C. (Dulwich and Pembroke)	1935
Griffiths W.H. (Charterhouse and St John's)	1946–8
Grimes A.D.H. (Tonbridge and Pembroke)	1984
Grimshaw J.W.T. (King William's, Isle of Man and Emmanuel)	1934–5
Grimston F.S. (Harrow and Magdalene)	1843–5
Grout J. (Private and St John's)	1838, 1839
Hadingham A.W.G. (St Paul's and Jesus)	1932
Hadley R.J. (Sanfield CS and St John's)	1971–3
Hale H. (Hutchins School, Hobart and Trinity)	1887, 1889–90
Hales J. (Rugby and Trinity)	1855–6
Hall J.E. (Ardingly and Sidney Sussex)	1969
Hall P.J. (Geelong GS and Sidney Sussex)	1949
Hammersley W.J. (Private and Trinity)	1847
Hammond O. (Bury St Edmunds and Emmanuel)	1855–7
Handley E.H. (Harrow and Trinity Hall)	1827
Harbinson W.K. (Marlborough and St John's)	1929
Hardy J.R. (Charterhouse and Peterhouse)	1829
Harenc E.A.F. (Naval College, Portsmouth and Magdalene)	1841
Harper L.V. (Rossall and Christ's)	1901–3
Harris J.E. (Sheffield Collegiate School and Gonville & Caius)	1859
Harrison W.P. (Rugby and Jesus)	1907
Hartopp E.S.E. (Eton and Trinity)	1841–2
Harvey J.R.W. (Marlborough and Christ's)	1965
Hawke Hon. M.B. (Eton and Magdalene), captain in 1885	1882–3, 1885

Hawkins H.H.B. (Whitgift and Trinity)   1898–9
Hayes P.J. (Brighton and Downing)   1974–5, 1977
Hays D.L. (Highgate and Selwyn)   1966, 1968
Hayward W.I.D. (St Peter's, Adelaide and Jesus)   1950–1, 1953
Haywood D.C. (Nottingham HS and Jesus)   1968
Hazlerigg A.G. (Eton and Trinity), captain in 1932   1930–2
Heath S.D. (King Edward's, Birmingham and Trinity)   1988
Helm G.F. (Marlborough and St Catharine's)   1862–3
Hemingway W. McG. (Uppingham and King's)   1895–6
Henderson S.P. (Downside, Durham U and Magdalene), captain in 1983   1982–3
Henery P.J.T. (Harrow and Trinity)   1882–3
Hewan G.E. (Marlborough and Clare)   1938
Hewitt S.G.P. (Bradford GS and Peterhouse)   1983
Hignell A.J. (Denstone and Fitzwilliam), captain in 1977–8   1975–8
Hill A.J.L. (Marlborough and Jesus)   1890–3
Hill-Wood W.W. (Eton and Trinity)   1922
Hind A.E. (Uppingham and Trinity Hall)   1898–1901
Hoare A.M. (Private and St John's), captain in 1846 but did not play against Oxford owing to
    illness   1844
Hobson B.S. (Taunton and St Catharine's)   1946
Hodgson E.F. (Eton and St John's)   1836
Hodgson K.I. (Oundle and Downing)   1981–3
Hodson R.P. (QEGS Wakefield and Downing)   1972–3
Holliday D.C. (Oundle and Christ's)   1979–81
Holloway N.J. (Leys and Jesus)   1910–2
Hone N.T. (Rugby and Trinity)   1881
Hone-Goldney G.H. (Eton and Trinity Hall)   1873
Hooper A.M. (Latymer Upper and St John's)   1987
Hope-Grant F.C. (Harrow and Trinity)   1863
Hopley F.J.V. (Harrow and Pembroke)   1904
Hopley G.W.V. (Harrow and Trinity)   1912
Horne E.L. (Shrewsbury and Clare)   1855, 1857–8
Horsman E. (Rugby and Trinity)   1827, 1829
Hotchkin N.S. (Eton and Trinity)   1935
Howard-Smith G. (Eton and Trinity)   1903
Howat M.G. (Abingdon and Magdalene)   1977, 1980
Howland C.B. (Dulwich and Clare), captain in 1960   1958–60
Hughes G. (Cardiff HS and Queens')   1965
Hughes O. (Malvern and Clare)   1910
Hughes T.F. (Private and Trinity Hall)   1845
Human J.H. (Repton and Clare), captain in 1934   1932–4
Human R.H.C. (Repton and Emmanuel)   1930–1
Hume A. (Eton and King's)   1841–2
Hunt R.G. (Aldenham and Pembroke)   1937
Hurd A. (Chigwell and Clare)   1958–60
Hutton R.A. (Repton and Christ's)   1962–4
Huxter R.J.A. (Magdalen College School and St Catharine's)   1981

Imlay A.D. (Clifton and Emmanuel)   1907
Ingram C.P. (Westminster and Trinity)   1854
Insole D.J. (Sir George Monoux, Walthamstow and St Catharine's), captain in 1949   1947–9
Ireland J.F. (Marlborough and Trinity), captain in 1911   1908–11
Irvine L.G. (Taunton and Sydney Sussex)   1926–7

Jackson E.J.W. (Winchester and Pembroke)   1974–6
Jackson F.S. (Harrow and Trinity), captain in 1892–3   1890–3
Jagger S.T. (Malvern and Clare)   1925–6
Jahangir Khan (Lahore and Trinity Hall)   1933–6
James R.M. (St John's, Leatherhead and Trinity)   1956–8

Jameson T.E.N. (Taunton, Durham U and Emmanuel)   1970
Jarrett D.W. (Wellington, Oxford U and St Catharine's)   1976
Jarvis L.K. (Harrow and Trinity)   1877–9
Jefferson R.I. (Winchester and Corpus Christi)   1961
Jeffery G.E. (Rugby and Trinity)   1873–4
Jenner C.H. (Eton and Trinity Hall)   1829
Jenner H.L. (Harrow and Trinity Hall)   1841
Jenner-Fust H. (Eton and Trinity Hall), captain in 1827   1827
Jenyns G.F.G. (Private and Emmanuel)   1849–50
Jephson D.L.A. (Manor House, Clapham and Peterhouse)   1890–2
Jessop G.L. (Beccles, Cheltenham GS and Christ's), captain in 1899   1896–9
Johnson G.R. (Bury St Edmunds and Clare), captain in 1855   1855–7
Johnson P.D. (Nottingham HS and Emmanuel)   1970–2
Johnson P.R. (Eton and Trinity)   1901
Johnstone C.P. (Rugby and Pembroke)   1919–20
Jones A.O. (Bedford Modern and Jesus)   1893
Jones R.S. (Chatham House, Ramsgate and Trinity)   1879–80
Jones-Bateman J.B. (Winchester and Gonville & Caius)   1848
Jorden A.M. (Monmouth and Fitzwilliam), captain in 1969–70   1968–70
Judd A.K. (St Paul's and St Catharine's)   1927

Kaye M.A.C.P. (Harrow and Pembroke)   1938
Keigwin R.P. (Clifton and Peterhouse)   1903–6
Kelland P.A. (Repton and St Catharine's)   1950
Kemp G.M. (Mill Hill, Shrewsbury and Trinity)   1885–6, 1888
Kempson S.M.E. (Cheltenham and Gonville & Caius)   1851, 1853
Kempson W.J. (Rugby and Trinity)   1855
Kemp-Welch G.D. (Charterhouse and Sidney Sussex), captain in 1931   1929–31
Kendall M.P. (Gillingham GS and Jesus)   1972
Kenny C.J.M. (Ampleforth and Trinity)   1952
Kerslake R.C. (Kingswood and St Catharine's)   1963–4
Khanna B.C. (Lahore and Peterhouse)   1937
Kidd E.L. (Wellington and Pembroke), captain in 1912   1910–3
Killick E.T. (St Paul's and Jesus)   1928–30
King F. (Dulwich and Christ's)   1934
King R.T. (Oakham and Emmanuel), captain in 1849   1846–9
Kingdon S.N. (Eton and Trinity)   1827
Kingston F.W. (Abingdon House, Northampton and Pembroke)   1878
Kirby D. (St Peter's, York and Emmanuel), captain in 1961   1959–61
Kirkman M.C. (Dulwich and St Catharine's)   1963
Kirwan J.H. (Eton and King's)   1839
Knatchbull-Hugessen Hon. C.M. (Eton and King's)   1886
Knight R.D.V. (Dulwich and St Catharine's)   1967–70
Knightley-Smith W. (Highgate and St John's)   1953
Koe B.D. (Eton and Gonville and Caius)   1838

Lacey F.E. (Sherborne and Gonville & Caius)   1882
Lacy-Scott D.G. (Marlborough and Peterhouse)   1946
Lagden R.B. (Marlborough and Pembroke)   1912–14
Lancaster O.P. (Lancing and Jesus)   1880
Lang A.H. (Harrow and Trinity)   1913
Lang R. (Harrow and Trinity)   1860–2
Langley J.D.A. (Stowe and Trinity)   1938
Latham P.H. (Malvern and Pembroke), captain in 1894   1892–4
Latham T. (Winchester and St John's)   1873–4
Lawrence A.S. (Harrow and Trinity Hall)   1933
Lea A.E. (High Arcal GS and Churchill)   1984–6
Leake W.M. (Rugby and St John's)   1851–4
Lee F. (Rugby and St John's)   1860

Lee J.M. (Blackheath Proprietary, Oundle and St John's)	1846–8
Leith J. (Private and Trinity)	1848
Lewis A.R. (Neath GS and Christ's), captain in 1962	1960–2
Lewis L.K. (Taunton and Pembroke)	1953
Littlewood D.J. (Enfield GS and St John's)	1978
Lockhart J.H.B. (Sedbergh and Jesus)	1909–10
Long F.E. (Eton and King's)	1836
Long R.P. (Harrow and Trinity)	1845–6
Longfield T.C. (Aldenham and Pembroke)	1927–8
Longman G.H. (Eton and Trinity), captain in 1874–5	1872–5
Longman H.K. (Eton and Trinity)	1901
Longrigg E.F. (Rugby and Pembroke)	1927–8
Lowe R.G.H. (Westminster and Trinity)	1925–7
Lowe W.W. (Malvern and Pembroke)	1895
Lowry T.C. (Christ's College, Christchurch, NZ and Jesus), captain in 1924	1923–4
Lucas A.P. (Uppingham and Clare)	1875–8
Luddington H.T. (Uppingham and Jesus)	1876–7
Lumsden V.R. (Munro College, Jamaica and Emmanuel)	1953–5
Lyon M.D. (Rugby and Trinity)	1921–2
Lyon W.J. (Torquay and Trinity)	1861
Lyttelton 4th Lord (Eton and Trinity)	1838
Lyttelton Hon. Alfred (Eton and Trinity), captain in 1879	1876–9
Lyttelton Hon. C.F. (Eton and Trinity)	1908–9
Lyttelton Hon. C.G. (Eton and Trinity)	1861–4
Lyttelton Hon. Edward (Eton and Trinity), captain in 1878	1875–8
Lyttelton Hon. G.W.S. (Eton and Trinity)	1866–7
Macan G. (Harrow and Trinity Hall)	1874–5
McAdam K.P.W.J. (Prince of Wales, Nairobi, Millfield and Clare)	1965–6
MacBryan J.C.W. (Exeter and Jesus)	1920
McCarthy C.N. (Maritzburg College, S. Africa and Pembroke)	1952
McCormick J. (Liverpool, Bingley and St John's), captain in 1856	1854–6
McDonell H.C. (Winchester and Corpus Christi)	1903–5
McDowall J.I. (Rugby and Fitzwilliam)	1969
MacGregor G. (Uppingham and Jesus), captain in 1891	1888–91
Machin R.S. (Lancing and Clare)	1927
Mackinnon F.A. (Harrow and St John's)	1870
McLachlan A.A. (St Peter's, Adelaide and Jesus)	1964–5
McLachlan I.M. (St Peter's, Adelaide and Jesus)	1957–8
MacLeod K.G. (Fettes and Pembroke)	1908–9
MacNiven E. (Eton and Trinity)	1846
Mainprice H. (Blundell's and Jesus)	1906
Majid Khan (Aitchison College, Lahore, Punjab U and Emmanuel), captain in 1971–2	1970–2
Makinson J. (Huddersfield, Owen's College and Clare)	1856–8
Malalasekara V.P. (Royal College, Colombo and Fitzwilliam)	1966–7
Mann E.W. (Harrow and Trinity), captain in 1905	1903–5
Mann F.G. (Eton and Pembroke)	1938–9
Mann F.T. (Malvern and Pembroke)	1909–11
Mann J.E.F. (Geelong and Corpus Christi)	1924
Manners-Sutton Hon. J.H.T. (Eton and Trinity)	1836
Mansfield Hon. J.W. (Winchester and Trinity)	1883–4
Maples W. (Winchester, Haileybury and Trinity)	1839
Marchant F. (Rugby, Eton and Trinity), captain in 1887	1884–7
Marlar R.G. (Harrow and Magdalene), captain in 1953	1951–3
Marriott C.S. (St Columba's and Peterhouse)	1920–1
Marriott H.H. (Malvern and Clare)	1895–8
March J.F. (Amersham Hall and Jesus)	1904
Marshall H.M. (Westminster and Trinity)	1861–4
Marshall J.H. (King Edward VI, Birmingham and Trinity)	1859

Marshall J.W. (King Edward VI, Birmingham and Trinity)   1855–7
Martin M.T. (Rugby and Trinity)   1862, 1864
Martineau L. (Uppingham and Trinity)   1887
Massey W. (Harrow and Trinity)   1838–9
Mathews K.P.A. (Felsted and Clare)   1951
Maule W. (Tonbridge and Gonville & Caius)   1853
May P.B.H. (Charterhouse and Pembroke)   1950–2
May P.R. (Private and Pembroke)   1905–6
Meetkerke A. (Eton and Trinity)   1840
Mellor F.H. (Cheltenham and Trinity)   1877
Melluish M.E.L. (Rossall and Gonville & Caius), captain in 1956   1954–6
Meryweather W.S.T.M. (Charterhouse and Trinity)   1829
Meyer R.J.O. (Haileybury and Pembroke)   1924–6
Meyrick-Jones F.M. (Marlborough and Trinity)   1888
Micklethwait F.N. (Eton and Jesus)   1836
Micklethwait S.N. (Shrewsbury and Magdalene)   1843
Middleton M.R. (Harrow and Gonville & Caius)   1987
Miller M.E. (Prince Henry GS, Hohne, W. Germany and St John's)   1963
Mills J.M. (Oundle and Corpus Christi), captain in 1948   1946–8
Mills J.P.C. (Oundle and Corpus Christi), captain at Lord's in 1982   1979–82
Mills W. (Harrow and St John's)   1840–3
Mischler N.M. (St Paul's and St Catharine's)   1946–7
Mitchell F. (St Peter's, York and Gonville & Caius), captain in 1896   1894–7
Money W.B. (Harrow and Trinity), captain in 1870   1868–71
Moon L.J. (Westminster and Pembroke)   1899–1900
Morcom A.F. (Repton and Clare)   1905–7
Mordaunt H.J. (Eton and King's)   1888–9
Morgan J.T. (Charterhouse and Jesus), captain in 1930   1928–30
Morgan M.N. (Marlborough and Downing)   1954
Morris R.J. (Blundell's and Trinity Hall)   1949
Morrison J.S.F. (Charterhouse and Trinity), captain in 1919   1912, 1914, 1919
Morse C. (Dedham and Trinity)   1842–4
Morton P.H. (Rossall and Trinity)   1878–80
Moses G.H. (Ystalyfera GS and Emmanuel)   1974
Moylan A.C.D. (Clifton and Downing)   1977
Mubarak A.M. (Royal College, Colombo, Sri Lanka U and Christ's)   1978–80
Mugliston F.H. (Rossall and Pembroke)   1907–8
Mulholland H.G.H. (Eton and Trinity), captain in 1913   1911–13
Murray D.L. (Queen's Royal, Trinidad and Jesus), captain in 1966   1965–6
Murrills T.J. (Leys and Emmanuel), captain in 1976   1973–4, 1976

Napier G.G. (Marlborough and Pembroke)   1904
Nason J.W.W. (University School, Hastings and Queens')   1909–10
Naumann J.H. (Malvern and King's)   1913, 1919
Nelson R.P. (St George's Harpenden and Gonville & Caius)   1936
Newton S.C. (Victoria College, Jersey and Corpus Christi)   1876
Nevin M.R.S. (Winchester and Emmanuel)   1969
Nicholson J. (Rugby, Harrow and Trinity)   1845
Norman C.L. (Eton and Trinity)   1852–3
Norman F.H. (Eton and Trinity), captain in 1860   1858–60
Norris D.W.W. (Harrow and Selwyn)   1967–8
Norris W.A. (Eton and Trinity)   1851
Northey A.E. (Harrow and Trinity)   1859–60
Noyes S.O. (RGS High Wycombe and Homerton)   1988
Nunn F. (Bury St Edmunds and Emmanuel)   1859

O'Brien R.P. (Wellington and Corpus Christi)   1955–6
Oddie H.H. (Eton and Trinity)   1836
Odendaal A. (Queen's College, Stellenbosch U and St John's)   1980

Olivier E. (Repton and Trinity Hall)   1908–9
Onslow D.R. (Brighton and Trinity)   1860–1
Orford L.A. (Uppingham and Clare)   1886–7
Ottey G.P. (Rugby and St John's)   1844–7
Owen-Thomas D.R. (King's College School, Wimbledon and Emmanuel)   1969–72

Page C.C. (Malvern and Clare)   1905–6
Palfreman A.B. (Nottingham HS and Emmanuel)   1966
Palmer C. (Uppingham and Clare)   1907
Palmer R.W.M. (Bedford and St Catharine's)   1982
Parker G.W. (Crypt, Gloucester and Selwyn), captain in 1935   1934–5
Parker H. (Maidstone and Corpus Christi)   1839
Parker P.W.G. (Collyer's GS and St Catharine's)   1976–8
Parry D.M. (Merchant Taylors' and St Catharine's)   1931
Parsons A.B.D. (Brighton and Corpus Christi)   1954–5
Partridge N.E. (Malvern and Pembroke)   1920
Pathmanathan G. (Royal College, Colombo, Sri Lanka U, Oxford U and Darwin) 1983
Patterson W.S. (Uppingham and Trinity), captain in 1877   1875–7
Paull R.K. (Millfield and Selwyn)   1967
Pawle J.H. (Harrow and Pembroke)   1936–7
Payne A.U. (St Edmund's, Canterbury and Jesus)   1925
Payne M.W. (Wellington and Trinity), captain in 1907   1904–7
Payton W.E.G. (Nottingham HS and Emmanuel)   1937
Pearman H. (King Alfred's, St Andrews U and Churchill)   1969
Pearson A.J.G. (Downside and Jesus)   1961–3
Peck I.G. (Bedford and Magdalene), captain in 1980–1   1980–1
Pelham A.G. (Eton and King's)   1934
Pelham Hon. F.G. (Eton and Trinity), captain in 1866–7   1864–7
Pell O.C. (Rugby and Trinity), captain in 1847   1844–7
Penn E.F. (Eton and Trinity)   1899, 1902
Pepper J. (Leys and Emmanuel)   1946–8
Perkins H. (Bury St Edmunds and Trinity)   1854
Perkins T.T.N. (St John's, Leatherhead and Jesus)   1893–4
Perry J.N. (Ampleforth and Trinity)   1987–8
Phillips E.S. (Marlborough and Pembroke)   1904
Pickering E.H. (Eton and St John's), captain in 1829   1827, 1829
Pickering W.P. (Eton and Trinity Hall)   1840, 1842
Pieris P.I. (St Thomas', Colombo and Queens')   1957–8
Pigg H. (Abingdon House, Northampton and Emmanuel)   1877
Plowden H.M. (Harrow and Trinity), captain in 1862–3   1860–3
Pointer G.A. (St Dunstan's and St John's)   1987–8
Pollock A.J. (Shrewsbury and Trinity), captain in 1984   1982–4
Ponniah C.E.M. (St Thomas', Colombo and Emmanuel)   1967–9
Ponsonby Hon. F.G.B. (Harrow and Trinity)   1836
Pontifex C. (Private and Trinity), captain in 1853   1851–3
Pope C.G. (Harrow and Trinity)   1894
Popplewell N.F.M. (Radley and Selwyn)   1977–9
Popplewell O.B. (Charterhouse and Queens')   1949–51
Potter A. (Private and St John's)   1879
Powell A.G. (Charterhouse and Magdalene)   1934
Powys W.N. (Private and Pembroke)   1871–2, 1874
Prest E.B. (Eton and Trinity)   1850
Prest H.E.W. (Malvern and Pembroke)   1909, 1911
Preston B. (Westminster and Gonville & Caius)   1869
Pretlove J.F. (Alleyn's and Gonville & Caius)   1954–6
Price D.G. (Haberdashers' Aske's and Homerton), captain in 1986–7   1984–7
Prideaux R.M. (Tonbridge and Sidney Sussex)   1958–60
Pringle D.R. (Felsted and Fitzwilliam), captain in 1982 but did not play against Oxford owing
    to Test selection   1979–81

Pritchard G.C. (King's, Canterbury and Gonville & Caius)	1964
Pryer B.J.K. (City of London and St Catharine's)	1948
Pyemont C.P. (Marlborough and Magdalene)	1967
Ramsay R.C. (Harrow and Trinity Hall)	1882
Ranjitsinhji K.S. (Rajkumar College, India and Trinity)	1893
Ratcliffe A.T. (Rydal and Trinity)	1930–2
Raymond-Barker H.B. (Winchester and Gonville & Caius)	1844
Raynor G.S. (Winchester and St John's)	1872
Reddy N.S.K. (Doon School, India and St John's)	1959–61
Rees-Davies W.R. (Eton and Trinity)	1938
Reynolds E.M. (Royal Institution, Liverpool and Emmanuel)	1853–4
Richardson H.A. (Tonbridge and Trinity)	1867–9
Richardson J.M. (Harrow and Magdalene)	1866–8
Riddell R.H. (Clifton and Sidney Sussex)	1926
Riley W.N. (Worcester GS and St Catharine's)	1912
Rimell A.G.J. (Charterhouse and Magdalene)	1949–50
Rippingall S.F.(Rugby and Peterhouse)	1845
Roberts F.B. (Rossall and Jesus)	1903
Robertson W.P. (Harrow and Trinity Hall)	1901
Robins R.W.V. (Highgate and Queens')	1926–8
Robinson J.J. (Appleby and St John's)	1894
Rock C.W. (Launceston GS, Tasmania and Clare)	1884–6
Roe W.N. (Clergy Orphan School, Canterbury and Magdalene)	1883
Roebuck P.G.P. (Millfield and Emmanuel)	1984–5
Roebuck P.M. (Millfield and Emmanuel)	1975–7
Romilly E. (Bury St Edmunds and Trinity Hall)	1827
Roopnaraine R. (Queen's RC, Guyana and St John's)	1965–6
Rose M.H. (Pocklington and Christ's)	1963–4
Ross N.P.G. (Marlborough and Selwyn)	1969
Rotherham G.A. (Rugby and Trinity)	1919
Rought-Rought D.C. (Private and Emmanuel)	1937
Rought-Rought R.C. (Private and Emmanuel)	1930, 1932
Roundell J. (Winchester and Magdalene)	1973
Rowe F.C.C. (Harrow and Trinity)	1881
Rowell W.I. (Marlborough and Jesus)	1891
Viscount Royston (Harrow and Trinity)	1857
Russell D.P. (West Park GS, St Helens and St John's)	1974–5
Russell S.G. (Tiffin and Trinity), captain in 1967	1965–7
Russom N. (Huish's GS and St Catharine's)	1980–1
St John E. (Private and Downing)	1829
Salter H.W. (Private and Clare)	1867–9
Savile Hon. A. (Eton and Trinity)	1840
Savile G. (Eton, Rossall and Magdalene)	1868
Saville S.H. (Marlborough and Trinity), captain in 1914	1911–14
Sayres E. (Midhurst and Trinity)	1838–41
Schultz S.S. (Uppingham and Jesus)	1877
Scott A.M.G. (Seaford Head and Queens')	1985–7
Scott A.T. (Brighton and Trinity)	1870–1
Seabrook F.J. (Haileybury and St John's), captain in 1928	1926–8
Seager C.P. (Peterhouse, Rhodesia and Jesus)	1971
Seddon R. (Bridgnorth GS and St John's)	1846–7
Selvey M.W.W. (Battersea GS, Manchester U and Emmanuel)	1971
Sharpe C.M. (Private and Jesus)	1875
Shaw V.K. (Haileybury and Emmanuel)	1876
Shelmerdine G.O. (Cheltenham and Christ's)	1922
Sheppard D.S. (Sherborne and Trinity Hall), captain in 1952	1950–2
Sherwell N.B. (Tonbridge and Gonville & Caius)	1923–5

Shine E.B. (King Edward VI School, Saffron Walden and Selwyn)	1896–7
Shirley W.R. (Eton and Pembroke)	1924
Shirreff A.C. (Dulwich and Pembroke)	1939
Short R.L. (Denstone and Emmanuel)	1969
Shuttleworth G.M. (QEGS Blackburn GS and King's)	1946–8
Silk D.R.W. (Christ's Hospital and Sidney Sussex), captain in 1955	1953–5
Simonds H.J. (Eton and King's)	1850
Sims H.M. (St Peter's, York and Jesus)	1873–5
Singh S. (Khalsa College, Punjab U and Christ's)	1955–6
Sinker N.D. (Winchester and Jesus)	1966
Sivewright E. (Eton and Trinity)	1829
Slack J.K.E. (University College School and St John's)	1954
Smith A.F. (Harrow, Wellington and Downing)	1875
Smith C.A. (Charterhouse and St John's)	1882–5
Smith C.S. (William Hulme's GS and Christ's)	1954–7
Smith D.J. (Stockport GS and St John's)	1955–6
Smyth R.I. (Sedbergh and Emmanuel)	1973–5
Snowden W. (Merchant Taylors', Crosby and Emmanuel), captain in 1974	1972–5
Southwell H.G. (Harrow and Trinity)	1852–3
Spencer J. (Brighton & Hove GS and Queens')	1970–2
Spencer R. (Harrow and St John's)	1881
Spiro D.G. (Harrow and Trinity Hall)	1884
Stacey F.E. (Eton and King's)	1853
Stanning J. (Rugby and Trinity)	1900
Stedman H.C.P. (Private and St John's)	1871
Steel A.G. (Marlborough and Trinity Hall), captain in 1880	1878–81
Steel D.Q. (Uppingham and Trinity Hall)	1876–9
Steele H.K. (King's College, NZ and Corpus Christi)	1971–2
Stevenson M.H. (Rydal and Christ's)	1949–52
Stogdon J.H. (Harrow and Trinity)	1897–9
Stow M.H. (Harrow and Trinity), captain in 1869	1867–9
Streatfield E.C. (Charterhouse and Pembroke)	1890–3
Studd C.T. (Eton and Trinity), captain in 1883	1880–3
Studd G.B. (Eton and Trinity), captain in 1882	1879–82
Studd J.E.K. (Eton and Trinity), captain in 1884	1881–4
Studd P.M. (Harrow and Clare), captain in 1939	1937–9
Studd R.A. (Eton and Trinity)	1895
Subba Row R. (Whitgift and Trinity Hall)	1951–3
Surridge D. (Richard Hale, Southampton U and Hughes)	1979
Sutthery A.M. (Uppingham, Oundle and Jesus)	1887
Swift B.T. (St Peter's, Adelaide and Gonville & Caius)	1957
Sykes W. (Private and Emmanuel)	1844
Tabor A.S. (Eton and Trinity)	1872–4
Taylor C.G. (Eton and Emmanuel), captain in 1838–9	1836, 1838–9
Taylor C.R.V. (Birkenhead and Trinity)	1971–3
Taylor T.L. (Uppingham and Trinity), captain in 1900	1898–1900
Templeton C.H. (Winchester and Trinity)	1827
Thackeray F. (Eton and Gonville & Caius)	1838–40
Thomas A. (Winchester and Trinity)	1838
Thomas F.F. (Eton and Trinity)	1886–9
Thompson J.R. (Tonbridge and St John's)	1938–9
Thompson W.T. (Private and Jesus)	1836
Thomson R.H. (Bexhill and Christ's)	1961–2
Thornewill E.J. (Harrow and Trinity)	1856
Thornton C.I. (Eton and Trinity), captain in 1872	1869–72
Thwaites I.G. (Eastbourne and Gonville & Caius)	1964
Tillard C. (Repton and Clare)	1873–4
Tindall M. (Harrow and St Catharine's), captain in 1937	1935–7

Tobin F. (Rugby and St John's)	1870–2
Tomblin A.C. (Uppingham and Emmanuel)	1857
Tomlinson W.J.V. (Felsted and Emmanuel)	1923
Topham H.G. (Repton and Jesus)	1883–4
Toppin C. (Sedbergh and St John's)	1885–7
Tordoff G.G. (Normanton GS and St John's)	1952
Townley T.M. (Eton and Trinity)	1847–8
Trapnell B.M.W. (University College School and St John's)	1946
Tremllen J.M. (Bradfield and St Catharine's)	1987–8
Tremlett T.D. (Eton and King's)	1854
Trevelyan W.B. (Rugby and Gonville & Caius)	1842–3
Tuck G.H. (Eton and Trinity), captain in 1865	1863–6
Tufnell N.C. (Eton and Trinity)	1909–10
Turnbull M.J. (Downside and Trinity), captain in 1929	1926, 1928–9
Turner J.A. (Uppingham and Trinity)	1883–6
Turner J.B. (Blackheath and Gonville & Caius)	1841
Turner R.J. (Milfield and Magdalene)	1988
Urquhart J.R. (King Edward VI School, Chelmsford and Emmanuel)	1948
Valentine B.H. (Repton and Pembroke)	1929
Varey D.W. (Birkenhead and Pembroke)	1982–3
Vernon H. (Harrow and Trinity), captain in 1852	1850–2
Vincent H.G. (Haileybury and Jesus)	1914
Wait O.J. (Dulwich and King's)	1949, 1951
Walker A. (Westminster, Magdalene and Trinity)	1864–6
Walker F. (Private and Trinity)	1849–52
Walker J. (Private and Trinity), captain in 1848	1847–9
Ward A.R. (Private and St John's), captain in 1854 but did not play against Oxford owing to illness	1853
Ward H.E. (Bury St Edmunds and Jesus)	1870–1
Warner W.S.O. (Higstead, Torquay and Trinity)	1867–8
Warr J.J. (Ealing County GS and Emmanuel), captain in 1951	1949–52
Warren C. (Oakham and St John's)	1866
Watts H.E. (Downside and Peterhouse)	1947
Webb R.H. (Eton and Christ's)	1827
Webster J. (Bradford GS and St Catharine's)	1939
Webster W.H. (Highgate and Pembroke)	1932
Weedon M.J.H. (Harrow and Magdalene)	1962
Weigall G.J.V. (Wellington and Emmanuel)	1891–2
Weighell W.G. (Bedford GS and Jesus)	1866, 1868–9
Wells C.M. (Dulwich and Trinity)	1891–3
Wells T.U. (King's College, NZ and King's)	1950
Weston J.S. (Rugby and Emmanuel)	1851–2
Wheatley O.S. (King Edward's, Birmingham and Gonville & Caius)	1957–8
Wheelhouse A. (Nottingham HS and Emmanuel)	1959
White A.F.T. (Uppingham and Pembroke)	1936
White A.H. (Geelong and Jesus)	1924
White H.S. (Bury St Edmunds, Brighton and Jesus)	1852
White R.C. (Hilton College, S. Africa and Jesus), captain in 1965	1962–5
Whitfield H. (Eton and Trinity)	1878–81
Whymper F.H. (Eton and Trinity)	1849
Wilcox D.R. (Dulwich and Pembroke), captain in 1933	1931–3
Wild J.V. (Taunton and King's)	1938
Wilkenkin B.C.G. (Harrow and Trinity)	1956
Wilkin C.L.A. (St Kitts GS and Pembroke)	1970
Wilkins-Leir E.J.P. (Marlborough and Trinity Hall)	1858
Willard M.J.L. (Judd and Corpus Christi)	1959–61

Willatt G.L. (Repton and St Catharine's), captain in 1947	1946–7
Wills T.W. (Rugby) (T.W. Wills had been entered at Cambridge but he never came into residence)	1856
Wilson C.E.M. (Uppingham and Trinity), captain in 1898	1895–8
Wilson C.P. (Uppingham, Marlborough and Trinity)	1880–1
Wilson E.R. (Rugby and Trinity), captain in 1902	1899–1902
Wilson F.B. (Harrow and Trinity), captain in 1904	1902–4
Wilson G. (Harrow and Trinity)	1919
Wilson T.W. (Repton and King's)	1869
Windows A.R. (Clifton and Jesus)	1962–4
Wingfield W. (Rossall and Trinity)	1855–7
Winlaw R. de W.K. (Winchester and St John's)	1932–4
Winter A.H. (Westminster and Trinity)	1865–7
Winter C.E. (Uppingham and Trinity)	1902
Winter G.E. (Winchester and Trinity)	1898–9
Winthrop S. (Rugby and St John's)	1829
Wood G.E.C. (Cheltenham and Pembroke), captain in 1920	1914, 1919–20
Wood H. (Sheffield Collegiate School and Sidney Sussex)	1879
Woodroffe K.H.C. (Marlborough and Pembroke)	1913–14
Woods S.M.J. (Brighton and Jesus), captain in 1890	1888–91
Wookey S.M. (Malvern and Emmanuel)	1975–6
Wooller W. (Rydal and Christ's)	1935–6
Wright C.C.G. (Tonbridge and Pembroke)	1907–8
Wright C.W. (Charterhouse and Trinity)	1882–5
Wright P.A. (Wellingborough and Jesus)	1922–4
Wright S. (Mill Hill and Emmanuel)	1973
Wroth H.T. (Uppingham and St John's)	1845
Wykes N.G. (Oundle and Queens')	1928
Yardley N.W.D. (St Peter's, York and St John's), captain in 1938	1935–8
Yardley W. (Rugby and Trinity), captain in 1871	1869–72
Young R.A. (Repton and King's), captain in 1908	1905–8

VII World Wars' Roll of Honour

First World War

OXFORD	CAMBRIDGE
Bird W.S.	Arnold A.C.P.
Boswell W.G.K.	Colbeck L.G.
Brandt D.R.	Cowie A.G.
Cunliffe, Sir Foster	Crawley E.
Curwen W.J.H.	Davies G.B.
Fisher C.D.	Driffield L.T.
Hatfeild C.E.	Eyre C.H.
Lagden R.O.	Goodwin H.J.
Lewis R.P.	Hopley G.W.V.
Raphael J.E.	Howard-Smith C.
Shaw E.A.	Lang A.H.
Tuff F.N.	Moon L.J.
Wright E.L.	Napier G.G.
	Nason J.W.W.
	Penn E.F.
	Phillips E.S.
	Roberts F.B.
	Woodroffe K.H.C.

Second World War

OXFORD	CAMBRIDGE
Ballance T.G.L.	Ashton C.T.
Butterworth R.E.C.	Blake J.P.
Chalk F.G.H.	Farnes K.
Dixon E.J.H.	Grimshaw J.W.T.
Legge G.B.	Human R.H.C.
Matthews M.H.	Kemp-Welch G.D.
Pershke W.J.	Nelson R.P.
Rücker P.W.	Winlaw R. de W.K.
Scott K.B.	
Tindall R.G.	
Walker D.F.	
Whitehouse P.M.W.	

VIII Blues who have won Test caps

	Test debut	Tests played		Test debut	Tests played
ENGLAND			Edmonds P.H.	1975	51
OXFORD			Farnes K.	1934	15
Bosanquet B.J.T.	1903	7	Gay L.H.	1894	1
Carr D.B.	1951	2	Gibb P.A.	1938	8
Cowdrey M.C.*	1954	114	Gilligan A.E.R.	1922	11
Evans A.J.	1921	1	Greig I.A.	1982	2
Fane F.L.	1905	14	Griffith S.C.	1947	3
Foster R.E.	1903	8	Hill A.J.L.	1895	3
Fry C.B.	1895	26	Hutton R.A.	1971	5
Harris Hon. G.R.C.	1878	4	Insole D.J.	1950	9
(later 4th Lord Harris)			Jackson F.S. (later Sir Stanley)*	1893	20
Hartley J.C. (later Colonel)	1905	2	Jessop G.L.*	1899	18
Holmes E.R.T.	1934	5	Jones A.O.	1899	12
Jardine D.R.	1928	22	Killick E.T.	1929	2
Knight D.J.	1921	2	(later the Reverend)*		
Legge G.B.	1927	5	Lewis A.R.	1972	9
Leslie C.F.H.*	1882	4	Lucas A.P.	1878	5
Leveson-Gower H.D.G.	1909	3	Lyttelton The Hon. A.	1880	4
(later Sir Henry)			MacGregor G.*	1890	8
Marks V.J.	1982	6	MacKinnon F.A.	1878	1
Mitchell-Innes N.S.*	1935	1	(later 35th Chief of MacKinnon)		
O'Brien T.C.*	1884	5	Mann F.G.	1948	7
Palairet L.C.H.	1902	2	Mann F.T.	1922	5
Nawab of Pataudi (Snr)	1932	3	Marriott C.S.	1933	1
Peebles I.A.R.*	1927	13	May P.B.H.*	1951	66
Philipson H.	1891	5	Mitchell F.	1898	2
Royle V.P.F.A.	1878	1	Moon L.J.	1905	4
Smith A.C.	1962	6	Parker P.W.G.	1981	1
Smith M.J.K.	1958	50	Pringle D.R.*	1982	14
Stevens G.T.S.*	1922	10	Ranjitsinhji K.S.	1896	15
Tavaré C.J.	1980	30	Robins R.W.V.	1929	19
Townsend D.C.H.	1934	3	Schultz S.S. (later Storey)	1878	1
Tylecote E.F.S.	1882	6	Selvey M.W.W.	1976	3
Warner P.F. (later Sir Pelham)	1898	15	Sheppard D.S.	1950	22
Webbe A.J.	1878	1	(later the Rt Reverend)*		
			Smith C. Aubrey	1888	1
CAMBRIDGE			(later Sir C. Aubrey)		
Absolom C.A.	1878	1	Steel A.G.*	1880	13
Allen G.O. (later Sir George)	1930	25	Studd C.T.*	1882	5
Allom M.J.C.	1929	5	Studd G.B.	1882	4
Bailey T.E.	1949	61	Subba Row R.	1958	13
Barber R.W.	1960	28	Tufnell N.C. (later Colonel)*	1909	1
Bligh Hon. I.F.W.	1882	4	Turnbull M.J.	1929	9
(later 8th Earl of Darnley)			Valentine B.H.	1933	7
Brearley J.M.	1976	39	Warr J.J.*	1950	2
Bromley-Davenport H.R.	1895	4	Wilson C.E.M.	1898	2
Brown F.R.	1931	22	(later the Reverend)		
Calthorpe Hon. F.S.G.	1929	4	Wilson E.R.	1920	1
Chapman A.P.F.	1924	26	Wood G.E.C.	1924	3
Dawson E.W.	1927	5	Woods S.M.J.	1895	3
Dewes J.G.*	1948	5	Wright C.W.	1895	3
Dexter E.R.	1958	62	Yardley N.W.D.	1938	20
Doggart G.H.G.*	1950	2	Young R.A.*	1907	2
Druce N.F.	1897	5			
Duleepsinhji K.S.	1929	12			

	Test debut	Tests played
AUSTRALIA		
CAMBRIDGE		
Woods S.M.J.*	1888	3
SOUTH AFRICA		
OXFORD		
Fellows-Smith J.P.	1960	4
Melville A.	1938	11
Owen-Smith H.G. (later Dr)*	1929	5
Pithey D.B.*	1963	8
van der Bijl P.G.V.	1938	5
van Ryneveld C.B.	1951	19
CAMBRIDGE		
McCarthy C.N.*	1948	15
Mitchell F.	1912	3
WEST INDIES		
OXFORD		
Kentish E.S.M.*	1947	2
CAMBRIDGE		
Alexander F.C.M.	1957	25
Cameron J.H.	1939	2
Grant G.C.	1930	12
Grant R.S.	1934	7
Murray D.L.*	1963	62

	Test debut	Tests played
NEW ZEALAND		
OXFORD		
Donnelly M.P.*	1937	7
CAMBRIDGE		
Lowry T.C.	1929	7
INDIA		
OXFORD		
Baig A.A.*	1959	10
Divecha R.V.	1951	5
Hafeez A.H. (later Kardar)*	1946	3
Nawab of Pataudi (Snr)	1946	3
Nawab of Pataudi (Jnr)*	1961	46
CAMBRIDGE		
Jahangir Khan (later Dr)	1932	4
PAKISTAN		
OXFORD		
Burki J.	1960	25
Kardar A.H.	1952	23
Imran Khan	1971	70
CAMBRIDGE		
Majid Khan	1964	63

* Test player before or during undergraduate career.

IX Test captains

(Chronological in order of debut as Test captain)

ENGLAND

1878–9	Lord Harris
1882	Hon. I.F.W. Bligh
1886	A.G. Steel
1888–9	Sir C. Aubrey-Smith
1895	Lord Hawke
1895–6	Sir T.C. O'Brien
1898–9	P.F. Warner
1905	Hon. F.S. Jackson
1907	R.E. Foster
1907–8	F.L. Fane
1907–8	A.O. Jones
1912	C.B. Fry
1922–3	F.T. Mann
1924–5	A.E.R. Gilligan
1928–9	A.P.F. Chapman
1929–30	Hon. F.S.G. Calthorpe
1929–30	A.H.M. Gilligan
1932–3	D.R. Jardine
1936–7	G.O. Allen
1937	R.W.V. Robins
1948	N.W.D. Yardley
1948–9	F.G. Mann
1950–1	F.R. Brown
1951–2	D.B. Carr
1954	D.S. Sheppard
1955	P.B.H. May
1959	M.C. Cowdrey
1961–2	E.R. Dexter
1961–2	M.J.K. Smith
1972–3	A.R. Lewis
1976	J.M. Brearley

SOUTH AFRICA

1904	F. Mitchell
1947	A. Melville
1955	C.B. van Ryneveld

WEST INDIES

1930–1	G.C. Grant
1939	R.S. Grant
1957–8	F.C.M. Alexander

NEW ZEALAND

1927	T.C. Lowry

INDIA

1946	Nawab of Pataudi (Snr)
1967	Nawab of Pataudi (Jnr)

PAKISTAN

1952–3	A.H. Kardar
1962	Burki J.
1982	Imran Khan

X Some great University batsmen

BY GERALD BRODRIBB

This survey covers the University career records of the most successful batsmen. The names all represent attractive batsmanship of highest quality. First, a list of those who scored 2000 runs at an average of 45 – a fair performance for what is usually over a period of three years.

	Years	Inns	Not out	Runs	Top score	Average	Hundreds
M.P. Donnelly (Ox)	1946–7	43	6	2400	154*	64.86	9
H. Ashton (Cam)	1920–2	43	8	2258	236*	64.51	7
P.B.H. May (Cam)	1950–2	57	12	2881	227	64.03	9
D.S. Sheppard (Cam)	1950–2	62	5	3545	239*	62.19	14
J.G. Dewes (Cam)	1948–50	62	8	3247	212	60.12	7
J.H. Human (Cam)	1932–4	48	8	2205	158*	55.12	10
G.H.G. Doggart (Cam)	1948–50	56	8	2599	219*	54.14	7
Majid Khan (Cam)	1970–2	52	4	2545	200	53.02	9
Nawab of Pataudi (Snr) (Ox)	1928–31	59	5	2744	238*	50.81	9
A.M. Crawley (Ox)	1927–30	63	5	2914	204	48.56	9
N.S. Mitchell-Innes (Ox)	1934–7	78	8	3319	207	47.41	9
E.T. Killick (Cam)	1927–30	59	3	2534	201	45.25	8
N.F. Druce (Cam)	1894–7	51	4	2121	227*	45.12	7

* not out

Sheppard's 14 centuries is a record total, as also is the 7 centuries he scored in 1952.

A high aggregate depends much on the opportunity to play, and in the 1950s and 1960s the Universities had more extensive fixtures than before, some batsmen having over thirty innings in a season. The highest aggregates over 2500 runs have been:

J.M. Brearley (Cam) 1961–68, 4310 runs at an average of 38.48
D.M. Sheppard (Cam) 1950–3, 3545 at 62.19
N.S. Mitchell-Innes (Ox) 1934–7, 3319 at 47.41
E.R. Dexter (Cam) 1956–8, 3298 runs at 37.90
J.G. Dewes (Cam) 1948–50, 3247 at 60.12
A.A. Baig (Ox) 1959–62, 3182 runs at 35.35
A.R. Lewis (Cam) 1960–2, 3167 at 42.22
M.J.K. Smith (Ox) 1954–6, 3009 runs at 41.21
A.M. Crawley (Ox) 1927–30, 2914 at 48.56
P.B.H. May (Cam) 1950–2, 2881 at 64.03
E.J. Craig (Cam) 1961–3, 2879 runs at 39.98
M.C. Cowdrey (Ox) 1952–4, 2848 runs at 42.49
Nawab of Pataudi (Snr) (Ox) 1928–31, 2744 at 50.81
G.H.G. Doggart (Cam) 1948–50, 2599 at 54.14
Majid Khan (Cam) 1970–2, 2545 at 53.02
E.T. Killick (Cam) 1927–30, 2534 at 45.25

(Brearley played for four seasons between 1961 and 1964, and also played five innings in 1966, and four more in 1968 – a very long career. Sheppard's total of 3545 is the best for the more usual three-season period.)

Others who passed the 2000 mark are: E.W. Dawson, K.S. Duleepsinhji, H.J. Enthoven, N.W.D. Yardley, P.A. Gibb for Cambridge; G.T.S. Stevens, N.M. Ford, F.G.H. Chalk, R.C.M. Kimpton and the Nawab of Pataudi (Jnr) for Oxford.

The making of 1000 runs in a University season is rare. The first to reach it was T.C. Lowry in 1923. Since then it has been achieved 35 times, including twice each by Brearley, Sheppard, Smith, Craig, Dexter and Lewis. Totals of 1200 runs have been gained by the following.

	Years	Inns	Not out	Runs	Top score	Average
D.S. Sheppard (Cam)	1952	23	3	1531	239*	79.05
A.R. Lewis (Cam)	1962	31	3	1365	148	48.75
E.J. Craig (Cam)	1961	32	4	1342	208*	47.92
J.M. Brearley (Cam)	1964	26	3	1313	169	57.08
R.M. Prideaux (Cam)	1960	34	0	1311	140	38.55
Nawab of Pataudi (Snr) (Ox)	1931	16	2	1307	238*	93.25
A.R. Lewis (Cam)	1960	32	2	1307	125	43.56
P.B.H. May (Cam)	1951	23	6	1286	178	71.44
G.H.G. Doggart (Cam)	1949	24	5	1280	219	67.36
J.G. Dewes (Cam)	1950	20	4	1262	212	78.87
M.P. Donnelly (Ox)	1946	22	2	1256	142	62.80
E.R. Dexter (Cam)	1958	32	2	1256	114	41.86
Nawab of Pataudi (Jnr) (Ox)	1961	24	2	1216	144	55.27
Majid Khan (Cam)	1970	23	1	1216	200	55.27
E.R. Dexter (Cam)	1957	32	1	1209	185	39.00

Once again the Cambridge names dominate the lists.

Some very high seasonal averages have been obtained, the highest being those shown below.

	Years	Inns	Not out	Runs	Top score	Average
Nawab of Pataudi (Snr) (Ox)	1931	16	2	1307	238*	93.25
D.S. Sheppard (Cam)	1952	23	3	1581	239*	79.05
J.G. Dewes (Cam)	1950	20	4	1202	212	78.87
R.E. Foster (Ox)	1900	13	1	930	171	77.50
D.R. Pringle (Cam)	1982	10	3	521	127	74.42
P.B.H. May (Cam)	1952	17	4	958	171	73.60
E.L. Kidd (Cam)	1913	15	3	866	150	72.16
P.B.H. May (Cam)	1951	23	6	1286	178*	71.44

Despite many successful seasons, individual scores of 200 are comparatively rare. The total is 33, 19 by Cambridge and 14 by Oxford. Below are scores of over 225.

281	K.J. Key (Ox)	v	Middlesex	Chiswick Park	1887
264*	G.J. Mordaunt (Ox)	v	Sussex	Hove	1895
254*	K.S. Duleepsinhji (Cam)	v	Middlesex	Cambridge	1927
239*	D.S. Sheppard (Cam)	v	Worcester	Worcester	1952
238*	Nawab of Pataudi (Snr) (Ox)	v	Cambridge	Lord's	1931
236*	H. Ashton (Cam)	v	Free Foresters	Cambridge	1920
236	E.R.T. Holmes (Ox)	v	Free Foresters	Oxford	1927
233*	J.S.F. Morrison (Cam)	v	MCC	Cambridge	1914
231	J.L. Bryan (Cam)	v	Surrey	Oval	1921
228	T. Bowring (Ox)	v	Gents of England	Oxford	1908
227*	N.F. Druce (Cam)	v	C.I. Thornton's XI	Cambridge	1897
227*	P.B.H. May (Cam)	v	Hampshire	Cambridge	1950
227	D.S. Sheppard (Cam)	v	West Indies	Cambridge	1950

Another notable feat of batting is to score two hundreds in a match. Those who have achieved this are the following.

R.E. Foster (Ox)	128 and 100*	v	A.J. Webbe's XI	Oxford	1900
M. Howell (Ox)	115 and 102	v	H.D.G. Leveson-Gower's XI	Eastbourne	1919
W.K. Harbinson (Cam)	130 and 103*	v	Glamorgan	Cambridge	1930
Nawab of Pataudi (Snr) (Ox)	165 and 100	v	Surrey	Oval	1931
A.T. Ratcliffe (Cam)	130 and 104*	v	Surrey	Oval	1932
J.H. Human (Cam)	110 and 122	v	Surrey	Oval	1933
R. de W.K. Winlaw (Cam)	115 and 109	v	Glamorgan	Cardiff	1934
R.C.M. Kimpton (Ox)	101 and 106	v	Gloucester	Oxford	1936
D.S. Sheppard (Cam)	143 and 126	v	Middlesex	Cambridge	1951
A.C. Smith (Ox)	145 and 124	v	Hampshire	Bournemouth	1959
R.M. Prideaux (Cam)	102 and 106	v	Somerset	Taunton	1960
Nawab of Pataudi (Jnr) (Ox)	106 and 113*	v	Yorkshire	Oxford	1961
Imran Khan (Ox)	117 and 106	v	Nottinghamshire	Oxford	1974
R.J. Boyd-Moss (Cam)	139 and 124	v	Oxford	Lord's	1983

It is rare for University batsmen to be concerned in big stands, but on five occasions stands of over 300 have been recorded.

340	7th wkt	K.J. Key and H. Philipson	v	Middlesex, Chiswick Park	1887
331*	2nd wkt	W.K. Harbinson and E.T. Killick	v	Glamorgan, Cambridge	1929
429*	2nd wkt	J.G. Dewes and G.H.G. Doggart	v	Essex, Cambridge	1949
343	1st wkt	J.G. Dewes and D.S. Sheppard	v	West Indies, Cambridge	1950
349	1st wkt	J.G. Dewes and D.S. Sheppard	v	Sussex, Hove	1950

In spite of the apparent dominance of Cambridge batsmen, due perhaps to the excellence of the Fenner's pitch, the average cost of runs per wicket works out at about 25 runs for each side, and the rate of scoring is equally level.

This survey should have included most of the great batsmen who achieved success while at the University, but others developed fully only in later life, the most obvious examples being C.B. Fry and Ranji. University cricket may at present be of a lower standard, but if England potential can still be found, even if only occasionally, then surely the continuance of University first-class cricket can be fully justified?

Bibliography

Abrahams H.M. and Bruce-Kerr J., *Oxford versus Cambridge*, Faber and Faber 1931.

Altham H.S. and Swanton E.W., *A History of Cricket*, 2nd edition, Allen and Unwin 1938.

Bailey P., Thorn P. and Wynne-Thomas P., *Who's Who of Cricketers*, Newnes Books in association with the Association of Cricket Statisticians 1984.

Bailey T.E., *Wickets, Catches and the Odd Run*, Collins Willow 1986.

Batchelor D.S., *C.B. Fry*, Phoenix House 1951.

Betham J.D., *Oxford and Cambridge Scores and Biographies*, London, Simpkin Marshall; Sedbergh Jackson 1905.

Bolton G., *History of the Oxford University Cricket Club*, Holywell Press 1962.

Brooke R.W., *Collins Who's Who of English First-Class Cricket 1945–1984*, Collins Willow 1985.

Cochrane A.J.H., *Records of the Harlequin Cricket Club, 1857–1926*, Eyre & Spottiswoode 1930.

Cowdrey M.C., *MCC: The Autobiography of a Cricketer*, Hodder and Stoughton 1975.

The Cricketer, 8 July 1933, Vol. XIV No. 10 pp. 290–1.

Fifty Years of Sport at Oxford, Cambridge and the Great Public Schools, arranged by the Rt Hon. Lord Desborough of Taplow, KCVO. Vols. I and II Oxford and Cambridge edited by A.C.M. Croome. Southwood 1913. Cricket in Vol. I pp. 83–189.

Ford W.J. *A History of the Cambridge University Cricket Club, 1820–1901*, Blackwood 1902.

Fry C.B., *Life Worth Living*, Eyre & Spottiswoode 1939.

Glover W., *The Memoirs of a Cambridge Chorister*, Hurst and Blackett 1885.

Grayson E., *Corinthians and Cricketers*, Naldrett Press in association with World's Press Work 1955.

Green B., *The Wisden Book of Obituaries*, MacDonald Queen Anne Press 1986.

Holmes E.R.T., *Flannelled Foolishness*, Hollis & Carter 1957.

Imran Khan, *Imran*, Pelham Books 1983.

Lewis A.R., *Double Century*, London, Hodder & Stoughton 1987.

Marlar R.G. 'The Universities in the Wisden Century', pp. 697 *et seq.* of *Wisden Cricketer's Almanack*, vol. 100, 1963.

Peebles I.A.R., *Batter's Castle*, Souvenir Press 1958.

Pycroft J., *Oxford Memories*, Bentley 1886.

Ranjitsinhji K.S., *The Jubilee Book of Cricket*, Edinburgh and London, Blackwood 1897.

Steel A.G. and Lyttelton, the Hon. R.H., *Cricket*, Badminton Library 1888.

Swanton E.W. (ed.), *The World of Cricket*, Michael Joseph 1966.

Swanton E.W. and Woodcock J.C. (eds.), *Barclays World of Cricket*, Collins 1980.

Swanton E.W., Plumptre W.G. and Woodcock J.C. (eds) *Barclays World of Cricket*, Collins Willow 1986.

Warner P.F., *Long Innings*, Harrap 1951.

Wilson F.B., *Sporting Pie*, Chapman and Hall 1922.

Wingfield Digby A., *A Loud Appeal*, Hodder 1988.

Wisden Cricketers' Almanack, 1864 to present.

Acknowledgements

The authors acknowledge with thanks the valuable personal contributions of Sir George Allen, J.M. Brearley, A.H. Broadhurst, J.F. Burnet, J.H. Cameron, J.A. Claughton, Cyril Coote, M.C. Cowdrey, M.A. Crawley, J.G.W. Davies, G.P.S. Delisle, S.J.G. Doggart, A.R. Duff, R.A. Fletcher, C.A. Fry, G. Goonesena, D.M. Green, J.W. Greenstock, S.C. Griffith, Dr P.M. Hayes, J.H. Human, D.J. Insole, D.W. Jarrett, C.J.M. Kenny, A.R. Lewis, V.J. Marks. R.G. Marlar, J.C. Marshall, R.C. Martin, Mrs Mary Maxwell, P.B.H. May, M.E.L. Melluish, H.A. Pawson, Dr S.R. Porter, D. Russell, A.P. Singleton, M.J.K. Smith, R.G. Stainton, C.J. Tavaré, J.R. Thompson, R.S. Thompson, D.C.H. Townsend, M.M. Walford, J.J. Warr, S.D. Weale, O.S. Wheatley, R.C. White, Rev. A. Wingfield Digby, Rev. S.M. Wookey.

The authors and publisher also acknowledge the following sources for the illustrations which appear in the book: Gillman and Soame Ltd, Patrick Eagar, MCC, Bill Smith Sports Photography, and Sport and General Press Agency.

Index

Index

Index